DATE DUE

		DISCARD	
APR 3 0 2010			
			4 2008

A Shostakovich Companion

A SHOSTAKOVICH COMPANION

Michael Mishra

PRAEGER

Westport, Connecticut
London

Library of Congress Cataloging-in-Publication Data

Mishra, Michael.
  A Shostakovich companiaon / Michael Mishra.
    p. cm.
  Includes bibliographical references (p.   ) and indexes.
  ISBN 978-0-313-30503-0 (alk. paper)
    1. Shostakovich, Dmitrii Dmitrievich, 1906–1975. 2. Composers—Soviet
Union—Biography. 3. Shostakovich, Dmitrii Dmitrievich, 1906–1975—Criticism and
interpretation. 4. Music—Soviet Union—History and criticism. I. Title.
  ML410.S53M64 2008
  780.92—dc22
  [B]   2007043983

British Library Cataloguing in Publication Data is available.

Library of Congress Catalog Card Number: 2007043983
ISBN: 978-0-313-30503-0

First published in 2008

Praeger Publishers, 88 Post Road West, Westport, CT 06881
An imprint of Greenwood Publishing Group, Inc.
www.praeger.com

Printed in the United States of America

∞™

The paper used in this book complies with the
Permanent Paper Standard issued by the National
Information Standards Organization (Z39.48-1984).

10 9 8 7 6 5 4 3 2 1

COPYRIGHT ACKNOWLEDGMENTS

The author and publisher acknowledge permission to quote from the following:

Isaak Glikman, *Story of a Friendship: The Letters of Dmitry Shostakovich to Isaak Glikman, 1941–1975*, trans. Anthony Phillips. Ithaca: Cornell University Press, 2001. U.S. and Philippines copyright © Cornell University Press. Used with permission. Rest of the world copyright © Faber and Faber. Used with permission.

Elizabeth Wilson, *Shostakovich, a Life Remembered*, original edition. Princeton: Princeton University Press, 1994. Copyright © Princeton University Press. Used with permission.

Solomon Volkov, *Testimony*. New York: Harper and Row, 1979. Copyright © HarperCollins. Used with permission.

The first half of Chapter 11 is a slightly modified reprint of James Morgan, "Interview with 'The Nose': Shostakovich's Adaptation of Gogol." In Andrew Wachtel, *Intersections and Transpositions: Russian Music, Literature, and Society*. Evanston: Northwestern University Press, 1998, 111–37. Copyright © Northwestern University Press. Used with permission.

The first half of Chapter 15 is an expanded reprint of "Shostakovich and the Passacaglia: Old Grounds or New?" *The Musical Times*, 141 (Spring 2000). Copyright © *Musical Times*. Used with permission.

Chapter 16 is a modified reprint of Richard Burke, "Film, Narrative, and Shostakovich's Last Quartet," *The Musical Quarterly*, 83 (1999), 413–29. Copyright © Oxford University Press. Used with permission.

Musical examples (Alban Berg). Copyright © European American Music. Used with permission. See Musical Examples Permissions page for details.

Musical examples (Shostakovich). Copyright © G. Schirmer. Used with permission. See Musical Examples Permissions page for details.

Every reasonable effort has been made to trace the owners of copyrighted materials in this book, but in some instances this has proven impossible. The author and publisher will be glad to receive information leading to more complete acknowledgments in subsequent printings of the book and in the meantime extend their apologies for any omissions.

CONTENTS

III. ANALYZING SHOSTAKOVICH

IV. ASPECTS OF SHOSTAKOVICH

Photo essay follows page 312

PREFACE

The year 2006 marked the 100th anniversary of the birth of Dmitry Dmitryevich Shostakovich. And an impressive anniversary it was. The twelve months between December 2005 and November 2006 saw at least seven academic conferences devoted to the composer (one in Italy, two in the USA, three in England, and one in Germany), a "Shostakovich on Film" season in London, and symphony and string quartet *integrales* all around the world. Indeed, the scope of the celebrations would almost prove a match for the other major composer anniversary of 2006, the 250th anniversary of the birth of Mozart. Yet it did not take an anniversary to tell us something that has been apparent for at least the last few years: no composer wholly of the twentieth century currently enjoys a higher standing amongst audiences of classical music, at least in the West. In North America, for example, Shostakovich was the ninth most frequently performed composer of orchestral music (of all periods) in the 2001–2002 season, and the tenth most frequently performed in 2004–2005, an impressive showing, especially for a twentieth-century composer. In the seasons incorporating the anniversary, Shostakovich ranked sixth (2005–2006) and fifth (2006–2007).[1]

Reasons for this popularity are not hard to find. More than any other twentieth-century composer, Shostakovich reignited the favorite forms of the classical and romantic eras (even, occasionally, of the baroque), imbuing them with compelling musical relevance and couching them in a mostly accessible musical language: symphonies that renewed the tradition of Beethoven and Mahler; string quartets that renewed the tradition of Beethoven and Bartók; and operas and song cycles that gave a new, contemporary slant on the great nineteenth-century Russian tradition of literary humanism. Indeed, given the Mahler boom that had started in the

1960s, it was perhaps inevitable that Shostakovich, Mahler's natural symphonic heir, would come to enjoy a boom of his own twenty-or-so years later.

Although Shostakovich's current standing is readily explainable in these purely musical terms, it cannot be denied that his profile has also received a substantial boost over the years by the controversies linked to *Testimony*, the memoirs that he purportedly dictated to the musicologist Solomon Volkov between 1971 and 1974. Published in 1979, four years after the composer's death and three years after Volkov's defection to the USA, *Testimony* presented Shostakovich not as the "faithful communist servant" familiar from his speeches, articles, and interviews, but as an angry, bitter man looking back over decades of personal grief and societal calamity, a man who had despised Stalin, a man who told Party officials what they wanted to hear in order that he could simply get on with his life.

The *Testimony* controversy began as a simple and somewhat predictable Cold War spat. To the Soviets, Volkov was a traitorous opportunist who had concocted his malicious presentation of a Soviet hero to feed a gullible Western audience hungry for anti-Soviet propaganda. For Westerners, however, *Testimony* would provide compelling new context for Shostakovich's music, much of which seemed to embody the very same traits found in the book—bitterness, irony, even sarcasm. With the subsequent collapse of the Soviet Union and the dismantling of the Shostakovich-the-loyal-communist myth, the "Cold War" element of the *Testimony* debate would quickly fizzle out. But other questions remained, and still remain, hotly contested. Although it is now clear that Shostakovich detested the Communist Party for at least a good part of his life, is it really appropriate to consider him a "dissident," given that he willingly accepted all the trappings and privileges that went with his "establishment" status and that unlike, say, Rostropovich, Solzhenitsyn, or Sakharov, he was not prepared to risk the dangers of speaking out in the face of government oppression and injustice? Then there is the music itself; to what extent should it be read as political commentary? But the issue that has been most responsible for fanning the flames of the "Shostakovich Wars," as they have come to be dubbed, for occasionally turning hotly contested debate into downright acrimonious mudslinging, is the now famous allegation, posited within weeks of *Testimony's* October 1979 publication, that Volkov had been less than candid about how he had assembled the book. And this allegation came not from the Soviet Union but from Western scholars who had noticed passages in *Testimony* that bore remarkable similarity to passages in previously published Soviet sources.[2]

The Shostakovich scholar Elizabeth Wilson has recently suggested that the "Shostakovich Wars" have "held up rather than promoted the advance of Shostakovich scholarship."[3] Of course, we cannot turn the clock back and put this to the test. We cannot know how Shostakovich scholarship might have developed had the environment been less fractious. But one thing is certain: over the past three decades or so, Shostakovich commentary has tended to focus more on the composer's life and his complex relationship with Soviet cultural politics than it has on his music. This is not a criticism, simply a statement of fact. Indeed, much

valuable information has emerged in the comparatively short time since Shostakovich's death, and now, in 2008, we can place the music itself in better perspective
than we could twenty, or even ten years ago. But it is hard not to agree, at least in
part, with Wilson's assessment. With the "Shostakovich Wars" so focused on politics and on *Testimony*, the music has often emerged as secondary, seemingly valued
more for its role as "supporting evidence" for this or that political theory than for
its own intrinsic worth.

Nevertheless, it would be wrong to hold the "Shostakovich Wars" entirely responsible for the paucity of analytical writing. In the introduction to his analysis
of Shostakovich's Second Piano Trio, Patrick McCreless forces us to consider a
rather wider range of culprits:

> Whether this rejection stems from theorists' finding the music structurally uninterest-
> ing, from their taking offence at the notion of "tonal" twentieth-century art music,
> from their being scared off by the language and cultural distance that separates us
> from the music of Shostakovich and other Soviet composers, from the overriding
> sense that one cannot deal with this music without coming to grips with its extramus-
> ical content, or from the fact that the currently dominant analytical theory of tonal
> music (Schenkerian theory) discounts the "cyclic," cross-movement relations that are
> so prominent in Shostakovich's symphonies and chamber works, the fact remains that
> the music thus far has been resistant to any inroads by what is now rather derisively
> called the "analytical formalism" of Anglo-American theory.[4]

McCreless wrote this in 1995. Since then, there have been encouraging signs.
Analytical writings can be found scattered across symposia such as David Fanning's
Shostakovich Studies (1995),[5] Rosamund Bartlett's *Shostakovich in Context* (2000),[6]
and Laurel Fay's *Shostakovich and His World* (2004),[7] and the last couple of years
have seen two full-length, single-work studies—Fanning's volume on the Eighth
Quartet (2004) and Pauline Fairclough's on the Fourth Symphony (2006).[8] These
join Fanning's 1989 study of the Tenth Symphony, for fifteen years the sole English-
language publication dedicated to the analysis of a single work of Shostakovich.[9]
There has also been an upsurge in the number of academic dissertations dedicated
to analysis—several are listed in the Bibliography in this volume. In the last two
or three years, as new avenues of study (both analytical and archival) have opened
up, the "Shostakovich Wars" have shown signs of abating, though the battle over
the transparency of Volkov's methods continues to simmer.

With *A Shostakovich Companion*, I hope to take another step, this time within
the context of a life-and-works volume. Following an overview of Shostakovich
reception history in Part I (Chapters 1–3), Part II (Chapters 4–10) focuses on the
evolution of Shostakovich's musical language—the stylistic eclecticism and independence of his early years, the very personal development of certain musical
forms, his highly characteristic use of modes, and his progression from the predominantly symphonically conceived works of his early- and mid-maturity to the
sparer and more narratively conceived works of the later period. This focus on
evolution dictated the decision to present works chronologically rather than by

genre, thus facilitating comparisons between musically connected works, often of different genres—the Fifth Quartet (1952) and Tenth Symphony (1953), for example. Interwoven with and supporting this discussion of musical style is a biography of Shostakovich, including analysis of his up-and-down relationship with Soviet cultural politics.

Following Part II's single-author account of Shostakovich's evolution, Part III (Chapters 11–16) presents a multi-author collection of analytical writings, a collection whose diversity is manifested not just in the topics themselves but in the analytical techniques brought to bear. James Morgan, for example, uses techniques of literary analysis to consider Shostakovich in the role of operatic dramatist. Morgan examines the composer's construction of libretti for *The Nose* and *The Lady Macbeth of the Mtsensk District*, comparing them with their literary source materials. David Haas' chapter, by contrast, is the most theoretical study here. Haas proposes a "Shostakovich mode" on the basis of the prevalence of certain scale structures found in the Fourth and Fifth Symphonies and, in particular, the op. 34 Preludes for Piano. This "Shostakovich mode" is not a mode in the conventional sense, i.e., one with a given tonal center, but a construction that is more akin to the Schoenbergian "vagrant sonority," a scalar pitch collection that is not necessarily related to the tonic of the moment. Although Haas considers only these works from the mid-1930s, his proposed mode's compatibility with the octatonic scale and, by extension, with the intervals that constitute the composer's famous "DSCH" monogram would give it a wider use in later works, though by that point the "vagrant sonority" quality has given way to something more traditionally modal, as the pitch collection more often centers itself onto the surrounding tonic.

Shostakovich's most significant innovation in terms of formal design was the "sonata-arch" structure. Although the "sonata-arch" was most often found in his symphonic first movements, certain compositional features associated with it (for example, the "gradually emerging" recapitulation) would find their way into other genres and forms. My own study shows the "sonata-arch" as manifested in the first movement of the Fifth Symphony, the work in which this form could be said to have reached its first maturity.

Two chapters that do consider genre—though genre based on compositional technique rather than performance format—are Andrew Grobengieser's on the Twenty-Four Preludes and Fugues, op. 87 and Lyn Henderson's on the passacaglia and serialism. Grobengieser discusses both the usefulness and the pitfalls of the analytical concept of "model" and goes on to show how this term can be meaningfully used with respect to Shostakovich's cycle, both intrinsically and with reference to the *locus classicus* of the prelude and fugue concept, Bach's *Well-Tempered Clavier*.

Aside from the Piano Quintet, whose first two movements also carry the titles "Prelude" and "Fugue," op. 87 would constitute Shostakovich's only engagement with that particular eighteenth-century pairing. By contrast, another baroque form, the passacaglia, would preoccupy Shostakovich for his entire career. Even excluding a couple of formative attempts at ground-bass composition (the opening of the Second Symphony and a short scene in *New Babylon*), this preoccupation would last over four decades and manifest itself across the board in symphonies, concertos, solo instrumental works, chamber music, opera, and song cycles. Lyn Henderson considers the changing role of this form in Shostakovich's music, arguing that while a progressively stronger engagement with baroque manners can be felt in the passacaglias written up to 1951 (culminating in the Twelfth Prelude of op. 87), the later examples (starting with the Sixth Quartet of 1956) would seek "a radically new orientation," one in which the melodic aspect of the ground would become more important. Although Shostakovich was a latecomer to serialism and his flirtation with it was short-lived, his treatment of the note-row as a melodic/expressive device rather than as a structural determinant à la Schoenberg would, in a sense, parallel the new melodic orientation of his passacaglias.

If James Morgan's chapter at the start of Part III analyzes compositional thinking from a literary and dramatic point of view, Richard Burke's at the end considers another "non-musical" aspect, Shostakovich's use of cinematic technique in the service of musical narrative. However, in applying his analysis not to a cinematic or even a stage work but to a concert work, the deeply private Fifteenth Quartet no less, Burke shows the psychological and dramaturgical connections that, for Shostakovich, could happily exist between works of blatantly different aesthetic and musical spheres.

Part IV (Chapters 17–19) considers three independent but vitally important aspects of Shostakovich's life: his association with the Soviet film industry, his career as a pianist, and his legacy as a teacher. It is certainly easy to dismiss Shostakovich's film scores. Even taking into account the vastly different requirements of film versus concert music, they can hardly be said to rank with the symphonies or string quartets in the quality of their musical invention, though the score to *Hamlet* comes the closest. But with almost forty film scores composed over a four-decade period, this genre would form, whether Shostakovich liked it or not, an important part of his output. John Riley explores the peculiarly "parabolic" trajectory of Shostakovich's film career, a career that started promisingly with the experimental *New Babylon* and *Alone*, but that became all too easily compromised as the film genre itself became increasingly co-opted for propaganda purposes and increasingly constrained by the shackles of Socialist Realism. If Shostakovich's film scores from the high-Stalinist period have more than a whiff of hackwork about them, a more individualistic approach to cinematic musical narrative would return in his later years, with the Shakespearean masterpieces *Hamlet* and *King Lear*.

For almost his entire life, Shostakovich maintained a close connection to the piano. Although his career as a performing artist in the conventional sense was over by about 1930, he would continue to tour extensively, performing and recording his own works, until ill health forced him to retire from the stage in 1966. His playing was certainly something of an acquired taste: "His innate capacity for piano-playing was phenomenal," wrote the conductor Nikolai Malko, "but at the same time it was not quite a 'pianistic' capacity."[10] There was a brittleness, an approach to the instrument that was, as the violinist Yakov Milkis put it, "like a xylophone ... [a] sarcastic, dry staccato,"[11] a reflection perhaps of the nervous, clipped manner of his speech. Nevertheless, as Sofia Moshevich argues, the commonly held view of Shostakovich's playing—frantic tempi combined with shallow phrasing and an indifferent approach to tone—is not always supported by the evidence on his recordings, many of which possess unique musical insights.

Finally, Louis Blois gives an overview of the Shostakovich legacy, as manifested by those who studied with him formally as well as those who fell more generally within his sphere of influence. As Blois, quoting Shostakovich's student Yury Levitin, reports, Shostakovich's teaching style was "unobtrusive." He taught with neither dogma nor ceremony but with respect, even humility, towards his students, no matter what their ability. Intensely aware of the potentially corrupting nature of power, Shostakovich had no time for professorial hubris. Indeed, he was not afraid on occasion to let his students influence him.[12] His coming to serialism in 1967, for example, may very well have been influenced by two of his students, Levitin and Boris Tchaikovsky, both of whom had composed serial works in the previous year.

It was certainly all-too-easy to fall under Shostakovich's spell, as a listen to, say, the first movement of Khrennikov's First Symphony, the scherzo of Sviridov's Piano Trio, or, most notoriously, sections of Gadzhyev's Fourth Symphony will attest.[13] Not surprisingly, for many Soviet composers in the 1970s and 1980s, the desire to escape from the looming shadow of Shostakovich was quite palpable. Yet there was certainly no sense of conformity to be found amongst the major composers that followed in Shostakovich's wake, e.g., Boris Tishchenko, Boris Tchaikovsky, Galina Ustvolskaya, and, though not strictly speaking a student, Mieczysław Weinberg. These figures would demonstrate diverse responses to the Shostakovich legacy. In the case of Tishchenko, Tchaikovsky, and Weinberg, it was usually the incorporation of specific Shostakovichian compositional devices into music that occupied quite different aesthetic spheres. In the case of Ustvolskaya, an initially very close attachment to Shostakovich's style (for example, her Concerto for Piano, Strings, and Timpani) would eventually lead to a complete rejection. With what we know of Shostakovich's own teaching style, we must believe that such diversity is exactly as he would have wished it.

Inevitably, considerations of cost and space have placed a limit on the use of musical examples. Examples are included where the text absolutely demands their presence. Elsewhere, though I acknowledge that full aural comprehension of a particular point might require access to a score, I have tried to write in such a way that the larger concept remains attainable for readers without such access.

***

I would first like to thank all the authors who contributed to Parts III and IV of this volume for their contributions and for their patience through the editing process. I would also like to thank Allan Ho, John Riley, and Constance Dee for many years of conversations about Shostakovich and for the encouragement they have given; Emmanuel Utwiller and Irina Antonovna Shostakovich for their hospitality at the Centre Chostakovitch in Paris, and for kindly providing the photographs in this volume; Olga Digonskaya at the Shostakovich Family Archive in Moscow for helping clarify some archival issues; James Harkey, Megan Bethel, and Kris Pineda for their preparation of the musical examples; Tatyana Buzina for translations of certain Russian sources; the students who have taken my Shostakovich seminar over the years for an often enlightening exchange of views and ideas; administrative, music department, and music library staff at Southern Illinois University Edwardsville for their support; the four (!) Acquisitions Editors at Greenwood, who have shown extraordinary patience over the last ten years. A thought also for my long-since departed, Shostakovich-loving grandfather. In particular, it was his Melodiya pink-label LP of Mravinsky conducting the Eleventh Symphony that first grabbed the imagination; a white-hot performance made, ironically, even more so by the crude Soviet engineering and those famously impossible crackly surfaces. Finally, the biggest thank-you must go to my wife Jenn, whose tolerance for a part-time husband over the years has been a vital ingredient in bringing this book about. Although she probably won't want to hear the name Shostakovich for a while, it is to her that *A Shostakovich Companion* is dedicated.

Michael Mishra
Edwardsville, Illinois
July 2007

ABBREVIATIONS

Sources

Collected Works — *Sobranie sochinenii v soroka dvukh tomakh* [Collected Works in 42 Volumes] (Moscow: Muzyka, 1979– 1987)

New Collected Works — *Novoe sobranie sochinenii* [New Collected Works in 150 Volumes] (Moscow: Izd-vo DSCH, 2001–)

DSCH Journal — *DSCH Journal*, published 1994–present. Volumes denoted by Arabic numerals

DSCH — Newsletter of the former Shostakovich Society (UK), Published 1987–1992. Volumes denoted by Roman numerals

Izd-vo — Izdatelstvo [Publisher]

Organizations and Archives

ASM — Assotsiatsiia sovremennoi muzyki [Association of Contemporary Musicians]

FEKS — Fabrika ekstsentricheskogo aktera [Factory of the Eccentric Actor]

Narkompros — Narodnyi komissariat prosveshcheniia [People's Commissariat of Enlightenment]

RAPM — Rossiiskaia assotsiatsiia proletarskikh muzykantov [Russian Association of Proletarian Musicians]

RGALI — Rossiiskii gosudarstvennyi arkhiv literatury i iskusstva [Russian State Archive of Literature and Art, Moscow]

RTsKhIDNI   Rossiiskii tsentr khraneniia i izucheniia dokumentov
                                       noveishei istorii [Russian Center for the Preservation
                                       and Study of Documents of Contemporary History]
TsGALI   Tsentral'nyi gosudarstvennyi arkhiv literatury i
                                       iskusstva [Central State Archive of Literature and Art,
                                       Moscow]
TRaM   Teatr Rabochikh Molodezh [Theater of Working
                                       Youth]

Score Locations
Fig. 17   Rehearsal figure 17
Fig. 17, b2   Second bar of 17

A NOTE ON TRANSLITERATION

The question of transliteration is fraught with dilemmas: whether to choose a literal letter-for-letter system, or one that better reflects Russian pronunciation as perceived by the English-speaking reader; how best to balance the needs of the scholar wishing to pursue sources for further research against those of the more general reader who may become irritated by "exotic" spellings of familiar names (e.g., Iurii, Meierkhol'd, or Prokof'ev). Most commonly used in music are the Library of Congress (LoC) and the Gerald Abraham/*New Grove Dictionary of Music and Musicians* systems. In common with many authors, I have adopted one of these (in this case, LoC) and created a two-tier system in response to the conflicting demands of the potential readership.

The bibliography, citations in endnotes, and list of abbreviations will adhere strictly to LoC in transliterating Russian source citations. (Where a Russian author has written in English or where a Russian work is translated into English, the transliteration of the author's name used by the respective publisher is reproduced here.) The main text, together with non-citational portions of endnotes, will follow LoC with the following modifications:

Cyrillic	Strict LoC–bibliography and citations	Modified LoC–text
e (at the start of a word, after a hard/soft sign, or after a vowel)	e (Evtushenko, Nikolaev)	ye (Yevtushenko, Nikolayev)
e (when pronounced "yo")	e (Fedor, Kovalev)	yo (Fyodor, Kovalyov)
чев (at the end of a name)	chev (Shcherbachev)	chov (Shcherbachov)
ий (at the end of a name)	ii (Dmitrii, Musorgskii)	y (Dmitry, Musorgsky)

Cyrillic	Strict LoC–bibliography and citations	Modified LoC–text
ю	iu (Iudina)	yu (Yudina)
я	ia (Iavorskii, Sovetskaia)	ya (Yavorsky, Sovetskaya)
кс	ks	x (for the following names: Maxim, Maximilian, Alexander, Alexandra, Alexei, Felix) ks (all other names and words)
ъ/ь (hard/soft sign)	' (muzykal'naia)	sign omitted (muzykalnaya)

Exception: Where standard spellings of well-known names have become firmly established, these are used in the text in preference to modified LoC, e.g., Glière, Koussevitsky, Khachaturian, Meyerhold, Prokofiev, and Tchaikovsky. However, the more correct "Musorgsky" is slowly gaining popular acceptance alongside the more standard "Mussorgsky" and is thus used here.

PART I

SHOSTAKOVICH RECEPTION

Michael Mishra

CHAPTER 1

SHOSTAKOVICH RECEPTION HISTORY

Soviet art and progressive art worldwide has suffered a great, irreplaceable loss. Dmitry Shostakovich, the great composer of our time, a Deputy of the Supreme Soviet of the USSR, Hero of Socialist Labor, People's Artist of the USSR, recipient of the Lenin and State Prizes of the USSR, has died at the age of 69. A true son of the Communist Party, a noted State and public figure, the artist Dmitry Shostakovich dedicated his entire life to the development of Soviet music, to strengthening the ideals of socialist humanism and internationalism, and to the struggle for peace and the friendship of nations.[1]

With these words, the world was officially informed of the death of the composer Dmitry Dmitryevich Shostakovich. Since the designated role of the artist in Soviet culture was as unashamedly social and political as it was artistic—in Stalin's notorious phrase, the writer was "the engineer of human souls"[2]—the official tone of the obituary, published in the state organ, *Pravda*, comes as no surprise. Every bit as imposing as the obituary itself, the associated list of eighty-five signatories opened with First Secretary Leonid Brezhnev and worked its way through the great and the good of the Communist Party and the Soviet musical establishment.

The notice appeared in *Pravda* on 12 August, a full three days after the composer's death—the delay apparently caused by the need to obtain approval of the obituary's wording from Brezhnev himself, who was on holiday at the time.

Shostakovich was without doubt the greatest composer to have lived his entire adult life under the Soviet regime and, as can be judged from the obituary, was to all appearances a staunch believer in Communism and in the integrity of the Soviet system. He assumed a vast array of Composers' Union and other official responsibilities, and in return was the recipient of a host of awards and honors. Yet, his relationship with the Party was not an easy one. *Pravda's* infamous 1936 condemnations of his opera *The Lady Macbeth of the Mtsensk District* ("Muddle Instead of Music") and his ballet *The Limpid Stream* ("Balletic Falsehood"),[3] the government's 1948 purges against "formalism," and the 1962 controversy over the Thirteenth Symphony were the most notorious incidents, although there were others. His critics accused him of negativism, of elitist isolationism, and of worshipping the false prophet of Western modernism, although in the case of the Thirteenth Symphony, it was not the music but the political tone of its texts (an exposé of, among other things, Soviet anti-Semitism) that riled. While the Party was attempting to engineer human souls through its "life-affirming" doctrine of Socialist Realism—essentially mass art carrying optimistic propaganda about Socialist construction—Shostakovich was creating his altogether different vision of reality, one of brooding introspection, irresolvable tragedy, and biting satire.

But ideology was not the only motivation behind the attacks against Shostakovich. Jealousy was also a factor. During the 1948 "anti-formalism" purges, Andrei Zhdanov, Stalin's commissar for culture and instigator of the purges, made a point of attacking not only the "formalist" composers themselves but also the critics, musicologists, and conservatories, whose "sycophantic" pandering to those composers had continued to enable them. Ironically, Zhdanov had a point. As the composer Mikhail Meyerovich recalls: "You could tell a Shostakovich pupil a mile off; they all wore glasses, both those who needed them and those who didn't. They imitated his jerky movements and stuttering manner of speech."[4] But of course, the accusation was deeply unjust; a supremely modest man, Shostakovich could hardly be held accountable for the fawning behavior of some of his students. But in the terrible atmosphere of that anti-formalist witchhunt, the justness of an accusation made little difference. Zhdanov knew his business, and the attack had the desired result; composers who had resented the Shostakoviches and Prokofievs over the years seized the opportunity to join the officially sanctioned feeding frenzy, grandstanding before their peers and superiors with for-the-record displays of Party loyalty.

The long-term psychological toll that these traumatic events placed upon Shostakovich was incalculable. Yet, it should be noted that his public rehabilitation following both the 1936 and 1948 scandals actually took place quite quickly, at least in comparison with certain other disgraced figures, many of whom would never regain their livelihoods. In the former case, the official rehabilitation came less than two years later with the Fifth Symphony; in the latter, the process began just over a year later, with Stalin's personal intervention to lift the ban that had been

placed on certain Shostakovich works, in preparation for the composer representing the Soviet Union at the Cultural and Scientific Congress for World Peace in
New York. In "forgiving" Shostakovich so quickly on each occasion, the Party continued to demonstrate its power, this time using the proverbial carrot to replace
the stick. Yet, in a very real sense, the Party needed Shostakovich as much as
he needed them. Whether in the arts, in sports, or in aeronautics, the one thing
the Soviet government craved above all was international prestige. As the Soviet
Union's one truly internationally famous composer, Shostakovich was in a unique
position to provide that prestige and fly the flag of Soviet musical achievement
around the world. Of course, there was also Prokofiev. But Prokofiev, fifteen years
Shostakovich's senior, had been educated under the tsarist system and had left Russia immediately after the Revolution, spending the next decade-and-a-half living
abroad before returning back in 1934. A man of suspiciously "European" tastes,
Prokofiev was never quite looked upon as "one of us."

Yet, even as Shostakovich's fortunes resurged, especially in the slightly more liberal environment that emerged after Stalin's death in 1953, Soviet culture itself
would continue to cocoon itself in its bubble of denial. In 1958, for example, the
Central Committee published a Resolution partially rescinding the 1948 Resolution against formalism. As an admission of Party fallibility, the new Resolution
was certainly a landmark. Yet the text was as limited as it was tepid, stating only
that "errors" had arisen from "the cult of personality," i.e., the undue influence of
Stalin. It made no mention of the 1936 condemnation of *Lady Macbeth* and
avoided altogether the real problem, namely the bankrupt doctrine of Socialist Realism itself. Indeed, a year later, in 1959, Shostakovich's biographer David Rabinovich would reaffirm the correctness of "Muddle Instead of Music," stating that
without such a severe rebuke, "the process of liberation from the fetters of modernism would have been a longer and more painful one, and [Shostakovich] would
have had greater difficulty in stepping over the border-line between youth and
maturity."[5]

By the time of Shostakovich's death in 1975, all animosity had been put aside,
or at least had been whitewashed out of official memory. The obituary spoke in
the blandest, most official terms of his achievements, making no mention at all of
his tribulations. The multi-honored Shostakovich, the acknowledged doyen of
Soviet composers, was accorded a state funeral and was buried at the national cemetery at Novodevichy. At the memorial service, Composers' Union chief Tikhon
Khrennikov proudly parroted a statement that Shostakovich had made to a journalist in Los Angeles in 1959: "first and foremost, I am a Communist."[6]

Even after Shostakovich's death, the inability of Soviet culture to unshackle itself
from its Stalinist past would continue to be embarrassingly apparent. During the
1980s, the Soviet publisher Muzyka made the first attempt at a "complete" Shostakovich edition—the forty-two volume *Collected Works*. Even though fifty years had
now passed since "Muddle Instead of Music," the original version of *Lady Macbeth*
would still be treated as a pariah, Muzyka publishing the opera in 1985 only in its
officially sanctioned and "cleaned up" revised version, *Katerina Izmailova*. True, in

his public pronouncements, Shostakovich had declared that only this later version should be performed, and notwithstanding a debate on the purpose of a scholarly critical edition, one could possibly justify Muzyka's decision on these grounds. But what is particularly telling is that the four-and-a-half page Editor's Note accompanying the score contains not a word about the scandal surrounding the opera and the fact that it had been banned for twenty-seven years. Instead, the reader is treated to the derisorily bland, and slightly misleading, statement: "Dmitry Shostakovich decided to revise his opera in the mid-fifties with a view to its new production."[7] (Shostakovich's re-workings were initially for his own private study, not for the purposes of revival.) Not surprisingly, this "pre-*glasnost*" thinking would infect Muzyka's other editorial decisions—the 1985 score of the two Cello Concertos, for example, appears without the dedications to the exiled Rostropovich,[8] while the 1987 edition of the First Symphony would continue the Soviet practice whereby every score of this Symphony published post-1929 would omit the name of the dedicatee, Shostakovich's boyhood friend Mikhail Kvadri, who had been shot by firing squad in 1929 during Stalin's first round of repressions. That dedication would finally be reinstated in the 2002 *New Collected Works* score.[9]

Western Reception

In the West, Shostakovich had made a great impression with his First Symphony. Almost immediately after its Leningrad premiere in 1926, foreign conductors and orchestras were clamoring to get their hands on it. Yet, by the 1930s, many Western writers were getting ready to give up on a composer who, in their minds, had conspicuously failed to live up to his early promise. Even prior to *Pravda*'s 1936 excoriation, Western critics were lambasting *Lady Macbeth* for its "crude infantilism." The *New York Times* critic Olin Downes, for example, wrote that the score was "flimsily put together."[10] Stravinsky, also witnessing the 1935 production at the Metropolitan Opera, was—perhaps not surprisingly given his vociferously anti-Communist views—even more scathing:

> The work is lamentably provincial, the music plays a miserable role as illustrator, in a very embarrassing realistic style. It is in recitative form with interludes between the acts—marches brutally hammering in the manner of Prokofiev, and monotonous— and each time the curtains were lowered, the conductor was acclaimed by an audience more than happy to be brutalized by the arrogance of the numerous communist brass instruments…. *Lady Macbeth* is not the work of a musician, but it is surely the product of a total indifference toward music in the country of the Soviets. How good that I am not going there![11]

Although *Pravda*'s attack was the result of a complex array of domestic political forces, forces that even to this day we struggle to understand fully, looking at the phenomenon from a global perspective, the attack could almost be viewed as, in essence, a parroting of the complaints that Western critics had already been putting forward. All that differed was the blame: the likes of Downes and Stravinsky viewed Shostakovich's failings as the inevitable result of a communist cultural mindset; *Pravda*, just as inevitably, blamed the "degenerate" Western influence.

In general, it was not until the late 1950s and early 1960s that Western critics began seriously to consider Shostakovich's place in the larger context of Western classical music, in particular his role as the inheritor of the Tchaikovskian and Mahlerian tradition of tragic symphonism. Yet, although few in the West saw Shostakovich as an active cheerleader for Stalin, few doubted either his commitment to the larger cause of Soviet communism. Moreover, to a certain segment of Western opinion, there was something rather enthralling about that peculiarly Soviet notion of Citizen-Artist—serious writers and musicians operating at the very heart of society rather than at its periphery, a periphery that Western modernism had seemed to have pushed to its most far-flung limits. For those in the West who had felt dispossessed by the ever greater abstruseness of musical modernism during the 1950s and 1960s, the Soviet experiment seemed highly promising. And Shostakovich was seen, at least by his supporters, as that experiment's vindicator—a man who responded to criticism, unjust though many Western critics were now acknowledging that criticism to have been, in a way that balanced his own aesthetic needs with those of the State; a composer who, at his best, was both profound and accessible, a rare achievement indeed in mid-twentieth century music. As Aaron Copland, no fan of Shostakovich, admitted, "one of [Shostakovich's] most remarkable attributes [is that] he has made the music of a living composer come fully alive for a world audience."[12]

But not all were convinced. For many in the West, Stalinism had emasculated the once precocious Shostakovich, turning him into a vapid, if highly skilled *routinier*, a puppet and prize exhibit of the Soviet system. Gerald Abraham, discussing the Fifth Symphony, Shostakovich's first major work after the 1936 condemnations, certainly had reservations:

> But to what does it all amount musically? Not, surely, to very much. The second movement, which comes most dangerously near to the old grotesque, malicious Shostakovich (and has had to have its mildly parodic element explained away as of a quite different type from the old), is merely tame; the harmonic banality has extracted any possible sting.... It is all recognizable as Shostakovich; but it is Shostakovich exorcised—and he was certainly much livelier in the days when the devil possessed him. The devil caused some repellant antics but he never allowed his victim to be merely dull.[13]

These sentiments were echoed thirty years later by the pianist and musical philosopher, Glenn Gould:

> [Shostakovich's First Symphony] is as lucid, imaginative, and joyously autobiographical as a first symphony ought to be. It is an extraordinary work—one in which this teen-ager sampled without inhibition the cultural reservoir of Western music, dipped cautiously into the expressionistic extravagance of Gustav Mahler, borrowed a bit of

the motoric rhythms of the neoclassicists, sampled the double-entendre pivot chords of the early Schoenberg, and whipped all of this up into a confection that chronicles the adolescence of a young man of such prodigious gifts that he might reasonably have been expected to become the great one of the coming generation. That he did not become so may be counted as one of the genuine tragedies of twentieth-century music. Shostakovich today is occupied with Symphony No. Fourteen or so. He turns out works which no longer speak with the intensity of Mahler because there is no longer anything that he wishes to be intense about. The rhythmic propulsion of the earlier works has turned into the incessant pulsing of an organism, fatigued and overworked and trapped by a treadmill of historical delusion which shows no signs of relinquishing its incessant demands of productivity. The skillful ambiguities of Schoenbergian double meaning have become frigid and tawdry, stylized clichés embarrassing in their frequency. All that remains is the occasional moment of some strange ecstatic adagio (Shostakovich, like all real symphonists, always had a sense of adagio) to indicate what might have been.[14]

If Shostakovich the Citizen-Artist represented the great hope for Western seekers of "socially relevant" music, his name barely registered at all in progressive circles or in Western academia, where many were beholden to the young Pierre Boulez's famous declaration that any musician who had not felt the necessity of serialism was "useless."[15] In such circles, Shostakovich was viewed as intellectually several rungs below the Greats of the twentieth century—Schoenberg, Stravinsky, or Bartók. (Ironically, Schoenberg had once dubbed Shostakovich "a real composer"[16] who possessed "the breath of [the] symphonist."[17]) In 1993, Boulez himself would remark, "the vogue for Shostakovich astonishes me. I would give his entire output for some little Stravinsky pieces like the Three Clarinet Pieces or the [Four] Russian Songs."[18] Later, in 2000, he opined: "It's like olive oil, you have a second and even third pressing, and I think of Shostakovich as the second, or even third, pressing of Mahler."[19] And this is positively tame compared with recent comments from the English composer Robin Holloway, who described Shostakovich's music as:

> Battleship grey in melody and harmony, factory-functional in structure; in content all rhetoric and coercion, exercises or instructions in communal lament and celebration, rendered by portentous slow music and mirthless fast music, nearly identical from work to work, coarsely if effectively scored, executed with horrifying fluency and competence, kept unflaggingly going after its natural cut-off point had passed; music to rouse rabbles, to be seen from far away like slogans in letters 30 feet high, music without inner necessity.[20]

Within the more radical Soviet and East European circles in the 1960s and 1970s, Shostakovich fared little better. According to Penderecki, Polish composers, many of whom were high modernists, viewed Shostakovich with suspicion both for his intellectual conservatism and for his connections to the Soviet regime, though Penderecki himself would later come to consider Shostakovich the greatest symphonist of the twentieth century.[21]

Testimony

In 1979, four years after Shostakovich's death, the musical world was ambushed by the publication of *Testimony*, the alleged memoirs of the composer "as related to and edited by" Solomon Volkov, a musicologist/journalist who had been working as an editor at the Composers' Union's official organ, *Sovetskaya muzyka*. Volkov had purportedly interviewed the composer between 1971 and 1974, and had shaped the chapters of *Testimony* out of what he described as a "mound of shorthand notes"—Shostakovich apparently did not like the presence of tape recorders.[22] In June 1976, ten months after the composer's death, Volkov emigrated to America. Amid protests from the Soviet copyright agency and the Shostakovich family,[23] *Testimony* was published in October 1979 and enjoyed an immediate *succès de scandale*. It has since sold around half a million copies in twenty languages, though not, as of 2007, in Russian.

Beginning with its explosive opening page—"Looking back, I see nothing but ruins, only mountains of corpses"[24]—*Testimony* set about dismantling the official "loyal communist" figure that had been peddled for so long. The Shostakovich who emerged from its pages was, for the most part, a bitter, angry man. If *Testimony* was to be believed, the balancing act that Shostakovich had appeared to perfect over the years was not, as those brought up on the legend of Citizen-Artist had believed, some principled reconciliation of his own musical needs with those of the State. Rather, it was a simple survival tactic: read pronouncements praising the Party, sign documents as required, produce the occasional piece of *agitprop*, and you can "live a year or two in peace" composing the music that really matters.[25]

For many Soviet émigré musicians, several of whom had known Shostakovich personally, *Testimony* was a vindication of their own experiences. The conductor Kirill Kondrashin, who had been close to Shostakovich during the 1960s and 1970s, and who had later defected to Holland, stated:

> It was with the greatest agitation that I read Shostakovich's memoirs, prepared by Solomon Volkov. Much of what comes as a surprise to the Western reader was not a surprise for me. I knew many things and guessed many others; but there were new things in it even for me, things that made me look at some of his works differently.[26]

The Soviet response to *Testimony* was predictable enough. In December 1978, a year before publication, the Party Central Committee resolved to "describe [it] as an anti-Soviet forgery that discredits the name of a great composer ... [and] to take additional measures to familiarize Soviet and Western society with the truthful political and creative views and pronouncements of D.D. Shostakovich."[27] These "measures" would include a four-record set of Shostakovich's speeches (released in October 1979, the same month as *Testimony*),[28] a volume of collected speeches and articles in Russian (1980)[29] and in English translation (1981),[30] and a weighty denunciation of *Testimony* ("Pitiful Forgery—Concerning the So-Called

Memoirs of D.D. Shostakovich") that appeared in the November 1979 issue of *Literaturnaya gazeta*, signed by five former Shostakovich students: Venyamin Basner, Kara Karayev, Karen Khachaturian, Yury Levitin, Boris Tishchenko—plus Mieczysław Weinberg (Moisei Vainberg):

> The noble and pure image of our great compatriot and great composer was touched by the dirty hands of a certain Solomon Volkov.... People who knew our teacher are struck by Volkov's monstrous attempt to draw a portrait of "another" Shostakovich by piling one lie upon another.... If we are to believe Volkov, Shostakovich, the modest, reserved man of goodwill his contemporaries knew was an envious misanthrope who denigrated his colleagues with unconcealed malice.... It is utterly impossible for upright people to imagine a man hating his society and vilifying the best masters of its culture, accepting gratefully with all his heart a tribute of recognition from this society (and all these masters), joining the Communist Party, and devoting his time to his duties as a Deputy and other public duties (and devoting it generously, as everybody well knows).[31]

In fact, the evidence suggests that only two of the six signatories, Basner and Tishchenko, had any first-hand knowledge of *Testimony* at the time they signed the denunciation, knowledge that, in any case, had hardly been garnered in the most reliable manner; according to Basner's daughter, Yelena, a representative from the Composers' Union—an institution maligned in the book—visited the two men and spent an "entire day" reading the book out loud, translating into Russian as he went.[32]

The sense that *Testimony* was indeed "too bad to be true," with Shostakovich lashing out at all and sundry, would also disturb many Western readers. Yet, such negativity was not inconsistent with the experience of those who knew the composer during the final years of his life. The musicologist Marina Sabinina, for example, described him as: "Gloomy, reserved, and unsociable. Completely different than he'd been in the 1940s, 1950s, and 1960s."[33] And like most of us, Shostakovich's opinions on certain matters did indeed change over the course of his life. As his son Maxim often liked to say: "At breakfast, Shostakovich would vigorously dispraise Tchaikovsky's ineptness at thematic development; at dinner, he'd claim to like nothing better than *Pique dame*. So if you only have breakfast with Shostakovich, you don't know him; wait until dinner."[34] And so, where the forty-something Shostakovich had once insisted that his young son go and see Prokofiev's *War and Peace* ("a masterpiece of true genius"),[35] it was not inconceivable that the sixty-something Shostakovich might have felt differently:

> I am rather cool about Prokofiev's music now and listen to his compositions without any particular pleasure.... Prokofiev sacrificed essential things too often for a flashy effect.... I listen and remain unmoved. That's how things are now. Once it was different; but this was a long time ago.[36]

***

Testimony would inevitably force a reappraisal of Shostakovich's long legacy of speeches and articles, and cast doubt on some of the traditionally accepted explanations of his music. The most famous *volte-face* concerned the Fifth Symphony. Composed in 1937, the Fifth had been touted as Shostakovich's repentance for the formalist "errors" exposed by *Pravda* the previous year; it had even carried the composer-approved designation "A Soviet Artist's Creative Reply to Just Criticism." At the time, Shostakovich had stated, "the symphony's finale resolves the tense and tragic moments of the preceding movements in a joyous, optimistic fashion."[37] But readers of *Testimony* were treated to something altogether different:

> What exultation could there be? I think it is clear to everyone what happens in the Fifth. The rejoicing is forced, created under threat, as in *Boris Godunov*. It's as if someone were beating you with a stick and saying, "Your business is rejoicing, your business is rejoicing," and you rise, shaky, and go marching off, muttering, "Our business is rejoicing, our business is rejoicing." What kind of apotheosis is that? You have to be a complete oaf not to hear that.[38]

There were many other instances where the Shostakovich of *Testimony* either directly contradicted earlier official statements or revealed hitherto concealed facts or opinions. In 1944, for example, he had spoken of his plans to celebrate Russia's forthcoming victory against the Nazis:

> I have a dream—common, I should think to every Soviet artist—of creating a large scale work which will express the powerful feelings we have today. I think that the epigraph to all our work in the next few years will be the simple but glorious word, "Victory." In these days of decisive battles, and in the coming years of peace, the people will demand vivid, inspiring music which will embody the heroism of the Great Patriotic War and the nobility and moral beauty of our nation ...[39]

In the winter of 1944–1945, Shostakovich did indeed embark on a heroic symphony, his Ninth, which would appear to have fallen in line with the statement above. But it was quickly abandoned, replaced by a much smaller-scale and decidedly anti-heroic Ninth Symphony the following summer. *Testimony* explains:

> Everyone praised Stalin, and now I was supposed to join in this unholy affair. There was an appropriate excuse. We had ended the war victoriously; no matter the cost, the important thing was that we won, the empire had expanded. And they demanded that Shostakovich use quadruple winds, choir, and soloists to hail the leader. All the more because Stalin found the number auspicious: the Ninth Symphony.... I confess that I gave hope to the leader and teacher's dreams. I announced that I was writing an apotheosis. I was trying to get them off my back, but it turned against me. When my Ninth was performed, Stalin was incensed. He was deeply offended, because there was no chorus, no soloists. And no apotheosis. There wasn't even a paltry dedication. It was just music, which Stalin didn't understand very well and which was of dubious content.[40]

In fact, the aborted "heroic" Ninth Symphony was not the first instance of a large-scale patriotic work promised by Shostakovich failing to materialize. In the

late 1930s, for example, he had announced plans for a monumental song-symphony based on Mayakovsky's iconic poem, *Vladimir Ilyich Lenin*. *Testimony*
explained:

> This is a special form of self-defense in the Soviet Union. You say that you are plan-
> ning such-and-such a composition, something with a powerful killing title. That's so
> that they don't stone you. And meanwhile you write a quartet or something for your
> own quiet satisfaction. But you tell the administration that you are working on the
> opera *Karl Marx* or *The Young Guards*, and they'll forgive you your quartet when it
> appears. They'll leave you alone. Under the powerful shield of such "creative plans"
> you can live a year or two in peace.[41]

Discussing Shostakovich's legacy of speeches and articles, Volkov, in his preface
to *Testimony*, quipped that "People from a more intimate circle could even tell
which 'literary adviser' of the Composers' Union had stitched together which article."[42] Or, as Maxim put it: "I never saw my father write down any speeches or
statements. They were brought to him all prepared from the Composers' Union,
and he just signed them or delivered the speech as written for him."[43] Of course,
Shostakovich was not a professional writer, and often sought the services of a
trusted associate. But even then, interference was the norm. Daniil Zhitomirsky,
who ghostwrote for Shostakovich on four occasions during the 1950s,[44] recalls his
preparation for a Shostakovich speech on Beethoven:

> I arrived at his place with the typed text. On my heels high-ranking characters from
> the Committee on Arts appeared. I read "Shostakovich's Speech," and then, looking
> very wise, they discussed it. As it turned out, many things were missing in this speech.
> Not about Beethoven himself, but about the attitude in the USSR regarding Beetho-
> ven and successive ties, and, of course, about the theme "Beethoven and revolution."
> I kept on taking notes. D.D. sat in the remotest and darkest corner and kept silent.
> His speech "was being created by the government"! Later on, I sat at the typewriter....
> I made various haphazard additions from memory until three o'clock in the
> morning.... Out of politeness [D.D.] looked at my typed sheets, amusingly scratched
> the back of his head, and then took his leave: "Thank you, thank you, it's excellent!"
> That was the whole "collaboration."[45]

Although most commentators in the West understood that Shostakovich, like
any figure in Soviet public life, had to watch his words, there had, prior to *Testimony*, been little overt acknowledgment of the sheer extent to which his verbal
output had been managed. Indeed, for those wedded to the legend of Citizen-
Artist, there was nothing at all incongruous about Shostakovich's statements
espousing the civic values of the Soviet political and cultural system. As for Shostakovich, he never failed to bristle at the apparently ignorant and insensitive questions posed to him at Western press conferences. At the 1962 Edinburgh Festival,
for example, he was asked to state his position on Zhdanov's 1948 Resolution.
Mstislav Rostropovich, who was with the composer, remembers Shostakovich's

response—"Yes, yes, yes, I agree. And not only do I agree, but I'm *grateful* to the Party because the Party taught me." Rostropovich reports that, following this display of self-abasement, Shostakovich turned to him and muttered, "That son of a bitch! How could he dare ask that question? Doesn't he understand that I can't answer it?"[46] One Westerner who did catch on to Shostakovich's predicament, however, was Alexander Werth who, as early as 1949, recognized that Shostakovich's responses to Zhdanov in 1948 "cannot be taken at their face value. They are the words of a great artist, utterly bewildered by what was happening, and making all sorts of irrelevant comments."[47]

***

Testimony's revelations were largely corroborated during the 1980s by Soviet émigrés who knew the composer, and they would be increasingly validated in the post-Soviet 1990s by non-émigrés able to speak freely for the first time. Further research has corroborated *Testimony* on many of those stories once thought questionable,[48] while seemingly controversial opinions—those about Prokofiev, for example—have come to be better understood as "of their time." Meanwhile, the old image of Shostakovich, an image manufactured by decades of Soviet propaganda, has now been resoundingly discredited. It is now generally agreed that: 1) Shostakovich harbored resentment towards the Soviet system for much or possibly all of his adult life; 2) he was forced to wear a "mask of loyalty"[49] behind which he was able to preserve a surprising degree of personal and musical integrity; and 3) several of his works contained, at least as part of their make-up, reflections of the Soviet Union's tragic times and maybe even commentaries on the evil and stupidity that created them, "sermon[s]," as Henry Orlov has put it, "to open his compatriots' eyes on themselves and their true situation, to make them think for themselves and shake off their complacency, to try to raise their sense of dignity and civic duty."[50]

Yet, no one studying the subject can fail to have noticed the "Shostakovich Wars" that have raged on and off over the past decade or so, battles that have turned the composer into one of the most controversial subjects in all musicology. There are essentially three areas of contention, though as so often happens with such debates there has been a tendency for these distinct areas to get conflated and confused, resulting in grotesque misrepresentations of opinion and, inevitably, an escalation of the rancor. The first issue is the debate over musical hermeneutics, which in the wake of *Testimony's* publication tended to center around discussion of "pro-Soviet" versus "anti-Soviet" interpretations of certain works, but which later, especially under the influence of Ian MacDonald's controversial 1990 book, *The New Shostakovich*, would explode into a more general politicization of Shostakovich's output. The second point of contention concerns the character of Shostakovich the man. Was he, as recently described, a "moral beacon,"[51] a man who, given the impossibility of open dissent during the Stalin era, nevertheless fought injustice whenever and to whatever extent he could? Or was there an element of cowardice or complacency in his make-up, one that caused him to make compromises that, especially in the post-Stalin era, he possibly did not have to make? In this regard, we seem to have developed what the composer and Shostakovich specialist Gerard McBurney has called a "special anxiety" about Shostakovich, an anxiety that not just the meaning but also the quality and, ultimately, the value of his music might in some way depend on the way he lived his life, an anxiety that, Wagner excepted, we seem not to have developed with any other composer.[52]

But the most bitter controversy concerns *Testimony* itself. Of course, there are the inevitable questions that arise with a memoir such as this. What effect might the passage of time have had on Shostakovich's recollection of events? Indeed, as Volkov himself is the first to admit, *Testimony*, like any memoir, represents only a snapshot of its subject's thoughts and feelings: "What Shostakovich felt and thought at the time of the premiere of the Fifth Symphony I don't know, you don't know, he didn't know at the time he dictated to me in *Testimony*. What is in *Testimony* is an expression of Shostakovich's views and opinions at that time.... a summary of his life.... not a contemporary diary."[53] Beyond this, some have even wondered whether Shostakovich may have been indulging, consciously or subconsciously, in a death-bed, guilt-expiating revision of his own image for the sake of posterity.[54] But the most serious and disturbing charge concerns the book's very authenticity. According to Volkov, *Testimony's* material had derived solely from first-hand interviews with Shostakovich.[55] But shortly after publication, Simon Karlinsky and subsequently Laurel Fay discovered passages, amounting to entire pages, which had appeared to have been lifted without attribution from previously published sources.[56] With Volkov's probity in question, *Testimony* would come to be disavowed by many scholars, even by some who would otherwise concur with the book's overall presentation of Shostakovich's character.

The issues of personal character and musical interpretation affect our perception, or "reception," of Shostakovich and his music, and the remainder of this chapter will be devoted to these matters. The debate over *Testimony's* authenticity is an altogether separate matter, and its resolution, should there ever be one, should not at this point materially affect our view of Shostakovich. Chapter 3 contains a brief history of this debate.

Shostakovich the Man: Dissent, Compromise, and Guilt

For Shostakovich, or indeed for anyone occupying a prominent cultural position in the Soviet Union, ghostwritten speeches and coerced signatures were a fact of life. When Shostakovich's name appeared underneath a piece of official prose, people, especially the intelligentsia of his own generation, "understood." Yet, his seemingly blasé willingness to read anything and sign anything, even denunciations, was not so easily comprehended by the younger generation of dissidents that was emerging in the 1960s and 1970s.[57] As for his joining the Communist Party in 1960, the composer Sofiya Gubaidulina stated: "our disappointment knew no bounds.... It made me realize that a man may be able to endure hunger and withstand political crushing, yet be unable to overcome the temptation of a 'carrot'. Shostakovich was defeated by a 'carrot'!"[58]

The problem, inevitably, was the generation gap. By the 1960s, the times had changed, but Shostakovich's psyche, formed in the crucible of the Great Terror, had not. Alexander Solzhenitsyn realized this when, following the 1968 Soviet invasion of Czechoslovakia, he had contemplated a petition, a terse three-sentence text ending with the line "I am ashamed to be Soviet!," to be signed by seven influential figures, including Shostakovich. But upon deciding that "the shackled genius Shostakovich would thrash about like a wounded thing, clasp himself with tightly folded arms so that his fingers could not hold a pen," and that the others would demand so many compromises to the text as to render it impotent, Solzhenitsyn abandoned the idea.[59] Yet, although Shostakovich was not, and could never have been, a dissident along the lines of a Sakharov or a Solzhenitsyn, friends and associates attest to his ability to detach himself from his ordeals and convey his disdain to sensitive ears. Daniil Zhitomirsky, for example, had always been struck by the lack of enthusiasm, even the apparent lack of intelligence, emanating from Shostakovich's mouth as he delivered his speeches. Was this genuine irritation on Shostakovich's part, carefully orchestrated irony, or a bit of both?

> In private, D.D. spoke in an amazingly lively and expressive manner. He had his own style of speech: short sentences, that almost sounded like aphorisms, in which all the unnecessary terms had been deleted; and his sentences always hit the mark, as does a sniper; his enunciation was extremely precise, each word and even individual sounds (including consonants) were endowed with a meaningful significance. The specific expressiveness of his speech lay in the humour and sarcasm that emanated from an unruffled seriousness.... From official rostrums, D.D. spoke quite differently. Here is one quote from my diary during the '50s: "Listened to his address with a growing irritation, but also with sympathy. How alien and artificial to him was the text he was reading: trite newspaper stock-phrases, verbosity, and textbook-like quotes. And how he read all this! Patter, total absence of punctuation, no caesuras, total absence of meaningful intonation ... Like an almost illiterate schoolboy answering a question by reading from his crib-sheet something that was way beyond his understanding. But there was also something that was pure artistic parody. As if he were denouncing both himself in his role of official orator and, from a general point of view, the entire practice of propagandistic speeches 'from a piece of paper'."[60]

An alternative strategy seemed to involve just the opposite, a ridiculously enthusiastic engagement with the objects of the composer's scorn. To quote Lev Lebedinsky:

> Without fail he attended every possible ridiculous meeting of the Supreme Soviet, every plenary session, every political gathering, and even took part in the agitprop car rally. In other words, he eagerly took part in events which he described as "torture by boredom." He sat there like a puppet, his thoughts wandering far away, applauding when the others applauded. Once I remember him clapping eagerly after Khrennikov had made a speech in which he had made some offensive remarks about Shostakovich. "Why did you clap when you were being criticized," I asked. He hadn't even noticed![61]

It is instructive here to cite Ian MacDonald who invokes the writings of the Polish poet Czesław Miłosz, who speaks of *ketman*:

> a form of pretence resorted to by anyone who, while harbouring thoughts of his own, wishes nevertheless to remain alive.... *Ketman*, an Iranian word, stood for the practice of Sufi mystics under orthodox Islam of at once hiding their heresy and mocking the establishment by professing orthodoxy in the most pedantically elaborate detail (and, where it was safe to do so, carrying their shows of solemn conformism to the point of absurdity).[62]

Although Shostakovich's spirit was to some extent broken by his life's ordeals, and though these ordeals had forced him to develop various coping strategies, he was at the same time a genuinely punctilious man with a deep-rooted sense of civic duty, and it should be acknowledged here that this might in part have accounted for his extraordinary diligence in Party matters. Nevertheless, his "shows of solemn conformism to the point of absurdity" were familiar enough to those who knew him well. A striking display can be found in the oft-cited letter to Isaak Glikman, dated 29 December 1957, in which Shostakovich describes the festivities celebrating the fortieth anniversary of the Soviet annexation of Ukraine:

> Dear Isaak Davydovich!
> I arrived in Odessa on the day of the nationwide holiday celebrating the 40th anniversary of the founding of Soviet Ukraine. This morning I went out in the streets; you will understand of course that on such a day as this, one cannot stay at home. In spite of the weather, which was rather gloomy and foggy, all Odessa was on the streets. Everywhere were portraits of Marx, Engels, Lenin, Stalin, and also Comrades A.I. Belyayev, L.I. Brezhnev, N.A. Bulganin, K.Ye. Voroshilov, N.G. Ignatov, A.I. Kirilenko, F.P. Kozlov, O.V. Kuusinen, A.I. Mikoyan, N.A. Mukhitdinov, M.A. Suslov, Ye.A. Furtseva, N.S. Khrushchev, N.M. Shvernik, A.A. Aristov, P.A. Pospelov, Ya.E. Kaliberzin, A.P. Kirichenko, A.N. Kosygin, K.T. Mazurov, V.P. Mzhavanadze, M.G. Pervukhin, N.T. Kalchenko.
> The streets are filled with flags, slogans, banners. All around can be seen beaming smiles on radiantly happy Russian, Ukrainian, and Jewish faces. On every side can be heard joyful exclamations hailing the great names of Marx, Engels, Lenin, Stalin, and also those of Comrades A.I. Belyayev, L.I. Brezhnev, N.A. Bulganin, K.Ye. Voroshilov, N.G. Ignatov, A.I. Kirichenko, F.P. Kozlov, O.V. Kuusinen, A.I. Mikoyan, N.A. Mukhitdinov, M.A. Suslov, Ye.A. Furtseva, N.S. Khrushchev, N.M. Shvernik, A.A. Aristov, P.A. Pospelov, Ya.E. Kaliberzin, A.P. Kirilenko, A.N. Kosygin, K.T. Mazurov, V.P. Mzhavanadze, M.G. Pervukhin, N.T. Kalchenko, D.S. Korochenko. Everywhere one hears the accents of Russian and Ukrainian speech, as well as from time to time the foreign tongues of those progressive representatives of mankind who have come to Odessa to salute Odessans on their great holiday. I myself walked the streets until, no longer able to contain my joy, I returned home and resolved to describe to you, as best I might, Odessa's National Day of Celebration.
>
> Do not, I beg you, judge me too harshly.
> I kiss you warmly,
> D. Shostakovich[63]

This letter is pure *ketman*. Its show of "solemn conformism" reaches its climax of absurdity with the recitation *à la Pravda* of the names of the twenty-seven luminaries who were being honored, as was the norm on these festive occasions, with portraits and eulogies. And if that were not enough, Shostakovich subjects Glikman to a second recital of the list, with one slight alteration.[64] The satire is obvious, and yet, in the not unlikely event of the letter being intercepted and inspected, the text itself is unimpeachable. Two decades earlier, Shostakovich had penned something similar to his close friend Ivan Sollertinsky. The letter's purpose was to express his serious and, as it would turn out, justified concerns about the reception of his ballet *The Limpid Stream*. But Shostakovich concludes:

> That's the end of the gloomy part of this letter. Today I had the enormous pleasure of attending the closing session of the Congress of Stakhanovites. On the podium I saw Comrade Stalin and Comrades Molotov, Kaganovich, Voroshilov, Ordzhonikidze, Kalinin, Kosior, Mikoyan, Postyshev, Chubar, Andreyev, and Zhdanov. I heard speeches from Comrades Stalin, Voroshilov, and Shvernik. I was utterly captivated by Voroshilov, but when I heard Stalin speak I completely lost all sense of proportion, joined the entire hall full of people shouting "hurrah," and could not stop applauding him.... Naturally, today is the happiest day of my life: the day on which I have seen and heard Stalin.[65]

Of course, any act of "solemn conformism" can be justified as *ketman*. The principal virtue of *ketman* is stealth, making its presence hard to prove and impossible to disprove. So, are we guilty of invoking *ketman* simply to fend off awkward moral questions? The musicologist Richard Taruskin believes we may actually have gone one step further, not only by fabricating a mythic image of the Brave Shostakovich but also, to put it crudely, by attempting to make Shostakovich look more like "us," or at least "us" as we would wish to think of ourselves were we in his situation.[66] Taruskin goes on to reject the idea of Shostakovich-as-dissident on the grounds that "though mercilessly threatened [he] never suffered a dissident's trials," unlike, say, Sakharov and Solzhenitsyn.[67] For Taruskin, dissidence is necessarily a post-Stalinist phenomenon; since open dissent was simply not possible during the Stalin years, at least if one wished to survive, to claim Shostakovich as a dissident is to express a historical impossibility, however well intentioned. Taruskin's disapproval is, perhaps ironically, shared by Volkov, who has described the characterization of Shostakovich-as-dissident as a "falsification."[68]

If we agree with Taruskin that "dissidence" has a meaning that is precise and limited—the *open* expression of dissent—and that the popularly promoted idea of "secret" dissidence is, by definition, oxymoronic, we may instead prefer, as David Fanning does, Mark Aranovsky's characterization of Shostakovich as *inakomyslyash-chii*,[69] which Fanning describes as "literally 'the otherwise-thinker', which implies something rather stronger than the Western 'non-conformist' but not so strong as 'dissident' in the narrow sense."[70] In choosing this term, we acknowledge that Shostakovich did not so much fight against the prevailing cultural politics as place himself spiritually outside them, preserving his own musical independence and integrity. Ultimately, though, whatever we make of the semantics, our evaluation of Shostakovich and his actions (or lack of actions) is meaningful only if carried out with as complete an understanding as possible of what his options were, at least as he perceived them, at any given time.

Taruskin goes on to vilify the nonchalance with which many "comfortably situated post-Soviet intellectuals and celebrities" seem to have reinvented themselves, and wonders whether *Testimony*, if authentic (which he doubts), was simply another example—the embittered, possibly self-loathing, composer who "ended his career a multiple Hero of Socialist Labour [wishing], late in life, to portray himself in another light."[71] Yet, Shostakovich was the very opposite of the guilt-free "Teflon" types that Taruskin vilifies. Guilt pursued him to the end of his life, and disclosures of that guilt go back several years prior to his purported interviews with Volkov: his tear-ridden confession to his family upon joining the Party—this from a man not given to lachrymose outbursts; his admission to Isaak Glikman that "My nerves cracked up, I gave into [Pospelov, the Party official charged with recruiting him]"; his remarks to Lebedinsky ("I am scared to death of them.... From childhood I have been doing things that I wanted *not* to do.... I've been a whore. I am and will always be a whore"[72]) and to Edison Denisov ("I've been a coward all my life"[73]); his plea to his wife, Irina, never to ask him about his Party membership; or his request to the musicologist Henry (Genrikh) Orlov in 1960 not to quote from his repertoire of published statements or speeches ("I showed lack of courage, was faint-hearted"[74]).

Perhaps the ultimate manifestation of the convergence within Shostakovich of dissent, conformism, guilt, and the sheer will to survive was the Thirteenth Symphony, which he composed in 1962, two years after his recruitment into the Party. Through the texts of the young dissident poet Yevgeny Yevtushenko, Shostakovich created in the five movements of his symphony a searing indictment of Soviet life: anti-Semitism ("Babi Yar"); faceless bureaucracy ("Humor"); economic mismanagement ("In the Store"); state terror ("Fears"); and conformism in the name of self-preservation ("A Career"). Not only did "Babi Yar" contain Shostakovich's first open attack against Soviet anti-Semitism—previous works like the song cycle *From Jewish Folk Poetry* had dealt with the topic implicitly rather than explicitly—it was also the first publicly aired work of Shostakovich in which his indictment of the Soviet system was not woven into some complex, semantically multilayered web. Where in previous works, Shostakovich had called upon tragedies or struggles of the distant past to hint obliquely at present-day problems—even the Thirteenth Symphony's fourth movement, "Fears," opens with the line "Fears no longer exist in Russia"—"Babi Yar" would force its Soviet audience to come to terms with a specific act of evil that had taken place within its lifetime, on its soil. And so, less than two years after Shostakovich had committed his greatest compromise to his own principles by joining the Party, he had found the courage to speak out. As one district Party secretary was overheard to say, "This is outrageous, we let Shostakovich join the Party, and then he goes and presents us with a symphony about Jews."[75]

The subsequent history of the Thirteenth Symphony is well known. Following the two premiere performances, which the authorities had made clumsy but futile efforts to stop, the Symphony was officially "discouraged," allowed only in a revised text in which reference to Russian and Ukrainian complicity at Babi Yar was removed. Shostakovich initially opposed the revisions, since the topic of complicity was at the very heart of the movement, but he eventually conceded in order to ensure the survival of the Symphony and this, his most public indictment against anti-Semitism. Such compromise was, of course, the very thing that was railed against in the Symphony's finale ("A Career"). Yet, ironically, in that witty moment in the finale in which Shostakovich engineers a momentary confusion over the two Tolstoys (is it the great Lev or is it the "other" one, presumed to be the Party hack, Count Alexei?), the composer appears to point the finger at least partly at himself and the compromises that he had had to make over the course of his career, a piece of self-indictment seemingly reinforced by his subsequent re-use of the same music in his autobiographical skit, *Preface to the Complete Collection of my Works, and Brief Reflections on This Preface* (1966; see Chapter 9). As Malcolm MacDonald has put it, "The question is raised (and it is surely infinitely to Shostakovich's credit that he could raise it): if Shostakovich is like Tolstoy, is he more of a Lev or a Count Alexei?"[76]

There is no doubt that, for good reason or not, Shostakovich was wracked with guilt for a good part of his later life. But as that indignant district Party secretary perhaps realized, Shostakovich used the Party for his own ends, usually altruistic, as they used him for theirs. A combination of musical authority, international renown, a sense of civic duty that was absolutely genuine, and a loyalty to the Party that was probably not, had made him all but indispensable to both Party and dissenter alike.

Characterizing Shostakovich's "Enemies"

One of Shostakovich's favorite stories was of an incident that occurred at his dacha shortly after the 1948 Resolution against formalism. Recalling the incident to Marina Sabinina, he described how one of his fellow dacha residents had become irritated by some music playing over the loudspeakers:

> "They publish the Party's special Resolution. They rave against the formalists. But those formalists simply will not give up! Just listen to that racket coming over the radio!" He then brusquely switched it off. Let me tell you, Marina Dmitrievna, I was on cloud nine from sheer delight! It was Tchaikovsky's Sixth Symphony![77]

Since *Testimony*, we have learned much about those in charge of cultural affairs, and have enjoyed many anecdotes of how musicians were able to "get one past" the authorities—something that would certainly have been easier to do in music than in the other arts. As Maxim once stated: "I have always played his music the true way, even in Russia.... It was lucky for me that the functionaries there who control music understand nothing about it."[78] We have even read about Shostakovich's own supposed dodges, writing the coda of the Fifth Symphony, for example, so as to exhibit its "true," dissident meaning to the sympathetic intelligentsia while going straight over the heads of the easily duped Party idiots, who would hear only the tub-thumping D major "optimism" on the surface. But who exactly were these "idiots," and how can we know what they really heard? Given the atmosphere of terror in which, ultimately, everyone was a pawn and no one was indispensable, was it always possible to distinguish between stupid people and people forced by fear to act stupidly?

A case in point is Georgy Khubov's well-known March 1938 review of the Fifth Symphony. A Party-line journalist attempting a serious, non-technical analysis of the Symphony in *Sovetskaya muzyka*, Khubov walked a tightrope. He would certainly have been aware of the official paranoia surrounding the premiere as well as the initial disbelief that Shostakovich had so quickly "reconstructed" himself since "Muddle Instead of Music." Consequently, he would have understood that an overly positive review may have fueled the paranoia rather than kill it. He also knew that his praise for Shostakovich could not eclipse his praise for the Party. Early in the review, he notes that the Fifth "could appear only as a result of the wise and just, truly bolshevist criticism spearheaded by *Pravda* which castigated the formalist chaos, falsity, trickery and crude naturalism in art."[79] The review is chock-full of such *Pravda*-style cliché, Khubov's insights filtered through, and ultimately disfigured by, the prescribed language of Soviet aesthetics. The analytical agenda is clear; "national character and realism" constitute "the principal aesthetic criteria in the analysis of a work of art."[80]

But the description of the finale—"not so much bright and optimistic as it is severe and terrifying"—shows that Khubov was no dim-witted hack.[81] Of course, his observation was not meant as a compliment. As a Party man, the only acceptable tragedy was "optimistic tragedy": "Genuine tragedy (in art) can be expressed only in a great, internally intense struggle where the decisive role is played by a lofty life-affirming idea which determines the 'brightening up' in the very outcome of the struggle ('catharsis')."[82] With Khubov hamstrung by his own agenda, it becomes well nigh impossible to tell if his disapproval of the "severe and terrifying" coda was 1) genuine aesthetic disapproval by Khubov the critic; 2) genuine political disapproval by Khubov the committed Party-liner; 3) a politically expedient way of covering his tracks, protecting the composer and maybe even himself from the potentially lethal force of his own observation; or 4) some combination of the above.

And what of Stalin himself? Was he the culturally illiterate poseur portrayed, for example, in *Testimony's* tragicomic description of the 1943 national anthem contest, or the lumbering oaf depicted in Shostakovich's political skit *Rayok*?[83] Volkov, for one, does not think so. He believes that Stalin's love of classical music was genuine and, to a degree, informed, and considers Shostakovich to have underestimated him in this respect. The problem is that while the only opinion that ultimately mattered was indeed Stalin's, it was his political rather than his personal opinion that counted. For example, as Volkov points out, Stalin's renaming of the Moscow Art Theater as the Gorky Art Theater was once questioned by an official who pointed out that it was really Chekhov's rather than Gorky's theater. Stalin himself even preferred Chekhov to Gorky, but understood that as the nominal godfather of Socialist Realism, Gorky carried the greater political weight.[84] With his political instincts overruling his personal preferences (an ironic case perhaps of Stalin becoming a pawn in his own system), the extent of Stalin's "philistinism" is, like Khubov's, almost impossible to gauge.

Interpreting the Music

Since the publication of *Testimony*, and the concomitant discrediting of the composer's legacy of speeches and articles, nearly every Shostakovich composition has come under the microscope in the search for new meanings. *Testimony* itself mostly avoided musical discussion, but its handful of pointed remarks, set against the backdrop of the book's "revisionist" context, was enough to fuel the subsequent debates. Indeed, those remarks have themselves become almost icons of Shostakovich reception history: the Fifth Symphony's "forced" rejoicing,[85] the "portrait of Stalin" in the Tenth,[86] or the "Leningrad that Stalin destroyed and that Hitler merely finished off" in the Seventh.[87]

In the early 1980s, there was much talk of "orthodox" and "dissident" interpretations of Shostakovich's music. Critics compared conductor A's "post-*Testimony*" performance of the Fifth Symphony, with its "forced rejoicing" in the coda, versus conductor B's "pre-*Testimony*" interpretation, complete with "real rejoicing" at the end. Writing in 1984, Norman Lebrecht opined:

> [The defection from the USSR of musicians close to Shostakovich] gave rise to two diametrically opposed styles of interpreting his music, "Shostakovich East" and "Shostakovich West." "His symphonies are like a secret history of Russia," says Rostropovich. "The finale of the Fifth, for example, is all about torture and suffering … But Soviet conductors, like [Yevgeny] Svetlanov, play it as if it were joyful, a triumph of their society. That is the official Soviet view." "I have always played his music the true way, even in Russia," insists Maxim Shostakovich. "It was lucky for me that the functionaries there who control music understand nothing about it." When Maxim Shostakovich and Svetlanov performed the Eighth Symphony on successive nights in London late last year, the very fish in the Thames could have told the difference."[88]

Lebrecht's article, written for a national newspaper, captured perfectly the spirit of the early post-*Testimony* era, even if the comments now seem a bit simplistic— the two opposing camps of interpretation, "Shostakovich East" (i.e., pre-*Testimony* or "orthodox") and "Shostakovich West" (post-*Testimony*, "dissident," or "revisionist"), and the rather disturbing implication that only those Russians who defected to the West could possibly have been on the correct ideological wavelength. But even during those early years, cautions were being sounded. The literary philosopher Christopher Norris, an unabashed supporter of the "Citizen-Composer" theory and someone who continues to this day to believe in Shostakovich the loyal communist,[89] may not have been entirely unbiased in his writings, but his general comment concerning the way in which preconceptions can manipulate the ear was certainly well made:

> It has long been a favourite device of literary critics to domesticate otherwise disturb-ing or subversive texts by discovering subtle ironies at work, thus allowing them to "mean" more or less whatever the critic would wish upon them. A similar ploy has been refined over the years by Western commentators on Shostakovich. Anything which sounds, to the innocent ear, like straightforward Socialist Optimism can always be interpreted as forced rejoicing crude enough to deceive the idiot Party watchdogs but grasped straight away by sharp-eared Western critics. The technique was devel-oped to a high point of subtlety long before it found triumphant confirmation in the Shostakovich "memoirs"…[90]

In 2000, Lebrecht revisited the topic, his former bipolar approach ("Shosta-kovich East" and "Shostakovich West") now expanded:

> There are four ways of conducting a Shostakovich symphony. The official Soviet method, happily a thing of the past, involved much oom-pah and precious little ru-bato. The dissident school, led by such defectors as Rostropovich, Kyril Kondrashin and Shostakovich's son, Maxim, leaned too much the other way and seemed to be underscoring every other phrase with political intent. Certain Western conductors—Stokowski, Haitink, Karajan—achieved a kind of musical Finlandisation, which acted as if the USSR did not exist, and the symphonies were performable as a Mahlerian extension. The fourth method, now prevalent, is the messiest. Its proponents are con-ductors who grew up under the hammer and sickle. They knew the compromises Shostakovich had to make, and experienced his music in more shades than propagan-dist black and white. The approach of Jansons, Gergiev, and Järvi combines text with subtext in a way that echoes the original interpreters, Mravinsky and Sanderling, but adds post-Soviet undertones.[91]

What was often forgotten in the post-*Testimony* furor was the fact that perception of dissent or subversion in Shostakovich's music was indeed documented long before *Testimony*, and not just by the "usual suspects"—Norris' "sharp-eared Western crit-ics" or émigré musicians "overplaying" the anti-Soviet card. The party-line critic Georgy Khubov was certainly neither of these, yet, as we have already noted, his partly "revisionist" view of the Fifth Symphony, published in *Sovetskaya muzyka* no less, dates from March 1938, a few months after the work's premiere. Yevgeny Mra-vinsky was another "establishment" figure and also, by his own admission, not a conductor who tended "to search for subjective, literary and concrete images in music which is not by nature programmatic."[92] But in 1967, he wrote:

> I interpret the Ninth Symphony as a work directed against philistinism, a primary "symphonic assault" that ridicules complacency and bombast, and the desire to rest on one's laurels.… Moreover, the element of forced and labored gaiety in the finale

express, not the composer's own feelings, but those of his antithesis—the smug, impudent philistine who is essentially indifferent to everything.[93]

Indeed, Yakov Milkis, a violinist in Mravinsky's Leningrad Philharmonic, recalled a rehearsal of the Ninth in which "he objected to the character of the sound in the celli and double basses when they play in unison with the trombones. 'You have the wrong sound. I need the sound of the trampling of steel-shod boots.' (We knew that he wasn't referring to ordinary soldiers, but to the KGB forces.)"[94]

***

Although the terms "orthodox" and "dissident" have been part of the Shostakovich reception landscape for nearly three decades, defining what they actually mean in performance terms has proven more problematic. Something of a bellwether in this regard has been the controversy surrounding the tempo of the Fifth Symphony's coda—in performance, anywhere between quarter = 76 and 216. Even though this enormous discrepancy is partly explainable as a simple editorial problem (see Chapter 6), it would become almost axiomatic in the post-*Testimony* era that a conductor's tempo for the Symphony's grand D major peroration indicates a political stand: a faster tempo signifying orthodox Soviet triumphalism, a slower tempo *Testimony's* "forced rejoicing." Now given that in this particular case, the anecdotal evidence would suggest that Shostakovich intended the slower tempo—the autograph score is lost—the question might seem moot. Nevertheless, underlying this debate have been some disturbing assumptions about the relationship between performance and "meaning."

One such assumption is that musical decisions in Shostakovich performance must necessarily be read as the result of political intention. Lebrecht, in the second of his two articles (above), referred to the "official Soviet method" of conducting Shostakovich, involving "much oom-pah and precious little rubato," versus the "dissident" school, which "underscore[ed] every other phrase with political intent." But how do we know that the rubato of the latter school was indeed "political"? How do we know that the excess of "oom-pah" in the former school was not simply the result of insensitive conducting or even, in the case of recorded performances, those famously garish Melodiya recording balances, things that had nothing to do with politics?

Another assumption upon which the Shostakovich interpretation "industry" seems to have been built is that a performance can "prove" a composer's intent. Ian MacDonald wrote, "The first blow [in favor of *Testimony*] was administered by a new record of the Fifth Symphony [Rostropovich's] in which the reading stridently concurred with the sour view of the work taken in *Testimony*."[95] Rostropovich's view is certainly sour. In his performance, the coda grinds towards its conclusion shackled by ball and chain, the whole edifice ultimately collapsing in exhaustion under its own weight. But even if such a performance reflects *Testimony's* commentary (which, as argued below, is questionable), the idea that any interpretation of a piece can be "proven" simply by creating a seemingly compatible performance represents not only a disingenuous twisting of logic, but also an unrealistic expectation of what music—which in general is a suggestive rather than an attestive art—actually has the power to do.

Given, then, that performance has the power to suggest, if not actually to prove, an interpretation, the question then arises: what exactly does or should "forced rejoicing" sound like? The aforementioned concept of *ketman* hinged on its "shows of solemn conformism." In other words, that which is to be parodied must first be mastered ("in the most pedantically elaborate detail") if the parody is to be successfully pulled off. If the end of the Fifth Symphony represents forced or insincere rejoicing, then it must surely to an extent sound like the real thing if the deception is to go unnoticed. Although Leonard Bernstein in 1959 would not have been privy to ideas of forced rejoicing, it is ironically his hectoring performance (at quarter = 216, faster even than the incorrect "fast" marking of 188 found in certain editions, over twice as fast as either Mravinsky or Rostropovich, and almost three times as fast as Yakov Kreizberg's recent recording) that has that quality of mindless optimism, the timpani making the crudest possible spectacle of its cadential figures. On the other hand, Rostropovich's performance, cited by MacDonald for its concurrence with *Testimony*, ends on a grim note that sounds nothing like rejoicing, real or forced. Rather, it brings to mind Rostropovich's own remark, made to Norman Lebrecht (see above): "The finale of the Fifth … is all about torture and suffering." Rostropovich's wife, the soprano Galina Vishnevskaya, has stated her interpretation of this coda, one that also seems to describe Rostropovich's performance:

> Beneath the triumphant blare of the trumpets, beneath the endlessly repeated A in the violins, like nails being pounded into one's brain—we hear a desecrated Russia, violated by her own sons, wailing and writhing in agony, nailed to the Cross, bemoaning the fact that she will survive her defilement.[96]

***

If the musical debates during the 1980s focused on the meaning of certain key Shostakovich works and how that meaning might be brought out in performance, the debates during the 1990s were dominated by Ian MacDonald's book, *The New Shostakovich*, which took the by-then accepted notion of Shostakovich as a chronicler of his times and controversially used it as a springboard for an unashamedly metaphorical approach to musical commentary. For example, on the basis of a passage in *Testimony* discussing Shostakovich's feelings of betrayal following "Muddle Instead of Music" and the expression of those feelings in the last pages of the Fourth Symphony, MacDonald came up with this description of the quirky *divertissement* that precedes those last pages:

> A little strutting promenade for bassoons and giggling piccolo leads us into the hall where thrumming harps call the conference to order. A wan waltz (the composer?) enters and sits dejectedly while flute and piccolo trill the opening remarks in a mood of schoolboy hilarity soon dispelled by three table-thumping chords across the full orchestra. The dismal subject of the two-note figure [which MacDonald dubs the

"Stalin" motive] is now raised by the horns and seconded by the violas, over another brooding pedal-point.... An opinionated bassoon now takes the floor ...[97]

Of course, one can no more disprove such commentary than prove it, though it should be noted in this particular case that Shostakovich was not, as MacDonald implies, present at any of the local Composers' Union discussions of "Muddle." Certainly, Shostakovich loved to satirize his foes. Marina Sabinina, for example, recalls him in 1950 sitting in the Conservatory from which he had been dismissed two years previously. As some professors walked past, he "started to imitate their smug, obsequious and fawning behavior, their pompous manners of speech."[98] And the deflation of bureaucratic self-importance through musical parody would form the very essence of works like *The Nose* or *Rayok*. Yet, it is one thing to identify an essential characteristic of Shostakovich's musical persona, quite another to use it as a yardstick, the filter through which all works are analyzed and evaluated. In *The New Shostakovich*, works would frequently be judged according to their "ironic" or "dissident" credentials. MacDonald would criticize the Eighth Symphony, for example, because he felt that the absolutely critical (for Shostakovich) element of satire was lacking, leaving the listener with only "tragic earnestness" and "howls of demented noise,"[99] descriptions that, ironically, came close to the Party-liner Viktor Belyi, who in 1948 had attacked the Eighth for its "repulsive" tendencies and its "urge to express one-sided tragic experiences."[100]

Ultimately, overly metaphorical interpretations of Shostakovich's music run the danger of simply replacing the crude old pro-Soviet "verities" with new, equally crude, anti-Soviet ones, while "agenda-based" criticism—does a piece of music stack up to the reviewer's pre-set criteria?—usually diminishes rather than enhances our view. It is an approach that Volkov claims to reject,[101] and one that Mac-Donald himself was apparently moving away from towards the end of his life. As Raymond Clarke points out in his posthumous revision of *The New Shostakovich* (2006), MacDonald acknowledged that he wrote the book primarily as a polemic, "a reaction against the rigidly conformist image of Shostakovich prevalent in the years preceding *Testimony*."[102] Whether such rigid conformism did in fact exist is highly arguable.[103] Nevertheless, Clarke, "reflecting [MacDonald's] own later wishes,"[104] would drop some of the more fanciful programmatic images, including the Fourth Symphony description quoted above, and tone down others, such as the critique of the Eighth Symphony, a work that MacDonald was beginning to warm to towards the end of his life.[105] Ironically, though, it was MacDonald himself who had wisely suggested in the original edition, "if the Shostakovich of 1973 is to be believed over the Shostakovich of 1937, the Fifth Symphony must speak for itself—with reference to its background, but without *depending* on it."[106]

A Multi-Layered Interpretation

In the end, any discussion about "meaning" must confront that essential, but almost impossible-to-answer question: what level of compatibility exists between audience reception and authorial intent? It is certainly fascinating and, it could be argued, productive to debate whether we hear in the Fifth Symphony's coda forced rejoicing, real rejoicing, agonized "wailing and writhing," as Vishnevskaya puts it, or perhaps even stoicism, "the determination of a strong man to BE," as Maxim Shostakovich has put it.[107] But are these multiple layers of meaning necessarily the result of specific, definable ambiguities manufactured by Shostakovich himself? Or have they simply accrued as a result of seventy years of audience reception? Shostakovich's friend Flora Litvinova recalls him in 1970 reflecting upon his music and how he had had to "resort to camouflage."[108] This would imply at least some "layering" on his part. But how much? Volkov, for one, believes that while Shostakovich's music is ironic, that irony is not the result of a contrived pro-Soviet/anti-Soviet layering: "No: he addressed himself as he felt, musically, and the resulting message was in itself ambiguous."[109] Or, as Gerard McBurney has put it, "The pressures that produce a musical language are far more subtle; they exist at a level of eruption."[110]

It is instructive to return to that prankish 1957 letter from Shostakovich to Glikman describing the celebrations in Odessa. Most commentary, including Glikman's own, focuses on the letter's satire. But there are other character traits that can be observed here. For example, the pedantic cataloging of the twenty-seven political luminaries can be read as a product of what Laurel Fay has dubbed Shostakovich's "actuarial streak,"[111] an obsession with counting, cataloging, and book-balancing, something that would manifest itself in things like his football diary in which he meticulously cataloged statistics of teams and results, an obsession that Iain Strachan believes may have extended to the manipulation of opus numbers, keys, and even musical phrase lengths in order to satisfy certain mathematical and numerological precepts—perfect squares, the Pythagorean 3-4-5 triangle, Fibonacci sequence, Gematria, etc.[112] Another Shostakovichian trait demonstrated in this letter is what Elizabeth Wilson has called a "morbid fascination, albeit abhorrence, with power and political intrigue,"[113] a trait manifested in his ability to remember the names, positions, and activities of even minor Party functionaries. And a third trait can be traced back to Shostakovich's association in the late 1920s with that troupe of anarchic intellectuals, the so-called Factory of the Eccentric Actor (FEKS), something of a former-day Monty Python. Among their interests—shared, incidentally, by Python—was something one might term "list" humor; the comic sketch that, stripped to its essentials, amounts to nothing more than a pedantic, pseudo-erudite list of objects, people, or places. Shostakovich, along with his friend Sollertinsky, delighted in such antics, and the fact that his beloved "list" humor could be so easily converted into a serious *Pravda*-style report would surely have been a source of delicious irony.

The letter to Glikman is, of course, a trifle, yet we have identified four currents of personality that may have collided (or, to use McBurney's term, "erupted") to create the letter: the satirization of *Pravda*, the "actuarial streak," the fascination with power, and FEKS-style "list" humor. Analyze a string quartet or a symphony, and the network of stimuli is more complex, the dangers of simplistic cause-and-effect ascriptions more obvious. A relatively simple example is the five-note horn call in the Tenth Symphony's third movement. In 1994, it was revealed to be a musical encoding of the name of Elmira Nazirova, a former student for whom Shostakovich had had something of an infatuation. Yet, prior to this discovery, it was generally considered to have been a quotation of one of Shostakovich's favorite works, the opening of Mahler's *Das Lied von der Erde*, a reference reinforced by the use of the same instrument as Mahler (the horn) and by the fact that Shostakovich's movement would end on that same strange tonic added-sixth chord (C-E-G-A) as *Das Lied*. Both interpretations provide fertile ground, yet "Elmira" has now become pre-eminent. One factor here is our natural tendency to reject, sometimes unthinkingly, older scholarship as it becomes apparently supplanted by the new. And "Elmira" satisfies to an even greater extent than *Das Lied* our yearning for specificity, our fascination with codes, not to mention the potential for a "romantic" linkage with Shostakovich's DSCH monogram, also present in this movement. Of course, this says more about us, the audience, than it does about Shostakovich or about the act of composition, for we will never be privy to the precise nature of the "eruption" that created this particular musical moment. And the real danger of forcing an "either/or" judgment is that we will miss the pun altogether, the idea that two important currents in Shostakovich's life could be so succinctly consolidated into one five-note motif, something that, once discovered, must surely have delighted that supreme ironist.

Considering the impact of "Elmira" upon previous perceptions of the movement, David Fanning asks:

> Does that mean that is what the music means? If so, what did it mean before? Nothing? Of course, it meant something and now it means something—expanded. But, apart from that musical pun, it means what it always meant, which is something strange, something which makes the music explore itself.... It's like a body in search of a soul. That hasn't changed. It's just that now we know a little more about what was on the composer's mind.... Anything a composer says about what was on his or her mind at the time is only a partial representation of the truth. And the truth comes out in performance and is untranslatable.[114]

The discovery of quotations and codes enriches our understanding of the Tenth Symphony. Or at least, it enriches our understanding of Shostakovich, for we cannot definitively assert that a composer's thoughts at the time of composition, whether simple or complex, necessarily equate either in part or in full to the "meaning" of the composition that subsequently emerges. Fanning's reference to the music "explor[ing] itself" alludes to the fact that the strangely disembodied Elmira/*Das Lied* horn call leads subsequently into the movement's most introspective, soul-searching area, a musing upon the first movement material from which it, the third movement, is derived; a literal searching for roots. One might characterize Fanning's observation as "internally programmatic," one that indeed tells a story, but a story that is intra- rather than extramusical, a story derived from the

Symphony's own structural and psychological processes, one enriched but not replaced by subsequent extramusical discoveries—formalism in the original and most meaningful sense of the word.

Let us end this brief discussion of multivalence by returning to that contentious Fifth Symphony coda and its infamous 252 repeated As that Vishnevskaya likened to "nails being pounded into one's brain." Those repeated As and the harmonic collisions that result as the melody in the trumpet and trombone hits B-flat (see Chapter 13) can be read in terms of political conflict, as Vishnevskaya and many others do, or they can be felt simply as gestures of musical conflict that cloud and provide agonizing tension to the D major ending. But recently, it has been suggested that the Fifth Symphony, a work that like the Tenth has come to be viewed for its lofty combination of high symphonism and political/philosophical statement, may also, like the Tenth, have had a female muse lurking in its background. In 1967, the musicologist Lev Mazel found a connection between the first movement's second subject and the refrain ("L'amour! L'amour!") of the Habanera from Bizet's *Carmen*.[115] In 2000, Alexander Beneditsky reported a more extensive network of *Carmen* references in the Fifth Symphony, and connected this to Yelena Konstantinovskaya, the student translator with whom Shostakovich had been having an affair in the mid-1930s. In 1936, the year before the Fifth Symphony, Konstantinovskaya had married the Spanish film director Roman Carmen, assuming his surname.[116] Furthermore, the Russian nomenclature for the note "A" is "lya" (derived from "la"), and it has been suggested that the 252 As in the finale's coda represent a reiteration of the name "Lyalya," the popular diminutive for Yelena, a form that Shostakovich himself is known to have used.[117]

Beneditsky concludes that the Fifth Symphony can be read as "a love song," one that reflects the "freedom to love" and, ultimately, "the freedom to be a human being."[118] If these observations are correct, our previous, already complex experience of the Fifth Symphony is enriched, though again, as with Elmira and the Tenth Symphony, it is not replaced. But more than that, these observations force us to consider a more complete picture of Shostakovich than our sometimes rather singular focus on the political aspects grants us. We are reminded that the *Lady Macbeth* scandal was not the only traumatic event for Shostakovich during the mid-1930s, and that his pain over an unattainable love may have infused the Fifth Symphony with as much of its pathos as his pain over his professional predicament or, indeed, the larger tragedy that was unfolding in the outside world.

CHAPTER 2

ON SHOSTAKOVICH

Personal Character

He never tried to seek revenge from anyone for what they had said about him and, in my view, this was the most appropriate behaviour, because the impact this had on people was much stronger than if he had taken some kind of action against them.[1] (Irina Shostakovich, composer's third wife)

I advise you to envy Mozart, Beethoven and Tchaikovsky. Yet to envy Koval, Muravlyov and so on is really not worth it, however lucky these wretches may be sometimes.[2] (Shostakovich to composer Edison Denisov)

I was astonished by Shostakovich's remarkable forbearance, as he listened to the remarks directed at him. He never objected, never complained about those who insulted him, and certainly he never protested to the authorities in charge, as did other composers. Unlike them, he generally appeared bewildered by praise, and the exaggerated enthusiasm of ladies simply annoyed him.[3] (Izrail Nestyev, musicologist)

He was a very punctual and reliable person. He never went in for excuses like: "I was late, the alarm didn't go off." If he said 9 o'clock, it was 9 o'clock.[4] (Galina Shostakovich, composer's daughter)

When we were still children he taught us the social code. We shouldn't telephone anyone after 10 o'clock in the evening or before 10 o'clock in the morning.... Just because someone said "Come and see us," it didn't mean we were invited. We should be invited for a certain day and at a certain time. Supposing he himself invited one of his friends for lunch, for example Khachaturian and his wife, the lunch would be relaxed, with jokes and laughter, but it couldn't go on and on: if it started at 3 pm, it should be over by 5 pm. And all of his friends understood this very well.[5] (Galina Shostakovich)

Back at home, he never used to walk about in pyjamas or a track-suit. He was always in a shirt and trousers when it was warm and wore a suit in winter. He had no casual clothes for wearing at home. I never remember seeing him in a dressing-gown, right up until the very end.[6] (Galina Shostakovich)

My father never failed to send ... greetings telegrams and birthday cards. He would always keep an eye on whether the postal service was working properly. Whenever we got to the dacha near Moscow, he would send himself a card to check that it arrived and also how long it took.[7] (Galina Shostakovich)

Dmitri Dmitriyevich only let it be known to his most intimate circle of friends that he listened to the BBC. I was always struck by a detail, typical of his punctiliousness: after listening, he was always careful to tune the radio back to the bandwave of Radio Moscow—just in case anybody bothered to check![8] (Venyamin Basner, composer and friend)

I sat next to him and he seemed to me the most nervous human being I've ever seen. He went through absolute hell under Stalin.... We would be there talking, and then he'd be very warm and friendly, and suddenly the head of what they call the Composer's Union would appear in the background and immediately he'd freeze up like that. I felt very badly and awfully touched, because I liked him.[9] (Roger Sessions, American composer)

His face was a bag of tics and grimaces: he would either twitch his lower lip, or unexpectedly blink, or keep correcting his glasses or stroke his hair, which, as a result, was in a state of permanent chaos. While talking, he would insert a lot of asides, "so to say," "a kind of," "you understand," which often had no connection at all with the sentence he was uttering at that given moment.... When he sat at his desk or at a table, he would always nervously drum at it with his fingers, or, pressing his left palm to his cheek, he would tap various rhythms with his fourth and fifth fingers.[10] (Krzysztof Meyer, Polish composer and musicologist)

He would write to me and be dying for me to reply, but whenever I turned up in person, after ten minutes he quite often asked me to leave. But then he would rush off down the street, write to me, or ring me up and tell me he had been looking for me....He couldn't talk to me quietly even for a moment. He would be constantly lighting cigarettes, getting up to open the window, sitting down again, and then getting up again to walk about. After a few minutes his complex personality would start to make me feel quite strange. (Elmira Nazirova, student of Shostakovich)[11]

It is difficult to choose the right word to define Shostakovich's gift for helping people discreetly. It was not just his tact, but his deep-seated fear of causing offence that qualified his charity.... My husband [Weinberg] once asked Dmitri Dmitriyevich if he could borrow a small sum of money.... They agreed that Weinberg would collect the sum from him the following afternoon at three. The next morning Dmitry Dmitriyevich rang to tell me that, as it happened, he himself would be in the vicinity of our flat, and to ask if I was going to be in. He arrived shortly, cash in hand. This was typical of his courtesy. He did not wish to humiliate anyone who had asked him for some favour; rather, he tried to save them from such embarrassment.[12] (Natalya Vovsi-Mikhoels, friend)

One day when we were out sightseeing, a so-called 'poet' who had had far too much to drink decided to attach himself to us. When he heard he was talking to Shostakovich, he immediately started to recite his poems to us. It was incredibly hot, and we should have left. Shostakovich was very uptight, and yet he stayed and listened to the very end, because he could not bring himself to hurt the man's feelings.[13] (Elmira Nazirova)

Can you imagine what Chekhov's reaction would have been had he known that his wife would expose him in front of honest people? She should be ashamed of herself, publishing all the intimate details of their life together. Chekhov was right in nicknaming her the Aktrissulya. What these actresses won't do to please the public ... [who] want to know whether the goings on in famous people's bedrooms are the same as in everybody else's, or whether they get up to something more inventive.[14] (Shostakovich, as quoted by Flora Litvinova, friend)

He is a frail, fragile, introverted and incredibly spontaneous and pure child.... He is [also] tough, caustic, probably strong, despotic and not very kind.... This is the combination you have to appreciate in him.... This is a wise man and, of course, a very genuine one.[15] (Mikhail Zoshchenko, poet and satirist)

I remember visiting him once at his home and finding a militiaman there who had come from Gorky.... When eventually the man left, Shostakovich spent nearly half an hour laughing and imitating his salutes, bows, and mannerisms.[16] (Krzysztof Meyer)

Tomorrow is my sixty-second birthday. At such an age, people are apt to reply coquettishly to questions such as "If you could be born over again, would you live your sixty-two years in the same way?" "Yes," they say, "not everything was perfect of course, there were some disappointments, but on the whole I would do much the same again." If I were ever to be asked this question, my reply would be: "No! A thousand times no!"[17] (Shostakovich to friend Isaak Glikman)

You ask if I would have been different without "Party guidance"? Yes, almost certainly. No doubt the line that I was pursuing when I wrote the Fourth Symphony would have been stronger and sharper in my work. I would have displayed more brilliance, used more sarcasm, I would have revealed my ideas openly instead of having to resort to camouflage.... But I am not ashamed of what I have written, I like all my compositions. "A child may be crippled and lame, but he's dear to his parents all the same."[18] (Shostakovich to Flora Litvinova)

Composing

An old hack will harp on about his "creativity" and his "unique personal themes." Shostakovich, on the other hand, is never offended when asked to write exactly one minute thirteen seconds of music, and when told that he must fade the orchestra to make way for dialogue at the twenty-fourth second, and bring it up again at the fifty-second to synchronize with a cannon shot. Art that is specially commissioned and functional does not necessarily have to be bad art![19] (Grigory Kozintsev, film director)

Any prelude and fugue by Bach can be played in any tempo, with any dynamic nuances or without them and it will be beautiful anyway. This is how music should be written, so that no rascal can spoil it.[20] (Shostakovich to an unknown correspondent)

Mitya had a natural facility and wrote very fast, but in addition he was incredibly hard working. He wrote out his music in full score straight away. He would then take his scores to lessons without having even played them through. I always found it amazing that he never needed to try things out on the piano. He just sat down, wrote out whatever he heard in his head and then played it through on the piano. He never demanded or appeared to need silence in order to compose.[21] (Zoya Shostakovich, the composer's younger sister)

I worry about the lightning speed with which I compose. Undoubtedly this is bad. One shouldn't compose as quickly as I do…. It is exhausting, rather unpleasant, and at the end of the day you lack any confidence in the result. But I can't rid myself of the bad habit.[22] (Shostakovich to composer Vissarion Shebalin)

My father always said, "I think long; I write fast."[23] (Maxim Shostakovich, composer's son)

Musical Analysis

I'm not generally very talkative. I don't like engaging in analysis and conversation about works I have heard, and I'm not good at it. All I do is listen to music that is presented to me. I either like it, or I don't. That's all.[24] (Shostakovich to Isaak Glikman)

"Critical Analysis" is a foreign concept to Shostakovich. If he likes the essential drift of a film, then, like an ideal spectator, he is so engrossed by the life of the screen that he cannot be distracted to formulate judgements in cold blood.[25] (Grigory Kozintsev)

Interpretation

No matter what I asked or suggested about the Sonata's text, Shostakovich always listened to my every word with his undivided attention and, as a rule, agreed with any new performance details which were new for him, and even those which went against his own notations in the score. Of course, these were relatively insignificant "corrections" of his masterful compositions. Nevertheless, many much less talented composers are also much less flexible. I recall, for example, that I asked him to allow a *crescendo* instead of the indicated *diminuendo* in the last bars of the Sonata's third movement—this was another of my interpretive attempts to "break away from the numbness." And Dmitry Dmitriyevich agreed to do so.[26] (Daniil Shafran, cellist)

[Shostakovich] allow[ed] their fantasy free play.... I was amazed how readily he accepted our interpretation, including my somewhat risky "imaginative" pedal techniques.[27] (Yevgeny Shenderovich, pianist)

These days I have given up consulting Dmitri Dmitriyevich about tempi. If I do he sits down at the piano and plays the passage almost twice as fast as it could possibly be correct to perform it.[28] (Yevgeny Mravinsky, conductor)

We composers always tend to play our music too fast.[29] (Shostakovich to Benjamin Britten)

"Mravinsky was conducting [Shostakovich's] Fifth Symphony.... After the performance Constantin Silvestri came up to Shostakovich in the conductor's room and asked what he thought about the tempo[s]. Shostakovich answered that the tempos were superb. Then, Silvestri showed him the score and said: "How come? The tempos indicated in the score do not match those in today's performance." Shostakovich answered somewhat sheepishly: "The tempos in my score are also correct ones."[30] (Gennady Rozhdestvensky, conductor)

Teaching

He had pupils of all kinds, including ones that were ignorant or without talent. He treated them with a gentle irony, but he never said a harsh word to them. Somehow he was able to affect them in such a way that even the most hopeless of them began to soar a little....You couldn't learn from him if you expected wrath and upbraiding; you had to listen carefully to his self-effacing remarks.[31] (Mikhail Meyerovich, composer)

Football (Soccer)

Shostakovich was a rabid fan. He comported himself like a little boy; leapt up, screamed, gesticulated.[32] (Mikhail Zoshchenko)

Shostakovich disliked bad temper, aggressive or foul play on the pitch. He loved it best when the game was open, honourable and chivalrous. He found intensely moving the selfless absorption and even ecstasy with which the great players strove to achieve the apparently impossible task of putting the ball between the posts. What attracted Shostakovich to football, I believe, was an idealized vision of the game.[33] (Isaak Glikman)

Shostakovich was a ... very keen and fussy referee. Once when the composers were playing particularly badly and the ball kept landing in the apple trees, [he] blew a sharp blast on his whistle. He said: "If you go on messing about like this, both teams will be disqualified for life."[34] (Rodion Shchedrin, composer)

CHAPTER 3

THE *TESTIMONY* DEBATE

It was Simon Karlinsky who first raised the question of *Testimony's* authenticity in November 1979, a month after the book's release:

> One is perplexed … to read two pages on Igor Stravinsky which are a verbatim repro-
> duction of a statement by Shostakovich published in the Soviet Union in 1973 in a
> collection of essays on Stravinsky edited by Boris Yarustovsky. Beginning identically,
> the texts in *Testimony* and in the collection of essays then diverge and go their separate
> ways. Similarly the section on Mayakovsky is almost identical with Shostakovich's
> brief memoir of him published in *Mayakovsky as Remembered by His Contemporaries*
> (Moscow 1963), except that the passages depicting the cordial contacts between the
> poet and the composer have been replaced in *Testimony* by memories of hostility and
> rudeness.[1]

The following year, Laurel Fay revealed five more recycled passages. Believing that it was "utterly inconceivable that the composer had memorized his previously published statements and then reproduced them exactly in his conversations with Volkov," Fay suspected foul play.[2] According to Volkov, Shostakovich had read the typescript, signing "Chital [Read]. D. Shostakovich" at the top of the first page of each chapter. Significantly, each of the seven recycled passages discovered between Karlinsky and Fay constituted the first page of its respective chapter (Chapters 2–8). In other words, the text above which Shostakovich's signature actually appeared was, in each case, a recycled passage. Was it possible, then, that Volkov had presented the composer with previously published articles for his approval and then replaced the main body of those articles (i.e., everything beyond the "approved" page 1) with new texts that he, Volkov, had fabricated? Fueling this theory was the fact that each of the recycled passages consisted entirely of blandly factual, uncontroversial material and corresponded to almost exactly one page of text, after which the chapter's tone would radically alter. (Admittedly, Fay was comparing the original Russian sources against *Testimony* as published in English, which made comparisons of page length somewhat approximate.) Fay also challenged the veracity of some of *Testimony's* content, and wondered whether Volkov, in the preface to the book, had not inflated his personal credentials vis-à-vis Shostakovich.

Connected to the question of authenticity was a debate over the book's genesis. At the time of *Testimony's* publication, the composer's widow, Irina, claimed that Volkov met Shostakovich on only "three maybe four occasions" and wondered how this could have elicited enough material for "such a thick book."[3] In 2000, she would restate this opinion: "They met on three occasions; each time the meetings lasted for two or two and a half hours, not more, for a longer talk tired Shostakovich."[4] Although Volkov, in his preface, did not state the number of meetings that he had with Shostakovich, his description of how the two men collaborated had certainly implied many more than three.[5]

Over the next two decades, debates about *Testimony* centered not so much on its authenticity—Fay's findings had come to be accepted as more-or-less conclusive—but rather to what extent a less than transparent presentation ultimately mattered. Some, like Malcolm Brown, Richard Taruskin, and Fay herself, took the view that a book processed from potentially contaminated data had to be rejected in its entirety as a matter of course, even if that meant the sacrifice of potentially valid and valuable material. But others, for example Ian MacDonald, concluded that the questions of provenance, troubling though they were, were not sufficiently critical to deflect from the book's "essential truth,"[6] a truth that would reveal itself even more strongly with the 1994 publication of Elizabeth Wilson's book, *Shostakovich: A Life Remembered,*[7] in which many ex-Soviets who had known Shostakovich presented pictures of him that, at the very least, sat a lot closer to *Testimony* than to the old, official Soviet view.

The subject of authenticity *per se* was not broached again until 1998. In their book, *Shostakovich Reconsidered*, Allan Ho and Dmitry Feofanov argued that Fay's doubts about Volkov's credentials and indeed some of her questions about *Testimony's* material and its genesis had arisen in some cases from a misreading of the text, and in other cases from a lack of proper perspective.[8] Countering Irina's statement that Shostakovich and Volkov had met on only three or four occasions, they cited Shostakovich's friend, Flora Litvinova, "who recalls the composer himself telling her that he had been meeting 'constantly' with a young Leningrad musicologist."[9] And, while acknowledging that the signatures in Chapters 2–8 do indeed appear over recycled material, Ho and Feofanov pointed to Chapter 1, where the composer's signature appears not over anodyne statements of the type that open the other chapters but over that unequivocal expression of contempt, a statement that could not possibly have been recycled from any official Soviet publication: "Looking back, I see nothing but ruins, only mountains of corpses."[10]

Ho and Feofanov answered many of Fay's charges and cleared up several misunderstandings. But there remained the issue of the seven recycled passages. Drawing on support from scholars in the field of memory study, they argued that for someone of Shostakovich's superior musical and verbal memory, an asset that had been well documented by those who knew him, the verbatim recitation of a page's worth of text from memory would not have been particularly remarkable. But was the issue in fact *Shostakovich's* memory? If Volkov had, as he put it, shaped his "mound of shorthand notes" into the chapters of *Testimony*,[11] then the way the text ultimately read was determined by Volkov, not Shostakovich. Only with reference to these shorthand notes, now unfortunately lost, might we have an inkling of how the finished typescript compared with the words as they came out of Shostakovich's mouth and, therefore, of how the recycled passages appeared: from Shostakovich himself, the conscious or possibly subconscious result of his extraordinary memory; or from Volkov's unscrupulous organization of the text.

For two decades, Volkov had kept silent, a decision that for many only added fuel to the suspicions he was hiding something. However, in 1999, with the authenticity debate now back in the spotlight, he made a rare public appearance. He declared once again that *Testimony* contained only first-hand material obtained directly from Shostakovich, and that the recycled passages would have been delivered to him as such by Shostakovich, the composer's extraordinary memory being the only plausible explanation. Volkov stated that although he had been working as an editor at *Sovetskaya muzyka* at the time of the *Testimony* interviews, he was not familiar with any of the previously published pieces, and that had he recognized them, he would not have used them. He also stated that the authenticating signatures were not his idea but Shostakovich's.[12]

In 2000, Laurel Fay was able to examine what she described as "an exact copy of the *Testimony* typescript used in making the published English translation," a copy now in the possession of the Shostakovich Family Archive in Moscow.[13] She discovered that Shostakovich's signature authenticating Chapter 1 does not in fact appear on the first page of the typescript but on the third. Moreover, handwritten repaginations that appear on this typescript suggest that the chapter had originally started there on page 3, and that the two pages that became pages 1 and 2 were added to the front later.[14] Thus, Shostakovich's signature had not been placed, as originally assumed, over the inflammatory material of what would become page 1 (the "mountains of corpses," etc.), but instead over what Fay discovered was yet another recycled passage, an excerpt from Shostakovich's dryly factual "Autobiography" of 1927, a piece that had been republished in *Sovetskaya muzyka* in 1966. In other words, it now appeared that in all eight of *Testimony's* chapters, Shostakovich's authenticating signatures had been placed exclusively over recycled material.[15] As already noted, Fay in 1980 had to conduct her comparisons using the published English version of *Testimony*. Now, with a Russian typescript, she was even more struck by the resemblance between it and the original sources:

> In seven cases out of eight, they reproduce exactly the layout and punctuation of their original published sources. Furthermore, the quoted material on these signed pages is confined to and precisely circumscribed by the length of a single typed page of the

Russian text. In every case, the direct quotation ceases abruptly—even breaking off in mid-sentence—the moment one turns to the next page. Beyond the first page, the texts diverge, sometimes radically.[16]

In their response (publication forthcoming), Ho and Feofanov question the provenance of Fay's Moscow typescript. They point out that copies of the original Russian typescript were circulated in 1979 by Harper & Row under strict conditions to a limited number of people: principally Henry Orlov, from whom Harper and Row had commissioned an authentication report;[17] and Antonina Bouis, Heddy Pross-Weerth, and Seppo Heikinheimo, translators of the American, German, and Finnish versions, respectively. Orlov, Bouis, Pross-Weerth, and *Testimony's* senior editor, Ann Harris, remember their copies as clean, with Shostakovich's signatures clearly at the start of chapters, and with no sign of repaginations, paste-ins, or handwritten alterations. However, Heikinheimo has admitted to having flouted Harper and Row's conditions by showing the manuscript to around fifty people, resulting in the creation of several unauthorized copies. Heikinheimo had already started editing the manuscript, and these copies bear his alterations. According to Ho and Feofanov, the Heikinheimo manuscript contains "the editorial emendations mentioned by Fay" and duplicates the non-textual marks that can be seen in Fay's published examples—"specks on the page, borders resulting from photocopying, etc." And the first signature in Heikinheimo's altered text appears, as it does in Fay's copy, on the third page of Chapter 1. Ho and Feofanov conclude: "Because of the very limited number of people who ever had access to the original typescript and the care with which it was handled, we believe that [Fay's] Moscow typescript is merely another copy of Heikinheimo's altered text."[18]

And so the mystery of *Testimony's* authenticity is, as of 2007, still ongoing. We now know more about the journey traveled by the original typescript and possibly by some of its (altered) derivatives. But the question of the recycled passages remains open. The claims and counterclaims about the book's genesis notwithstanding, there are, in the end, only two items of evidence that will help solve this mystery: 1) the original Russian typescript that was submitted by Volkov to Harper and Row; and 2) Volkov's shorthand notes made at the time of the interviews. The former was sold by Volkov in 1998 to a private collector. If it ever becomes available for examination, the relationship between it and the Moscow typescript examined by Fay will finally become clear. However, even this original typescript remains ultimately a secondary source, given that it was "shaped" from the shorthand notes. As previously stated, these notes are now lost. And the opportunity to come closer to Shostakovich's conversations with Volkov has probably been lost as well.

PART II

THE LIFE AND STYLISTIC EVOLUTION OF SHOSTAKOVICH

Michael Mishra

CHAPTER 4

YOUTH, REVOLUTION, AND FAME (1906–1926)

"I do not think it is of great interest to know which Gymnasium I went to, or what my marks were for Handwriting."[1] Thus wrote the twenty-year-old Dmitry Shostakovich. In fact, throughout his life the composer was reluctant to reminisce over his seemingly happy but, as he insisted, unremarkable childhood, and seemed bemused that anyone else would show the slightest interest. Certainly, his description of himself as unremarkable is backed up by his younger sister, Zoya, who describes a very normal, if occasionally dreamy, young boy:

> [Apart from his outstanding musical gifts], he was a normal boy, although somewhat reserved and introspective. He liked nature. He enjoyed going for strolls, but he was always listening to something. If we went mushrooming, it was me who found them and Mitya who picked them. He could stand right on top of a mushroom and not notice it. He was somewhat absent-minded. Yet he was a wonderfully kind and cheerful child. He was full of mischief and good spirits in the first years of his life, and indeed he remained so until they started beating the fun out of him.[2]

Shostakovich was born into the Russian liberal intelligentsia. His father, Dmitry Boleslavovich Shostakovich (1875–1922), had been an inspector at the Office of Weights and Measures. In 1908, he was hired to run the estates of his friend Adolf

Rennenkampf, but at the end of the First World War returned to Weights and Measures as its deputy director. The composer's mother, Sofya Vasilyevna Kokoulina (1878–1955), was a housewife and amateur musician. She had been a student at the St. Petersburg Conservatory and was her son's first piano teacher. Born on 25 September 1906 (12 September in the old style calendar), Dmitry Dmitriyevich was flanked by two sisters: Mariya (1903–1973), who would become a pianist and teacher, and Zoya (1908–1990), who became a veterinary scientist.

Amateur music making was a staple of the Shostakovich household, with Dmitry *père* often entertaining the family with gypsy romances. Yet, if his "Autobiography" of 1927 is to be believed,[3] the young Shostakovich drew little conscious inspiration from this. His interest in music may well have been piqued after attending a performance of Rimsky-Korsakov's *The Tale of Tsar Saltan* in early 1915, but the crucial factor appears to have been the commencement of piano lessons that summer. Not only would he prove prodigiously gifted on the piano, but within a year, he had penned his first composition, *The Soldier (Ode to Liberty)*, and over the next three years would write approximately thirty pieces, mainly for piano. Most were programmatic "poems" (*In the Forest, The Noise of the Train, Thunderstorm*, etc.), and a few were of contemporary topical interest—*The Soldier (Ode to Liberty)*, *Hymn to Freedom*, *Revolutionary Symphony*, and *Funeral March* ("In Memory of the Fallen Heroes of the October Revolution"). He also tried his hand at a mini-opera (*The Gypsies*, after Pushkin) and ballet (*Rusalochka*, after Hans Christian Andersen's *The Little Mermaid*). Later, in 1925, the nineteen-year-old Shostakovich would destroy nearly all of these compositions in what can only be interpreted as an attempt to close the door on his childhood.[4]

***

To what extent the eleven-year-old Shostakovich witnessed the tumultuous events of 1917, and to what extent he was conscious of their significance, is debatable. He was certainly present at the mass funeral procession held on 23 March to bury the victims of the February Revolution, that "bloodless" uprising that had resulted in Alexander Kerensky's short-lived liberal workers government in Petrograd. Sofya Shostakovich's sister, Nadezhda, recalls that "The Shostakovich family was there in the crowd and the children had climbed to the top of an iron fence surrounding an old churchyard."[5] As they made their way through the streets, mourners sang the revolutionary march, "You Fell a Victim," a tune that Dmitry reproduced at the piano on returning home that evening. Some time after that event, he wrote his *Funeral March* ("In Memory of the Fallen Heroes of the October Revolution"). In January 1918, following Lenin's dissolution of the Constituent Assembly (in which his Bolshevik delegates had been a minority), a peaceful gathering of protesters defending the Assembly was fired upon by Bolshevik troops. Later that month, Shostakovich played his *Funeral March* at a memorial service for the slaughtered.[6] In April, he would refer to it as his "Funeral March in Memory of Shingaryov and Kokoshkin," two democrats murdered in the January massacre.[7]

Shostakovich's relationship to other events, however, is less certain. For example, he claimed to have witnessed the slaying of a small boy by a policeman at a street demonstration during the February 1917 uprising, a sight that allegedly haunted him for the rest of his life; in 1927, he even dedicated an episode of the Second Symphony to the memory of that little boy. However, his school friend Boris Lossky disputes this, believing it impossible that Shostakovich's parents would have allowed their ten-year-old son onto the streets during an uprising. Lossky thinks that Shostakovich may have mentally appropriated an incident in which his older sister Mariya, returning from school, witnessed a demonstration in which a boy was slain by a policeman.[8] Also questionable is the claim that Shostakovich witnessed that iconic moment of the Revolution, Lenin's arrival at St. Petersburg's Finland Station on 3 April 1917 and his famous midnight speech atop an armored car, a story that would provide the composer with useful fodder decades later. His sister Zoya clearly recalls him running home "in raptures, saying that he had seen Lenin."[9] Again Lossky disagrees, insisting that the young Dmitry would not have been out on the streets that late,[10] although, as Elizabeth Wilson has suggested, he might have been accompanied on this occasion by his Bolshevik uncle, Maxim Kostrykin.[11] (Incidentally, the Shostakovich of *Testimony* acknowledges being present at the event, but appears to remember it only through second-hand reportage—"*They say* that the major event in my life was the march down to the Finland Station."[12] The slaying of the young boy is recalled more positively.)

Even more confusion prevails regarding Shostakovich's education, a confusion exacerbated by the renaming of schools under the new Bolshevik nationalization system. From 1915, he was a pupil at Mariya Shidlovskaya's school (officially known as The Commercial School), a relatively new institution catering to the children of the intelligentsia. According to his curriculum vitae written in 1926, he studied there until 1918, whereupon he transferred to Gymnasium No. 13 (the former Stoyunina Gymnasium) run by Boris Lossky's grandmother. In 1919, he transferred back to Shidlovskaya, now renamed School No. 108.[13] However, Shidlovskaya/School 108 had closed in 1919. More credible is Lossky's account. According to him, Shostakovich stayed at Shidlovskaya for one more year following its renaming in 1918. He then transferred to Stoyunina (which, confusingly, Lossky gives as Soviet School No. 10) in 1919, the same year he started at the Petrograd Conservatory, and studied concurrently at both institutions for what would appear to have been two years before finally giving up his general schooling to concentrate on music. Lossky also disputes the biographer Sofya Khentova's contention that Shostakovich was forced to leave Stoyunina, completing his general education at the School No. 8 while continuing to study at the Conservatory.[14]

***

During the post-Revolutionary period, students at the Petrograd Conservatory were placed according to musical level rather than age. Pursuing joint studies in piano and composition, the thirteen-year-old Shostakovich found himself with peers several years his senior. Yet he stood out, and not just because of his youth. His ability to absorb the precepts of four-part writing, keyboard harmony, and aural dictation was apparently extraordinary. Critical too was the interest taken in his composition by his piano teacher, Leonid Nikolayev, a far cry from the disparaging stance adopted by his former teacher, Ignaty Glyasser. An occasional composer himself, Nikolayev sought to cultivate in his piano students not just technical skill, but a holistic aesthetic understanding of music.

Shostakovich's official composition teacher was Maximilian Shteinberg, son-in-law of Rimsky-Korsakov and perpetuator-in-chief of the Rimskian tradition. A highly conservative figure, Shteinberg emphasized core academic values and discouraged experimentation. The relationship between teacher and student was mostly cordial and always respectful, but Shostakovich felt stifled by Shteinberg's narrowly academic approach. Responding to a questionnaire conducted in 1927, two years after his graduation in composition, he reflected upon his education:

> At the conservatory, they taught me "scheme," not "form."... [I was told], "once you've composed several principal and subordinate themes, we'll pick the best principal theme and make a transition to the best subordinate theme; and this way we will have an exposition." ... Not a word was uttered about the expressive character of the musical line, about relaxation, tension, and dialectical development. But the following answer came: given a principal and a subordinate theme, and if you have a tonic and know how to manage modulation and voice-leading, then the development will come very easily. I am now convinced that the development is indeed the hardest part of sonata form. Given the two themes (or theme groups), the exposition always has something of an architectonic structure, but the development must absolutely be dynamic and dialectical.[15]

In the end, Shostakovich's intellectual curiosity and his desire, manifested at a remarkably young age, to be beholden to no one school of thought or composition prompted him to supplement his formal academic experiences. He joined the so-called "Fogt Circle," a group of predominantly modernist composers (including Vladimir Deshevov and Pyotr Ryazanov) that met weekly during the early 1920s under the leadership of Vladimir Shcherbachov in order to share their works and explore contemporary foreign music. Ironically, it was Shcherbachov that the Conservatory would turn to in 1923 for help in reforming its composition department.

It was the poet Mayakovsky who perhaps best encapsulated the nation's cultural agenda during this period with his poems "Order to the Armies of Arts" (1918) and "Order No. 2 to the Armies of Arts" (1921). These utilitarian, pseudo-militaristic harangues exhorted artists to rid themselves of their bourgeois pretensions, their "fig leaves of mysticism": "Give it up! Forget it. Spit on rhymes and arias and the rose bush and other such mawkishness from the arsenal of the arts."[16] Its academic conservatism notwithstanding, the Conservatory was a vital hub of post-Revolutionary creative activity. Here, Mayakovsky's order to "Drag the pianos out onto the streets" was being taken literally at its word,[17] with small ensembles (including pianos) touring the city on lorries, stopping at factories or military barracks to give short performances.

The aftermath of the Revolution had witnessed the severest hardships. The city's limited fuel resources had been commandeered for military purposes, leaving the Conservatory unheated through the harsh winters; Leo Arnshtam once recalled a performance of Beethoven's Ninth Symphony where the singers engulfed themselves in a vaporous fog each time they opened their mouths, and in which "several formless layers of thermal underwear" were discernable underneath the conductor's tails.[18] Compounded by the year-round food shortages, these conditions took their toll on many students, not least the none-too-robust Shostakovich. In 1921, the Conservatory's director, Alexander Glazunov, and the composer's godmother, Klavdia Lukashevich, appealed, successfully, to Anatoly Lunacharsky, the head of the People's Commissariat for Enlightenment (Narkompros), for increased rations for the sickly teenager. Lukashevich wrote:

> From lack of nutrition—he almost never has any milk, eggs, meat, sugar, and only very rarely butter—our dear young boy is very pale and emaciated. He shows signs of nervous disorder, and what is more terrible, he has severe anaemia. The hard Petersburg autumn is approaching, and he has no strong footwear, no galoshes and no warm clothes.... He gets a school ration, the so-called "talented" ration, but lately it has been so miserable that it cannot possibly save him from hunger ... he is issued with two spoons of sugar and half a pound of pork every fortnight.[19]

It is important here to acknowledge Glazunov's efforts. Although no fan of Shostakovich's music—he once described it as "revolting"—he nevertheless realized the young man's extraordinary potential.[20] For his part, although he never considered Glazunov a great composer, Shostakovich never forgot his kindness and vision, and spoke of him always with affection.

***

It has long been believed that Shostakovich's first opus under Shteinberg's tutelage was the Scherzo for Orchestra, op. 1, and that it was composed in the autumn of 1919, within weeks of his admission to the Petrograd Conservatory. However, recent research suggests that it may actually have been written almost two years later in 1921.[21] This would place it after the Eight Preludes for Piano, op. 2, and make it roughly contemporaneous with the Theme and Variations for Orchestra, op. 3 (1921). Regardless of its exact composition date, the somewhat dry and sequence-bound nature of the Scherzo gives it away as the work of a student, albeit a talented one. The same can be said for the Theme and Variations, with its conservative theme (a regularly phrased twenty-four bar melody with the occasional Schubertian harmonic tinge) and its somewhat predictable transformations—the theme audibly close to the surface most of the time. Yet, it is a more ambitious piece than the Scherzo and explores a wider palette of texture and style. Shostakovich had been very taken with the music of Tchaikovsky during this period, something that comes out in the delicately chattering woodwind (reminiscent perhaps of an early Tchaikovsky symphony) in the second variation, or in the rumbustious scoring of the finale. One oddity, given the rhythmic squareness that pervades most of the piece, is the mixed meter effect in the dance of variation 10 (Fig. 28; also in the coda). Notated in a 12/16 time signature, each bar is asymmetrically divided into 5/16 plus 7/16. Although mixed meter would become a common enough sight in Shostakovich, the rather Bartókian manner with which it is employed here, with asymmetrical divisions operating within an otherwise regular time signature, is unusual and not a path that Shostakovich would pursue further. The perfumed romanticism of variation 11 (reminiscent of Szymanowski or Suk) would represent another cul-de-sac. In fact, apart from a brief moment of multi-part string *divisi* in variation 5 (Fig. 13), the work portends very little, stylistically, of the future Shostakovich. He himself described it as "completely unsuccessful" and too heavily indebted to Glazunov.[22] Nevertheless, the theme-and-variations form would preoccupy Shostakovich for much of his career. Later in life, his advice to young composers was inevitably, "Begin with some variations."[23]

In the *Three Fantastic Dances*, op. 5, for piano, composed between 1920 and 1922, we start to hear some of the quirky wit and flare for characterization that would soon become a staple of Shostakovich, even if the musical style itself is not yet developed. In fact, the main melody of the first dance has more than a whiff of Spain about it, sounding not unlike a Turina or Albeniz miniature.

The *Two Fables of Krylov*, op. 4, (1922) shows the emergence of a more individual voice, one that explores beyond the basic functionalism of the earlier pieces and that, more than any work prior to the watershed First Symphony, ventures onto the periphery of "real" Shostakovich. In the second song, "The Ass and the Nightingale," the fifteen-year-old already shows his feel for irony. Following the *echt*-Russian introduction (foreshadowing parts of the Thirteenth Symphony or *The Execution of Stepan Razin*), the ass declares to the nightingale: "They say you've got a great talent for singing. I'd very much like to hear you sing."[24] In Shostakovich's setting, the ass makes his plea in a lumbering monotone, with the none-too-discreet accompaniment of that most unlovely of beasts, the contrabassoon, an instrument that Shostakovich would turn to in the future for moments of gruff satire. Meanwhile, the nightingale begins to "display her artistry" and "fill the glade with dainty trills" with a shimmering delicacy not usually associated with Shostakovich. With hindsight, this song—with the ass judging the artistry of the nightingale—seems eerily prescient of Shostakovich's own experiences of life under the Soviet regime. (Coincidentally, Mahler's song "Lob des hohen Verstandes" ("In Praise of Lofty Intellect") from *Des Knaben Wunderhorn* had used a similarly surreal conversation and competition between animals to satirize the judgments of philistines.)

***

In 1922, tragedy hit the Shostakovich family with the death of Dmitry senior from pneumonia. He was forty-seven. The composer's mother, Sofya, was forced to find work, but her periods of employment would be short-lived. Things got worse still in the spring of 1923 when Shostakovich was diagnosed with lymphatic tuberculosis. He was, nevertheless, able to play his graduation recitals in June, with his neck still bandaged, though the conductor Nikolai Malko notes that Shostakovich failed to answer a single question in the statutory political ideology exam.[25] The rest of the summer was spent convalescing at the Black Sea resort of Gaspra, a trip financed by the sale of one of the family pianos. There, he enjoyed the therapeutic effects of the warmer climate, the sea air, and not least, his first girlfriend,

Tatyana (Tanya) Glivenko. Although their physical separation—Glivenko lived in Moscow—ensured that future encounters were relatively sporadic, their relationship would last at least until her marriage to another man in 1929, possibly even until the birth of her first child in 1931. It was to Glivenko that Shostakovich dedicated his short, romantically lyrical, First Piano Trio, op. 8 (1923).

Some insights into the late-teenage Shostakovich can be gleaned from his letters to both Glivenko and his mother, though, not untypically for an adolescent, opinions could change drastically from one week to the next. One minute, the seventeen-year-old expresses disgust to Glivenko over "pornographic" trends in modern ballet;[26] two weeks later, he is deriding Tolstoy's plea for chastity in *The Kreutzer Sonata* as "filth."[27] His feelings on love, sex, marriage, and family reveal a tantalizing mix of traditional and progressive values, as witnessed in this 1923 letter to his mother:

> Love is truly free. Promises made at the altar are the worst thing about religion. Love can't last forever. Of course the best thing imaginable would be a total abolition of *marriage*, of all fetters and duties in the face of love. But that is utopian, of course. Without marriage there can be no family, and that really does spell disaster. But at any rate that love should be free—that much is indisputable. And Mother dear, I want to warn you that if I ever fall in love, maybe I won't want to marry. But if I did get married and if my wife ever fell in love with another man, I wouldn't say a word; if she wanted a divorce, I would give her one and I would blame only myself.... But at the same time there exists the sacred calling of a mother and father. So you see, when I really start thinking about it my head starts spinning. Anyway, love is free![28]

Shostakovich's late-teenage political views are equally hard to pin down. The earlier letters to Glivenko (1923–1924) suggest, often in the brusquely intolerant manner typical of that period's youth, a certain Revolutionary orthodoxy. He sympathizes with the plight of German Communists and chastises the selling-out of Revolutionary values at home under the New Economic Policy (NEP).[29] Such sentiments more or less disappear by about 1925, but, as Ian MacDonald points out, between 1923 and 1925, Shostakovich had endured a certain amount of jealousy from his fellow Conservatory students—there was even a move to have his financial assistance removed—and there may well have been an element of self-protection about these expressions of political orthodoxy. But inconsistency can be found even here. One moment, he solemnly bemoans the death of Lenin; shortly after, he is mocking the cultism that had turned the city of Peter (St. Petersburg/ Petrograd) into the city of Lenin (Leningrad) by addressing two letters from "St. Leninburg,"[30] and musing in a third, "If I become as great a man as Lenin, when I die will the city be named Shostakovichgrad?"[31] Of course, what Shostakovich was deriding was the cult of Leninism rather than Lenin himself; as MacDonald points out, "such disapproval could have been made from almost anywhere on the political spectrum."[32] But in the prevailing climate, even these gently ironic digs at the cult of Leninism may have rendered Shostakovich a political "unreliable."

***

Upon his return home from his Black Sea convalescence, Shostakovich pursued his playing career while continuing his studies in composition. He also made his debut as a cinema pianist in December 1923.[33] In the spring of 1924, he applied for admission to the postgraduate piano course at the Leningrad Conservatory, but was turned down. Precisely why is unclear—the official reason was "immaturity." Although Nikolayev generously offered to continue teaching him privately, *gratis*, Shostakovich viewed the Conservatory's rejection as his opportunity to free himself altogether from the pedantic Shteinberg and promptly applied to the composition department at the Moscow Conservatory. Nikolai Myaskovsky was certainly no radical, but the department that he headed in Moscow was considerably more progressive than Shteinberg's. Shostakovich was overjoyed that the Moscow professors accepted his Piano Trio in lieu of the sonata form exam and admitted him straight into the Free Composition class, something he believed the "stupid formalists" in Leningrad would never have done.[34]

That the move to Moscow did not, in the end, take place can be put down to the relationship between Shostakovich and his mother. In truth, although he loved her dearly, part of him had relished the chance to escape from her fretting and occasionally domineering manner. But in the two years since the death of his father, he had come to see himself as her protector. The dedication of his career, in part, to his mother's welfare can be seen in his letters to her, which were frequently peppered with such phrases as "Don't you worry, Mother. We are going to have a good life."[35] With the move to Moscow abandoned, Shostakovich continued in the composition class in Leningrad. In the autumn of 1924, he embarked on the task assigned to the 1925 graduating class: a symphony. In the winter, he resumed on a more regular basis the cinema employment that he had tried in 1923. It was work he would quickly come to detest.

April 1925 saw a second attempt to move to Moscow, though for different reasons. By this time, the allure of the "old" professors of the Moscow Conservatory had evaporated, Shostakovich now describing Myaskovsky as "tak[ing] the cake when it comes to gloominess,"[36] an opinion that the volatile eighteen-year-old would again change within a few months. His feelings towards "the horrid town of Moscow" were not entirely favorable either. For Shostakovich, the city's "stuffy streets," and "wretched little Moscow river and its church of Christ the Savior" paled in comparison to the splendor of his hometown. His negative impression of Moscow was only reinforced after a concert of his works given there on 24 March 1925 met with a mixed reception.[37] However, he had by this time built up a small support network of contemporary Moscow musicians—Vissarion Shebalin, Mikhail Kvadri, and Lev Oborin, amongst others. It was Kvadri, for example, who introduced him to Marshal Mikhail Tukhachevsky, a national figure (and an amateur violinist and violin maker) who would become one of Shostakovich's chief supporters during the late 1920s and early 1930s. But the main attraction was a figure whom Shostakovich first met during that March 1925 visit, the "scientific theorist" and composer Boleslav Yavorsky.

Yavorsky represented the very opposite of Shostakovich's world. His musical ideas (e.g., his concept of "modal rhythm"), cultural outlook, and bohemian, homosexual lifestyle were all eye-openers to the musically and socially conservative young composer. The Shostakovich family may have been of liberal-minded, *intelligent* stock, but they remained traditional in matters of behavior and lifestyle. Shostakovich himself admitted to being "infected by conservatism," and valued the efforts of Yavorsky ("the only real musician in Moscow and Petrograd—the only ray of light in the darkness of the modern musical world") to rid him of it.[38] Ian MacDonald notes:

> In the months after his meeting with Yavorsky, his letters [to Glivenko] become lighter, more scabrous and, on sexual subjects, easier-going. At the same time, he reports himself casting off his conservative traits and "becoming more of a modernist" (a key composition for him in this respect being the Scherzo from [the Prelude and Scherzo for String Octet] op. 11). By 1926, the transformation is complete: he is enjoying Ehrenburg's picaresque satires, reading erotic French novellas, and teasing Tanya with tales of his sexual conquests."[39]

This second attempted move to Moscow was also aborted, once again out of consideration for his mother. But Yavorsky had made his mark. At the start of 1925, with three movements of the symphony composed, Shostakovich had been floundering. His medical ailments, his depression over the serious illness of his friend Volodiya Kuvcharov, and the pressures of cinema work (which included having to sue the manager of the Bright Reel for non-payment) were all conspiring against him. But his encounters with Yavorsky in March had revived his spirits. Upon his return home from Moscow, work proceeded quickly on the finale. The symphony was presented to the Conservatory faculty in May and was fully orchestrated by July.

***

Although hardly modernistic, Shostakovich's First Symphony challenged head-on the didactic style of Shteinberg. The composer at one point even described it as a "symphony-grotesque," possibly to spite his teacher who had frequently criticized his fondness for grotesquerie.[40] The work possesses a Stravinskian spareness of utterance and sonority, with tutti passages brighter and less weighted than they would later become. The humor is quick, pointed, and quirky, though without the heavy satire that would become part of Shostakovich's armory by the decade's close, or the grim irony that would come later still. Specifically, it is the Stravinsky of *Petrushka* that comes to mind, with its quasi-balletic waltzes (cf. Shostakovich's first movement second theme) and its piano obbligato. Unlike Stravinsky's ballet about a puppet, Shostakovich's First Symphony carries no program, but there is a cartoon-like quality to many of its gestures, particularly in the first two movements: the opening, for example, with its furtive duet of hide-and-seek between the trumpet and bassoon, its mock-dramatic pauses, and its scurrying pizzicato figures; or the opening of the scherzo, with the lumbering double basses comically arriving at their destination a beat or so after the cellos, despite having started at the same time and playing the same music. It is no surprise that the filmmaker Mikhail Tsekhanovsky would later ask Shostakovich to compose the soundtrack for his cartoon *The Tale of the Priest and His Servant Balda*.

This cartoonish skittishness is also reflected by a mercurial approach to tonality. Throughout the first movement's relatively long introduction, all hint of tonic is avoided. When we finally "settle" into the first theme (Fig. 8), a semblance of the advertised F minor is obtained, but this wry little march continues to wriggle in and out of barely hinted keys. The second theme waltz may be more stable tonally, with a very classical relative major (A-flat) relationship to the first theme. But it is less settled metrically; it is notated to make the second beat of the bar feel like the first, which in turn results in a jolt when the waltz's final four bars, a chattering staccato eighth-note figure, assumes a "normal" metrical placement (Fig. 14, b5).

That the short development section is emotionally less momentous than developments in the later symphonies is no surprise given Shostakovich's inexperience and the movement's relatively lightweight source material. Yet, it does provide a satisfying intensification over the exposition. Shostakovich may have rued his teacher's emphasis on "scheme" rather than "form," but it would not appear to have stymied his ability to create a genuinely "dynamic and dialectical" symphonic development. One characteristic often found in the developments of the later symphonies is a canonic presentation of exposition material, usually towards the development's climax, and usually in the brass (e.g., Fifth Symphony, first movement, Fig. 32, b4; fourth movement, Fig. 11, b2). Although this does not quite happen here in the First Symphony, the short passage at Fig. 29, a canonic presentation of the introduction in the trumpets, violins, and woodwind, does provide a brief foretaste.

Another foreshadow of Shostakovich's later symphonies is the reverse-order recapitulation. The movement's introduction and its two main themes (Figs. 8 and 13) are recapitulated in palindrome—second theme (Fig. 32), first theme (Fig. 38), introduction (Fig. 43)—giving the movement as a whole an arch shape. The only kink in the palindrome is a brief, four-bar, pseudo-reprise of the first theme (albeit in D minor; Fig. 30, b2) as the development subsides in preparation for the reprise of the second theme at Fig. 32. (In later symphonies, such distortions to the palindrome will have a more profound effect, creating a more complex tension between the progressive/sonata and regressive/palindrome/arch forces—see Chapter 13.)

The second movement scherzo is based on the traditional three-part model (scherzo-trio-scherzo). The trio theme, a remote, almost chant-like melody for flutes, returns as a crazed, high-kicking burlesque towards the end of the scherzo reprise. This procedure, namely the reprise of a trio theme modified to the scherzo environment, would be employed by Shostakovich in several later scherzos, e.g., the Fourth and Sixth Symphonies. If the First Symphony's first two movements reflect the teenage Shostakovich and his love of Stravinsky, they also bring to bear the influence of Shostakovich the cinema pianist: the pauses-for-effect, the quasi-improvisational character of the Symphony's introduction, and, in the scherzo, the presence of the piano itself. In fact, Shostakovich had used a piano obbligato in the work he had completed immediately prior to starting on the Symphony, the second orchestral Scherzo, op. 7. With a feel for the grotesque not found in the earlier Scherzo op. 1, op. 7 could be viewed as a warm-up to the First Symphony in general and to its scherzo in particular. In both works, Shostakovich relies heavily on simple parallel octave textures in the piano, a characteristically brittle sonority that would later predominate in his two piano concertos.

Commentators often point to a stylistic divide between the Symphony's first two movements and its last two. Certainly, the slow third movement places us in a world neither explored nor predicted by the Symphony's first half. The Tchaikovskian oboe melody and the Brahmsian string figurations that accompany it have no parallel elsewhere in this, or indeed any other Shostakovich symphony. This unusually romantic spirit lasts at least until the movement's first climax, and is heard most powerfully in the lead-up to Fig. 4, where a passionately reaching violin melody, a slow, tense, chromatically descending bass line, and throbbing horn sextuplets combine in a moment of unashamedly Tchaikovskian pathos. Similarly, the military-funereal fanfare heard in the trumpet and snare drum immediately before Fig. 3 functions like a Tchaikovskian "fate" motif, recurring ever more ominously as the movement progresses.

If the plaintive oboe is given the lead in the slow movement and in the slow introduction to the finale (the latter doubled by the flute), the clarinet, which had opened the main portions of the first and second movements, takes back control to launch the whirlwind main theme of the finale. Yet, for all its dash and its building of orchestral momentum, the attempt to create a dazzling finale is constantly frustrated, persistently undercut by one intrusion or another. The entire operation is eventually brought to a screeching halt; at Fig. 35, the timpani hammers out, unaccompanied, an inverted version of the third movement's fanfare figure. The remainder of the movement represents a return to the pathos and, later on, the material of the third movement. As for the last-minute F major fanfares at the Symphony's close, these are more blusterous than triumphant, and are swiftly axed down by the work's final gesture—a short, decisive unison F (the "majorness" taken away) in only the lower instruments.

Although there is an emotional and, to some extent, stylistic divide between the Symphony's two halves, there are also unifying factors. A descending three-note chromatic motive, often extended and/or inverted, generates nearly every main theme in the Symphony. And although the more modernistic orchestral textures of the first half cede for the most part to more traditionally romantic textures in the second, the use of trumpet and percussion-dominated fanfares in all four movements, as well as the piano in three movements, provides at least some consistency of sound world.

The First Symphony was clearly Shostakovich's breakthrough. It was his first "individual" piece, unencumbered by the academicism of Shteinberg or Glazunov. It stood in relation to his conservatory training rather as his film accompanying— loved by some for its fresh, improvisational style, and detested by others for the same reason—stood in relation to the prefabricated mood-pieces that were then the cinematic norm. It looked forward to its successors in ways already described, but would ultimately prove to be a unique statement, capturing some sound worlds that would never again be explored by Shostakovich—the eerily magical combination of violins (open strings plus harmonics), triangle, and low-register piano at the end of the scherzo being perhaps the most striking. When he did look over his shoulder, it was not to his "grandfather *in academe*," Rimsky-Korsakov (apart, perhaps, from the strange inclusion of that Rimskian relic, the contralto trumpet in F), but to the archrival of the Rimsky clan, Tchaikovsky. Later, the cellist Mstislav Rostropovich would report that, as a teacher in the 1940s, Shostakovich preached the virtue of "pure" sounds *à la* Tchaikovsky over the "mixed" sounds favored by Rimsky-Korsakov.[41]

***

The Symphony was presented to the Conservatory during the summer of 1925, but it would be almost a year before its famous public unveiling. Worryingly for Shostakovich, the intervening period saw no new composition. He fretted that his symphony would turn out to be a five-minute wonder and that he would be condemned to a life of cinema work, becoming "a musical machine able to portray at the drop of a hat 'happy meetings of two loving hearts'."[42] Of course, for a student graduation piece to receive any kind of public premiere outside the confines of the Conservatory, let alone a venue as lavish as the Leningrad Philharmonic, was highly unusual. But, upon the recommendations of Shteinberg and Yavorsky, the conductor Nikolai Malko promised at least to consider the Symphony. Impressed by what he saw, Malko agreed to take it on.

Although almost beside himself with excitement, Shostakovich kept his nerve and sense of purpose, rejecting the concerns of Malko and Shteinberg over tempi and orchestration, even testing some of the tempi out on professional musicians to establish their playability.[43] He also rejected Glazunov's advice to re-harmonize the distinctive cadential progression in bars 5–8 in the first movement. At first, he agreed to the change ("Of course, I did not dare argue, my respect and love for Glazunov were too great, and his authority was indisputable"), but shortly before the first rehearsal changed it back, much to Glazunov's displeasure.[44] As Malko later wrote: "The fact is that he knew exactly what he wanted when he wrote his score. The first sounds that issued from the orchestra confirmed the correctness of his imaginations, and he had no reason to make any fuss."[45] It was only later that Malko observed "something in his make-up, stemming from his unsettled and nervous nature, that seemed to interweave his dignity and his bright and observant mind with a petty and silly vanity, mischievousness, and a bent for tomfoolery."[46]

The Symphony's premiere on 12 May 1926 was a sensation. The scherzo was encored, and the nineteen-year-old Shostakovich, who had not slept the previous night, was almost dizzy with disbelief. For the rest of his life, the composer would celebrate three days each year: his birthday, New Year's Day, and 12 May. Within a year of the premiere, the Symphony was published, and within two years it had been taken up by Bruno Walter and the Berlin Philharmonic and by the

Philadelphia Orchestra under Leopold Stokowski. If the First Symphony brought any grief for Shostakovich, it was over his relationship with the man generally considered Russia's leading musicologist and supporter of new music, Boris Asafyev. Initially, Asafyev had shown interest, but constantly turned Shostakovich away on the pretext of being too busy. (Shostakovich's fear of rejection—a fear that made him unable to directly ask Malko to consider his symphony, despite the fact that he was actually in Malko's conducting class at the time—stemmed largely from this experience.) Asafyev did eventually support the work, but then stayed away from the premiere because of an apparent disagreement with Yuliya Veisberg, the head of the concert's sponsoring organization, the Leningrad Association for Contemporary Musicians (LASM)—Veisberg's cantata, *The Twelve*, was also on the program. For Shostakovich, Asafyev's vanity was unforgivable: "Not to come and hear my symphony *on principle* because of his relationship with Veisberg, and so on, is the height of stupidity and formalism."[47] Relations between the two would be superficially repaired, but Asafyev's seemingly opportunistic attacks on Shostakovich, both in 1936 and 1948, would cause the composer later to remark, "I have met many good people and many bad people in my life, but never anybody more rotten than Asafiev."[48]

CHAPTER 5

THE MODERNIST AND THE ICONOCLAST (1926–1931)

If Shostakovich's compositional flame had waned somewhat between the First Symphony's completion in July 1925 and its premiere the following May, the second half of 1926 would witness a resuscitation of his creative energy. Although a couple of attempts to write a piano concerto came to nothing,[1] October saw the completion of his First Piano Sonata. Also that autumn, Shostakovich was admitted to the Leningrad Conservatory's postgraduate course in composition, though his study was more nominal than actual; the submission of an annual report was all that was required to keep his student status active and enable him to draw his stipend, which he continued to do for the next three-and-a-half years. He also took up a part-time position teaching score-reading at the Central Music Technicum, a school run by some of his old Fogt Circle friends.

***

With hindsight, we have come to view Shostakovich's First Symphony both as a unique document of his youth and as a piece that over the long term influenced works such as the Fourth and Fifth Symphonies. But in the short term, the First bore little fruit. Over the next couple of years, Shostakovich would relinquish that mix of Tchaikovskian romanticism, circus grotesquerie, and indeed any of the trappings of traditional symphonism contained in his First Symphony, and explore instead the path of high modernism. The second of the Two Pieces for String Octet, op. 11, provided some clues, but the new direction was confirmed in the two piano works that followed: the single-movement First Piano Sonata, op. 12 (1926) and *Aphorisms*, op. 13 (1927).

Prokofiev's Third Piano Sonata (1917) had been making the rounds in Leningrad at about this time—indeed, it had been in Shostakovich's own repertoire since his conservatory days. Prokofiev's heavy motoric rhythms (e.g., the 12/8 meter of his first movement) and dissonant harmonies clearly influenced Shostakovich in his almost self-consciously virtuosic Sonata. As Ronald Stevenson has put it, Shostakovich's Sonata is almost a celebration of the piano as machine, a *Hammerklavier* manufactured by "carpenters and engineers," one that glories in "pounding chords and slashing *glissandi*."[2] (At his first demonstration of the work to friends, Shostakovich reportedly injured his finger, leaving blood stains on the keys.[3]) The most glaring "pounding chord" is a cluster containing the consecutive pitches A, B-flat, B, C, C-sharp, and D reiterated, tremolo, right before the start of the *Lento* (bars 205–208). At the end of this tremolo pounding, the cluster, located just below the bass staff, chimes out in all its cavernous murk. But the sound is neither stopped nor allowed to decay naturally. Rather, Shostakovich specifies a controlled *diminuendo* through repeated pedal changes, creating a "wah-wah" effect. Stephenson points to two putative influences here: the American composer Henry Cowell and the Russian-American Leo Ornstein, both of whose music was known in Russia in the mid-1920s.

The Sonata would represent Shostakovich's one and only engagement with the Prokofiev-like rhythmic-constructivist aspect of 1920s modernism. Yet that influence of Prokofiev, even Prokofiev at his most hard-hitting, actually attenuates the Sonata's modernism to a degree. There are several places where a tonal reference can be felt, no matter how fleeting or ambiguous. As David Fanning points out, for example, each of bars 21–25 of the first movement, though thoroughly atonal, starts with C major harmony.[4] Meanwhile, the *Lento* even contains a semblance of melody, albeit reminiscent of Scriabin or, at times, Prokofiev at his most acidic. That the Sonata perplexed its audiences is understandable, especially in the light of expectations raised by the First Symphony. Nevertheless, both it and the brutally terse and sardonic character pieces that comprise *Aphorisms* stop short of the unbridled modernism that Shostakovich would unleash in his Second Symphony and his opera, *The Nose*.

***

Back in March, Shostakovich had decided to quit his cinema position, mainly because he detested the work itself, but also because it had become an impediment to his piano career. In what could have been a significant boost to that career, he was selected as one of five pianists representing the USSR at the First Chopin International Piano Competition in Warsaw in January 1927. However, his disappointment at receiving only an "honorable mention" at the competition (something he later blamed on an attack of appendicitis that he suffered on the eve of the competition and that plagued him through the course of the event) was a major factor in his eventual decision to concentrate on composition. (Incidentally, permission to travel to Poland had depended on his passing a newly mandated Marxist Methodology exam. Having failed a similar exam in 1923, he was apprehensive, though he clearly considered the whole thing a joke, telling Yavorsky that "The Exam in ~~Holy Scriptures~~ Marxist Methodology ... fills me with horror, because I am almost sure I won't pass it."[5] During the exam, Shostakovich was disqualified after he and another student burst into laughter while a third candidate attempted to answer a question on the social and economic differences between

Liszt and Chopin. He was allowed to re-sit, and pass, the exam the next day. At his request, the student whose exam he had sabotaged was also allowed to re-sit.)

With its lack of audience appeal, the Piano Sonata hardly helped to improve the dire family finances, which had already been set back by Shostakovich's retirement from the cinema and which was now looking still more vulnerable as he became increasingly pessimistic about his piano career. It was under these circumstances that he accepted a commission in March 1927 from Lev Shulgin of Agitotdel to create a work celebrating the upcoming tenth anniversary of the Revolution.[6] The result, replete with "Happy Birthday" quotation,[7] was the *Symphonic Dedication "To October,"* redesignated a few years later as the Second Symphony ("Symphonic Dedication: 'To October'"). The Symphony would employ a single-movement design comprising a longish orchestral prelude and a short choral finale, a formula that was quite common for this type of dedicatory work.[8]

The period's two prevailing cultural currents were experimentalism and proletarianism. Representing the former, the Moscow-based Association of Contemporary Musicians (ASM) advocated Western-style modernism, yet also fought for the preservation of the Russian and European high-art tradition. Founded in 1923, and initially affiliated to the International Society for Contemporary Music, its members included radicals, such as Mosolov and Roslavets, as well as more conservative composers, such as Myaskovsky. Later, the independent Leningrad ASM (LASM) attracted figures as diverse as Shteinberg, Shcherbachov, and Shostakovich—though Shostakovich, soon fed up with the organization's infighting and inbred leadership ("an object lesson in how the heirs of Rimsky-Korsakov snatch at power"[9]), resigned after only a few months, following Shcherbachov into the rival Circle for New Music. At the opposite pole stood the three proletarian musical organizations: the Russian Association of Proletarian Musicians (RAPM, founded 1923); the Association of Revolutionary Composers and Musical Workers (ORKiMD, founded 1924); and the Production Collective of Moscow Conservatory Students (Prokoll, founded 1925). RAPM was the best known of the three, and the most politically powerful, but it was Prokoll that would come to boast the leading composers of the proletarian movement—Viktor Belyi, Alexander Davidenko, Marian Koval, and Boris Shekhter—at least until 1929, when the four defected to RAPM.[10] Though infighting was rife here too (ORKiMD, for example, was founded as a breakaway group by certain disgruntled RAPM members) and though the three groups did not necessarily agree on their methods (Prokoll, in particular, viewed itself as the purveyor of more sophisticated music than either RAPM or ORKiMD), they were, broadly speaking, fighting towards the same goals: the elimination of "rightist," "anti-Revolutionary" bourgeois influences (i.e., the high-art traditions that ASM was fighting to preserve), the creation of specifically proletarian musical forms (principally the mass song), and the extension of proletarian philosophy into the fields of musical criticism and music education. Complicating matters still further, however, was the fact that many ASM members were also committed proletarians, "leftists" who upheld Revolutionary values but who believed in the elevation of the worker to the heights of culture and opposed

RAPM's "race to the bottom." Artistic futurists espousing revolutionary music for revolutionary times, their advocacy of industrial, or "constructivist," elements (e.g., the famous sheet metal effects in Mosolov's *The Iron Foundry*) was both a demonstration of their proletarian credentials and an application of ASM's avant-garde agenda. As LASM's publication, Novaya muzyka, put it, "Proletarian masses, for whom machine oil is mother's milk, have a right to demand music consonant with our epoch, not the music of the bourgeois salon, which belongs in the era of the horse and buggy and of Stephenson's early locomotive."[11]

Between the Circle for New Music and the Central Music Technicum, Shostakovich had surrounded himself with Leningrad's most progressive musical thinkers—to which could be added Yavorsky in Moscow. Under their (particularly Shcherbachov's) influence, he developed a new, self-propelling linear style ("ultrapolyphony") freed from the dictates of harmonic progression. The Second Symphony opens with a deliberately murky texture in the strings, created by the gradual superimposition of lines of ever-accelerating note values. The result, a polyrhythmic texture played out against an unchanging basic pulse—a "stationary accelerando," as it is sometimes dubbed—could be considered a prototype for the clustered, micropolyphonic textures of Ligeti or Penderecki decades later. Joseph Darby has dubbed this technique "systematic ultrapolyphony": "a 'mathematical' approach to polyphony in which a quasi-serial system of composition affects the musical structure. Note for example the rhythm and bowing patterns [at the beginning—up to Fig. 4, b2]."[12] The other instance of ultrapolyphony in the Second Symphony, using a non-mathematical approach that Darby calls "unsystematic ultrapolyphony," is the section of thirteen-voice free counterpoint beginning at Fig. 29, as striking a depiction of organized chaos as can be found anywhere in music, and something that David Haas has suggested "could be interpreted as a protracted exercise in idiomatic improvisatory writing of the sort Shcherbachov required of his students, here raised to the level of *tour de force*."[13] Even more than its atonality, the ultrapolyphony was the Second Symphony's most strikingly modernist feature. It was this "absolute emancipation from any kind of 'verticality'" that constituted Shteinberg's main complaint against his student's work.[14]

The choral finale, a setting of Alexander Bezymensky's *agitprop* poem, "To October," brings a sudden change of style. The extreme atonality and the ultrapolyphony are abandoned, other than during a brief recall of the Symphony's opening just before the end (Fig. 95). A characteristic RAPM touch here is the *deklamatsii* in which the praises of Lenin and the Revolution are shouted in street-demo style between the various sections of the choir (Fig. 94). Yet, it has to be said that, for all its efforts to emulate the RAPM-style mass song, this choral finale is surprisingly ungrateful vocally, uncertain tonally, and unmemorable melodically, lacking those very qualities that would seem *de rigueur* for this type of music. The principal culprit was probably a lack of inspiration. Shostakovich detested Bezymensky's crudely propagandistic texts—to Shulgin, he complained about their lack of "melodious quality";[15] to his girlfriend Tatyana Glivenko, he simply described them as "abominable."[16]

Just as the relationship between the "experimental" and "proletarian" camps was more complex than at first appears, so too was the relationship between the Symphony and the two camps themselves. The proletarian influence, at least in its populist (as distinct from "leftist") guise, was not just confined to the choral finale. It governed the very form of the Symphony, a form whose roots were not so much in any musical predecessors (the genre of "choral symphony" notwithstanding), but in proletarian mass theater, in particular, the so-called "mass spectacle" that had been popular during the Civil War. A creation of the Proletkult,[17] the mass spectacle was a large-scale outdoor re-enactment of Revolutionary themes, involving sometimes thousands of performers—musicians, dancers, actors, acrobats, gymnasts, military personnel, etc. The genre fell into decline around 1920, mirroring the decline of Proletkult itself, but was revived on an even larger scale for the Revolution's tenth anniversary in 1927,[18] and enjoyed a brief second wave. Despite its extreme diversity of content, the Proletkult mass spectacle had adhered to a standardized chronological depiction of the three "phases" of the Revolution: the darkness of the pre-Revolutionary past, the struggle of Revolution, and the ultimate triumph of the working man. Although the "second wave" of mass spectacle would pay less attention to Revolutionary chronology, playing up instead the cult of the present—as Katerina Clark notes, "events shift back and forth thematically from war to industrialization to revolution.... [with] frequent travesties of chronology ... and temporal reversal such that recent times act upon the past"[19]—it was the original form that influenced Shostakovich's Second Symphony: murky, confused clusters at the opening leading to the "struggle" of the thirteen-part ultrapolyphony, leading in turn to the celebratory "worker's" finale.

It was not only the Symphony's structure that was influenced by the mass spectacle. Although its "ultrapolyphony" may have been formed under the influence of Shcherbachov, the idea of the chaotic interplay of unrelated lines, as in that passage of thirteen-part counterpoint, also had its roots in the mass spectacle, where disparate elements were often pitted against each other to underline specific points within the story. For example, the spectacle *The Storming of the Winter Palace* had the Communist hymn "Internationale" (representing the revolutionary forces) progressively drown out the "Marseillaise" (the bourgeoisie), an effect worthy of Ives.[20] Of course, even regardless of these contrivances, the sheer reality of coordinating thousands of performers over large outdoor areas would inevitably have created its own brand of ultrapolyphonic chaos.

One of the prevailing artistic forces during the mid-1920s, and not just in Russia, was Industrialism, something that had been enthusiastically embraced in certain ASM quarters, and that was now being heavily featured in the second wave of mass spectacles with their pyrotechnic displays—another example of commonality between the two rival camps. The Second Symphony's famous "industrial" moment comes with the blast of the factory hooter "in F-sharp" just before the entrance of the chorus—the score sanctions an orchestral substitute (three trombones) if a hooter is not available. The hooter was Shulgin's idea, though Shostakovich made a point of visiting a factory for research and testing purposes. Although effective in context, it remains something of a token gesture. Neither this nor the awkwardly lyr-ical setting of Bezymensky's "industrial" passages (e.g., "Factory chimneys stretching up to the sky") quite convinces the listener of Shostakovich's industrialist credentials. The aesthetic of "iron and steel" modernism was certainly embraced more convinc-ingly by Prokofiev, in his Second Symphony or the ballet *Pas d'Acier*, or even briefly by Shostakovich himself in the First Piano Sonata, than it was here in Shostakovich's Second Symphony—though even Prokofiev's best efforts paled alongside such mon-strosities as Arseny Avraamov's *Symphony of Hooters* (*Simfoniya gudkov*, 1922), per-formed at the port in Baku and featuring multiple choirs, cannons, foghorns, batteries of artillery guns, machine gun divisions, factory sirens, steam whistle machines, and conductors wielding flags and firing pistols.

The Second Symphony may have been a self-conscious exercise in musical mod-ernism, but that did not preclude the presence of more historical forces. The opening's systematically accelerating lines (quarter notes, eighth, triplet-eighth, six-teenth, etc.) could almost be read as an atonal, ultrapolyphonic adaptation of spe-cies counterpoint. Moreover, the very use of counterpoint to represent conflict goes back centuries, as does the particular use of sparring between different sec-tions of a choir to imitate crowd scenes. Compare the *deklamatsii* at the end of the Symphony with the *turba* choruses in, say, Bach's *St. Matthew Passion*, where call-and-response between the two antiphonally placed choirs depicts the anxiety of the crowd. And although the Second was not designated a symphony until the early 1930s, comparisons with the *locus classicus* of choral symphonies, Beethoven's Ninth, inevitably come into play. Shostakovich's *Schlußchor*, described by Richard Taruskin as "a RAPM stereotype, replaying the closing gestures of Beethoven's Ninth as street harangue, accompanied by a rhythm-band orchestra,"[21] empha-sizes, like Beethoven's, the theme of brotherhood, though reinterpreted for a Soviet context. Meanwhile, the "pre-Revolutionary" darkness and confusion at the Sym-phony's start seems to echo Beethoven's misty, formative opening.

Despite a structure that owes more to the proletarian mass spectacle than to the symphony, aspects of traditional symphonism can be detected, albeit modified to serve the work's dramatic purpose. Sections here are delineated by tempo and texture changes rather than by theme or tonality. Nevertheless, what becomes one of the few identifiable themes in the choral finale does make several fragmented appearances earlier on. Joseph Darby calls it "a kind of 'foredevelopment' in which components of the theme are varied before it is presented in full—reversing the traditional state-ment-development formula common to symphonic music. The October theme, as it were, struggles into being during the second and fourth episodes before being stated in full during the chorus."[22] Traditional technique is thus reversed rather than rejected. The "October" theme itself (Example 5.1) presents a melodic shape that would come to be something of a Shostakovich trademark—a "wedge" formed by the alternation of a constant pitch with an ascending or, as here, descending line. Incidentally, the "October" theme would make a return thirty-five years later in Shostakovich's other Lenin-inspired symphony, the Twelfth, where it forms the main theme of the finale, "The Dawn of Humanity."

Example 5.1

These thematic foredevelopments are also paralleled tonally. The Symphony's final destination, B major, is foredeveloped by appearances of its dominant (F-sharp) at two pivotal moments—the enharmonically equivalent G-flat major chord at the close of the first *Allegro* (Fig. 24), and the factory hooter announcing the chorus (Fig. 69). In neither instance is B major actually implied, but the facts that both instances occur at structurally important points and that they represent about the only oases of tonality in the Symphony's orchestral prelude inevitably endow upon them a degree of tonal signification. Like the thematic foredevelopment, this tonal pre-emption pays homage both to traditional symphonic technique—the Beethovenian teasing of the listener in the earlier stages of a work with a tonality that will become important later on—and to the proletarian mass spectacle, in which a *Leitmotiv* often acted as a beacon of hope throughout the stages of oppression/struggle, achieving its full flowering in the final stage of victory.

For all that it sheds light on the cultural influences of the day, the Second Symphony remains, ultimately, an uneven achievement—"thesis and antithesis denied culminatory synthesis," as David Fanning has put it.[23] And assessing the impact of those influences is not a straightforward matter, given their frequent cross-pollination. We have already noted the diverse sources of the Symphony's ultrapolyphony (Shcherbachov and the mass spectacle) and of its occasional industrialism (ASM "leftism" and proletarianism). David Haas, for one, rejects the simplistic notion of ASM versus RAPM, and considers an important difference between the Leningrad modernists and their counterparts in Moscow:

In the end the Second seems not a work of imitation or emulation, but merely a full length demonstration of the fact that Shostakovich had "moved closer" to the linearist aesthetic in such a way as to fulfill minimum conditions, without abandoning his own creative path. On no account should it be considered a work of opportunistic conciliation between the warring RAPM and ACM [ASM] aesthetics, as [Gerald] Abraham seems to imply. While Bezymensky was indeed a RAPP poet, no RAPM composer would have relinquished clear downbeats and strophic setting for the odd meters, extreme ranges, free arioso passages, and complicated counterpoint of Shostakovich's choral writing. By the same token there do not appear to be any stylistic affinities between Shostakovich's work and the music of the Moscow-based ACM [ASM] composers ... [who] were more concerned with the continued exploration of Late Romantic chromaticism or the development of systematic atonal alternatives, rather than linear tension, the varieties of melos, and the possibilities of nonschematic form.[24]

Shostakovich's picking and choosing from the various currents around him was simply another exercising of the independence that he had declared for himself back in his early Conservatory days. The composer Yury Tyulin, a member of the Shcherbachov circle, described Shostakovich's ability "to use his memory selectively,"[25] even early in his student career: "During this time of crisis, when the split between teaching of a scholastic dogma and real compositional practice was at its most extreme, Mitya Shostakovich felt as free as a fish in water. He absorbed only what was useful to him, both within his study course and outside it."[26] Indeed, another friend of the time, the musicologist Mikhail Druskin, has even questioned the extent and importance of the associations with Shcherbachov and Asafyev, believing that Shostakovich essentially stood apart from their spheres of influence.[27] On this point at least, David Haas disagrees, citing Shostakovich's earlier involvement in Shcherbachov's informal discussion sessions (the Fogt group) and his following of Asafyev and Shcherbachov out of LASM and into the Circle for New Music.[28] Shostakovich's independence was also fueled by his Conservatory training, though for perhaps unexpected reasons. Of course, a certain amount of rebellion against the strict dogma of Shteinberg's teaching was to be expected. Earlier, Shostakovich had joined the Fogt group specifically for an alternative outlet, and his First Symphony certainly demonstrated an independent mind. But his Conservatory training had also ingrained within him a deep sense of craft, which appears to have bolstered his independence by strengthening his immunity to faddishness. As Druskin put it, "[Shostakovich] did not succumb to passing fashion or temporary enthusiasms for new music, but accepted them with discrimination.... [He] was also not touched by the polemics in the literary world ... [and] the furious arguments about 'constructivism' and 'urbanism' which were supposed to reflect the spirit and requirements of the age."[29]

***

Of the friendships and musical associations that Shostakovich made during this period, one would stand out. In the spring of 1927, he struck up a friendship with Ivan Sollertinsky. Linguist, historian, and philosopher, Sollertinsky dazzled Shostakovich with his erudition, his articulacy, and his razor-sharp and coruscating wit. The musically untrained Sollertinsky had also become a self-made musicologist, establishing himself as one of Russia's most influential musical thinkers and advocates; his Leningrad Philharmonic pre-concert talks became significant events in their own right. Nikolai Malko, for one, believed that Sollertinsky's knowledge of the history and sociology of music was actually superior to Shostakovich's.[30] His advocacy of Mahler in particular would have a profound effect. As they very quickly recognized in each other a kindred spirit, their friendship, described by the composer's sister Zoya as "insane,"[31] developed like wildfire. No friendship in Shostakovich's life would have quite the intensity of this one, and it is perhaps no surprise that composition of the bitingly acerbic *Aphorisms* should have exactly coincided with the onset of this friendship. Malko, who had already noted a degree of brattiness in Shostakovich's behavior, wrote:

> Jokes ran riot and each tried to outdo the other in making witty remarks. It was a veritable competition. Each had a sharply developed sense of humor; both were bright and observant; they knew a great deal; and their tongues were itching to say

something funny or sarcastic, no matter whom it might concern. They were each quite indiscriminate when it came to being humorous, and if they were too young to be bitter they could still come mercilessly close to being malicious.[32]

Sollertinsky was influential in Shostakovich's choice of material for his first opera, *The Nose* (1927–1928), based on Gogol's story of the same name. For Shostakovich, laboring on the Second Symphony, spinning his wheels in the mire of Bezymensky's dull verses, Gogol's satire about a nose that becomes detached from its owner, the Collegiate Assessor Kovalyov, only to show up in the breakfast roll of Kovalyov's barber, Ivan Yakovlevich, and subsequently take up a life of its own provided a delicious diversion. Operatic imports such as Prokofiev's *The Love for Three Oranges*, Berg's *Wozzeck*, and Krenek's *Jonny spielt auf* were being premiered in Russia (1926, 1927, and 1928, respectively), but *The Nose* would be the first attempt at a domestically produced, modernist opera, as well as the first Soviet opera of any standing not to employ a Revolutionary or "Soviet" theme. Like Hindemith's contemporary *Neues vom Tage*, *The Nose* presented itself as "anti-opera," or at least anti-Romantic-opera, rejecting nineteenth-century precepts of musical delivery and, indeed, musical primacy. For Shostakovich, it was the text and its delivery on stage that was paramount, something evidenced by his rejection of that mainstay of romantic opera, the aria, and his development instead of an arioso/recitative style of delivery—"living language," as Sollertinsky would call it,[33] or "symphonized" speech, as Boris Asafyev later termed it.[34] The opera's frequent use of mixed meter, for example, was conceived not so much "musically," but as a tool to disarm lyricism and cantilena, and promote instead the natural rhythms and patterns of speech (e.g., Chapter 11, Example 11.1). It was for this reason that Shostakovich so strongly opposed the concert-version preview that took place in June 1929 at the Leningrad Malyi Theater in advance of the staged premiere in January 1930. In a letter to the theater's director, Nikolai Smolich, written shortly before that preview, he wrote: "*The Nose* loses all sense to me if it is viewed only from the musical standpoint. For its musical component is derived exclusively from the action.... I repeat once more: the presentation of *The Nose* in concert performance will be its death."[35]

Shostakovich's treatment of the text (in conjunction with Georgy Ionin, Alexander Preis, and, to a lesser extent, the satirist Yevgeny Zamyatin) is discussed in Chapter 11. Although he denied exaggerating the opera's comic elements, arguing that he had followed Gogol's own serious, deadpan style,[36] almost every facet of its composition seems to have been calculated for maximum satirical impact. It is officialdom that bears the brunt of Shostakovich's most biting commentary—the pompous Kovalyov, the bureaucrats whom he tries to enlist to help retrieve his nose, even the clergy. In perpetrating its satirical mission, *The Nose* turns every precept of traditional vocal technique on its head, with its disjunct writing, extreme ranges, and frequently grotesque modes of delivery—the shrill nagging of Praskovya Osipovna; the arrogant but ineffectual policeman whose high E-flats go above and beyond the virile heroism of the tenor "high C" into a realm of ridiculous effeminacy.

The Nose is as brutally atonal as anything from the period, with ultrapolyphony occasionally rearing its head, such as during the barber Ivan Yakovlevich's dash down the riverbank, the counterpoint reflecting his accumulating panic as he tries to get rid of the severed nose found earlier in his bread roll. Orchestrally, the satire is played out through the astringent sonorities of a chamber orchestra, though one featuring an unusually heavy percussion battery, a group that comes into its own, literally, in the entr'acte (Act 1, no. 4) for nine unpitched percussion instruments—perhaps the ultimate example of music that makes no sense divorced from the stage action. The film director Grigory Kozintsev would later describe his impressions of the work on stage:

> Vladimir Dmitriev's sets spun and reeled to the sounds of rollicking galops and dashing polkas; Gogol's phantasmagoria was transformed into sound and colour. The particular imagery of Russian art that was linked to urban folklore—the signs of taverns, shops and picture booths, cheap dance orchestras—all burst into the kingdom of *Aida* and *Il Trovatore*. Gogol's grotesque raged around us; what were we to understand as farce, what as prophecy? The incredible orchestral combinations, texts seemingly unthinkable to sing ... the unhabitual rhythms ... the incorporating of the apparently anti-poetic, anti-musical, vulgar, but what was in reality the intonation and parody of real life—all this was an assault on conventionality.[37]

Perhaps the one place where the "assault on conventionality" is put on hold is in the relatively traditional fugato that constitutes most of the orchestral interlude between Scenes 5 and 6. It is, as Levon Hakobian has put it, "the only island of relative stability and order that survives the all-crushing typhoon of the absurd.... the place where, having acquired a specific quality surrounded by 'opposite value signs,' the longing of a real artist for true values crawls into the music of this absurdist opera."[38] Shostakovich's ability to hold in reserve a mode of expression that is alien to the overall tone of a work, and then deploy it to make a searing dramatic point, would come to fruition in his next opera, *The Lady Macbeth of the Mtsensk District,* in which, despite a musical context that is far less avant-garde, Katerina's fourth act aria still would stand out as the alien mode, lyrically expressive rather than expressionistic, crowning her as the only genuinely human entity among the caricatures that constitute the rest of the cast.

***

From the purely musical perspective, *The Nose* would represent the culmination of Shostakovich's brief flirtation with the avant-garde. But his general interest in experimental art forms continued for a while longer. In 1929, he completed his first film score, *New Babylon,* and collaborated with the stage director Vsevolod Meyerhold on his production of Vladimir Mayakovsky's comedy *The Bedbug.* Shostakovich's association with Meyerhold dated back to the end of 1927, when the stage director had invited the young composer to work as a music director in his theater. He spent the first two months of 1928 in Moscow working for Meyerhold, living with the director and his actress wife, Zinaida Raikh. Although his embrace of artistic industrialism had never been more than lukewarm,

Shostakovich was intrigued by Meyerhold's theories of "biomechanics," a constructivist approach to acting that promoted physical expressivity through economy of motion. Premiered on 13 February 1929, *The Bedbug* was an instant hit. But the increasingly vociferous guardians of the proletarian interest would attack the play for its dangerously esoteric direction, its unusual sets (by the "Kukryniksy" group in the first half of the play and the constructivist painter Alexander Rodchenko in the futurist second half), and its scabrous musical score.[39] Yet, *The Bedbug's* audience popularity kept it in production for at least a couple of years. Shostakovich's other experimental project, the film *New Babylon*, which premiered in March 1929, was not so lucky.

New Babylon's directors, Grigory Kozintsev and Leonid Trauberg, belonged to the so-called Factory of the Eccentric Actor (FEKS), a group of iconoclasts dedicated to the debunking of bourgeois art forms or, as their impudent manifesto put it, to the "electrification of Gogol"—a reference to Lenin's famous 1920 call for the "electrification of the whole country." In contrast to the increasingly nationalistic proletarian culture of the late 1920s, FEKS' cultural loyalties were unashamedly American—Charlie Chaplin and Buster Keaton were its heroes. But the topic of *New Babylon,* the fall of the Paris Commune of 1871, was a story that had come to occupy a special place in communist lore and one that had taken on almost mythic proportions after Lenin had requested that he be shrouded in the Communard flag upon his death. Not surprisingly, Kozintsev's and Trauberg's breathlessly avant-garde treatment of this iconic story, together with Shostakovich's outrageously debunking score—the whole thing exacerbated, it should be said, by a series of technical problems (audio/visual co-ordination and inconsistent running speeds—see Chapter 17)—was denounced in many quarters as a sacrilege. *New Babylon* was withdrawn shortly after its release.

***

In 1928, Stalin had inaugurated his First Five-Year Plan, a manically ambitious program of industrialization and agricultural collectivization designed to bring the Soviet Union's lagging industrial performance up to Western standards. The period between 1928 and 1932 would also witness the unstoppable ascendancy of proletarian culture, with RAPM and its literary counterpart RAPP (Russian Association of Proletarian Writers) given *carte blanche* to transform or destroy institutions and practices deemed alien to the proletarian state, a power they exercised with thuggish zeal.

Central to this Cultural Revolution was a program of public smear campaigns and show trials designed to root out and expose "wreckers" of the Five-Year plan and whip the nation into a state of fear and paranoia. In the first of these campaigns, the Shakhty trial of 1928, fifty-three mining engineers from the Shakhty district were arrested and charged with conspiracy. Three of the accused were German. Concocting its "evidence" from accident reports and disciplinary claims, the trial concluded that German "imperialists" were plotting to sabotage the mines. The trial was carried out in full public view. In fact, with over 100,000 witnesses called to testify, the public itself became an integral part of the show.

The Shakhty trial would give Stalin the excuse he had been looking for to pursue his campaign of "vigilance" against the professional classes and whip up anti-Western sentiment.[40] He would dub 1929 "The Great Turning-Point" (*velikii perelom*). With his opposition (principally Trotsky, Zinovyev, and Kamenyev) neutralized, and his consolidation of power all but complete, the Cultural Revolution could go into high gear. There were campaigns against Boris Pilnyak and Yevgeny Zamyatin, heads, respectively, of the Moscow and Leningrad branches of the Authors' League, the literary equivalent of ASM; Pilnyak's sin was to publish his banned pro-Trotskyist novel, *Mahogany*, in Germany, while Zamyatin's famous anti-utopian novel, *We* (1921), was proving far too prophetic for comfort. Also that year, the liberal Anatoly Lunacharsky was removed from the head of Narkompros and replaced by the hardliner Andrei Bubnov. In December, the Party decreed that all production of literature be consolidated under the aegis of RAPP.[41] Meanwhile, in the musical world, 1929 saw the defection of leading figures from both Prokoll (Production Collective) and ORKiMD (Association of Revolutionary Composers and Musical Workers)—people like Belyi, Davidenko, Koval, and Shekhter—to the more powerful RAPM, as well as the folding of ASM's journal, *Contemporary Musician*. Joseph Darby reports that of the seven musical journals in circulation at the start of 1929, only three, all rigidly proletarian, made it to the end.[42] ASM itself effectively ceased functioning the following year, and officially disbanded in 1931. Shostakovich was profoundly affected by the events of 1929. He was dismissed from his part-time post at the Choreographic Technicum, where he had been teaching theory since the beginning of the year, and his friend, the pianist Mariya Yudina, was fired from her position at the Conservatory on the grounds of spreading religion. Most horrific of all was the arrest and execution of the composer Mikhail Kvadri, for alleged anti-Revolutionary activities. Shostakovich had dedicated his First Symphony to Kvadri; in typical Soviet fashion, all editions of the Symphony published after 1929 would excise the name of its dedicatee.

As previously noted, *New Babylon* and *The Bedbug* had proved controversial at their respective unveilings in early 1929. But Shostakovich now had the upcoming premiere of *The Nose* to worry about. Although this unashamedly modernist opera might have flown in 1927 as Shostakovich was embarking on it and when ASM was alive and flourishing, the deterioration of the cultural climate put it now in a much more precarious position. Eyebrows were certainly raised at the concert-version preview held in June 1929. Over the next few months, Shostakovich attempted to convince the public of the importance of contemporary and innovative Soviet opera. On 14 January 1930, four days before the staged premiere, he and Sollertinsky went to discuss *The Nose* at a short presentation of selected scenes for a worker's audience. Sollertinsky attempted to assuage the assembled gathering, telling them that the opera's revolutionary modernism "will be difficult for the opera buff accustomed to Italian opera, but understandable to the worker."[43] But these exercises in damage control made no difference. Following the premiere on 18 January, *The Nose* was blasted as "the infantile sickness of leftism" in an article entitled "The Handbomb of an Anarchist."[44] Although he could have hardly been surprised by the negative reaction, Shostakovich was still crushed by it. He remained adamant that "the path followed by *The Nose* is a correct one," but in April asked director Zakhar Lyubimsky to take it out of production, as it was not being received as he had hoped.[45] *The Nose* would receive a few more performances over the next year, but was eventually taken out of production, not to be seen again in Russia until 1974.

***

Against this increasingly hostile background, Shostakovich took every opportunity to mouth publicly his commitment to the proletarian cause. His annual reports to the Conservatory spoke of his allegiance to the mass audience and of his respect for its judgment. In his report dated 31 October 1929, he discussed the Second Symphony. Even back in the more liberal climate of 1927, its ultrapolyphony had not been well received in proletarian circles. Now, in the report, he tried to justify it as a consciously political device: "I attempted to depict the zeal of struggle and victory. Here I introduced it as an instrumental system of ultrapolyphony.... This device places "To October" on the side of the working public."[46] Whether Shostakovich had actually believed this at the time of the Symphony's composition is hard to tell, since the attachment of the "October" label onto anything modernistic or "Revolutionary" had been so widespread. His comments connecting ultrapolyphony with the "working public" certainly have a whiff of retroactive face-saving about them, similar to Sollertinsky's using the complex modernism of *The Nose* ("difficult for the opera buff accustomed to Italian opera") to flatter his audience of workers. Nevertheless, backing up his words with deeds, Shostakovich's output over the next couple of years would indeed be dominated by projects that, in theory at least, could be described as "proletarian-approved": the Third Symphony (1929, serving also as Shostakovich's postgraduate diploma piece), the ballets *The Golden Age* (1929–1930) and *The Bolt* (1930–1931), and three incidental scores for productions by the Theater of Working Youth (TRaM): Bezymensky's *The Shot* (1929), Gorbenko and Lvov's *Virgin Soil* (1930), and Pyotrovsky's *Rule, Britannia!* (1931).

Like its predecessor, the Third Symphony (subtitled "The First of May") depicts a key event of the Soviet calendar and attempts a single-movement fusion of episodic orchestral prelude with closing *agitprop* chorus (texts this time by Semyon Kirsanov). Yet, the tendency to view the Second and Third Symphonies as a pair is somewhat misleading. In the first place, the musical language of the Third is a good deal less avant-garde. Although this is most obvious in the orchestral prelude, where the ultrapolyphony and extreme atonality of the former symphony are nowhere to be heard, it can also be felt in the choral finale, in which the simple lines and swaggering, march-like character emulate proletarian mass song more convincingly than did the tortuous setting of Bezymensky's "To October." Yet, while the Third Symphony tamed the musical language of its predecessor, it would further the principle of episodic construction. Thematicism, employed, albeit somewhat idiosyncratically, in the Second Symphony, is completely rejected in the somewhat ramshackle Third, where themes pass by the listener like floats at a parade, with no repetition or recapitulation. Joseph Darby refers to "a principle of continuous variation—a dialectical approach to composition that perpetually synthesizes new and old material to generate new themes."[47]

Shostakovich himself described the Third Symphony as "of an entirely different order" to the Second, noting "In 'To October' struggle plays a self-sufficient role, while the 'May symphony' expresses, as much as possible, the mood of a public holiday of peaceful construction."[48] How sincere was this description is again open to question. The Symphony is certainly chock full of street imagery—mass songs and marches, "oom-pah" brass bands. But the frenzy into which Shostakovich occasionally whips his material is frankly more terrifying than festive; as with so many later works, e.g., the finale of the Sixth Symphony, the dividing line between "festive" and "frenetic" is perilously thin. (Perhaps wisely, Shostakovich abandoned his original idea to feature a wooden ratchet simulating machine-gun fire.)

Although he had been loosely associated with TRaM since 1927, it was not until 1929 that Shostakovich began an active collaboration. Founded in Leningrad in 1925, TRaM's mission was a theater in which, as its director Mikhail Sokolovsky put it, "the working lad plays himself."[49] However, Sokolovsky quickly realized the limitations of his cadre of part-time, untrained factory workers, and in 1927 put TRaM on a more professional footing. Its productions became more ambitious. They starred theatrically talented workers who had traded in their jobs for a full-time stage career, and employed professional writers (e.g., Adryan Pyotrovsky) and composers (e.g., Shostakovich and Vladimir Deshevov). By 1932, TRaM would boast a nationwide network of three hundred municipal branches plus a network of factory cells (*tramyada*).

Despite its popularity, TRaM was beset with problems. The cultural mismatch between its professional writers and its workers-turned-actors often created friction. Indeed, the very employment of writers and composers from the intelligentsia was viewed in some quarters as a sell-out of TRaM's proletarian principles. And, like the unashamed pro-Americanism of FEKS, TRaM's pro-Western outlook (particularly toward the German avant-garde) put it increasingly out of step in an age when the Bolshevik fervor of international brotherhood was itself being increasingly drowned out by the crude drum of nationalism. And TRaM's collectivist philosophy, which specifically denied its works and productions the power to mobilize, was becoming a liability in this increasingly authoritarian age. Katerina Clark writes:

> The directors sought to break down the identification between actor and character by having their actors critique their roles even as they were acting them. . . . They aimed to present a conflicted and multilayered account of reality such that no single and coherent account of anything should be presented; its opposite should always be there simultaneously. A TRaM script was to present no conclusions to its audience as a guarantee of true collectivity (no overriding voice). There should, the group maintained, be no finality, a characteristic they identified with a Marxist account of the dialectic whereby all would be in a state of contradiction, of becoming. There was even to be no final version of the script.[50]

Its problems notwithstanding, TRaM still counted as a proletarian organization and Shostakovich's collaboration in three of their productions gave him some political cover. That said, he did seem to have had at least a modicum of affection for the organization. In his 1931 "Declaration" against Soviet proletarian culture (see below), he would specifically exclude TRaM from his criticisms. Lest this be interpreted as disingenuous self-justification, it should be noted that Shostakovich also explicitly berated his own ballets *The Bolt* and *The Golden Age*.

***

From the earliest days of Bolshevik power, the arts had been exploited for their propaganda potential. This exploitation went into full gear with the Cultural Revolution as it used the arts to promote the First Five-Year Plan and its associated campaigns against wreckers and bourgeois "corruption." Alexander Ivanovsky's ballet, *Dinamyada*, was one in a line of "morality" works that popped up during this time to promote public vigilance. In January 1929, *Dinamyada* had been awarded first prize in a competition to find a new ballet on a contemporary theme. It tells the story of a Soviet football team, Dynamo, visiting the imaginary country of Fashlandiya (Fascistland—although this name was later dropped) during an industrial exhibition. A local dancer attempts to lure the captain of the Soviet team, but to no avail—the team proves immune to the entreaties and provocations of the capitalist opposition. Wholesome Soviet values triumph over bourgeois sleaze.

By spring 1929, a somewhat reluctant Shostakovich had been brought on board to provide the score, his reservations about the ballet (now renamed *The Golden Age*) possibly outweighed by the chance to incorporate into his work one of his major passions: soccer. Rehearsals were plagued with difficulties, a major stumbling block being the unfamiliarity of the classically trained dancers with the choreographic requirements of a contemporary score saturated with popular urban dance. But the premiere a year-and-a-half later (October 1930) was a great audience success. Shostakovich's brilliantly illustrative music was a hit—catchy marches and songs to depict the Soviet athletes in all their moral rectitude, and "degenerate" bourgeois genres (foxtrots, tangos, cancans, etc.) to depict the capitalist enemy, with wickedly salacious cabaret music for the attempted seduction of the Soviet captain. Although Shostakovich enjoyed the success, he was at the same time dismayed by this "anti-artistic" project and its sidelining of musical values. In what seemed like a shift of priorities since *The Nose*, he wrote, "I am now more than ever convinced that in every piece of music theatre the music must play the main, and not the supporting role."[51] However, the more immediate problem to face *The Golden Age* was the virulent ongoing campaign against light music being waged by RAPM. Within days of the premiere, the ballet was attacked for "insinuat[ing] the ideology of the western pigsty onto the stage."[52] But audience popularity won the day, at least for a short while. The ballet survived into 1931, receiving new productions in Kiev and Odessa, before it was finally removed.

Ironically, Shostakovich himself had been ostensibly supporting RAPM's campaign against light music, as witnessed by his uncharacteristically harsh, dogmatic article in *Proletarsky muzykant*, published in March 1930, seven months before the ballet's premiere. Singling out gypsy romances—ironically, the very music his father used to sing at the family's musical soirees—he had called for "an appropriate resolution completely forbidding the publication and performance of light music."[53] Maybe he did it to insulate himself from RAPM's attacks against *Tahiti-Trot*, his 1927 orchestration of Vincent Youmans' *Tea for Two*, famously done from memory in forty-five minutes as a bet with Nikolai Malko. Or it may have been, as Joseph Darby has suggested, a way to distance himself from the financial scandals that were then rife in the light music business.[54] Either way, Shostakovich's rant was clearly a smokescreen; he had always appreciated and would continue to appreciate good quality light music, often using the phrase "Bach to Offenbach" to characterize his tastes.

Although rehearsals for *The Golden Age* during the early part of 1930 had been proving difficult, that did not stop Shostakovich from accepting a second ballet commission that February, even if he did find the libretto of Viktor Smirnov's *At the New Machine* somewhat less than enthralling. He wrote sarcastically to Sollertinsky:

> The subject is most topical. There is a machine. It has gone wrong (problem of wear and tear on materials). They fix it (problem of amortization), and at the same time buy a new one. Finally everybody dances around the new machine. Apotheosis. All of this takes up three acts.[55]

The story was subsequently reworked to incorporate an industrial sabotage theme. The new libretto (renamed *The Bolt*) told of Lyonka Gulba (literally "lazy reveler"), a sacked factory worker. Lyonka seeks vengeance and convinces his apprentice Goshka to throw a bolt into the factory's new machine, bringing both the machine and the department to a halt. Boris, a young communist accused by Lyonka, is arrested for the crime, but, in true "morality" style, Goshka confesses, Lyonka is unmasked, and the factory resumes operations.

Shostakovich treated this inane material in the only honest way that he could, creating a satirical send-up of the whole subject of sabotage, most memorably perhaps in "The Bureaucrat," with its wrong-note tomfoolery and its comically polarized bassoon/piccolo duet. *The Bolt* would represent the pinnacle of a particular brand of satire that had had it roots in the cartoonish grotesquerie of the First Symphony and had taken in *New Babylon* and *The Golden Age*. But *The Bolt* and *The Golden Age* are also transitional works, sitting midway between the heavy satire of the mid-to-late 1920s (*Aphorisms* and *The Nose*) and the light music of the early-to-mid 1930s (the revue *Declared Dead*, the ballet *The Limpid Stream*, even the incidental score to *Hamlet* and the First Piano Concerto).

According to one of *The Bolt*'s set-designers, Tatyana Bruni, the ballet's success seemed assured, at least judging by the response at the public dress rehearsals.[56] But *The Bolt* would not make it past its opening night on 8 April 1931.[57] Critics objected that upstanding workers and wreckers alike had been characterized dramatically and musically in the same negative way, and that important national issues were being mocked. Although he had embarked on this project with serious misgivings, the sensitive Shostakovich was still disturbed at the outcome. Publicly, he admitted that "*Raymonda* and *Coppelia* seem like works of Shakespeare compared to the dramaturgy of *The Bolt*,"[58] but in a letter to his friend Vissarion Shebalin, he was keen to place his ballet into what he considered its proper perspective, noting that although *The Bolt* may indeed have been "shit," next to Davidenko (RAPM's leading figure) it was "pure Beethoven."[59] Following the ballet's withdrawal, revisions were promised, but none materialized. Other than the staging of some excerpts in 1976, it would not be seen again until the Bolshoi's 2005 "premiere," though, like *The Golden Age*, portions of its deliciously debunking music would be made familiar through concert suites.

The Bolt was quickly followed by yet another stage work, the music-hall revue *Declared Dead*.[60] Composed in the summer and autumn of 1931, and premiered in October, this "light-music circus entertainment in 3 acts" was yet another attempt to capitalize on the "morality" bandwagon. A typical "trial-between-love-and-duty" tale dealing with the responsibilities of a Soviet citizen during an air-raid drill, *Declared Dead* featured a light, witty score not dissimilar in style to *The Bolt*. On stage, meanwhile, the famous bandleader, Leonid Utyosov, a figure much admired by Shostakovich, played with his "Tea-Jazz" (*teatralnyi dzhaz*) band. In the end, *Declared Dead* went the way of *The Golden Age* and *The Bolt*. The public loved it, while the critics again complained of the flippant treatment of serious issues. After the first season, the show was taken off.

***

By the autumn of 1931, Shostakovich had reached an impasse and a crisis of confidence. His achievements over the previous year or two had amounted to two problematic ballets, a failed music-hall revue, three productions for TRaM, and a symphony (the Third) in which he had clearly not yet found a convincing voice. But one work does stand out—his 1930 score for Kozintsev's film, *Alone (Odna)*. Certainly, the music is uneven in quality and eclectic in style. It has its share of *Bolt*-isms: knockabout galops, satirical polkas, organ-grinder waltzes, and the odd bit of Stravinskian grotesquerie. It features sentimental ballads (e.g., the unashamedly Verdian duet with chorus, "Stay with us") as well as atmospheric depictions of the Steppes and the Altai region—"oriental" music reminiscent of Borodin or Ippolitov-Ivanov. And with the newly fashionable theremin depicting the howling wind in "The storm breaks," Shostakovich pays homage to the cinematic innovations of the day.

But the musical importance of *Alone* lies in its foreshadowing of certain elements of Shostakovich's mature style. His discovery of Mahler, for instance, which would bear more significant fruit a few years later with the Fourth Symphony, can be vaguely heard in the *Wunderhorn*-like melody in the second half of "In Kuzmina's Hut," the effect heightened by the earthily Mahlerian scoring for two oboes. In the melody's final phrase, the scoring of a military "trumpet" rhythm for a woodwind instrument (in this case, oboe) is again very Mahlerian. Meanwhile, the polarized string scoring in "Calm after the Storm," a "middle-less" texture of high violins against low cellos and basses, looks forward several decades to Shostakovich's late style. But perhaps the most important of these forward glimpses is the long oboe recitative in "Bai Takes the Schoolchildren to the Sheep Pasture," the longest sustained passage of recitative that Shostakovich would ever write, outside the slow movement of the Second String Quartet. This type of recitative, featuring a solo instrument playing a chromatically inflected prolongation of the slow-moving harmony under- neath, would become a staple of Shostakovich's later music, particularly between the late 1930s and mid-1940s. Although the recitative in *Alone* is atonal, with non- functional supporting harmony, its influence on the later examples is clear enough.

***

Shostakovich's carefully worded reports to the Conservatory, his dubious participation in RAPM's campaign against light music, and, of course, his own proletarian-styled compositions show that he had quickly learned the art of sur- vival in the Cultural Revolution. Yet, he was all too aware of the consequences of RAPM's hegemony. Back in 1929 he had warned: "Critics must possess the high- est musical culture ... but not all of our critics get it."[61] By the early autumn of 1931, the Cultural Revolution had reached its peak. Shostakovich, whose own compositional crisis of confidence was also coming to a head at about this time, finally threw caution and political expediency to the wind, launching a series of diatribes against the proletarian forces and its dismal achievements. In November, he described the "catastrophic" state of Soviet music in his "Declaration of a Composer's Responsibilities." Although not mentioning RAPM by name, Shosta- kovich placed the blame on an "applied" musical culture in which composers, himself included, had been prostituting themselves at the service of inferior stage and screen productions:

> For a long time, all work in every dramatic theatre and sound film has been simply cranked out (I exclude from this list only the work at TRaM). Music there plays the role of accenting "despair" and "delight." There are certain "standard" tricks in music: a rap on the drum in announcing a new character, the "cheerful" and "fiery" dance of positive characters, a foxtrot for "decay," and "cheerful" for a happy ending. This is the "material" for the composer's creativity. It is impossible ... to reduce the role of music toward the bare adaptation of the tastes and creative methods of the theatre, which are often terrible and disgraceful ("Hypothetically Murdered" at the Music- Hall). It has resulted in a real lack of compositional individuality.... The theatre that is currently being built by the leadership and workers has recently manufactured two clear aims: 1) music in opera or ballet should assist pleasant digestion and 2) to create favorable conditions for a tenor to show effective notes, and a ballerina—for some turn. By being covered with a fig leaf—this falsely understood slogan about mastery of the classical heritage—the theatre makes its most harmful business by reviving all sorts of "Judases," "Corsaires," and similar trash. With regard to Soviet music produc- tions, we have seen perfectly disgraceful methods at work here ("Red Poppy," "Ice and Steel," "Black Ravine," "Bolt," and "The Golden Age").[62]

Shostakovich went on to assert that operas and ballets should be composed in- dependently of a particular theatre or producer. "The theatre should exist only to accept (or not accept) and stage operas and ballets in ready shape when we bring them to the theatre for consideration."[63] He announced that he would fulfill his obligation to the Vakhtangov Theater's production of *Hamlet*, but that he was canceling and returning his advance for *Negro* and *The Concrete Sets*: "I do not have enough strength to 'depersonalize' myself and carry on mechanically.... I announce to all of my future 'customers' from the dramatic theatre and sound film that I am breaking from these fronts of music for the next five years."[64] In a December follow-up, Shostakovich specifically targeted RAPM for the "helpless, illiterate" offerings of its leading figures: Koval's *Songs about the Red Flag* ("absolutely pitiful") and Davidenko's opera *Downslope* ("light pulp," "perfectly pitiful").[65]

Ironically, despite Shostakovich's seemingly principled railing against "applied" culture, his own stage and screen work continued unabated. In fact, he was already in the thick of his second opera, *The Lady Macbeth of the Mtsensk District*, at the time of the "Declaration." Was he simply feigning indignation in order to justify his withdrawal from *Negro* and *The Concrete Sets*? To be fair, the real target of his ire was not stage work per se but rather the whole culture of "commissioning," and *Lady Macbeth*, at least, was not a commissioned work. Nevertheless, Shostakovich was learning some skills that would be essential to his survival in the decades to follow, mastering the art of uttering in public certain half-truths about his future creative activities. A few months later, he announced plans for a choral symphony on the theme "from Karl Marx to our own days," a project that would never come to fruition and that was possibly nothing more than an insurance policy to protect himself from the possible fallout from his "Declaration."

As 1931 drew to a close, the West was treated to a rare glimpse of the young Shostakovich via a now-famous *New York Times* interview. An interview with the foreign press would have been carefully monitored by Party officials, and, needless to say, Shostakovich did not regale his interviewer, Rose Lee, with gripes about RAPM. Instead, he attributed his tiredness to three years with "no real vacation and not much relaxation." Mouthing the standard Party line, he advocated music as an "organizing force," while declaring that "Beethoven's Third awakens one to the joy of struggle" and that Scriabin is "our bitterest musical enemy." As Lee noted, "There was something alarming in the assurance of this young man, disposing of the past with no more apparent effort than a twitch of the fingers and a curl of his short upper lip."[66] But although Shostakovich had no doubt been coached for the occasion, it should be noted that some of the opinions expressed—his animosity towards Scriabin and his indifference to Wagner—would be consistently reiterated both in public and in private throughout much of his life.

CHAPTER 6

RISE AND FALL, FALL AND RISE
(1932–1937)

The latter half of 1931 had seen the beginning of a backlash against the Cultural Revolution, as the demoralization of Soviet culture was now becoming apparent not only to the long-disgruntled intelligentsia but to elements within the Party and even within the proletarian organizations themselves.[1] In September, the Party acknowledged that proletarian music education had been a "superficial, harebrained scheme,"[2] while in December, Narkompros reported that the Moscow Conservatory (which, in a fit of proletarian fervor, had in 1930 been renamed the Felix Kon Higher School of Music) placed "little emphasis ... on musical techniques, or on the significance of appreciating musical heritage" and promoted a "vulgarization of the Marxist analysis of music."[3] Given that the conservatories had been decimated by the more-or-less enforced departure of its leading figures, people like Asafyev, Shcherbachov, Myaskovsky, and Gliere, this should have come as no surprise.

Bold and risky though they undoubtedly were, Shostakovich's November "Declaration" and his subsequent comments in December can, in hindsight, be seen as part of the emerging backlash. On 23 April 1932, that backlash would come to a head with a Central Committee Resolution ("On the Reformation of Literary-Artistic Organizations") liquidating all creative organizations, including RAPP and RAPM, and mandating the formation of state-controlled Unions (Writers' Union, Composers' Union, etc.). In the words of the Resolution, the proletarian organizations had become "too narrow and ... an obstacle to the serious development of artistic work."[4] At a gathering of composers later that day, the chief of Narkompros, the proletarian hardliner Andrei Bubnov, made what must have seemed like a stunning admission: "With mass song alone, you cannot go far. There is a need for Soviet opera, Soviet Symphonies, and chamber music and light music."[5]

The Resolution was keenly received by the artistic community. Indeed, it was one of the major factors in Prokofiev's eventual decision to return back to Russia from France, something he had been flirting with since the mid-1920s. Shostakovich, too, expressed his appreciation, describing RAPM as having been "in no way occupied ... with questions on the education of fellow-travelers—it was only abuse, abstraction, and demagoguery in opinion, sticking labels and nicknames on fellow-travelers and their works."[6] In fact, four weeks after the Resolution, Shostakovich would spring his own "revenge" on that despised organization with his impertinently scatological send-up of RAPM leader Davidenko's mass song, *They Wanted to Beat Us*, inserted into his incidental music to Nikolai Akimov's iconoclastic, swashbuckling production of *Hamlet*.[7] But as Shostakovich, Prokofiev, and scores of other composers would in time learn, the Resolution was not entirely what it appeared to be.

Stalin's First Five-Year Plan (1928–1933) to collectivize Soviet agriculture and centralize the economy had been both an economic disaster and a human tragedy. Millions of peasants had been deliberately starved to death in the name of a scheme that would fail to achieve any of its grotesquely bloated targets.[8] In the event, the Plan was terminated in 1932, though in true Soviet style this disaster was turned into a public relations victory—"The Five-Year Plan in Four Years," bragged the official report.[9] Although the full horror of Stalin's atrocities was kept under wraps, there were enough dissenting voices within the Party—perhaps most notably the Leningrad Party boss Sergei Kirov—that even Stalin realized the vulnerability of his position if improvements in the lives of ordinary people were not appearing to take place. The Second Five-Year Plan, published in 1933 with rather more modest targets, inaugurated a two-year period of economic liberalization, the so-called "Second NEP." Meanwhile, 1934 saw the initial drafting of a Soviet Constitution, published in 1936, promising improved civil rights and even a hint of democracy. Stalin's famous slogan, coined towards the end of 1935, "Life has become better, life has become happier," became the obligatory mantra of the period.

Stalin also understood that his survival depended upon a *nomenklatura*, or "interested class"—people whose privileged positions depended upon his survival and whose loyalty he could thus take for granted. That was why the storm troopers of RAPP and RAPM had enjoyed his backing. For as long as they were useful in bullying the intelligentsia, they received preferential treatment. But their time was now up. There was no longer a place for the "cult of the ordinary" in Stalin's new age of authoritarianism, social conservatism, and "socialist heroism." This new world of grandiose Five-Year Plans needed high art that was ambitious, yet traditional—not the "agitational" short-forms of the 1920s but epic masterpieces (novels, symphonies, operas, ballets) worthy of their nineteenth century forebears; not mechanized post-Revolutionary modernism but "red romanticism," expressing "the writer's emotional involvement with the reality he is describing, his predictions and dreams for the future."[10] Cultural leadership had to be wrested away from the "workers from the bench" (as the saying went) and given back to the intelligentsia, i.e., the old enemy. And the Resolution of 23 April 1932 would be the primary mechanism to bring this about.

***

Shostakovich had spent part of the spring of 1932 finishing his score for Akimov's production of *Hamlet* and would spend part of the autumn on his score to the film *The Counterplan*, yet another of those ubiquitous "industrial sabotage" pieces. As successful as the latter was—the "Song of the Counterplan" became a pop hit in its own right—this piece of unashamed Socialist Realism was certainly no panacea for the compositional doldrums Shostakovich had been experiencing for the past two or three years. It was, rather, his second opera, *The Lady Macbeth of the Mtsensk District*,[11] that would set him down the path of compositional maturity. Composed between October 1930 and December 1932, *The Lady Macbeth of the Mtsensk District* was an adaptation of Nikolai Leskov's 1864 short story of the same name. In Leskov's novella, a bored and frustrated merchant's wife, Katerina Izmailova, murders her way out of her oppressively provincial and patriarchal surroundings to clear the way for a new life with one of the Izmailov estate workers, Sergei. She kills her father-in-law, Boris, her husband, Zinovy, and her child nephew. Exiled for their crimes, Katerina and Sergei join the convict trail to Siberia. On the trail, Sergei drops her for another convict, Sonyetka. At the end, Katerina kills both herself and her rival. Although it had rather fallen out of view, Leskov's tale had been making something of a comeback during the late 1920s, thanks in part to a 1927 film adaptation. Shostakovich's interest was likely further piqued by the fact that a 1930 re-publication of the novella had featured illustrations by his recently deceased friend Boris Kustodiyev.

Leskov had narrated his story in an almost brutally matter-of-fact style, succinct and non-judgmental. By contrast, Shostakovich, together with his co-librettist Alexander Preis, would give this "tragedy-satire," as he termed it, an unmistakable angle, one overtly sympathetic to Katerina. Through careful changes to the plot and through his musical characterization, he attempted to present Katerina not as an inherently evil woman, but as a victim forced into her vile acts by her surroundings, surroundings that appear even more oppressive in the opera than they are in the novel. For example, the police are now given their own scene in which, even before their murder investigation begins, their brutality, stupidity, and corruptness are plain for all to see. (Although the opera was, of course, touted as a commentary on the oppressiveness of rural Tsarist life, the insertion of this particular scene may well have had relevance in the context of the emerging Stalinist police state.) Discussion of the Shostakovich/Preis libretto, as it relates to Leskov, can be found in Chapter 11. The extent to which Shostakovich succeeded in his avowed goal can perhaps be gauged by a comment made to him by "an outstanding musician" at rehearsal: "[the opera] ought to be named *Juliet of the Mtsensk District* or *Desdemona of the Mtsensk District*, because Lady Macbeth was an energetic woman whereas in my opera she was a gentle and suffering woman arousing compassion and sympathy rather than fear."[12]

Shortly before its completion, Shostakovich described *Lady Macbeth* as the first of a planned trilogy of operas "about the fate of women in Russia at different epochs."[13] A year or so later, that projection would expand to a "Soviet *Ring of the Nibelung*—an operatic tetralogy about woman, in which *Lady Macbeth* will be analogous with *Das Rheingold*."[14] The remaining three operas would be based on Revolutionary or Socialist Realist feminist themes, Shostakovich declaring, "This is the leading motive of my daily reflections and will be for a decade to come."[15] Although it is impossible to tell how his operatic career might have developed were it not for the events of 1936, Shostakovich's unusual specificity and insistent tone raise the suspicion that these may indeed have been "political" promises for official consumption, akin to the promised but never delivered choral symphony on the theme "from Karl Marx to our own days." The Soviet Union had always prided itself on its progressive stance towards women, at least until Stalin's mid-1930s push for traditional family values. Completion of a "feminist" operatic tetralogy could have earned Shostakovich political capital.

Lady Macbeth's raw-nerved drama would meet its match in a score combining the lurid naturalism and violent eroticism of Strauss' *Salome* or Berg's *Wozzeck* with a heavy dose of music-hall satire. Yet, Shostakovich, who had so recently complained about music's subordinate role in contemporary stage works, was also keen to distance himself from his former "anti-operatic" tendencies. In particular, the primacy of the word, which had been one of the central tenets of *The Nose*, was usurped by a more traditional "music first" approach. To this end, he abandoned the recitative/arioso style of *The Nose*, stressing instead that "there should be singing" and that "all the vocal parts in *Lady Macbeth* are in the nature of cantilena, songful."[16] He also stressed *Lady Macbeth's* "symphonic" nature. Although he was likely using the term to describe the opera's continuous and vital orchestral fabric rather than to connote symphonic process in the usual sense, there would nevertheless be signs here of a new "symphonic" profundity—none more so perhaps than the passacaglia that constituted the entr'acte between Scenes 4 and 5, Shostakovich's first serious attempt at a device that would become such a fixture in his later writing. (His one previous attempt was a rather basic ground, lasting about forty seconds, in *New Babylon*.)

Another connection to "traditional" opera cited by commentators is the use of leitmotif, though Shostakovich himself categorically denied it.[17] David Fanning, for example, has identified four main sets of leitmotifs that he believes represent, respectively, "force," "sleeplessness," "male sexual inadequacy," and "Katerina's self-assertion."[18] The "force" motif, identified as such by others also,[19] is particularly notable and crops up in many other Shostakovich works.[20] It comprises two entities: the first contains within it, or, as in Example 6.1, consists solely of, a dotted rhythm or some variant thereof; the second is a simple two-note figure that, more often than not, reiterates the same pitch. Example 6.1 shows the motif as it appears in the fanfare from the police entr'acte between Scenes 7 and 8.

Example 6.1

Fanning points out that "the fact that this motif starts with such a strongly accented downbeat as well as finishing with those two accented notes enables it to function equally well as a beginning of a phrase or a conclusion,"[21] although in practice, the motif often appears not so much as the departure or arrival point of some longer phrase but as its own self-contained phrasal entity. In some cases, simple repetitions or variations of the motif aggregate to create longer phrases. The example above demonstrates this, though the so-called "invasion theme" from the Seventh Symphony (1941) is even more striking in this regard (Example 6.2).

Example 6.2

Occasionally, Shostakovich would use the reiterated two-note figure independently of the dotted rhythm, but still within a highly forceful context, e.g., the Fifth Symphony finale (Fig. 111, b7), where the reiterated figure provides an emphatic termination to the movement's first section.

If *Lady Macbeth* was Shostakovich's passport to maturity, it was also, thrillingly, a work of its time. Shostakovich's output between 1930 and 1932 had been overwhelmingly slanted towards "light music" (and would continue to be for the next couple of years), and he had no compunction about allowing this influence into this, his first tragic masterpiece. Here, the "Soviet Rossini" (as he had sometimes been dubbed) and the "Soviet Beethoven" sit incandescently, if not always comfortably, cheek by jowl. The opera's "music-hall" moments include the Gogolian musings of the Priest before he delivers his requiem for the murdered Boris (Scene 4), the Shabby Peasant's paean to the joys of alcohol (Scene 6), the scene at the police station (Scene 7), and the taunting of the Ismailovs' cook Aksinya (Scene 2), the latter, incidentally, a reworking by Shostakovich of the "Bacchanalia" from *Declared Dead*.

The opera's famous erotic moments also have their share of music-hall vulgarity. During the notorious sex scene with Katerina and Sergei, Shostakovich drives along the action with a raucous galop—no transcendental Wagnerian eroticism here. But then this is overtly a "sex" scene, and one with more than a hint of brutality, not a "love" scene. (The association of the galop with sadism is reinforced elsewhere—the aforementioned molestation of Aksinya as well as the flogging scene immediately following Sergei's conquest of Katerina.) At the climax come the infamous trombone glissandi—upwards to portray Sergei's tumescence, then downwards to portray the opposite. If the upward glissandi are somehow integrated into the galop's frenetic fabric, the post-climactic downward glissandi are pure comedy, a moment of "nudge-nudge" humor in which our attention is unceremoniously, if briefly, ripped away from the plot as we are forced to laugh at the twenty-five-year-old composer's unblushing smuttiness.

Yet, for all this, Shostakovich did not view the opera as primarily sexually driven. He was as critical of those audience members who, seemingly, were in attendance only for gratuitous titillation as he was of those whose prudery prevented any serious appreciation of the opera. He would be horrified, for example, by the "provincial" reaction at an April 1933 preview that he gave in Sverdlovsk in which his audience questioned whether an opera written "in our heroic times" should feature sexual intercourse "taking place all the time."[22] He would also be concerned that the performances themselves set the right tone, that Sonyetka, for example, should not degenerate into "a female vampire, a hoity-toity courtesan, or a worldly coquette," but should remain a "simple, flirtatious girl, without any demoniacal side to her."[23]

The aforementioned sex scene sits on a knife-edge between heavy expressionism and music-hall comedy. In fact, this "knife-edge" between seemingly incongruous elements provides the basis for much of the opera's conflicts and ironies. For example, the scene between Boris and the estate laborers (Scene 1) provides a wonderfully uneasy balance, this time between Musorgskian grand opera and musical comedy. Boris chides the laborers for showing no "sadness or longing" at their master's (Zinovy's) imminent departure. The laborers retort indignantly, "We do!," with a full-throated chord of A-flat major, the opera's first choral/orchestral tutti and its first overtly "grand" gesture. The laborers then proceed to bemoan the dreariness of life without the master and to plead for his quick return. The parallel with the Prologue of Musorgsky's *Boris Godunov*, where the idle crowd assembled outside Novodevichy monastery is castigated by the cudgel-wielding police officer ("What's wrong with you? Have you turned to stone?") and then falls to its knees to plead for Boris' attention, is inescapable.

> **Musorgsky (crowd):** "To whom are you abandoning us,/Our Father!/Oh, to whom are you leaving us,/Benefactor!/We are all your orphans,/Quite defenseless . . .
>
> **Shostakovich (laborers):** "Why are you leaving us, master,/Why? Why?/To whom are you abandoning us?/ To whom? To whom?/Without the master life will be boring,/Boring, depressing and unhappy . . .

In both operas, the response to orders and threats from above is laced with irony—a case of "forced rejoicing," to use *Testimony's* famous phrase. But where Musorgsky's crowd sublimates this irony into a pliant chorus of the pleading and the downtrodden, the Izmailov estate laborers, after their grand A-flat outburst, do their "pleading" with a drinking song. Courtesy of Shostakovich, *Boris Godunov* plunges headlong into *La Traviata*.

Following the poisoning scene (Scene 4), Shostakovich takes up again the Musorgskian reference to pleading and abandonment. Once the priest declares Boris dead, Katerina starts wailing: "Oh, Boris Timofeyevich,/Why have you left us?/To whom have you abandoned Zinovy and me?/What will Zinovy and I/Do now without you?" But now, Shostakovich appropriates not just the text from Musorgsky's chorus but the music as well, as Katerina launches into a falsely hysterical rendition of Musorgsky's theme, to a ridiculous accompaniment of bassoons and piccolo (later E-flat clarinet)—her crocodile tears over the loss of her sad, sadistic father-in-law, Boris, perhaps passing commentary, in some perverse way, on the evils of Tsar Boris himself.

The influences upon Shostakovich over the course of his life were, of course, many: Stravinsky, Hindemith, and Berg in his younger years; Mahler, Musorgsky, Beethoven, Bach, and possibly Britten later on. Yet, it would not be a stretch to assert that no single work in the repertoire—not *The Well-Tempered Clavier*, not *Das Lied von der Erde*, not even *Wozzeck*—cast as long a shadow down the path of Shostakovich's career as did *Boris Godunov*, a work that Shostakovich would himself re-orchestrate in 1939. In addition to its influence on *Lady Macbeth*, echoes of Musorgsky's great opera would be heard in portions of Shostakovich's Fifth and Eleventh Symphonies. Even more specifically, the first few notes of the aforementioned crowd theme would provide the basis for the "invasion" theme in the Seventh Symphony (see Example 6.2, above) and the first theme in the Eighth.

***

Shostakovich completed *Lady Macbeth* in December 1932 and dedicated it to his new wife, Nina Vasilyevna Varzar, whom he had married that May. Their relationship, which had been developing since their first encounter in 1927, had caused consternation at home; Shostakovich's ultra-protective mother did not initially take too kindly to Nina. A further complication was Shostakovich's continuing involvement with Tatyana Glivenko. Although Glivenko married in 1929, Shostakovich had continued to believe in a future with her, a belief that only faded with the birth of her first child in 1931. In other words, Shostakovich was true to the sentiments he had expressed back in 1923 to his mother. Then, he had decried the institution of marriage as an impediment to free love, but had defended "the sacred vocation of parenthood."[24]

A physicist by profession, Nina was a strong, independent woman who would prove the very embodiment of the ideal partner outlined by Shostakovich in that adolescent letter—a loving wife and devoted mother, but professionally and sexually independent. The couple had agreed to an open marriage, not unusual in Russia for those who came of age during the 1920s, though the result was still turbulent. In 1934, Shostakovich began an affair with a student translator, Yelena Konstantinovskaya, telling her, "I am dreaming of you falling in love with me and becoming my wife ... in spite of me being more or less married."[25] In 1935, the Shostakoviches filed for divorce, though a hasty remarriage was arranged upon the news of Nina's pregnancy, yet another testament to the accuracy of Shostakovich's teenage prediction—"I have only now realized and fathomed what a remarkable woman she is, and how precious to me," he would tell Sollertinsky.[26] The birth of Galina in 1936 and Maxim in 1938 brought some stability, though the open arrangement in matters sexual would continue. In later years, Nina's strength and her organizational abilities were a life-saving foil for her emotionally more fragile husband. To what extent Shostakovich saw Nina's strong, vibrant personality in the character of Katerina—his own somewhat idealized operatic vision of Katerina, that is—we can only speculate. But *Lady Macbeth* was undoubtedly the work that he most associated with Nina. Not only was it dedicated to her, but it was also the work that would preoccupy him in the immediate aftermath of her untimely death in December 1954.

***

Lady Macbeth would eventually open in January 1934, thirteen months after its completion, in two parallel productions, one in Leningrad, one in Moscow. For Shostakovich, much of 1933 was spent with the negotiations and eventual supervision of these productions, but the first half of the year saw two completed works, the Twenty-Four Preludes for piano, op. 34, and the First Piano Concerto. Both pieces—and to these, one should add the Cello Sonata of 1934—were written in part to revive a piano career that had now ground to a halt. Shostakovich had not performed in public since 1930 and was keen to resume at least some level of concert activity, though he had long since abandoned any thoughts of a full-time solo career. More importantly, though, these three works announced Shostakovich's return, after a seven-year hiatus, to the world of non-programmatic concert music.

Composed between December 1932 and March 1933, the Preludes can be viewed as an "update" of *Aphorisms*. Less overtly iconoclastic and more nuanced in their ironies, they were modeled after Chopin's Twenty-Four Preludes, op. 28. Shostakovich follows Chopin's journey through the twenty-four keys—clockwise around the circle of fifths, incorporating both major and relative minor (C major, A minor, G major, E minor, etc.). And although Shostakovich will hardly go down in history as a miniaturist, his ability to portray fleeting impressions and, perhaps more crucially, complete a full-fledged musical argument in highly compressed time periods proves almost the equal of the nineteenth-century master. Yet, his engagement with the Romantic miniature comes through a neoclassical filter. Keyboard textures are spare and comic gestures abound, most of which arise from quirky tonal juxtapositions. In many of the Preludes, the tonic is abandoned immediately after the initial phrase or phrase period, with the rest of the Prelude spent on a search-and-rescue mission for the lost tonality, often to uproarious effect. This skittishness is enhanced by a frequent use of pitch collections (usually scales) that conflict with the tonality of the moment, a technique discussed in Chapter 12.

The shorter Preludes are often particularly striking in this regard. In the most extreme example, the whirlwind D major Prelude (No. 5), the music goes off the tonal rails at the end of the fourth bar and does not return to "the upright position" until the curt D major cadence at the very end. That final surprise is set up by a left hand line that, in the four bars leading up to the cadence, proclaims itself in B-flat minor. And while the left hand is attempting this diversion, the last three bars in the right hand feature nothing but unadulterated D major scales. This dual-track method of tonal preparation—a (relatively) long final approach to the tonic in one hand subverted by a non-prepared, instantaneous arrival at the tonic in the other—gives the music its quirky irony. Other Preludes present different slants on the same concept. Unlike the D major Prelude, the 42-bar long F-sharp minor Prelude (No. 8) does touch upon its tonic on several occasions towards the end—bars 25, 29, and 35. But in bar 36, F-sharp minor suddenly disappears, to return only as a last minute cadence (see Chapter 12, Example 12.6). Something similar happens in the B major Prelude (No. 11), which even has a tonic presentation of the first theme ten bars before the end. The A-flat Prelude (No. 17), on the other hand, presents the one "opposite" (as Levon Hakobian might characterize it),[27] the single instance of non-ironized Romantic pastiche, the one Prelude where, for all its perfumed chromaticism, the tonic is never threatened. Perhaps not coincidentally, this Prelude turns out to be gesturally the most Chopinesque of the set—a romantic, rubato-laden slow waltz, marked *espressivo amoroso*.

After the scabrous wit, sarcasm, and heavy-fisted iconoclasm that had characterized much of Shostakovich's writing between 1926 and 1932—whether in *Aphorisms*, *The Nose*, *The Golden Age*, *The Bolt*, *Declared Dead*, *Lady Macbeth*, or the incidental score to *Hamlet*—the First Piano Concerto, scored for piano, strings, and trumpet obbligato, would see a return to the more benevolent, knockabout circus wit that had characterized the First Symphony. In retrospect, the First Symphony and First Piano Concerto can be viewed almost as respective book ends framing that seven-year exploration of "extreme" humor and non-concert forms. Although the Concerto's first movement starts with a Prokofiev-like lyricism (after the one-bar introductory tease and the deadpan quotation of Beethoven's *Appassionata* Sonata, that is), the second subject already displays some of the madcap circus style that will come back in the finale. Appearing in the classically expected key of E-flat (relative to the work's tonic, C minor), that second subject indulges in various comic "wrong-note" antics, the flat sixth (C-flat) being a favorite. (The First Piano Concerto (1946) of Shostakovich's student German Galynin was certainly written under this influence.) In the recapitulation, Shostakovich reprises only the second part of this second theme, but then uses that as the basis for a new theme, also in the circus style—one of the first examples of the type of thematic transformation that would be such a critical factor in Shostakovich's recapitulations from the mid-1930s on.

The circus buffoonery comes to a head in the fourth movement sonata-rondo finale (A-B-A-C-A-B-coda). Like the first movement, the finale starts with "serious" music, this time, a spiky, agitated theme that, like its very different first movement counterpart, seems Prokofiev-inspired. Yet, to an even greater extent than the first movement, the opening theme is not what ultimately resonates in the memory. It is quickly hijacked—first by the brash trumpet quotation from Haydn's Piano Sonata No. 33 (D major, Hob. xvi/37) that concludes the first subject group (Fig. 51, b7), then by the assortment of music hall and circus-like tunes that constitute the second subject group (starting Fig. 52, b2), and finally by the rondo's central theme (Fig. 63), a quotation, played by the trumpet accompanied by strings *col legno*, of the English nursery song "Poor Jennie sits a-weeping"— incidentally, the fourth time in as many years that Shostakovich had employed this tune.[28] In this latter theme, the piano is the comedian, whose sole function is to bang out a single chord, *fff*, in what may be an attempt to outdo Haydn's *Surprise*

Symphony. (Incidentally, the chord itself—B-sharp, D-sharp, F-sharp, A-sharp—may sound like "wrong-note" humor, yet it is harmonically functional in the context of the E to D-flat modulation that is taking place at this point.) Although the initial "A" theme does return in most of the expected sonata-rondo places, its function becomes ever more subordinate to the high-wire circus acts that occupy the rest of the movement.

The choice of sonata-rondo for a concerto finale emphasizes Shostakovich's neoclassical intentions, though even this is subverted in humorous ways. The ever-decreasing importance of the "A" theme, the movement's only "serious" music, is one. The placement of the cadenza, in which the grand classical-style cadence onto the dominant chord and accompanying trill occurs not after the cadenza but before it, is another. The cadenza itself, which subsequently shoots off in an entirely different key from that prepared by the dominant chord, pulls out yet another quotation, Beethoven's *Rondo a capriccio* ("The Rage over the Lost Penny"). As Shostakovich wrote the following year, "I want to defend the right of laughter to appear in what is called 'serious music.' When listeners laugh at a concert of my symphony music, I am not in the least shocked—I'm pleased."[29]

Of course, the First Piano Concerto is not all hi-jinks and circus acts. The inner two movements possess a lyricism, even at times a romanticism, which had not been fully felt in his music since the First Symphony's slow movement—though, of course, *Lady Macbeth* and the Preludes, op. 34, had witnessed a move in this direction. Yet, the lyricism in the Concerto is of a nature different from that in the Symphony—simpler, less feverish, less Tchaikovskian. The cool, high-lying violin line at the start of the slow second movement looks forward to the lyrical portions of Shostakovich's Seventh Symphony, while the piano's conclusion to that opening melody, before it goes off into its own material, is written in that "innocent" lyrical style that Shostakovich would later employ in his oratorio *The Song of the Forests* or the Second Piano Concerto.

If the finale's sonata-rondo structure was a tribute to a Classical archetype, the same might be said about the second movement. With its slow outer sections flanking a faster, more agitated center, it is reminiscent of a type of slow movement, the *Romanza*, occasionally found in Mozart.[30] Meanwhile, the recitative-like third movement, in essence a short prelude to the fourth movement finale, creates a mini-drama between piano and strings similar in concept to, if wholly different in character from, the slow movement of Beethoven's Fourth Piano Concerto.

Shostakovich had originally conceived the work as a trumpet concerto. He then revamped it as a double concerto for piano and trumpet, before eventually consigning the trumpet to an obbligato role. In the first movement, the trumpet functions as little more than a commentator. In the exposition, it takes up one of the piano's second subject melodies and subsequently provides some closing flourishes. It contributes hardly at all in the development, but comes back to close the movement. Its role expands in the second movement, where it plays the reprise of the main melody following the movement's central section, and so acts as a counterweight to the violins, which played this melody on its first appearance. Silent in the third movement, the trumpet comes into its own in the finale. Although still not an equal partner to the piano, it initiates ideas to a greater extent than in previous movements, and is even given its own theme ("Poor Jennie"), shared with neither the piano nor the orchestra.

***

As intended, the Piano Concerto put Shostakovich back on the concert platform. But this and other activities—for example, his work during the winter of 1933–34 on the incidental music to Pavel Sukhotin's play *The Human Comedy* (based on Balzac)—were overshadowed by the premiere of *Lady Macbeth*, the opera that had by this point been over three years in the making. It opened on 22 January 1934 at the Leningrad Malyi Opera (Malegot). Two days later, billed as *Katerina Izmailova*, it opened in Moscow. By all accounts, Vladimir Nemirovich-Danchenko's Moscow production was a grander affair than Nikolai Smolich's in Leningrad. Shostakovich certainly enjoyed the quality and professionalism of the Moscow forces, though he felt that Smolich's less frilly production, with its greater satirical immediacy, came closer to his own conception.[31] In the first year, the opera was given some fifty times in Leningrad ("standing room only with increased prices," as Shostakovich liked to boast[32]), while 1935 would see performances in Europe (Zagreb, Ljubljana, Bratislava, Copenhagen, Stockholm, Prague, Zurich, London) and the Americas (Cleveland, New York, Philadelphia, Buenos Aires), as well as the opening of a second Moscow production, this time at the Bolshoi.

Lady Macbeth's violence and sympathetic portrayal of a murderess were, inevitably, not to everybody's taste. But for the most part, this was not dwelt upon. Public and critics alike were thrilled by the enormous talent on display; the press missed no opportunity to squeeze maximum political capital from what it saw as "the result of the general success of Socialist construction, of the correct policy of the Party."[33] Shostakovich was praised for having "torn off the masks and exposed the false and lying methods of the composers of bourgeois society,"[34] and for his "Soviet" interpretation of Leskov's novella that exposed, as Leskov himself could not, pre-Revolutionary moral corruption as the story's true culprit. Shostakovich had not enjoyed a sensation like this since the First Symphony.

The overtly political way in which *Lady Macbeth* was being touted in Russia did not go unchallenged abroad. Following the performances in New York in early 1935, the fiercely anti-Soviet Stravinsky described being "brutalized by the arrogance of the numerous communist brass instruments,"[35] while *New York Times* critic Olin Downes deplored the libretto as "Communistic." Yet, although he found the score "flimsily put together,"[36] Downes was, like many in the West, enthralled by the opera's theatrical impact.

Although Shostakovich had, as already noted, encountered some "provincial" attitudes towards *Lady Macbeth's* eroticism, this aspect had not crippled its success amongst Soviet critics—at least, not at this point. However, Western commentators were not so forgiving. *New York Sun* critic, William J. Henderson, dubbed

Shostakovich "without doubt the foremost composer of pornographic music in the history of the opera,"[37] while in Philadelphia, the Clean Amusement Association of the City of Brotherly Love lobbied to have *Lady Macbeth* banned altogether. One foreign admirer not stricken by coyness was Benjamin Britten:

> Of course it is idle to pretend that this is great music throughout—it is stage music and as such must be considered. There is some terrific music in the entr'acts. But I will defend it through thick & thin against these charges of "lack of style." People will not differentiate between style & manner. It is the composer's heritage to take what he wants from where he wants—& to write music. There is a consistency of style & method throughout. The satire is biting & brilliant. It is never boring for a second— even in [concert] form. . . . The "eminent English Renaissance" composers sniggering in the stalls was typical. There is more music in a page of MacBeth than in the whole of their "elegant" output![38]

***

With *Lady Macbeth* now up and running, the public could finally witness that "knife-edge" that Shostakovich had been grappling with throughout the early 1930s; the juxtaposition of the music hall and the deadly serious, the interaction of the young Shostakovich (the "Soviet Rossini") with the more mature (the "Soviet Beethoven"). Shostakovich's compositions in 1934 would be primarily of the "light music" variety—probably the final year of his career for which this was true. In February, he composed his three-movement First Suite for Jazz Orchestra— as delightful a refutation of RAPM's egregious 1930 campaign against light music as it is possible to imagine. Of course, the movement's titles (Waltz, Polka, and Foxtrot) indicate that what was being offered was not jazz in the conventional Western sense, but "Tea-Jazz" (*teatralnyi dzhaz*)—dance hall or café music of the type that Leonid Utyosov's band in particular had made popular. Although not composed for Utyosov, the First Suite is scored for a typical dance band—saxophones, trumpets, trombone, percussion, piano, Hawaiian guitar, solo violin, and solo double bass.

In addition to the completion of the incidental music to *The Human Comedy*, 1934 also saw Shostakovich's impish score to Mikhail Tsekhanovsky's cartoon, *The Tale of the Priest and his Servant, Balda*. The film was never completed and, as Derek Hulme reports, only 165 feet of it survived the 1941 bombing of the Leningrad Film Studio.[39] However, Shostakovich's Suite survives, and in the short extant footage ("Scene in the Bazaar"),[40] we can hear the composer's quick-wittedness, his own penchant for cartoonery, put to excellent use.

Also composed mainly in 1934 was Shostakovich's score to Fyodor Lopukhov and Adryan Pyotrovsky's ballet, *The Limpid Stream* (premiered in Leningrad in June 1935). A typical story of Socialist construction, *The Limpid Stream* tells of the arrival of artists at a collective farm in the Kuban region, and of the subsequent struggles and eventual reconciliation between them and the resident farm workers. Once again, Shostakovich had found himself with an uninspiring ballet libretto. "Ignominious failure" is how he described it to Sollertinsky after its first performances in Leningrad, adding "that has always been precisely my attitude to it from the very first."[41] For his part, Sollertinsky admitted that the music, though "lively [and] full of temperament," "lack[ed] inner unity."[42] Like the previous ballets, *The Limpid Stream* would enjoy greater acclaim with audiences than amongst the critics.

Although Sollertinsky would revise his opinion somewhat after seeing the superior production in Moscow that opened in November 1935, his perception of the ballet's lack of unity should hardly have come as a surprise given that ten of its forty-four numbers were recycled—eight from *The Bolt*, two from the Suite for Jazz Orchestra. Of course, this was not the first time that Shostakovich had dipped into his reservoir of earlier works: *New Babylon* and *The Bedbug* had shared two numbers, *Lady Macbeth* and *Declared Dead* had one number in common, as had *Declared Dead* and *The Tale of the Priest and his Servant, Balda*. But nowhere was the recycling more blatant than in *The Bolt* (taking from *The Bedbug, Alone, The Golden Age,* and *New Babylon*), the incidental music to *Hamlet* (using material from *Rule Britannia!, Declared Dead, The Golden Age,* and *Alone*), and *The Limpid Stream*. Possibly, Shostakovich was trying to salvage music from works that had fallen out of the repertoire. But his recycling of entire numbers, not to be confused with his propensity for melodic self-quotation, does in many cases seem to have been little more than a time-saving device for a hassled and uninspired composer. In his 1931 "Declaration," he had complained about the careless "cranking out" of music, yet it was only after *The Limpid Stream* that he finally made good on his promise to cut back on work for the stage, and it is probably no coincidence that his practice of wholesale recycling for the most part came to a halt at this time (though it would be revived in his 1958 operetta, *Moscow, Cheryomushki*).

* * *

The most important work of 1934 was the Cello Sonata, composed in August and September, and premiered in December. Devoid of "light music" influences, the Sonata represented the first full flowering of a somewhat neoclassical lyrical style that had been tentatively emerging through the early 1930s, a style that had been briefly witnessed in the slow movement of the First Piano Concerto and in some of the op. 34 Preludes. In fact, the Cello Sonata is possibly the most completely lyrical non-vocal concert work that Shostakovich would ever write, an assertion that, ironically, holds whether one shares David Rabinovich's opinion of the work as a "sudden ray of sunshine" or Ian MacDonald's view of it as "strained, sardonic, and distinctly bitter."[43] As for the neoclassicism, this was manifested not just in the cut of the Sonata's melodies but in some of the formal aspects too—for example, the scherzo-trio-scherzo-coda form in the second movement, not to mention the decidedly old-fashioned exposition repeat in the first, a feature that would later grace the similarly neoclassical first movements of the Ninth Symphony (1945) and the Third Quartet (1946). Yet, although the Sonata's first movement looks backwards in certain formal and stylistic respects, it would also function as an important step in Shostakovich's development of a "sonata-arch" form, a journey that had started back in the First Symphony (see Chapter 13).

Following a second movement that is styled as a high-voltage version of the Mahlerian *Ländler*, the slow third movement presents a funereal elegy. It opens with a wandering, tonally unstable introduction—the first six bars in the cello form a nine-note row, with the piano adding a tenth note—before B minor establishes itself in bar 20, right before the entry of the main theme. Although initially disconcerting within the lyrical context of the Sonata as a whole, this could actually be viewed as an "updating" of the chromatically wandering introductions of Haydn or Beethoven—another aspect of the work's neoclassicism.

The main melody (bar 21) is new, yet there is a whiff of familiarity about it. If the contour of its first notes (descending major second followed by a rising major second) is not enough to conjure memories of the first movement's second subject, the three-note monotone figure that pervades most of the piano accompaniment surely is, and it is this that gives the elegiac melody its funereal undertone. The movement contains no contrasting second theme; it is, rather, based upon a slow intensification and development of this one melody. Although the introductory material does indeed return twice, it does so both times as a structural delineator rather than as a contrasting theme per se. The first reappearance, an extended version starting at bar 57, puts the brakes on the previous intensification of the main theme and subsequently ushers in the tonic B minor reprise of that theme (bar 72, now without the "funereal" three-note figure), the second reappearance constitutes the movement's coda.

With its sonata rondo construction (ABACABA) and pseudo-Mozartian main theme, the fourth movement finale provides yet another nod to the classicists, though at a mere four or four-and-a-half minutes long (or three-and-a-half minutes in Shostakovich's own recording with Rostropovich!), it is actually rather dwarfed by its typical Mozartian counterpart. Yet, although on the surface, there would barely seem time for more than a routine, "textbook" run-through of the rondo's seven sections, Shostakovich creates a surprisingly dynamic movement. The presentation of the third "A" section in F minor (as opposed to the expected D minor tonic) and the stormy, disfigured transformation of the subsequent "B" section extends the developmental character of the preceding "C" section into what would, in the classical model, be considered the recapitulation, and thus creates a more fully dynamic sonata rondo presentation than the movement's brevity would seem to allow. Here, it is the fourth and final "A" section that feels like the true point of recapitulation. Over the next couple of decades, Shostakovich would explore further the integration of his own developing brand of symphonism into the highly stylized classical sonata rondo structure, e.g., in the finale of the First Violin Concerto (1948).

For the most part, the Sonata features simple parallel-octave (or two-octave) piano writing of the sort that would later become a staple in Shostakovich. On the other hand, though hardly interventionist, the piano writing is not above the odd moment of virtuoso bluster, particularly in the finale. Such moments remind us that for all its predominating lyricism, the Cello Sonata was written, like the Piano Concerto and the Preludes before it, in part to put Shostakovich the pianist back on the circuit.

∗∗∗

Less than a month after the watershed Resolution of 23 April 1932, the Organizing Committee of the fledgling Union of Soviet Writers had held its First Plenary Session. Taking its cue from the founding philosophies of Marx, Engels, and Bakhtin, the Committee proposed the literary method of Socialist Realism, which it defined as the "represent[ation of] reality in a truthful fashion, given that reality is in itself dialectical."[44] Later that year, the Union's journal, *Literaturnaya gazeta*, reiterated the method's dialectical, flexible nature: "The formula does not, of course, mean that all writers are obliged to write in the same way."[45] But at the Union's First Congress in August 1934, though some delegates continued to advocate flexibility and diversity within the "guiding line" of Socialist Realism, it was the altogether more doctrinaire stance of Andrei Zhdanov that eventually won out. Reiterating Stalin's view that the Soviet writer must be an "engineer of human souls,"[46] Zhdanov demanded that literature must above all display Party-mindedness (*partiinost*):

> In the first place, it means knowing life so as to be able to depict it truthfully in works of art, not to depict it in a dead, scholastic way, not simply as "objective reality," but to depict reality in its revolutionary development. In addition to this, the truthfulness and historical concreteness of the artistic portrayal should be combined with the ideological remolding and education of the toiling people in the spirit of socialism. This method in *belles lettres* and literary criticism is what we call the method of socialist realism. Our Soviet literature is not afraid of the charge of being "tendentious." Yes, Soviet literature is tendentious, for in an epoch of class struggle there is not and cannot be a literature which is not class literature, not tendentious, allegedly non-political.[47]

With this, Zhdanov not only put paid to the possibility of a flexible approach to Socialist Realism, but in his advocacy of "reality in its revolutionary development" actually opposed those founding principles of Marx and Engels. Where they had believed that "the writer is not obliged to obtrude on the reader the future historical solutions to the social conflicts pictured,"[48] the Zhdanov doctrine demanded "no conflict" (i.e., non-dialectical) literature that celebrated only positive social and political trends, showing clearly tomorrow's solutions to today's problems—in other words, selective reporting. The next few years would see a flurry of "Party-minded" Five-Year-Plan and Stakhanovite novels—hyperventilating, red-romantic prose celebrations of industrial and agricultural "overachievement."[49] In music, celebrations of the Five-Year-Plan could be heard in any number of "topical" symphonies and song-symphonies, the latter essentially an expansion of the old proletarian mass song into something of symphonic pretensions—Stalinist "Beethoven Ninths" high on political posturing and low on symphonic competence. Yet, amid this onslaught of blindly (and blandly) affirmative, "no conflict" art, certain elements, at least in the musical community, would fight for an alternative path.

One such figure was Sollertinsky. In the dark years of the Cultural Revolution, and against all the odds, Sollertinsky had managed to keep the flame of symphonism alive. Shrewdly, his 1929 article, "The Problem of Soviet Symphonism," had put less emphasis on symphonic language, with all its attendant bourgeois associations, and had instead played up the politically fashionable topics of "collectivism" and "dialectics" and their relationship to the symphonic process. In so doing, Sollertinsky was able to pull off something of a coup. "If a work could be described as symphonic," writes Pauline Fairclough, "then, assuming Sollertinsky's claims were accepted, no other apologia would be necessary. Music that was 'symphonic' would be inherently relevant, in spite of its abstract language."[50] Post-1932, however, this tactic would make less sense, given the re-emergence of Romantic cultural values, and would indeed create something of a dilemma for Sollertinsky's 1932 study of Mahler.[51] As Fairclough points out, the study is a web of self-contradiction, with Sollertinsky attempting to play up Mahler's proletarian/collectivist credentials while simultaneously declaring him a role model for the new, post-Resolution requirements of high art and heroism.[52]

Held in the shadow of the August 1934 Writers' Congress, the Composers' Union's Discussion on Soviet Symphonism took place between 4 and 6 February 1935. Like their literary counterparts, the composers at the Discussion struggled to find sense in a maze of ill defined, yet politically loaded concepts. The idea of "formalism," for example, the supposed antithesis of Socialist Realism, was being defined as "form for form's sake," "art for art's sake," "form at the expense of content," or, as it would later be defined by the Moscow Composers' Union chief, Nikolai Chelyapov: "the sacrifice of the ideological and emotional content of a musical composition to the search for new tricks in the realm of musical elements—rhythm, timbre, harmonic combinations."[53] But what exactly did this all mean? Was a work formalist simply because it lacked ideological content? Shostakovich reflected:

> I have heard many fine words on [topicality and content] yesterday and today, but unfortunately I am not able to say that I learned anything or had the question made clearer to me.... For a time it was oversimplified: it seemed that if you write a verse, that's content, [but if you] don't write a verse—that's formalism. Now they are beginning to state seriously that this issue rests not only in verses but also in music. But I repeat—this issue is too complicated, and it is impossible to give recipes for writing music with content.[54]

Two months later, Shostakovich would again attack the simplistic and indiscriminate use of the "formalist" label. Responding to allegations that he had succumbed to formalism, he retorted, "To brand any work as formalistic on the grounds that its language is complex and perhaps not immediately comprehensible, is unacceptably frivolous."[55] At the Discussion itself, in a speech that was depressingly reminiscent of his 1931 "Declaration," Shostakovich attacked the poor quality of contemporary Soviet symphonism, complaining that its achievements had been generally "exaggerated." He singled out the much-feted song-symphonies of Lev Knipper, describing them as "wretched and primitive."[56] He also called for re-established contacts with the West and for seminars on the music of Berg, Weill, and others,[57] a repeat of a similar call he had made the previous year,[58] and something that would have been unthinkable in the rabidly anti-Western atmosphere of the Writers' Congress. Other speakers out of step with the Zhdanov "no conflict" doctrine included the composer Konstantin Kuznetsov, who proposed a symphony that would conclude "in a depressed, slow vein (Adagio)" with "the weariness and subdued quality of Tchaikovsky's symphonism,"[59] and, of course, Sollertinsky, who continued to advocate a Mahlerian symphonic model, with its conflict-laden dialectics and its unashamed incorporation of popular genres.

That such dissent could be aired at all was one of the benefits of music's "lesser" status compared to literature. Unlike the Writers' Union, the Composers' Union did, at this stage at least, enjoy a degree of autonomy. Indeed, of the four creative Unions (Composers, Writers, Artists, and Architects), it was the Composers' Union—at that point still existing only in municipal (Moscow, Leningrad) and Republican (Armenia, Georgia, Ukraine, Azerbaijan) forms—that enjoyed the greatest autonomy from the Party.[60] Whereas the 1934 Writers' Congress had been a prestigious international showcase, attended and addressed by key Party figures and widely covered in the press, the Discussion on Soviet Symphonism received little notice outside the specialized columns of *Sovetskaya muzyka*. Pauline Fairclough has contrasted the "tightly controlled and monitored" Writers' Congress with the "rambling and unofficial" Discussion—the latter replete with "Shebalin's sarcastic comments, Sollertinsky's jokes, and Shostakovich's ironic observations."[61] The difference in status between music and literature, at least at this point, can perhaps be gauged by Stalin's dismissal in 1935 of the case of the arrested composer Nikolai Strelnikov: "We'll put this case aside. Don't let's trouble the musicians."[62]

For Shostakovich, the Discussion proved mostly worthless. He was attracted to Sollertinsky's proposals, but his search for a "symphonic credo," as he called it, was still ongoing. It had been five years since his last symphony, ten since his last successful symphony—a fourth symphony had been started back in late 1934, but was quickly aborted.[63] At first glance, his very next work following the Discussion, the aphoristic, workshop-like *Five Fragments* for small orchestra, could not have been further removed from symphonic concerns. In the single day (9 June 1935) that it took to pen this nine-minute work, Shostakovich entered instead the world of the Stravinskian miniature, using it as a base from which to pursue a variety of strands, some of which, however, would bear fruit in the upcoming Fourth Symphony. The Nielsenesque counterpoint of solo wind instruments that constitutes the first Fragment would be heard in the coda of the Fourth Symphony's first movement—compare the oboe's undulating fourths sandwiched inside a discord (Fig. 1, b6) with Fig. 108, b2–3 of the Symphony—as well as in parts of its scherzo. The second Fragment is a grotesque march with Mahlerian overtones, while the glacial third Fragment, with its sparse string writing and tolling harp, throws us forward to the Fourth Symphony's bleak coda. In fact, with its three-and-a-half octave space between cellos and violins at the start, it provides a glimpse of textures more associated with Shostakovich's late (post-1966) style. The fourth Fragment returns to the world of the first, and the fifth takes on yet another Mahlerian archetype, the *Ländler*, though the gypsy fiddle of Stravinsky's *L'histoire du soldat* also lurks in the background. Such a *Ländler* for solo violin would find its way into the Fifth Symphony's scherzo, though without the iconoclastic accompaniments found here in the Fragment—snare drum, then solo double bass. The *Ländler* itself had recently featured in the Cello Sonata and would appear again in several portions of the Fourth Symphony. In fact, a four-bar quotation from this Fragment can be found in the Symphony's finale—cf. fifth Fragment, Fig. 24, b4 and Fourth Symphony, Fig. 195.

Three months later, in September 1935, Shostakovich embarked for a second time on his fourth symphony, but now with the confidence to embrace Sollertinsky's model. The almost psychedelically ferocious, take-no-hostages symphony that emerged constituted the fiercest declaration of independence from a world dominated by Five-Year-Plan novels and "topical" song-symphonies. Yet, given that Sollertinsky's ideas for a Mahlerian-type symphony had gained at least some currency at the 1935 Discussion, and given that the Discussion had not reached any concrete conclusions as to the form the new Socialist Realist symphony should take, Pauline Fairclough argues that "there is no reason to suggest that [Shostakovich] was acting in defiance of Party or Composers' Union guidelines."[64] This is an important point to keep in mind as we come to consider the explosive and seemingly irrational events of 1936.

***

The second Moscow production of *Lady Macbeth* opened on the smaller stage of the Bolshoi theater on 26 December 1935. Directed by Smolich, it ran concurrently with Nemirovich-Danchenko's production. On 17 January 1936, Stalin attended the Bolshoi production of Ivan Dzerzhinsky's opera *The Quiet Don*. At the end, he granted Dzerzhinsky an audience and praised him for his achievements in the field of Socialist Realist opera. Nine days later, on 26 January, Stalin returned, this time to see contemporary Soviet musical theater's most acclaimed work, *Lady Macbeth*. That morning, Shostakovich received a phone call demanding his presence at the performance, a call that, according to his friend Levon Atovmyan, who was present at the time and who would accompany Shostakovich that evening, had given him a "funny feeling."[65]

For reasons that may only be guessed, a decision was made to augment the orchestra with extra brass for that night's performance. By all accounts, that, along with the unusually feverish conducting of Alexander Melik-Pashayev, contributed to a particularly overwrought performance of the already raw-edged opera, a fact noted by the author Mikhail Bulgakov, Atovmyan, and Shostakovich himself.[66] The tenor Sergei Radamsky, who sat beside Shostakovich that evening, reported agitation and laughter amongst the dignitaries in the government box (Zhdanov, Vyacheslav Molotov, and Anastas Mikoyan—Stalin himself was invisible, seated, as was his custom, behind a curtain). As the evening went on, Shostakovich became increasingly tense.[67] In the event, and in stark contrast to Dzerzhinsky's experience the previous week, no invitation to meet Stalin was forthcoming. In fact, sources disagree on whether Shostakovich even took a bow at the end of the performance.[68] When exactly the government dignitaries walked out is also disputed,[69] though Stalin's comment upon leaving the theater box was reportedly "It is noise, not music."

That night, following the performance, Shostakovich left for Arkhangelsk. Still rattled, he complained to Atovmyan: "Why was it necessary to reinforce the band, to exaggerate the noise level? What was all this, Melik-Pashayev with his excessive "shish-kekab" temperament? Did he have to spice up the entr'acte and the whole scene like that? I should think those in the government box must have been deafened by the volume of the brass. I have a bad premonition about this."[70] Two days later, on 28 January, at the Arkhangelsk railway station, Shostakovich picked up a copy of that day's *Pravda*, only to have his worst fears confirmed. There, on page three, appeared the article that would become the definitive document of Stalinist musical criticism, the unsigned editorial "Muddle Instead of Music: On Shostakovich's Opera *Lady Macbeth of the Mtsensk District*":

> From the first minute, the listener is shocked by deliberate dissonance, by a confused stream of sounds. Snatches of melody, the beginnings of a musical phrase, are drowned, emerge again, and disappear in a grinding and squealing roar. To follow this "music" is most difficult; to remember it, impossible.... Here we have "Leftist" confusion instead of natural, human music. The power of good music to infect the masses has been sacrificed to a petty-bourgeois, "formalist" attempt to create originality through cheap clowning. It is a game of clever ingenuity that may end very badly.... The composer apparently never considered the problem of what the Soviet audience expects and looks for in music. As though deliberately, he scribbles down his music, confusing all the sounds in such a way that his music would reach only the effete "formalists" who had lost their wholesome taste. He ignored the demand of Soviet culture that all coarseness and wildness be abolished from every corner of Soviet life.... *Lady Macbeth* is having great success with bourgeois audiences abroad. Is it not because the opera is absolutely unpolitical and confusing that they praise it? Is it not explained by the fact that it tickles the perverted tastes of the bourgeoisie with its fidgety, screaming, neurotic music?[71]

Theories abound over the identity of "Muddle's" author. Over the years, David Zaslavsky (*Pravda's* then chief editor) and Zhdanov have been touted as the likeliest candidates. But it has also been generally assumed that the author, whoever it was, was merely a front for the "real" author, Stalin himself. That the editorial emanated from the highest Party echelons was publicly acknowledged by Zhdanov in 1948, and the recent publication of secret memos sent to Stalin by informants working for the NKVD (the People's Commissariat for Internal Affairs, a forerunner of the KGB) has revealed that Stalin's hand was actually suspected by several people at the time.[72] The editorial's disproportionate emphasis on sex, something that had not until now been much of an issue in Soviet reviews, certainly bore the fingerprints of the notoriously prudish dictator. And words like "simplicity," "clarity," and "muddle," liberally strewn throughout the editorial, were also well-known Stalinisms. *Testimony's* words are worth noting here, if only because they conflict with Solomon Volkov's own views of Stalin's intelligence and literacy:

> It might have been written down by the well-known bastard Zaslavsky, but that's another matter entirely. The article has too much of Stalin in it, there are expressions that even Zaslavsky wouldn't have used, they were too ungrammatical. After all, the article appeared before the big purges. There were still some fairly literate people working at *Pravda* and they wouldn't have left in that famous part about my music having nothing in common with "symphonic soundings." What are these mysterious "symphonic soundings"? It's clear that this is a genuine pronouncement of our leader and teacher. There are many places like that in the article. I can distinguish with complete confidence Zaslavsky's bridges from Stalin's text.[73]

No matter who ultimately put pen to paper, the content and, to some extent, verbiage of "Muddle Instead of Music" was unmistakably Stalin's. But how had the whole episode arisen in the first place? Possibly, Stalin had no prior agenda other than to see a much-feted opera by a leading Soviet composer who had also been proving himself useful in the all-important area of cinema. Another view is that the visit was instigated by enemies of Shostakovich (who knew exactly what Stalin's reaction would be) in an effort to get the opera taken off.[74] Recent evidence, however, suggests that the entire event was not so much the doing of an anti-Shostakovich faction, but the product of an internal Party power struggle into which Shostakovich had unwittingly become embroiled. On the basis of newly released material from the Central Party Archive and the Russian State Archive of Literature and Art, Leonid Maximenkov believes that the scandal was the by-product of the rivalry between Platon Kerzhentsev, the head of the newly formed Committee for Artistic Affairs (formed, incidentally, on 17 January, the day that Stalin visited *The Quiet Don*), and Viktor Gorodinsky, head of the Party Central Committee's Music Section:

> The first two years of the Committee [for Artistic Affairs] are crucial to the history of Soviet culture: it instituted artistic censorship, enforced in part by the program of socialist realism; put the life of the artist in a straitjacket of financial dependence; and created a system of perks and "table of ranks." At the same time, however, there were bodies within the Party structure that supervised the arts. . . . The head of the Central Committee's music section, Viktor Gorodinskii, had been spearheading a campaign to create Soviet opera. As part of his efforts to support revolutionary music (for example, that of Shostakovich), he recommended the composer to head the Academic State Opera Theatre. Kerzhentsev felt threatened by Gorodinskii's campaign and brought Stalin to see *Lady Macbeth* on 26 January 1936. Two days later, a denunciatory, unsigned editorial appeared in *Pravda*. The editorial had, in fact, been written by Kerzhentsev. . . . [whose] skill in shaping cultural policy resided in his understanding of the interconnections between the demands of socialist realism and those of the Stalinist cult of personality.[75]

If Kerzhentsev was indeed the architect of Stalin's visit, it is possible that the augmented brass section that night might have been deployed in a deliberate attempt to guarantee Stalin's ire. This, though, remains speculation.

Other than its overemphasis on matters sexual, two things about "Muddle Instead of Music" are worth noting. The first was its unblushing reversal of previous official opinion. Back in 1934, the opera's introduction of a "Soviet" perspective into Leskov's apolitical story was praised. Now, it was being used as ammunition: "The story of Leskov has been given a significance it does not possess."[76] Furthermore, the opera that in 1934 had "exposed the false and lying methods of the composers of bourgeois society"[77] now "tickle[d] the perverted tastes of the bourgeoisie with its fidgety, screaming, neurotic music."[78] The second oddity was the implication that *Lady Macbeth* appealed only to an exclusive set of ideologically twisted aesthetes and intellectuals. Of course, admission of the truth, that the opera's successful two-year run in multiple productions had been the result of its mass appeal, would have rather nullified the point that *Pravda* was trying to concoct.

***

Shostakovich's emotional state as he was faced with the most blistering, and the most public, indictment of his work yet can only be imagined. Shortly after, he would subscribe to a press-cutting service so that he could compile a scrapbook with every article and editorial published against him—something that his friend Isaak Glikman at the time felt to be "a self-indulgent piece of masochism,"[79] but which Ian MacDonald views as an act of "brilliant thinking" by a man who "needed to gather data about his situation fast."[80] Yet, in the musical community at large, the initial response to "Muddle Instead of Music" was not one of great urgency. *Lady Macbeth* received only one further performance at the Bolshoi, but there was no special sense of crisis at the concurrent Nemirovich-Danchenko production, where the opera played for a further five weeks. (Nemirovich-Danchenko himself maintained, somewhat wishfully perhaps, that had Stalin attended his less satire-laden production instead of Smolich's, his reaction would have been less hostile.[81]) As Laurel Fay points out, critics were attacked by the press "for their insufficiently thoughtful attention to the issues raised by the 'Muddle' editorial. In Leningrad especially, some musicians expressed disagreement with the tendentious article, mistakenly assuming that the position advanced by *Pravda* might leave room for debate."[82]

On 6 February, nine days after "Muddle," *Pravda* published a second denunciation. Entitled "Balletic Falsehood," this critique of *The Limpid Stream* accused Shostakovich of creating "painted peasants on the lid of a candy box":

> The music is without character, it jingles, it means nothing. The composer apparently has only contempt for the national songs.... The authors of this ballet, the composer, and the producers apparently think that our public is not demanding, and will accept everything concocted by opportunists and high-handed men. In reality, it is only our music- and art-critics who are not discriminating. They will often praise undeserving works.[83]

Shostakovich immediately instigated a meeting with Kerzhentsev. Kerzhentsev's memo to Molotov and Stalin, dated 7 February, reads:

> I indicated to [Shostakovich] that he should free himself from the influence of certain obliging critics like Sollertinsky, who encourage the worst aspects of his work, created under the influence of Western expressionists. I advised him to follow the example of Rimsky-Korsakov and go around the villages of the Soviet Union recording the folk songs of Russia, Ukraine, Belorussia and Georgia, and then select from them the hundred best songs and harmonise them."[84]

With the publication of "Balletic Falsehood," the musical community finally whirred into action, hastily convening meetings in Leningrad and Moscow. Boris Asafyev described the *Pravda* articles as "a warning [that] has come at exactly the right time,"[85] while former *rapmist* Viktor Belyi noted "an abundance of deeply principled and truly Party-minded remarks about the development of Soviet music."[86] Shostakovich resisted the pressure to attend, fearing that the meetings would degenerate into the ritual mud-slinging familiar from the show trials of the late 1920s and early 1930s. And so it would prove. Kabalevsky, for example, pronounced Shostakovich's Piano Concerto, Twenty-Four Preludes, and Cello Sonata as the music of a "very bad composer;"[87] Lev Knipper (whose music Shostakovich had criticized at the previous year's Discussion on Soviet Symphonism) regaled his audience with anecdotes of Shostakovich's personal failings.[88] Others, meanwhile, attempted to characterize Shostakovich as not so much a culprit but a victim of certain corrupting influences, principally Sollertinsky. In fact, Maximilian Shteinberg, describing Shostakovich as "the best of all my students," placed the blame on the modernists with whom the young composer had associated in the mid-1920s, even before Sollertinsky had appeared on the scene.[89]

A few did stand in Shostakovich's defense. Shcherbachov abstained in the otherwise unanimously carried resolution of censure, despite the fact that he was no fan of *Lady Macbeth*. Myaskovsky too, though his own aesthetics were far removed from the world of *Lady Macbeth*, supported Shostakovich for standing against the "paucity and primitivism that might otherwise reign in music today."[90] Support also came from the composers Andrei Balanchivadze and Vissarion Shebalin, and from Meyerhold, Marshal Mikhail Tukhachevsky, and the author Maxim Gorky, one of the founding fathers of Socialist Realism. Writing to Stalin, Gorky asked: "What does this so-called "muddle" consist of? Critics should give a technical assessment of Shostakovich's music. But what the *Pravda* article did was to authorize hundreds of talentless people, hacks of all kinds, to persecute Shostakovich. . . . You can't call *Pravda's* attitude to him 'solicitous.'"[91] Gorky's letter was especially remarkable, since he of all people would surely have recognized the editorial's Stalinesque terms and phrases, not least the very word with which he took issue: "muddle." But the relationship between the two men had always been unusual. As one of Stalin's closest advisors, Gorky's opinions held a certain amount of sway. Yet, as many Soviet figures would learn to their cost, "close" did not necessarily mean "trusted." Three months after his letter defending Shostakovich, Gorky was dead, believed murdered on Stalin's orders, although there is no evidence linking his fate directly to this letter.

Allegations of Shostakovich's "formalism" had been surfacing on and off throughout the 1930s. But the two *Pravda* editorials now brought to public view a debate that had hitherto been mostly contained within musical circles. Exposed in the general press, a composer had now joined the ever-growing ranks of "wreckers." The spirit of tolerance that the 1932 Resolution had appeared to promise was singularly failing to materialize. Describing the long-term effect of "Muddle Instead of Music," Isaak Glikman would later write:

> And so the campaign against Shostakovich as the composer of *Lady Macbeth* proceeded on its seamlessly successful way not only in Leningrad but all over the country. The musical community brilliantly learned the part assigned to it, and earned top marks in subservience and anti-sedition witch-hunts. It abdicated from all opinions and convictions of its own, accepting a newspaper article inspired by Stalin as the fount of unquestionable truth which rapidly acquired the status of holy writ. The disgraceful diatribe found its way into Conservatoire courses on the history of music. Teachers quoted from it, expounded on its significance, analysed its content, bowed down in superstitious reverence before its superior wisdom. It continued to resonate far beyond its time.[92]

***

The *Lady Macbeth* scandal would affect Shostakovich not just psychologically, but also financially. Although never extravagant, Shostakovich had over the past two or three years come to enjoy a more comfortable standard of living—a combination of *Lady Macbeth's* success and the marginally more liberal economic climate of the so-called Second NEP. He had become a regular partaker in the "Restaurant Life," a scene that in the 1920s he had professed to despise. As Ian MacDonald put it, Shostakovich, though always skeptical, had been "sucked gradually into the *nomenklatura*—and he was rather enjoying it."[93] But in the months following the *Pravda* scandals, his income took a nosedive. The effects were exacerbated by the birth of the Shostakovichs' first child, Galina, in May 1936.

Events notwithstanding, Shostakovich continued work on his Fourth Symphony. As the *Lady Macbeth* scandal broke, he was into the third movement finale, though exactly where in the movement is not known. By April, the Symphony was finished. Over the next few months, Shostakovich played it on the piano for visiting guests, including Otto Klemperer, who had expressed interest in conducting it on an upcoming South American tour. The premiere was scheduled for 11 December, but at the last minute, following several rehearsals under the Austrian conductor Fritz Stiedri, the Symphony was withdrawn. It would not be heard again, at least in its orchestral guise, until 1961.

The cause of the withdrawal has never been definitively explained. In his public statements, Shostakovich cited his own dissatisfaction with parts of the Symphony. It was an explanation that he stuck to; revisiting the topic twenty years later, he described the Fourth as "a very imperfect, long-winded work that suffers—I'd say—from 'grandiosomania.'"[94] However, the fact that he would eventually present the Symphony in 1961 exactly as he had left it in 1936 would rather cast doubt on that particular piece of self-evaluation. Another version blames the cancellation on the incompetence of Stiedri. "It was a shambles," remarked the conductor Alexander Gauk. "Stiedri obviously did not understand the music, and the orchestra played messily. It was quite depressing."[95] For Western readers, it was *Testimony* that first threw up Stiedri as the main culprit, though there he is portrayed not as a "remarkable, inspired conductor ... [who] was not able easily to enter the world of a symphony that was more or less alien to him" (to quote the conductor Gavriil Yudin[96]) but simply as incompetent, lazy, and cowardly:

> Besides, Stiedry's rehearsals weren't merely bad—they were outrageous. First of all, he was scared to death, because no one would have spared him either.... Secondly, Stiedry didn't know or understand the score, and he expressed no desire to grapple with it. He said so straight out. And why be shy? The composer was an exposed formalist. Why bother digging around in his score?[97]

More recently, new layers have been added to the mystery. Gavriil Yudin relates that Shostakovich simply acted upon well-meaning advice given to him by a (unnamed) Party official.[98] Isaak Glikman, meanwhile, describes something more coercive. According to Glikman, the Leningrad Composers' Union chief, Vladimir Iokhelson, and a local Party official, Yakov Smirnov, visited the director of the Philharmonic, Isai Renzin, demanding that the performance be cancelled. To save embarrassment, Renzin asked Shostakovich to withdraw the work. Glikman states that the officials' decision was fueled by the persistent rumors spread by the musicians themselves that Shostakovich had defied criticism and composed "a symphony of diabolical complexity and crammed full of formalist tendencies." Glikman also refutes the accusations of Stiedri's incompetence, claiming that Shostakovich thought highly of him.[99]

Whatever the truth or truths surrounding the cancellation, Shostakovich's public criticism of the Symphony's "grandiosomania" was clearly a convenient explanation made under very difficult circumstances, although the turning towards greater musical economy in the Fifth Symphony the following year might indicate, at least at some level, a partial agreement with that public assessment. Nevertheless, Shostakovich continued to believe passionately in the Fourth, whatever its faults. Given its status as a politically suspect work by a now-disgraced composer, Shostakovich could very easily have purged it from his *oeuvre* by designating the following symphony, i.e., the Fifth, as the Fourth, thus obscuring the "real" Fourth and covering over its tracks with the newer work. Instead, he reserved the Fourth's place in the canon until such time as it could be publicly aired.

* * *

Notwithstanding earlier remarks about Shostakovich's 1930 score to *Alone* or, for that matter, his attempted two-piano transcription of the first movement of

Mahler's Tenth Symphony from the late 1920s,[100] the Fourth Symphony was essentially the first, and perhaps the most important, product of Shostakovich's Sollertinsky-inspired love affair with the music of Mahler. The influence can be witnessed in a number of ways, although it should be said at the outset that very little of Shostakovich's music, in the Fourth Symphony or elsewhere, actually sounds like Mahler.

At the most general level, the Symphony marked Shostakovich's first engagement with the sheer scale, both temporal and orchestral, posited by Mahler. With its quadruple winds (three bassoons) plus ancillaries, eight horns, and an expanded percussion section, the scoring was to be Shostakovich's largest in a symphony. Running at approximately 60–65 minutes, the Fourth was just over twice as long as the First, up to that point his longest symphony. Yet, more important than its length, or its mass, or even its status as "epic" was its irrepressible, outsize personality, its Mahlerian, all-embracing aesthetic which, in one and the same breath, encapsulated both high and low art in a symphonic context; a personality that allowed, for example, the finale's central *divertissement*, a satirical, vaudevillian collection of waltz, polka, and galop, to sit unblushingly in the middle of a movement that starts with a funeral march and ends in drained purgatory. Such ironic juxtaposition of the tragic and the tawdry was the very essence of Mahler—and the very last thing sought by the commissars of Soviet culture in their quest for heroic "masterpieces."

The first movement was Shostakovich's first attempt at sonata-form composition in a symphonic work since the First Symphony eleven years earlier. As discussed in Chapter 13, its structure can be related both to sonata movements that preceded it (i.e., the First Symphony and the Cello Sonata) and to those that followed it (the Fifth, Eighth, and Tenth Symphonies). Yet, defining how exactly this sonata movement works has proved problematic, the movement's sheer complexity throwing up a startling array of analytical interpretations. The start of the development, for example, has been variously placed at Fig. 19, b3 (Tim Souster),[101] Fig. 31 (Hugh Ottaway),[102] Fig. 40 (Eric Roseberry),[103] Fig. 47, b11 (Karen Kopp),[104] and what is surely the most logical placement, Fig. 51 (Joseph Darby,[105] Pauline Fairclough,[106] Richard Longman,[107] Bill Stanley,[108] Richard Taruskin[109]). Accordingly, this yields an exposition lasting anything from 159 bars (about five minutes long) to 477 bars (about thirteen minutes).

One problem here is the defining of tonality, with much of the Symphony (and in particular, the first movement) operating, as David Haas puts it, "on the fringes of tonality."[110] In considering the key of the first movement's second subject (Fig. 31; see Chapter 12, Example 12.3), Haas points to six authors, who between them come up with eight different explanations. And though the eight explanations all revolve around either A or E as the tonal center, both the melody and the accompaniment use only pitches of the D minor scale (rising melodic). Haas' identification of what he calls a "Shostakovich mode," prevalent also in the op. 34 Preludes, is an attempt to deal with a tonal language in which the actual perception of tonic often clashes with the "tonic" implied by the collection of pitches used (see Chapter 12). Discussing the movement's tonality more generally, Richard Longman writes:

> Harmonically there is little reinforcement of this structure; beside the sense of departure and return to C minor, there are few clearly focused or extended harmonic centres. A parallel with arch-form may be suggested, whereby the harmony takes functionalism as its point of departure and return, but slips into non-functionalism for extended structural paragraphs. This is perhaps partially compensated for by the ascendance of rhythm as the steering factor in the musical progression, to the point of employing harmony as a percussive resource.[111]

Another problem is the apparent surfeit of superficially unrelated themes. As one theme moves quickly into (or collapses quickly onto) the next, the listener can be forgiven for thinking that the exposition is over long before Fig. 51. Certainly, the jackbooted march that starts the movement, the seemingly rambling lyrical theme at Fig. 7, b3, the pseudo-baroque set of figurations at Fig. 14, the inflated brass contrapuntal variation on the movement's opening at Fig. 19, and the woodwind *danse macabre* at Fig. 24—all this before we even get to the exposition's second area at Fig. 31—provide enough food for thought. Compounding the problem is the fact that contained within all this superficial diversity over the course of the 477-bar exposition is a considerable amount of real development of the movement's two main themes, development that, as Pauline Fairclough points out, provides more in the way of traditional thematic working-out than does much of the actual development section.[112] Although this movement is aesthetically nowhere close to the typical Soviet symphony of the mid-1930s, Fairclough notes that the idea of the "developmental exposition" was something that Shostakovich may have commandeered from his contemporaries.[113]

Following this "developmental exposition," the development section proper emerges more as a series of set-piece character variations: a polka on the first theme; a savage four-voice fugato on the first theme (later famously jeered by Marian Koval as the releasing of four "formalistic 'serpents'" that would make "the great Bach turn in his grave"[114]); and a sardonic waltz based on the second theme. Yet, the sheer brute force of the fugato carries all before it, injecting the development section with a momentum that the label "character variations" perhaps does not fairly connote. The subsequent re-transition, and the effect that the thematically re-characterized reverse-order recapitulation has on our perception of the movement as a whole, is discussed in Chapter 13. In the coda, the mechanically forlorn first theme reprise in the solo bassoon gives way finally to obsessive, almost totemic, repetitions of the Mahlerian falling-fourth "cuckoo" idea heard earlier in the movement (e.g., Fig. 40, b3). Here at the end, the English horn intones the repeating descending and ascending fourth (G down to D and back) for sixteen bars, piledriving through anything that stands in its way. It willfully clashes against the D-flat minor harmony at Fig. 107, the first theme snippet at Fig. 108, the phantasmagoric tone-cluster at Fig. 108, b2, and even the closing tonic C minor chord.

The second movement scherzo was Shostakovich's first symphonic attempt at a Mahlerian *Ländler*, although a precursor can be found in the Cello Sonata. Mahler's examples tended to fall into two types. The *Ländler* scherzos in his First, Fifth, Sixth, and Ninth Symphonies are earthy and deliberate, recalling their peasant roots; those in the Second, Fourth, and Seventh are generally less rhythmically emphatic, with more delicate, occasionally pointillistic, textures. Of course, the boundaries are fluid; Mahler frequently incorporated elements of both types into the same movement. But the point is worth making, especially since a similar differentiation can be discerned with Shostakovich. The Fourth Symphony's scherzo is based on slurred, undulating, "swimming" sixteenth-note passages akin to those in the third movement of Mahler's Second, whereas the Fifth Symphony's scherzo is, despite a very similar tempo, more robust in character and sound, more reminiscent of Mahler's First.

Although the first movement, understandably, has garnered the most attention from investigators of the Fourth Symphony's tonality, the scherzo contains some idiosyncrasies of its own, even though in general it is the more tonally grounded of the two movements. The reprise (Fig. 130) presents the opening material as a bitonal fugato in the strings (D minor and A minor). Even more striking is the subsequent stretto presentation in the woodwind (Fig. 139). With successive entries only two beats apart (later closing up to one beat) in D minor, E-flat minor, E minor, and F minor, Shostakovich creates a quadratonal ultrapolyphonic texture worthy of the Second Symphony. There are important differences, of course. The fact that the polyphony is imitative and involves a definable theme (the movement's main theme, no less) makes it, at least superficially, more comprehensible to the listener than the unprepared free counterpoint of the earlier work.

A Mahlerian funeral march opens the third movement finale. Specifically, it would appear to be a parody of the funeral march from Mahler's First Symphony (a march that is itself a parody), one that "distorts" Mahler's perfect fourth bassline vamp into a tritone. The iconoclasm extends to the melody itself, with the bassoon's clipped rhythms creating a *Petrushka*-like, "mechanical" funeral, a character that only intensifies when the oboe takes over for the theme's second strain (Fig. 153, b3) and the three bassoons and contrabassoon act as the "rhythm section." Although Shostakovich subverts Mahler's beloved perfect fourth vamp at the start of the march, the "correct" version can be heard at this second strain, and is highlighted elsewhere.

The march's climax is perhaps more a parody of Bruckner than Mahler—note the reiterated fast string figurations in the lead-up (Fig. 158) and the pseudo-Brucknerian harmonic progression in the brass at the climax itself (Fig. 160). However, this climax is short-lived, perhaps because Shostakovich knows that the entire funeral march episode is, ultimately, not a self contained entity but an introduction to a larger movement, and that this funeral material will return, to even more catastrophic effect, later on. Considering the transition from the march into the main *Allegro*, Richard Longman points to another Mahlerism, namely the foreshadowing at the end of a section fragments of the theme with which the next section will begin, the fragment acting as the bridge. In this case, the end of the funeral march reiterates a descending minor third, the same interval with which the *Allegro* starts. A comparable moment in Mahler can be found in the first movement of the First Symphony, where the reiterating descending fourths at the end of the slow introduction become the opening interval in the subsequent *Allegro*.

After the harrowing journey through the opening funeral march, the psychotically disfigured collection of popular set-pieces that form the movement's central *divertissement*, and the overt "pre-Resurrection" allusion to Mahler's Second Symphony in the cellos and basses (compare Fig. 237 with Fig. 2 in the finale of Mahler 2, both in C major),[115] we arrive at one of the most astonishing codas in the repertoire, a two-part affair in which a savage onslaught of C major collapses onto a stunned, numbed C minor death-watch. If the blaze of attempted acclamatory glory that is the C major onslaught is indeed a subversion of the "resurrection" promised only moments earlier, it could also be, as Richard Taruskin believes, a reference to the final "Gloria" chorus of Act 1 of Stravinsky's *Oedipus Rex*.[116] Both present chorale-like figures (as, indeed, does the Resurrection ode, "Auferstehen," in Mahler 2), and in both cases the first phrase starts on a tonic chord, moves through a discord, arriving onto dominant-ninth harmony. David Fanning suggests that Stravinsky's ironic context may have had a message for Shostakovich too:

> But Stravinsky's "Gloria" is not the entirely straightforward paean it seems. It is more than a little tinged with dramatic irony, since the crowd's acclamation is based on ignorance of Jocasta's misdeeds. In addition, it follows hard on Oedipus's hearing (but not understanding) of Tiresias's pronouncement of his doom and (at least in the composer's own recording) on the narrator's explanation of the true state of affairs. The acclamation is therefore one in which ignorance (the crowd's) and knowledge (the audience's) are fused. Does Shostakovich's allusion mean that something of this ironic dimension transfers to his coda?[117]

The irony is heightened by the fact that, as Fanning puts it, "C-major acclamations were in the air in the Soviet Union at the time."[118] Fanning cites the codas of the first movement of Shebalin's Third Symphony (1933) and the finale of Gavriil Popov's First (1935), and observes that C major was also "a key of choice . . . for the Party-affirming Mass Song."[119]

Yet, for all its raucous assertiveness, the C major of the Fourth Symphony's coda is decidedly not the C major of the mass song. Even without foreknowledge of the eventual collapse into the minor mode, this is clearly C major under stress, constantly threatened by minor-mode elements, putting up a brave fight (or, at least, a display of bravado) before eventually ceding. Certainly, this C major should be less likely confused for an apotheosis than the D major coda at the end of the Fifth Symphony would come to be. As Table 6.1 shows, each recurrence of the chorale's second phrase presents a new attack on the "majorness" of the C tonic:

Table 6.1
Relationship of Chorale's First and Second Phrase to C Major

Fig. 238	Chorale first phrase	C major
Fig. 239	Chorale second phrase	C major
Fig. 240	Chorale first phrase	C major
Fig. 240, b8	Chorale second phrase	C major with lowered seventh (+ lowered second toward the end)
Fig. 241	Chorale first phrase	C major
Fig. 241, b7	Chorale second phrase	C major with lowered third and seventh

The Mahlerian second strain of the movement's opening funeral march then returns at Fig. 242 (quoting the oboe theme from Fig. 153, b3) in that favorite Mahlerian scoring: a unison mixture of flutes, oboes, and clarinets, *a4* (Shostakovich adds an E-flat clarinet), the element of struggle exacerbated by the fact that this scoring, potent yet in what is dynamically the softest section of the orchestra, must fight to be heard above the fray—Shostakovich wisely omitting the heavy brass here. This in turn sets the stage for the main return of the funeral march (Fig. 243), blazing in the brass, rather as a first movement theme might return to crown the end of a Bruckner or Elgar Symphony. But, unlike those composers, there is here no glory or exultation. Accompanied by minor-second wailing in the horns *a8*, the funeral march presents itself in all its splenetic and tragic force, worlds away from the detached, ironic, *Petrushka* funeral with which the movement started. Eventually burned up by its own fury, the music collapses, felled by one catastrophic blow of the tam-tam, into the coda's desolate second phase in C minor. (This shattering, tam-tam driven collapse, whose roots lay perhaps in the shipwreck episode of Rimsky-Korsakov's *Scheherazade*, would become a Shostakovich specialty—the first movement of the Eighth Symphony, the last movement of the Eleventh, or the film score to *Hamlet* providing the most spectacular examples.)

In the Fourth Symphony's final minutes, we see a slow sapping of whatever residual life force managed to survive the impact. The ostinato pedal-C heartbeat, related possibly to the end of Tchaikovsky's *Pathétique* Symphony, eventually "flatlines," losing its pulse altogether (Fig. 259). Violins and violas rummage through the wreckage of one of the movement's *divertissement* themes, while the horn, then the flute, and finally the trumpet ponder the perfect-fourth-plus-tritone figure (here, G-C-F-sharp) from the funeral march's second strain. At each attempt, the trumpet gets stuck agonizingly on the F-sharp, never resolving to the G so desperately sought by the surrounding C minor harmony. This phase contains yet another reference to Mahler's Second Symphony. A few bars from the end of Mahler's first movement, a C major chord is held in the winds; its third then turns tragically downwards while the two outer notes are sustained (Example 6.3a).[120] Shostakovich disturbs the harmony—Mahler's pure C major chord is turned into a cloudy C half-diminished seventh with a superimposed major element (enharmonically respelled as F-flat)—but the connection is clear enough (Fig. 249; Example 6.3b).

Example 6.3a

Example 6.3b

In the Symphony's closing moments, Shostakovich introduces a celesta, an instrument that would for him often signify valediction, and a choice that was possibly inspired by Mahler's celesta in the closing stages of the valedictory "Abschied" from *Das Lied von der Erde*, avowedly Shostakovich's favorite Mahler score. After obsessively repeating a C minor arpeggio, rather as a person in shock might mumble a phrase over and over, the celesta finally lands on D, clouding the Symphony's C minor ending in a shroud of uncertainty.

***

Aesthetically, the expressionist Fourth Symphony could not have been further removed from the parade of Socialist Realist symphonies being peddled during the period. Yet, in some respects it does mimic, even as it subverts, the narrative ideals of the Stakhanovite epic. The historian Boris Gasparov points to the "images of industrial clatter and the relentless rhythms of labor" in the Symphony's first theme and to the strident trills in the upper woodwinds at the very start, which recall "an alarm clock or a factory siren whose piercing sound proclaims the beginning of a new day of labor."[121] Images of alarm clocks, waking up, and starting the day were very common in the Stakhanovite literature. Gasparov invokes the opening of that most famous of Stakhanovite epics, Valentin Katayev's *Time, Forward!* ("The alarm clock rattled like a tin of bonbons"),[122] as well as Shostakovich's hit "Song of the Counterplan" from the film *The Counterplan*, in which industrial labor is treated quite literally as the national religion: "Don't sleep, wake up, curly-head,/with the tolling of its factory bells,/the country is arising in glory to meet the coming day!"[123] And Shostakovich had already treated us to an ironic use of the "wake up" theme in *Lady Macbeth* as the Izmailov estate laborers swagger in during Boris' dying moments: "See, the dawn is breaking/The sky is getting lighter/Mustn't waste time like this/Hey, to work, and quickly, fellows/The barns await us, that's for sure/And the flour that feeds us waits/Our master's fierce and cruel/Just like a crocodile."[124]

Gasparov also compares the narrative mode of the Fourth Symphony, its splintered style and disjunctive alternations of extremes, with that of the Socialist Realist novel:

> The hero of a socialist realist novel . . . is capable of a full range of thoughts and emotions. The only thing he seems not to be capable of is experiencing them simultaneously. . . . However hectic the circumstances in which its heroes find themselves, their infantile lack of memory allows them to enjoy an undisturbed wholeness of self, be it total happiness or total suffering, at every given moment. Hence the effortlessness with which they shift from excruciating pain to small pleasures, from crushing fatigue to a renewed burst of energy, from the tragic to the jocose. These shifts may seem abrupt to an observer, yet they appear natural under the compartmentalized conditions of human consciousness projected by the narrative to the novel's peculiar world.[125]

Gasparov contrasts this with the Fifth Symphony, in which "Shostakovich's new symphonic narrator possesses an intense inner life; the very pain inflicted upon him confirms his humanity, because he responds to it with meditation and mourning, not [the] Pavlovian reactive impulses [of the Fourth]."[126]

* * *

Given its violence, its dissonance, and its total rejection of Socialist optimism, the real mystery of the Fourth Symphony is, as Laurel Fay has observed, "not why it was withdrawn but how it came as close to performance as it did."[127] Firstly, it is important to dispel the oft-promoted assertion that Shostakovich withdrew the Symphony in direct response to the *Lady Macbeth* scandal, an assertion that is clearly refuted by the chronology of events. Not only had Shostakovich continued to work on the Symphony in the aftermath of the *Pravda* articles, but he had then submitted it for rehearsal with a view to performance. Certainly, in retrospect, the Leningrad Philharmonic's acceptance of the score does seem surprising; this was after all exactly the type of conflict-laden, Mahlerian symphony that Sollertinsky had been advocating over the years, and therefore exactly the type of work that might in mid-1936 (as opposed, say, to late 1935) have been viewed with suspicion now that Sollertinsky himself had come in for criticism. Nevertheless, the fact remains that both Shostakovich and the Philharmonic continued to consider the Fourth Symphony viable right until the end of 1936, nearly eleven months after "Muddle Instead of Music." How had Shostakovich come to exhibit such confidence? Did he honestly believe that the Symphony would not offend? Or was it simply defiance? Much later, Levon Atovmyan would recall Shostakovich demonstrating if not active defiance then at least a certain bullish indifference: "I don't write for the newspaper *Pravda*, but for myself. I basically don't think about who will say what about my work, but write about what moves me, what has sprouted in my soul and mind. As for how they evaluate the symphony, that is the business of critics, who get paid for it."[128] Such a comment would certainly justify Mark Aranovsky's use of the term *inakomyslyashchii* to describe Shostakovich, connoting a spirit of independence rather than active dissidence.[129]

The withdrawal of the Fourth Symphony attests ultimately to the fact that the political climate at the end of 1936 was dramatically different from that at the start. Certainly, we must not underestimate the far-reaching psychological damage that the January and February editorials inflicted upon Shostakovich, and there can be no question of the fear that prevailed at the subsequent discussion meetings. Yet, the fact that several dissenting voices (e.g., Shcherbachov or Myaskovsky) were heard, however faintly, suggests that the political terror had not yet maximized its grip. And if the story of the Fourth Symphony is a reliable guide, we can see that it was still believed possible, even in mid-1936, to declare one's independence, at least in the field of music. It was during that summer, however, that things started to accelerate. Two months after the liquidation of Maxim Gorky in June, Stalin unleashed his campaign to rid the nation, once and for all, of the so-called "oppositionists" to his rule.

The pretext for the purges was the assassination twenty months earlier (1 December 1934) of the Leningrad Party chief, Sergei Kirov. Kirov's popularity had always irked Stalin. It is now generally believed, though it has never been proven, that Stalin himself masterminded the murder, not only to get rid of Kirov, but then to use the subsequent "investigation" to link the crime to a larger conspiracy of "traitors." This, in turn, would give him the opportunity to round up any and all enemies upon whom he could stick even the remotest charge of guilt by association. Within days of the murder, over a hundred former White Guards had been charged, secretly tried, and executed for their part in a "foreign conspiracy" to murder Kirov. A few weeks later, however, attention had turned to a "Leningrad center" of Stalin oppositionists. On 28 and 29 December, fourteen members of this "center," including the actual assassin, Leonid Nikolayev (not Shostakovich's former piano teacher!), were tried and, according to the published transcript of the trial, confessed not only to Kirov's murder but to a conspiracy to murder several Party leaders, including Stalin himself, and to replace the leadership with their own allies, including the former Trotskyites Zinovyev and Kamenyev. All fourteen were immediately shot, though in what was clearly a face-saving exercise, an obscure tangential connection with the White Guards was concocted to justify the previous executions. In January 1935, Zinovyev, Kamenyev, and others were imprisoned for their indirect involvement, with Kamenyev's sentence increased at a further trial in July. However, in the year between July 1935 and August 1936, on the surface a year of relative calm, Stalin had been, behind the scenes, amassing and concocting information to implicate Zinovyev and Kamenyev more directly. In trials held between 19 and 24 August 1936 ("The Case of the Trotskyite-Zinovyevite Terrorist Center"), Zinovyev, Kamenyev, and five others were charged with preparing and perpetrating the murder of Kirov and of conspiring to assassinate Party leaders Stalin, Voroshilov, Zhdanov, Kaganovich, Ordzhonikidze, Kosior, and Postyshev. A further nine people were charged with the latter crime. All sixteen were found guilty and shot.[130] The Great Terror was now under way.

Was the Fourth Symphony's purgatorial ending, then, the clinching factor in the decision to have it withdrawn? It is a view that is perhaps obliquely suggested in a remark made by Shostakovich to the conductor Boris Khaikin in 1937: "I finished the Fifth Symphony in the major and fortissimo.... It would have been interesting to know what would have been said if I finished it pianissimo and in the minor?"[131] In one of her earlier articles, though not in her book on the Fourth Symphony, Pauline Fairclough takes this hint on board: "Had Shostakovich's own personal situation been easier, his symphony could have been performed, provided that it had ended at rehearsal 243 [i.e., before the return of the funeral march and the subsequent collapse into C minor] rather than 259."[132] It is indeed likely that the Fourth Symphony's parched *pianissimo* minor key coda would have been politically unacceptable by late 1936. But in reality, the fatal blow had probably already been struck much earlier in the Symphony. Those rumors of "diabolical complexity" and "formalist tendencies" buzzing around Leningrad at the time of rehearsal would surely have applied at least as much to the Symphony's first movement juggernaut, with its screaming twelve-note clusters and its infamous tear-away fugato as to anything in the finale. And given the extent to which this first movement dominates the Symphony, it is doubtful that any C major apotheosis in the finale, never mind the traumatized C major that Shostakovich actually gives us, could have rescued it.

***

The end of 1936 saw three compositions: the incidental music to Alexander Afinogenov's play *Salute to Spain*, the score to the film *The Return of Maxim* (the second of the "Maxim" trilogy), and the *Four Pushkin Romances* for bass and piano. The first two, both commissioned, would provide some much needed income during this tense and financially lean time. For the film, Shostakovich donned the requisite Socialist Realist mantle, though the culminating Funeral March, composed in an otherwise typical "Russian Revolutionary" style, does inject a Mahlerian hue into its earlier stages, Shostakovich providing an echo of the Fourth Symphony's funeral march. More significant was the *Four Pushkin Romances*, written to commemorate the one hundredth anniversary of the poet's death. In the tradition of the Romance, that favorite genre of nineteenth-century Russian composers, Shostakovich created a lyrical score, shorn of expressionistic tendencies. Its mix of lyricism and gravitas and, as Gerard McBurney has put it, its "new way of making each phrase grow out of the one before,"[133] would provide Shostakovich with his entry point to the Fifth Symphony.

The *Romances* also represented a breakthrough in terms of its political state-ment. Although possibly not his first protest against Stalinism (at least if we believe *Lady Macbeth's* police scene and the Fourth Symphony's coda to fall into that category), the *Romances* did, at the very least, constitute Shostakovich's first musically expressed stand against the defamation of artistic integrity by political power, a stand taken less than a month after the forced withdrawal of the Fourth Symphony. In the first song, "Rebirth," Shostakovich appears to replay Pushkin's own controversial relationship with Tsar Nicholas I in order to point the finger at a latter-day "barbarian artist," Stalin himself:

A barbarian-artist, with a sleepy brush,
Blackens over a picture of genius.
And his lawless drawing
Scribbles meaninglessly upon it.

But with the years the alien paints
Flake off like old scales;
The creation of genius appears before us
In its former beauty.

Thus do delusions fall away
From my worn-out soul,
And there spring up within it
Visions of original, pure days.[134]

As is now well known, the finale of the supposedly "redemptory" Fifth Sym-phony written a few months later would contain two musical quotations from "Rebirth," quotations associated with the poem's first line (the "barbarian artist") and its last ("visions of original, pure days"). But, because the *Romances* were not premiered until 1940 and not published until 1943, these quotations would have gone unnoticed, other than by close associates of the composer, for several years fol-lowing the Symphony's premiere. The implications of the two quotations are dis-cussed below. However, it should be noted here that the Symphony actually contains a third quotation from the Pushkin Romances, this time from the start of the second song, "Jealousy." The song's introductory figure, an upward minor-ninth leap followed by a downward minor-second resolution that accompanies the words "Weeping bitterly, a jealous girl was scolding a young man," is mimicked by the first violins in the third bar of the Symphony's first theme (Fig. 1, b3; see Chapter 13, Example 13.3b). In Shostakovich's later orchestration of three of the *Romances* this figure is played by a solo violin. (The figure had also been heard four bars before the end of the piano Prelude, op. 34, No. 3, and also constitutes one of the leading ideas of Mahler's Fifth Symphony, where at one point it is heard in a solo violin.)

* * *

By 1937, the Great Terror had reached the peak of its frenzy. If the previous year had provided a taste of things to come with the arrests of Shostakovich's friend Galina Serebryakova and his former lover Yelena Konstaninovskaya (the for-mer imprisoned for twenty years, the latter released within a few months), a horrifying catalogue of events during 1937 would leave the composer in a highly vulnerable state: the arrests of his uncle Maxim Kostrykin and his brother-in-law, Vsevolod Frederiks; the exile of his sister, Mariya, to Central Asia; the sentencing of his mother-in-law, Sofya Varzar to hard labor; and the arrest and execution of his friend and confidant Marshal Mikhail Tukhachevsky. One of the nation's top military men, but also an amateur violinist and violin-maker, Tukhachevsky had been a friend of the composer since 1925. In May 1937, he was arrested and executed as part of the purge on the Red Army. Inevitably, as the witch-hunt made the rounds, associates of the accused were trawled in. In November, the music theorist Nikolai Zhilyayev was arrested for his association with Tukhachevsky. He was executed two months later. Zhilyayev had also been a mentor to Shostakovich and had been one of the first to view the scores of the *Four Pushkin Romances* and the Fifth Symphony. Connected to both Tukhachevsky and Zhilyayev, Shostakovich certainly had reason to fear for his own life. Decades later, the composer Venyamin Basner would claim that Shostakovich was questioned by the NKVD regarding his relationship with Tukhachevsky, though no corroboration of this interrogation exists.[135]

In April 1937, Shostakovich started work on his Fifth Symphony. Most sources give 20 July as the completion date, though the Shostakovich archivist Manashir Yakubov has recently provided evidence to suggest that composition continued into September, possibly even October.[136]

It was with the Fifth Symphony that Shostakovich's experiments with a sonata-arch form reached its maturity. More dramatic than the first movement of the First Symphony, less sprawling than that of the Fourth, the opening movement of the Fifth Symphony would for the first time hold in near perfect balance the progressive nature of sonata form and the cyclic nature of the arch structure. An analysis of this movement, as well as its motivic and procedural relationships with the Symphony's later movements, appears in Chapter 13.

Hugh Ottaway describes the second movement scherzo as "a relaxation: a genial, outward-looking scherzo and trio, formally unremarkable but well made, and in character and function comparable with the waltz movements in the symphonies of Tchaikovsky.... There is genuine gaiety here, and a sense of fun rather than satire."[137] Compared to the first movement, the scherzo is indeed formally unremarkable and does represent a relaxation in terms of structural and harmonic complexity. But the entrance of the cellos and basses at the start of the movement, crashing into the tense, rarified air held in suspension from the end of the previous movement, could hardly be described as "genial." And although there are certainly moments of Tchaikovsky (in particular, the balletic theme at Fig. 53), the movement overall seems more attuned to the Mahlerian *Ländler* than the Tchaikovskian waltz.

Nevertheless, Ottaway's remarks do, implicitly at least, point to the shift in Shostakovich's style from the overt, debunking satire of the late 1920s to the more nuanced, if often bitterly ironic style that would dominate from the mid-1930s on. Such irony would find its way into many different musical contexts, though not surprisingly it is particularly prominent in scherzo-type movements, and in many cases, such as here in the Fifth Symphony, the framework is provided by the

Mahlerian *Ländler*. Less fleeting than a Beethoven scherzo, earthier than a minuet, the *Ländler* seems particularly conducive to humorous or ironic underlining. With its inherent lilt, distortions of its natural rhythmic character take on a subversive quality; in this respect, the heavier rhythmic accentuation in the Fifth Symphony's scherzo has the greater potential for ironic subversion than its more fluid Fourth Symphony counterpart. Take, for example, the coda's recall of the trio theme. In the trio itself, a gypsy-fiddle melody (see Example 6.4b) is presented in a natural *Ländler* character, with the stress on the first beat of the bar and perhaps, depending on the performance, a very slight hesitation on the upbeat to the first phrase; in short, the very essence of Mahlerian *Gemütlichkeit*. On its return in the coda, however, this character is subverted by a snarling accent on the second beat. Add to this the "squeezing" of the original melodic intervals and the whole thing takes on a sour flavor, though this is quickly dismissed by the final four bars. (It is somewhat reminiscent of the coda of the scherzo of Beethoven's Seventh Symphony, where a four-bar fragment of the trio theme, in a rather sinister harmonic transformation, is swiftly negated by the decisive closing chords.)

Another device suggestive of irony, particularly within the context of the *Ländler*, is the use of string portamento. A portamento moving from a strong beat to a weaker one tends to dissipate energy in a wistful manner, as in the above-mentioned trio theme in its original appearance in the solo violin. Moving in the opposite direction, from a weak beat to a stronger one, portamento tends to exaggerate the music's guttural irony (e.g., Fig. 61, b2–3). Such portamento within a *Ländler*-type setting can also be found in the Fourth Symphony; not in the scherzo, but towards the end of the first movement's development, at Fig. 81, b6 (violins), and Fig. 86, b7–10 (cellos), the latter almost identical to one in the scherzo (bar 55) of the Cello Sonata, another *Ländler*-type movement.

The perception of irony is also affected by timbre. The E-flat clarinet that introduces the main theme of the Fifth Symphony's scherzo, with its trills and grace notes, inevitably brings up comparisons with Berlioz' *Symphonie fantastique*; Mahler too had capitalized on the sardonic potential of this instrument, for example, in the *Ländler* scherzo of the Second Symphony. By contrast, the comedic role of the bassoon and contrabassoon, those mainstays of Shostakovich's earlier iconoclastic writing, is now somewhat attenuated.

Placing the scherzo second rather than third in the order of movements would become the norm for Shostakovich, at least in his symphonic writing. In only three symphonies—9, 12, and 15—does the scherzo appear in its more traditional place, following a slow second movement, and it is notable that these three are the only symphonies whose first movements attempt something like a traditional sonata-allegro structure. By contrast, the scherzo comes second in Symphonies 1, 4, 5, 6, 7, 8, 10, 11 (if the second movement can be called a "scherzo"), and 13, and in every case, except for the First Symphony, it functions as an emotional safety valve to a long, intense first movement, sometimes even perpetuating motivic ideas from that opening movement, as here in the Fifth Symphony (see Chapter 13).

The other effect of this "reversal" is to shift the symphony's psychological center of gravity towards its slow movement. In such works as Beethoven's Ninth, Bruckner's Eighth, or Mahler's Fourth, it is not just the length and the profundity of their slow movements that make them the center of gravity of their respective symphonies. It is also the fact that there is no scherzo separating them from their finales, that the slow movement has direct access, so to speak, into the symphony's culminating material. And so it is with Shostakovich's Fifth, whose intense *Largo* third movement, written in only three days, constitutes the work's emotional core. Of course, this is not just a question of placement. What so moved the Leningrad audience, many of them to tears, at the premiere was the simple, naked outpouring of tragic meditation and lyricism in this, Shostakovich's first symphonic slow movement in twelve years.

Like Mahler in the *Adagietto* of his Fifth Symphony, Shostakovich explores the textures of *divisi* strings—here, violins *a3*, violas *a2*, and cellos *a2*. And this is not the only echo of Mahler's *Adagietto*. Both Shostakovich's first theme and Mahler's entire movement are scored for strings only. Shostakovich omits Mahler's harp, though his second subject at Fig. 79 and again at Fig. 94 has the harp as the sole accompanying instrument, the latter appearance closest imitating Mahler's strings and harp texture. And both movements start with a halting, rising three-note anacrusis. Mahler's anacrusis is an integral part of the melody, returning every time the melody returns. Shostakovich's, on the other hand, never returns despite several recurrences of the theme. However, transformations of it can be heard later on, principally a retrograde version that forms the basis of the third theme at Fig. 84 (opening: F-sharp-G-sharp-C-sharp; Fig. 84: C-G-F)

If the more flowing second subject at Fig. 79 takes the movement, temporarily, into clearer vistas, the third subject at Fig. 84 does the opposite. A tense woodwind quasi-recitative (oboe, then clarinet, then flute) hovering preciously over a barely flickering violin tremolo, this represents the movement's, indeed the Symphony's, point of maximum stasis. Later, it forms the core of the movement's tragic climax (Fig. 90) and eventually provides the coda its point of resolution (Fig. 96).

Many have read religious associations into this third theme. Klaus Meyer believes it to be a direct quote of a Jewish cantorial (*chazanut*) "Amen" cadence.[138] Timothy Jackson concurs, arguing that "the character of Jewish synagogue chant is preserved at rehearsal 84 and 86. Like the Jewish chant, the melody in its entirety is monophonic and constructed from small motivic elements, which are repeated with slight variations (centonization)."[139] And regarding the aforementioned retrograde relationship between the movement's opening anacrusis and this theme, Jackson considers the possibility that it was the latter that influenced the former, rather than vice-versa.[140] Such a "reverse" interpretation of thematic influence is certainly feasible, especially given the pivotal role of this third theme in the movement as a whole. And this would certainly not be the only time that Shostakovich appeared to shape his own material with at least one eye on an upcoming quotation—the Ustvolskaya quotation in the Fifth Quartet and the *William Tell* quotation in the Fifteenth Symphony come to mind. Here in the Fifth Symphony, the influence could possibly be said to

extend back to the second movement. One of the characteristics of the centonization to which Jackson refers is pitch alliteration, something that can be found
not only at the start of this third theme (each phrase starting on the same note,
C; Example 6.4a) but also back in the second movement's trio (each phrase starting on E; Example 6.4b).

Example 6.4a

Example 6.4b

The point of maximum stasis, and of maximum tension, within this highly
charged third theme area comes with the extraordinary string cadence at Fig. 86
(Example 6.5a), separating the initial oboe and clarinet versions of the "chant"

Example 6.5a

Example 6.5b

from the succeeding flute version. In Richard Taruskin's words, "the imitation is so literal that you can almost hear the string instruments intone the *vechnaya pamyat'* (Eternal Remembrance), the concluding [Russian Orthodox] requiem hymn."[141] Its modalism and its dense *divisi* string texture seem to echo yet another famous work of profound meditation, Vaughan Williams' *Fantasia on a Theme of Thomas Tallis* (1910). The string *divisi* was a favorite sonority of Shostakovich at such moments, vertical intensity compensating, as it were, for horizontal stasis. The opening of the Eleventh Symphony, for example, derives much of its atmosphere from this texture. An even closer cousin to the string cadence at Fig. 86 (Example 6.5a) can be found in the second movement of the Fifteenth Symphony, at the point at which the first theme makes its other-worldly return following the movement's devastating climax (Fig. 75; Example 6.5b). Note in both cases the limited melodic contour of the individual voices as well as the use of multi-octave (in this case dominant) pedals, two features typical of Shostakovich's *divisi* writing.

The movement's two climactic paragraphs (Figs. 89 and 90) make their devastating impression not by contrapuntal thematic combination, as in the first movement, but rather by the almost hysterical intensification of earlier ideas. For example, the tremolo, originally a single-strand *pianissimo* wisp of sound accompanying the third theme (Fig. 84), is here (Fig. 89) intensified both harmonically, through a two-part texture, and orchestrally, with the piano adding a brittle edge to the violins and violas. Meanwhile, the melody, a fragment derived from Fig. 78, is intensified by the strained tessitura of cellos and bassoons, and the brittle xylophone. The even more harrowing second paragraph of the climax (Fig. 90) continues and extends the extreme cello tessitura.

As the climax burns itself out, the first theme, or rather repeated fragments of it, returns at Fig. 93 in C minor, the remotest key possible from the movement's F-sharp minor tonic. It is the stunned response to the devastation of the movement's climax, similar to the aftermath of the climax of the Fifteenth Symphony's slow movement (see Example 6.5b, above) with its *divisi* texture and suspended harmonies. Technically, this could be considered a recapitulation, leading as it does to reprises of the second and third themes, and some commentators who are wedded to a sonata-form analysis of this movement label it so.[142] But although it is possible to draw up a sonata-like plan of events based on surface features, the profile of musical tension and release here works more along the lines of a Bruckner slow movement than sonata principles.[143]

The tense, desolate coda recalls the first movement's coda with its valedictory use of the celesta, though here it combines with the sound of harp harmonics, a characteristic Shostakovich doubling in moments of "post-massacre" stillness (e.g., the Eleventh Symphony's second movement, following the massacre scene). However, unlike the first movement's coda, which thematically returns to the movement's roots, this coda is based upon the desolate third subject, the theme that has in many respects been the lynchpin of this movement. On one level, this ensures that the movement closes with its most harmonically stable theme, the stability reinforced by the final chords in the tonic major. Yet, lingering in the background is the theme's previous associations, for the tense tremolo that in one form or another has always accompanied this theme is still present at the very end; its continuing agitation felt above the resolution of the final chords.

On the heels of this barely flickering flame of F-sharp major, the finale's opening D minor chord crashes in, a contrast rendered even starker by the strident trills in the high woodwinds that effectively turn the D minor chord into a bitonal "Schreckensfanfare." Even the scoring for woodwinds, brass, and timpani is reminiscent of Beethoven's famous Ninth Symphony "Schreckensfanfare." Following the brutal introductory brass quotation of "A Barbarian Artist" (see above), the first main theme enters (Fig. 98) with a hammering accompanimental ostinato reminiscent of the ostinato that drove the first theme of the Fourth Symphony. Analyzing that earlier ostinato, Richard Longman writes:

> Shostakovich often uses the third alone to define his tonal orientation; that is, he omits the fifth from the triad. For example, the first subject of the Fourth Symphony's first movement is delivered over pounding chords of C plus E-flat, followed by B plus D, and so forth: the percussive rhythmic assertion both substitutes for the complete triadic definition, and underlines the tonal fragility in its absence.[144]

Longman's observation applies equally here. In fact, the similarities between these two passages extend to the themes themselves; both start with a two six-teenth-note anacrusis and both rely on a scalar figure, with similar rhythms, to connect the end of their respective first phrases with the start of their second (compare Fourth Symphony, Fig. 1, b5 with Fifth Symphony, Fig. 99). And both themes contain a pronounced, flamenco-like triplet figuration. Example 6.6 shows the triplet as it appears in the Fifth Symphony. Its resemblance to the "trill motive" from the second movement is unmistakable (see Chapter 13), as is its occurrence in many other Shostakovich works, where it almost invariably suggests a devilish mood—for example, the third movement of the Eighth Quartet, the scherzo of the Thirteenth Symphony ("Humor"), or the scherzo of the Viola Sonata. When used orchestrally, it is more often than not given to the high woodwinds, those traditional purveyors of grotesquerie. (The first theme of the Fourth Symphony, where it appears in lumbering trumpets and trombones, is a notable exception.)

Example 6.6

This finale is composed in two large sections (the second beginning at Fig. 112) plus a coda (from Fig. 121). However, like the slow movement, it has lured several writers into a sonata-type analysis, wherein the second theme is given at Fig. 108, development at Fig. 112, recapitulation at Fig. 121, and coda at Fig. 131. But the music from Fig. 121 lacks the structural synthesis generally associated with the term "recapitulation." Another problem lies in the idiosyncratic function of the so-called "second theme" at Fig. 108, which is in fact not an opposing theme to the first group, but a transitional theme whose sole purpose is to bridge the move-ment's two large sections. It is heard towards the end of the first part (Fig. 108) and at the start of the second (Fig. 112, b3). Once its bridging function is ful-filled, Shostakovich dispenses with it, other than as an occasional accompanimen-tal fragment (Fig. 114, b8; Fig. 115, b6; Fig. 124; and Fig. 128). One proponent of the sonata analysis, Preston Stedman, cites one of these fragments, the six-note fragment at Fig. 128, as the reprise of "theme 2," forcing onto it a status it clearly does not possess.[145]

At Fig. 102, towards the end of the finale's second section, there appears the second of the *Pushkin* quotations. As a slow transformation of the finale's first theme grinds away in the cellos and basses, the first violins soar over it with a minor 2nd/ octave figuration (Example 6.7) that in the *Pushkin Romances* accompanied the words "visions of original, pure days." This figuration emerges as a variant of another minor 2nd/octave figuration that was introduced back at Fig. 116, b7, Shostakovich again appearing to fashion earlier material in the light of a subsequent "import."

Example 6.7

Unlike the recently discovered "barbarian-artist,"[146] this second *Pushkin* quotation has long been acknowledged. English-speaking readers first encountered it in David Rabinovich's 1959 biography, a work that, incidentally, was never published in Russian, only in an English translation by George Hanna, where the passage read: "And the waverings pass away/From my tormented soul/As a new and brighter day/Brings visions of pure gold." On the basis of this, Rabinovich/Hanna concluded that "in the finale, the present day completely overcomes earlier doubts and waverings, the former romantic isolation."[147] However, "visions of pure gold" was a misleading translation of the verse's final words ("videnya pervonachalnykh, chistykh dnei"), words better translated as "visions of original, pure days," a very different proposition. In their eagerness to push the forward-looking doctrine of "reality in its revolutionary development," Rabinovich/Hanna had perverted the backward-looking nostalgia of Pushkin's text. Read correctly, the intent is clear: not the promise of future gold, but a desire to return to a former and better time.

Pushkin's dream is quickly shattered by distant percussion, a growling horn pedal, and a return to D minor (Fig. 121). The "original, pure days" are not to be. The coda replays the movement's opening material as a grim, slow-motion march, slowly building up and leading into the final onslaught of D major (Fig. 131). This D major peroration has been subject to the most extreme range of interpretation, with a performance tempo ranging from quarter = 216 (Leonard Bernstein) down to quarter = 76 (Yakov Kreizberg).[148] The hermeneutic issues that have sprouted from this are discussed in Chapter 1, but it should be reiterated that such variation is due, at least in part, to a mundane editorial discrepancy— the metronome indication appears in some editions as quarter = 188 and in others as eighth = 184 (i.e., quarter = 92).[149] It seems almost certain that the slower marking is the correct one, though we must rely on anecdotal evidence here since the manuscript score is lost. The conductor Sir Charles Mackerras notes: "at a meeting with Shostakovich which I had in Moscow, he sang it quite a lot slower when I questioned him on this very point. Naturally at this meeting we did not discuss feelings or hidden messages, but stuck to practical matters such as tempi, orchestration and editorial mistakes. He was quite specific that the tempo of the Finale should be slow and not fast."[150] The composer's son, Maxim, concurs,[151] and it is at least worth noting that Yevgeny Mravinsky, the conductor of the Symphony's premiere, consistently performed the coda at a slower speed. Nevertheless, Shostakovich's flexibility in this regard can be gauged from his seemingly confused remarks to the conductor Constantin Silvestri (see Chapter 2) or, indeed, from his letter to the conductor Mark Paverman, in which he wrote: "I was very taken with the [1959] performance ... by the talented Leonard Bernstein. I liked it that he played the end of the finale significantly faster than is customary."[152]

Leaving aside for the moment extra-musical considerations, several have doubted the finale's ability to function as a viable *symphonic* conclusion. Preston Stedman, for example, describes it as "another of Shostakovich's 'festive' concluding movements which is short on organic growth and rationality and long on repetition and frenzy."[153] He is referring no doubt to the sequential passages starting at Figs. 102, 102, b8, and 107, in which Shostakovich's powers of melodic invention and development are admittedly not at their peak. However, in Stedman's case, some of the disappointment appears to have stemmed from his misplaced structural expectations (discussed above). The D major ending, in particular, has been portrayed by many as something of a *Deus ex machina*, a last-minute attempt to resuscitate the movement's momentum—in his diary, Myaskovsky describes it simply as "bad."[154] Yet, these criticisms recede to an extent if the D major ending is heard as part of a longer "re-characterizing" coda that begins back at Fig. 121 rather than as a last-minute rescue for a recapitulation that was not fulfilling its function. The coda as a whole emerges as harmonically more varied than the D major peroration alone would suggest, and provides an organic transition from the movement's slow central section to its final chords. With this in mind, and leaving other considerations aside, it is the slower tempo that perhaps allows the final pages to extend more organically from the previous material and give the coda as a whole greater structural cogency.

The hermeneutic debates surrounding this conclusion—"real" rejoicing, "forced" rejoicing, not to mention its possible reference to Shostakovich's former lover Yelena Konstantinovskaya—are discussed in Chapter 1 and need not be rehearsed here. Meanwhile, the internal evidence points to an inseparable mingling of tragedy and defiance—the anguished injection of minor subdominant harmony at Fig. 133, creating a clash between B-flat in the melody and the ongoing A pedal, or the stoic grinding out of D major chords in a broad augmentation of the Symphony's hallmark anapaest rhythm at Fig. 134 (both elements discussed in Chapter 13). At the very end, the major mode itself implodes, with the removal of the F-sharp. To the accompaniment of the timpani ostinato (tonic-dominant), the orchestra unleashes its final gesture, a unison D. A cymbal crash is heard at the start of that D, but four beats later, the only percussion left is the "dull," non-metallic timpani, bass drum, and snare drum. Thus, for this final gesture Shostakovich first removes one source of brightness, the F-sharp, then the other source, the sound of metallic percussion.[155] In the bar prior to this unison D, the timpani, reinforced by the bass drum, hammer out the tonic-dominant ostinato as the rest of the orchestra look on in silence. The musicologist Inna Barsova, who sees images of death in the movement as a whole,[156] writes:

> Shostakovich's sudden "stripping down" to the kettledrums striking fourths in the third bar from the end, when the massive chords stop, creates the sinister effect of the lid of a coffin being nailed down. Mahler never allowed the kettledrums to sound alone in his apotheoses. He did write a solo for the bass drum, however, at the beginning of the finale of his Tenth Symphony, and Shostakovich was familiar with the facsimile of this score.[157]

Does pessimism here win out over defiance? Perhaps not. The composer's son, Maxim, writes:

> Fadeyev once said that he was scolding someone in the finale. My father replied, "It was not just scolding. The hero is saying, 'I am right. I will follow the way I choose.'" It says again and again, "No. You will not be able to do anything to me." It is not happiness. It is not victory. It is the determination of a strong man to BE.[158]

***

Conducted by a young and little-known Yevgeny Mravinsky, the Fifth Symphony's premiere on 21 November 1937 was a triumph and an unforgettable experience for those present. Public expressions of genuine emotion and humanity had become such rare commodities at a time when artificially whipped-up merriment was the order (literally!) of the day, that to be able simply to *feel* again in public was itself an overwhelming experience. The applause at the end lasted for over half an hour, with the composer brought back for seemingly endless curtain calls. Yet, in a paranoid atmosphere in which audience "over-enthusiasm" could so easily be construed as a "demonstration," Shostakovich had to be careful. Vissarion Shebalin recalls that "Ivan Ivanovich (Sollertinsky) was very worried ... he and my wife had to use all means at their disposal to restrain D.D. from walking out on stage too often, and they dragged him away."[159]

Within days of the premiere, a short review penned by composers Anatoly Alexandrov and Vasily Nechayev appeared in *Muzyka*. Regurgitating the same formula that had once been used to receive *Lady Macbeth*, they concluded that "A work of such philosophical depth and emotional force could only be created here in the USSR."[160] But, as Shebalin and Sollertinsky had indeed feared, the predominant reaction in official circles to the Fifth Symphony was not rejoicing but panic. The conductor Alexander Gauk, who had attended the premiere, recalled a conversation he overheard the following day:

> I heard [Shatilov, director of Music Repertoire Committee] recounting to another official his version of the Symphony's Leningrad premiere. He belittled its enormous success, saying that it had been a put-up job arranged by Shostakovich's Moscow

friends, who had gone up to Leningrad for this very purpose. At this point I interrupted and said that I too had been at the concert, and that six- or seven-odd people from Moscow could hardly have been capable of inciting the 2,500-odd Leningraders present.[161]

Similarly, the then managing director of the Leningrad Philharmonic, Mikhail Chulaki, tells of a subsequent Leningrad performance attended by Party officials V. N. Surin and Boris Yarustovsky.[162] Their brief was to establish the cause of Shostakovich's new success:

> After the concert ... [Yarustovsky] made a constant stream of snide remarks, shouting to make himself heard over the noise in the hall: "Just look, all the concert-goers have been hand-picked one by one. These are not normal concert-goers. The Symphony's success has been most scandalously fabricated," and so on in this manner. In vain did I, as director of the Philharmonic, try to convince the rabid official that the public attending the concert had bought tickets at the box-office in the normal manner ... For some time, echoes of the "symphonic scandal" stirred up by the two officials continued to reach Leningrad. I had to write explanations, fill in questionnaires and prove the absence of a criminal.[163]

The conspiracy theories were partially allayed following a special performance of the Symphony laid on for Leningrad Party activists. In the ensuing discussion, the work was dubbed "an optimistic tragedy," a term probably derived from Vsevolod Vishnevsky's 1933 play, "An Optimistic Tragedy," and one that would become a common moniker in Soviet cultural discourse. It was in essence a spin on "reality in its revolutionary development," but one that coyly admitted tragedy into Soviet art. Resolvable tragedy, that is. The concept was exploited further in Alexei Tolstoy's review, published on 28 December in *Izvestiya*. Comparing the Fifth Symphony to "the formation of a personality," Tolstoy described a philosophical quest in which the first movement's "psychological torments" give way to the finale's "enormous optimistic lift." Treating the Soviet audience as a monolithic entity with "organically" pre-conditioned responses, the review was a typical piece of hagiography, chock-full of *Pravda*-style clichés: "Our audience is organically incapable of accepting decadent, gloomy, pessimistic art. Our audience responds enthusiastically to all that is bright, clear, joyous, optimistic, life-affirming."[164]

Throughout those final weeks of 1937, Shostakovich offered very little comment. But in January 1938, he finally jumped on the optimistic tragedy bandwagon with his "own" article, "My Creative Response," published in *Vechernyaya Moskva*. Rehashing Tolstoy's tragedy-to-triumph drama ("Very true were the words of Alexey Tolstoy, that the theme of my symphony is the formation of a personality"), Shostakovich concluded that "The symphony's finale resolves the tense and tragic moments of the preceding movements in a joyous, optimistic fashion."[165] The article had begun with the words, "Among the often very substantial responses that have analyzed this work, one that particularly gratified me said that 'the Fifth Symphony is a Soviet artist's practical creative answer to just criticism'."[166] The author of that "gratifying" phrase was never identified, but Shostakovich's apparent concurrence caused the Symphony for many years to be saddled with the unfortunate slogan, "A Soviet Artist's Reply to Just Criticism." Years later, Shostakovich confirmed to the musicologist Genrikh (Henry) Orlov that "My Creative Response," like so many articles of its type, had been scripted by government officials and that he, Shostakovich, had "fainthearted[ly]" acquiesced.[167] This recent revelation by Orlov would appear to end speculation that Shostakovich possibly coined the slogan himself and then attributed it to some unnamed author with whom he could then be seen to "concur." Solomon Volkov believes that the author of the famous phrase was Stalin himself. Volkov points to the fact that the phrase, given pride of place at the head of the article, appeared in boldface in the newspaper, standard practice for Party directives and slogans. In Volkov's opinion, the fact that the article does name Tolstoy indicates that "the author of the formula about the 'constructive creative response' *wished* to remain unnamed. The authoritative tone of the statement, its familiar stylistic idiosyncrasies, and the fact that it gave Shostakovich 'particular joy' (in those days a ritual reaction to any speech by Stalin) all point to Stalin as its author."[168]

So how, in this schizophrenic environment of denunciations, rehabilitations, ghostwriters, and conspiracy theories, did the Fifth Symphony come to function as its composer's redemption? Richard Taruskin argues that as part of the Party's carefully calculated stick-and-carrot system of punishment and reward, Shostakovich's return to grace was "foreordained" in advance of the premiere. Sometime in the early autumn of 1937, Shostakovich and Nikita Bogoslovsky had presented the Symphony to the Leningrad Composers' Union in a four-hand piano arrangement. Taruskin writes: "Thanks to the system of *pokazï* (peer reviews) and the need for securing performance clearance from the Committee on Artistic Affairs, Shostakovich's work was known on high before its public unveiling. Its status as apology and as promise of a personal *perestroyka* was a conferred status, bestowed from above as if to show that the same power that condemned and repressed could also restore and reward."[169]

Such stick-and-carrot practices were common. But in the case of the Fifth Symphony, there is still the question of the conspiracy theories: if, as Taruskin argues, the Symphony's status was indeed conferred before the fact, why was the triumph of the work's first performances cause for suspicion? Like Taruskin, Volkov believes that the redemption of Shostakovich was managed from the top. But Volkov argues that the decision to bring him back into the fold came only after the premiere, once the conspiracy theories had been put to rest and once Stalin had taken soundings from advisers like Tolstoy and Nemirovich-Danchenko and even from the Party activists present at the special performance. Once everything was in place, the green light could be given for the publication of Tolstoy's article on 28 December, which in turn would set the stage for Shostakovich's January article, thus completing the redemption ritual. Although Volkov's theory takes into account the role of the "conspiracy" questionnaires and reports, there does remain the possibility that these conspiracy theories may, like the rehabilitation itself, have been cooked up in advance, expressly to be unleashed after the premiere in order to discourage premature optimism and to remind the public who was in charge.

Unlike Taruskin or Volkov, Ian MacDonald argues that, far from being carefully scripted, the redemption of Shostakovich was nothing more than a face-saver, hastily arranged *a posteriori* by panicked officials:

> What, on the face of it, appears more likely is that an undertow of jealous grumbling from Shostakovich's rivals in the Composers' Union had, by mid-December 1937, coincided with a basic uncertainty among the cultural *apparat* over what to make of the Symphony, thereby creating a need for a fully considered official position on the work.... Far from being the "foreordained" redemption of a temporarily disgraced artist, the evidence ... suggests rather that the response of the *apparat* to Shostakovich's Fifth was a hasty botch designed to make a world-famous composer (upon whom they could not then lay a finger) seem part of their stupid world of bumpkin ideology.[170]

In March 1938, two months after "My Creative Response," Georgy Khubov's review of the Fifth Symphony appeared in *Sovetskaya muzyka*. His conclusion was predictable enough: "Such a work as Shostakovich's Fifth Symphony could appear only as a result of the wise and just, truly bolshevist criticism spearheaded by *Pravda* which castigated the formalist chaos, falsity, trickery, and crude naturalism in art."[171] Yet, he also criticized the *Largo* for employing "an expressionist exaggeration to show us numbness, a state of spiritual apathy, where the will is destroyed, where the victorious force is destroyed." And his impression of the finale was "not so much bright and optimistic as it is severe and terrifying."[172] The complexities and paradoxes of Khubov's review are discussed in Chapter 1; all that need be noted here is that the perception of a less-than-optimistic finale, commonly touted as a post-*Testimony* revelation, was in fact on record, in the Composers' Union journal no less, only four months after the Symphony's premiere.

CHAPTER 7

MATURITY (1938–1947)

Shostakovich entered 1938 with good cause for optimism. He was now established as a mature composer, and was starting to make a name for himself as a pedagogue. Although he had held a number of teaching positions over the previous decade, his appointment in 1937 to the composition department at the Leningrad Conservatory raised his profile considerably. He relished the challenge, but at the same time felt, as Isaak Glikman put it, "fundamentally inadequate in this role."[1] Laurel Fay suggests that this insecurity may have been partly responsible for the idea, mooted during the spring of 1938, to take lessons with his old friend and mentor Boleslav Yavorsky.[2] In the event, the lessons never materialized. But what seems especially telling is that in the face of all the advice being hurled at him by the likes of *Pravda* and the Composers' Union, Shostakovich would turn instead for solace to this 1920s Leftist renegade, a "scientific" theorist who embodied all that was currently unfashionable. Shostakovich's desire to reconnect with his past, then, was possibly about more than just pedagogical insecurity.

At first glance, Shostakovich's output for 1938 seems meager—four short film scores,[3] the Second Suite for Jazz Orchestra,[4] and the First String Quartet. The films were a necessary evil, both financially (especially with the birth in May of the Shostakoviches' second child, Maxim) and politically, given the increasing role of film as a propaganda tool. Commenting on the film *The Friends*, Shostakovich mouthed the required platitudes, promising to make "a thorough study of the songs and music of the peoples of Chechnya, Ingushetia, and Kabardino-Balkaria," work he called "really captivating."[5] The Quartet, meanwhile, was initially conceived not so much as a work for publication but as a private study in chamber writing. In this brief and relatively simple work, one senses Shostakovich's relief after the traumas of the previous two years, the simple joy of being left alone to "write a quartet or something for your own quiet satisfaction," as the author of *Testimony* puts it.[6] But more significantly, the Quartet almost self-consciously engages with the past—not with Shostakovich's own past, as the attempt to re-establish links with Yavorsky might have signified, but with the world of Haydn, Beethoven, and Schubert.

Some years later, Shostakovich would describe the Quartet as being filled with "childhood scenes, somewhat naive, and bright moods associated with spring."[7] If the First Symphony had been, in the words of Glenn Gould, "everything a first symphony ought to be,"[8] then this work, with its vernal innocence and occasional acts of homage to Haydn, could perhaps be said to represent everything that a first quartet ought to be. Certainly, Shostakovich's description is more convincing than the similar one ("moods of spring, joy, youth") that he would offer up in relation to the Sixth Symphony.[9] Yet to describe the First Quartet only in terms of its C major innocence and spring-like moods would be to miss the tensions that underlie the work, tensions that creep in from the very start, where unsettling hints of E-flat minor in the upper parts (bar 2) clash against the cello's calm but insistent declaration of C major—its eight bars of rising C major scale almost a parody of what a C major work should be.

As with the Fifth Symphony (see Chapter 13), what is a small twist at the outset assumes a higher-level structural role later on. That passing suggestion of E-flat minor in bar 2 is later "elevated" into the E-flat (major) tonality of the second subject. The choice of the mediant for the second subject both here and in the finale lends a neo-Schubertian quality—not unlike the first movement of Shostakovich's previous chamber work, the Cello Sonata. Indeed, there is even something Schubertian (or Beethovenian) about the preparation of this key. The second subject's introductory vamp, a G ostinato in the viola, could very easily be construed as a tonic pedal in what would be the more traditional dominant key for the second subject. But at the onset of the theme itself, the cello enters a major third beneath the ongoing ostinato, illuminating the actual key of E-flat—this nonchalant insertion of a major third underneath a stated or implied harmony to provide a sudden turn in tonal direction aping a favorite tactic of the late Classicists.[10] The second subject itself is a playfully musing pseudo-*Ländler* for the cello, the most memorable element of which is a sardonic rising glissando, a gesture familiar from the scherzos of the Fifth Symphony and the Cello Sonata.

In the second movement theme and variations—a decidedly Classical choice— we witness another holdover from the Fifth Symphony, a tendency towards Neapolitan key relationships and Phrygian colorings, two related elements that would become almost defining features of Shostakovich's mature style. The theme and its first variation are presented in the viola in A minor, but when the first violin takes over at the start of the second variation (Fig. 17), the music shifts, immediately and without preparation, into the Neapolitan, B-flat minor, a key that itself becomes imbued with a Phrygian coloring with the C-flats in the second violin countermelody. At the movement's close, B-flat minor returns to inject some mischief into the final A minor cadence.

A Phrygian coloring (D in the key of C-sharp minor) also characterizes the opening of the scherzo's main theme. This fleeting, spectral scherzo (*con sordino* throughout and no dynamic louder than *piano*) rejects the Mahlerian *Ländler* scherzi of the Fourth and Fifth Symphonies. Rather, it looks forward to the Sixth Symphony (1939), the eighth-note ostinato that drives through much of the movement foreshadowing, in its muted way, the pile-driving ostinato that will dominate the middle section of that Symphony's scherzo. Another foreshadowing of the Sixth Symphony comes in the almost self-consciously Classical cadential rhythmic formula that ends the Quartet's finale (Example 7.1).

Example 7.1

As Example 7.1 shows, an anapaest rhythm is generated by tonic chords in the violins, *secco*, while the lower parts spin out a triadic ostinato. The end of the Sixth Symphony features something similar (*secco* chords tutti, triadic ostinato in the timpani), as do two works of the early 1940s: an extended and rhythmically modified version at the end of the Piano Quintet's scherzo (*secco* chords in the piano, triadic ostinato in the strings), and a slow-motion version at the end of the Second Piano Trio's opening movement.

A combination of procedural and stylistic cues from the Fifth Symphony and the Cello Sonata on the one hand and aspects of eighteenth-century composition on the other would make this modest First Quartet something of a trailblazer, for this particular combination of elements would come to define Shostakovich's style through the 1940s. In fact, almost every non-cinematic instrumental work written between the First Quartet (1938) and the Twenty-Four Preludes and Fugues (1950–1951) would feature the conscious incorporation of an eighteenth-century device: the theme-and-variation structures in the Second Piano Sonata (1943) and Second Quartet (1944); the passacaglias of the Eighth Symphony (1943), Second Piano Trio (1944), and First Violin Concerto (1948); the fugues in the Piano Quintet (1940, replete with preceding Prelude), Eighth Symphony, Third Quartet (1946), and First Violin Concerto; the pseudo-Haydnisms of the Ninth

Symphony (1945) and the Third Quartet; even the "massed violins soliloquizing a chaconne," as Richard Taruskin has put it, in the Seventh Symphony (1941).[11]

***

Shostakovich may have acquired for himself a degree of stability going into 1938, but he remained under no illusion: the consequences of miscalculation remained potentially severe. This was the culminating year of the Great Terror, the year in which Stalin completed his revenge on his old Trotskyite enemies. In March, Nikolai Bukharin and other "wreckers" were tried for their participation in the so-called Right-Trotskyite Bloc conspiracy. As always, a well-rehearsed press whipped up public hysteria:

> In all their voracious aspect, the heinous degenerates appear before the court of the people, accomplices of the fiend Trotsky, Bukharin, Rykov, Yagoda and other plotters of the "Right-Trotskyite bloc." This pack of bloody dogs wished to steal from the Soviet people all that they had achieved through decades of persistent and heroic struggle. These traitors to the Motherland wanted to dismember the Soviet country and sell it piecemeal to imperialist invaders.... The scoundrels will get their just deserts. The entire Soviet people will rally even more closely around the party of Lenin and Stalin, and, without mercy, sweeping off the face of the earth the degenerates of the human race, and will continue its victorious progress forward to the bright future, to communism.[12]

Admitting guilt by association, Bukharin's final plea came straight out of the Stalinist show-trial playbook: "I am guilty of the dastardly plan of the dismemberment of the USSR, for Trotsky was negotiating about territorial concessions, and I was in a bloc with the Trotskyites. This is a fact, and I admit it."[13]

In April, less than a month after the Bukharin trials, Shostakovich started work on a song-symphony based on the life of Lenin. At least, that is what the public was told in an announcement issued five months later in September: a new "Sixth" symphony "in at least four movements," to be based on Mayakovsky's poem, *Vladimir Ilyich Lenin*, supplemented by verses of the Kazakh poet Dzhambul Dzhabayev and the Dagestani poet Suleiman Stalsky. Progress reports continued into 1939, yet what was eventually premiered in November of that year was something altogether different; a three-movement, purely orchestral Sixth Symphony that had been composed between April and October. Yet, even as the new Sixth was taking shape during the summer of 1939, Shostakovich continued to release details of the "Lenin" Symphony, now slated as the Seventh. In August, he even gave details of its four movements: Lenin's Youthful Years; Lenin at the Head of the October Storm; The Death of Vladimir Ilyich; and Without Lenin on the Leninist Path.[14] The promises dragged on for another two years; only in 1941, with the onset of war, was the project officially abandoned.

As with the aborted "Karl Marx" project of 1931, it is hard to map the trajectory of Shostakovich's motivation. Was the work ever started? If so, was it driven more by sincerity or by opportunism, and when and why was it abandoned? Shostakovich's friend, Marietta Shaginyan, claims that it was shelved in April 1939, once work had started on the "real" Sixth,[15] but Laurel Fay believes that it continued to churn in Shostakovich's mind even after the completion of the Sixth.[16] Ian MacDonald, on the other hand, has speculated that the whole project may have been dropped as early as May 1938, one month after it was purportedly started and, ironically, four months before the initial September announcement.[17] Yet, whatever the facts, the one thing that is clear is that at some point opportunism did indeed set in, with Shostakovich activating the "smokescreen" ploy that he had learned over the years, stringing officials along with a project that had already been shelved—if, in fact, it had ever existed. Shostakovich did not take a cynical view of his public, but with the events of March 1938 resonating across the country, his wish to take out an extended insurance policy—a policy underwritten by the texts of Stalin's canonized "state poet" Mayakovsky no less—was certainly understandable.

***

The premiere of the Sixth Symphony in Leningrad on 21 November 1939 was well received,[18] but the critical shine did not last long. Disappointment over the "Lenin" Symphony aside, the main complaint, both at home and abroad, concerned the work's "lop-sided" structure—a first movement *Largo*, accounting for about seventeen of the Symphony's thirty minutes, followed by two short scherzos. Not that a three-movement structure *per se* was that peculiar; it was actually quite common amongst Soviet symphonies of the mid-1930s, but symphonies of that type worked mainly according to an unwritten but well-understood formula: a *moderato* or fast opening movement, a slow middle movement, and a *moderato* or fast finale.

But perhaps more than anything, it was the Symphony's very *raison d'être* that eluded listeners. Shostakovich's First had been cheered as a young man's symphonic debut—derivative in parts, yet shot through with an unmistakably fresh, promissory genius. And though the Second and Third Symphonies drew very mixed opinions, these two "murals for orchestra and chorus," as Henry Orlov once described them,[19] could easily be grasped as products of the helter-skelter late 1920s, their composer in part paying homage (whether earnestly or cynically) to that period's noisily competing cultural factions. As for the Fifth Symphony—in addition to its crucial political ramifications, it was understood as Shostakovich's first attempt to grapple with what had perhaps been the single most dominant force in Western Art music over the previous century or so, the Austro-German *grosse Symphonie*. And although the withdrawn Fourth did not at that point figure into the equation, with hindsight it would come to be read as Shostakovich's expressionistic epic, a symphonic *Lady Macbeth* driven in part by his new-found acquaintance with the works of Mahler. But what exactly was the Sixth Symphony? Where did it "fit"? Certainly after the Fifth's "philosophical" journey (however that may be interpreted), the only trip here seemed to be a half-hour descent from high seriousness to low comedy, one that defied "symphonic" definition.

The start of the Sixth Symphony plunges straight into a world of tortuous lyricism, and, not for the first time in a Shostakovich symphony, presents us almost immediately with an eighteenth-century artifact. If the Fifth Symphony's opening gesture brought to mind the baroque French Overture, the first subject of the Sixth (Fig. 4), though not a fugue subject, recalls that favorite gesture of eighteenth-century, "tortuously lyrical" minor key fugue subjects—the diminished seventh fall from the minor sixth degree (in this case G) down to the leading note (A-sharp) with eventual resolution to the tonic (B).[20] And this supplemented by a viola accompaniment that seems almost like an exercise in triplet species counterpoint. But perhaps the movement's most striking feature is its "inverse" distribution of musical activity and tension. Historically, the development section of a sonata-form movement represents the peak of the movement's tonal, harmonic, and contrapuntal intensity. The *Largo* of Shostakovich's Sixth essentially turns this experience on its head. Employing a tempo even slower than that of the already slow outer sections, the movement's center represents the area of least activity—recitative-like musings on a fragment of the movement's second subject, a theme that was already rather fragmentary to begin with. A precedent for this "redistribution" of sonata activity can be found in the first movements of Mahler's Sixth and Seventh Symphonies, whose central portions take the listener into a similarly rarefied world of spiritually charged contemplation. Mahler's woodwind birdcalls and distant Alpine cowbells, though not their associated *topos* of nature-spirituality, find their counterpart in Shostakovich's other-worldly woodwind recitatives.

The recitative was yet another icon of the eighteenth century to preoccupy Shostakovich during the late 1930s and early 1940s. Pioneered in the film *Alone* (1930), but used most famously in the Sixth, Eighth (1943), and Ninth (1945) Symphonies, and the Second Quartet (1944), the recitative was for Shostakovich a signifier of desolate introspection. In the symphonies, solo woodwind (two solo flutes in the Sixth, English horn in the Eighth, and bassoon in the Ninth) weave a hypnotic, rhythmically elastic, chromatically inflected thread around the strings' static harmony; in the Quartet, the first violin takes the role of the woodwind soloists. Comparison of these recitatives with their eighteenth century forebears, however, brings up something of a paradox. For a Handel or a Mozart, the recitative's purpose was to advance plot, or to let us in on conversation, with emotional reflection generally reserved for the ensuing aria or ensemble. With Shostakovich, it is just the opposite—his recitatives providing the soul-searching core of their respective movements while the "plot" is temporarily suspended.

In the first movement of the Fifth Symphony, the recapitulation's reduced activity came as a relief following the frenetic brutalization of the central development. Paradoxically, despite its "inversion" of activity, the same can be said here in the Sixth. The glacial tempo, recitatives, and the tense string pedals of the *Largo's* central section spellbind the listener into a condition of stasis and emptiness, a spell broken only when the horn announces the return to the recapitulation with its more relaxed (i.e., faster) motion. In other words, this movement's center generates the greatest intensity even though it displays the least activity—Shostakovich ultimately paying homage to traditional precepts of sonata form while superficially subverting them. The truncated recapitulation begins with the movement's introductory theme played over the first subject's accompaniment (Fig. 29). Once again, Shostakovich shows a predilection for dressing up one theme in the clothes of another. (Compare the recapitulation of the Fourth Symphony's first movement, where the second theme appears not only with the first theme's accompaniment, but with its orchestration too.)

The second movement is a spiritual descendant of the scherzo of Mahler's Seventh Symphony, by way of Shostakovich's own First Quartet. Although without the *Ländler* gait of the Mahler, or indeed other Shostakovich scherzos, it occupies the same spectral world, with its quick-fire juxtaposition of short melodic fragments and its wide registral leaps and plunges. Its mercurial nature is heightened by a frequently ambiguous approach to tonality—without being polytonal, the movement's opening theme contrives to imply simultaneously D minor, B-flat major, and G minor. The principal binding agent holding the movement together is the single-pitch sixteenth-note ostinato, which underpins the disparate melodic fragments and helps create psychological unity, while at the same time contributing its own specific energy. Such ostinato is deployed here to a greater extent than in any previous Shostakovich scherzo, except perhaps the First Quartet, and would soon be taken up again in the scherzos of the Piano Quintet (1940) and Second Piano Trio (1944).

A complaint often leveled at the Sixth Symphony concerns the consecutive placing of what are essentially two scherzo movements. Although a similar juxtaposition of scherzos would later occur in the Eighth Symphony and the Third and Eighth Quartets, those works seem to have escaped this particular criticism, probably due to the fact that their "paired" scherzos constitute, in each case, internal movements within five-movement structures. Yet, it is easy to overlook how different from each other the Sixth Symphony's two scherzos actually are. The spectral, nightmarish world of the second movement, with its relentless ostinati and its grotesque jabs, contrasts with the third movement, which wears, in its outer sections at least, a surface jollity, exemplified by the opening "William Tell" *saltando* figure in the violins. That this jollity might in fact constitute "forced rejoicing" (to steal *Testimony's* famous description of the Fifth Symphony) cannot be ignored, and nowhere more so than in the movement's disruptive central section, a jackbooted waltz with not a hint of a lilt. In the lead-up to its climax, the waltz assumes a flamenco rhythm, replete with that neurotically insistent, devilish triplet gesture previously discussed in the Fifth Symphony (see Chapter 6, Example 6.6). The climax itself provides the only real point of comparison with the second movement, with its drunken mixed meter, its percussion fusillade, and its quick collapse.

The late 1930s had seen a slight relaxation in the official attitude toward the genre of light music. Ian MacDonald, for one, believes that this was a result of Stalin's desire to normalize the Soviet Union's image with the West in preparation for a possible showdown with Hitler.[21] MacDonald describes the finale's manic coda as "light music with a vengeance" with its "high-kicking vulgarity imported about equally from Broadway and the Folies Bergères"[22]—to which one might add the Red Army Band. He also relates the jarring juxtaposition of the tragic and comic found within the Symphony as a whole to that same juxtaposition in Soviet society: though the Terror was, by 1939, slowing down, it remained the background behind which "happiness" was officially being peddled:

> The frosty ambivalence of this period ensured that, far from healing over, the split between public/diurnal and private/nocturnal life only pulled wider apart.... A puzzle to every commentator on its composer's output, the Sixth was particularly opaque to those Soviet critics at its 1939 première who, perplexed by its lack of a sonata-allegro first movement, dubbed it a "symphony without a head." To them, its long opening largo bore no discernable relation to the pair of short, fast movements which followed it, the work's two halves existing in schizoid isolation, apparently oblivious of and irreconcilable with each other. Why this should be so, the Soviet critics—stepping out of the concert hall and back into the psychotically fractured world of Stalinist society—simply could not imagine.[23]

Yet, it is not just Soviet critics who have had problems with the Sixth Symphony's "lop-sided" structure. Even MacDonald, about the only commentator in print to have attempted an interpretation of the Symphony's *raison d'être*, has expressed doubt over its ability to stand musically on its own two feet:

> The Sixth Symphony remains a piece whose lop-sidedness, whilst deliberate, vitiates its value as a work of art once divorced from its historical context. Both the Fourth and Fifth stand as musico-dramatic designs in their own right, independent of their background. That knowledge of this background charges these works with heightened meaning, altering perspectives on their designs in the most radical way, is purely contingent. Ultimately, they do not beg to be explained. The Sixth, its provocative originality notwithstanding, does.[24]

Although the Sixth Symphony's fortunes have improved considerably in recent decades, the sense that it is "one movement short of a full load" continues to haunt critics. Recalling the "symphony without a head," David Fanning writes that "The three-movement Sixth appears to lack a first movement altogether."[25] Others have speculated that it is the "third" movement that is missing. Roy Blokker, for example, argues that "we may speculate ... that in the planning stage the composer envisaged a long slow, or moderately slow, movement to be positioned between the two quick ones. This would have given the work a more satisfying balance and would, furthermore, have presented an overall pattern similar to that used in the symphonies which lie on either side of the Sixth."[26] But perhaps the most extreme example of second-guessing comes from Robert Dearling:

> Did the composer feel that it was necessary to produce a new symphony as a quick follow-up to the applauded No. 5 but, due to the immense amount of time he had wasted on the Lenin Project, he was reduced to issuing three unconnected movements? If so, perhaps the slow first movement is the only survival of his Lenin

labours. On the other hand—a more likely alternative—did he have a symphony ready but for some reason did not wish to release the second of its two slow movements, which would have taken third place in the design? If this were the case, what became of that second slow movement, and why, in any case, did he not withhold the Symphony until he had completed it with *another* slow movement?[27]

The first of these scenarios is, as Dearling acknowledges, not very likely, for there is no evidence, aside from the none-too-credible promotional puff put out by the composer, that he did in fact spent an "immense amount of time" on the Lenin symphony. And although the second scenario cannot be ruled out, it does seem to be rooted in the belief that a Shostakovich symphony must possess four movements; this despite the fact that only seven of the fifteen symphonies actually do. Dearling's reluctance to acknowledge a genuinely conceived three-movement symphony leads him to conclude, somewhat bizarrely, that "it really is necessary in performance to allow a generous pause between the Scherzo and Presto finale. Too prompt an entry of the latter weakens the effect of both movements."[28]

Despite its unusual though not unprecedented set up—Saint-Saëns' Second Piano Concerto provides one possible structural precedent—the Symphony does work. The first movement succeeds in its dual function, possessing, at the outset at least, all the expository force of the opening movements of the Fifth or Eighth Symphonies, matching their purposeful presentation of tragic material, albeit within a more lyrical framework, while its subsequent turn inwards gives it a "slow movement" character. Meanwhile, the contrast between the two scherzos is a significant one; their progression from manic to more manic creating a momentum that, though unusual, is in its way genuinely symphonic.

***

During the proletarian Cultural Revolution of the late 1920s, as "bourgeois" genres were being expunged from the cultural scene, two historic musical figures had remained more-or-less immune. The names of Beethoven and Musorgsky were frequently invoked as spiritual comrades-in-arms, fellow revolutionaries who had challenged the bourgeois traditions of their respective times. Political expediency aside, both composers were major forces in Shostakovich's life. Although he would not incorporate an audibly Musorgskian style into his own music until the late 1950s and early 1960s (with the Eleventh and Thirteenth Symphonies and *The Execution of Stepan Razin*), his engagement with certain Musorgskian aesthetic values was already well entrenched—the already noted connections between *Lady Macbeth* and *Boris Godunov*, for example. In 1939, the centenary of Musorgsky's birth, Shostakovich went one step further in this engagement, accepting a commission to re-orchestrate *Boris Godunov* for a Bolshoi Theater production. Although both of Musorgsky's own versions had been played in Russia, it was Rimsky-Korsakov's performing version that had held sway over the decades, as it would for most of the twentieth century. Like many, Shostakovich regarded Rimsky's smoothing out of Musorgsky's harmonic audacity and colorful sprucing up of Musorgsky's naturally monochrome orchestration as a betrayal of the Musorgskian ethos, even if it had been carried out with the best of intentions—to preserve and promote a masterpiece that might otherwise have remained in limbo. Shostakovich's objective was to return the opera to its roots, making "corrections" as needed to Musorgsky's orchestration but preserving the basic sound of the original. As he remarked in 1953, "Rimsky-Korsakov groomed, waved, and sluiced Musorgsky with eau de cologne. My orchestration is crude, in keeping with Musorgsky."[29] With the outbreak of war and the subsequent evacuation of the Bolshoi Theater to Kuibyshev, the intended 1941 production never went ahead. Shostakovich's version of *Boris Godunov* would not be premiered until 1959.

Shostakovich's final composition of 1939 was the *Suite on Finnish Themes*, an eleven-minute-long, seven-movement setting of Finnish folksongs for two singers and mixed chamber ensemble, completed on 3 December. Four days earlier, on 30 November, Stalin had invaded Finland (the so-called "Winter War") in an unprovoked act of aggression. It seems that the *Suite* had been designed as a publicity stunt to be used by what Stalin assumed would be the victorious Soviet occupying force; an olive branch of "respect" for the occupied country's native music. Shostakovich had been commissioned by the political division of the Leningrad military district to submit a Finnish work by 1 December, i.e., the day after the invasion. It is not known exactly when he received the commission, though he would clearly have had no idea of the *Suite's* intended purpose. But the embarrassing defeat of the Soviet forces put the kibosh on any "victory" performance. The score was hurriedly filed away at the library of the Leningrad Committee for Radio Broadcasting, though it eventually ended up in the hands of the musicologist Alexander Dolzhansky and was later purchased by the Shostakovich archive in Moscow. The premiere of the *Suite* in Finland in 2001 revealed a pleasant work, though one totally devoid of Shostakovichian character. The humor is mild and innocuous, any idiosyncratic folk character subsumed in all-purpose jollity.[30]

***

The composition of the Piano Quintet during the summer of 1940 was in part spurred by the desire of the Beethoven Quartet to perform with Shostakovich. And the benefit was reciprocal. In an explanation that was only partly tongue-in-cheek, Shostakovich, who declared himself a "dyed-in-the-wool wanderer," told Isaak Glikman that he had originally intended to compose a string quartet, but decided to include a piano part "so that I could play it myself and have a reason to go on tour to different towns and places. So now the Glazunovs and the Beethovens, who get to go everywhere, will have to take me with them, and I will get my chance to see the world as well!"[31] The Quintet was premiered in November of that year. It was well received and went on to win a Stalin Prize (first class) the following year. Yet, some critics were more circumspect. Moisei Grinberg, for example, complained of the "atmosphere of unhealthy sensation" surrounding the Quintet, its "stilted, singular new sounds resulting from abstract formal quests," its lack of "genuine beauty and strength," and its inability to "connect with the life of the people."[32]

Superficially, the Quintet's five-movement form recalls that of Mahler's Fifth Symphony. In both works, the five movements fall into a larger tripartite structure—a central scherzo flanked on each side by a pair of linked movements. In both works, the second movement follows *attacca* from the first, the fifth *attacca* from the fourth, with the central scherzo "detached" from its surroundings. What Shostakovich does not replicate is Mahler's distribution of weight within this superficially similar structure. Mahler's scherzo is central not just physically, but also psychologically. By a small margin the work's longest movement, it enacts the crucial transition from the death-ridden anguish of the first two movements towards the ecstatic *Adagietto* (an intermezzo in all but name) and the life-affirming finale, and thus emerges as the Symphony's center of gravity, a historically unusual role for a scherzo. Shostakovich's scherzo makes no such claims. Physically the shortest and compositionally the simplest movement in the Quintet, it deflects the work's weight towards the outer pairs of movements.

Shostakovich's continuing engagement with the baroque is clear from the very titles of the Quintet's opening pair of movements—"Prelude" and "Fugue." And for Shostakovich, "Prelude" was not just a convenient label, for he would take on board the very essence of that baroque genre, opening with a grand presentation of tonic harmony in the piano, replete with scalar flourishes and an assortment of typically baroque rhythms and figurations. In fact, like a baroque prelude, the entire four-minute movement is essentially a prolongation of the G tonic—although the baroque dance-like theme that follows this introduction does explore other pitch centers, the G tonic is never far out of earshot. The introductory material then returns, eventually culminating in a grand cadential "spinning out" of the sort frequently found at the end of a Bach prelude. And into those final string cascades embellishing the tonic (major) chord, Shostakovich injects the flattened second, A-flat. Although the Piano Quintet is generally not considered one of his "Jewish" pieces, the presence of this favorite Phrygian inflection (A-flat) together with the Picardy third (B-natural) in an otherwise minor-key context creates the Jewish *freygish* mode, a mode that will play an all-important role in the Second Piano Trio (1944).

The second movement Fugue would be the first of four fugues composed by Shostakovich during the 1940s. Along with the fugues in the finale of the Eighth Symphony, the first movement of the Third Quartet and the scherzo of the First Violin Concerto, it could be viewed as a preparation for the monumental set of Twenty-Four Preludes and Fugues, op. 87, that Shostakovich would pen in 1950-1951. Indeed, many of the traditional baroque fugal characteristics found in the op. 87 set can be found here, including a preservation of the tonic-dominant subject-answer axis, middle entry pairs separated by a fifth, and stretto in the movement's later stages (see Chapter 14). And the concept of prelude/fugue integration frequently found in op. 87 is also apparent here: the rising three-note figure in the Fugue's second bar, a figure that later takes on a life of its own, derives from the rising three-note groupings that form the aforementioned cascades at the end of the Prelude, while the Prelude's closing *freygish* inflections are replicated in the closing bars of the Fugue.

In other respects, however, this fugue is unusual. In the lead-up to the movement's central climax, Shostakovich suspends the fugue, replacing it with music

that, while based on the fugue subject, is more homophonic, more sharply rhythmic, more "gestural." Following the climax is a pseudo-cadenza for piano and then
cello, something that in a small way looks forward to the post-climax recitative in
the Eighth Symphony's first movement. The fugue eventually returns in stretto
(Fig. 34), paler, muted, and bereft of its initial momentum. And because the climax
has already passed, there is no pressure on the stretto to perform its usual climax-
building role. Rather than the more typical stretto whirlwind, we are drawn instead
to the sheer purity of counterpoint, first between the two violins, then between the
second violin and viola. The form of this movement may be somewhat unusual,
but it does serve a clear expressive goal—setting the inexorable momentum, texture,
and procedures of fugue into a larger psychological profile that, with its central climax and gradual withering away, is less typically "fugal" and more akin to a Shostakovich symphonic slow movement (that of the Fifth Symphony, for example).

The third movement scherzo is a fast *Ländler*. Its marked tempo (dotted half =
96) is roughly equivalent to the First Quartet and Sixth Symphony scherzos (96
and 88–96, respectively), but its gait is more earthy and its mood less mercurial.
The central trio section moves us geographically southwestward, with its pseudo-
flamenco style. Two features in particular stand out: the castanet-like rhythm of
three triplet-eighths followed by two quarter notes, where the triplet forms a melodic turn; and the melodic emphasizing of the Phrygian mode, especially the
characteristic fandango descending line 4-3-flat-2-1 at the end of a phrase, e.g.,
Fig. 53, b12–13. Following a modified, actually slightly extended, return of the
main scherzo material, the movement ends with a variant of the cadential figure
previously encountered in the First Quartet and Sixth Symphony (see Example
7.1 and subsequent remarks).

Shostakovich would revisit this type of scherzo in the Second Piano Trio
(1944). In fact, the rising scalar figure heard in the piano at the start of the movement, and upon which much of the movement is built, resurfaces in parts of that
later scherzo. As for the "flamenco" rhythms of the trio section, these would be
heard again in the trio of the Seventh Symphony's scherzo (1941)—both "flamenco" episodes based on the same sharp-side pitch center, highlighting their
nervy, high-strung character: G-sharp Phrygian in the Quintet and G-sharp *freygish* in the Symphony. Other connections that link all three of these scherzi are a
snappy dance-like rhythm consisting of a quarter followed by four eighth notes
(used in the Quintet and the Symphony as an ostinato with all five notes on the
same pitch) and a series of neurotically lurching *crescendi* created by quickly
retaken upbows, e.g., Fig. 50 in the Quintet (Example 7.2), Fig. 88, b3 in the
Symphony, and Fig. 37 in the Trio. It should be noted that, individually,
the above-mentioned attributes can be found quite often in Shostakovich: the
repeated-upbow gesture resurfaces in the Tenth Symphony's third movement (Fig.
129, b6), while the "castanet" rhythm can be heard in the central section of the
Sixth Symphony's finale and, with its rhythms modified for a duple meter environment, in the scherzos of the Eighth Quartet (second movement; see Chapter 9,
Example 9.6b) and Thirteenth Symphony (Example 9.6a), and the Overture to

The Gamblers together with its offspring, the scherzo of the Viola Sonata, to name but four examples.

Example 7.2

In keeping with the spirit of the first two movements, the fourth movement Intermezzo (*Lento*) appears initially to present yet another baroque favorite of Shostakovich, the passacaglia. That this movement is not in fact a passacaglia becomes apparent three bars into what would be the ground's second rotation, where the bass diverges from its original path. Nevertheless, the implacably processional nature of this bass line, with its square quarter-note rhythm and mainly stepwise motion, brings to mind many a baroque passacaglia. Shostakovich even indulges in the Purcellian passacaglia technique of "blurring" phrase boundaries—the first bar of the would-be ground's second rotation coinciding with the last, cadential, bar of the violin's opening melody. Indeed, the tempo, the walking bass, and the general melodic and rhythmic profile of the main melody are all reminiscent of another famous pseudo-passacaglia, the slow movement ("Air on the G-string") of Bach's Third Orchestral Suite. And an allusion to yet another work "in the olden style" occurs later at the movement's *appassionato* climax, where the layering of voices and heavy strong-beat triplets is heavily reminiscent of the fourth movement of Grieg's *Holberg Suite*.

The light, almost inconsequential tone of the Finale, with its gently wistful, slightly ironic mood, seems at odds with the weighty, serious tone of the rest of the work. Yet, although the movement's throw-away ending hardly strives for anything like the same transcendental quality, the finale as a whole can perhaps be viewed as an exercise for a type of finale that would later be perfected in the Eighth and Thirteenth Symphonies, where predominantly lightweight material becomes sublimated in the coda to achieve an enigmatic but highly poignant sense of resignation.

***

Shostakovich's heavy performing schedule meant that the first half of 1941 would see only one composition, the incidental music for Kozintsev's stage production of *King Lear*. Along with *Hamlet*, *Lear* was the Shakespeare work that most resonated with Shostakovich, and he would return to both works later in life. But overshadowing everything was the onset of war following the German invasion on 22 June. Over the course of the summer, Leningrad's major artistic institutions were evacuated—the Philharmonic to Novosibirsk, the Conservatory to Tashkent, the Kirov Theater to Perm. Shostakovich meanwhile tried to maintain as normal a life as possible in Leningrad, refusing an initial evacuation offer. He applied for military duty, but was turned down. Instead, he assisted in various civil defense projects as a member of the Conservatory's volunteer force, and was also nominally a member of the Conservatory's fire guard although, like most celebrities, was barred from actual fire-fighting service. By September, however, Leningrad was under siege. It would remain so for the next nine hundred days.

On the evening of the 17 September, Shostakovich played the two completed movements of his new Seventh Symphony at home to a circle of friends and colleagues. His friend Valerian Bogdanov-Berezovsky reports:

> We expected something extraordinary. And the extraordinary certainly happened, captivating and thrilling us.... After the overwhelming impression left by the first movement of the symphony, not a sound could be heard. Shostakovich then nervously opened a package of cigarettes and began smoking, thus creating a pause in the performance ... When [the second movement] was over, everybody simultaneously demanded a repeat performance of the second movement. But all of a sudden, an air raid siren sounded. Shostakovich suggested that we take only a short break—he had to take his wife and children, Galina and Maxim, to the bomb shelter—and then we would continue later on.[33]

The situation soon became untenable. On 1 October, Shostakovich, his wife, and his two children were moved to Moscow. Two weeks later, they began the arduous week-long train journey to Kuibyshev (formerly and latterly Samara), the residence of the evacuated Bolshoi Theater. The first week or so in Kuibyshev was spent on a classroom floor along with members of the Bolshoi.[34] Later, the Shostakoviches were allocated a separate room, and eventually, a two-room apartment.[35] With the improved conditions, Shostakovich was able to complete the fourth movement of the new Symphony—he had completed the third at the end of September, shortly before his evacuation. Nevertheless, he could not help but feel out of place in this relative cultural backwater. In particular, he missed the companionship of Sollertinsky (billeted in Novosibirsk) and Glikman (in Tashkent). Also preying on his mind was the safety of his mother and extended family, still awaiting evacuation back in Leningrad where food supplies had dwindled to dangerously low levels. In March 1943, after months of bureaucratic wrangling, Shostakovich was reunited in Kuibyshev with his mother and with his sister Mariya and her family.

The Seventh Symphony (the "Leningrad") received its premiere in Kuibyshev on 5 March 1942 with the Bolshoi Theater Orchestra under Samuil Samosud, who also led the Moscow premiere three weeks later. The first performance by Leningrad forces took place in July, with Mravinsky conducting the evacuated Philharmonic in Novosibirsk. But by far the most extraordinary performance was the one given in Leningrad itself by the All-Union Radio Orchestra under Karl Eliasberg on 9 August. The Radio Orchestra was the only ensemble to have remained in Leningrad during the siege. It had borne terrible losses over the previous year, and by the summer of 1942 was operating at about half strength. At eighty minutes, the Seventh was Shostakovich's longest symphony and, though not possessed of the gigantic orchestral complexity of the as yet unperformed Fourth Symphony, still required sizeable forces, including additional *banda* at climactic moments. Extra wind players were hurriedly conscripted from the front. Oboist Kseniya Matus remembers the first rehearsal:

> I grabbed my instrument and when I opened the case it also turned out to have dystrophy. All the pads had turned green, the valves had turned green. The oboe wouldn't play, but I took it as it was. And when I got to the hall I became frightened. Those I had known before the war were so emaciated. Some were covered with soot, their faces were blackened with smoke. They were hungry, and all dressed in I don't know what. But they came. Eliasberg stood up at the podium. He lifted his hands and they were trembling, and to my imagination, he was a wounded bird, whose wings are hurt and is about to fall. But he didn't fall.[36]

According to the clarinetist, Viktor Kozlov, the first rehearsals were only fifteen or twenty minutes long: "we were unable to hold our lips, we couldn't strain and our lips became weak. Slowly, the rehearsals became longer."[37] On the day of the performance, bombardment continued until about five o'clock. Additional shelling of German positions took place in order to silence the enemy during the concert.[38] The performance itself was a highly charged experience for performers and audience, with the bedraggled, emaciated orchestra presenting Shostakovich's gift to the city with all the power at their disposal. Kozlov observed:

> It's interesting that the Germans were sending out tickets for 9 August also saying that they were going to celebrate their victory at the Astoria hotel. It was precisely on that day that Shostakovich's 7th Symphony was performed to show them that the city was still alive and functioning. The audience received us very, very well. There was a lot of applause and standing ovations—one woman even gave the conductor flowers—imagine, there was *nothing* in the city then and yet this one woman found flowers somewhere.[39]

The Seventh was not just a domestic sensation. The Kuibyshev premiere, complete with Shostakovich's spoken introduction to the audience, had been broadcast internationally, and the Symphony's extraordinary story was making headlines around the world. Even before the premieres in Novosibirsk and Leningrad, a microfilm of the score stuffed in a tin box had been secreted out of the country and, in a scenario that reads like something out of a spy novel, flown from Kuibyshev to Tehran, driven to Cairo, eventually surfacing in London for use in the British premiere in June given by the London Symphony Orchestra and Henry Wood. Finally, it made its way to New York. On 19 July, it received its US premiere in an NBC studio broadcast with Toscanini conducting the NBC Symphony. The following day, the image of a steely eyed Shostakovich bedecked in fireman's helmet adorned *Time* magazine's front cover, along with the caption: "Amid bombs bursting in Leningrad he heard the chords of victory."[40] Given the somewhat conditional nature of his stint in the fire guard, the portrait, based on a posed photograph that had previously been making the rounds, was perhaps something of a fiction. Nevertheless, the image would turn the composer into a household name and an icon of US-Soviet anti-fascist solidarity,

In the USA, the competition to be "first" had been not altogether amicable. Leopold Stokowski, who was also under contract to NBC, had wanted the July premiere for himself. Upon hearing of this, Toscanini had written to Stokowski: "I was deeply taken by [the symphony's] beauty and its anti-Fascist meanings, and I have to confess to you, by the greatest desire to perform it. Don't you think, my dear Stokowski, it would be very interesting for everybody, and yourself, too, to hear the old Italian conductor (one of the first artists who strenuously fought against Fascism) to play this work of a young Russian anti-Nazi composer."[41]

Following the NBC studio premiere, Serge Koussevitsky gave the first American live concert performance of the Seventh Symphony at the summer music festival in Tanglewood on 14 August with the resident Berkshire Music Center Orchestra. But the Toscanini/Stokowski rivalry would flare up again in the negotiations for the upcoming concert season. Toscanini had scheduled three performances with the New York Philharmonic-Symphony for the middle of October and was determined not to be upstaged, especially not by Stokowski in Philadelphia. In a letter to the publishers Am-Rus Music, the Philharmonic-Symphony's management underscored Toscanini's "claim":

> I sincerely hope that you will protect the Philharmonic-Symphony Society from any other performances in this country before ours, with the exception of course of Tanglewood and the NBC. In other words, the Society would not like to have the Philadelphia Orchestra play this work in Philadelphia before October 14th. The Society agreed to pay you the fee that you have stipulated, but under no circumstances would we consent to any other orchestra in this country playing this Symphony in a regular concert series before the dates mutually agreed by us.[42]

In a pointed response, Am-Rus asked, "Against whom must the Philharmonic Orchestra under TOSCANINI be protected?," and defended the contract as pertaining only to a "first performance in New York City" and not the United States as a whole.[43] Again, Toscanini won—the performances in Philadelphia (under Eugene Ormandy rather than Stokowski) did not take place until the end of November, though, ironically, Toscanini's coveted New York Philharmonic-Symphony "premiere" would be pre-empted both by the Boston Symphony with Koussevitsky and by the Chicago Symphony with Frederick Stock.[44]

Perhaps the real irony here, though, was the fact that Toscanini did not actually care too much for the Symphony itself. In that letter to Stokowski, he had admitted that "I admire Shostakovich's music, but I don't feel such a frenzied love for it like you." Years later, after listening to the famous RCA recording of his NBC premiere, he was heard to ask, "Did I really learn and conduct such junk?"[45] Given the extraordinary circumstances, it was perhaps inevitable that the Seventh Symphony would become an institution, a work whose "story" and notoriety would quickly eclipse the music itself. Despite the enormous publicity put out by various Western governmental and political bodies and by the likes of *Time* magazine, critical reception of the *Leningrad* Symphony in the West was mostly negative, ranging from the mildly bemused Olin Downes, who described "sincere and competent music-making [but] thin in substance,"[46] to the downright hostile Ernest Newman, who wrote one of his most famous diatribes following a 1944 performance by the BBC Symphony Orchestra under Sir Adrian Boult. Having previously chided the BBC for their "sob-stuff propaganda on behalf of the symphony,"[47] Newman wrote:

> The result was to confirm the former impression of most of us that nothing at once so long-winded, so empty, so pretentious has been perpetrated in music within living memory. The dreadful thing takes some seventy minutes to perform; the amount of real musical thinking there is in it could have been accomplished in seventeen by a composer who understood his job. If you want to locate the work on the musical map, look for it somewhere within the seventieth degree of longitude and the last degree of platitude.[48]

The Seventh Symphony was Shostakovich's first full symphonic work in a major key. (Neither the one-movement Third Symphony, nominally in E-flat, nor the largely atonal single-movement Second Symphony that winds up in B are really "full" symphonic works.) Publicly touted by Shostakovich as a depiction of "people living a peaceful, happy life" prior to Hitler's invasion,[49] the first movement's exposition opens with a forthright, somewhat militaristic theme in C major. It is one of Shostakovich's plainest, most diatonic creations, though the F-sharp that dominates the third bar not only provides a moment of chromatic tension but, typically for Shostakovich, proves to be of structural importance later on. In keeping with the exposition's tone of forthright simplicity, the lyrical second theme is presented in G major, establishing a classical sonata form tonic-dominant relationship, something that has been quite rare in Shostakovich's music thus far,[50] but that will become more common in later works.

Compared to Shostakovich's previous symphonic expositions, this one is almost startlingly plain. But it is the movement's development section, dominated almost entirely by its repetitions *à la Boléro* of its infamous march theme, that has caused the real eyebrow-raising; a musical non-development, or even anti-development, that has become one of the most reviled passages in all of Western art-music— Bartók's unflattering parody of the march theme in his *Concerto for Orchestra* constituting perhaps the most famous piece of commentary on the subject. According to Shostakovich at the time, this was his depiction of war, or at least "the emotional impact of war."[51] The author of *Testimony* put in into a wider context: the "Leningrad that Stalin destroyed and that Hitler merely finished off,"[52] a view supported by Shostakovich's friend Flora Litvinova, who recalls him telling her that both the Seventh and Fifth Symphonies "were not just about Fascism, but about our system, or any form of totalitarian regime."[53] Although this section does rather stand apart from the rest of the movement, the theme itself (see Chapter, 6, Example 6.2), though externally "new," is in fact something of a conflation of earlier themes, even other Shostakovich melodic archetypes. For example, it is one of several Shostakovich melodies that are based on two-bar groups, where the first contains a dotted rhythm and the second contains two reiterated pitches (see Chapter 6). Furthermore, its melodic profile, or at least the first four notes of it, is based on the opening chorus of Musorgsky's *Boris Godunov,* a theme that Shostakovich had already quoted in *Lady Macbeth*. And as David Hurwitz points out, the quick-fire five-note rhythm that forms the basis of the snare drum ostinato accompanying the march theme can be heard in melodic, usually scalar, form in several places throughout the exposition's first subject (e.g., bars 10 and 11).[54]

This "invasion" episode falls into two parts: the initial "non-developing" half, containing the march theme followed by its eleven re-orchestrated repetitions (sometimes, though inaccurately, dubbed "variations"; Figs. 19–45); and a limited development of same, leading eventually into the recapitulation (Figs. 45–52). The march and its repetitions have, inevitably, been compared to Ravel's *Boléro*: the slow crescendo, the re-orchestrated repetitions (eighteen rotations altogether in the Ravel, twelve in the Shostakovich), the persistent snare drum ostinato, and the tear-away modulation at the end. Shostakovich himself remarked to Glikman that "critics . . . will damn me for copying Ravel's *Boléro*. Well, let them. That is how I hear war."[55] Later, he told Khachaturian, "Forgive me, will you, if this reminds you of Ravel's *Boléro*."[56] Of course, Shostakovich's (deliberately?) anonymous, earthbound, and obstinately diatonic theme, with its rigid phrase structure, is a world away from *Boléro's* seductive chromaticism and phrasal elisions. And nowhere is the flat-footedness of Shostakovich's theme—what Izrail Nestyev called a "monotonous Prussian march"[57]—more apparent than in the fourth iteration (Fig. 25), where the bassoon's idiotic copycat repetitions of the oboe's every phrase drag out the theme to twice its actual length—perhaps the one genuine example of self-sabotage in Shostakovich's output.

The second, "developing," part of the "invasion" episode announces itself with a sudden, unprepared modulation to A major, the most distant key from the theme's initial tonality of E-flat. This jarring modulation is also accentuated metrically: under the prevailing phrase structure, the new A major melody should arrive at Fig. 45, b2, but instead, it enters in the middle of Fig. 45 itself, two beats "early," creating a metrical distortion. The feeling here is of liberation, as the formerly earthbound melody is finally allowed to soar—the pulling away to the most distant possible key perhaps a symbol of this emancipation—though the melody, in essence a variant of the "invasion" theme, takes on a tragic-heroic quality, resulting from Shostakovich's characteristic choice of mode. While the orchestra hammers out chords of A major, the supplemental *banda* intones the melody, using notes of the A minor scale from the tonic (A) down to the fourth degree (D) and back. A combination mode is thus created in which the top portion of A minor is superimposed onto the bottom portion of A major (A, B, C-sharp, D, E, F, G, A), a pitch collection that can actually be heard as a scale a few bars later (Fig. 45, b8–9). Such a "half-and-half" combination mode should not be confused with genuine bimodality, where major and minor are used simultaneously, a device also favored by Shostakovich.

The ambiguous tragic-heroic flavor created by this combination mode recalls the bitter-sweet, "laughing through tears" quality of another dark/bright combination mode beloved of Shostakovich, the Jewish *freygish*, with its optimistic major third sitting poignantly within the darker Phrygian scale (see discussion of the Second Piano Trio, below). In fact, the major/minor combination mode can be found amongst the collection of Jewish and pseudo-Jewish modes in Shostakovich's 1948 song-cycle *From Jewish Folk Poetry*, for example, in the first ten bars of "Fussy Mummy and Auntie" (see Chapter 8), and the musicologist Timothy Jackson has suggested a Jewish, particularly a klezmer, quality at this point in the Symphony,[58] a suggestion that is rather reinforced by the orchestration—the thundering timpani and bass drum replaced at Fig. 45 by the almost klezmer-like sound of cymbals and tambourine.

Alongside the first movements of the Fifth, Eighth, or Tenth Symphonies, the development here seems crude in terms of its transformational processes. Yet, any development that follows, as this one does, almost ten minutes of obstinately non-developing material will register. And the accumulation of tension remains impressive, especially given the rhythmic discipline that Shostakovich has imposed upon himself. The developments in the first movements of the Fifth and Eighth Symphonies both contain march-like episodes, but in each case, the music eventually tears away from its militaristic thumbscrews with a headlong rush to the devastation and collapse that await at the start of their respective recapitulations. By contrast, the strict military rhythm here in the Seventh is preserved, even after Fig. 45 when the music does, in other respects, break loose. In fact, the power of this development could be said to derive not so much from its (rather limited) transformational processes but from the tension created between the forces of accumulation and hysteria (flutter-tongued brass and screaming woodwind trills) and the forces of militaristic discipline.

And what of the march theme itself? Apart from the aforementioned *Boris Godunov* allusion in its first two bars, the descending six-note scale that runs from the end of the sixth bar to the start of the eighth (pitch degrees 2, 1, 7, 6, 5, 4) appears to some listeners to be a quotation from "Da geh' ich zu Maxim" from

Léhar's *Merry Widow*, a tune that, with its reference to Maxim, was something of
an in-joke *chez* Shostakovich. Others find here an allusion to the start of Tchaikovsky's Fifth Symphony (end of the fourth bar to the start of the sixth—pitch
degrees 1, 7, 6, 5, 4, 3), or even to *Deutschland über alles* (6, 5, 4, 3, 2, (3), 1).
Ian MacDonald believes this to have been Shostakovich's attempt to fashion "a
tune that would sound German and Russian at the same time." Noting that the
theme's final appearance (Fig. 50) replicates the key of Tchaikovsky's melody as it
appears in his finale (E major), MacDonald speculates that the march is thus
marked "at the very peak of its hysteria, as Russian rather than German."[59] Ascribing authorial intent, a tricky matter at the best of times, is here made even more
difficult by a controversy over dating, for evidence suggests that the "invasion"
theme may actually have been composed before the War—a claim supported by
Lyudmila Mikheyeva (who states that Shostakovich played it to his students prior
to the War),[60] Galina Ustvolskaya,[61] and Lev Lebedinsky.[62]

Unusually for a major key movement, the recapitulation enters with the first
subject in the tonic minor (Fig. 52), perhaps bearing out Shostakovich's stated
view of the recapitulation as "a requiem for the war's victims."[63] And shorn of its
first two bars, the theme starts not with the resolute tonic C with which the movement began, but with the "diabolic" F-sharp of the movement's third bar. As in
the Fifth Symphony's first movement, tensions continue to run high during this
first theme reprise; a full sense of recapitulatory resolution is delayed. But that is
where the similarity ends, for the two movements go on to display entirely opposite responses to the "brutalization" of their respective developments. In the Fifth
Symphony, the first theme reprise collapses with one shattering blow (*con tutta
forza*), a swift, decisive action that clears the air for the reprise of the second
theme. The reprise itself, floating in the clear air of D major, resolves the tonal,
metrical, and harmonic-rhythmic issues raised in the exposition (see Chapter 13).
In the Seventh Symphony, by contrast, the music does not so much collapse as fizzle out (Fig. 56, b3), and the reprise of the second theme takes what was in the exposition a very stable theme and performs an act of dismemberment. There is a
moment of stability prior to the reprise, as the violins and flute sing a rarified
post-massacre threnody over a long string pedal (Fig. 58). But the key here is
F-sharp, the furthest possible key from the movement's C major tonic, and yet
another manifestation of the previously discussed tritone relationship. The first act
of dismemberment is the jettisoning of the original gently rocking accompaniment
to the second theme and its replacement by a limping figure that shakily alternates
between 3/4 and 4/4 time (Fig. 60). Four bars later, the second theme itself enters.
It is almost unrecognizable—pale, hesitant, and bruised in a solo bassoon, a world
away from its serenely confident exposition presentation in the first violins. The
key is F-sharp Phrygian, again a world apart from the original G major. When the
first subject eventually returns in C major (Fig. 66), it is almost in a trance. An
attempt to inject something of its original rhythmic energy (Fig. 67) leads
nowhere, and the movement ends with a whispered, almost throw-away, reference
to the "invasion" theme.

The second movement is a gently ironic scherzo with a not-so-gently ironic trio, the latter recalling several characteristically sardonic gestures previously discussed in the Sixth Symphony and Piano Quintet scherzos—the lurid grotesquerie of the E-flat clarinet, the "castanet" triplet, and the lurching repeated-upbow *crescendi*. Indeed, Shostakovich himself remarked on the similarity between this movement and the Quintet's scherzo.[64] The grotesque character also comes from Shostako-vich's swerving between one modal extreme and another—the sarcastic main E-flat clarinet melody in C-sharp Phrygian (Fig. 82, b8) versus the brief, "over-festive" brass theme in C Lydian (Fig. 90), for example—as well as his use of combination modes, such as the Lydian with a flattened seventh (Fig. 84). As previously mentioned, both the passage with the "castanet" triplets (Fig. 88) and the entire Piano Quintet trio (where this triplet figure predominates) are based on the same pitch center: G-sharp Phrygian in the Quintet and G-sharp *freygish* in the Symphony—although it could be argued that the latter is simply a prolonged dominant of the trio's prevailing C-sharp minor/Phrygian rather than a tonic in its own right, the type of "dominant scale" tonal deployment often found in Jewish or Balkan folk music.[65]

The musical language and orchestration of the Symphony's first two movements (and, for that matter, the finale) are very typical of Shostakovich's style of the period. So the baldly ascetic chorale at the start of the slow third movement, with its piquant close-harmony mixture of high-lying reeds, comes as something of a surprise. This "reediness" is most apparent at the very top of the texture, where Shostakovich doubles the E-flat clarinet and first oboe, a rather different proposition to his more typical doubling of E-flat clarinet with either piccolo or flute. The remaining high woodwind lines follow suit: second oboe doubles first clarinet, English horn doubles second clarinet, the reedy austerity heightened by the absence of any member of the flute family. At the other end of the spectrum, horns, bassoons, contrabassoon, and bass clarinet chime lugubriously, while a pair of tolling harps binds the two ends of the texture together. The harmonic language, too, is unusual for Shostakovich. Based mainly around dyads and partially constructed seventh and ninth chords—in most cases, it is the third that is missing—and abetted by those stark, reedy sonorities, it conjures an air of Stravinskian primitivism. The *Symphony of Psalms* comes to mind—perhaps not a surprise if *Testimony's* statement that the Seventh Symphony was written under the influence of the Psalms of David holds true.[66]

If such primitivism goes beyond the Shostakovichian mainstream, the pseudo-recitative that constitutes the response (Fig. 106; aptly described by Richard Taruskin as "massed violins soliloquizing a chaconne")[67] pulls us quickly back. The Stravinskian chorale returns at Fig. 107, now with an energized bass line derived from the pseudo-recitative. At Fig. 108, the violins attempt the recitative again, but this time the music settles, and a simple, elegiac melody emerges (Fig. 109). With its slightly faster, but rather turbulent central section (*Moderato risoluto*), the structure of the movement as a whole is reminiscent of the Mozartian *romanza*. Perhaps more pertinent, it is also a simplified version of Shostakovich's own symphonic "first movement moderato" form, with the recapitulation of the opening chorale coming as the high-strung dotted rhythms of this central theme continue unabated (Fig. 130). Indeed, this would be Shostakovich's first use of this characteristic structure outside a first movement context.

Aside from a long introduction, a carry-over from the end of the third movement, the C minor finale is based structurally on the Fifth Symphony's finale: two parts—one fast, one slow—plus a grand C major coda. And like the Fifth Symphony's famous, though less grand, D major conclusion, the coda has found itself the subject of the "sincerity" question: is it to be read as genuine triumph or hollow triumphalism? Yet, despite the formal and possibly hermeneutic parallels, the two finales are aesthetically quite different from one another. Here in the Seventh, the tone of public heroism courses through the entire movement. And where the slow section in the Fifth had veered between feverish intensity (e.g., the palpitating references to Tchaikovsky's *Romeo and Juliet*) and shadowiness, not to mention the "hidden" quotation from the *Four Pushkin Romances*, the slow section here seems more straightforward, a moment of contemplation before the final push.

At the end of the Symphony, the first movement's opening theme returns triumphantly in the brass (Fig. 207, b4). Regardless of the interpretation we place on that opening theme, its return here is a psychologically powerful moment, the theme rising from the ashes, as it were. Such cyclism, not to be confused with deeper-level inter-movement motivic development, had been rare in Shostakovich's concert music; the First Symphony is one exception, the Fourth Symphony, in spirit at least,[68] another. But the Seventh Symphony would inaugurate a two-decade period in which nearly all Shostakovich's concert works would be overtly cyclic (see Chapter 9, Table 9.1).

Yet, this cyclism does not preclude deeper motivic connections both within and between movements, the most prominent of which is a three-note figure comprising an ascending followed by a descending major second. This figure is first heard as the accompaniment to the first movement's second subject (D–E–D in the violas answered by G–A–G in the cellos; Fig. 6) and subsequently forms the first three notes of the "invasion" theme (E-flat–F–E-flat, see Chapter 6, Example 6.2)—as already noted, these pitches plus a fourth pitch, B-flat, derive from *Boris Godunov*. Additionally, the figure functions as the principal accompanying figure (B-flat–C–B-flat) to all but the first three and final two of the march's twelve rotations. A semitonal version of the motive (ascending and descending minor second) is later used as a tension builder, for example in the lead up to the recapitulation (Fig. 51). There, in the bass instruments, the motive G–A-flat–G (G being the dominant of the upcoming C minor recapitulation) is used to anchor a chromatically rising sequence, creating a typically Shostakovichian "wedge" shape that pulls further and further from the G. In the finale, a variant of this figure is used first to launch the main theme (Fig. 150), then to bring the first section to a close (Fig. 175), and finally as the basis for the long ascent to the coda (starting Fig. 189). In another inter-movement motivic connection, the slower middle section of the finale is based rhythmically on the first movement "invasion" theme, but modified into triple meter to create a characteristically Shostakovichian chaconne-like rhythm (♩ ♩. ♪‖♩ ♩ ♩).

***

Our discussion of Shostakovich's output between 1937 and 1941, i.e., from the Fifth to the Seventh Symphonies, has revealed two overriding musical characteristics. The first is an engagement with eighteenth-century forms (recitative, the prelude and fugue pair, theme and variations, etc.) and, to a lesser extent, eighteenth-century styles (the French overture launching of the Fifth Symphony or the characteristic diminished seventh drop in the first subject of the Sixth Symphony). Although there are earlier instances of such historical engagement (the Theme and Variations, op. 3, the recitative in *Alone*, or the passacaglia in *Lady Macbeth*), it was post-Fifth Symphony that these became a defining characteristic. The second feature is the use of modal inflections, in particular the Phrygian (darkening the minor context with its flattened second) and Lydian (brightening the major context with its sharpened fourth). These two "polarizing" modes in part define Shostakovich's brand of musical intensity, as do his "combination" modes, where elements of major and Phrygian (i.e., in the *freygish* mode), or major and minor, tug against each other within the same scale.

These characteristics would dominate for at least another decade, and would continue to be a factor in Shostakovich's later music. But one important work of the early 1940s stands somewhat outside this compositional orbit—the *Six Romances on Words of W. Raleigh, R. Burns, and W. Shakespeare* (often known as *Six Romances on Verses by English Poets*, reflecting the Russian tendency to interchange "English" and "British") for bass and piano, penned during the course of 1942. Here the melodic contours are noticeably simpler, with less inflected chromaticism. The second song, a bleak setting of Burns' "Oh wert thou in the cold blast," epitomizes the difference, Shostakovich eschewing his favorite polarizing modes and instead coloring the basic D minor tonality with a neutralizing Dorian inflection—neutral due to its placement between minor and major in the spectrum of modes.[69] With the Dorian mode lacking strong tendency tones, the music emerges as appropriately tensionless, all emotion subsumed in the barren wasteland of Burns' text ("Or were I in the wildest waste/Sae black and bare, sae black and bare/The desert were a paradise/If thou wert there, if thou wert there.")

More than any other work from this period, the *Romances* looks forward thirty-or-so years to Shostakovich's late style, where simplicity and melodic purity, bleaker, and with less overt passion, would become the order of the day. In fact, the cycle is probably most effective in Shostakovich's 1971 transcription (op. 140) for bass and chamber orchestra (not to be confused with his orchestration for bass and full orchestra, op. 62a, made in 1943), a seemingly natural fulfillment of the work's late-style prophecy. There, "Oh wert thou in the cold blast" is made doubly bleak with its brooding orchestration of cellos *a3*, double basses (divided at the end), solo viola, and timpani. In fact, it is highly reminiscent of the start of another famous blast of "cold water," Sibelius' Fourth Symphony, where a solo cello emerges from a black pool of divided cellos and basses.

The *Romances* may have been in some ways stylistically unusual, but in another respect, the collection bore an air of familiarity, for this was now the second time in two years that Shostakovich had presented settings of classic poetry with the apparent purpose of making a political statement—the *Four Pushkin Romances* of 1936 had just received its premiere the previous year. The first and third songs of the "English" cycle, "To His Son" and "MacPherson's Farewell,"[70] are replete with gallows references, and it is surely no coincidence that the opening theme of the latter would be used two decades later in Shostakovich's most famous work of protest, the Thirteenth Symphony, where the same impish melody portrays the power of humor over soulless authority.

The most potentially inflammatory song, however, was the fifth, a setting of Shakespeare's famous Sonnet 66, complete with the line that had become almost a rallying cry for the Soviet intelligentsia, "And art made tongue-tied by authority"—presented effectively if more prosaically in Boris Pasternak's translation as "and remembering that the mouth of thought is gagged." Pasternak himself used to deliver the Sonnet at underground poetry readings, usually shading that iconic line with a special color.[71] Shostakovich's setting, with its climax on the word "*rot*" ("mouth") and his establishment in the preceding line of dissonance in what is otherwise consonant music, leaves us in no doubt that for him too this line forms the crux of the Sonnet, though of course not even Shostakovich could have known that Shakespeare's very next line, "And Folly (Doctor-like) controlling skill," would be eerily prescient of Stalin's own doctor-related folly that would hit the Soviet Union a decade later. Incidentally, the 1971 orchestration reciprocates the cycle's influence on the Thirteenth Symphony, for the chime that ominously marks the start of "Babi Yar" now ushers in "Sonnet 66." (The musicologist Marina Frolova-Walker puts forward the interesting speculation that the reiterated pedal G that chimes throughout "Sonnet 66" might have been a pun on the song's dedicatee, Sollertinsky [G= "Sol"]. This would create an interesting parallel with the reiterated A at the end of the Fifth Symphony that may possibly have been a pun on Lyalya [Konstantinovskaya] – see Chapter 1).[72]

The sixth and final song, "The King's Campaign" (based on "The Grand Old Duke of York") provides a short and pithy coda to the cycle: "Up to the top of the hill/The King has marched his men/The King has come back down again/But without his band of men." As Richard Longman writes, "The black humour veils a bitter message: the leaders live to repeat their follies, while whole regiments disappear."[73]

***

The autumn of 1942 would prove particularly difficult for Shostakovich, with the deaths of the two most influential mentors of his adolescence, Nikolayev and Yavorsky. Shostakovich's depression was exacerbated by his own battles with typhoid that winter and the continuing boredom of life in Kuibyshev. He had been able to travel to Moscow in March and Novosibirsk in July to supervise performances of the Seventh Symphony, and to Moscow again in September to collaborate with the NKVD Song and Dance Ensemble on *Native Leningrad*, a show for which he had written incidental music, but a permanent move from his wartime home was not yet in the offing. He was also frustrated by his attempts to compose a new comic opera on Gogol's play, *The Gamblers*. He had started it on 28 December 1941, the day after completing the Seventh Symphony's finale (a juxtaposition that begs interesting questions), and had worked on it some more the following spring. But by November 1942, with only the overture and two scenes completed (these three items alone coming to about forty-five minutes of music), he had come to the realization that his original intent to set Gogol's words line-for-line was simply not feasible. He reluctantly aborted the project, although three decades later the overture would be reworked and given a new life as the scherzo of the Viola Sonata (1975).

Still in frail health, Shostakovich set about his Second Piano Sonata in January 1943, completing it in March at the Arkhangelskoye sanatorium, near Moscow. Dedicated to the memory of Nikolayev, the Sonata drew mixed opinions, with many finding the characteristic Shostakovich qualities of pathos and irony to be strangely muted. Even Emil Gilels, who later became one of the Sonata's greatest exponents, felt at the time that it "testifie[d] more to Shostakovich's wonderful technique than to the depth of thought which was characteristic of his last symphonies."[74] Incidentally, it is one of the few piano works, and without doubt the most important, that Shostakovich never recorded, though he performed it often in concert.

The Sonata is characterized by an uncompromising introspection, an economy of means, and a lack of virtuoso bluster. Typically for Shostakovich, the keyboard textures are spare, often confined to the simplest two-part writing. The first movement's first subject, in B minor, is a long-limbed theme built on an insistent, rather Schumannesque sequence of dotted rhythms. With the second subject also making heavy use of the dotted rhythms, the movement could be accused of rhythmic monotony. Yet, once the true function of the second subject is understood, the rhythmic consistency makes more sense. Presented *fortissimo*, this rather triumphalist E-flat Lydian second subject, accompanied by fifteen bars of repeated tonic-chord accompaniment (a characteristic familiar from the climax of the Seventh Symphony's "invasion" theme), is harmonically stable in a way that the formative, preparatory first subject is not, and thus impinges itself not as a contrast to the first subject but as an outgrowth of it.

The seemingly unorthodox tonal relationship between first and second subjects amounts to an enharmonically respelled mediant relationship (B minor to D-sharp), a favorite of Beethoven or Schubert. More interesting, though, is the way that this relationship plays out through the movement and through the Sonata as a whole. The heightened importance of the second subject in the exposition is reinforced in the recapitulation where, unusually, it is given in its original exposition key, E-flat. Sonata-form recapitulations traditionally present all themes in the tonic, i.e., the key of the exposition's first subject, a fact that tends to reinforce that subject's structural primacy. Here, however, Shostakovich allows his second subject to preserve its original tonal identity. Actually, it would be more accurate to say that the second subject is at least allowed to fight for its identity, for underneath its presentation in E-flat, the first subject continues to grind away in B minor. With hints of Hindemith or Stravinsky, such bitonality harks back to an earlier period in Shostakovich's work. But where he had traditionally used bitonality in an iconoclastic way to emphasize moments of "wrong note" absurdity, here it has a seriousness of purpose—genuine, internally driven conflict, not Gogolian incongruity. (Other moments of bitonality can be found in bars 132–133 of the first movement and in variation six of the third, the latter a canon pitching G minor against G-sharp minor.)

The second movement, too, seems stylistically atypical for Shostakovich. Eschewing the recitatives, the passacaglias and pseudo-passacaglias, and the Phrygian inflections otherwise favored during slow movements of this period, Shostakovich takes us unto a rarefied world that is almost Schoenbergian in its tonal and rhythmic intractability, its melodic cragginess, and its textural sparseness. Also unusual are the rapid pedaled arpeggios that creep in about two-thirds of the way through—this from a composer who was no fan of impressionism.

Purportedly a tribute to Nikolayev's love of theme-and-variations (not to mention Shostakovich's own interest in the form), the third movement finale is a set of nine variations on a thirty-bar theme. Of the theme itself, Alexander Tentser writes:

> The influence of Russian folk songs ("protyazhniye pesni," i.e., prolonged or stretched-out songs) is quite evident in the third movement. Delson compared this long and sad melody to the Russian "pritchet," a special type of song usually reserved for a serious purpose, such as the death of a close friend. The "pritchet" consists of a short melodic repetitive formula of asymmetrical structure (nine measures, ten measures, and eleven measures). Both the effect and the asymmetrical structure are atypical of Russian folk songs. Shostakovich appears to have consciously chosen this type of folk song to cast his third movement, as the tragic circumstances surrounding the composition of this work indicate. Another typical expressive device drawn from Russian folklore is the use of the flat second, fourth, and eighth steps in the important places of the melodic line as the line leaps up to these altered tones, falling back down again. This is a gesture typical of the "plach" (cry), another type of Russian folk song. In West European music we find similar gestures in the "lamento" phrases occurring in Italian opera.

It is in this finale that the relationship between B minor and E-flat reaches its culmination, for the most naggingly insistent of the altered tones mentioned by Tentser is the lowered fourth (E-flat, in the key of B minor), resolving down to the third, D (Example 7.3).

Example 7.3

We have already encountered several instances in which a small chromatic inflection at the outset would predict a larger tonal relationship later on—the F-sharp in the Seventh Symphony's opening melody, for example. In a sense, the Sonata reverses this system of tonal planning. Here, Shostakovich first presents the relationship between B minor and E-flat in its largest, most expansive guise, namely as the two main tonal areas of the first movement's exposition. Later, in the recapitulation, the relationship is "contracted," the two keys appearing simultaneously in the bitonal reprise of the second subject. And the process of contraction reaches its conclusion in the finale, where the relationship is lowered out of the domain of tonality down to the level of melody—the pitch E-flat chromatically inflecting a B minor melody.

What the Sonata presents, then, is three layers of tonal opposition: juxtaposition (the second key next to the first); superimposition (the second key playing bitonally against the first); and embedding (the second key melodically suggested within the first). This triple use can be found in other works, although the order may vary. In the Fifth Symphony's first movement, for example, we see embedding (the pitch E-flat presented within the opening D minor melody), followed by juxtaposition (E-flat minor as the movement's second key following D minor), and finally superimposition (the development's climactic dissonance pitching together the two keys). And we will see it in the Second Piano Trio (1944): an embedding of sorts (the first chromaticism of the first movement's *Moderato* is a brief tonicization of B-flat within an otherwise very diatonic E minor framework); juxtaposition (exposition starts in E minor, development starts in B-flat minor); a second juxtaposition (third movement in B-flat minor, finale in E major/minor); and superimposition (the climactic Fig. 91 in the finale where the pitch E clashes against the third movement's B-flat minor chord progression).

*****

The opportunity to relinquish Kuibyshev for good finally came in April 1943, when Shostakovich took up a teaching position at the Moscow Conservatory, now under the directorship of his friend Vissarion Shebalin. There, in July, he started on his Eighth Symphony, completing it over the next two months at the newly built retreat at Ivanovo. The Symphony was premiered by Mravinsky on 4 November. But although there were some positive press notices, with a few voices acclaiming it as superior to the Seventh, the work quickly fell off the radar. Its less populist tone, its uncompromisingly tragic character, and its enigmatic ending did not endear it to an audience still giddy from the brouhaha surrounding the Seventh Symphony, to a nation that was sensing for the first time the very real possibility of a wartime victory. A few months later, the Eighth Symphony came under attack. Shostakovich's private response to the criticisms was typically wry: "I am sure that it will give rise to valuable critical observations which will both inspire me to future creative work and provide insights enabling me to review that which I have created in the past."[75]

The Symphony opens with a forceful statement of a three-note melodic cell (*x*), C–B-flat–C. It is an inversion of the Seventh Symphony's three-note motive, although

A Shostakovich Companion

its status here in the Eighth is far more prominent—the introduction to the first movement, the respective first themes of all five movements, plus various other subsidiary themes throughout the Symphony are based on this motive, resulting almost in a "motto symphony" in the Russian mold of Tchaikovsky's Fifth or, perhaps more pertinently, Rachmaninov's First.

Following this imposing introduction, the first subject steals in at Fig. 1 in the first violins. Its first six notes comprise an inversion of *x* (C–D–C) followed by a transposed version of its prime form (G–F–G), meaning that the first four notes (scale degrees 1-2-1-5) also correspond to the first four notes of the Seventh Symphony's "invasion" theme (in turn a quotation from *Boris Godunov*), though this first subject's parched, numbed character could not be more different from the earlier work. As the melody proceeds along its tortuously winding course, it takes in other manifestations of *x*, especially around Fig. 2, and as the music intensifies further, a semitonal version becomes more prominent—e.g., D-sharp–E–D-sharp (Fig. 5) or F-sharp–G-F-sharp (Fig. 6, b10).

Aesthetically, the E minor second theme, also in the violins, somewhat more open in its expression than the first theme, though the unusual-for-Shostakovich 5/4 meter (unusual in that it lasts for the entire duration of the theme), exacerbated by the pulsating ostinato in the lower strings, means that the music emerges as simultaneously elegiac and agitated. The *x* motive is prevalent here also, for example, in the second bar (B–C–B; Fig. 8, b3). In fact, the first bar of this second subject comprises what might be described as a widening of *x* to encompass a larger interval (B–E–B), rather as Shostakovich would in his later twelve-note music widen the so-called "mordent exception" on repeated pitches (see Chapter 15). When a slightly altered version of this second theme presents itself in the violas and English horn at Fig. 11, its ten-bar run is made up almost exclusively of transformations, including widenings, of the *x* motive (bracketed in Example 7.4).

Example 7.4

After the in some ways tangential tracks taken by the "English" *Romances* and the Second Piano Sonata, the Eighth Symphony would resume the path that Shostakovich had been consolidating over the previous five or six years. Indeed, many have pointed, and not always in an admiring way,[76] to the obvious procedural and even thematic similarities between the first movement and its Fifth Symphony counterpart: the imposing introductory double-dotted figures deployed canonically between low and high strings, the chromatically searching first subjects, the more freely soaring second subjects together with their pulsating accompaniments, the brutalizing developments, and the tonal and gestural processes that govern their respective gradually emerging recapitulations. Yet, at the same time, it must be said that aesthetically, the two movements do make quite a different impression from each other, even when their surface landscapes seem similar. For example, where the leaping intervals that open the Fifth Symphony propel the music into immediate action, the forceful reiteration of the tonic in the Eighth's first two bars before the first minor sixth leap (the same interval that launches the Fifth Symphony, incidentally) lends its opening a more dogged intractability. The Eighth Symphony's first subject is more halting, at least in its initial stages, than its in some ways similar Fifth Symphony counterpart, while the 5/4 meter of its second subject lends the pulsating accompaniment greater agitation than the more regular, dactylic accompaniment to the Fifth's second subject.

In general, the Eighth Symphony operates on the longer fuse. In both works, the development proceeds by discrete stages, each stage playing off the last to effect a large-scale build-up of intensity. But where the development in the Fifth starts its process of acceleration from its outset, over half of the development (in terms of performance time) in the Eighth takes place at the *Adagio* tempo. Even the *Allegro non troppo* at Fig. 25 and the *Allegro* at Fig. 29 are imbued with a terrific resistive force, in contrast to the mostly forward hurtling found in the Fifth. Yet, although the Eighth Symphony's climaxes take longer to attain, once reached they assault the listener with a protracted, screaming intensity that goes beyond anything heard in the earlier work.

In this movement, Shostakovich provides yet another take on the gradually emerging recapitulation concept (see Chapter 13). Whereas in the Fifth Symphony, the collapse after the tutti presentation of the first theme (Fig. 38, b3) is quick and decisive, leading within six bars to the return of the second theme, here the return of the second theme after the tutti presentation of the introduction is held in abeyance by an agonizingly haunting thirty-nine-bar recitative for English horn over a tense string tremolo. It is as if the sheer destructive brutality of the development has created a huge musical "crater" in the landscape over which this seemingly timeless solo looms. As David Fanning puts it, this recitative "ponders on fragments of the first subject, its shell shocked numbness being about the only conceivable truthful response to the preceding horrors."[77] Although this would not be the first re-characterized theme to grace a Shostakovich recapitulation— previous examples include the disfigured bassoon rendition of the second theme in the first movement of the Seventh Symphony, or the numbed, halting version of the first theme in the Cello Sonata's first movement (see Chapter 13)—it would be the most extreme example of its type, with those fragments of first subject almost unrecognizable as such.

The recitative itself works on the same principle as the recitative in the Sixth Symphony's first movement—a chromatic elaboration of the fundamental accompanying harmony. Yet for all its desolation, there is over the course of its 39 bars an impressive control of what one might call long-term tonal release. The tremolo harmony follows a falling progression of tonic seventh chords based on E-flat (Fig. 34, b16), D (Fig. 36), and D-flat (Fig. 36, b12), arriving at the tonic C major for the return of the second subject (Fig. 38). Yet, constant through all this is a pedal G in the cello—consonant to the E-flat at the start of the progression, dissonant to the next two chords, "resolving" onto the C major chord of arrival. As Fanning shows, this harmonic descent is in fact an answer to a comparable harmonic ascent in the previous paragraphs, i.e., through the entire restatement of the introductory theme (starting Fig. 34).[78] Such "release" via a chromatic harmonic descent is reminiscent of the Fifth Symphony, where the bass-line descent, B–B-flat–A, in the latter stages of the first subject's reprise sets up the ultimate return to D major (Figs. 38 to 39; see Chapter 13, Example 13.1).

The second subject reprise in C major provides some comfort, just as the D major second subject reprise had in the Fifth Symphony. In the earlier work, this moment was greeted with the fresh sonority of the flute/horn duo. Here in the Eighth, the melody, an outgrowth of the previous recitative, continues to be borne by the English horn, its lamenting tones somewhat attenuating the feeling of "newness." However, unlike in the Fifth, the first theme does return in the coda in something like its original, i.e., non-inverted, melodic form (Fig. 44, b3). That, together with the *tièrce de Picardie* at the very end, gives this movement, which in most respects is even more harrowing than the first movement of the Fifth Symphony, at least a limited sense of resolution.

The epic first movement is followed by two scherzos. The march-like second movement is composed in what was becoming a favorite scherzo form of Shostakovich—a scherzo-trio-scherzo structure (with a coda), where the trio returns during the scherzo reprise, slightly modified to reflect the different environment. Written in the key of D-flat (Shostakovich's favorite Neapolitan relationship once again in evidence), the potential warmth, even mellowness, of the strings in that particular key is cruelly offset by the piercing sounds of the upper woodwinds and brass as well as by the movement's characteristically fractured, jagged rhythms that cut through like broken glass. The scoring of the very first bar illustrates this conflict—an imposingly sustained unison D-flat in the strings answered by a shrieking D-flat/F dyad in the upper woodwinds and brass (note in particular the very high clarinet scoring, not to mention the E-flat clarinet), the dyad made all the more hysterical by the wailing, lurching *crescendo*, an instruction conspicuously absent in the strings.

This second movement is based on the semitonal version of the *x* motive (initially D-flat–C–D-flat). If the brutal toccata-like third movement—even more fractured and jagged than the second—can be said to have a theme at all, it is a rhythmically augmented version of *x*, spat out mostly in the woodwind or brass above the mechanistic string ostinato that dominates the movement's outer sections. Here, the angularity is enhanced by the built-in octave displacements (Example 7.5).

Example 7.5

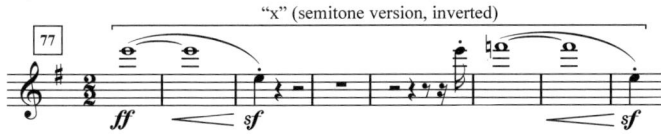

The movement's trio section, with its macho trumpet solo and breathless "oom-pah" brass and percussion accompaniment, almost throws us into the bullfighting ring. Although Shostakovich does not employ here the flamenco-type rhythm that he had used in, say, the scherzos of the Piano Quintet or Seventh Symphony, he does emphasize extreme sharp-side tonality, just as he did in the "flamenco" portions of those earlier scherzos. The sense of something exotic here is also provided by the highly modal melodic writing in the trumpet coming into conflict with the obstinate major triads in the accompaniment. Against F-sharp major triads, the opening trumpet phrase presents F-sharp Phrygian with a lowered fourth (the theorist Alexander Dolzhansky's "lowered Phrygian" mode)[79] and an oscillating fifth (D-sharp/D-natural). The second phrase, in an A-flat major harmonic context, is an A-flat Phrygian melody with an oscillating third (C-flat–C-natural) and raised fourth. Although this trio is based around simple scalar ideas, the *x* motive does show up in a cackling riposte in the first violins and violas that quickly alternates the semitonal version of *x* with the inverted semitonal version (Fig. 99, b8, et seq.). To add to the general sense of nastiness here, the motive is presented as a chain of "forbidden" parallel fifths.

Following the trio, the scherzo returns, compressed to about half its original length. But what is most striking are the muted sonorities. For the entire reprise, every instrument that can be muted is, even the timpani. On the one hand, the muted strings give the effect of a more choked vehemence. On the other, the muted brass brings a new snarl. The overall effect is at once more distant and more edgy. Even the ferocious culminating ostinato at the end of the movement (a *crescendo* from *ff*) is muted. After this "suffocated" *crescendo*, a blistering percussion artillery is unleashed, spilling *attacca* into the fourth movement. Only now are the mutes taken off, allowing the tutti onslaught that constitutes the new movement's first two bars to scream unhindered.

The fourth movement is a passacaglia, a form that had not been heard in Shostakovich since *Lady Macbeth*—the Piano Quintet's fourth movement being a near miss—but that would now appear with greater frequency. Although the movement is composed in 4/4 rather than the more usual, for a passacaglia, 3/4, Shostakovich does adhere to at least some of the baroque traditions of the form, for example, the initial rotation of the ground bass being presented unaccompanied, or the blurring of sectional boundaries through the deliberate misalignment of ground bass and upper voice phrases. As David Hurwitz writes, "The resulting rhythmic independence detaches the melody from its accompaniment and allows it to float, rootless, giving the movement a numb, drifting quality, representing a

devastatingly logical reaction to the preceding brutality."[80] Not only that but, as
Lyn Henderson points out (Chapter 15), the ground bass itself "exercises appreciably less harmonic control" on the upper voices than one might expect, resulting
in an "almost perpetual harmonic drift."

Each of the first two bars of the ground bass is built on the x motive, as are the
final three bars. Some of the free voices also show the influence of x, none more
so than the recitative-like threnody heard in the piccolo (Fig. 118, b3) and, later,
in the clarinet (Fig. 119, b9). In fact, at the end of the clarinet version, two clarinets isolate the "x" portion, reiterating it in their *chalumeau* register like a tolling
bell, ushering in the next bass rotation and, with it, what one might loosely dub
the movement's recapitulation (Fig. 121). Certainly, the recitative-like quality of
the woodwind solos in the previous "development" reinforces the feeling of "drift"
noted by both Hurwitz and Henderson, as do the mysterious flutter-tongued flute
chords that creep into the movement's latter stages.

From out of the fourth movement's final chord emerge, tentatively, the beginnings of the fifth movement finale. This finale is a modified sonata-rondo, a form
that would come to assume increasing importance for Shostakovich, resurfacing in
the finales of the Second Piano Trio (1944), Third Quartet (1946), and First Violin Concerto (1948). Here in the Symphony, the sonata rondo is best outlined as
A–B–A–C–Development–C–B–A–Coda, though other interpretations have been
expounded—David Hurwitz, for example, gives: A–B–A–C–Development
(fugue)–A–D–C–A.[81] By contrast, Robert Dearling's reading of the movement as
a theme with nineteen variations plus a coda gives no hint of the movement's
"symphonic" tension and release, its structure that is so clearly related to Shostakovich's first movement sonata forms.[82] Certainly, it could be argued that the movement's rather sectional unfolding of themes and the relationship of themes to each
other (principally through the x motive) do impart a certain variation-like quality,
but this finale remains worlds apart from the actual theme-and-variation structures
found in the finales of the Second Piano Sonata or Second Quartet, to give the
two chronologically closest examples.

The finale begins with an amiability that seems disconcertingly inconsequential
after the tragic tread of the preceding passacaglia. The opening bassoon melody is
based on the inverted x motive in its most "positive" form, i.e., using the major
second rather than the minor (C–D–C), and a certain wry humor is injected
through the limping, off-beat accompaniment in the second bassoon and contrabassoon. This is complemented by a cheeky subsidiary melody in the flute (Fig.
126), a melody that, in its more disjunct latter stages, could almost be a model for
the flute solo that would open the Fifteenth Symphony nearly thirty years later.
Following the more serious, if somewhat wistful, "B" theme (A minor; Fig. 129)
and the subsequent return of "A" (C major; Fig. 132), the "C" theme (Fig. 136)
emerges as a rough-hewn dance with "oom-pah" trombones and, later on, gypsy-
like, open-string-heavy double-stops in the violins. The material thus far might
seem out of place in the finale of what is one of the most harrowing symphonies
in the repertoire. But in creating such deliberately banal material, Shostakovich

provides perhaps a musical parallel to the human experience of trauma—the idea that trauma is often followed by a period of denial, a period characterized by mindlessly bustling activity and fake cheeriness.

It is not until the development that the movement assumes more gravity. The fugue that constitutes the development's first phase was the second of the four fugues that Shostakovich would compose during the 1940s in the run-up to his set of Twenty-Four Preludes and Fugues, op. 87 (1950–1951). Like the previously discussed second movement of the Piano Quintet, this fugue contains many of the baroque procedures that would later find their way into op. 87: an exposition alternating tonic and dominant level entries (strings; Fig. 141); paired middle entries (woodwind; Fig. 145); and a stretto (brass; Fig. 151). In the Piano Quintet, Shostakovich had broken the fugue mid-stream to create a climactic section and a post-climactic cadenza, resuming the fugue towards the end of the movement with an unusually becalmed stretto. Here in the Symphony, there is also a break between the middle entries and the stretto, though not as lengthy as in the Quintet. More importantly, the Symphony's stretto is a preparation for what will be the climactic second phase of the development; in other words Shostakovich is moving here towards the more traditional climax-building role of the stretto, a move that would be consolidated in the op. 87 set.

The development's second phase starts with a new theme (Fig. 154, b6). Vigorous march-like dotted rhythms and E-flat major tonality suggest an infusion of optimism. But it quickly turns grim—shades here of the first movement of Mahler's Sixth Symphony. In fact, this is one of the very few passages in Shostakovich that really does sound like Mahler, certainly more so than anything in the Fourth Symphony, which owes more to Mahler in its ethos, in its thematic allusions, and in certain areas of compositional procedure than in its musical language. This march leads to the movement's climax, a devastating tutti presentation of the first movement's introduction, similar to that heard at the first movement's climax, though now re-harmonized to even more brutal effect. In effect, Shostakovich strengthens the connection between the two movements by placing the recall in the finale at exactly the same structural point, i.e., the climax of the development section.

Unlike the first movement, where the post-climactic English horn solo created almost a new entity out of the first subject material, the recapitulation here preserves the themes in their more-or-less original form, even preserving their original pitch centers. There are two interesting twists, however. The first is the modal switching. The recap begins with the dance-like "C" theme. In the exposition, this theme was in E major; now it is in E minor. Correspondingly, the "B" theme reprise that follows, originally in A minor, is now in A major. The second twist is the new emphasis on solo instruments. The "C" theme, originally in the cellos doubled by bassoon and bass clarinet, is now presented by the bass clarinet alone, while the double-stopping first and second violins are replaced by a single instrument; in the "B" theme, a solo cello replaces mass cellos. As with the English horn solo in the first movement, the idea of individual voices picking out melodies from the devastated ruins only enhances the fragility of this recapitulation.

Following the reprise of the "A" theme, given in its original bassoon and, later, first violin guise, the movement comes to a close in a state of numbed luminescence as the violas and finally double basses pick out the Symphony's x motive, in its "positive" inverted major second version (C–D–C), accompanied by the mysterious sound of the low flute (an echo, perhaps, of the massed low flutes that began the first movement's development). Above all this, held for thirty-four bars, is a C major chord in the violins, creating a poignant conclusion that, though hardly joyful, provides at least a glimmer of hope. It is a type of ending that we will experience again in the Second Piano Trio (1944) and, especially, the Fifth Quartet (1952).

***

Though Shostakovich's Seventh Symphony would stand unchallenged as "the" iconic musical work of the war years, the general importance of music in promoting the wartime effort cannot be overstated. As Kiril Tomoff points out, the production of music was not just about inspiring those "fighting at the front and working in the rear," but also served a larger cultural point—"counter[ing] the Nazi claim that Soviet (or Russian, or Slavic, or non-Aryan) culture was subhuman and worthy only of complete eradication."[83] As part of the effort to promote the production of new music, competitions were held by various organizations. Of these, the most high-profile, and possibly the most bizarre, was the 1943 contest organized by Stalin to find a new Soviet national anthem. Held during the summer and autumn, the contest garnered several hundred entries, including submissions by Shostakovich alone as well as in collaboration with Khachaturian.[84] By the final round, an elaborate audition in which the leading contenders were performed by orchestra alone, chorus alone, and orchestra and chorus in combination, it became apparent that the front-runner was the anthem submitted by Alexander Alexandrov. But Stalin had found fault with Alexandrov's orchestration. In fact, Alexandrov had delegated this job to Viktor Knushnevitsky, and at the meeting between Stalin and the finalists began blaming Knushnevitsky for the inferior work. Shostakovich immediately objected and, according to Khachaturian, repeated "convulsively" the phrase "a composer should be able to orchestrate himself."[85] Creating a scene was generally not his way, but Alexandrov's abrogation of his responsibilities and his cowardly shifting of blame onto the hapless Knushnevitsky (who was not there to defend himself) offended Shostakovich to the core. In this, his first face-to-face meeting with Stalin, he would show remarkable courage and resolve. In the end, Alexandrov's anthem was chosen, though, ironically, Shostakovich's higher position in the "table of ranks" used to evaluate the relative merits of Soviet artists meant that he was actually paid the higher fee, despite losing to Alexandrov.[86]

***

In December 1943, Shostakovich embarked on his Second Piano Trio. In Russia, this genre had come to acquire an "in memoriam" connotation, for example, the trios by Arensky, Tchaikovsky, and Rachmaninov. And so it would prove with Shostakovich. A few days before the completion of the first movement the following February, Shostakovich received news of the tragic and untimely death of his mentor and closest friend, Sollertinsky, at the age of forty-one—this less than a year-and-a-half after the deaths of Nikolayev and Yavorsky. In August 1944, Shostakovich completed the Trio, dedicating it to Sollertinsky's memory. It was premiered on 14 November.

Shostakovich's fusion of eighteenth-century technique with his own peculiar strain of tragic ethos is nowhere clearer than at the very start of this Trio. On the one hand, this slow introduction is a strict baroque-style canon between three instruments. But it is the cello that forms the soprano voice, its parched, disembodied harmonics creating a sense of danger, seeming almost to foretell the tragedy awaiting in the Trio's third and fourth movements. Of course, the very inclusion of a slow introduction to a faster sonata-form first movement, unusual for Shostakovich, was itself a rather old-fashioned gesture, a nod in the direction of the Classicists. And as Haydn or Beethoven might have done, Shostakovich plants in the opening couple of bars seeds to the rest of the movement. In rhythm and melodic contour, the first bar of this slow introduction generates the first theme of the ensuing *Moderato*; the second bar, a falling four-note scalar figure, finds its way into a later stage of that first theme (Fig. 7, b4–7) as well as the entirety of the second theme, which is built on little more than a succession of falling scale patterns.

The first movement's main *Moderato* shows Shostakovich in a neoclassical vein, with predominantly lyrical melodies that are almost Haydnesque in character. Meanwhile, its tonal evolution demonstrates a familiar "conflict" between classical procedure and Shostakovichian idiosyncrasy. Superficially, this E minor movement functions classically, with the relative major, G, as the secondary key, just as the E major finale modulates to the classically expected dominant, B (with a flexible minor-based mode), for its second group. Yet, as already alluded to in the discussion of the Second Piano Sonata, it is another pitch, B-flat, and in particular the key of B-flat minor (the remotest key from the work's tonic), that presents itself as a rival secondary key in the first movement, and in fact turns out to be the real secondary pitch center of the Trio as a whole. It first appears shortly after the start of the *Moderato* (Fig. 7, b2), where B-flat major is briefly tonicized before a return, four bars later, to E minor. Towards the end of the exposition (Fig. 15) is a second B-flat major tonicization, this time within the context of the second subject key of G. This one is more pronounced; not only is it longer (eleven bars as opposed to four), it is harmonically more varied. It even allows brief departures from the B-flat base, hinting at other tonicizations, something that, ironically, strengthens rather than weakens the B-flat tonicization, since B-flat is now allowed to behave like a "real" key (i.e., one strong enough to permit temporary departures), something that was not possible with that shorter first tonicization.[87] The other appearance of B-flat is a few bars into the development (Fig. 18, b9), this time in its all-important minor mode.

Although not described by Shostakovich as such, the brilliant second movement scherzo was thought by Sollertinsky's sister to be "an amazingly exact portrait of Ivan Ivanovich, whom Shostakovich understood like no one else. That is his temper, his polemics, his manner of speech, his habit of returning to one and the same thought, developing it."[88] Its characteristics and its similarities to the Piano Quintet's scherzo have already been described in the discussion of that earlier work, though one difference here is that the trio section is a good deal less distinctive as a separate section than is usually the case with Shostakovich. This is perhaps compensated for by a greater than usual development of the main scherzo theme. This later scherzo might be considered a "turbo-charged" version of the earlier one, though to what extent remains controversial; the original Muzgiz-based editions give a tempo of *Allegro non troppo* (dotted half = 108), a tempo slightly faster than the Quintet's scherzo (96). The later Muzyka *Collected Works* gives *Allegro con brio* (132), a substantially different proposition. Shostakovich's two recorded performances lean heavily towards the latter interpretation.

The elegiac third movement passacaglia, with all of that form's historic connotations of death and burial, was in all likelihood Shostakovich's musical response to the loss of Sollertinsky. Above the stoic chords in the piano emerges a mournful canon between the violin and cello, a canon that lasts for about half the movement. Like the slow movement of the Fifth Symphony, this passacaglia comes almost as a mid-work reappraisal, taking it to a new, more personal realm of experience. The key is B-flat minor, bringing that secondary pitch center hinted at in the first movement to fruition. However, while the piano's rotating chord progression (see Chapter 15, Example 15.3) begins solidly enough in B-flat minor, its eighth and final bar reminds us of the Trio's E minor heritage, landing on a dyad of B-natural and D; only at the very last moment does Shostakovich rescue the ground from the beckoning allure of E minor and return it to B-flat minor for its next rotation. In other words, the relationship between E minor and B-flat minor here reverses, or reciprocates, that heard in the first movement. At the ground's final appearance, that concluding E minor twist becomes the entryway into the E major finale.

The fourth movement finale, a grotesque, "dance of death" rondo, was Shostakovich's first attempt at an overtly Jewish musical idiom. The style would be characterized by the use of Jewish modes or derivatives thereof, klezmer-type "oompah" accompaniments (e.g., the string parts in Example 7.7), and the use of the so-called iambic prime—chains of slurred eighth or sixteenth note pairs, where the first note of a pair repeats the last note of the previous pair and where the second note of a pair is usually a major or minor second higher or lower than the first, creating something akin to the *lamento* effect of successive appoggiaturas (e.g., the fourth bar in the piano in Example 7.7).

The "A" section of this modified rondo presents two themes, and with them the two most common Jewish modes. The first of these, the *freygish* mode, raises the third degree in what is otherwise a Phrygian scale. Shostakovich also raises the seventh degree (i.e., D-sharp), a commonly encountered chromaticism in this particular mode. The incursion of one of music's brightest modes (major) into one of its darkest (Phrygian) results in the characteristically Jewish augmented second interval between the mode's second and third degrees and, with it, the "laughing through tears" quality so often associated with Jewish music, although in this particular case, Shostakovich does not exploit the full melodic richness that this interval traditionally provides—while the melody dwells often on the lowered second (F-natural), the major third (G-sharp) appears melodically only in the eleventh of the twelve bar period, although it is prevalent in the accompanying piano harmony. The effect of this "attenuation," enhanced by the violin's dry pizzicato presentation, is to turn this rich Jewish mode into something skeletal and empty, a true "dance of death" (Example 7.6).

Example 7.6

The second of the "A" themes (Fig. 66) is written in the Jewish Altered Dorian mode (based on C). Here, the fourth degree of the Dorian scale is raised, the augmented second now falling between the third and fourth degrees (Example 7.7).

Example 7.7

Following a return to the first "A" theme, the "B" group presents two themes, a soulful cello melody in a 5/8 meter in B minor (Fig. 71) and another Jewish theme (Fig. 75) in B *freygish*. These two themes are allied to each other to a greater extent than the two themes of the "A" group. Not only do they have the same tonal center, they are in a constant state of interaction with each other, both here and in the subsequent development. The two "A" group themes by contrast are almost invariably presented separately, interacting only towards the climactic stages of the development.[89]

At the peak of the movement's heart-wrenching climax, the B-flat minor chord progression from the slow movement bursts forth, this time as a fast, rippling piano arpeggiation underneath the pedal E held in the strings (Fig. 91). Although not quite the full-on bitonal clash between primary and secondary tonalities witnessed in the Second Piano Sonata, this nevertheless represents the peak of their interaction, and paves the way for the cyclic return of the first movement's main theme (Fig. 92). After the recalled material has played itself out, the two "A" themes return. We have already noted the sense of emotional "dismemberment" that Shostakovich achieved in the recapitulation stages of the first movements of the Seventh and Eighth Symphonies and the Cello Sonata. Here in the Trio, a similar process takes place. The first Jewish theme appears in the piano, scored organum-like in parallel fifths (Fig. 99), the hollowness exacerbated by the *col legno* accompaniment in the strings at the repeat (Fig. 100). The second Jewish theme makes an impassioned final outburst, violently cutting off the previous one in its final bar (Fig. 101), something that it had not done at the start of the movement. Yet, the disposition here is also more sickly: the simple tonic accompanimental chords now replaced by obstructionist half diminished sevenths; the previous Altered Dorian mode darkened through a lowering of the sixth degree; and the new nauseous, lurching *crescendi* in the violin and cello. Towards the end, Shostakovich brings back the sound of string harmonics with which the Trio began, followed by a final recall of the passacaglia progression, back in its original block-chord formation (Fig. 105). Like the Eighth Symphony, the Trio closes in the major mode—a tearful glimmer of hope after a tragic journey.

***

Shostakovich was neither Jewish nor of Jewish descent, and, as far as we know, he was not particularly interested in the Jewish religion *per se*. Yet, his consciousness of the centuries-long plight of the Jews, and of their status as a persecuted minority in the Soviet Union, was profound. As he once recalled, "My parents considered anti-Semitism a shameful superstition, and in that sense particularly I was given a very good upbringing."[90] The musicologist Timothy Jackson goes as far as to suggest that Shostakovich's "Jewish" music arose not just out of sympathy with the Jewish people, but out of an actual sense of self-identification: "the composer as Jew."[91] It is a compelling thesis; the reappearance of the Trio's Jewish theme (from Example 7.7) sixteen years later in Shostakovich's overtly autobiographical Eighth Quartet would seem to validate it. But others disagree. Marina Ritzarev, for instance, believes that Shostakovich's "philosemitic expression" was always at a one-step remove[92]; Esti Sheinberg, although acknowledging Shostakovich's affinity to the suffering of the Jewish people and to the particular ability of Jewish music, so laden with irony, to express that suffering, believes that Shostakovich's ultimate goal was not simply the expression of Jewishness, but the expression of the very irony of human existence.[93]

For Jackson, the first hint of Shostakovich's musical "self-identification" had come with the Fifth Symphony (1937), where what appears to be an allusion to cantorial chant can be heard in the slow movement (Fig. 84)—isolated, vulnerable music written when Shostakovich himself was at his most isolated, vulnerable, or, as Jackson puts it, "Jewish." But it was with the Second Piano Trio that Shostakovich unequivocally exposed his Jewish "persona"—and not with *chazanut* quotations, the significance of which would have been comprehended only by a small minority, but with folk-inspired, klezmer-inflected music that the larger world would instantly recognize as Jewish. And the timing was no coincidence; by 1944, the world had finally got a grip on the tragedy that had befallen Europe's Jews. Shostakovich was distraught not only by the news of the Holocaust but also by the worsening anti-Semitic climate at home. The Jews may have been a natural ally in the fight against fascism—the government had even set up a Jewish Anti-Fascist Committee in 1942 to raise money in the West for the war effort—but sympathy for them was hardly universal.

Ironically, 1942 had also seen the start of a new anti-Semitic campaign, one that would last until Stalin's death eleven years later. The first target of the campaign was the arts. In a secret report compiled in August 1942 ("The Selection and Promotion of Personnel in the Arts"), Agitprop's chief, Georgy Alexandrov, complained about the preponderance of "non-Russian people (mainly Jews)" running the Bolshoi (where it was noted that ten of the twelve senior musical and executive posts were occupied by Jews), the Moscow Philharmonic, the Moscow and Leningrad Conservatories, and the art and literature departments of *Pravda*, *Izvestiya*, *Vechernyaya Moskva*, *Literatura i iskusstvo*, and *Muzgiz*.[94] Unlike the show trials of the 1930s, this campaign unfolded mostly behind closed doors. Subsequent firings of high-profile Jews, e.g., the Moscow Conservatory's Director, Alexander Goldenveizer or the Bolshoi's Chief Conductor, Samuil Samosud, were explained away as "retirements" due to age or ill-health. Nevertheless, it is clear that by 1944 Shostakovich had some inkling of what was going on; the previous September he had protested the attempted dismissal, on racial grounds, of Moscow Conservatory professor Yevgeny Guzikov.

Shostakovich's conscience was profoundly shaped by these national and international events, but other more local events may also have spurred the emergence of a "Jewish" persona at around this time. In 1943, he had met and befriended the composer Mieczysław Weinberg, a Polish Jew who had fled his homeland following the extermination of his family in 1939. A composer with a strong attachment to his heritage, Weinberg had produced his first cycle of *Jewish Songs* in 1943 (the title of which had been forcibly changed to *Children's Songs* in order to receive performance permission) and a second cycle in 1944. And with Weinberg the son-in-law of Solomon Mikhoels, the famous actor who was also the director of the Jewish Theater in Moscow and head of the Jewish Anti-Fascist Committee, the friendship would give Shostakovich a privileged insight into Soviet Jewish life.

A more hands-on encounter with the Jewish musical idiom would come with Venyamin Fleishman's klezmer-inflected one-act opera, *Rothschild's Violin*. A former student of Shostakovich, Fleishman had died on active service in 1941 during the siege of Leningrad, leaving his opera incomplete. Shostakovich had been sufficiently impressed that in February 1944, he took it upon himself to complete and orchestrate it. Yet another possible influence, suggested by the musicologist Judy Kuhn, was the noted Russian scholar on Jewish music, Moisei Beregovsky, who in 1944 defended his doctoral dissertation on Jewish instrumental folk music at the Moscow Conservatory, where Shostakovich was teaching.[95] And finally, it is worth considering the role of the Trio's dedicatee, Sollertinsky, who was not, as is sometimes claimed, Jewish, but who may have been responsible through his advocacy of Mahler for planting a Jewish musical seed in Shostakovich. Noting Sollertinsky's origins in what had been the heavily Jewish-populated town of Vitebsk, and his subsequent contributions to the culture of Leningrad, Marina Ritzarev writes:

> Sollertinsky must have developed into a powerful advocate of the Jewish impact on European culture, as evident from his studies on Mahler (1932), Offenbach (1933), and Schoenberg (1934). Setting the tone for the attitude to Jews among intelligentsia circles, he was probably perceived by Shostakovich as a kind of link between pure "Russianness" and the other peoples and cultures, in which the cultural image of Jews was seen in the Judeo-Christian tradition as contributing to the basic values of humanity and civilization. It is possibly such thoughts and feelings that . . . rose to the surface when [Shostakovich] worked on his Second Piano Trio in memory of Ivan Sollertinsky."[96]

***

Premiered alongside the Second Piano Trio in November 1944 was the Second Quartet, composed that summer. Like the Piano Quintet four years earlier, the titles of the Quartet's movements would carry echoes of a previous age: Overture, Recitative and Romance, Waltz, and Theme with Variations. If the First Quartet had paid homage to Haydn, the Second launches with all the confidence and tonal focus of early Beethoven. Actually, its first five bars have neither major nor minor leanings (the three modally defining pitches—the sixth, the seventh, and especially the third—are all conspicuous by their absence), yet they possess an unmistakably major-key feel, created perhaps by the unplayed C-sharp vibrating sympathetically within the stack of open fifths (A and E) outlined by the three lower instruments. Ironically, when the first modal definer does appear (the G-sharp in bar 6), it not only confirms the major mode, but appears to take on an even brighter hue, the Lydian raised fourth within the D tonality that is misleadingly suggested in bar 5.

Challenging the "symphonies are public, quartets are private" cliché, the Fitzwilliam Quartet's violist Alan George writes that in the case of Shostakovich, "such a division is really only skin-deep, as can be seen by their reciprocal influence: the earlier quartets tend to be symphonic in conception, with the last symphonies becoming more rarified and inward."[97] And the "symphonic" quality of the Second Quartet is not just a matter of textural density, although the work certainly has its share of "orchestral" moments. It is also about the incorporation of specifically Shostakovichian symphonic procedures. In this case, it is the Eighth Symphony of the previous year that provides the inspiration. We shall later encounter other quartet/

symphony "pairs": Ninth Symphony (1945)/Third Quartet (1946); Fifth Quartet (1952)/Tenth Symphony (1953); Thirteenth Symphony (1962)/Ninth Quartet (1964); Fifteenth Symphony (1971)/Fourteenth Quartet (1973); even the highly symphonic First Violin Concerto (1948)/Fourth Quartet (1949).

Upon its return in the recapitulation (Fig. 22), the opening theme's original full-sail confidence is disfigured melodically (the introduction of the modally flattened second and, a few bars later, fifth), harmonically (the supporting "root position" open fifths of the exposition inverting themselves to less supportive "second inversion" open fourths), and rhythmically (the confident first-beat attacks of the accompaniment in the exposition giving way here to third-beat jabs).[98] Although Shostakovich does not here go for the reverse-order recapitulation found in the Fifth and Eighth Symphonies, preferring instead the more traditional sonata deployment of themes, the idea of developmental tensions spilling over into the recapitulation, an idea that Shostakovich pursued in the Fifth, Eighth, and, to an extent, Seventh Symphonies, had now found its way into the quartet medium. And in this particular case, it is not just a general sense of "developmental tensions" spilling over. Two of the three modifications listed above, the modal flattening and the weak-beat jabs, actually derive from the very end of the development (Fig. 21). If the First Quartet had diverted away from Shostakovich's epic symphonism to pursue a dialogue with Haydn, the Second would take that exploration of the classical style and reincorporate it back into the Shostakovichian mainstream.

The influence specifically of the Eighth Symphony can also be felt via certain allusions. Shortly before the start of the recapitulation (Fig. 20), the viola plays an almost direct rhythmic quote from the Symphony's second movement (Fig. 53, b9). Compare also the almost identical contrapuntal usage of this figure that subsequently occurs between the viola and cello in the Quartet (Fig. 20, b6) and between piccolo and first bassoon/contrabassoon in the Symphony after Fig. 56. Also, compare the rhythmic/textural structure of the chords in the Quartet (Fig. 25) with those in the Symphony's fifth movement (Fig. 161).

The Eighth Symphony's influence becomes even more striking in the second movement Recitative. Like the Symphony's great English horn recitative, the first violin here plays a melodic prolongation of the accompanying harmony, now clashing with, now resolving onto the harmony sustained in the lower strings. So, at the start, a dominant seventh chord in B-flat is held, hypnotized in a tense third inversion, while the melody emphasizes those dissonances that tug at the chord's root (F) and fifth (C): G-flat to F, D-flat to C, and, to a lesser extent, B-natural to C. In the second paragraph, the melody emphasizes A-flat to G and D-flat to C in a C major harmonic context, while the third paragraph returns to the harmony of the first. The movement's central Romance, meanwhile, with its cantilena and its mobile accompaniment, provides a foil to the hushed concentration of the outer Recitative sections. Yet, it is integrated to the Recitative by a process of transformation by which the theme (if one can use that term) of the Recitative becomes that of the Romance—the rhythmic/melodic contour with which the Recitative opens is gradually modified at Fig. 32, b3 and again during the transition at Fig. 34, b4 until it becomes the opening melody of the Romance.

Perhaps the most surprising influence of the Eighth Symphony's first movement comes in the Quartet's third movement Waltz. Up to this point, Shostakovich's scherzi, at least as found in the symphonies and chamber music, had fallen into two formal types. The first follows the classical model of scherzo-trio-scherzo plus, in most cases, a coda. Examples include the First Quartet, the Fifth and Seventh Symphonies, and the third movement of the Eighth Symphony. In the otherwise similar second type, the scherzo's reprise combines in its later stages with elements of the trio, e.g., the Fourth and Sixth Symphonies, and the second movement of the Eighth. In both types, though, the central trio is a musically separate entity that acts as a foil to the main scherzo. But here in the Second Quartet, the trio is jettisoned in favor of a development of the scherzo material, replete with the techniques of "brutalization" familiar from Shostakovich's larger symphonic developments. (In this respect, the Piano Trio was perhaps a halfway house—there, the trio, although not entirely jettisoned, was certainly shorter and less distinctive than usual, while the main scherzo material was subject to slightly more extended development.)

Typically, the recapitulations that follow Shostakovich's "brutalizing" developments present the movement's opening material (either its introduction or its first theme) in a new, more turbulent context. And so it is here; when the main scherzo theme returns in the tonic at Fig. 77, the originally simple waltz accompaniment above the cello melody is now angular (pizzicato and *fortissimo*) and dissonant. As the theme unfolds over the next fifteen bars, the accompaniment "unwinds," descending in pitch and relaxing harmonically. At Fig. 78, the music becomes, for a few bars at least, similar to its original presentation.

Following a short introduction in which the E-flat minor of the scherzo is transformed over seventeen bars into its polar opposite, A minor, the fourth movement finale presents a set of variations on a fourteen-bar melody. The phrase structure of the fourteen bars is 4+4+6, the asymmetry exacerbated by the expansion of the second group's final bar from a 4/4 to a 3/2 meter. Like the finale of the Second Piano Sonata (the phrase structure of which is similarly idiosyncratic), the first few variations are treated "classically," with the original melody in its fourteen-bar entirety largely in the foreground. In the classical theme-and-variation style it was not unusual for the theme to recede or even disappear temporarily over the course of later variations, leaving in its place a harmonic "shadow." Shostakovich, too, observes this procedure beginning with the melodic fragmentation of the fourth variation (Fig. 99, b2). It is also at this point that the original phrase structure shows signs of disintegrating. In fact, with their increased tempo and melodic fragmentation, the next several variations, starting with the fifth (Fig. 101), behave rather like a typical Shostakovich first movement development. Although the boundaries between variations remain discernable, the momentum that connects them is of a higher order than in the movement's earlier stages. At the climax (Fig. 115), Shostakovich does something that would become typical of climactic points in his symphonic developments, namely a replay of an earlier, usually slower, theme (in this case, the movement's introductory theme) underneath the frantic ongoing activity. The remaining variations (from Fig. 116) represent a winding down, though the comparatively untroubled mood of the theme as it had been originally presented never quite returns. Instead, a hushed, disquieting intensity takes over, with the final variation (Fig. 123) reminiscent of the Fourth Symphony's coda, with its high violin musings and throbbing low string ostinato. The coda (Fig. 128) returns us to the movement's introduction, leading to a final, declamatory, harmonized statement of the movement's main theme and a defiantly somber final cadence. Of course, minor-key finales are unusual for major-key works. The Seventh Symphony finale was a rare exception, although even that was capped by a rousing C major coda. Here in the Second Quartet, by contrast, there is no *tierce de Picardie*, the confident A major of the Quartet's opening now a world away.

Incidentally, the final variation is not the only allusion to the Fourth Symphony to be found in the Second Quartet; at Fig. 67 in the third movement, there is a three bar quotation from the Symphony's finale (Fig. 181). It is certainly tempting to speculate the extent to which the unperformed "problem child" was on the composer's mind during this period. Laurel Fay points out that in 1942, shortly before his death, Boleslav Yavorsky had written to Shostakovich expressing the hope that the Fourth Symphony would soon see the light of day.[99] In 1945, Shostakovich and Weinberg would perform the two-piano version of the Fourth Symphony at the Composers' Union. The score of that transcription would be published in 1946.

***

With the government's wartime energies focused on the military effort rather than on "building Socialism," its interference in artistic matters had receded somewhat. Without in any way understating the horrific brutality that the War inflicted on the Russian people or the profound sympathy and concern that Shostakovich had for his fellow citizens, wartime life for artists was in this one small but significant respect improved in comparison with the pre-war Terror years. With grief now an allowable commodity, the masks of Socialist optimism could to an extent be dropped; the dictum "truth is the first casualty of war" ironically turned on its head. But in the final year or so, as Stalin sensed the possibility of victory, the propaganda machine began to be re-stoked. Shostakovich's remarks from November 1944 were typical:

> I have a dream—common, I should think to every Soviet artist—of creating a large scale work which will express the powerful feelings we have today. I think that the epigraph to all our work in the next few years will be the simple but glorious word, "Victory." In these days of decisive battles, and in the coming years of peace, the people will demand vivid, inspiring music which will embody the heroism of the Great Patriotic War and the nobility and moral beauty of our nation . . .[100]

Within weeks of these remarks, the "large scale work" had begun to unfold. By the early months of 1945, Shostakovich was demonstrating the opening section of his new, choral Ninth Symphony to friends and colleagues—"victorious major music in a vigorous tempo," according to Rabinovich.[101] Isaak Glikman reports hearing "about ten minutes" of it at the end of April ("magnificent in its sweep, its pathos and its irresistible movement"[102]). But Shostakovich abandoned the work shortly after, telling Glikman that he was dissatisfied with parts of it and that the pressure of composing a choral Ninth symphony, with all the attendant historical connotations, had become too much.[103] (The story that he allegedly told Solomon Volkov in the early 1970s was rather more blunt: "I couldn't write an apotheosis to Stalin, I simply couldn't."[104]) Of course, this was not the first time that a promised grand patriotic work had mysteriously "disappeared," although unlike, say, the proposed "Lenin" symphony, there is at least some evidence of his having started the piece. Actually, Genrikh (Henry) Orlov states that Shostakovich later reported having made two false starts on the Ninth Symphony; so, despite the similarities of their descriptions, it cannot be said for certain that what Glikman heard and what Rabinovich reported upon were necessarily the same thing.[105] Moreover, an autograph manuscript dating from January 1945, containing 322 bars (about twelve minutes) of a symphony in E-flat minor (i.e., contradicting Rabinovich's report of "major music"), has recently been discovered. According to the archivist Olga Digonskaya, material from that manuscript is also to be found in a sketch for an unfinished sonata for violin and piano dating from June 1945 as well as in the much later Tenth Symphony.[106]

What replaced the much anticipated *magnum opus* was a short, almost neoclassical Ninth Symphony for orchestra alone, composed in July and August 1945 and premiered in November. Its reception would follow an all-too-familiar trajectory. Initially, the Ninth was praised for its transparent textures, its clarity, and its simple beauty.[107] But at the Composers' Union discussions in December, it was attacked for its un-heroic, even anti-heroic, tone—the old charge of "light music" surfacing once again. The Symphony was subsequently nominated for a Stalin Prize (Second Class)—its failure to win the award was probably the result of a secret memo sent to Malenkov urging the Symphony's withdrawal from consideration.[108]

Stylistically, much of the Ninth Symphony's first movement does indeed sound like latter-day Haydn with its classically clipped rhythms, its discrete approach to phrase structure, and its wit. Orchestral textures are more chamber-like than in previous Shostakovich symphonies—one has to go all the way back to the First Symphony to find anything on a similar textural scale, although the sense in that earlier work of the young composer experimenting with daring instrumental sonorities is not quite replicated here. This was also the first Shostakovich symphony to contain a straightforward classical sonata-form first movement, with no "arch" processes or gradually emerging recapitulations, the classicism even extending to an exposition repeat. Structurally, it is perhaps closer to Haydn than to Mozart. As so often with Haydn, the second theme appears almost at the end of the exposition, giving it more the status of a closing theme, though (also like Haydn) the importance of that theme becomes apparent as the development unfolds.

What gives the Ninth Symphony its characteristic flavor is the use of witty incongruity within "congruous" boundaries, not quite the same thing as the overtly "wrong-note" styles found in Shostakovich's earlier pieces of iconoclasm, such as *The Bolt*. An example of the tension between congruous and incongruous can be found in the last few bars before the first movement's second subject (Example 7.8). On the one hand, the octave E jump at the end of the rising scale is a typical classical period "pre-second subject" half cadence, implying A as the new key. But then, the trombone's cadential figure is not the expected E–A but F–B-flat, moving the whole edifice up a semitone in the blink of an eye. Yet, as impertinent and disconcerting as that is, the F is in fact a congruously logical continuation of the rising scale, and is of course the entrance into the "correct" second subject key for a symphony in E-flat major, namely B-flat. This idea of a harmonic approach that is both "right" and "wrong" at the same time is, again, rather Haydnesque.[109]

Example 7.8

To his credit, Shostakovich is not one to play the same joke twice (unless one counts the exposition repeat). At the corresponding moment in the recapitulation, we get the same rising scale, and the same octave E drop, although this time with E major harmony. However, instead of continuing up a semitone to F, the trombone subverts our expectations and drops a semitone to E-flat, preparing A-flat as the key of the second subject. Such humor through misdirection is, of course, an old theatrical trick, and in this case it reveals yet another "incongruity," namely A-flat as the new key rather than the expected tonic E-flat. But even this could be viewed as a tonal elevation of the brief visits to subdominant or flat-side keys sometimes found in Classical period recapitulations. And for the trombone, the excursion to A-flat is a vindication of its pestilent behavior earlier on in the recapitulation, where it rudely throws around its cadential E-flat–A-flat figure in an attempt to throw us off. As for the expected E-flat tonic, this does not arrive until the clarinet's final statement of the first subject (Fig. 24), although it is subsequently lost in the coda, regained only in the final four bars.

With its wistful, gently rocking clarinet melody, the second movement *Moderato* is perhaps as close to Prokofiev as Shostakovich would ever get—Prokofiev in his vein of acidic lyricism, that is, not the "iron and steel" Prokofiev that Shostakovich had emulated in his First Piano Sonata. The *Moderato* tempo marking (quarter = 208) is crucial to the wistful character, and indeed Shostakovich objected to performances that tried to evince out of this music a more traditional slow movement or play it too straight.[110] Written in a sonatina form—the form that would soon become a favorite of Shostakovich, particularly in string quartet first movements—it presents an unusual contrast between an almost exclusively woodwind first subject and an almost exclusively string second, though the wind chorale/string pseudo-recitative in the Seventh Symphony's slow movement had presented a similar contrast of monoliths. As the pulsating second subject in the strings gathers momentum, however, it is joined by a variant of the first subject in the oboe and clarinet (Fig. 37).

Following the brilliant third movement scherzo, complete with a high-octane version of Shostakovich's flamenco-type trio (the trumpet providing some toreador-style bravado), the Symphony starts to accumulate darker undertones. The fourth movement bassoon recitative that follows on, *attacca*, from the scherzo wrests us away from the world of neoclassical brilliance and back to a more familiar Shostakovichian pathos. It would be the last of the four great Shostakovich recitatives from 1939–1945, and proceeds according to the same principle as the others—a solo instrument spinning out, in a seemingly free rhythm, a melodic prolongation of slow moving harmonies; the chords themselves held suspended in the accompanying strings. Yet, there is a difference. In the other examples, the ethereal sound of the flute (Sixth Symphony), the anguished, serious tones of the English horn (Eighth Symphony), and the overtly impassioned, possibly even Jewish-inflected,[111] sound of the violin (Second Quartet) reflected perfectly the tragic sentiment being expressed in each case. Moreover, each instrument was capable of handling, without ironic connotation, the wide registral demands that Shostakovich placed upon it. But as the bassoon strains to reach into its highest register in the Ninth Symphony's recitative, the emerging pathos is of an altogether more ironic kind, an irony heightened when, at the end of the movement, the bassoon slips slyly into the finale's jaunty first theme. Although the recitative gives the listener pause for thought—it constitutes, after all, the only genuinely slow music in the entire Symphony—its status as transition from one *scherzando* movement (the third) to another (the fifth) places it in a different light to the other examples. And the irony is, if anything, further heightened by the low brass fanfares that introduce, and later interrupt, the recitative; fanfares whose inflated pomp and emptily rhetorical sequences render them surprisingly devoid of portent or potency. Was this an attempt to inject some "seriousness" into the Ninth Symphony, or a deliberate deflating of a culture whose grandiosity and sense of self-importance was reaching farcical new heights?

The Symphony's most biting irony is reserved for the finale, whose coarse-edged polka tune is the very antithesis of grandiose victory. Although this movement is in sonata form, its evolution is highly idiosyncratic. The rather tight-lipped exposition presents the two main themes, mostly at a *piano* dynamic and with a seemingly deliberate lack of symphonic momentum. Not unusually, the early stages of the development play with fragments of those themes, but the effect is, if anything, still more remote. Only about a third of the way into the development does the music start to gather momentum, though even this falls under the watch of increasingly ominous tuba and low horn pedals. The momentum increases further at the *Pochissimo animato* in preparation for the big return, tutti and *fortissimo*, of the first theme at the start of the recapitulation. This is clearly the moment that the movement has been gearing up towards, the moment at which the theme, stifled in the exposition and development, is finally allowed to let rip. Yet, having reached this point, Shostakovich severely truncates the recapitulation, presenting a bare-bones play-through of the first and second themes (the latter, incidentally in the key of A-flat, reminiscent of the first movement), shorn of all transitional and subsidiary material. Barely allowed to get into its stride, this recapitulation comes to an abrupt halt after only forty-nine bars (compared to the exposition's 160, an extreme truncation even by Shostakovich's standards), giving way to a nervous, high-speed coda. Humor does get the last word, though, with the scrambling for the correct key in the Symphony's final moments—only in the penultimate bar does the music find its E-flat tonic. In the Symphony as a whole, the musical material is of an ironic nature. But in this movement, it is as if Shostakovich is also parodying the very conventions of sonata form, with all of its associations with the great symphonies of the past. Whether the deflation of the form through its simplistically routine, non-transcendent recapitulation carried a message that went beyond the purely musical can only be a matter for speculation.

In the context of the Shostakovich cycle, the Ninth Symphony stands out almost as a deliberately "anti-epic" work, even disregarding the attendant political contexts and expectations. Sandwiched between the epic Eighth and Tenth Symphonies, it is, if one may borrow Schumann's famous description of Beethoven's Fourth Symphony, the "slender Grecian maiden between two Nordic giants." Yet, the Symphony does connect into "mainstream" Shostakovich in other ways. The finale's exposition, for example, contains rondo characteristics (the first subject area takes on an ABA form before moving to the second subject area at Fig. 77), something that will be found increasingly in the concertos and chamber music. Meanwhile, the placement of recapitulation second subjects in keys other than the tonic, such as occurs in both of the outer movements, also looks forward to some of the later quartets.

***

The shadow of the Eighth Symphony, which had been so clearly felt in the Second Quartet, would extend, at least in one respect, to the Third Quartet, composed between January and August 1946. The Third Quartet's distribution of its five movements would follow almost exactly that of the Eighth Symphony: a sonata-style movement; two scherzos; a slow pseudo-passacaglia (the main theme of which even resembles that of the Symphony's actual passacaglia); and a rondo finale. From the stylistic point of view, however, it is the Ninth Symphony that would exert the stronger influence. The first movements of the Ninth Symphony and the Third Quartet both launch with a Haydnesque first violin melody with simple rhythmic accompaniment in the other strings, and both continue with a neo-classical sense of style and scale, even down to the exposition repeat, though in Shostakovich's opinion at least, the Quartet movement should be played "gently, not with verve."[112] Thematically, the two movements share other similarities, for example, the rhythmic contour of the openings of their respective second subjects.

Breaking up the otherwise very classical diatonicism of the opening phrase is the seemingly odd collection of notes in its third bar. The four notes (E-flat, A-flat, and D-flat in the first violin; B-natural in the second violin) are one note short of forming a totally complementary set to the work's F major tonic. In the short term, they charm the ear, vaguely threatening modulation, although the ongoing tonic pedal in the cello keeps F major firmly in view. In the long term, however, these pitches will prove structurally important.

Unusually, the development takes the form of a fully worked out fugue, yet another nod to the eighteenth century. The introduction of counterpoint or the intensification of previous counterpoint in a movement's development section was, of course, standard practice for composers of sonata-form movements in all eras. Even the use of fugato or fugue itself was not uncommon, as we have already seen in the first movement of Shostakovich's Fourth Symphony or the finale of the Eighth. But devoting a movement's entire development section to a full fugue is highly unusual—the finales of Beethoven's Piano Sonata No. 28 and Bruckner's Fifth Symphony are two of the few examples that come to mind. The fugue here in the Third Quartet is based on the movement's first theme with its countersubject taken from a small fragment of the exposition's codetta, although several commentators view it as a double fugue, for example, Richard Longman and Christopher Rowland.[113] Others, such as Eric Roseberry, hear a single subject.[114] In reality, it falls into something of a gray area; the material that accompanies the first answer enjoys a higher profile than one normally expects from a countersubject but, as the fugue progresses, shoulders less responsibility than might be expected if it were indeed a separate second subject. A comparison with the genuine double fugue that Shostakovich would write in the scherzo of the First Violin Concerto less than two years later is enough to make the point.

Double fugue or not, the challenge for a composer attempting to incorporate a fugue into a sonata development is the realization of not just one step-up of intensity (from sonata exposition to sonata development), but two (sonata exposition to fugue exposition to fugue development). At the start of the development, Shostakovich gives us a five-part fugal exposition of the main subject with a mostly conventional sequence of entries—based around, respectively, E, B, E, B, and C-sharp. But, unusually, the ensuing fugal development contains a new series of complete entries—A-flat (Fig. 16), A-flat (Fig. 16, b4), E-flat (Fig. 17), B-flat (Fig. 18), plus an incomplete entry on D-flat (Fig. 19) truncated to four bars in preparation for the repeated two-bar versions in the cello (A-flat, from Fig. 20) that constitute the retransition. What is notable is that three out of these four development keys (A-flat, E-flat, and D-flat) derive from the movement's strange chromatic third bar.

With the fugue development comprising only complete entries (other than the final one at Fig. 19), Shostakovich breaks with conventional wisdom, and indeed with his own typical practice, because almost every bar in this development bears witness to the movement's main theme in its complete and original form. Such a move would seem to militate against the requisite stepping-up of intensity, but

Shostakovich finds other ways. Following the fugue exposition's predictable timing
of entries—second entry after seven bars, third entry after ten, fourth entry after
seven, fifth entry after ten—the development throws this macrorhythm out of kil-
ter, with entries after three-and-a-half, five-and-a-half, six-and-a-half, and four-
and-a-half bars, respectively—the presence of the half-bars continually teasing the
listener's metrical reference. And the subject's relationship with the countersubject,
already prone towards bitonality in the fugue exposition, becomes even more dissonant in its development.

The retransition into the recapitulation is short and harmonically concise,
although its function has misled at least one commentator.[115] At Fig. 20, the cello
presents a two-bar fragment of the main theme in the key of A-flat, bringing the
fugal development back to the key in which it started. In this key, the final note
of the fragment is C. Shostakovich prolongs this note for nearly two bars, giving it
the status of a pedal point, repeating the process three bars later. The C becomes
the dominant pedal for the upcoming recapitulation at Fig. 21. (Something similar will occur with the retransition of the F-sharp minor fugue of op. 87; see
Chapter 14.) In fact, the first two bars of the recapitulation also function as a final
quasi-stretto for the fugue, giving the briefest of glimpses into the canons and aug-
mentations that would have typically been found in the late stages of a Shostakovich symphonic development. In other words, we have, in miniature, a typically
Shostakovichian example of developmental tensions bleeding over into the recapitulation. Not surprisingly, given its unusual prevalence in the development, the first
theme is severely curtailed in the recapitulation (twenty-two bars long compared
to fifty-three in the exposition).

Following the pattern set by the Eighth Symphony and, for that matter, the
Sixth, Shostakovich presents two consecutive, although contrasting, scherzi. The
second movement's aggressive triadic ostinato in the viola reminds us, albeit in
slow motion, of the triadic viola ostinato that starts the Eighth Symphony's third
movement. Meanwhile, the heavy, chordal hammer blows in the third movement
look forward to the more brutal of Shostakovich's later scherzos—the Eighth and
Tenth Quartets and the Tenth Symphony. However, as Richard Longman points
out, the unsettled alternation of meter, not to mention the more ironic dance style
of much of this third movement, gives it ultimately a less relentless impression.[116]
The fourth movement's quasi-passacaglia apes the Eighth Symphony's passacaglia
in both rhythm and gesture. Here, seven rotations are separated by what Richard
Longman terms "interludes,"[117] each interlude related either to the first interlude
or to the quasi-passacaglia theme.

The fifth movement finale engages with yet another historic form, the rondo.
But as in the finale of the Eighth Symphony, Shostakovich fuses that eighteenth-
century form with his ongoing approach to symphonism, creating an "arch-rondo"
structure with reverse thematic appearance following a central crisis climax: A–B–
A–C–A–Climax (quasi-passacaglia theme)–C–B–A, with the final A functioning as
the coda. The climax, though very short, brutalizes to some degree the fourth
movement pseudo-passacaglia theme, and even includes a few bars of typically

Shostakovichian canon (Fig. 107, b2). And, like the Eighth Symphony's finale, the return of the jaunty "C" theme is presented in a transformed version, in this case a pale reflection (A minor, *con sordino*) of its former A-major self (Fig. 111). As it progresses, the major creeps back in, misleading the listener to expect a resumption of a normal rondo. But, as in his symphonic examples, Shostakovich's reverse-order recapitulation signifies not resumption but unraveling. By the time the "A" theme makes its final appearance, *Adagio*, it is fragmented; a lone voice (the first violin) playing over twenty-six bars of sustained tonic harmony.

The Third Quartet presents an unusual journey. Its first movement asserts itself in Shostakovich's "quartet" style: a more-or-less straightforward sonata-allegro containing themes of a decidedly classical cut; a form whose structural ebb and flow follows the classical model rather than that of Shostakovich's more prevalent "symphonic" first movement *Moderato*. Likewise, the rondo finale promises to bring the Quartet to a classically influenced conclusion. But later in the movement, Shostakovich's symphonic *Moderato* begins to wield its influence, diverting the rondo's course, bringing it to a close of introspective resignation following a tragically turbulent climax.

Like the Second Piano Trio and the Eighth Symphony, the Third Quartet closes by musing on thematic fragments over a tonic pedal. All three works feature the sound of soft pizzicato chords, while the Quartet and the Trio also use violin harmonics to generate a disembodied sound. Meanwhile, the first violin's fragmentation, its rests and fermatas create a pseudo-recitative over the harmonic pedal in the other instruments. Essential to the Second Quartet's Recitative was the choice of chromatic tendency tones pulling towards their resolutions. There, over the first chord (V7 of B-flat), the flat second and flat sixth scale degrees pulled down, while the raised fourth pushed up. Here, at the end of the Third Quartet, over an F major tonic chord, the very same intervals are at work, coincidentally resulting in exactly the same set of pitches. With this final gesture, Shostakovich brings to a close not just the Third Quartet, but a linked tetralogy—the Eighth and Ninth Symphonies, and the Second and Third Quartets.

***

With the Nazis defeated, Stalin's reputation, not to mention his ego, had inflated to mythic proportions. Whatever small amount of cultural liberalization had occurred during the War had quickly come to an end as the newly emboldened, but no less paranoid, dictator sought a new scapegoat with which to reinforce his grip. In the past, those scapegoats had included the intelligentsia, industrial "wreckers," and Trotskyites. Now, Stalin's greatest worry was America's burgeoning power and the ideological "contamination" of Russian troops by the Western Allies alongside whom they had fought. And so a new campaign was spearheaded to promote Russian nationalism. Crucially, the emphasis was on Russian, not Soviet, nationalism. Although himself a Georgian, Stalin had a distrust of non-Russian Soviets that was almost as deep-seated as his distrust of the West. A two-pronged plan was developed: a series of campaigns against certain nationalities, something that had already begun with his wartime deportations of Ossetians and Ingush, not to mention the quietly brewing anti-Semitic activities; and a purge of Soviet culture. To spearhead the latter, he appointed Andrei Zhdanov, who had been one of the founding architects of Socialist Realism back in the mid-1930s. That, together with his quietly bullying demeanor, made him the ideal man for the job.

Zhdanov turned first to literature. It was the field he knew best and was, with the exception of film, the most important in terms of its propaganda potential. His primary target was two Leningrad-based literary journals, *Zvezda* and *Leningrad*, and two of its most prolific contributors, the satirist Mikhail Zoshchenko and Anna Akhmatova, the poet whose powerful combination of mysticism and eroticism had earned her the label "half nun, half harlot." Following Zhdanov's investigations, the Central Committee published its Resolution, "On the Journals Zvezda and Leningrad," on 14 August 1946. The Resolution attacked the journals for their "spirit of cringing servility before everything foreign" and for their apolitical stance. It ordered the closure of *Leningrad* and placed *Zvezda* under the control of the Central Committee's Directorate of Propaganda. As for Zoshchenko and Akhmatova, they were treated to a typical Soviet-style character assassination.

> Zoshchenko has long specialized in writing empty, vapid, and vulgar things, in spreading putrid nonsense, vulgarity and indifference to politics, so as to mislead our young people and poison their consciousness.... Zoshchenko portrays Soviet order and Soviet people in a freakishly caricatured way, slanderously presenting Soviet people as primitive, lacking culture, stupid, with narrow minds and tastes and tempers. The spiteful hooligan-like image Zoshchenko has of our reality is accompanied by anti-Soviet attacks. Giving the pages of "Zvezda" over to such literary pretenders and riff-raff as Zoshchenko was especially intolerable.... Akhmatova is a typical exponent of empty, frivolous poetry that is alien to our people. Permeated by the scent of pessimism and decay, redolent of old-fashioned salon poetry, frozen in the positions of bourgeois-aristocratic aestheticism and decadence—"art for art's sake"—not wanting to progress forward with our people, her verses cause damage to the upbringing of our youth and cannot be tolerated in Soviet literature.[118]

Both were expelled from the Writers' Union. Akhmatova would be partially rehabilitated in 1950 with her volume of poems glorifying Stalin. The less politically savvy Zoshchenko never recovered, descending into a life of poverty and alcoholism, though, according to Shostakovich's friend Flora Litvinova, the composer quietly provided him material support.[119]

Having placed his stamp on the literary world, Zhdanov turned to theater and film. The Resolution, "On the Repertoire of Dramatic Theaters and Measures for Improving it," was published on 26 August, and "On the Film *A Great Life*" on 4 September. Ominously for Shostakovich, criticism of his Ninth Symphony was resurfacing at about this time. An article by Izrail Nestyev published on 30 September, though praising the high moral tone of much of Shostakovich's music, criticized the Ninth Symphony's disengagement from the grand issues of the day, a criticism that was taken up a few days later at the Plenum of the Composers'

Union Organizing Committee.[120] Coming as they did amid those portentous events in literature and film, these criticisms would not be forgotten.

The following year, 1947, saw an increase in Shostakovich's non-composing obligations. In addition to his duties at the Moscow Conservatory, he was reappointed professor at the Leningrad Conservatory, taking over the composition class of his former teacher, Shteinberg, who had died at the end of 1946. He was also appointed chairman of the Leningrad Composers' Union and was elected as one of Leningrad's Deputies to the Supreme Soviet of the RSFSR (Russian Federation). Although now settled in Moscow, where he would remain for the rest of his life, he still considered Leningrad his spiritual home. His obligations there, and the fact that his mother had returned there following the wartime evacuation, allowed him to maintain connections with his beloved "Peter." Nevertheless, the frequent commuting between the two cities took a toll on his composition; 1947 would see only the score to the film *Pirogov*, the cantata *Poem of the Motherland*, and the first two movements of the First Violin Concerto.

Shostakovich carried out his official obligations diligently. Although by this point, he was less than enamored with the Party, and although he would complain about the more tiresome aspects of the Deputy position (dealing with residents' housing problems, arbitrating disputes between neighbors, etc.[121]), his overriding sense of civic duty ensured his commitment. But with hindsight, we can see that this flurry of civic and political activity represented possibly the first attempt by the Party to turn Shostakovich into something like an official state composer. Prokofiev notwithstanding, Shostakovich was now the nation's pre-eminent composer, and his potential value as a mouthpiece in Stalin's new cultural war was incalculable. Appointing him to administrative and political posts was one way of bringing him into the fold. Dangling "carrots" was another: in 1947, on Stalin's orders, the composer was rewarded with two new accommodations, a large duplex apartment in Moscow and a dacha in Bolshevo, a picturesque area on the outskirts of the city. He was also awarded the Order of Lenin in December 1946 and made a People's Artist of the RSFSR in November 1947.

The year 1947 marked a double celebration: the thirtieth anniversary of the Revolution and the 800th anniversary of the city of Moscow. The festivities would provide Shostakovich a chance to demonstrate his loyalty, return favors, and perhaps make amends for the Ninth Symphony. But with his energies focused on the Violin Concerto, his sole anniversary contribution that autumn was *Poem of the Motherland*, a hasty assemblage of popular and Revolutionary material, including a recycling of his former hit, "Song of the Counterplan." It was poorly received; for the second time in two years, an uninspired Shostakovich had failed to deliver.[122] And he was not alone. Prokofiev's most important work that year, the dark, turbulent Sixth Symphony, was hardly celebration fare, and his anniversary offerings (*Festive Poem, "Thirty Years,"* and *Flourish Mighty Land!*) carried little conviction. Myaskovsky's Choral Nocturne, *Kremlin by Night*, also missed the mark, as did Khachaturian's Third Symphony (*Symphony-Poem*), with its dizzying mix of hyper-triumphalism, 1920s-style "iron and steel" modernism, and exotic lyricism.

With such lack-luster offerings emanating from the leading figures, much hope was placed in a new opera, *The Great Friendship*, by the relatively unknown Georgian, Vano Muradeli. Premiered in Stalino (Donetsk) in September 1947, it quickly became a hit and was soon in production across Russia. It had what seemed like a good "Soviet" story—a celebration of Sergo Ordzhonikidze (1886–1937), the Commissar who established Soviet power in Georgia in the early 1920s—and a tuneful oriental-romantic style, a sort of watered-down Borodin. It is certainly hard to imagine how such a musically innocuous work would, within a few months, find itself at the center of the most inflamous brouhaha in Soviet musical history, the "antiformalism" purges of 1948.

As with other "flashpoint" events in Soviet cultural history, for instance, the 1936 denunciation of *Lady Macbeth*, interpreting the chain of events that led up to Zhdanov's "antiformalism" purges is not a straightforward matter. One school of thought is that the purge against composers was predestined—the inevitable extension of Zhdanov's 1946 purges in literature, theater, and film—and that Muradeli's opera was merely a convenient scapegoat, something to get the ball rolling. However, even prior to its September 1947 unveiling, *The Great Friendship* had already been causing concern in higher Party echelons, not so much for its "formalism" as for the libretto's historically "inaccurate" portrayal of the relationship between the Russian majority and the Lezgin minority. In December, Dmitry Shepilov sent a memo to Zhdanov, complaining not just about the libretto's inadequacies but about the general lack of interest in heroic Soviet opera and the unhealthy emphasis on abstract forms such as non-programmatic symphonies and chamber music. A special closed performance of *The Great Friendship* was held for senior Party members on 5 January 1948, and a discussion meeting was convened the following day. Attending the meeting, amongst others, were Shepilov, Zhdanov, senior administrators of the Bolshoi Theater, the conductor and several of the cast, as well as Muradeli and his librettist. Though the discussion focused at first on the opera itself, Muradeli's response would open the proverbial can of worms, as he blamed his admitted shortcomings on, as Kiril Tomoff puts it, "a stifling professional organization and training program that favored originality over melodic composition"[123]—in other words, the undue influence of formalists. For Zhdanov, no doubt emboldened by his prior crackdowns on literature, theater, and film, it was time for action.

CHAPTER 8

"DSCH" (1948–1953)

Less than a week after the special performance of *The Great Friendship*, Zhdanov convened an extraordinary meeting of composers and musicians at the Party Central Committee (10–13 January 1948).[1] This meeting would constitute one of the most infamous moments in Soviet cultural history. In his opening salvo, Zhdanov went straight for Muradeli's opera, describing it as "frequent[ly] cacophonous" and "alien" to the folk styles of the Northern Caucasus, and attacking the libretto's "historical inaccuracies."[2] But the hapless Muradeli was merely the hors d'oeuvre. *The Great Friendship* duly censured, Zhdanov got down to what over the previous few days had become the larger issue, namely the hounding of "formalists"— Shostakovich, Prokofiev, Myaskovsky, Khachaturian, Kabalevsky, and Shebalin. Zhdanov compared their music to "a dentists' drill or a musical gas-wagon, the kind the Gestapo used,"[3] and accused them of abandoning the "true" Soviet forms of opera and folksong, and concentrating only on "elitist" symphonic and chamber compositions.

Yet, as Zhdanov knew only too well, the Party had been supporting these "formalists" for years. During the 1940s, Shostakovich had been awarded, *inter alia*, three Stalin Prizes and a dacha together with 60,000 rubles for "fittings," and only two months before the conference had been made a People's Artist of the RSFSR.[4] In his opening speech, Zhdanov suggested that the Party had relied too much on the judgments of the Composers' Union: "an oligarchy, where everything is run by a small group of composers, and their faithful retainers—I mean music critics of the boot-licking kind—and where everything is a million miles away from real creative discussion, criticism, and self-criticism."[5] However, in his closing speech, he effectively contradicted that assertion, arguing instead that the Party had understood all along that the recipients were not "free of faults" but conferred the prizes anyway as an act of good faith: "We were patient, and waited for you to choose the right road. Now, clearly, the Party has had to intervene."[6]

Contradictions aside, Zhdanov's rabble-rousing speeches served their intended purpose, unleashing the deep reservoir of jealousy that had been festering in the middle ranks of the Composers' Union. Ivan Dzerzhinsky, who in the 1930s had enjoyed considerable success with his opera *The Quiet Don*, responded that young composers wrote only to please the likes of Prokofiev, Shostakovich, or Myaskovsky: "whether the public (or even the composer himself) likes the work is quite unimportant."[7] As he had a few days earlier, Muradeli blamed his failures on the "pro-Western," "pro-formalist press," to which Shostakovich would later retort that "[Muradeli] talked as if he had consciously written a bad opera, i.e., that he knew exactly how to write a good opera, but that because he was badly taught, he still wrote a bad one."[8] However, it was the writers of popular songs (the so-called *melodisty*) who had the biggest axe to grind. Though they had, for the first time, been granted Union membership during the war, they had always felt like second-class citizens. As Kiril Tomoff points out, it was fortuitous for Zhdanov that the *melodisty* tended to be culturally more conservative, and hence more loyal to the Party, than their "serious" music counterparts.[9] The comments of the folksong composer Vladimir Zakharov, egregious and insulting though they were, reflected the sentiments of many of those present:

> There are still discussions round the question whether Shostakovich's Eighth Symphony is good or bad. Such a discussion is nonsense. From the point of view of the People, the Eighth Symphony is not a musical work at all; it is a "composition" which has nothing to do with musical art whatsoever.... The whole of our people are now busy carrying out the Five-Year plan. We read in the papers of heroic deeds in factories, on collective farms, and so on. Ask these people whether they really love Shostakovich's Eighth or Ninth Symphony, and a whole lot of other symphonic works—as the press claims they do.... During the blockade of Leningrad, when people were dying of hunger in the factories, they asked for folk songs to be played to them on the gramophone, not Shostakovich's Seventh Symphony![10]

Although Zakharov's rant did not escape without comment—Shostakovich chided him for his "not very thoughtful" words, and Shebalin mocked his "sweeping statements" and pretensions of "papal infallibility"[11]—the authority of Zhdanov inevitably prevailed. Published the following month on 10 February, the official Central Committee Resolution ("On V. Muradeli's Opera, *The Great Friendship*") would state:

> This [formalist] music is characterized by the negation of the chief principles of classical music, by the preaching of atonality, dissonance and disharmony, all of which are supposedly signs of "progress" and "innovation" in the development of musical form. These composers reject the essential foundations of the musical work, such as melody; instead, they take delight in chaotic and neurotic sonorities, turning music into cacophony, an anarchic piling-up of sounds.... Many Soviet composers, in pursuit of a misconceived notion of "innovation," have removed themselves from the artistic tastes

and demands of the Soviet people. These composers flout the best traditions of Russian and Western classical music; they reject those traditions as "antiquated," "old fashioned," and "conservative," and they arrogantly persecute those composers who have made a conscientious attempt to assimilate and develop the devices of classical music, calling them "primitive traditionalists" and "epigones."[12]

The Resolution named the six "formalists" cited at the meeting, but with one twist—Kabalevsky's name was now replaced by that of Popov, seemingly the result of a behind-the-scenes deal. Four days later, on 14 February, Glavrepertkom, the repertoire division of the Committee for Artistic Affairs, published the official list of works now banned from performance. For Shostakovich, this covered the Sixth, Eighth, and Ninth Symphonies, Piano Concerto [No. 1], Two Pieces for String Octet, Second Piano Sonata, *Six Romances on Verses by Raleigh, Burns, and Shakespeare*, and *Aphorisms. Poem of the Motherland* also appeared although it was later crossed out. Also censored were selected works of Prokofiev, Myaskovsky, Khachaturian, Shebalin, Popov, Krein, Feinberg, Polovinkin, Belza, Peiko, Weinberg, and Levitin.[13]

Recently, the musicologist Leonid Maximenkov has suggested that Zhdanov's purges may have been more than just ideologically motivated. Muradeli had been in charge of the Composer's Union's financial division, Muzfond, which since 1941 had given out over 13 million rubles in assistance to the likes of Shostakovich, Prokofiev, Khachaturian, and Shebalin, in other words, the most prominent members of the Union's Organizing Committee. Although it was Muradeli's deputy, Levon Atovmyan, who was responsible for the actual disbursement of funds, Maximenkov believes that Muradeli was being punished in part for Muzfond's culture of profligacy and cronyism.[14]

The aftermath of the Resolution saw the firing of the Union's Organizing Committee (which included Shostakovich), along with the removal of Mikhail Khrapchenko from the chairmanship of the Committee for Artistic Affairs and of Kabalevsky from the editorship of *Sovetskaya muzyka*. Previously, the Composer's Union had enjoyed at least a certain amount of autonomy from the Party. In fact, other than its Organizing Committee, formed in 1939, it had hardly existed as a national entity at all, concentrating its efforts rather on the local branches (Moscow Composers' Union, Leningrad Composers' Union, etc.). Following the shake-up, the Union's structure would more closely reflect that of the Writers' Union, an organization that had always been hardwired into the Party Central Committee. The restructuring of the Composers' Union would also see the meteoric rise to power of its new Secretary-General, the thirty-four year old composer Tikhon Khrennikov. Although the more senior Boris Asafyev would hold the ceremonial position of Chairman until his death the following year, it was Khrennikov who would be responsible for the day-to-day running of the Union. Ambitious, doctrinaire, and hardly shy about wielding his power,[15] Khrennikov would preside over the Union's affairs for the next forty-three years.

The role of Khrennikov, who died in 2007, continues to be fiercely debated. Khrennikov himself admits that he was out of his depth in 1948. Referring to his maiden speech in April 1948, he claims that "it was not me who wrote [the speech]. It was written in the central committee of the Communist Party, and everybody knows it. But I had to read it out at the Congress."[16] He also acknowledges the advisory role of Viktor Belyi. In the words of Kiril Tomoff, Belyi helped Khrennikov "negotiate the tricky line between public discipline and private protection of professional colleagues during the early days of his tenure atop the Composers' Union."[17] Later on, however, although Khrennikov was under no illusion as to his role—to relate Party dictates to the Union membership—he would frequently assert the Union's professional autonomy in interpreting and carrying out those dictates, something that would occasionally put him into conflict with his political masters at the Committee for Artistic Affairs.[18] His support for the Union's Jewish members during the "anti-cosmopolitan" campaign of 1949–1953 was a case in point.

Held between 19 and 25 April, the First All-Union Congress of Soviet Composers, taking place fourteen years after its Writers' Union counterpart, was Khrennikov's chance to show that he had "arrived." Tracing the career of Shostakovich, he attacked the "cold linearity" and the "abstract play with rhythm and timbre" in the Second Symphony and *Aphorisms*, "the banal, vulgar, and meaningless" ballets, and the "unhealthily exaggerated expressionism" of the operas. He paid the requisite homage to the Resolution of April 1932, and singled out the late Ivan Sollertinsky (a "troubadour of modernism") for creating an atmosphere conducive to "formalistic experimentation."[19] Of course, these were all old complaints. But even where Shostakovich's music had clearly been in-sync with the national mood, for example, the iconic, Stalin prize-winning Seventh Symphony, Khrennikov was not above a bit of revisionism:

> The musical thought of this composer was far better suited to depicting the evil images of Fascism and the world of subjective reflection than expressing the positive heroic images of our times. During the War, Shostakovich did not attempt to bring himself closer to the musical language of the people. Thus, the abstractness of its intonations and the cosmopolitanism of its language stand in the way of the Seventh Symphony's lasting popularity with the Soviet people.[20]

Khrennikov's speeches were a demonstration, if any were needed, of the depth to which the cultural debate had sunk. Of course, the honesty of Socialist Realism, at least as Zhdanov had defined it back in 1934, was always questionable. But what had started in 1932 as a debate-worthy, if unashamedly political philosophy had now become little more than a buzzword: if an artistic work was officially liked, it was Socialist Realism; if not (for any one of a variety of reasons), it was formalism. And it does not require hindsight to see this. Alexander Werth, living in Moscow at the time and writing shortly after the events in question, described the discussions of the period as "gibberish,"[21] and reported the "strongest mental reservations" of the French Communist Party and the "perturbed and embarrassed" reaction in Poland and Czechoslovakia.[22] And despite Zhdanov's claim of renewed Party vigilance, artistic decisions would continue to be every bit as capriciously made post-Resolution as they had been before.[23]

***

For Shostakovich, these events would evoke painful memories of 1936, though in many ways the strains were now heavier. For a start, fewer people were willing to stand in his defense, at least publicly, and the vilification in the press, both general and musical, was if anything more vicious—the expansive three-issue diatribe, "The Creative Path of D. Shostakovich," penned by the newly appointed editor of *Sovetskaya muzyka*, the former *rapmist* Marian Koval, perhaps taking the prize for outright spite.[24] Over the course of the year, Shostakovich would endure everything from neighbors hurling rubbish over the fence at the Komarovo dacha to his dismissal in the autumn from his positions at the Moscow and Leningrad Conservatories.[25] It is notable however, that like other disgraced composers, Shostakovich was not expelled from the Composers' Union. This contrasted with, say, the expulsions of Akhmatova and Zoshchenko from the Writers' Union in 1946.

In 1936, Shostakovich had managed to distance himself from the attacks; a single meeting with Kerzhentsev was his only serious attempt to face his detractors in person. But by 1948, the stakes had risen. His international reputation and the extent to which he was now associated with the cultural/political machinery (Chairman of the Leningrad Composers' Union, Deputy to the Supreme Soviet of the Russian Federation) mandated his participation in the orgy of "creative discussion, criticism, and self-criticism," to use that favorite Zhdanovian phrase. Speaking at February's General Assembly of Soviet Composers, he cycled through the required platitudes, admitting to have "overestimated the depth of my creative reconstruction," and praising the Central Committee for having "clearly and definitively shown that there are no signs of national character in my works—no signs of that great spirit of the people." He closed by urging composers "to give their best efforts to the cause of realizing this wonderful Resolution."[26] As for April's All-Union Congress, Shostakovich would later recall to the musicologist Marina Sabinina how his speech had been thrust into his hand as he made his way up to the stage. Sabinina recalls his description:

> "And I got up on the tribune, and started to read out aloud this idiotic, disgusting nonsense concocted by some nobody. Yes, I humiliated myself, I read out what was taken to be 'my own speech'. I read like the most paltry wretch, a parasite, a cut-out paper doll on a string!!" This last phrase he shrieked out like a frenzied maniac, and then kept repeating it.[27]

Whatever façade Shostakovich adopted in public, his private feelings about the events of 1948 were later—though it is not quite certain how much later—given vent in a skit for four soloists, chorus, and piano, entitled *As an Aid to Students: The Struggle between the Realistic and Formalistic Tendencies in Music*. Better known as *Antiformalist Rayok*, or simply *Rayok* ("Peepshow"), this work is a scabrous send-up of a Central Committee meeting. It features four characters: the

Chairman; I. S. Yedinitsyn (translated roughly as Mr. One), an obvious take-off of Iosif Stalin with his lumbering, circuitous speeches and his habit of posing questions that he then clumsily attempts to answer; A. A. Dvoikin (Mr. Two), a parodying of A. A. Zhdanov's obsession with elegance and refinement, "musical gas chambers," and "authentic" *lezghinkas* (a reference to *The Great Friendship*); and D. T. Troikin (Mr. Three), a reference to D. T. Shepilov, Zhdanov's successor who, speaking at the Second All-Union Congress of Soviet Composers in April 1957, famously mispronounced Rimsky-Korsakov as Rimsky-KorSAkov, much to Shostakovich's amusement. The chorus plays the part of the Congress delegates, wholeheartedly agreeing with every idiotic platitude emanating from the platform.

Rayok is pure farce. It features popular songs like "Kamarinskaya" and "Kalinka," while Yedinitsyn's speech is sung to the tune of "Suliko," apparently Stalin's favorite Georgian folksong. Both the score and the written foreword indulge in a complex network of puns, while the foreword's unflattering references to certain musicologists and party functionaries attest to Shostakovich's love of scatological humor.[28]

The sections featuring Troikin were penned immediately after the April 1957 Congress, and a finale, in which the chorus urges "vigilance," was added in the mid-1960s. The dating of the rest, however, is uncertain. Manashir Yakubov, curator of the Shostakovich archive, believes that *Rayok* was started sometime in 1948 in the aftermath of the Zhdanov purges. Isaak Glikman also claims to have heard sketches in the summer of 1948.[29] Shostakovich's friend Lev Lebedinsky, however, insists that the 1957 Congress inspired the whole thing (except the finale).[30] Lebedinsky also claims authorship of the sung libretto, a claim Yakubov disputes. Laurel Fay, meanwhile, questions whether *Rayok* should be viewed as a "composed" work at all, and suggests that the popular genre of *kapustnik*, the party skit that over time would be supplemented and embellished in performance, might provide the more useful model. Needless to say, whether "composition" or "skit," the incendiary *Rayok* was strictly "for the drawer." It was premiered (minus the finale, which was only discovered a few months later) in Washington DC in 1989.

***

As Shostakovich endured the trauma of the Zhdanov conference in January, work on the Violin Concerto's third movement provided the one oasis of sanity. The movement was finished within a week of the conference, and the fourth movement finale was completed in March. Indeed, there is a parallel here with 1936. When "Muddle Instead of Music" hit the streets, Shostakovich was in the midst of his Fourth Symphony. Yet, he had soldiered defiantly and uncompromisingly on, completing the Symphony with no concession to *Pravda's* "words of wisdom." Now, twelve years later, he would again emerge from the surrounding noise artistically undimmed. All brooding introspection and barbed wit, the Violin Concerto was pure Shostakovich. As for the composer's skill at verbal doublespeak, this too remained undimmed; asked shortly after the February resolution what the Concerto was going to be "about," he told Shepilov (then deputy head of Agitprop), that it was about "the preparation for the spring sowing campaign."[31] The

Violin Concerto would be the first of four works composed between 1948 and 1952 that would not receive their premieres until after the death of Stalin in 1953.

Unlike Shostakovich's previous concertante work, the First Piano Concerto, the Violin Concerto was symphonic in conception—almost a symphony with violin obbligato. Its unusual four-movement format was maybe an attempt to adapt a symphonic model to a concerto setting; with its slow-fast-slow-fast ordering, the Fifth Symphony in particular comes to mind. Also unusual is the absence of cadenzas within movements. Instead, a single long cadenza forms the bridge between the third movement and the finale, almost qualifying as its own movement—something Shostakovich would formalize in the First Cello Concerto (1959), where the cadenza would be separately banded. Although it would be a stretch to consider the Violin Concerto a one-movement work, the placement of the cadenza about three-quarters of the way through the Concerto reflects the placement that one would expect to find within an individual movement. And it is not just its location that marks it as a "global" cadenza. Its content too is global, featuring themes from all four movements.

This was Shostakovich's first concerto involving anything like a full orchestra, although even here certain idiosyncrasies obtain. There are no trumpets. Even more unusually, the score includes tuba while omitting trombones, an idiosyncrasy it shares with another famous Russian violin concerto, Prokofiev's First. As a result, tutti climaxes take on a distinctive hollowness compared to Shostakovich's middle-period symphonic scores, though the sound is still recognizable as Shostakovich. In general, the woodwinds and horns have the lion's share of the dialogue with the solo violin; the orchestral strings are less melodic, more accompanimental. Particularly distinctive is a contrabassoon-dominated woodwind combination, where that instrument (in conjunction with bassoons and/or bass clarinet) combines with either oboes or clarinets in their middle-to-higher register, creating a distinctive sonority that is at once gruff and sour (e.g., first movement, Fig. 5, and scherzo, Fig. 29), a sonority not so frequently encountered in the symphonies. These characteristics would carry over into the Second Violin Concerto (1967) and both Cello Concertos (1959, 1966), all of which eschew trumpets and lower brass, and all of which take advantage of that peculiar contrabassoon-dominated wind sound. In other words, like many nineteenth- and twentieth-century composers, Shostakovich conceived a somewhat different orchestral palette for his concertos than for his symphonies.

The bleak first movement "Nocturne" presents two parallel melodic strains. The first, in the low strings, launches the movement; the second, in the solo violin, enters four bars later. The latter adds a touch of lyricism to the austere intervallic quest of the former, but essentially the two strains form an evenly matched counterpoint. If the Fifth Symphony was in fact a model for the Concerto, the Symphony's first movement seems to have inspired certain processes in the "Nocturne." The low string opening is a rhythmic variant of the Symphony's low string dotted figure and even preserves its first pitches, that favorite Shostakovich head motif—scale degrees 1, flat-6, 5. And, as in the Symphony, this opening music functions as a ritornello, binding together the disparate sections of the movement's first subject area. It reappears at Fig. 3, b2 (with a "preview" at Fig. 3); at Fig. 5, b2; and can be heard at Fig. 1, b6 embedded in the solo melody, in effect binding the two strands of that opening two-part counterpoint even closer together. Such embedding is also to be found in the Symphony (see Chapter 13).

The Fifth Symphony's influence continues into the second subject. In both works, the new theme emerges in the Neapolitan—B-flat (predominantly major) to the Concerto's A minor tonic, E-flat minor to the Symphony's D minor tonic. In both cases, the new key is flagged early in their respective movements with the initial chromatic pitch of the respective first subjects—the B-flat in the solo violin (Fig. 1, b2) in the Concerto, the E-flat in the first violins (Fig. 1, b2) in the Symphony. And in both cases, despite this early telegraphing of the new key, the actual modulation does not occur until the last minute following a return—a tonal ritornello, so to speak—to the movement's tonic (Fig. 5, b7 in the Concerto; Fig. 8 in the Symphony), though in this respect the Concerto's four-bar transition is not quite as abrupt as the Symphony's one-note, instant modulation.

Although the poignant entrance of the second subject in a translucent B-flat major registers as new, the theme soon begins to accumulate attributes, especially rhythmic, of earlier themes. And with the fast evaporation of the major-key translucence, we are quickly plunged back into the darker world of the exposition's first half. The only extended area of contrast is the codetta, which is based on the second subject but with rarified quartal harmony (Fig. 11) and otherworldly sonorities—that favorite Shostakovich doubling of celesta with harp harmonics (Fig. 12, b5), and the "late period" polarized scoring of double basses versus violins and violas (Fig. 13).

Following a short development, in which the second subject material is intensified along with a triplet figure from the codetta, the recapitulation, like that of the Fifth Symphony, emerges in stages, beginning with a reversal of the movement's opening two-part counterpoint: at Fig. 17, b7, the violin reintroduces the original low string ritornello; at Fig. 18, the double basses intone the violin's opening melody from Fig. 1. At only five bars long, this area of first subject reprise is even shorter than its Fifth Symphony counterpart, and its transitional nature even more pronounced.

If the first movement owes its construction to that of the Fifth Symphony, the biting, sardonic second movement scherzo in B-flat minor (another manifestation of the Neapolitan relationship) recalls the scherzo of the Sixth. It may not be as tonally mercurial, but its tempo and rhythmic carriage are similar, and its distinctive opening flute and bass clarinet duo are reminiscent of a similar passage in the Sixth (Fig. 68). Structurally, it is modeled after the scherzos of the First, Fourth, Sixth, and Eighth Symphonies—scherzo, trio, scherzo reprise incorporating in its later stages elements of the trio, and coda. However, it is thematically more prolific than those earlier examples, with the main scherzo incorporating an initial theme in B-flat minor, a second area in the Neapolitan, B major (Fig. 33; often misidentified as a transposed version of Shostakovich's DSCH monogram), and a third area back in B-flat minor (Fig. 37). Add to that the klezmer-like trio in a modally flattened E minor (Fig. 42) plus the fact that the opening theme turns out to be two themes working in tandem—the aforementioned woodwind duo and a violin accompaniment—and this scherzo becomes the bearer of no fewer than five main themes.

This thematic generosity reaches its full potential at the reprise, a double fugue drawing in several of the movement's primary and subsidiary ideas. The idea of fugue-as-recapitulation is still more unusual than the fugue-as-development found in the Third Quartet's first movement, though fugal elements had been found in the reprise of the Fourth Symphony's scherzo. Yet, this double fugue could perhaps be viewed simply as the natural expansion of the two-part "invention" texture at the start of the movement, or even as Shostakovich's answer to the eighteenth-century culminating fugue. It ends with a dizzying, one-beat-apart, three-voiced stretto on the scherzo's opening woodwind idea (Fig. 62).

Following the fugue are short reprises of the "klezmer" theme (Fig. 65) and the "misidentified DSCH" idea (Fig. 66, b7 and Fig. 67). However, the pitch structure of the latter is now modified to render what is generally considered Shostakovich's first DSCH quotation, albeit in transposed form—starting on F-sharp at Fig. 66, b7, and on A-flat at Fig. 67. Crowning the contrapuntal *tour de force*, the movement's coda is a short two-part canon (Fig. 68).

The plundering of eighteenth-century soil continues with the third movement passacaglia (see Chapter 15 for further discussion). Here, the violin grieves more openly than in the first movement, and the relationship between it and the ground bass creates an altogether different kind of tension to the first movement, where the violin was concerned less with "pulling away" from the bass line than with contrapuntally weaving with it. The stentorian horn fanfares that open the passacaglia return at the end, now hushed in the solo violin. Growing out of this is the cadenza, a five-minute process of gradual unfolding and acceleration, taking in the opening of the first movement (cadenza bars 19–21), a foretaste of one of the finale themes (bars 51–62 and 72–76), another transposed DSCH motif (double-stop starting on C-sharp and E, respectively, bars 77–78), and a reference to the scherzo's opening (bars 85–88). It climaxes with a ringing quotation of the scherzo's "klezmer" theme (bars 98–100), after which an ever-accelerating series of scale passages whips up momentum for the *burlesca* finale, which follows *attacca*.

Reportedly described by Shostakovich as reflecting the "joy of a man who has just been released from a concentration camp"[32]—a far cry indeed from the "spring sowing campaign" line that he had given to Shepilov—the rowdy finale is cast in that favorite form of Classical-period concerto finales, the sonata-rondo. Yet, even this, the most stylized of Classical forms, falls under the spell of Shostakovich's symphonism. The start of the recapitulation (Fig. 102), for example, not only continues to wrestle with ideas from the development, i.e., the unsettling, chromatically serpentine bass ostinato, it also contorts the bright opening melody (E–A–B–A) into something that is both darker (E–A–B-flat–A, distilling the Concerto's previous assortment of Phrygian/Neapolitan relationships) and, with triple meter replacing duple meter, more akin to a wild *danse macabre*. Meanwhile, at the height of the development (Fig. 100), the passacaglia ground is brought back, another favorite Shostakovich device. But unlike other places where this happens, the Sixth or Tenth Quartets for example, the intent here seems satirical—the ground squawked out in a two-part canon involving high clarinets, horn, and xylophone. Later, a manically brutalized version of the ground in the violin opens the *Presto* coda (Fig. 107). Only in the coda's final lap (Fig. 109, b9) does the ground, pealing in the horns over the rest of the orchestra, regain something of its former dignity.

***

A few weeks after the Concerto's completion, Shostakovich found himself immersed in a newly published volume of translated Jewish (Yiddish) traditional folk songs.[33] By August 1948, he had set eight of its poems for soprano, contralto, tenor, and piano, and by the start of October, the cycle *From Jewish Folk Poetry* was orchestrated. Later that month, three more songs were added, although apparently not orchestrated,[34] creating an eleven-movement work: "Lament for a Dead Infant"; "Fussy Mummy and Auntie"; "Lullaby"; "Before a Long Separation"; "The Warning"; "The Abandoned Father"; "Song of Want"; "Winter"; "The Good Life"; "The Young Girl's Song"; "Happiness."

From Jewish Folk Poetry would constitute Shostakovich's most substantial exploration of the Jewish folk-musical idiom. With its use of Jewish modes, klezmer "oom-pah" accompaniments, and iambic primes (see Chapter 7 for explanations), the result is a typically Jewish fusion of dance and *lamento*. Yet, reflecting his approach to modes in general, Shostakovich's treatment of the Jewish modes would prove to be somewhat eclectic. The aforementioned "klezmer" theme in the Violin Concerto's scherzo, for instance, is not actually based on klezmer modes at all (see below). In fact, in all three "Jewish" works of the period—the Concerto, the song cycle, and the Fourth Quartet (1949)—the border between Jewish modes and Shostakovich's own characteristic modal preferences is remarkably fluid; the following examples should be read more as a series of representative observations than a list of categories or definitions.

1. **Pure Jewish modes**. Rare, but can be found in bars 14–16 of "Lullaby" (A-flat *freygish*) or between Figs. 97 and 98 towards the end of the Fourth Quartet (D *freygish* with one brief chromatic moment at Fig. 97, b5).

2. **Mixed Jewish modes**. For example, the introduction of an altered Dorian element (raised fourth) into what is otherwise a *freygish* melody, as in first half of the coda of "A Young Girl's Song" (A–B-flat–C-sharp–D-sharp–E–F–G). Such mixtures are often found in authentic klezmer music.

3. **Introduction of Jewish elements into Western modes**. For example, the insertion of an altered Dorian element (raised fourth) into a Phrygian melody during the introduction and opening line of "Lullaby," or in the introduction to "A Young Girl's Song" (in both cases C–D-flat–E-flat–F-sharp–G–A-flat). This particular scale will often employ the raised seventh, e.g., the highly charged duo lament in bars 11–14 et

seq. of "Fussy Mummy and Auntie" (E-flat–F-flat–G-flat–A–B-flat–C-flat–D), or a similar passage towards the end of the Fourth Quartet (D–E-flat–?–G-sharp–A–B-flat–C-sharp; Fig. 96–Fig. 96, b6). The raised seventh doubles the potential for "Jewishness" because the resultant mode now contains two of the highly characteristic augmented second intervals (between the third and fourth and between the sixth and seventh degrees). Neither of the abovementioned examples really takes advantage of this, but the similarly constructed melody that introduces "The Warning" does.

4. **Western modes mixed with Shostakovich-style modal alterations, creating pseudo-Jewish colorings**. Particularly prevalent is the Phrygian mode colored with Shostakovich's beloved lowered fourth, where the "Jewishness" arises from the augmented second between the fourth and fifth degrees. For example, the opening two bars of "Lament for a Dead Infant" (B–C–D–E-flat–F-sharp–G); or the first appearance of the "klezmer" theme in the First Violin Concerto's scherzo (Fig. 42; E–F–G–A-flat–B). In the third and fourth bars of the latter, Shostakovich further colors the mode by introducing the lowered fifth (B-flat), oscillating with the "real" fifth (B-natural). In another fabricated mode, the top half of a natural minor scale is attached to the bottom half of a major scale, something already observed in the Seventh Symphony (see Chapter 7). For example, the first ten bars of "Fussy Mummy and Auntie" (E-flat–F–G–A-flat–B-flat–C-flat–D–D-flat); or the reprise of the Concerto's "klezmer" theme, this time with an oscillating seventh (Fig. 65; B-flat–?–D–E-flat–F–G-flat–A-flat–A-natural).

5. **Harmonic alterations**. For example, the oscillating major/minor third in the accompaniment at the start of "Lullaby," and in bars 25–27; or at the tenor's first entrance in "Before a Long Separation," bars 14-17. As discussed above, the opening of "The Warning" introduces an altered Dorian element (raised fourth) plus a raised seventh into a D Phrygian melody. However, the accompaniment also features the lowered fourth (G-flat) played simultaneously with the raised fourth (G-sharp), creating a tantalizing fusion of Western mode, Jewish coloring, and Shostakovichian predilection (D–E-flat–F–G-flat–G-sharp–A–B-flat–C-sharp). Interestingly, the first six pitches of this collection reveal the first six notes of an octatonic scale, something that would be a frequent occurrence in later Shostakovich.

***

The First Violin Concerto, *From Jewish Folk Poetry*, and the Fourth Quartet (1949) would make the period between late 1947 and 1949 the most musically "Jewish" period in Shostakovich's career. (As a postscript, one could add the F-sharp minor Prelude and Fugue from op. 87 [1950]). We have already noted the factors that had led to the composition of the Second Piano Trio in 1944. But what was the cause of this new intensification of "Jewish" activity?

Zhdanov's calling-to-arms at the Party Central Committee was not the only ominous event of 13 January 1948. Earlier that day had come the news that Solomon Mikhoels had been killed in a car accident in Minsk the previous evening. Although nothing could be proven at the time—it was highly dangerous even to talk about such matters—suspicions of foul play circulated immediately.[35] The Jewish Anti-Fascist Committee (JAC) that Mikhoels had headed up, though originally set up with the government's blessing in 1942 to raise funds for the War effort, had since reinvented itself as a Jewish-rights organization in response to rising post-war anti-Semitism, and had become an increasing thorn in Stalin's side. Mikhoels' daughter, Natalya Vovsi-Mikhoels, reports that at the gathering of mourners at the family apartment on the evening of 13 January ("an endless stream of stunned and frightened people"),[36] "Shostakovich spoke . . . of how 'this' had started with the Jews but would end up with the entire intelligentsia."[37] Only later would the suspicions be confirmed: Mikhoels had indeed been murdered on Stalin's orders, the car accident a staged cover-up.[38]

As discussed in Chapter 7, an official campaign of anti-Semitism had been brewing behind the scenes since 1942. However, the subsequent shutting down of the JAC in November 1948—it was accused of a post-war plot to annex part of the Crimea as an autonomous Jewish republic—followed over the next three months by the arrest of about a hundred of its members plus many other Jewish intellectuals finally brought the campaign out into the open. By February 1949, the stage was set for a full-scale assault against "rootless cosmopolitans," complete with smear campaigns and 1930s-style show trials, culminating in the infamous "Doctors' Plot" of 1952–1953, a fantasy cooked up by a paranoid-delusional Stalin who believed that a group of doctors, mostly Jewish, was conspiring to poison him.

So when, and how, did these events impinge themselves into Shostakovich's consciousness and his music? The first "Jewish" piece of this period was the scherzo of the Violin Concerto. This movement was completed in December 1947, prior to Mikhoels' death. But what may be significant is the quotation of the scherzo's "klezmer" theme in the Concerto's cadenza, composed in January 1948 in the immediate aftermath of the "accident." Although this long cadenza would use material from all four movements, it is the single anguished outburst of the "klezmer" theme towards the end that constitutes its climax, bestowing upon that theme a greater significance than it ever had in the scherzo, where it had been essentially one theme among several.

Was the "klezmer" outburst in the Concerto's cadenza, then, a requiem to Mikhoels? We can only speculate. On the other hand, most writers agree that *From Jewish Folk Poetry*, composed between August and October 1948, was indeed a deliberate act of solidarity with the increasingly persecuted Jewish population and, as such, represented considerable personal risk for the composer. Recently, however, Laurel Fay has argued that since the cycle was composed before the disbanding of the JAC in November and the public unleashing of the anti-Semitic campaign the following February, it could not possibly have been conceived as a reaction or protest. In Fay's opinion, to believe that it was is the result of misreading the chronology of events and/or a late twentieth-century Western desire to mythologize Shostakovich into a more courageous figure than he actually was. Instead, Fay believes that *From Jewish Folk Poetry* was an attempt to answer the Party's call to explore the folk music of the "nationalities," a directive that Shostakovich fulfilled by turning quite naturally and innocently to an ethnic idiom (i.e., Jewish) with which he had already enjoyed success. Fay concludes that it was only with the public explosion of anti-Semitism in February 1949, and with the song cycle already completed, that Shostakovich realized the situation into which he had inadvertently got himself: "It was his rotten luck that of all the available nationalities, great and small, he just happened to pick the wrong 'folk' as his inspiration."[39]

As Fay rightly states, Shostakovich in August could not have foreseen the closure of the JAC in November or the subsequent press hysteria. She is also correct in pointing out that Shostakovich had made no attempt to hide the work and indeed performed it on a number of occasions to private audiences over the final months of 1948. In other words, *From Jewish Folk Poetry* was not composed, as is so often assumed, "for the drawer." Yet, as his above-quoted response to the death of Mikhoels back in January makes unambiguously clear, Shostakovich was certainly not "in the dark" about the official campaign of anti-Semitism that had been ongoing since 1942. And the fact that *From Jewish Folk Poetry* was not written "for the drawer" is, as an explanation of Shostakovich's motives, somewhat misleading. An examination of his behavior with regard to the song cycle shows something rather more complex—determination mingled with apprehension, a mix somewhat reflective of the status of Jewish culture itself during 1948.

Since the War, Jewish culture had been dangling precariously over what Joachim Braun terms the "borderline between the 'permitted' (*de jure*) and the 'anti-Soviet' (*de facto*)."[40] Supporting Jews was always risky, yet Stalin himself had been pretending to do just that throughout much of 1948—the lavish funeral and the official accolades heaped posthumously onto Mikhoels, the recognition in May of the new state of Israel (the Soviet Union was the first country in the world to provide full legal recognition), and the public celebration in September of the arrival of Israel's first ambassador, Golda Meir. In other words, as Braun puts it, "Soviet Jewish culture, although endangered, had not yet been anathematized."[41] Indeed, Stalin's hypocritical fawning may, ironically, have made it slightly easier, even as late as the autumn of 1948, to present a Jewish work, provided of course that it heeded the usual criteria for ethnic music: 1) an accessible, "non-formalist" musical language; and 2) texts that rejected ethnic isolationism and emphasized the happy lives of the nationality in question and their "harmonious," "fraternal" coexistence amongst the peoples of the Soviet Union.

Although the urban folk style of *From Jewish Folk Poetry* would easily satisfy the first criterion, Shostakovich's choice of texts, with their topics of death, exile, anti-Semitism, poverty, and winter, hardly satisfied the second. The first performance was at Shostakovich's birthday party on 25 September 1948, where friends were treated to, in the words of Vovsi-Mikhoels, "what we dared not ever express in conversations."[42] As she describes it, Shostakovich rubbed his hands nervously and announced, "I have here, you might say, some new songs," hardly the image of a man innocently going about the Party's business. Shostakovich's caution, even fear, was understandable, yet his determination to have the cycle publicly performed was just as strong, as was demonstrated by what happened next.

October saw the addition of three songs. The first contrasts the narrator's previous life of poverty and sorrow with his new happy life on the *kolkhoz* (collective farm), the second is a paean to "the beauty of my land," and the final song celebrates the fulfillment of the dreams of a Jewish cobbler's wife. Of course, an optimistic ending to an otherwise tragic work is not in itself unusual and need not betoken insincerity. But here, the added songs seem not quite of a piece with the original eight. There is certainly Jewish inflection to be found in this final group, but it is altogether more diluted. It is particularly striking, for instance, that in the "The Good Life," the only hint of Jewish inflection comes as the narrator recalls the cramped, damp basement in which he once lived. Although Braun perhaps exaggerates the purely musical differences between the original and final groups, his analysis is revealing of the larger aesthetic point:

> The first (1–8) presents genre scenes, the second (9–11) presents pronouncements and slogans; the text of the first is based on folkloric elements and uses folk lexemes, that of the second exploits features of art song and uses the vocabulary of Soviet mass songs; the first uses the dialogue form typical of Jewish folk songs, the second eschews this structure; the first approximates stylized Jewish folk music, with ample use of "speech intonations," while the second reflects a mixture of the conventional *melos* of the Soviet mass song and the Russian art song.[43]

As Braun concludes, "these differences create the sense that these two groups of songs are independent of, indeed alien to, one another."[44] He also points out that where the original volume of poetry used verses about war and labor to make a transition from the initial tragic poems to the final happy ones, Shostakovich's jump from the tragic group to the happy group is as jarring as the stylistic differences between them. All told, then, the motivation behind the "tacked-on" final group would appear to have been more opportunistic than artistic.

Possibly revealing too are the titles of the songs themselves. The autograph score of the orchestral version of the first eight songs, dated 1 October, names each song by its first line, as had the original volume of poems. However, the autograph score of the piano version of all eleven songs, dated 1 August to 24 October, gives each song a new title. Daniil Zhitomirsky refers to a private performance on 18 December, at the end of which was an "animated conversation and collective devising of new names for the songs."[45] Given that the titles by which we now know the songs (listed above) are consistent with those found in the autograph piano score completed on 24 October, it would seem either that any new names devised in December did not in the end supersede those created in October or that Zhitomirsky was mistaken and that this "collective devising of new names" in fact took place in October. The point, however, is that the new titles may have constituted yet another ploy to increase the cycle's acceptability—firstly by making them less Jewish sounding ("Oi, Abram!" becomes "Before the Separation"; "My Sheindl is in bed" becomes "Winter"), and secondly by making more explicit the "fraternal" spirit of that later group ("Oh, open fields" becomes "The Good Life"; "I boldly took my husband's arm" becomes "Happiness").

Shostakovich, then, entered 1949 with a work that now went some small way toward fulfilling that second criterion. In a letter dated 22 January, he told Kara

Karayev of his plan to present it "in about ten days."[46] We do not know if this presentation (presumably at the Composers' Union) took place, but the explosion of anti-Semitism in February would in any case have scotched further progress; *From Jewish Folk Poetry* would not be publicly aired until 1955. Nevertheless, Shostakovich's introduction of damage-limitation measures in the autumn of 1948 does not square with someone who realized only in February 1949 that he had picked the "wrong folk." That he desired a way out of his dire personal situation in 1948 is not in question. And the fact that for much of that year a work based on Jewish folk themes, although dangerous, could under certain conditions have satisfied the Party's "nationalities" directive may very well have crossed his mind. But there is no evidence to suggest that the fulfillment of that directive was the driving force. If it were, it is unlikely that he would have so blatantly rejected one of the directive's two prime requirements, only "correcting" himself later, and not very convincingly, with the "fraternalist" poems, afterthoughts in every sense of the word. Much later, Shostakovich would face a similar situation with the Thirteenth Symphony, and would again choose the same path, accepting a compromised version of Yevtushenko's "Babi Yar" text so that a vital political document might survive.

***

The other work of the period that would lay dormant until after Stalin's death was the Fourth Quartet, written between April and December 1949, but not premiered until December 1953. As Laurel Fay points out, even without its "Jewish" finale, penned as the anti-Semitic campaign was reaching new heights, the elitist stigma now attached to the string quartet medium itself made the work's "for the drawer" status virtually a foregone conclusion, something confirmed when the Beethoven Quartet presented it at the Committee for Artistic Affairs in May 1950.[47] Interestingly, the cellist Valentin Berlinsky recalls the Borodin Quartet performing the work at the Ministry of Culture, the post-1953 successor to the Committee for Artistic Affairs, for the purpose, successful as it would turn out, of securing a commission and fee for Shostakovich.[48]

The 1960s would see a move away from full sonata structures in the opening movements of Shostakovich's quartets. Those of the Seventh, Ninth, and Tenth, for example, are all written in sonatina form (sonata form without development). Also in sonatina form, the opening movement of the Fourth Quartet foreshadows this move, although one idiosyncrasy here is that neither the exposition nor the recapitulation contains much in the way of a secondary area. The movement opens, as do many of Shostakovich's quartets, with a rather classical sounding melody with the occasional chromatic inflection. As it expands both dynamically and chromatically, it pulls ever harder against a tonic (D) drone in the viola and cello, a drone that plays non-stop for sixty-four bars. In fact, the first area could be said to be made up entirely of a sixty-four-bar prolongation of the opening D major harmony, an idea that seems more Wagnerian than Shostakovichian, though in fact it is closely related to the recitative style that so preoccupied Shostakovich earlier in the decade—the same chromatic weaving around a pedal, though now metered and propelled.

Following a short transition (Fig. 8), the movement's secondary area, such as it is, functions more as a codetta and retransition. Starting in B minor (Fig. 9), the graceful triple meter second subject glides into E minor eleven bars later. However, the E pedal that is set down in the viola and cello at this point becomes the new accompanying drone for the reprise of the first theme back in the tonic, D major (Fig. 10, b3). The recapitulation explores the same thematic material as the exposition, but the replacement of the tonic-D drone with the supertonic E casts a disturbing shadow. Meanwhile, the melody itself is recast from duple into triple meter (a hangover from the exposition's second subject) and from the major mode to the Phrygian. Interestingly, these are the same three modifications—the introduction of a dissonant drone, the change to triple meter, and the modal flattening—that were heard at the recapitulation of the Violin Concerto's finale; individually, these modifications can be heard elsewhere in Shostakovich's output.

Dominated by violin cantilena, the second movement takes us back to the world of the Second Quartet's "Romance." Its lyricism can almost be viewed as a flowering of what had been the very short second subject area of the previous movement. Meanwhile, the insistent two-quarter note ostinato accompaniment (on beats one and two) is reminiscent of the Violin Concerto's passacaglia ground bass. When the opening theme returns (Fig. 30), it is harmonized in B-flat rather than F minor, despite laying at the same melodic pitch level, and thus creates, albeit very briefly, a typically Shostakovichian moment of disorientation at the start of this reprise.

The lyricism continues into the third movement scherzo. Although the opening is Shostakovichian in its rhythmic pointedness and its flat-fourth and flat-second nudging, and although the trio is in part propelled by his favorite dactylic rhythm, the movement as a whole is gentler than usual for a Shostakovich scherzo, an impression reinforced by the use of muted strings throughout, as well as by those moments of pure melody, such as the two-octave "unison" for first violin, viola, and cello at Fig. 39, where explicit harmonic tension and rhythmic ostinato are temporarily suspended.

The transition to the finale is provided by a chant-like viola soliloquy. Each phrase is based on a modally flattened C (in one case lowering every scale degree except for the C), with each arriving on the tonic C "resting tone." However, each arrival onto the tonic is differently harmonized—C major (Fig. 54, b9), C minor (Fig. 55), A-flat major (Fig. 55, b5), and finally A minor (Fig. 56 et seq.)—each chord providing its own *tinta* to the resting tone. Again, we can hear the influence of the Shostakovichian recitative, with its modal melodic weaving around the scherzo's tonic pitch, C. The A minor harmony to which the final phrases gravitate provides the pivot for the modulation to the finale's tonic, D. At the climax of the finale's development, the soliloquy returns as an impassioned unison statement, rerunning the modulation from C to D as a preparation for the recapitulation.

Two of the modes from the latter part of this "Jewish" finale have been discussed above. However, the initial presentation of the "Jewish" theme (Fig. 58) is, for its first eleven bars, written in a pure Dorian mode, its Jewish connotation emerging only through the "oom-pah" accompaniment and iambic primes. It is not until the twelfth bar that Shostakovich introduces two Jewish modal colorings: the descending harmonic minor scale (Fig. 58, b12–13) which, though not itself a Jewish mode, contains the characteristically Jewish augmented second; and the raised fourth indicative of the Jewish altered Dorian mode (Fig. 59, b6–7).

This "Jewish" finale could be said to represent a two-fold culmination. Locally, it is a natural outgrowth of the recitative-inspired first movement—as Judy Kuhn has pointed out, there is a connection between the chromatic inflections of Shosta-kovich's recitatives and those of the Jewish modes, and the "pseudo-recitative" lines that tug against the pedal drone in the Quartet's first movement are certainly a case in point.[49] Globally, the finale represents the culmination of Shostakovich's "Jewish" period, whether defined as a two-year span taking in the First Violin Concerto and *From Jewish Folk Poetry* or as a five-year span beginning with the *Rothschild's Violin* completion and the Second Piano Trio. And with its translu-cent, *morendo*, major-key close, the Fourth Quartet's journey ends in much the same way as the Trio's—a shaky glimmer of hope following a bittersweet Jewish journey.

***

With the Cultural Revolution of 1928–1932 and the *Pravda* attacks of 1936, Shostakovich had learned to master the art of dual personality in the cause of sur-vival. But nowhere was the "two Shostakovich" syndrome more pronounced than in the years following the 1948 purges. With the First Violin Concerto, *From Jew-ish Folk Poetry*, and the Fourth Quartet all consigned to, if not having been written for, "the drawer," Shostakovich's premieres over the next few years would be re-stricted, with the notable exception of the Twenty-Four Preludes and Fugues, to films and choral works, mostly of a political nature. These were the necessary articles of "atonement." Politically and economically, they were essential to his survival.

Two such works were composed in 1949, the oratorio *The Song of the Forests* and the score to one of the most outrageously hagiographic films in the history of cinema, Mikhail Chiaureli's *The Fall of Berlin*. The former was a celebration of Stalin's grandiose plan to afforest the Russian Steppes, the latter a fictitious story of how Stalin conquered Berlin at the end of the War (see Chapter 17 for discus-sion of the film). Both featured nauseatingly obsequious libretti by Yevgeny Dolmatovsky.

Shostakovich detested the oratorio's texts ("If Stalin said 'It will be,' we'll answer the leader, 'It is'") but was able to don the requisite folk-lyrical style, a testament to his professionalism. Admittedly, its Stalinist associations make fair evaluation almost impossible. Yet, although hardly first-rate Shostakovich, as an example of a neo-romantic choral ballad, it is musically well crafted, melodically appealing and, as Myaskovsky noted, superior to the dozens of other similar works that were being churned out at around this time.[50] This, though, could hardly have been any consolation to Shostakovich. According to Galina Ustvolskaya, "After the premiere ... we went to the hotel Evropeiskaya, where he was living at the time, and he started sobbing with his face in a pillow.[51]

The following year saw the predictable pay-off. Both the film, for which Shosta-kovich had provided an appropriately tub-thumping score, and the oratorio were awarded Stalin Prizes (First Class). Yet, in the spring of 1949, before composition had started on either work, the process of rehabilitation through public recan-tation had already got underway, and in an international arena. Between 25 and 27 March, the Cultural and Scientific Congress for World Peace was held at the Waldorf-Astoria Hotel in New York. As a member of the Soviet delegation, Shos-takovich duly delivered "his" indictment of American policies as well as his thanks for the Party's guidance and criticisms: "The criticism brings me much good. It helps me bring my music forward."[52]

Shostakovich had been a reluctant participant. In February, he had refused Molo-tov's request to join the delegation, but his name was placed on the list anyway. On 7 March, he appealed for help, partly on health grounds, asking that Nina be allowed to accompany him in the event that he would be required to make the trip.[53] That the trip was by this point a foregone conclusion can perhaps be gauged by a secret memo dated 10 March, warning against performing the Eighth and Ninth Symphonies in the USA and rejecting Shostakovich's suggestion for a concert with the Beethoven Quartet (the Piano Quintet, Second Piano Trio, and a string quartet) due to the political "unreliability" of certain of its members. The Fifth and Seventh Symphonies, the suite from *The Young Guard*, and a selection of songs were recommended instead.[54] When Shostakovich received the famous phone call from Stalin on 16 March,[55] he again objected, telling Stalin that he could not legitimately represent the Soviet Union abroad while his works languished unperformed at home, and that in any case he was physically not up to the journey. That same day, Stalin rescinded the repertoire ban of February 1948 and restored to Shostakovich and his family access to the Kremlin Hospital, a privilege that had been removed following the 1948 Resolution.[56] And Shostakovich went to America.

Stalin's decision to lift the ban was revealing. For all his hatred of the West, he still fretted about his image there. Shostakovich, meanwhile, had demonstrated his own power. Although the phone call itself was highly stressful—he later recalled how he had "imagined with horror" the questions with which he would be bombarded in the USA, and how he had "blurted out" to Stalin that he was sick—his objections had clearly registered.[57] We do not know whether Stalin' s lifting of the ban was a direct result of the phone call, or whether he had already decided on this in advance. Either way, despite the fact that the American trip was probably unavoidable, Shostakovich had realized its potential as leverage, a lesson that would prove useful in the future.

Ironically, though the lifting of the repertoire ban came directly from Stalin, performing institutions would be slow to re-embrace works that had been so recently condemned; the Eighth Symphony, for example, would have to wait another seven years to be performed. In fact, the fear that had spread throughout the musical community was such that even works not banned by Glavrepertkom had been largely shunned. A memo drawn up by the Committee for Artistic

Affairs on 5 March, less than two weeks before Stalin's call, would reaffirm the list of banned works from the previous year. But it also made a point of listing works approved for performance (First and Second Quartets, Second and Third Symphonies, Second Piano Trio) as well as those considered Shostakovich's "finest" (First, Fifth, and Seventh Symphonies, Piano Quintet, plus unspecified film scores and songs).[58] Khrennikov's aforementioned rant against the Seventh Symphony would seem not to have affected the official view of the work as one of Shostakovich's "finest."

The trip itself gave Shostakovich his first experience of celebrity American-style. For the publicly diffident, camera-shy composer, this would have been a traumatic experience even without the heavy political baggage that he was shouldering. His stock in America may have fallen a bit since those heady days when conductors were fighting to premiere the Seventh Symphony and his face stared out of the front cover of *Time* magazine, but "Shosty" was still the most recognized and feted of the Soviet delegates. The then head of the Writers' Union, Alexander Fadeyev, noted that a drugstore where the composer had stopped to buy aspirin quickly put up a "Dmitry Shostakovich shops here" sign in its window.[59] Shostakovich's celebrity status was sealed at the Congress' close, when he performed the scherzo of his Fifth Symphony on the piano in front of 18,000 people at Madison Square Garden.

But not all was plain sailing. Each day saw anti-Soviet protesters outside the hotel. Stravinsky, resident in California, famously snubbed the event by refusing to sign a telegram of welcome: "Regret not to be able to join welcomers of Soviet artists coming [sic] this country. But all my ethic and esthetic convictions oppose such gesture."[60] When asked if he would agree to a debate with Shostakovich, he replied: "How can you talk to them? They are not free. There is no discussion in public with people who are not free."[61] Following the Congress, the Soviet delegation, which had been scheduled to participate in other activities, was summarily sent home by order of the US State Department.

At the sessions, Shostakovich was his typically nervous, twitchy self. The composer Nicolas Nabokov reports:

> I watched his hands twist the cardboard tips of his cigarettes, his face twitch and his whole posture express intense unease. While his Soviet colleagues on the right and left looked calm and as self-contented as mantelpiece Buddahs, his sensitive face looked disturbed, hurt and terribly shy. I felt … that he wanted to have it over with as quickly as possible, and that he was out of place in this crowded room of rough, angry people, that he was not made for public appearances, for meetings, for "peace missions." … When after several trying and ludicrous speeches, his turn came to speak he began to read his prepared talk in a nervous and shaky voice. After a few sentences he broke off and the speech was continued in English by a suave radio baritone.[62]

The crowning moment came when Nabokov, a virulently anti-Soviet émigré and friend of Stravinsky, asked if "he, personally, the composer Shostakovich, not the delegate of Stalin's Government, subscribed to the wholesale condemnation of

Western music as it has been expounded daily by the Soviet Press and as it appeared in the official pronouncements of the Soviet Government."[63] As Nabokov knew only too well, there was no way that Shostakovich was going to divorce in public his personal opinions from those of the Party. Shostakovich replied that he did indeed denounce those who, like himself, had deviated down the path of formalism. Many have criticized Nabokov for unnecessarily humiliating an already broken man. Some have accused him of being a Stravinsky plant. Nabokov himself claims that he had no choice; he did it not to humiliate the "wretched" Shostakovich but to expose the entire event for the fraud that it was.

***

The Song of the Forests, *The Fall of Berlin*, and the ritual atonement in New York helped Shostakovich's rehabilitation over the course of 1949. In what was a mixed blessing, the next few years saw the resumption of many of the duties that the events of 1948 had forced him to relinquish, not to mention the acquisition of some new ones. In 1949, he was placed on the organizing committee for Stalin's seventieth birthday; in 1950, he was named to the Soviet Committee for the Defense of Peace. Altogether happier was a trip to East Germany in July 1950 to participate in the events commemorating the bicentennial of Bach's death. In Leipzig, he served on the jury of the First International Bach Competition, where he was particularly taken with the winner, Tatyana Nikolayeva. Her performances would inspire him to embark upon a cycle of twenty-four preludes and fugues that October.

The culmination of a decade-long exploration of eighteenth-century forms, the Twenty-Four Preludes and Fugues, op. 87, was also a catharsis for Shostakovich. As he told his former student Yury Levitin: "I have decided to start working again, so as not to lose my qualifications as a composer. I am going to write a prelude and a fugue every day. I shall take into consideration the experience of Johann Sebastian Bach."[64] The cleansing power of the first C major prelude—what David Fanning has called "a return to the musical womb"—is intensely moving, and it is possibly not a coincidence that Shostakovich's Haydnesque First Quartet, which also followed a period of trauma, was written in that same cleansing key.[65] At the Composers' Union discussion in May 1951, Shostakovich declared that it was not necessary to perform the entire cycle from beginning to end, arguing that "it might even harm the work, as it is indeed difficult to comprehend."[66] In his own performances, he usually played groups of four or six Preludes and Fugues. (A discussion of op. 87 appears in Chapter 14.)

That discussion would prove as traumatic as any Shostakovich had to endure. He was blasted for regressing back into formalism after the promising signs of *The Song of the Forests*. Kabalevsky reportedly described op. 87 as a "grave miscalculation," and theorist Sergei Skrebkov called it "ugly." Nikolayeva and the pianist Mariya Yudina defended it, with Yudina attacking the "armchair theoreticians" for their stereotyped and shallow criticisms. Responding to the charge that Shostakovich had fallen into his old satirical habits, she thundered: "If indeed there are . . . instances of caricature, tell me what's wrong with that? Maybe some of us deserve to be caricatured. And indeed life is far richer and more varied than the recipe provided by Comrade Skrebkov. He couldn't even write a single prelude and fugue."[67] Throughout the ordeal, reportedly, Shostakovich sat hunched over, his head sometimes hanging between his knees. In the end, op. 87 was neither banned nor encouraged. Individual preludes and fugues were performed throughout 1951. In 1952, Nikolayeva presented the cycle at the Committee for Artistic Affairs, this time to a more positive reception, and at the end of that year, she gave its public premiere.

***

Although the period between 1948 and 1953 saw the starkest polarization between Shostakovich's serious music and his works of political atonement, there was one work that, possibly, was able to bridge that gaping chasm. Composed in early 1951, *Ten Poems on Texts by Revolutionary Poets* was a tribute to the aborted uprising of 1905. Scored for chorus *a cappella*, a first for Shostakovich, this underrated work shows a remarkable mastery of forces. Possibly the absence of an orchestra freed him to explore the individuality of the choir; his treatment of, say, the second song, Yevgeny Tarasov's "One of Many," demonstrates a level of polyphonic freedom comparable to the string quartets and a flair for dramatic vocal characterization of which the composer of *Belshazzar's Feast* might have been proud. The settings also display a uniquely Russian approach to choral sound— something of the sort had been heard in the Second and Third Symphonies. The work would occupy a special place in Shostakovich's heart; he was particularly sensitive to criticisms made against it.[68] It was awarded a Stalin Prize, though its Second Class ranking seems ironic, if hardly unexpected, in the light of the First Class ranking given to *The Song of the Forests*.

This new choral mastery was partly a matter of maturity, but was perhaps also inspired by the texts themselves. With their themes of tyranny and oppression, these pre-Revolutionary poems, written between 1870 and 1917, struck a far more responsive note with Shostakovich than the banal, hagiographic lines of Bezymensky, Kirsanov, or Dolmatovsky. But although these texts from Revolutionary history were politically unimpeachable, in an era when the achievements of Stalin were being exalted over those of the ever-more distant and dispensable Lenin, there was perhaps something slightly seditious about their use. With its references to human rights and murderous tyrants, *Ten Poems* makes a striking statement, sandwiched as it is between *The Song of the Forests* and *The Fall of Berlin* on the one side, and the cantata *The Sun Shines over Our Motherland* (1952) and Chiaureli's Stalinist propaganda film *The Unforgettable 1919* (1951) on the other. Drawing on a previous era of Russian history, Shostakovich would rely on his audience to draw the appropriate latter-day inferences. Six years later, he would adopt the same strategy in the Eleventh Symphony, whose second movement was based musically on the sixth of the *Ten Poems*, Arkady Kots' "9 January."

If the *Ten Poems* was the high point en route to Shostakovich's rehabilitation— an outwardly politically correct text set to high quality music—the low point was undoubtedly his 1952 cantata *The Sun Shines over Our Motherland*, based once again on a text of Dolmatovsky. With its military and industrial imagery ("The proletarians fought for their cause—it was their last and decisive battle"; "We decorate the country with gigantic construction sites ... Electric power stations grow up along Russian rivers as lighthouses of the great truth."),[69] Shostakovich's pale and banal score matched Dolmatovsky's text cliché for cliché, with its predictable "stirring" marches, its saccharine children's chorus, and its quasi-religious fervor. In fact, the cantata proved so dismal that even the likes of Ivan Dzerzhinsky could muster little enthusiasm.[70]

***

Written concurrently with *The Sun Shines over Our Motherland*, but standing in stark opposition to it, was the Fifth Quartet, completed in November 1952. Like its predecessor, it would not be aired until after Stalin's death. However, where the Fourth Quartet looked forward to Shostakovich's quartet style of the late 1950s and early 1960s (e.g., in its use of a sonatina-form first movement), the Fifth Quartet would return to the symphonic style of the Second and Third. Indeed, it would represent the culmination of that particular type of Shostakovich quartet.

In comparison with the Fourth Quartet's first movement, whose exposition was essentially the single-minded pursuit of the opening theme and a prolongation of its tonic harmony, the exposition of the Fifth's first movement positively bubbles with ideas. This surfeit is matched by the restlessness, particularly rhythmic, of the themes themselves. The opening never quite seems to establish its rhythmic footing; a later subsidiary theme of the first subject area swerves unpredictably from duple to triple pulse (Fig. 6, b3); and most of the second subject and codetta is infected by a Brahmsian two-against-three cross-rhythm. But the real contrast with the Fourth Quartet is the development, omitted entirely in the earlier work. Here, 151 bars of full-fledged intensification prove a match even for the Third Quartet's fugal development. At the climax (Fig. 29), Shostakovich introduces a quotation from the Sonata for Clarinet, Violin, and Piano by Galina Ustvolskaya. The composer's romantic interest in this former student is well known, and the quotation has come in for much commentary.[71] Unlike other quotations of personal significance (for example, DSCH and "Elmira" in the Tenth Symphony—see below), this one is not "framed." Yet, given that that might not have been possible in this restlessly symphonic movement without an unacceptable sapping of momentum, the quotation has still been positioned to be maximally intrusive, as the brutalization of earlier material comes to a head.

The most striking feature of Ustvolskaya's theme is its insistent pitch repetition, the six consecutive quarter-note Ds in its second and third bars, and the eleven Ds a few bars later. It is particularly striking in the context of the quotation, as the violins hammer out Ustvolskaya's obsessively static melody above the turbulent development of Shostakovich's own material. Yet, some of Shostakovich's earlier material also relies on repetition, for example, at Fig. 3. In fact, that particular theme is exploited in the development in the bars leading up to the Ustvolskaya quotation (from Fig. 25); the quotation actually emerges quite naturally from it. Paradoxically, then, Ustvolskaya is both an intrusive force and a logical goal, leading one to wonder to what extent Shostakovich had the quotation in mind when fashioning his exposition material.

In the Fourth Quartet's first movement, we noted the disruption that Shostakovich engineered at the start of the recapitulation. Here in the Fifth, the disruption at the corresponding point is of an altogether higher order, if shorter-lived. Example 8.1a shows the start of the movement, while Example 8.1b shows the start of the recapitulation. In the latter, the viola attempts to reassert its layer of the first subject in the tonic, even setting down the opening tonic note B-flat, something that was originally the cello's responsibility. But the other instruments are uninterested: the violins play their opening material in the wrong key (D-flat, perhaps telegraphing the "wrong" second subject key to follow), while the cello abandons its simple tonic-setting function in favor of double-stopped

Example 8.1a

Example 8.1b

dissonances of uncertain tonal purpose. Add the lurching *crescendi* and the desta-bilizing fourth-beat accents, and it is clear that developmental tensions are still alive and attempting to subvert.

After four bars, the violins and cello drop their subversive games and the tonic is established, at least for long enough to convince us that the recapitulation has, in fact, emerged. Later portions of the recapitulation either divert away from the expected tonic (e.g., the D-flat major rendition of the second subject) or else distort tonality itself where the exposition had been tonally clear (compare, for instance, Fig. 35 with Fig. 1). In fact, B-flat major is never convincingly established again until just before the coda.

With that coda comes a return of the Ustvolskaya quotation (Fig. 49), now muted and coy, in the first violin. As the movement winds down, Ustvolskaya gets the last word. However, tensions do not evaporate entirely. The gentle, added-sixth "tonic" pizzicato chords (B-flat–D–F–G) that introduce the quotation (Fig. 48, b4) and then accompany its closure (Fig. 55) shroud the coda in mystery. At the end, the first violin high F that has been hanging in space for twenty-six bars cre-ates a bridge into the next movement, which follows seamlessly on.

Contrasting with the open lyricism of the Fourth Quartet's slow movement, the Fifth's slow movement is bleak and withdrawn. The strings are muted throughout, and Shostakovich uses mostly single and double octave unison textures amongst the three upper instruments to render a cold, wiry sonority. Nowhere is the sense of unease more apparent than at the outset, as the aforementioned violin F, conso-nant to the first movement's B-flat major, refuses initially to resolve into the new B minor environment. And by the time it does resolve to F-sharp several bars later, the tonality has already started to wander. Only in the two interruptive *Andantino* sections is a more lyrical and richly textured style allowed to blossom, though even here the dotted rhythms provide a certain funereal imagery.

At the end of the movement, the high violin F-sharp creates a bridge to the third movement finale, where an even more elaborate, "reverse" version of the process heard at the beginning is played out via a forty-nine-bar-long introductory "dissolve" from B minor back to B-flat major (see Chapter 16). After that long introduction, the finale's *Allegretto* takes off with unexpected insouciance, although the idea of the enigmatic, superficially light-hearted finale to an otherwise restless or even tragic work was by now a familiar one in the Shostakovich *oeuvre*. What such innocence does not prepare the listener for is a development section even more tumultuous than the first movement's. Once again, the Ustvolskaya theme appears at the climax (Fig. 109). In the aftermath, it is treated to its own mini-sec-tion, where it is presented in Shostakovich's "shell-shocked," post-brutalization manner (Fig. 115). Accompanying the quotation is a series of sharp, angry anapes-tic chords in the lower strings (from Fig. 117, b5), which the musicologist Arkady Klimovitsky has speculated spell out the syllables "Mi-tyen-ka," one of the affec-tionate diminutives, along with the more common "Mitya," by which Shostako-vich was known.[72] This speculation has received a mixed reception. David Fanning, although he does not explicitly endorse it, does accept it as a possibility[73]; Elizabeth Wilson finds it a bit "far fetched."[74] If true, however, the autobiographical significance of combining an angry Shostakovich with a withdrawn, fragile Ustvolskaya becomes obvious.

As in the first movement, the recapitulation here emerges gradually. The first theme reappears, disfigured in B Phrygian, from out of the ruins of the Ustvolskaya theme, with the accompaniment skirting around G minor. However, the fact that B Phrygian shares four of its seven scale degrees (C, D, G, and A) with the expected B-flat major results, ironically, in a melody whose very disfigurations offer the way back. If the primary pillars of B Phrygian (B, E, and F-sharp) stand in defiance of the attempted tonic, those secondary members (C, D, G, and A) pull the music back down "from within." Tonally, this gradual emergence of B-flat from out of the jaws of B Phrygian can be viewed as a flashback to the B minor/ B-flat major "dissolve" at the start of the movement, just as the tutti return of the viola soliloquy before the start of the recapitulation in the Fourth Quartet's finale had replayed the tonal progression (C minor to D Dorian) heard at the start of that movement.

The playful *Allegretto* does eventually resume, but the Fifth Quartet ends, like the Third and Fourth Quartets before it, in quiet, poignant resignation.

***

A small but significant diversion for Shostakovich during the genesis of the Fifth Quartet was the *Four Monologues on Verses by Pushkin* for bass and piano, which he composed over a four-day period in October 1952. His previous Pushkin-inspired work, the *Four Pushkin Romances* (1936), had been a vehicle for some political and autobiographical revelations, and the same could possibly be said here too. The first song, "Fragment," although not written in a Jewish idiom, could be viewed as a postscript to *From Jewish Folk Poetry*, with its description of life in the Jewish hut and the fear of the midnight knock at the door. Meanwhile, another familiar Shostakovich *topos*, exile, can be found in the third song, "Deep in Siberia's Mines." Although the title, *Monologues*, may have been used to distinguish it from the earlier *Romances*, it is possible that it was also designed to reflect, as Dorothea Redepenning has suggested, their more declamatory and confessional nature.[75]

Although the cycle does not carry a dedication, Shostakovich gave the manuscript, together with that of the Fifth Quartet, to Ustvolskaya. As Elizabeth Wilson asks, "Would it be fanciful to suppose that the Pushkin monologues came at a time when there was a break (if perhaps only temporary) in Shostakovich's and Ustvolskaya's close sentimental relationship, that the former was banned from the latter's life, sent into exile?"[76] Apropos to this supposition is the fourth song, "Farewell," and the second, "What Does My Name Mean to You?," which bemoans the day when the author's name will be all but forgotten by his once beloved. Wilson further speculates that the idea of "my name" is prefigured in the opening three-note pattern in the piano left hand (E-flat–C–D), a formative manifestation of the DSCH motif that would burst forth a year later in the Tenth Symphony and that also appears, in a hidden form, in the Fifth Quartet (see below).

Several commentators also note a "quotation" of this second song in the first movement of the Symphony. However, although the song (in particular, the piano part) contains similar stepwise writing, also in a moderate triple meter context, this hardly amounts to a quotation. Nevertheless, the very act of prefacing the Tenth Symphony, Shostakovich's first symphonic work in eight years, with the *Four Pushkin Monologues* is possibly significant in that it parallels the prefacing of that other "landmark" symphony, the Fifth (1937), with the *Four Pushkin Romances*.

***

That Shostakovich had not composed a symphony since 1945 was indicative of the crisis that had been brought on by the 1948 Resolution. It was becoming clear that the emphasis on cantatas and oratorios, a direct result of the Resolution, was backfiring, as evidenced by the dismal achievements of even the best composers. In February 1953, three months after the ill-received premiere of *The Sun Shines over Our Motherland*, Party-line musicologist Georgy Khubov decried the neglect of "monumental, heroic" symphonies.[77] Not only had it been eight years since the last Shostakovich symphony, it had been six years since the last Khachaturian symphony, eleven years for Khrennikov, and nineteen years for Kabalevsky. Only Prokofiev had delivered recently with his Seventh Symphony (1952), though the labels "monumental" and "heroic" do not readily apply there. Khubov was in essence repeating the call that had been heard back in 1932: re-engage with epic genres to reflect the heroism of the age and counter the surfeit of "proletarian" forms. Three months after Khubov's speech, a secret memo was sent to Central Committee member Pyotr Pospelov complaining about the dearth of Soviet opera. It accused Shostakovich of "ideological vacillation" and of lacking the willpower to face the challenge of opera, choosing instead the easier path of cantatas and film scores. It also criticized the Ministry of Culture and the Composers' Union for their lack of guidance.[78]

***

We will probably never be able to fully absorb the scale of emotion that gripped the nation following Stalin's death on 5 March 1953. During his twenty-five year rule, he had achieved mythic status—"Leader and Teacher," "Great Gardener," "Friend of Children," "Friend of the Sciences." He had brought the country into the industrialized twentieth century. He had conquered Nazism. That the patient, smiling, avuncular Stalin—no deranged Hitlerian or Mussolinian rhetoric here— had not just presided over but had actually orchestrated one of the most brutal terror sprees in history was for the man or woman in the street inconceivable, especially since the "culprits" had already been exposed, most famously Stalin's security chief during the Great Terror, Nikolai Yezhov—that period had even become known as the Yezhovshchina. At the news of Stalin's death, the outpouring of grief by ordinary people was genuine. And the sense of denial a few years later, as the crimes of the *vozhd* began to be exposed, just as palpable.

Yet, among those connected to the higher echelons of power, there had always been suspicion. Flora Litvinova described Shostakovich as expressing relief at the dictator's demise, though it was with "no sense of euphoria." He did not trust the new ruling troika of Molotov, Malenkov, and Beriya, and scoffed at Beriya's promised reforms: "How can you believe such deliberate lies. . . . *Beriya*, who personally cut up corpses and flushed them down the toilet, now wants people to believe that he has grown wings."[79] Still, he knew that, ultimately, it was Stalin who had controlled the political and cultural climate. The unveiling on 13 November 1953 of the Fifth Quartet, after a year languishing in the drawer, was a testament to that, as was the premiere the following week (22 November) of the Tenth Symphony. Composed during the summer and autumn of 1953,[80] the Tenth announced Shostakovich's return to symphonic writing. A *grosse Symphonie* of predominantly tragic cut, it emerged as an unequivocal challenge to all that the 1948 Resolution had stood for.

***

Shostakovich's mastery of the quartet medium had evolved out of his symphonic experience. The influence of the Eighth Symphony (1943) on the Second (1944) and Third (1946) Quartets, and the Ninth Symphony (1945) on the Third Quartet have already been noted, and one could perhaps also pair the First Violin Concerto (1948) and Fourth Quartet (1949). The Fifth Quartet and Tenth Symphony form another "pairing," though this time the quartet came first. In fact, 1953 would mark a dividing line in Shostakovich's career: up to this point, he had composed ten symphonies and five quartets; hereinafter, he would pen ten quartets and five symphonies. But let us not overstate this. Although the Tenth Symphony would indeed be profoundly influenced by the Fifth Quartet, it also represents the culmination of the Shostakovich *grosse Symphonie*, perhaps the last great example of its type by any composer, and as such owes at least as much to the Fifth and Eighth Symphonies. And there is certainly nothing chamber-like here; the permeation of Shostakovich's orchestral textures by his chamber style would still be more than a decade away.

Although the Tenth Symphony's first movement represents the culmination of structural processes heard in the first movements of those two earlier symphonies, the musical material could not be more different. Where those earlier works opened with highly "gestural" music, e.g., the imposing dotted rhythms of their respective introductions, or the quasi-operatic line of the Fifth Symphony's first subject (particularly its second strain, Fig. 3), the Tenth Symphony, with its rhythmically undifferentiated and melodically "cooler" opening, does not. David Fanning describes the "non-physical" character of the Tenth Symphony's introduction as "tak[ing] on a virtually archetypal quality—at the most essential level, 'thought.'"[81] These expansive and tonally exploratory opening paragraphs eschew the dramatic "stage setting" of the earlier symphonies, preferring simply to lay down, in a sober but intense way, the essence of the journey to follow.

True to character, the first theme (Fig. 5) "grows out" of the introduction to an even greater extent than in the Fifth and Eighth Symphonies. It is based on the essential features of the introduction—the simple two-voice counterpoint, the unifying pedals, and the stepwise minor third motion—yet at the same time subtly asserts its own identity. It is tonally more settled, and although rhythmically it continues to rely on the introduction's limited collection of quarters, halves, and dotted halves, it shapes these into more lyrical patterns at a slightly more flowing tempo (quarter = 108 instead of 96)—the songlike half-quarter rhythm particularly prevalent. Meanwhile, the introduction's most characteristic rhythmic features—hemiolas, general pauses, and repeated cadential figures—temporarily disappear. And in the context of a highly sensitive movement in which the smallest changes make a difference, the introduction of the clarinet, following 106 bars of purely strings, registers significantly. The second theme (Fig. 17; Example 8.2a) widens the movement's emotional arc a little more with its slinky, muted dance rhythm (the tempo moved up another notch to 120) and its hints of bitonality in the accompaniment, but preserves the minor third motion, now contained within Shostakovich's favorite wedge shape, and brings back the hemiola.

The development, too, has a flavor different from those of the two earlier symphonies, even though its techniques are similar in principle. The process of fragmentation familiar from the earlier works is also at work here, yet we are less aware of it. For instance, at Fig. 35, the Symphony's opening two bars function naturally, almost imperceptibly, as the bass line to the trumpets' intoning of the second subject, as they do again at Fig. 41, though with a different pitch relationship between bass line and melody. When the horns and trumpet enter with an inversion of the movement's opening bar, riding on top of the second subject in the strings and woodwinds, they create a perfectly integrated descant voice (Fig. 41, b4). And whereas in the Fifth and Eighth Symphonies the sense of fragmentation is heightened by the ever-accelerating tempi, with bits of themes flashing past in an increasingly hectic montage, in the Tenth the development is marked at a single tempo (quarter = 108), creating a very different framework for tensions to unfold. Preserving the majesterial triple-meter tread of the movement as a whole, the development moves unhurriedly, yet inexorably, like a huge passacaglia—though of course without the ground bass.

In the Fifth and Eighth Symphonies, the recapitulation is announced with a slamming of the brakes and a powerful, tutti presentation of the first theme (in the case of the Fifth Symphony) or introduction (in the case of the Eighth). Though developmental tension continues to run high and is not fully resolved until the entrance of the respective second subjects, the sheer heraldic force of these tutti presentations is mightily impressive. In the Tenth, by contrast, there are no show-stopping gestures. There is perhaps a touch of rhetoric at Figs. 44 and 45, but even this is relatively subtle, a brassy "hemiola ritardando" where note values are broadened but the underlying pulse is not. Since this development had not been subject to the accelerations of the earlier symphonies, there is no need, indeed no room, for brake slamming. In any case, this movement's "non-gestural" material would seem to militate against such treatment – a rhetorical, tutti presentation of such haunting, cerebral music seems utterly unimaginable.

Instead, the reprise of the introduction appears in the Neapolitan, F minor, full-force but without fanfare, in the low strings and bassoons (Fig. 47, b2). At the same time, the upper strings play a countermelody based on the eighth note figuration from Fig. 8, thus rendering a recapitulation that appears to start from two different exposition points at once. Yet, throughout it all, there is no arrest of the developmental process, nor for that matter is there any sign of the tonic itself, until the return (tonic major) of the second subject at Fig. 57. This is indeed the most gradually emerging of Shostakovich's gradually emerging recapitulations. As if to confirm the long-awaited arrival, the second subject reprise is tonally more stable than its exposition counterpart; all hint of bitonality is expunged and the clarinets in thirds provide a reassurance of sorts compared with the exposition's solo flute. Any reassurance is short-lived, though. Following a baleful, chorale-like woodwind setting of the movement's introductory theme, the coda ends with the cold, otherworldly musings of two piccolos.

The first movements of the Fifth and Eighth Symphonies provide the obvious model for the first movement of the Tenth. But there is perhaps another influence looming in the background. In its ability to sustain a twenty-minute unfolding of lyrically conceived, un-rhetorical, triple-meter material, an ability that would appear to be quite rare given the paucity of such movements in the symphonic repertoire, the first movement of the Tenth Symphony is reminiscent of that of Brahms' Second. Emotionally, the two are far apart, but their cumulative momentum, the way in which they "move," is similar. They open at a similar tempo, with simple figures based on half and quarter notes. In both cases eighth-note motion is delayed (bar 44 of the Brahms; bar 107 of the Shostakovich), and in both cases it is introduced in the first violins and continues the combination scalar/arpeggio lines that have predominated from the outset. Both introduce one-bar general pauses: before Fig. 1 and Fig. 4 in the Shostakovich; bars 32 and 36 in the Brahms. In fact, the soft timpani roll with which Brahms fills his pause is replicated by Shostakovich when his opening material returns in the coda (Fig. 65, b3). Both movements make use of hemiola to provide rhythmic broadening in the earlier stages and to generate tension later on, e.g., the dissonant, brassy passages leading into the climax of the respective development sections (Brahms, letter G et seq.; Shostakovich, Figs. 44, 45, and especially 46).

Like the second movements of the Fifth and Eighth Symphonies, the scherzo of the Tenth cuts into the tense, still air hanging over from the previous movement's coda. But its whirlwind savagery, impressive even by Shostakovich's standards, is a world apart from the Fifth Symphony's galumphing *Ländler* or the Eighth's sadistic meat-grinding march. And at around four minutes long, it is also considerably terser. Indeed, to have attempted to sustain such brutality for much longer would probably have weakened its impact. Possibly, the need to unleash fury here is greater than in the other two scherzos because the pent-up tension at the end of the first movement is greater (mainly the result of the movement's comparative lack of tension-releasing gestures) than it had been in the other two symphonies. There is, of course, the now famous description, attributed to Shostakovich in *Testimony*, that the movement was "a musical portrait of Stalin, roughly speaking."[82] Although ascribing authorial intent so definitively is always a tricky matter, several commentators have noted a connection between the scherzo's main theme and the "Storming Zeyelovsky Heights" music from the Stalinist paean, *The Fall of Berlin*.

Stalin or no Stalin, this movement exudes impotent rage. Although there is plenty of fire and fury, there is also a hollowness, a feeling of wheel spinning. The nineteen bars of axe-wielding tonic B-flat minor chords at the movement's opening are a case in point. They are all in first inversion, which does not diminish the brutality, but does render it rather empty. Although some limited harmonic variety creeps in from bar 20, the double basses are stuck on D-flat for the first fifty-eight bars. With very few root position tonic chords, the movement is kept in a febrile state of flux. The central trio section, if one can call it that, provides no let up (Fig. 79) with its chromatic tail-chasing melody in thirds (violins, violas, and cellos) and sporadic slashing chords in the brass and timpani. But the double basses' whirlwind sixteenth note ostinato, scored unusually high for the instrument, is at once furious and weak, with the accented lower G at the beginning of each bar sounding like desperate stabbing rather than a firm foundation.

Although not in sonata form, this scherzo does feature one characteristic of Shostakovich's "brutalizing" developments, namely a forceful replay of the first theme in augmentation in the low brass (plus, in this case, cellos, basses, and bassoons) following the trio (Fig. 87). Unlike other such occurrences (e.g., the outer movements of the Fifth Symphony or the first movement of the Eighth), it is presented in unison rather than canon, although the offset horn and trumpet countermelody provides a pseudo-canonic effect. This augmentation draws together even closer the relationship (i.e., the rising scalar third) between the main theme of the scherzo and the opening of the first movement.

Following this barnstormer, the wry *Allegretto* third movement attempts a resumption of sanity. It moves in a dance-like manner, though it is a somewhat stiff, awkward dance. Its angular character comes into its own with the marionette-like second subject (Fig. 104), which also constitutes the first appearance in a Shostakovich work of the DSCH motif in its prime form. As is well known, the motif is a musical representation of Shostakovich's monogram, дш (in English, "D.Sh"), in the German transliteration, "D.Sch," which in German nomenclature yields D–Es–C–H, or in English, D–E-flat–C–B. Although its autobiographical significance was openly acknowledged by the composer, its origin remains unclear.[83] The scherzo of the First Violin Concerto had featured two transposed versions (see above), and as Louis Blois points out in Chapter 19, that Concerto was written in the wake of the First Piano Concerto of Shostakovich's student German Galynin, a work that contains two "conspicuously exposed utterances" of DSCH, also transposed. Whether a connection or a coincidence, Galynin's framing of the two "utterances" looks forward to Shostakovich's own presentations, which tend similarly to stand in relief from the surrounding texture.

Musically, the most striking aspect of DSCH is its interval structure and potential for harmonic ambiguity, with its two minor seconds (D to E-flat and C to B) and encompassing diminished fourth (B to E-flat). Its most natural operating environment, what David Fanning calls its "'home' key,"[84] is C minor—it is perhaps not surprising that the autobiographical Eighth Quartet, based on the DSCH motif, should be in that key. Yet, both at the end of the Tenth Symphony and at the climax of its third movement (Fig. 132, b3), it functions almost as comfortably within the tonal center of E—anchors being the leading note D-sharp (notated as E-flat) and the dominant B, the latter emphasized by the downward-pulling flat sixth, C-natural. And at its first appearance, back at Fig. 104 in the third movement, the context is a modally altered G major—D and B are part of the tonic triad, with the dominant D again emphasized by the flat sixth, E-flat. Additionally, there are instances where the motif is not meant to fit, and is written against the prevailing tonality, such as the F major context at Fig. 127 in the third movement.

After a short development of the "DSCH" subject (Fig. 106), the first subject returns (Fig. 110). This is followed by the next piece of the autobiographical puzzle, a lone horn call on the pitches E–A–E–D–A that forms the basis of the movement's third area (Fig. 114). The horn call seems oddly disruptive, an attempt perhaps to inject a "statement" into a movement that has up to this point seemed lacking in import. Musically, too, the call seems to breathe "air from another planet"; as David Fanning points out, its open intervals seem alien to the conjunct melodic motion that dominates the rest of the Symphony.[85] However, as has often been noted, the call almost replicates the opening notes (E–A–E–D–E–A; also horns) of Mahler's *Das Lied von der Erde*, a known favorite of Shostakovich. More recently, the Azerbaijani composer Elmira Nazirova has revealed that it is a musical cipher on her name; using a mix of conventional and solfege nomenclature, "Elmira" is represented as E–La–Mi–Re–A, i.e., E–A–E–D–A. Nazirova had studied with Shostakovich between 1947 and 1948 and over the next few years became something of a confidante. She reports that a letter from the composer, dated 29 August 1953, states his intention to incorporate her name into a piece of music.[86]

Unlike the short development of DSCH back at Fig. 106, where the motif was paraded through various transpositions, the subsequent development of "Elmira" amounts to stubborn repetitions, always at the same pitch, intermingled with reminiscences of the first movement's introduction (most obviously, Fig. 115) and a melody in the flute and piccolo that, although new, also seems molded out of the first movement's thematic substance (Fig. 117, b7). However, the antepenultimate and penultimate statements of Elmira add the pitch E before the final A, thus lining the theme exactly with *Das Lied von der Erde* (Figs. 118 and 119). The final statement in this section of the movement returns Elmira to her original form (Fig. 120).

The first subject returns again (Fig. 121) followed by the second (Fig. 127), the latter paving the way for a gradual *crescendo* and *accelerando* towards the movement's climax. The climax itself brings a convergence of the movement's "internal autobiography" (a reference to the first movement in the bass line at Fig. 132) and its two external autobiographical references, DSCH and Elmira. It is certainly tempting to formulate scenarios based on Shostakovich's deployment of these two characters at the climax—the frantic, circular repetitions of DSCH thrashing about in the violins, violas, and cellos, fighting against other musical lines in the rest of the orchestra versus the unopposed, stentorian blasts in the horns, now *a4*, of Elmira. In the disintegration that follows, DSCH collapses via a descending sequence (Fig. 136). If Elmira reigns supreme at the climax, the tables are turned somewhat in the sparse coda, as DSCH gets the last word, a tentative word it should be said, after Elmira's final muted horn whisper.

Ironically, though this third movement is in the DSCH "home" key of C minor, the DSCH motif itself is, with two exceptions, avoided during the movement's C-based portions. One exception is the low flute lead-back to the first subject at Fig. 109, b5; the other is at the movement's close where it appears over an almost impressionistic, expanded tonic major chord—C–E–G–A. This concluding yet inconclusive chord is exactly the same chord that Mahler used to bring his "Abschied" ("Farewell"), the final movement of *Das Lied von der Erde*, to a close, thus drawing our attention back to the parallel between the Elmira theme and *Das Lied*. In fact, this strange chord is the same added-sixth harmony that we noted towards the end of the Fifth Quartet's first movement (B-flat–D–F–G) accompanying the Ustvolskaya quotation. These two consecutive works, the Fifth Quartet and the Tenth Symphony, could thus be said to create an autobiographical triangle: DSCH, Elmira, and Ustvolskaya, with *Das Lied von der Erde* as the unifying factor. And, taking into account Elizabeth Wilson's above-quoted thoughts vis-à-vis Ustvolskaya and the *Four Pushkin Monologues*, it is notable that the final song of the *Monologues*, "Farewell," should parallel the title of Mahler's final song, "Abschied."

The fourth movement finale opens with a slow introduction, a feature shared by only four other symphonic fast movements in Shostakovich's output: the first movement of the Twelfth and the finales of the First, Fourth, and Fifteenth. Its tentatively generative nature parallels the slow introduction of the Fifth Quartet's finale. The two movements have little else in common, though the "pronounced rondo characteristics" (as David Fanning puts it)[87] of the Symphony's sonata form finale can to an extent be found in the Quartet's finale—principally in the short restatement of the first subject just before the development (Fig. 94).

If the first movement represented the culmination of the brooding Shostakovich symphonic *moderato*, the main *Allegro* of the finale deals with the horrors of previous movements, both musical and extramusical, via a traditional, high-kicking, festive Russian finale of the sort found in Tchaikovsky's Fourth Symphony or Borodin's Second. As the development reaches its climax, it picks up cues from the scherzo—the snare drum rhythm and the rising scalar minor third (Fig. 183, b9). If the scherzo was indeed a "portrait of Stalin," then the ultimate crushing of this pile-driving figure by the all-stops-out, unison rendition of DSCH at Fig. 184 rather explains itself.

The recapitulation (Fig. 185) provides a sweep through all the exposition's themes, starting with the slow introduction material sped up to fit the ongoing *Allegro* tempo. If the slow introduction gets the double-speed treatment, the ensuing bassoon rendition of the first theme emerges in a lumbering half-speed augmentation—the bassoon once again Shostakovich's favorite "re-characterizing agent"[88]—while the village-band percussion keeps the beat. This burlesque is quickly superseded by the original "full-speed" clarinet version at Fig. 194. The coda is an orgy of DSCH: the strained shrill high-register horns, *a4* (Fig. 202) followed by an imposing rendition for low brass, cellos, basses, and bassoons (Fig. 203), a scoring that suggests a connection with the augmented presentation of the scherzo's main theme at Fig. 87, and finally the timpani, daubing DSCH onto the orchestra like graffiti–the ultimate act of personal defiance.

Aside from the importance of DSCH to the Tenth Symphony *per se*, the motif provides yet another link back to the Fifth Quartet. Although the Quartet does not use DSCH, a reordered version, C–D–E-flat–B (i.e., "CDSH"), is presented quite conspicuously at the very opening (see bracket in Example 8.1a). This "CDSH" version is also the basis for the main themes of the Symphony's first and third movements (E–F-sharp–G–D-sharp and C–D–E-flat–B, respectively) and the scherzo of the First Violin Concerto (B-flat–C–D-flat–A), i.e., the movement in which the DSCH motif, transposed, was first mooted. Another reordering, "DCHS," can be heard in the Quartet's finale (Fig. 115, b2; A–G–F-sharp–B-flat) and in the first movement of the Symphony (Fig. 28, b5; D–C–B–E-flat).

Returning to the question of the "tonality" of DSCH, two observations are worth making. First, the three abovementioned "CDSH" appearances in the Tenth Symphony and First Violin Concerto, although not the appearance in the Fifth Quartet, constitute scale degrees 1–2–3–7 of their respective movements (E minor, C minor, and B-flat minor, respectively), a tonal patterning that Shostakovich would return to for the main theme of his 1967 symphonic poem *October* (C minor). Secondly, when placed in scalar order, i.e., "HCDS," the DSCH motif forms the first four notes of the "Shostakovich Mode" proposed by David Haas in Chapter 12, and, by extension, the first four notes of the octatonic scale. This observation will become particularly relevant with the quartets of the 1960s (see Chapter 9, Examples 9.5 and 9.8).

There are yet further thematic links between the Tenth Symphony and the Fifth Quartet. For example, the second subject of the Symphony's first movement (Example 8.2a), although representing a melodic "wedge" quite common in Shostakovich, is presaged almost exactly in the finale of the Quartet (Example 8.2b).

Example 8.2a

Example 8.2b

Another link appears in Example 8.3a (Quartet, finale) and Example 8.3b (Symphony, first movement).

Example 8.3a

Example 8.3b

***

The Tenth Symphony's predominantly tragic cast and its failure to "reflect our Soviet reality" created the predictable flap, especially amongst those for whom the 1948 Resolution was still holy writ. At the 1954 Stalin Prize discussions, Khrennikov rejected the Symphony and its "neurotic spasms" as the work of a "frightened intellectual" and instead nominated *The Sun Shines over Our Motherland*, though even his advocacy could not secure an award for the cantata.[89] But others, like Khachaturian, stood up for the Symphony–though understanding that things do not change overnight, Khachaturian played it safe and resorted to the "optimistic tragedy" moniker,[90] the time-honored euphemism that had been used in the official response to the Fifth Symphony. Euphemisms aside, however, it was clear that the ice was starting to crack.

CHAPTER 9

THE STATE COMPOSER: COMPROMISE AND DISSENT (1954–1965)

Like most composers, Shostakovich suffered his share of dry spells: 1925–1926, in the immediate wake of the First Symphony; 1929–1931, as he struggled to find a way forward from his brief fling with modernism and deal with the demands of the Cultural Revolution; or 1938, as he regrouped himself after the personal and political traumas of the previous two years. But the "fallow" period of the mid-1950s was more serious, at least in his mind. Between the Tenth Symphony (1953) and the Sixth Quartet (1956), he wrote no substantial concert works, his output comprising the Concertino for Two Pianos (1953), three film scores (*Song of the Great Rivers* (1954), *The Gadfly* (1955), and *The First Echelon* (1955–1956)), two lightweight song cycles (*Five Romances on Verses of Yevgeny Dolmatovsky* (1954) and *Spanish Songs* (1956)), and the *Festive Overture* (1954), a last-minute work to celebrate the thirty-seventh anniversary of the Revolution, knocked off, according to Lev Lebedinsky, in just a few hours, while a non-stop stream of couriers delivered pages of the score back to copyists at the Bolshoi Theater, where it was to be premiered.[1] By 1956, a distressed Shostakovich was heard to complain, "I will soon start to feel like a Rossini ... [who] wrote his last composition at the age of forty, after which he lived until the age of seventy without composing another note."[2]

Political post-trauma was as likely a cause as any for this sudden dearth, at least initially. With the death of Stalin and Shostakovich's cathartic unleashing of persona in the Tenth Symphony, the lighthearted Concertino for Two Pianos that followed possibly represented the same need to return to simplicity as the First Quartet had following the Fourth and Fifth Symphonies and their associated political traumas. But at the end of 1954, tragedy of a more immediate kind would hit Shostakovich. On 4 December, his wife Nina died suddenly while on assignment in Yerevan. She was forty-five and had just been diagnosed with cancer of the colon. Although their marriage had been occasionally stormy, Nina had been everything that Shostakovich had needed—a loving, though sexually independent wife who understood "the sacred calling" of parenthood.[3] She had been his organizer and protector, controlling the flow of visitors to the apartment, fending off the unwelcome ones. Her death would also hit the family financially, necessitating Shostakovich to take on an exhausting performing schedule. And in the wake of Khrushchov's mass release of political prisoners, which began in 1954, the Shostakovich apartment became, as Maxim put it, "like a small hotel for people who came back."[4]

***

Although 1955 saw little in the way of original composition, it did witness the premieres of two of the works that had been languishing in the drawer since 1948: *From Jewish Folk Poetry* (premiered in January) and the First Violin Concerto (premiered in October). Back in 1948, the song cycle's final lines, "Doctors, doctors are what our sons have become," seemed innocent enough. Now, in the aftermath of the "Doctors' Plot" of January 1953, those lines had taken on a tragic significance. Natalya Vovsi-Mikhoels recalls the premiere, in particular the moment when the announcer introducing the song cycle explained that one of the songs, "Lullaby," with its references to exile in Siberia, "all took place in Tsarist Russia":

> With that he left the stage. There was animation in the hall and people barely restrained themselves from laughing. For a long time after that Dmitri Dmitriyevich loved to repeat, "It all took place in Tsarist Russia, it all took place in Tsarist Russia."[5]

These premieres, along with the resumption of his own performing activities, were not the only demands on Shostakovich's time during 1955. In the days following Nina's death, he had found himself thinking again about *Lady Macbeth*, the opera that he had dedicated to her over twenty years earlier. As a private exercise, and in contradiction of his usual practice of not returning to a work once it had been completed, he had set about rewriting some of the vocal parts that he had now come to feel were awkward or unduly extreme in range. He told Isaak Glikman: "Don't imagine that I am doing this with the theatre in mind. I'm no longer interested in whether the opera gets another production or not; it's had quite enough mud and abuse thrown at it already."[6] But this professed indifference evaporated a few weeks later when it became known that the Leningrad Malyi Opera (Malegot) was contemplating a revival. Shostakovich went into full gear, enlisting Glikman to create a revised libretto. After a successful audition before Malegot's artistic board in March 1955, the company agreed to a production the following season.

The new score would tone down the more salacious elements of the original—excising, for instance, the infamous trombone glissandi—in an effort to make Katerina appear less sexually voracious and more maternal. In his notes to Glikman, Shostakovich wrote:

> I think that on pages 161–162 we have to find other words for Katerina Lvovna, suggesting something other than her desire for a passionate kiss. Instead of the night of

rapture they have just spent or are still spending, they should reflect Sergey's brutal flogging of the previous day. So the situation could be that Sergey is still getting over his beating and Katerina Lvovna is tending to him.

Pages 169–170: again we should play down the idea of the insatiable female. Page 171: her complaint that Sergey is sleeping "while her loving lips are so close" must also go. On the contrary, she should be happy that he is asleep or going to sleep: it means that he is recovering from his thrashing.[7]

Conventional wisdom has it that these changes were politically motivated. Certainly, Shostakovich had to proceed with caution. The post-Stalin "Thaw" was proving a touch-and-go affair and *Lady Macbeth* remained dangerous territory.[8] But there may have been other reasons behind the softening of the opera's tone. The Shostakovich of 1955, a recently widowed forty-eight year old bearing sole responsibility for his teenage children—children whom he was always concerned to protect from his own predilection for "colorful" language—was a very different man from the at times brash twenty-five year old who was not inclined to spare his audience from life's seamier aspects. All of this perhaps goes some way to explaining Katerina's new maternal instincts. But in any case, Shostakovich had already started to tone down certain elements of the opera even prior to 1936 (as witnessed in the 1935 piano/vocal score, for example).[9] Although *Lady Macbeth* was indeed a highly sexual opera, Shostakovich even back then had been concerned that the eroticism not become the driving force, and was distressed by the occasionally rowdy way the opera's erotic moments had been received by the audience—a mix of prudish disapproval on the one hand and unconcealed prurient glee on the other.

Notwithstanding Malegot's approval, permission still had to be obtained from the Ministry of Culture. Ominously, the audition did not take place until March 1956, towards the end of the season in which the opera had been slated, something that Glikman believes to have been a deliberate ploy. Glikman characterizes the requisite post-audition discussion that took place at Shostakovich's apartment as little more than a rehash of the old accusations of formalism, with Georgy Khubov, Dmitry Kabalevsky, and Mikhail Chulaki all noting how the lessons of "Muddle Instead of Music" had still not been learned. Glikman spoke in the opera's defense, but Khubov constantly interrupted him with "shrill interjections."[10] Maxim Shostakovich adds, "I looked at those disgusting people and regretted that I didn't have the catapult that I once used in Komarovo against my Father's assailants."[11] While all this was playing out, Shostakovich sat at the other end of the room in silence, his blank expression punctuated with the occasional "grimace of pain."[12] When, at the end, his opinion was solicited, he "declined to speak and with astounding self-control thanked his colleagues 'for their criticisms'."[13] Permission to produce the opera was denied.

***

The rejection of *Lady Macbeth* was yet another blow to Shostakovich's tattered psyche, which was also dealing with the death of his mother a few months earlier on 9 November 1955, only eleven months after Nina. Perhaps nothing was more telling of Shostakovich's psychological state at this time than his sudden and, as it would turn out, disastrous marriage in July 1956 to Margarita Kainova, a teacher and Komsomol activist. Various stories exist of exactly how the two got together, but all point to Shostakovich proposing within a day or two of their first meeting, an impulsive act committed by a man trying desperately to inject some normality back into his life. But Margarita's attempts to do just that met with resistance, especially from Shostakovich's children. According to his secretary at the time, Zinaida Gayamova, Margarita constantly tried to "re-educate" Shostakovich and showed little understanding of his needs.[14] Two years later, he would admit that Margarita was a "complete stranger."[15] In 1959, they divorced. Shostakovich's hastiness in affairs of the heart during this time can also be gauged by his two proposals of marriage to Galina Ustvolskaya—the first soon after Nina's death, the second after his divorce from Margarita. Both were rejected.

If Shostakovich's personal life was in ruins, a glimmer of hope in the outside world came on 25 February 1956 when, at the now famous "secret" session of the Twentieth Congress of the Communist Party, Nikita Khrushchov delivered the news that many had suspected but that no one had dared voice openly: that the twenty-five year reign of terror carried out in the name of Socialist Construction had indeed been orchestrated by Stalin himself. Citing Stalin's "intolerance, his brutality and his abuse of power," Khrushchov described a dictator paralyzed by his own egotism, one who "often chose the path of repression and physical annihilation, not only against actual enemies, but also against individuals who had not committed any crimes against the Party and the Soviet Government." Khrushchov condemned the "cult of the individual," whereby a single person had been able to hold, unchecked, "immense and limitless power."[16] That term, "cult of the individual" or "cult of personality," would quickly be adopted as the standard euphemism for Stalin.

***

If Shostakovich's marriage to Margarita in July was an attempt to restart his personal life, the Sixth Quartet, composed in August, was quite possibly his attempt to do the same for his composition. Reinforcing a sense of "new beginning," the Sixth begins in a Haydnesque vein, the classicism emphasized by the parallel thirds and the repeated quarter-note pedal ostinati that pervade much of the first movement, not to mention the procedure of repeating the first theme immediately after the first mini-tutti (Fig. 4). But though the Sixth would be Shostakovich's most lightweight quartet since the First, it would nevertheless absorb issues raised by its larger brethren. For example, that initially innocent Haydnesque melody very quickly undergoes chromatic distortion with a piece of "wrong-note" humor at the first cadence (bar 12), where Shostakovich's beloved Neapolitan relationship is heard as an injection of A-flat (in particular, a cello line of F–A-flat–E-flat) into the otherwise pure G major air—a small piece of mischief that, in true Shostakovich style, wreaks more serious havoc later.

Like the corresponding moment in the Fifth Quartet, the recapitulation begins with one instrument (in this case, the first violin) attempting to recapture the tonic while the others derail the process, this time by a strange "cadential" alternation of tonic G major and Neapolitan A-flat harmony (Fig. 21, b5), a development, so to speak, of the "wrong note" accident of bar 12. Adding to the derailment, the violin theme is dislocated by half a bar, while the accompanying cadences provide an implied overlay of a 3/2 meter against the prevailing 4/4. A dislocation of a different type follows the reprise of the second subject. Presented in E-flat minor (a Neapolitan move from the exposition's D major), this second subject reprise ends with an E-flat ostinato in the viola. As the first subject establishes itself for the last time, that E-flat ostinato continues, providing a "false dominant" pedal, while the two violins attempt to start the theme in the tonic G (Fig. 30). But within a couple of bars, they too take on Neapolitan shadings. Only at Fig. 31 does the E-flat ostinato resolve onto D, giving the recapitulation's first unimpaired view of G major—an example of the "gradually emerging" recapitulation being deployed just as successfully in the classically cut Sixth Quartet as in works of a more epic disposition.

One last piece of Neapolitan mischief making appears at the movement's closing cadence, a strange mix of A-flat and G, underpinned by the aforementioned cello line from bar 12 (Example 9.1). Although succinctly summarizing the movement's main G/A-flat conflict, it makes for an enigmatic final cadence. Even stranger is the return of this cadence, with the same cello line, at the end of every movement, almost like a signature. Recently, David Fanning has pointed out that the high point of this "yawn" of a cadence reveals a possibly unique instance of DSCH aligned vertically: "It would be possible to dismiss this cryptic version of the DSCH signature as non-intentional, were it not for its anomalous prominence—it is reiterated at the end of each movement, as if to reinforce its quasi-leitmotivic quality—and for its chronological proximity to other works that include unmistakable DSCH signatures (i.e., the Tenth Symphony and Eighth Quartet)."[17]

Example 9.1

In keeping with the Quartet's scaled-down mood, the middle two movements, a scherzo and a slow passacaglia, are gentler, less intense than previous Shostakovich examples. The passacaglia in particular, with its layering of lyrical lines, is more songlike and less inexorably tragic than usual. Possibly the fact that it is in 4/4 meter rather than the usual (both for Shostakovich and for his Baroque precursors) 3/4 diminishes that sense of inexorable tread.

Other than that strange "signature" cadence at the end of each movement and the tense return of the passacaglia at the finale's climax (in its original third movement key, B-flat minor and, incidentally, in a triple meter; Fig. 80), the Sixth Quartet is not cyclic to the extent of, say, the Seventh or Ninth Quartets. Yet, there is certainly a whiff of the first movement to be heard in the finale, whose first and second subjects are both based on rising three-note anapests similar to the Quartet's opening. The jaunty second subject (Fig. 69) in particular is reminiscent, with its duple meter and its succession of staccato quarter notes following the anapest, a connection reinforced in the reverse-order recapitulation where this theme is introduced by a stuttering one-note ostinato in the cello that is mildly reminiscent of the very start of the Quartet (Fig. 84).

Although this finale is not as emotionally searching or momentous as that of the Fifth Quartet, it does share certain characteristics. Both are marked *Allegretto* (dotted half = 63 in the Fifth Quartet; 69 in the Sixth) and move in a similar waltz-like way, with primarily conjunct, legato motion and with an emphasis on a two-note upbeat that creates, in conjunction with the following downbeat, an anapest. Both have an element of sonata rondo, returning the first subject towards the end of the exposition. And both feature a momentous quotation at the climax of their respective development sections: the return of the Ustvolskaya theme in the Fifth, and the return of the slow movement ground bass in the Sixth.

Like the Fifth Quartet (and indeed the Third and Fourth), the Sixth ends *morendo*. But where in those highly charged earlier quartets (or the Eighth Symphony, for that matter), there is a process of emotional disintegration towards the end as the music withdraws ever-inwards, the basic motion (and emotion) in the Sixth proceeds relatively unhindered until six bars towards the end, where everything comes to a halt to pave the way for that by-now obligatory tag, that strange cadential progression that caps every movement in this quartet. It is a comparatively low-key ending to what has been, by Shostakovich's standards, a low-key quartet.

***

By the mid-1950s, Shostakovich's rehabilitation was more-or-less complete, if not *de jure* then certainly *de facto*. Yet, the official vortex into which he was being sucked was starting to take a psychological toll. On 24 September 1956, the day before his fiftieth birthday, a gala was held in his honor. Glikman reports:

> He was already dreading the flood of congratulatory speeches, awash with hypocritical insincerity. As he confided to me when I came to Moscow the day before his birthday, he knew that the very people who had tormented him would throng to kiss him, contorting their features into a mask of devoted admiration.... Shostakovich sat on the

stage surrounded by bouquets of flowers, his face resembling that of a man condemned to death by verbal assault. He did his best to look interested while speaker after speaker droned on with addresses which were, to him, devoid of interest or value.
At the conclusion of each peroration the orator attempted to kiss the hero, but I
observed the dexterity with which, apparently accidentally, he contrived to elbow away
all those who particularly repelled him."[18]

By the winter of 1956–1957, Shostakovich's compositional muse had begun
to take hold again. The first fruit was the Second Piano Concerto, written for
Maxim and premiered on his nineteenth birthday in May 1957. Not surprisingly, the Concerto was on a modest scale, with a straightforward solo part, with
Shostakovich's trademark two-part, two-octave piano texture to the fore. Ian
MacDonald has described it as "a jeu d'esprit, full of private jokes (such as the
scale-exercises in its finale) and, aside from a beguiling Tchaikovskian andante,
little else."[19] Easy to dismiss, the Concerto is that rarest of beasts: a Shostakovich work that seems genuinely cheerful. Its optimism is not defiant, cautious,
febrile, or bombastic. Instead, unforced, uncomplicated joy pervades in the outer
movements, and simple heartfelt tenderness in the middle slow movement,
whose theme is somewhat reminiscent of the slow movement of Beethoven's
Emperor Concerto.

MacDonald also asserts that the Concerto was written "with at least one eye on
sweetening the Soviet authorities" at what was for Shostakovich a financially lean
time.[20] Certainly, the Concerto could be viewed as "Young Pioneer" music—that
genre of optimistic, "edifying" music for the nation's youth, most famously exemplified by Kabalevsky's Third Piano Concerto of 1952, the so-called "Youth" Concerto.[21] But it is surely also about simple communication from father to son. For
Shostakovich, a concerto or a sonata was a document of friendship, fashioned with
the qualities of its dedicatee in mind. Discussing Shostakovich's cello music, for
example, Gerard McBurney writes:

> The 1934 Sonata was composed for the small-scale talents of Viktor Kubatsky, and
> the difference shows in the music's relative simplicity and gentle lyricism. The cello
> parts in much of the chamber music were for the Beethoven Quartet's Sergei Shirin-
> sky, an accomplished team player but—to judge by what survives on recordings—not
> one for drama or virtuosity. The concertos for Rostropovich are unimaginable without
> those qualities. Both depend spectacularly on the power and almost operatic heroism
> of Rostropovich's bowing, as it is today and especially as it was in earlier days.[22]

This may very well explain why neither the First Piano Concerto (written for his
own small-boned, brittle style) nor the Second (written for his nineteen-year-old
son) have the scale or emotional range of the concertos written for Oistrakh or Rostropovich. Because Shostakovich himself was an active performer, collaborations
with virtuoso pianists, the sort that might have inspired a more ambitious work, were
more limited.

***

Between late March and early April 1957, the Composers' Union held its Second All-Union Congress. Reaction against the Zhdanov purges had been slowly mounting—this Second Congress was far less dogmatic and vindictive in tone than the 1948 First Congress had been. Yet, in true Thaw fashion, it was only "the cult of personality," not the doctrine of Socialist Realism itself, that was placed under the microscope. Indeed, Socialist Realism continued to be touted as the way forward. Dmitri Shepilov, the Central Committee minister for ideology, echoed his predecessor Zhdanov's call for elegance and refinement in music, invoking the figures of Glinka, Tchaikovsky, and Rimsky-Korsakov. He also struck out against the pernicious influence of jazz, with its "wild cave-man orgies" and "explosion of basic instincts and sexual urges."[23]

At the Congress, Shostakovich was elected to the Union's Secretariat, another step in the process of reeling him into the official fold. In public, he dutifully read the speech that Daniil Zhitomirsky had prepared for him. In private, he took Shepilov's speech and gleefully threw it, complete with its infamous "Rimsky-KorSAkov" mispronunciation, into his satirical skit, *Rayok* (see Chapter 8 for questions of dating).

***

Since 1955, Shostakovich had been hinting at plans for a new symphony commemorating those who had paved the way to the Revolution, but it was not until the summer of 1957 that composition of the Eleventh Symphony ("The Year 1905") began in earnest, the work appearing in time for the fortieth anniversary of the Revolution. The most overtly narrative of Shostakovich's symphonies, the Eleventh tells of the failed uprising of 9 January 1905 (old-style calendar) in which a peaceful gathering of unarmed workers in front of the Tsar's Winter Palace, petitioning for improved human rights, was gunned down in cold blood by troops protecting the palace. Premiered in October 1957, the Eleventh was rapturously received for its "realistic" qualities. It received a Lenin Prize in 1958.

As an inheritor of the *narodny* tradition, Shostakovich was empathetic to the 1905 uprisers, and the Eleventh Symphony was no doubt a sincere depiction of events and aspirations. Yet, although the plan as expressed in 1955 was to deal with pre-Revolutionary topics, by the time of the Symphony's composition two years later, the world had witnessed the all-too-similar 1956 Hungarian uprising in which peaceful protesters in Budapest's Parliament Square were gunned down in a show of Soviet-backed governmental force. Inevitably, the Eleventh Symphony acquired an additional resonance, not just for the audience but for Shostakovich as well. When the choreographer Igor Belsky produced his ballet *Eleventh Symphony* in 1966, Shostakovich reportedly urged him not to forget when the work had been written.[24] Debating which interpretation takes precedence, 1905 or 1956, is ultimately moot, for as with so many "either/or" questions with Shostakovich, the answer probably turns out to be "both." Shostakovich was acutely aware of the dictum that those who don't learn from history are in danger of repeating it, and it is that tragic inevitability of history repeating itself that is perhaps the larger theme of the Eleventh Symphony.

Like the Second and Third Symphonies, the Eleventh is narrative-driven. The Second Symphony had had its structure dictated by that of the post-Revolutionary mass spectacle, while the free-wheeling Third, in which no theme is ever repeated, was an attempt to reflect the random succession of parades observed on a public holiday. The Eleventh does not employ the single-movement format of those earlier works, but with all four movements connected *attacca*, and with its heavy use of cyclism, it emerges *de facto* as a single-movement work where the structure of individual movements and the larger relationship of movements to one another are driven solely by the narrative. This distinguishes it from, say, the Seventh Symphony, where Shostakovich had attempted to hold the narrative elements in a balance with more formal symphonic considerations. The famous "invasion" theme, for example, certainly had a narrative function (however one chooses to read it), and may even have been deliberately designed to impede symphonic progress. But ultimately, it was still required to work within the context of a sonata form movement; after the invasion has been and gone, there is still a recapitulation to set up and deliver. The Eleventh Symphony, on the other hand, makes no such attempt to balance narrative with traditional symphonic process.

Shostakovich paints here on a broad, almost cinematic canvas. The first movement, "Palace Square," is an intensely still, bleak depiction of the vast snow-covered square; the opening's parched five-octave spread of open fifths, G and D, has bows barely moving over the string. As pure sonority, it is potently atmospheric. But that extraordinary heaviness of spirit is also generated from the melodic line, with its limited conjunct motion that is constantly being pulled back to its opening note D, as if lacking the energy to go further. Before the events unfold, Shostakovich injects commentary via two popular Revolutionary songs: "Listen!" ("The autumn night is as black as treason, black as the tyrant's conscience . . ."; Fig. 8); and "The Prisoner" ("The night is dark, try to catch the passing minutes; but the prison walls are strong, the gates are closed with iron locks . . ."; Fig. 15, b8). The quotations circle the G minor tonic ("Listen!" in A-flat and "The Prisoner" in F-sharp minor), and thus parallel tonally what the movement's opening phrases impress melodically, namely the heavy magnetic pull of a central pitch. In fact, the "Palace Square" theme itself, essentially a ritornello, exerts its own gravitational pull on the movement as a whole, because nearly all the movement's events, whether the two Revolutionary quotations or the interspersed muffled timpani triplets and brass fanfares (e.g., Figs. 1 and 2, or Figs. 4 and 5), eventually melt back into it. In fact, "Palace Square" will turn out to be the magnetic center for the Symphony as a whole.

Those timpani triplets, and to a lesser extent the brass fanfares, serve as an important motivic generator for the Symphony as a whole. The triplet motif first appears as a gently ominous pulsation (*piano pesante*) immediately following the opening statement of "Palace Square" (Fig. 1; Example 9.2). The triplet rhythm is echoed in the muted brass fanfares that immediately follow (Fig. 2) and again in the "Listen!" quotation (Fig. 8), yet another example of Shostakovich appearing to contrive earlier material around the needs of an upcoming quotation. As

Example 9.2 shows, this motif affirms the movement's tonic, G minor. Although the C-flat, if read as B-natural, possibly hints at G major, the larger voice-leading refutes this, at least for now. The C-flat is heard as just that; a "dissonant" diminished fourth pulling down to the minor third, not a "consonant" major third in its own right.[25] Indeed it is the pitch structure of this motif, even more than the rhythm, that will most resonate over the course of the Symphony.

Example 9.2

The second movement, "9 January," depicts the protest and the ensuing massacre, and is based thematically on Shostakovich's 1951 choral setting of Arkady Kots' poem "9 January," which formed the sixth of his *Ten Choruses on Texts by Revolutionary Poets*. Two portions of that setting are recalled here: "Our Tsar, Our Little Father," which forms most of the movement's first section; and "Bare Your Heads" (Fig. 41). "Palace Square" returns as a flashback in the winds just before the massacre (Fig. 69). At the fugato depicting the massacre, the timpani triplet motif from the first movement is split into its rhythmic and melodic components (Fig. 71). The former manifests itself as a gunshot triplet in the snare drum, the latter as the start of the fugato subject itself, the pitches transposed to A, C, and D-flat. At Fig. 85, the heavy artillery is unleashed: a fractured, brutalized version of "Palace Square" fired out in triplets by the orchestra over a ferocious percussion ostinato, alternating with the timpani giving the fugato subject. The massacre ends with an intoning of "Bare Your Heads" over the percussion fusillade (Fig. 89). It comes to an abrupt halt, leaving in its wake a ghostly recall of "Palace Square," now back in the strings, with the melody and most of its accompanying pedals set into a gentle but eerie trilling motion to conjure the icy wind blowing over the corpses and the carnage. Adding an extra frisson, the melody here is doubled by the celesta, Shostakovich's favorite instrument of "farewell."

The third movement, "Eternal Memory," a requiem for the slaughtered, uses the "timpani triplet" motif, G–C-flat–B-flat, as the basis for the simple cello and bass pizzicato accompaniment to the G minor viola elegy, a quotation of the song "You Fell as a Victim," while the central section quotes from "Welcome the Free Word of Liberty" (Fig. 106). Like the massacre in the second movement, this elegy reaches its climax with a recall of "Bare your heads" (Fig. 113). At Fig. 114, while the timpani and trumpet pound out octave D triplets, the strings recombine the triplet rhythm with the G–C-flat–B-flat melody to create a forceful ostinato, giving us, in essence, a slow-motion reminiscence of the massacre. As Roy Blokker puts it, "In remembering our dead comrades, the music seems to say, let us not forget how and why they died."[26]

The finale, "Tocsin," promises vengeance against the perpetrators, and quotes from several more Revolutionary songs—"Rage You Tyrants!" (opening), "Boldly,

Comrades, On We March" (Fig. 129, b5), and the Polish song, "Varshavianka" (Fig. 140)—as well as a worker's march from Sviridov's opera *Ogonki* (Fig. 145, b13). After the ensuing cataclysm, "Palace Square" returns one last time to introduce the extended, plaintive English horn lament on "Bare Your Heads." "Our Tsar, Our Little Father" returns at the end of the lament and, together with "Bare Your Heads," forms the basis for the coda (Fig. 167).

In the coda, a triplet-based ostinato in the timpani and snare drum underpins the rest of the orchestra as it struggles to wrest G major from out of the jaws of G minor. The two moments when the orchestra lands on a resounding G major chord (Figs. 178 and 178, b8) suggest a defiant ending to tragic events, similar to the D major chords at the end of the Fifth Symphony (even down to the anapest rhythm, cf. Fig. 134 in the Fifth). The final moments have the tubular bells pealing out the melodic component of the timpani triplet motif, but with Shostakovich now putting into action the alternative reading suggested back at the motif's very first appearance in the first movement: the pitch C-flat is now written as B-natural. The Symphony ends in a battle between G major and G minor as the tubular bells (representing the Tocsin of the finale's title) alternate B-natural with B-flat over the unison tutti G. On the page, it is the B-flat, representing G minor, that gets the last word, but with the acoustic hangover that inevitably occurs with such bells, the Symphony in effect ends, as it began, in modal uncertainty.

In addition to its various transformations, the "timpani triplet" motif gives rise to a further consideration. As already discussed, the opening pitches of the second movement fugato subject (A, C, D-flat) are based on this motif. Yet, as the subject unfolds, it reveals a mode: A–B-flat–C–D-flat–E-flat–E-natural. The first five notes follow David Haas' proposed "Shostakovich mode," based on A (see Chapter 12), and the set of six notes follows the octatonic scale. Basing his theory on music from the early-to-mid-1930s, Haas stresses that the note upon which a "Shostakovich mode" is based is not usually the tonic of the moment. What is significant about this fugato subject is that the mode is in fact based on the prevailing tonic (i.e., A). In other words, the "Shostakovich mode" has now evolved from a "vagrant sonority" pitch collection into an actual mode. This particular phenomenon, together with a cementing of the relationship between the "Shostakovich mode" and the octatonic scale, will become more prevalent as we enter the 1960s.

***

The 1957 Second Composers' Union Congress had marked a small step in the direction of liberalization. On its heels, in June 1958, came a new Central Committee Resolution, "On the Correction of Errors in the Evaluation of the Operas *The Great Friendship, Bogdan Khmelnitsky,* and *From All One's Heart.*" Expressing regret over the treatment of those "gifted composers, Comrades Prokofiev, Shostakovich, Khachaturian, Shebalin, Popov, Myaskovsky, and others" during the antiformalist purges of 1948, the Resolution blamed Stalin's "subjective attitude to certain works of art" and the "very adverse influence" exercised by Molotov, Malenkov, and Beriya.[27] But just as Khrushchov's landmark "secret speech" had skirted around the problems of Communism itself—its purpose was to show Stalin's "distortions" of the "correct" Leninist line—this tepidly worded Resolution continued to push the virtues of Socialist Realism, confining its criticisms to the problems of "personality."

Although Shostakovich's own rehabilitation had effectively taken place several years earlier, he was still offended by the refusal of this new text to condemn outright the Resolution of 1948. Galina Vishnevskaya remembers him sarcastically proposing a toast "to the great historical Decree 'On Abrogating the Great Historical Decree,'"[28] while Marina Sabinina recalls his anger over the lives that had been wrecked by the 1948 Resolution:

> "I was called up to see a certain 'high-up official.' They, you see, are now interested, as to how they can somehow "correct" the Central Committee's famous Decree of 1948. *Correct it*!! Correct the very thing that carried off Myaskovsky to his grave, broke Prokofiev, and poisoned the lives of many young, talented musicians, and opened up careers for all kinds of filthy trash. Do you know that I visited Nikolai Yakovlevich Myaskovsky literally on the eve of his death, about two days before he died. He lay in bed, terribly emaciated, pale and weak, and suddenly he gasped in a barely audible whisper: 'As I lie here, I keep thinking, could it possibly be that everything I did and taught was 'against the People'? Perhaps there is some bitter truth in it after all, and we were indeed on the wrong path.' You understand, this most noble, modest of men lay there dying, tortured by these thoughts, torn apart by doubts, seriously looking for a grain of truth in that illiterate, revolting document! I answered this high-up official, saying, 'No, nothing should be corrected, the only thing is to revoke the Decree, *revoke* it.'"[29]

***

For Shostakovich, the greater part of 1958 was devoted to two stage works, the operetta *Moscow, Cheryomushki* and an orchestration of Musorgsky's opera *Khovanshchina* for a film production directed by Vera Stroyeva. The operetta, later designated a "musical comedy," was Shostakovich's first stage work since his ballet *The Limpid Stream* (1935)—excluding, that is, the aborted opera *The Gamblers* and his scores of incidental music. Noviye Cheryomushki, literally "New Bird-Cherry Trees," was an actual Moscow suburb of experimental, non-communal, high-rise housing co-operatives, one of many that went up in the late 1950s and throughout the 1960s. Offering an escape from the miseries of the *kommunalki*, single-family apartments in these projects were much sought after, though their often dodgy construction would soon become the butt of jokes. Shostakovich's operetta literally hit close to home, with its humorous look at the trials and tribulations of daily living—housing shortages, city government corruption, landlord/tenant relationships, and a bit of romance. It was, as Ian MacDonald put it, an "'allowable' satire of the kind that would later be tolerated by the authorities in the magazine *Krokodil*,"[30] though Gerard McBurney draws attention to the fact that it was also "part of a nationwide campaign to talk up the new building programs. In other words, it was [also] a work of propaganda."[31]

For the most part, *Moscow, Cheryomushki* steers a course between the traditional sentimental Russian romance on the one hand and something approaching Broadway on the other, with perhaps a dash of Gilbert and Sullivan thrown in—in her song lamenting how she had spent too much of her youth "studying books" rather than "attending to her looks," Lidochka the museum guide cannot help but come across as a latter-day Modern Major General, knowledgeable yet utterly clueless ("I know the dates of the Magna Carta and the form of a sonata" . . .). Shostakovich's first completed stage work since the mid-1930s, *Moscow, Cheryomushki* would revert back to his old habit of wholesale quotation and self-quotation, using material from previous stage works (*The Bolt* and *Declared Dead*) as well as a miscellany of Russian folk and popular songs. In fact, Lidochka's lament was set to the most famous Shostakovich tune of all, his 1932 hit "The Song of the Counterplan." Perhaps this orgy of quotation was indeed a case of laziness in the face of a less than enthralling project or, in the case of "Counterplan," an attempt to wring just a few more miles out of an old potboiler. But, as McBurney argues, it is hard not to find something mischievously subversive about a song that "had been rammed down the throats of whole generations of Soviet children—in school, Pioneer camp, and youth group—as they were taught the virtues of social (and socialist) conformity and sad, conformist, unworldly figure of Lidochka.[32]

For Shostakovich, *Moscow, Cheryomushki* was a quick earner at a financially lean time, though it may in part have been done as a return favor to the conductor Grigory Stolyarov, who had led Nemirovich-Danchenko's 1934 production of *Lady Macbeth*. Certainly, *Moscow, Cheryomushki* lacks some of the trenchant iconoclasm of Shostakovich's best light music from the 1930s. Yet, in the right performance its irrepressible zest can hardly fail to raise a smile, or even a laugh. Admittedly, Shostakovich himself found little to smile about. He begged Isaak Glikman not to attend the premiere, describing it as "boring, unimaginative, stupid."[33] His opinion later softened following the release of the film version (1963; entitled simply *Cheryomushki*), with revised libretto and score.

The orchestration of *Khovanshchina* was certainly the more satisfying project. Left unfinished and, apart from two small portions of Act III, unorchestrated by Musorgsky, *Khovanshchina* had for all practical purposes existed only in the version edited and orchestrated by Rimsky-Korsakov. As in his earlier *Boris Godunov* reorchestration, Shostakovich returned the opera's sound world back to something more authentically Musorgskian, and restored the harmonic rough edges that Rimsky had smoothed out, though he generally adhered to Rimsky's dramaturgical decisions even in places where they clearly ran counter to Musorgsky's stated intentions. In fact, Rimsky's "positive" ending, clearly overriding Musorgsky's stated wishes, is made even more so here by Shostakovich. (In 1913, Stravinsky had attempted to rectify Rimsky's misjudgment with his own arrangement of the final chorus.)

Stroyeva's film was released in 1959 (coincidentally, the year of Shostakovich's *Boris Godunov* premiere), and a stage production followed in 1960. Since then, Shostakovich's score has become more-or-less the standard performing version—unlike the

Boris orchestration, which has essentially been rendered obsolete, other than as an item of historical interest, by the increased acceptance of Musorgsky's two original versions.[34]

* * *

If the Sixth Quartet had represented a scaling-down in a medium that Shostakovich had hitherto been developing along rather symphonic lines, the same could be said about the First Cello Concerto, composed during the summer of 1959 and premiered by its dedicatee, Mstislav Rostropovich, on 4 October. It is less epically symphonic than the First Violin Concerto, and scales down the orchestration still further by removing all brass, save for a solo horn obbligato. This sparer orchestral approach could be read as a preview of Shostakovich's later style, although it could also have been simply a way of eliminating the balance problems that often arise with cello concertos.

Indicative of the Concerto's neoclassical nature, the sardonic first movement is cast in a straightforward sonata form. Its construction, and to an extent its character, is based on simple repetitions and limited developments of short cells, principally the four-note cello motif with which the Concerto opens. The motif itself is a quotation from the "Procession to Execution" from Shostakovich's score to the film *The Young Guard* (1948)—the cello's up-tempo presentation of the motif here, not to mention the witty rejoinders in the woodwind (complete with that contrabassoon-dominated sound that Shostakovich seemed to reserve for his concertos), are perhaps a telling example of his gallows humor. The movement's "cellular" construction applies even in the development section and, like the orchestration, could be viewed as a forerunner to his later style (the Eleventh Quartet, for instance), though Eric Roseberry describes this as "as much neo-baroque as neo-classical in its elaboration of a single idea-mood, its regular pattern-making, its structural element of ritornello and limited key scheme which lacks the faster harmonic change of the Beethovenian development section."[35]

Throughout the Concerto, the solo horn is something of a Sancho Panza to the cello's Don Quixote. Sometimes it announces, sometimes it picks up the cello's "leftovers," but most of the time it sits silent. Like the trumpet in the First Piano Concerto, the horn here is never placed in dialogue with the main solo instrument—it is always one step removed. Its varying roles in the first movement typify its roles in the Concerto as a whole. Silent in the exposition, it is then heard several times throughout the development blasting out the opening motif as a kind of ritornello separating the various stages of that section. Later, it asserts itself still further firstly by setting up a false recapitulation and then by leading both halves of the second subject reprise.

Although less intense than the First Violin Concerto's passacaglia, and without the domestic intimacy of the Second Piano Concerto's slow movement, the Cello Concerto's ternary-form second movement shares their occasional moments of unashamed romanticism, a quality generally avoided in the symphonies and quartets of the period, where the lyricism tends to be sparer and less yielding. And like those other two slow movements, this one opens with an orchestral introduction featuring Shostakovich's favorite chaconne-like rhythm, with the characteristic double emphasis on the first two beats of the second of the two-bar phrases. By contrast, the cello's opening theme is more folk-like in its lyrical simplicity and its reliance on pairs of more-or-less repeated one-bar cells. Following the movement's climax and collapse, that theme returns, played as harmonics, bringing to mind the pale, disembodied sound of the opening of the Second Piano Trio. The cello here alternates its phrases with the celesta, heightening the otherworldly quality.

In the First Violin Concerto, the cadenza had formed the link between the slow movement and the finale. The cadenza in the Cello Concerto fulfills a similar function. Although marginally shorter than the earlier one, Shostakovich designates the cadenza as its own movement. Like the earlier cadenza, it begins by musing over fragments of the immediately preceding slow movement. As it builds and accelerates, it draws in thematic fragments from the first movement. Unlike the Violin Concerto cadenza, it does not foreshadow finale material directly. However, given that the first movement theme that it does quote turns out to be the motivic supplier for each of the finale's main themes (e.g., Fig. 62, b11–12) and is itself returned later in the finale, an indirect link between cadenza and finale can be claimed.

In fact, the fourth movement finale is essentially designed as a reclaiming of that first movement theme and, indeed, key. Initially in G minor, this finale declares its independence, so to speak, refusing to conform to the Concerto's E-flat tonic; both the first and second appearances of the "A" theme in this attempted rondo are cast in G minor. The intervening "B" theme is a frenetic klezmer-like idea (Fig. 65), yet another link to the First Violin Concerto. Following the galumphing triple-meter dance that forms the "C" theme (Fig. 69), the "A" theme comes back, also now in triple meter (Fig. 75). At this point, the rondo starts to break down, as the return of the first movement theme progressively takes over, drowning out any attempt of the finale's material to re-establish itself. In fact, the only real foothold that the finale's material gets in this latter half is a self-mocking, bitonally cackling version in the woodwind (Fig. 80). And as the first movement asserts itself over the finale, so too does the Concerto's E-flat tonic, ousting the G minor "pretender."

Shortly after the start of the finale, Shostakovich satirizes Stalin's favorite song, *Suliko* (Fig. 63, b8–13), a tune he had also quoted in *Rayok*. There, it was lampooned not so much musically as by the crassly dim and lumbering libretto. Here in the Concerto, the tune itself is mercilessly mocked: the first five notes brutally hammered in the strings; the next three notes sneeringly answered several octaves higher, in the wrong key and in a bitter minor mode, in the woodwinds. This "disassembly" of *Suliko* was certainly complete enough for the quotation to have passed unnoticed by Rostropovich, who remained unaware of it until it was pointed out to him.

Incidentally, where the "klezmer" theme in the Violin Concerto was not actually constructed from Jewish modes, the one in the finale of the Cello Concerto is, though the mode in question, A *freygish*, conflicts with the perceived overall tonality, C-sharp. Furthermore, the very opening bars of the entire Concerto can be heard to outline the *freygish* mode in E-flat—the cello's first four notes (G–F-flat–C-flat–B-flat) and the responding E-flat major harmony in the woodwinds. Joachim Braun views the Concerto as a product of a mini-Jewish period that would also take in the Eighth Quartet (by way of its Second Piano Trio quotation) and the Thirteenth Symphony, the latter by way of its topic rather than its musical style.[36]

***

In the summer of 1959, Shostakovich had hinted that he was working on a new quartet. Following a short bout in the hospital in February 1960, he completed his Seventh Quartet in March. It is likely, although not absolutely certain, that this was the same piece that he had started the previous summer—as several commentators have pointed out, the dedicatee of the Quartet, his late wife Nina, would have been fifty in 1959, and so the work was in all likelihood conceived as an anniversary commemoration.[37]

Before discussing the Quartet, it is worth considering the role of cyclism in Shostakovich's music thus far. Since the early 1940s, he had been increasingly preoccupied with inter-movement cyclic connections, i.e., surface-level, obviously identifiable, recalls of earlier material (as opposed to the deeper-level motivic connections that may also run through a work). Indeed, twelve of the seventeen multi-movement instrumental concert works written between 1941 and 1960 contain such cyclic references, an extraordinarily high proportion (see Table 9.1).[38] Only the Second Piano Sonata, the Second Piano Concerto, the Ninth Symphony, and the Second and Fourth Quartets are free of such references.

As Table 9.1 shows, Shostakovich almost always reserved his cyclic recalls for his finales. Moreover, he was remarkably consistent in the placement and the manner of their deployment, usually presenting the recalls in the finale as a disruption to the development section's central climax (assuming some kind of sonata-related structure), after which the finale's own material would reassert itself, in some cases immediately, in other cases more gradually. Even where the recalls return again in the movement's coda (e.g., the Tenth Symphony or the First Violin Concerto) or, in the exceptional case of the Seventh Symphony, appear there for the first time, they may challenge or color the ongoing material, but they never topple it; in each case, the finale ends on the finale's terms. In the Sixth Quartet, because the finale ends the same way as the first movement, it could be argued that the finale's own material is, in the end, deposed by the cyclic recall. But given the disembodied, "tacked-on" nature of that cadence in each movement, this would be rather stretching the point.

However, the last three works listed in Table 9.1, the First Cello Concerto and the Seventh and Eighth Quartets, would see an intensifying of the cyclic relationship, with Shostakovich now allowing his recalls to have a more profound influence on the work's ultimate direction. As previously discussed, the recall of the first movement's main theme about two-thirds of the way through the finale of the Cello Concerto almost completely pushes aside the finale's own material. As a

Table 9.1
Use of Cyclism in Multi-Movement Instrumental Concert Works (1941–1960)[39]

Work	Cyclic Use
Seventh Symphony (1941)	Recall of two first movement themes in finale
Eighth Symphony (1943)	Recall of first movement climax in finale
Second Piano Trio (1944)	Recall of first movement in finale
	Recall of third movement passacaglia progression in finale
Third Quartet (1946)	Recall of third movement pseudo-passacaglia bass in finale
First Violin Concerto (1948)	Material from all four movements in third movement cadenza
	Recall of third movement passacaglia ground in finale
Fifth Quartet (1952)	Recall of first movement Ustvolskaya quotation in finale
Tenth Symphony (1953)	Recall of first movement introduction in third movement
	Recall of scherzo in finale
	Recall of third movement DSCH monogram in finale
Sixth Quartet (1956)	All movements end with the same cadential "signature"
	Recall of third movement passacaglia ground in finale
Eleventh Symphony (1957)	Palace Square theme in movements 1, 2, and 4
	Timpani triplet motif in movements 1 and 2
	Trumpet fanfare motif in movements 1, 2, and 4
	"Listen!" in movements 1 and 2
	"Our Tsar, Our Little Father" in movements 2 and 4
	"Bare Your Heads" in movements 2, 3, and 4
First Cello Concerto (1959)	Recall of first movement fragments in cadenza
	Recall of first movement in finale
Seventh Quartet (1960)	Recall of first movement in finale
	Recall of second movement in finale
Eighth Quartet (1960)	Recall of opening material in finale
	Recall of First Symphony quotation in finale
	DSCH motif used in all five movements

result, that movement's latter stages take on something of the first movement's energy, more straitjacketed and less carefree than the music had been up to that point. As we shall see in the discussion of its finale, the Seventh Quartet would take this concept of cyclic "influence" several steps further.

At only twelve minutes, the Seventh would be the shortest of Shostakovich's fifteen quartets. But where the Sixth Quartet had still employed some of the "symphonic" techniques of the earlier quartets, albeit in scaled-down circumstances, the Seventh in its quiet way looks forward to the less symphonic, more narrative, forms of late Shostakovich—"quiet," literally, for other than in the first half of the third movement, it rarely raises its voice above *mezzo piano*.

The first movement is in sonatina form, which immediately removes it from Shostakovich's world of epic symphonism—a simple nine-bar retransition is all that connects the end of the exposition to the start of the recapitulation, rather like a typical Rossini overture. However, the last two bars of this retransition see a switch from the movement's 2/4 meter to 3/8; the recapitulation first theme is then run in this new meter (Fig. 9). The first movement of the Fourth Quartet had also recast duple meter music into triple meter at the recapitulation. But in that case, the metrical switch, along with the modal recasting of the theme and the creation of a dissonant pedal, created a new layer of tension that would affect the subsequent course of the recapitulation. Here in the Seventh Quartet, the rhythmic recasting and the pizzicato presentation provide simple contrast rather than intensification; in all other respects the reprise is identical to the exposition, at least for the first thirty-five bars or so. The second theme reprise is then presented in the tonic in its original meter. The relationship between recapitulation and exposition in this movement then has little to do with the symphonic processes of sonata form. A more apt comparison might be the relationship between an eighteenth century character variation and its original theme.

The basic key of the second movement is D minor. However, the opening melody in the first violin corresponds, at least in its first few bars, to D Phrygian, though with the raised leading note, C-sharp, while the pitch content of the undulating second violin line (up to Fig. 18) forms an octatonic scale based on D, though again with C-sharp replacing the expected C-natural: D–E-flat–F–G-flat–A-flat–A-natural–B–C-sharp. In both cases, the C-sharp reflects Shostakovich's non-dogmatic approach to modes, and in the case of the octatonic scale, provides greater tonal stability. It is also notable that the first five intervals of this octatonic scale correspond to the first five intervals of the first movement's opening F-sharp minor theme, placed in ascending scale order: F-sharp–G–A–B-flat–C–C-sharp–D–E-flat (Example 9.3).

Example 9.3

The use of octatonic scale portions would become increasingly prevalent in Shostakovich's music throughout the 1960s, although it should be said that for the most part, the scale is used as an expressive or even destabilizing melodic device within a tonal context rather than as the basis for the type of genuinely octatonic music found in, say, Bartók or Messiaen. In this respect, it is comparable to Shostakovich's use of the twelve-note row later in the decade—maximally enhanced chromaticism rather than genuine serialism.

A mode of limited transposition, to use Messiaen's term, the octatonic scale comes in three forms. However, for a given tonic, such as the F-sharp of the Quartet's first movement, there are two forms, one starting with a minor second (Example 9.4a), the other starting with a major second (Example 9.4b). Both forms of the scale distort tonality to an extent. However, the presence in the first version of the tonic-dominant relationship (F-sharp to C-sharp in Example 9.4a) in addition to the tonic-tritone relationship (F-sharp to C-natural) helps stabilize tonality some-what. Shostakovich tends more often than not to go for the first version, possibly for its greater tonal stability, and possibly because it has built within it the lowered second degree (F-sharp to G-natural in the example below), one of Shostakovich's favorite modal inflections. The first five pitches of this version (Example 9.4a) also correspond to David Haas' proposed "Shostakovich Mode" (see Chapter 12), and the first four pitches correspond to a reordered DSCH ("HCDS").

Example 9.4a

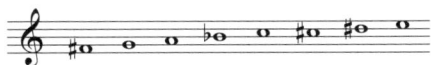

Example 9.4b

Eleven bars into the movement, the second violin's arpeggiated figure smoothes out into an undulating four-pitch melodic pattern, *x*, (F–G-flat–A-flat–B-double-flat), in other words, an octatonic/"Shostakovich Mode"/"HCDS" formation. Fol-lowing a short central section based on funereal dotted rhythms, and a severely truncated reprise of the first theme, *x* returns in the viola six bars before the end of the movement. In the penultimate bar, everything stops and the viola makes one final, unaccompanied, rhythmically augmented statement of *x* in descending scalar order (B-double-flat–A-flat–G-flat–F). The finale then explodes, *attacca*, with a raucous quasi-inversion (though still octatonic) of the first movement's opening theme played by the first violin, dissonantly accompanied by the second violin and cello. The viola responds calmly with its descending-scale rendition of *x* (now enharmonically rewritten as A–G-sharp–F-sharp–E-sharp) in an even larger augmentation. In both cases, the viola's isolation of *x* seems to frame it as a quota-tion, which is perhaps not surprising given that it is a derivative of DSCH. Fol-lowing a repeat of the outburst in the other three instruments, the viola uses the *x* figure, now ascending (F-sharp–G–A–B-flat), to launch into the savage fugue that will constitute the first half of this finale (Example 9.5).

Example 9.5

At the climax of the fugue, the main second movement theme is brought back in the viola and cello *in alt*, the tension heightened further by the rhythmically destabilizing ostinato in the first violin (Fig. 37). In other words, Shostakovich does here what he has done in most of the other works listed in Table 9.1, deploying a cyclic recall at a central, climactic moment in the finale. This leads immediately into a second cyclic recall, a tutti declamation of the first movement's main theme, scored in an angry, almost Bartokian quartal-based harmony. But what happens next is what sets the Seventh Quartet apart. The finale's material does indeed return, but severely transformed. A wan, muted, world-weary waltz, also based on the x figure, takes the place of the highly charged fugue. Of course, it could be argued that the transformation of something bold into something pale could merely be a familiar Shostakovichian, post-traumatic response following a passage of musical "brutalization," one that has nothing to do with cyclic recalls. But the choice of the waltz here, with its slowing of the tempo and its change into a triple meter, would appear to be a conscious attempt to bring the finale into line with the first movement in preparation for what will be a gradual takeover by the first movement. Initially, the first movement theme vies on an equal basis with the waltz, but gradually the waltz recedes from view, leaving only the skeleton of the first movement theme. In other words, the cyclic return actively instigates a change of course in the finale's own material, a change that eventually leads to its demise altogether—a demise that is more profound emotionally and psychologically than in the Cello Concerto. By the coda, the Quartet has returned to something like the place where it began. "Cyclic" here takes on its literal meaning: not just denoting a recall of previous themes, as in the other works in Table 9.1, but functioning literally as the adjective of "cycle"—a returning to the point of origination.

Thus, the Seventh Quartet takes on a narrative quality of journey and return that puts it in a different sphere from Shostakovich's previous symphonic and chamber works—although certain individual movements had possibly possessed this quality, e.g., the finale of the Fifth Quartet. And given that the four notes (x), whose octatonically based intervals had instigated the first movement's opening theme, would subsequently set up, through a series of connections, both main themes in the finale, that journey is characterized by a level of thematic integration that goes beyond almost anything in Shostakovich's previous output—another connection is the slow movement's chain of funereal dotted rhythms reappearing as the tail of the finale's fugue subject.

The Eighth Quartet would take the concept of transformative cyclic returns one stage further, for there the entire finale represents a return to the first movement, and actually explores further, delivering what the first movement attempted to deliver but was unable to—namely a fugue on DSCH. And in that Quartet, the famous autobiographical quotations, not to mention remarks that the composer made to his nearest and dearest, would provide "content" to the narrative. At first glance, the Seventh Quartet does not throw up ready-made associations like the Eighth does. But is it possible that the slurred arpeggiated figure in the second violin at the opening of the second movement is an allusion to the opening of Berg's Violin Concerto? Berg's opening solo entry presents an arpeggio on the violin's open strings—G, D, A, and E. Although open strings may or may not be the most desirable way to play the second violin line in the Shostakovich, the emphasis here on the notes D and A would seem to reinforce the connection. As already mentioned, the Seventh Quartet was dedicated to Shostakovich's first wife, Nina; 1959, the year the Quartet was probably begun, would have been Nina's fiftieth birthday and, ironically, was also the year that Shostakovich ended his disastrous marriage to Margarita. Which bring us to Berg's own famous dedication of his Violin Concerto—"To the Memory of an Angel"; the angel in this case being Manon Gropius, the daughter of the architect Walter Gropius and Alma Mahler, who had died at the even more untimely age of eighteen. In other words, is it possible that via an allusion to Berg, Shostakovich wished to introduce into the Seventh Quartet the topic of "death" or "love-death" or, even more specifically, the untimely death of a loved one? This is something that would appear to be reinforced fourteen bars into this second movement where the viola and cello quote the most famous "love-death" reference of them all, the opening to Wagner's *Tristan and Isolde*, scored in mysterious, almost medieval sounding, parallel fifths, and made still more mysterious by the aching slow glissando in both instruments, as they strive to reach their high point (Fig. 18). And those funereal dotted rhythms later in the movement seem to reinforce the idea of a memorial.

The Seventh Quartet would provide a prototype for the kind of cyclic, possibly autobiographical narrative that becomes apparent in the Eighth. In the Seventh Quartet, we have a fugue and a waltz based on the abovementioned *x* figure, the reordered, or "hidden," DSCH. In the Eighth, we also have a fugue and a waltz, but now based on the "real" DSCH (in the fifth and third movements, respectively). If the subject of the Eighth Quartet is the composer himself, that of the Seventh Quartet is possibly a combination of the composer (through the veiled, reordered DSCH motif) and Nina. Indeed, Nina would hardly be forgotten in the Eighth either, for one of the most poignant moments of that Quartet is the quotation in the fourth movement of Katerina's fourth act aria from *Lady Macbeth*, the ill-fated opera that Shostakovich had dedicated to Nina back in 1932 and that he had pulled down from the shelves in 1955 in the immediate aftermath of her death.

The Seventh Quartet, all twelve minutes of it, would represent a milestone, and not just because of its intensified treatment of cyclism and narrative—the work hints at a later Shostakovich style in other ways too. The restless mixed meter of the first and, to a lesser extent, third movements is one example. The frantic parallel minor second passage between viola and cello in the third movement fugue is another (Fig. 29, b5). Certain sonorities are also unusually modernistic for Shostakovich. In the first movement's recapitulation, for example, the first note (F-sharp) of each repetition of the first violin's descending pizzicato scale (excluding the very first run at Fig. 9) is doubled by the second violin playing the same pitch, *arco*, with a quick *diminuendo*, giving a pointillistic effect bordering on *Klangfarbenmelodie*, as the sharp pizzicato attack fades to the sound of the bow. Such effects, reminiscent of the Second Viennese School, would become more common with Shostakovich during the 1960s, i.e., during the period of his own flirtation with serialism. And we have already mentioned the bare, organum-like parallel-fifth treatment of the second movement's *Tristan* allusion—indeed, the *Tristan* allusion itself would also occur in several later works, e.g., the Fourteenth and Fifteenth Symphonies and the Thirteenth and Fourteenth Quartets. The Seventh Quartet is a tonal work, but it stood on the brink of a decade in which a certain amount of post-Schoenbergian modernism would infiltrate into Soviet composition. Nevertheless, its fleeting glimpses of modernism would not be replicated in the Eighth Quartet written four months later, or in the Twelfth or Thirteenth Symphonies (1961 and 1962, respectively). It would still be a few years before Shostakovich would face the challenges posed by Soviet modernism, and for that, he would largely have his own students to thank.

***

The years leading up to 1960 had seen a flurry of official activities at home and abroad, further cementing the public image of Shostakovich as, in essence, the State composer. The latest push appears to have been inaugurated with the aforementioned election to the Secretariat of the Composers' Union in 1957. In 1958, he visited Bulgaria and France in what would be his final overseas tours as a pianist, and collected awards in France, Italy, England, and Finland,[40] as well as the Lenin Prize for his Eleventh Symphony. He also chaired the First International Tchaikovsky Competition and was elected President of the USSR-Austria Friendship Society. In 1959, he attended the World Peace Council in Sweden, the Autumn Festival in Warsaw, and was one of six composers dispatched on a month-long, seven-city tour of the USA in October/November. There, he was made an honorary member of the American Academy of Arts and Letters and attended the US premiere performance and world premiere recording of the First Cello Concerto with Rostropovich, the Philadelphia Orchestra, and Eugene Ormandy. Although the experience was less fraught than the ill-fated 1949 trip, Shostakovich still stood out with his distracted, fidgety behavior. In the words of the American composer Roger Sessions, the "warm and friendly" Shostakovich would "freeze up" the moment Khrennikov appeared in the room.[41] As a young man, Shostakovich had relished travel. But now, not only was it more physically exhausting, the pressure to maintain the official facade was taking a psychological toll. As he told Glikman, "I would be better off sitting at home playing patience."[42] And apart from Oxford University, whose ancient traditions he rather enjoyed, the accumulation of honors was also of little value: "I am frightened that I will choke in an ocean of awards."[43]

The late 1950s also saw an escalation of Party-scripted "Shostakovich" speeches and articles, all saturated, needless to say, with high-flown rhetoric and obsequious praise for the all-wise, all-caring Party. As Ian MacDonald observed, the significance of culture as one of the major battlegrounds of the Cold War post-1956 meant that "Shostakovich . . . needed to be 'defused' as a figure of cultural controversy by formally bringing him into the Soviet fold."[44] With hindsight, we can see that this flurry of activity, not to mention the official rehabilitation of Shostakovich courtesy of the 1958 Resolution, was in all likelihood a preparation for the recruitment of the composer into the Party itself.

In 1960, Shostakovich was invited to serve as First Secretary of the newly formed Russian Federation (RSFSR) Union of Composers. Accepting the post would make him the highest ranking composer-official in the Russian Federation, and the second highest in the Soviet Union, after Khrennikov. Glikman reports that the appointment was Khrushchov's idea and was conditional upon Party membership. However, the latter is open to question since it was not until June, two months after taking up the post, that moves were made, at least officially, to induct the composer into the Party. A distraught Shostakovich told Glikman that the Central Committee official responsible for ensnaring him, P. N. Pospelov, had leaned on him incessantly, eventually wearing him down and breaking his resistance. According to Glikman, Shostakovich vowed not to attend the meeting that was being set up in Moscow at the end of June to induct him: "They'll only get me to Moscow if they tie me up and drag me there, you understand, they'll have to tie me up."[45] Lev Lebedinsky recalls events differently. According to him, Shostakovich had decided to take the train back to Moscow, and it was only through Lebedinsky's persuasion that he stayed in Leningrad, instead sending a telegram claiming to be ill.[46] Either way, the induction was postponed. But Shostakovich's mental state during those last days of June was apparent to both Glikman and Lebedinsky. Glikman wrote:

> The moment I saw him I was struck by the lines of suffering in his face, and by his whole air of distress. He hurried me straight into the little room where he had slept, crumpled down on to the bed and began to weep with great, aching sobs. . . . he managed through tears to jerk out indistinctly: 'They've been pursuing me for years, hunting me down . . .' Never before had I seen Shostakovich in such a state of hysterical collapse.[47]

While all this had been playing out during June, Shostakovich was finishing up *Satires*, settings of five poems of Sasha Chorny (real name Alexander Glikberg) for soprano and piano. The poems ("To a Critic," "Spring Awakening," "Descendants," "A Misunderstanding," and "Kreutzer Sonata") deal with philistinism and the foolishness of Utopianism; in fact, the theme of "misunderstanding" pervades the entire cycle. Given all that was going on around him, it is not surprising that Shostakovich was drawn to these recently republished poems, though of course he had long enjoyed the satirical writings of the likes of Krylov, Zoshchenko, and Ilf and Petrov. As a youth, Shostakovich had derided Tolstoy's plea for sexual chastity in "Kreutzer Sonata" (see Chapter 4). It is not difficult, then, to understand his attraction to Chorny's "Kreutzer Sonata," with its parody of Tolstoy's plea. Needless to say, this final song brings the inevitable quotation of Beethoven's sonata.

Chorny's biting commentaries meet their match with Shostakovich's pithy music. Contributing to the sense of cyclic unity here is the fact that each song starts the same way, with a quietly repeating single pitch chiming in the piano, a single pitch that then erupts into harmony—a different harmony for each song. Though the style does not particularly emulate *Lady Macbeth*, the juxtaposition of the achingly erotic and music-hall triviality in "A Misunderstanding" is suggestive of similar juxtapositions in the opera. At the suggestion of the work's dedicatee, Galina Vishnevskaya, Shostakovich added the subtitle "Pictures of the Past." This was, of course, not the first time, nor would it be the last, that he would use such a ploy to create a "respectable" distance from his own satirical or condemnatory creations so that, on the surface at least, the audience need not be embarrassed or disturbed out of their complacency—"It all took place in Tsarist Russia," as the commentator at the premiere of *From Jewish Folk Poetry* had so memorably put it. For Shostakovich, the subtitle "Pictures of the Past" was his "fig leaf" to "cover up the embarrassing parts."[48]

With the issue of Party membership deferred, if not resolved, Shostakovich spent the next two weeks in East Germany observing the filming of *Five Days, Five Nights*. Directed by his friend Leo Arnshtam, the film commemorated the wartime destruction of Dresden. Shostakovich stayed in the nearby spa town of Gohrisch, but visited Dresden to inspect the still devastated city for himself. Yet, little progress was made on the score; what emerged instead was the Eighth Quartet, composed in a three-day blitz between 12 and 14 July. On his return home, Shostakovich told his daughter Galina that the Quartet was an autobiographical work that he had decided to dedicate to himself,[49] a statement he repeated at around the same time to Glikman:

> Instead [of the film score] I wrote this ideologically flawed quartet which is of no use to anybody. I started thinking that if some day I die, nobody is likely to write a work in memory of me, so I had better write one myself. The title page could carry the dedication: 'To the memory of the composer of this quartet.'... It is a pseudo-tragic quartet, so much so that while I was composing it I shed the same amount of tears as I would have to pee after half-a-dozen beers. When I got home, I tried a couple of times to play it through, but always ended up in tears. This was of course a response not so much to the pseudo-tragedy as to my own wonder at its superlative unity of form. But here you may detect a touch of self glorification, which no doubt will soon pass and leave in its place the usual self-critical hangover."[50]

With Shostakovich now back from East Germany, he had to face once again the issue of Party membership. His induction as a provisional member of the Communist Party took place in September, with promotion to full membership the following year. Ultimately, there is no easy answer to the question "Was Shostakovich forced to join the Party?" As Laurel Fay has pointed out, he could hardly have contributed any more to the Party as a member than he had already been doing in the previous few years as a non-member, so from a practical point of view it made very little difference.[51] However, symbolically, the difference was enormous, and this episode would tie him in knots for the rest of his life. His reticence in discussing the matter extended even to the woman who would become his third wife, Irina Supinskaya, though he did once quip to Glikman during a bout in hospital that his ailments were probably God's punishment for joining the Party.[52]

***

With its heavy reliance on the DSCH motto and its miscellany of musical self-quotations and allusions,[53] the Eighth Quartet's autobiographical tone was hard to miss. But given that Shostakovich could hardly admit in public what he had told Galina and Glikman in private, there remained the question of what such autobiographical content actually meant. Perhaps conveniently, the week before the October 1960 premiere, Shostakovich described the Quartet as his response to the devastation that he had witnessed in Dresden, and announced that he was dedicating it to the memory of "the victims of war and Fascism."[54] Although it does not appear in Shostakovich's manuscript, this dedication would be printed into the published score. Whether this was done with Shostakovich's imprimatur is not clear. As for the autobiographical content, this could now be explained as an emblem of Shostakovich's identification with the victims, a reminder, as Yury Keldysh's pioneering review put it, "that the struggle against the dark forces of reaction has always been a basic theme in his work."[55]

So where does the "official" dedication stand in relation to the work itself? In essence, there are three possibilities: 1) the dedication was a ploy, a shield under which to hide this obviously tragic work—the "fascist threat" was still a hot political topic, and artistic works exposing its dangers were always welcome; 2) given that Shostakovich's own anti-fascism was completely genuine, the dedication constituted a belatedly applied second layer, a layer of convenience perhaps, but one that for Shostakovich neither jeopardized the tone or "meaning" of the music nor conflicted with his own personal beliefs; or 3) the Quartet was genuinely and integrally conceived as a semantically dual-layered piece commemorating both personal and universal suffering, only one of which, the latter, was safe to discuss in public. A fourth viewpoint, that the official interpretation constitutes the Quartet's only layer, can probably be discounted given Shostakovich's aforementioned private comments.

Although we will probably never know exactly how this issue evolved in Shostakovich's mind, one small anomaly is worth pointing out. Shostakovich's dedications were nearly all personal in nature—usually family members, friends, teachers, or fellow musicians. Public dedications were rare. In fact, aside from the Eighth Quartet, there would be only four such examples: the Seventh Symphony and the incidental music to *Native Leningrad* (both dedicated to the city and its people), and those two orchestral "megaphones," *Novorosiisk Chimes* (1960; "In Memory of the Heroes of the Great Patriotic War") and the *Funeral-Triumphal Prelude* (1967; "In Memory of the Heroes of the Battle of Stalingrad"), both intended for tape-recorded replay at outdoor city-square war memorials. Next to such blatantly public utterances, the deeply private Eighth Quartet makes a strange bedfellow indeed.

In each of Shostakovich's previous five-movement works, the Eighth and Ninth Symphonies and the Third Quartet, the third, fourth, and fifth movements had been linked, *attacca*. In the Eighth Quartet, all five movements are linked. The first movement opens with a stretto on DSCH, one whose slow but inexorable rhythmic carriage and pathetic tugging minor seconds bring to mind the C-sharp minor Fugue from the First Book of Bach's *Well Tempered Clavier* or the first movement of Beethoven's C-sharp minor Quartet, op. 131. One oddity is the sub-dominant answer of Shostakovich's fourth voice (first violin, bar 5), perhaps the influence of Beethoven's dominant-centered fugue, in which answers enter at the fourth; only with a fifth entrance in the viola (bar 8) does Shostakovich give the expected dominant answer. But it is the stretto treatment itself, something tradi-tionally associated with the end of a fugue rather than the start, which is perhaps the more significant indicator that traditional fugal unfolding is not on the agenda, at least not at this juncture. Indeed, by bar 12, the stretto has fizzled out in preparation for the first self-quotation, a wan rendition of the First Symphony's (originally playful) opening (Fig. 1, b3).

So what, then, is the purpose of eleven bars of fugue? Taking the long-range view, David Fanning sees it as one of a number of elements that Shostakovich leaves open or "failed" in the Quartet's earlier stages in order to resolve them later on. In this case, the aborted fugue in the first movement is resolved with the suc-cessful fugue in the last.[56] But there is possibly also a short-term reason for the use of stretto at the outset of the Quartet, for regardless of its fugal connotations, the stretto is also a highly effective way to create emotionally searing, "stacked" chromatic dissonance (e.g., the introductions of Mozart's "Dissonance" Quartet or Haydn's *The Creation*) while concurrently establishing the thematic identity of DSCH.

The main portion of the movement following the First Symphony quotation is given over to a series of arioso passages. The first of these (Fig. 2; an allusion to the first movement of Tchaikovsky's *Pathétique* Symphony) is reminiscent of the Shostakovich recitatives of the 1940s, with its chromatically decorated first violin line over a static drone and its quasi-cadential resolutions by semitone onto the various members of the C minor tonic chord (A-flat to G, F-flat to E-flat, and D-flat to C). The drone itself outlines an open fifth—octave tonic Cs in viola and cello and G in the second violin. The second arioso (Fig. 4; an allusion to the first movement of Shostakovich's Fifth Symphony) continues the C pedal in the viola and cello, but the second violin G pedal is now "activated" both melodically, par-ticularly its tugging A-flat to G motion, and rhythmically, with a dactylic figure that, sped up, will become the main rhythmic driving force behind the second movement, an example of one movement "informing" the next. In a partial nod to arch form, the third arioso (Fig. 7) returns us to the material of the first, while the movement ends with a return to the First Symphony quotation (Fig. 9, b6) and a final, non-fugal, musing on DSCH. Five bars before the end, the second violin intones the aforementioned dactylic oscillation between the dissonant A-flat and the consonant G over the open fifth pedal. However, in the movement's pe-nultimate bar, the A-flat is denied its resolution to G. Instead, it is reinterpreted as a held G-sharp, providing, via a *crescendo*, the plunge into the C-sharp minor sec-ond movement.

The second movement is often compared to the third movement of the Eighth Symphony with its obsessive, toccata-like stream of hammering quarter notes and its seemingly sporadic, slashing *sfff* chords. Yet the effect is quite different, the faster tempo rendering a wilder, more frenetic brutality compared with the meat-grinding juggernaut of the Symphony. Aside from the obsessive DSCH ostinati (e.g., Fig. 23), the movement's principal quotation is the Jewish dance theme from the finale of the Second Piano Trio. It is presented in the original Piano Trio key of C altered-Dorian, and the brittle two-octave spacing between first and second violins reflects the piano's similar presentation in the earlier work (Fig. 21). Although this quotation forms the trio section of the Quartet's scherzo, there is no relaxation. The underlying C minor harmony, which in the Piano Trio was given as a klezmer-like "oom-pah" rhythmic figure, is here presented as a hurtling triplet *arpeggiando* in the lower strings, sucking this dance theme into the vortex of the scherzo's ongoing ferocity.

Towards the end of the movement, Shostakovich replays the Jewish theme. But this time, its journey is more tortuous. Presented now in the viola and cello, it has to fight harder to be heard, since its registral placement puts it into collision with the violins' *arpeggiando* accompaniment, the latter now altered from the original C minor to a diminished seventh (C-sharp–E–G–B-flat). At first, the new harmony registers as a color change, as if we are looking at the same theme but through a different light or at a different angle. But it could be argued that the inconclusive harmony is a signifier of the fate of the theme itself, which, after accumulating a head of steam courtesy of its obsessively repeated one-bar cells (Fig. 34, b1–15), is brutally cut short right before its final cadence. After a tense general pause, the third movement barges its way in with a forthright statement of DSCH, unaccompanied in the first violin, setting up the *danse macabre* waltz rhythm that will come to define this movement.

Like the Eighth Symphony and Third Quartet, the Eighth Quartet features two consecutive scherzos. In all three cases, they occupy the respective second and third movements, and each scherzo tells its own story. In the Eighth Symphony, the contrast is perhaps between the force of human cruelty (second movement) and something more mechanically brutal (third movement); in the two quartets, the second scherzo acts as a shock absorber, as Fanning puts it, to the violence of the first.[57] In fact, the use of a waltz or *Ländler* to diffuse brutality was not uncommon in Shostakovich, e.g., the jackbooted waltz following the Fourth Symphony's wild first movement fugato, or even the succession of second movement (brutal scherzo) to third movement (marionette-like waltz) in the Tenth Symphony. Of course, the word "diffuse" should be read with caution. Saturated in irony, these waltzes usually leave behind more questions than answers.

This third movement's main waltz theme is based on DSCH (or, more specifically DDSCH, which Fanning believes is a play on the composer's full name, Dmitry Dmitriyevich Shostakovich[58]), and plays on the characteristic rhythm (quarter note followed by four eighths) of Saint-Saëns' *Danse macabre*. In fact, Fanning reports that at one of the Quartet's draft stages, Shostakovich had contemplated chords similar to Saint-Saëns' scordatura chords.[59] Also prevalent is

Shostakovich's favorite "castanet" triplet rhythm (e.g., Fig. 39, b5), often associated with moments of devilry; that figure had already occurred in the second movement (e.g., Fig. 23, b9) in a passage that would be quoted two years later in the scherzo of the Thirteenth Symphony in connection with the antics of Nasreddin Hodja (see Examples 9.6a and 9.6b). The trio section, meanwhile, takes what sounds like a new, duple-meter theme, but one that is in fact based on DSCH (Fig. 42, b4), and uses it as a springboard for a quotation from the first movement of the First Cello Concerto, a quotation given, ironically, to the first violin (Fig. 43). The cello, however, picks up the thread at Fig. 44 with a new, triple-meter theme, again based on DSCH, a theme whose gentle rocking motion is mitigated by its strained delivery in the upper reaches of the instrument.

The main scherzo material returns, though now presented *con sordino*. The mutes add a sense of remoteness, almost as if the life is slipping away from the movement. The sense of mystery is heightened by the cello high E with which the trio ended continuing to hang like a poison cloud over the opening melody for the next twenty-eight bars. The incomplete reprise of the trio that follows works in the opposite manner to that of the previous movement. There, the Jewish theme was abruptly cut off at the top of its *crescendo* immediately before what would have been its climax; here, the Cello Concerto quotation is simply left to fizzle out.

What is left is a single note, A-sharp, in the first violin, a note that hangs into the next movement. It continues to hang for twenty-one bars, unperturbed by the violent three-note outbursts that dominate this fourth movement. Constituting the most overtly gestural music in the entire Quartet, these outbursts, dissonant major second dyads in a heavy anapest rhythm, have, over the years, become the work's primary magnet for extramusical interpretation. Invariably viewed as the point at which the Quartet's *topos* (however that may be read) reaches its most graphic realization, these outbursts have been interpreted as bombs falling on Dresden (with the violin A-sharp drone representing the constant whine of aircraft), or the NKVD knock on the door in the middle of the night. The musicologist Harlow Robinson, meanwhile, believes that they represent the three taps under the table, the code purportedly used amongst the intelligentsia to warn of the presence of informers.[60] In musical terms, it is a brutalization of the anapest group of the Cello Concerto's second bar, a connection reinforced by the use of the Concerto's first bar as a slow, grinding three-note upbeat (usually E–C-sharp–G-sharp) to each of the subsequent outbursts.

Built into the Cello Concerto quotation is an additional reference, namely the piece upon which the Concerto's first theme is itself based, the "Procession to Execution" from *The Young Guard*. And this is no incidental "bonus." *The Young Guard* itself has direct relevance to the Eighth Quartet, since the heroes in that Procession sing what is to be Shostakovich's next quotation in this fourth movement, not a self-quotation this time, but the Revolutionary song "Zamuchen tyazholoi nevolei." (The title does not translate easily. "Tormented by Harsh Captivity" is probably the best translation—"nevolei" literally "unfreedom"—though "Tortured by Grievous Bondage" is also common.)

The ultimate goal of the finales of both the Cello Concerto and the Seventh Quartet was to reclaim their respective first movements. And so it is in the Eighth Quartet, only here the reclaiming process takes place over two movements. What the fourth movement reclaims is the first movement's use of long pedals, starting with that violin drone brought in from the previous movement, as well as its arioso style of thematic delivery. The two quotations here, "Tormented by Harsh Captivity" (Fig. 57, b13) and Katerina's fourth act aria from *Lady Macbeth* (Fig. 61, b16) are both played to the accompaniment of static pedals, just as the Fifth Symphony and Tchaikovsky *Pathétique* allusions had been in the first movement. Meanwhile, the fifth movement (*Largo*) reclaims the DSCH fugue that was so quickly aborted in the opening movement, playing it out, complete with countersubject and three expositions, the third of which (Fig. 70) replays, *con sordini*, the first movement's stretto, complete with the quirky second and fourth voice answers, at the subdominant and the subsequent "corrective" fifth voice at the dominant. It also replays three bars of the First Symphony quotation (Fig. 71, b5). Like the first movement, the Quartet ends with the oscillation between A-flat and G over the open fifth pedal (C and G), though now the final resolution to G is granted, bringing with it at least a tentative peace.

The Eighth Quartet's larger structure can be viewed in several ways. It can be seen as an arch in which the two outer movements, the aborted and the realized fugues on DSCH, respectively, flank the three inner ones. Or it can be viewed as an arch in which the first movement at one end and the "repossessing" fourth and fifth movements as a pair at the other flank the second and third movements. At the same time, the Quartet is also a two-part structure. The first part (movements 1–3) presents three self-quotations, and one allusion, in chronological order: First Symphony (1926); the allusion to the Fifth Symphony (1937); Second Piano Trio (1944); and First Cello Concerto (1959). The second half (movements 4 and 5) puts the process into reverse with quotations from the Cello Concerto and its subsidiary, *The Young Guard* (1948), *Lady Macbeth* (1932), and finally the First Symphony again—the bridge between the two halves provided by the transforming of the Cello Concerto quotation from a "familiar" guise in the third movement to the slow-motion, brutalized version in the fourth.

So, why did Shostakovich choose the quotations and allusions that he did to chart his autobiographical journey? Needless to say, any answers, as obvious as some of them may appear to be, remain speculative. Over the Quartet's first three movements, Shostakovich appears to choose a work of particular personal significance from each decade of his adult life. The First Symphony was the piece that catapulted him to international fame, the Fifth constituted his return to grace following the *Lady Macbeth* scandal, while the Piano Trio was the work associated with his closest friend, Sollertinsky, and marked the first of his encounters with the Jewish idiom. Admittedly, the Cello Concerto lacks such a ready-made explanation; it may simply have been Shostakovich's way of bringing the narrative up to date. Of course, the even more recent Seventh Quartet could also have served. Indeed, the Concerto's role as the supplier of the fourth movement's brutal anapestic outbursts and its motivic compatibility with the DSCH motif are also shared by the Quartet, though the direct thematic connection to *The Young Guard* may have been the decisive factor here.

In the Quartet's second half, the personal significance of *Lady Macbeth* needs no explanation. But aside from the fact that it is probably the most melodically "quotable" theme in the entire opera, the choice of Katerina's aria is very much in the spirit of the fourth movement, Katerina literally "tormented by harsh captivity" as she deals with her new life on the Siberian convict trail. Incidentally, this aria is given to the cello, reversing, so to speak, the earlier violin presentation of the Cello Concerto material, and leading many to wonder if this was indeed some kind of pun on "Sergei"—the subject of the aria and the name of the cellist (Shirinsky) of the Beethoven Quartet, the work's first performers. As Fanning points out, this fourth movement, with its references to *The Young Guard* and "Tormented by Harsh Captivity" and its infamous outbursts, takes us out of the personal domain of the first three movements (i.e., the Quartet's first part) and into an arena depicting communal suffering.[61] And this journey is somewhat paralleled by the journey of DSCH itself—prominent in the first three movements (particularly the third), less so in the "communal" fourth, and reinstated as the rightful subject in the fifth.

The Eighth is by far the most popular and frequently played of Shostakovich's quartets, and in all likelihood, the work's special set of circumstances and extramusical associations (whether interpreted in the "orthodox" or the "revisionist" manner) have contributed to this. Yet, for some, these associations have had a negative impact. Richard Taruskin, for example, writes:

> The Eighth Quartet is a wrenching human document.... But its explicitness exacts a price. The quotations are lengthy and literal, amounting in the crucial fourth movement to an inert medley; the thematic transformations are very demonstratively, perhaps over-demonstratively, elaborated; startling juxtapositions are reiterated till they become familiar. The work provides its own running paraphrase, and the paraphrase moves inevitably into the foreground of consciousness as the note patterns become predictable.[62]

For others, the Quartet's autobiographical content is not only effective at its own level but is artistically transcended, as it indeed has to be if it is to avoid mere bathos and hectoring coercion. David Fanning, for example, sees not just the work's autobiographical journey, but also its larger journey from the personal (movements 1–3), through the communal (movement 4) to the philosophical (movement 5): "Shostakovich's Eighth Quartet works its way from a concept of self bound up with suffering in the outside world to one that achieves—or at the very least strives for—inner liberation, by means of the power of creative thought."[63]

***

Back in the summer of 1959, Shostakovich had announced plans for a large-scale work to commemorate "the greatest man of our most complex epoch," Vladimir Ilyich Lenin.[64] According to the announcement, he wished to have the work ready in time for Lenin's ninetieth anniversary the following April. In the event, nothing materialized, but some sketches were drawn up during the summer of 1960, and in October Shostakovich announced the near completion of two movements and outlined the program for the work as a whole. The four movements of this new Twelfth Symphony would represent, respectively, the arrival of Lenin in Petrograd in April 1917, the events of 7 November, the Civil War, and the victory of the Revolution.[65] Interestingly, some of the sketches penned that summer reveal an apparently satirical spin on the subject; indeed, one sketch was based on the sarcastic little waltz that formed the song "Misunderstanding" from *Satires*, in particular the line, "He did not understand the new poetry."

It is certainly hard to reconcile this with the project's official importance, not to mention the concurrent ballyhoo surrounding Shostakovich's induction into the Party. Nevertheless, Lev Lebedinsky claims that Shostakovich expressly described the Twelfth Symphony as a satire of Lenin, and that it was only through Lebedinsky's persuasion that Shostakovich eventually ditched the idea and rewrote the symphony in a more conventional manner.[66] The Twelfth Symphony that was eventually premiered on 1 October 1961 (timed to coincide with Shostakovich's "elevation" to full Party membership) was subtitled "The Year 1917," with a somewhat revised program for its four movements: "Revolutionary Petrograd," "Razliv," "Aurora," and "The Dawn of Humanity." Lebedinsky, somewhat controversially, claims that the rewrite did not take place until only a few days before the first rehearsal, i.e., sometime during mid-to-late September. Regardless of whether even the prodigious Shostakovich could have achieved such a wholesale recomposition, together with the attendant rewriting of the orchestral parts, in "only a few days," the Symphony had already been performed in the obligatory two-piano preview at the Composers' Union on 8 September. Laurel Fay reports that the piece described in the Union's review would appear to match the Twelfth Symphony that was premiered on 1 October.[67] The date usually given for the Symphony's completion, 22 August 1961, would, then, seem more realistic than the claims of Lebedinsky.

Like the Second and Third Symphonies, the Eleventh and Twelfth are often thought of as a pair due to their association with Revolutionary subject matter. Yet, with both of these "pairs," these surface connections belie more significant differences. Like the Eleventh Symphony, the Twelfth projects its program through a four-movement, cyclic structure in which each movement follows *attacca* from the previous one, giving the effect almost of a single-movement work. However, the program itself is less specifically drawn than that of the Eleventh. And where the Eleventh had made use of actual Revolutionary folk material, the Twelfth presents original themes that are folk-like in their shape (i.e., they contain generally narrow contours, stepwise motion, and repeated "cellular" construction) but that have more in the way of symphonic heft. For example, the great striding theme of the Symphony's introduction, which David Hurwitz has compared to the start of Borodin's Second Symphony,[68] transforms magnificently into the tense first subject of the movement's main *Allegro*, and provides material elsewhere in the Symphony. And unlike the Eleventh's expansive narrative canvas, the Twelfth balances programmatic elements with symphonic structures, so that that first movement, for example, is composed in a relatively traditional sonata form, albeit with a rather sectionalized development. The Twelfth is Shostakovich's most traditionally "romantic" symphony, and in a highly Russian vein. At about forty minutes long, it is more compact than the Eleventh, and its smaller orchestral forces also suggest "Romantic" rather than "post-Romantic."

Ironically, however, it is the more "sprawling" seventy-minute Eleventh Symphony, a folk-tune laden, cinematographic canvas that rejects traditional symphonism, which is not only the more intensely atmospheric work but also the more coherent one. The Twelfth contains many moments of genuine beauty and tension, in particular the slow second movement, which combines deep contemplation (Razliv was Lenin's hiding place where he planned his strategy) with unsettling allusions to *Boris Godunov*.[69] But as the Symphony progresses, the nagging worry that its material may not be absolutely top-drawer comes ever more into the foreground. The percussion fusillade at the end of the third movement scherzo, depicting the Revolution's initial salvos from the battleship Aurora into the windows of the Winter Palace, seems crudely drawn, a pale reflection of the genuinely terrifying "massacre" percussion in the Eleventh Symphony. And it is hard from a musical point of view, let alone a programmatic one, to reconcile those warlike sounds at the end of the scherzo with the grandiose strains of the "October" theme (familiar from the Second Symphony) pronouncing the "Dawn of Humanity" at the start of the finale, wafting in nonchalantly in the horns like some *Deus ex machina*. Indeed, the finale is where the thinness of the musical material is at its most exposed and the platitudes start to mount, something that Shostakovich himself perhaps realized when he told Glikman that "the fourth [movement] does not look as though it is going to work. I am having great difficulty writing it."[70] At the end, we are treated to a rather clumsy quasi-deceptive cadence (tonic to flat-supertonic seventh), complete with *crescendo* on the "surprise" chord (Fig. 126). With one small harmonic modification on its final appearance, the stunt is replayed three more times before the "real" final cadence is sounded. Richard Taruskin's above-quoted comment on the Eighth Quartet ("startling juxtapositions ... reiterated till they become familiar") could not apply more here. At the Symphony's dress rehearsal, Lebedinsky recalls sitting with Shostakovich: "Shostakovich was holding my hand, and he kept asking, 'Is it really awful? ... It's terrible.'"[71]

Recently, Fumiko Hitotsuyanagi has speculated on the significance of a three-note cell, E-flat–B-flat–C, first heard towards the end of the first movement. There, it is heard on eight distinct occasions, always in the strings, pizzicato, and always set in relief from the surrounding material. It is heard five times in the second movement (also pizzicato, though enharmonically respelled—D-sharp–A-sharp–B-sharp) and twenty times in the finale, where it comes to the fore, finally being heard, tutti, in the coda's chain of cadences. Hitotsuyanagi believes that this cell constitutes a hidden "Stalin" motif.[72] Using the German notation system (Es–

B–C), and reading these German pitch names as Cyrillic letters, using the version of "E" that sounds "Yo," renders the English transliteration Yos. V. S., the initials of Yosif (Josef) Vissiarionovich Stalin. Hitotsuyanagi wonders if the Twelfth Symphony, purportedly dedicated to Lenin, is not more about the emergence of Stalin—the motif "hidden in the shadows" in the first movement, "subjugat[ing] the entire orchestra" in the last, with the latter indicative either of Stalin's "total victory and glorification" or of the "ultimate exposure of the crimes of the 'cult of personality.'" Incidentally, as Hitotsuyanagi also points out, this motif, transposed, corresponds to the fanfare heard in the police entr'acte between Scenes 7 and 8 in *Lady Macbeth* (see Chapter 6, Example 6.1), an observation that begs interesting questions.

***

One mystery of Shostakovich's output concerns what appear to have been two attempts at a Ninth Quartet made between the autumn of 1961 and the summer of 1962. According to Isaak Glikman, Shostakovich had told him at the beginning of October 1961 that he was working on a new quartet in *"style russe."*[73] A few weeks later, Shostakovich informed him that he had finished the work, but then burned it in "an excess of healthy self-criticism."[74] Then, in May 1962, he told his bride-to-be, Irina, that he had embarked on a new quartet. That summer, the Beethoven Quartet placed it on the schedule for the following season, and on 20 October, Shostakovich told *Pravda* of his intention to have it finished "in about two weeks." The next known reference to the work was in May 1964, when Shostakovich described the newly completed Ninth Quartet as "entirely different" to the one "written about two years ago," which had "been scrapped."[75]

In 2003, archivists discovered a manuscript containing 225 bars of music, entitled "9/I, op. 113," i.e., the first movement of a ninth quartet. In the foreword to the published score (2005), Olga Dombrovskaya and Olga Digonskaya offer conflicting explanations. Dombrovskaya believes it to be part of the "burned" quartet from autumn 1961, arguing that only a work dating from before April 1962 could have carried the designation "op. 113." After April, that number was taken by the forthcoming Thirteenth Symphony. Dombrovskaya also finds the musical style consistent with Shostakovich's *style russe* description. Digonskaya, however, believes that this manuscript is from the later attempt, arguing that it would appear to be part of an unfinished work (the designation "9/I" implying other movements), whereas Shostakovich claimed to have finished the 1961 quartet before he burned it. Digonskaya also asserts that once Shostakovich had decided to expand what was originally the single movement tone poem "Babi Yar" (composed in April 1962) into the Thirteenth Symphony, the opus number "113" became briefly available again, and could very well have been used for the quartet in May.[76]

***

During 1962, Shostakovich would attend festivals of his music in Edinburgh and Gorky. Meanwhile, his Party and Composers' Union duties seemed to multiply, further entrenching his "establishment" image. Yet, 1962 would also prove a year of revitalization. A significant factor was the premiere on 30 December 1961 of the long suppressed Fourth Symphony. Over the previous quarter of a century, the Fourth had enjoyed a limited circulation via Shostakovich's piano duo arrangement; it was known by certain students, and the score of the arrangement had been published in a limited edition in 1946, though it was banned and copies confiscated in 1948. Although he had periodically hinted at the need for revision, particularly of its last movement, Shostakovich was now adamant that the Symphony should be unleashed onto the public exactly as he had left it in 1936. His spirits, dampened by the recent failure of the Twelfth Symphony and by his perception of himself as a spineless compromiser, were once again electrified by the orgy of imagination that was the Fourth Symphony. According to the composer's secretary, Zinaida Gayamova, the one disappointment for Shostakovich was that Yevgeny Mravinsky, who over the years had conducted the premieres of Symphonies 5, 6, 8, 9, 10, and 12, seemed unenthused by the Fourth. In the event, the premiere was led by Kirill Kondrashin, who had "jumped at the prospect," and who acquitted himself brilliantly in this complex score.[77]

In 1961, Shostakovich had resumed teaching at the Leningrad Conservatory (his first such position since 1948) and, in 1962, took his third wife, the twenty-seven-year-old Irina Supinskaya, a literary editor for *Sovetsky kompozitor* whom he had known for about five years. In November 1962, he even plucked up the courage to make his conducting debut, leading the Gorky Philharmonic in performances of the *Festive Overture* and the First Cello Concerto with Rostropovich. Although he had declined an invitation back in 1942 from the New York Philharmonic-Symphony to conduct the Seventh Symphony ("Regretfully admit that I do not master the art of conducting"),[78] he seemed now to have had a change of mind. According to both Rostropovich and the then conductor of the Gorky Philharmonic, Izrail Guzman, Shostakovich displayed competence on the podium, though the orchestra had been prepared in advance by Guzman to play the Concerto by itself if necessary. Asked by Guzman after the concert whether he enjoyed the experience, Shostakovich replied "not in the slightest!"[79] It would be his first and last time on the podium.[80]

However, the biggest indicator of a newly emboldened Shostakovich was his willingness to risk one more confrontation with the authorities—a confrontation summarized by one indignant District Party secretary: "This is outrageous, we let Shostakovich join the Party, and then he goes and presents us with a symphony about Jews."[81]

Back in September 1961, *Literaturnaya gazeta* had published Yevgeny Yevtushenko's poem "Babi Yar," memorializing the ravine outside Kiev into which, over a two-day period at the end of September 1941, Nazi forces shot almost 34,000 Jews. Since the War, the "Jewish Question," as it was routinely dubbed, had been a constant source of embarrassment for the Soviet authorities. Those who tried to confront anti-Semitism would be accused of stirring up racial divisiveness and "insulting" the hardships that ordinary Soviet people had suffered during the War. In any case, as the authorities liked to boast, anti-Semitism was illegal under the Soviet constitution. But Yevtushenko had gone further, not just attacking anti-Semitism, but also implicitly condemning those who had prevented a memorial being erected at Babi Yar.

Yevtushenko's poem electrified Shostakovich. He read it within days of publication and immediately began setting it as a vocal tone poem. In a touching episode that tells much about his personality—gritty determination combined with diffident politeness—the composer called Yevtushenko to request permission to set the poem. Only after Yevtushenko replied positively did Shostakovich disclose that he had in fact already completed the work. He then decided to supplement "Babi Yar" with other Yevtushenko texts to create a Thirteenth Symphony ("Babi Yar"), for bass, male chorus, and orchestra. He chose "Humor," "In the Store," and "A Career," as, respectively, the second, third, and fifth movements. For the fourth movement, he commissioned from Yevtushenko a new poem, "Fears."[82] The Symphony was completed in July 1962, but its path to performance would be a perilous one.

The first setback involved the chosen bass soloist, Boris Gmyrya. During the War, the famous Ukrainian singer had remained in Kiev where he had performed under the auspices of the occupying German forces. Subsequently labeled a "collaborator," Gmyrya was particularly vulnerable to manipulation and blackmail. He had been allowed by the Ukrainian and Soviet authorities to continue his career, and indeed had been awarded both a Stalin Prize and the title People's Artist of the USSR during the 1950s. But he served at the pleasure of the authorities, and their wish that he not perform "Babi Yar" put an end to the matter.

Although sorely disappointed, Shostakovich understood Gmyrya's position. Altogether more mysterious was the behavior of Yevgeny Mravinsky. From the start, the conductor had been evasive. By the first week of October 1962, only ten weeks before the scheduled premiere, he had still not committed.[83] Finally, he declined. Various eyewitness accounts offer conflicting explanations. The composer Isaak Shvarts recalls:

> [He] was now experiencing certain doubts—something was inhibiting him. But as Mravinsky voiced them out loud, seeking [his second wife] Inna's advice, she put forward an irrefutable argument for a refusal to perform the work: Mravinsky never conducted choral works.... "You must only conduct pure music."[84]

Shvarts attributes Inna's advice to that fact that she had once been a Party activist and was "groomed in the school of Party thought."[85] But although not an active dissident, the patrician Mravinsky had always kept a certain distance from the Party. Why would he now be worried about such things? And as for the statement about choral music, it is certainly true that Mravinsky rarely conducted such works. In fact, other than a performance of Borodin's *Polovtsian Dances* in 1961, Mravinsky had not worked with a choir in ten years, although his biographer, Gregor Tassie, attributes this not so much to a lack of sympathy with the repertoire as to his poor relationship with Leningrad's choirs.[86] Back in 1949, Mravinsky had conducted the premiere of *Song of the Forests*.

Another eyewitness account comes from Alexandra Vavilina, a flautist in the Leningrad Philharmonic who would later become Mravinsky's third wife. She was present when Shostakovich phoned the conductor in October to discuss the Symphony, and reports that Mravinsky did not in fact refuse to conduct the work but had problems only with scheduling the premiere as soon as December.[87] Later on, Vavilina would disclose that Inna's terminal illness had just then been diagnosed and that it was Mravinsky's wish to devote his time to Inna that was the primary factor.[88] According to Tassie, the ultra-private Mravinsky felt unable to confide such deeply personal information to Shostakovich.[89] But Shostakovich, having already been stung by the conductor's unenthusiastic response to the Fourth Symphony the previous year, interpreted his actions and excuses as a betrayal. Relations between Shostakovich and Mravinsky would later improve, though how completely has been a subject of debate.

Shostakovich immediately offered the premiere to Kondrashin. As a precaution, two singers were prepared, Viktor Nechipailo and Vitaly Gromadsky. But days before the premiere, another hurdle would emerge. On 1 December, in what would turn out to be a curious replay of the 1936 Stalin/*Lady Macbeth* visit, Khrushchov attended an exhibition of modernist abstract art ("Thirty Years of Moscow Art") at the Manezh gallery. The remarks of the notoriously intemperate leader as he made his way around the exhibition, remarks that would positively dwarf "Muddle Instead of Music" in their personal viciousness, would spur a new anti-formalist crackdown on modern art.[90] A meeting of artists and Party leaders was held on 17 December, the day before the Symphony's premiere, to discuss this new crisis. At one point, Yevtushenko confronted Khrushchov with the subject of anti-Semitism, reciting the last two lines of "Babi Yar." Khrushchov retorted that "this poem has no place here," and that, in any case, anti-Semitism is not a problem. Yevtushenko continued: "We cannot go forward to communism with such a heavy load as Judophobia. And here there can be neither silence nor denial.... The whole progressive world is watching us and the resolution of this problem will even more greatly enhance the authority of our country."[91] (Khrushchov had a particular axe to grind in the case of Babi Yar: as First Secretary of the Ukrainian Communist Party Central Committee during the 1940s, it was he who had been responsible for rejecting the proposal to erect a memorial at the ravine.)

Events would take another turn for the worse at the following morning's dress rehearsal. Nechipailo, who was scheduled to sing the first of the two premiere performances, failed to turn up. Gromadsky was eventually found, but the rehearsal was again interrupted when Kondrashin took a phone call from Georgy Popov, the Russian Minister of Culture. The conductor was asked whether he had "any political doubts in relation to 'Babi Yar.'" He replied that he had none. Popov then asked whether the Symphony could be performed without its first movement. Kondrashin answered "no." Popov's response: "Well, do as you see fit."[92] Boris Schwarz describes the scene that evening:

> The government box remained unoccupied, and a planned television transmission did
> not take place ... the entire square [was] cordoned off by the police. Inside, the hall

was filled to overflowing ... The tension was unbearable. The first movement, *Babyi Yar*, was greeted with a burst of spontaneous applause. At the end of the hour-long work, there was an ovation rarely witnessed. On the stage was Shostakovich, shy and awkward, bowing stiffly. He was joined by Yevtushenko, moving with the ease of a born actor. Two great artists—a generation apart—fighting for the same cause—freedom of the human spirit. Seeing the pair together, the audience went wild.... (Contrary to custom) the texts were not printed in the programme.[93]

Clearly, the authorities had decided not to risk the damaging international publicity that would have arisen were it to appear that the doyen of Soviet composers had been muzzled. Both the premiere and the repeat two days later proceeded unhindered.[94] However, once the spotlight of the premieres had been removed, the authorities moved in quickly, banning further performances pending revisions to the text. The following month, Yevtushenko revised eight lines, two passages of four lines each, not, as Kondrashin has stated, for publication in a literary forum, but for the sole purpose of bailing out the Symphony. Contrary to Kondrashin's accounts,[95] the revision is to be found only in the Symphony's first published scores.[96] In typical Soviet fashion, the revised texts whitewashed over the specifically Jewish tragedy of Babi Yar, substituting instead generalized statements about brotherhood and antifascism:

Original (Fig. 2): "I imagine now that I am a Jew. Here I wander through ancient Egypt. And here, I am crucified on the cross and die, and still bear the marks of the nails." **Revised:** "I stand there as if at a wellspring. That gives me faith in our brotherhood. Here lie Russians and Ukrainians. With Jews they lie in the same earth."
Original (Fig. 24): "And I become like a long, soundless scream above the thousand thousands here interred. I am each old man shot dead here, I am each child shot dead here." **Revised:** "I think about Russia's heroic feats in blocking fascism's path. To the tiniest dewdrop, her whole essence and fate is dear to me."

Shostakovich initially opposed the changes, but eventually relented, for the Symphony was too important to abandon. Nevertheless, even with the revisions, performances were hardly encouraged. A secret Central Committee memo, dated 15 May 1963, urged the Ministry of Culture "to restrict performances ... and to establish a procedure for its availability."[97] Nevertheless, a few conductors would get away with performing the original version.[98]

***

As previously noted, Shostakovich had used the term "*style russe*" to describe the string quartet that he had written, and then purportedly burned, back in 1961. It was a term that he would use again in reference to his 1964 cantata, *The Execution of Stepan Razin*.[99] Although he did not, as far as we know, use it in connection with the Thirteenth Symphony, there is no doubt that this would indeed turn out to be the most "Russian" of Shostakovich's symphonies, sharing a very strong stylistic affinity to the cantata.

The term itself, "*style russe*," initially seems odd coming from a Russian composer, the use of the French in particular implying an element of estrangement. But what the term appears to have meant to Shostakovich, based at least on *Stepan Razin* and, by extension, the Thirteenth Symphony, was above all an engagement with Musorgsky. Of course, Musorgsky, and in particular *Boris Godunov*, had been a seminal influence almost from the start of Shostakovich's career. The thematic, dramatic, and philosophical influences of *Boris*, particularly its opening chorus, on *Lady Macbeth* and the Seventh and Eighth Symphonies have already been discussed (see Chapters 6 and 7). And, as Jeffrey Baxter points out, the Thirteenth Symphony's oppressive opening shares something of a kinship with the introduction to Boris' Act II aria, "Ah I am suffocating" (*Uf! Tyazhelo*).[100] But more than allusions, it is the Musorgskian "sound" that is so striking in the Thirteenth Symphony (and for that matter *Stepan Razin*)—orchestral sonorities that are at once gray and searing, the declamatory choral style, and the style of the word setting, with its rhythms and stresses rooted in the Russian language. It is perhaps not a coincidence that Shostakovich's next project after the Thirteenth Symphony would be a darkly brooding orchestration of Musorgsky's *Songs and Dances of Death*.

The most striking example of *style russe* in the Symphony's first movement is the Byelostok episode (see below), with its coarse whooping crowd effects (e.g., the chorus' opening jump at Fig. 5, b6, on the word "blood" (*krov*)) and oompah dance rhythms to depict the taunting mob, as it kicks and spits on the young Jewish boy. This music is highly Russian not only in effect, but also in content, for the closing part of this theme (Fig. 8, b7) is a quotation of the folksong "Akh vy seni, moi seni,"[101] a song that Shostakovich had used to uproarious, vaudevillian effect only a few years earlier in *Moscow, Cheryomushki* (Lidochka and Boris' duet), and that Stravinsky had used in the "Shrovetide Fair" tableau in *Petrushka*.[102] Here in the Symphony, Shostakovich's brassy scoring and series of insistent "squeeze-box" *crescendi* give a brutal edge to the tune, an edge that Elizabeth Wilson reads as a depiction of "misguided chauvinism."[103]

Many have expressed surprise that Shostakovich, who loved and was by this point highly experienced with the Jewish musical idiom, should have employed such an overtly Russian style in what would be his most outspoken diatribe against Soviet anti-Semitism. Joachim Braun has put forward one theory:

> The "Jewishness" of Shostakovich's music increased with the heightening of the abstractness of the musical form and the deepening of its esoteric meaning. The more hidden the meaning, the stronger is the ethnic coloring of the music, and the more intense is the Jewish musical idiom. Conversely, the more open and direct the meaning, the less Jewish is the music, and the more doubtful is its ethnic provenance.... In the Thirteenth Symphony, the text speaks an open language of resistance and there can be no doubt about the central concept of the composer. The specifically Jewish musical element is absent here and is, in fact, superfluous; it does not add anything to the clear intention of the text. On the contrary, the idiom is Russian: Russian chimes, Russian modes, etc.[104]

For Esti Sheinberg, the lack of "Jewishness" here provides a vindication of her theory that, for Shostakovich, the Jewish musical style was not ultimately about the Jewish experience, but was rather a fertile tool for the expression of a larger existential irony. And since there is no irony in "Babi Yar," a Jewish style would rather miss the point.[105]

Although Braun and Sheinberg have differing views on the function of the Jewish musical style in Shostakovich, they both agree that such a style would have been unnecessary in the context of "Babi Yar." But why the special adoption of the Musorgskian *style russe*? One factor was the connection that existed in Shostakovich's mind between Musorgsky, in particular *Boris Godunov*, and what Shostakovich frequently described as the theme of "civic morality," and it is notable that two close contemporaries of the Thirteenth Symphony, two works that also deal with the theme of conscience, *Stepan Razin* and his film score to *Hamlet* (1963), should occupy a similarly Musorgskian sound world. But "Babi Yar" was more than just a story with a moral. Yevtushenko's poem was a direct plea to the Russian people ("Oh my Russian people, I know you are truly internationalists") to reject the anti-Semites who had tarnished their good name. For Shostakovich, a composer for whom audience understanding was paramount—he always preferred that his vocal music be sung in the language of the country in which it was being performed[106]—couching such a plea in a Jewish musical language would not only have been superfluous or "missing the point," it would actually have attenuated the power of the message. A plea to Russians to renounce anti-Semitism had to be done in Russian, not Jewish terms. And in this first movement, this was a point that would be made not just stylistically but also structurally.

The first movement falls into three parts, corresponding superficially to a sonata structure, though one informed primarily by narrative rather than by symphonic considerations. Indeed, if we are to use sonata terminology here, the three parts are perhaps best labeled Exposition 1, Exposition 2, and Recapitulation, since that second section is not so much a development of material as a continuation of the narrative. In the B-flat minor opening, the chorus balefully announces the movement's premise: "There is no memorial at Babi Yar." The bass soloist then takes us chronologically through history's treatment of the Jews: The Exodus from Egypt and the Jew nailed to the cross (Fig. 2; both B-flat minor), the Dreyfus affair (Fig. 3; B minor), and the boy in Byelostok (scene of the 1906 pogrom) assaulted by a Russian mob "stinking of vodka and onions" (Fig. 5; G minor). The division of labor between soloist and male chorus is, on the whole, representative of that found throughout the Symphony. The soloist is a mostly first-person narrator, re-enacting the stories that he is telling—"Now I am Dreyfus," "Now I am a boy in Byelostok," etc. The chorus meanwhile declaims premises, as at the very opening, and plays the role of the crowd. (Later in the Symphony, it will also play the role of respondent, throwing in a piquant observation or ironic comment. Except for one notable moment in the third movement, the chorus sings in unison throughout, giving the text a singular, declamatory force that emphasizes the Symphony's timbral starkness.)

The second exposition returns to the opening material and key (Fig. 9), while the soloist temporarily removes himself from narrating in order to make his first moral plea to "Russia, my people," before bringing the narrative further up to date with an episode about Anne Frank (Fig. 13; E major). The truncated recapitulation starts with the opening material and key, now tutti and *fortissimo*, with screaming, swirling high woodwinds and strings (Fig. 21). The chorus then reiterates the situation at Babi Yar, while the remainder of the movement, split between soloist and chorus, resumes, and brings to a climax, the plea to the Russian people.

The relating of the episodes of Jewish history occupies an important place in this narrative version of sonata form—the greater part of the two expositions is given over to this. But these episodes, in the end, are just that—episodes. The key structural points, on the other hand—the opening material together with its return at the start of each of the two subsequent main sections, and indeed the entire recapitulation—concern themselves not with Jews or Jewish issues but with Russian attitudes, Russian behavior, and the Russian disgrace that "over Babi Yar there is no memorial." In other words, Shostakovich has shaped not just the musical language but also the very structure of the movement as a primarily Russian phenomenon.

The second movement, "Humor," presents the figures of Aesop and the legendary thirteenth-century satirist and prankster Nasreddin Hodja, a Till Eulenspiegel-like character who had stood up to gray and faceless authority. The movement is shot through with musical trickery (e.g., the opening in which the strings, playing triads in all manner of exotic keys, attempt to derail the winds, who are obstinately trying to stick to the point—in this case C major) as well as typically sardonic timbres (e.g., the two-octave doubling of the bass soloist and an E-flat clarinet at Fig. 39, or the *danse macabre*-like solo violin at Fig. 44). As Jeffrey Baxter puts it, the music "adroitly skip[s] in and out of keys, meters, and sections like the hero of the poem who skirts one near-miss after another in his best *Till Eulenspiegel* manner."[107]

Like *Till Eulenspiegel*, "Humor" is led to the gallows with the appropriate militaristic trappings, and yet, also like Eulenspiegel, still gets the final word. The procession begins (Fig. 53, b9) with military rhythms and a goose-stepping B-flat/E bass vamp, the latter possibly influenced by the tritone vamp in the funeral march that starts the finale of the Fourth Symphony, a work that had been premiered only the year before. And the gallows humor continues with a quotation from Shostakovich's own setting of "MacPherson before his Execution" from his *Six Romances on Words of W. Raleigh, R. Burns, and W. Shakespeare*. Burns' text reads: "Sae rantingly, sae wantonly, Sae gauntingly gae'd he; He played a spring, an danced it roun' Below the gallows-tree"—though here in the Symphony, the springing, dancing MacPherson melody is given the full *style russe* treatment, uproarious trombone glissandi and all. Towards the end, Shostakovich inserts a quotation from the Eighth Quartet's second movement, one that tellingly includes his favorite "diabolic" triplet figure (Symphony—Example 9.6a, Quartet—Example 9.6b).

Example 9.6a

Example 9.6b

The remaining three movements are played without a break. "In the Store" portrays the misery of Russia's women, forced to queue for scraps, shortchanged by an indifferent shopkeeper who is himself simply trying to make ends meet. The poet, outraged at the hardship these women are forced to endure, and by the callous cheating, himself steals from the shopkeeper. And so the cycle of misery continues. This movement contains the Symphony's single moment of choral harmony, a plagal cadence following a terse, brutal climax (Fig. 90, b4–5). Paradoxically, the effect of this sweetly sanctimonious Amen cadence on the words "their righteous hands" (and in the key traditionally associated with simple sanctimony, C major) is quite jarring to the ear by now attuned to bare unison writing.

Starting with a protracted tuba solo, the bleak fourth movement, "Fears," the poem written especially for the Symphony and which Shostakovich himself had a hand in revising, tells how fears "no longer exist in Russia." Compared to the forthright "Babi Yar," "Fears" would resort to the perennial Shostakovichian ploy of dressing up present-day tragedy in historical disguise. The fifth movement, "A Career," compares the "senseless" Galileo, persecuted for his heretic beliefs, with a fellow scientist who shared these beliefs but who publicly rejected them because he "had a family" to consider, and ends with the message, "I pursue my career by *not* pursuing it."

This finale has no climax in the conventional sense, but the defining moment comes with the chorus' invocation of "Shakespeare and Pasteur, Newton and Tolstoy, And Tolstoy." Why the strange repetition of Tolstoy, the only repeated line in the entire symphony (Fig. 140, b9–Fig. 141, b5)? To emphasize him over the others? Or to suggest a second figure by the same name? The answer comes immediately. "Lev?" [L'va?], asks the soloist. "Lev!," shouts the chorus, confirming that it is indeed the great Lev Tolstoy who is being invoked and not the "other" Tolstoy, presumed to be Count Alexei Tolstoy, that famous purveyor of red-romantic prose and government propaganda. It is a humorously ironic moment, especially given that Yevtushenko's original text contained only the simple statement, "Tolstoy . . . Lev!" For Yevtushenko, "Lev" was either an innocent afterthought, a realization that "Tolstoy" on its own might be ambiguous, or more likely a subtle but pointed aside, a knowing wink. However, by adding the second "Tolstoy" and a question, "Lev?," Shostakovich raised Yevtushenko's easily overlooked aside into a telling demonstration.

Four years later, Shostakovich would incorporate this "demonstration" into something more concretely autobiographical, his *Preface to the Complete Collection of My Works, and Brief Reflections on This Preface*. A three-minute skit for bass and piano, *Preface* finds Shostakovich reflecting, not too seriously, on his career. Amidst the lampooning of his official honors and titles, there appears a brief quotation from "A Career" (bar 29), from the very passage cited above, in which confusion over the two Tolstoys brings the movement's moral argument to a head. As Malcolm MacDonald has put it, "it reminds us that such honors are often the rewards for compromise, if not worse. The question is raised (and it is surely infinitely to Shostakovich's credit that he could raise it): if Shostakovich is like Tolstoy, is he more of a Lev or a Count Alexei?"[108]

Aside from the continuation of the undulating third movement theme (a typically Shostakovichian "wedge" shape) into the fourth movement, and its subsequent transformation to become the main theme of the fifth movement, the Thirteenth Symphony is not as obviously cyclic as its two predecessors. Possibly the presence of a text mitigated the need for associative musical mottos. Nevertheless, there are certain inter-movement connections here that help provide unity. The interval of the tritone, for example, can be heard at several levels. It is used melodically, as in the aforementioned vamp (E to B-flat) accompanying Humor's execution, and harmonically, as in the ominous fanfares scored in parallel tritones, over a tritone pedal, leading up to the first climax in "Fears" (Fig. 105). On a larger scale, the Symphony's tonal arc is based on a tritonal pull between the B-flat pitch center of the outer movements and E in the central movement describing the long-suffering Russian women. In fact, Richard Longman views E—a key often associated with radiance—as the "feminine" foil to the horrors of B-flat minor, given that E (with a Mixolydian coloring) is also the key for the first movement's Anne Frank episode.[109] Meanwhile, as Malcolm MacDonald has pointed out, the music depicting the women of the third movement, who "smell of onions, cucumbers, and 'Kabul' sauce" (Fig. 76, b2), bears noticeable resemblance to that depicting the "stink of vodka and onions" in the first movement's Byelostok episode.[110]

Another important inter-movement connection involves an instrument, the tubular bell. Its chilling, doom-laden sonority chimes at the very start of the Symphony and reappears with each return of the opening "Babi Yar" material—at the start of the second exposition, at the start of the recapitulation, and in the coda. In the scherzo, the bell is heard twice: at the line "Humor's severed head/Was stuck on a warrior's pike" (Fig. 47); and just before the end of the execution episode (Fig. 57, b4). Significantly, both passages are in the "Babi Yar" key of B-flat minor. And in the first passage, immediately after the reference to the "warrior's pike," the woodwinds parody the Babi Yar material, an effect that summons to mind Berlioz' witches parodying the executed protagonist in the *Symphonie Fantastique*. Silent in the third movement, the bell next appears in "Fears" after each of the two climaxes (Figs. 105, b9 and 114, b9), and returns at the very end of the Symphony to set an ambiguous seal on its wistfully resigned B-flat major farewell—that coda complete with Shostakovich's favorite instrument of "farewell," the celesta. The bleak clouds of Babi Yar may have evaporated, but the bell tolls as the lone voice of remembrance.

It is often suggested that Shostakovich's last three symphonies, 13–15, form a triptych—late-period works in which the topic of death is prevalent—just as the two previous symphonies, the Eleventh and Twelfth, had formed a natural pairing based on their Revolutionary subject matter. Yet, the Thirteenth is perhaps better viewed as part of the earlier group. Stylistically, its Musorgskian Russianness is much closer to its two predecessors, certainly to the Eleventh, than it is to the late 1960s modernism of the Fourteenth or the enigmatic fusion of modernism and neoclassicism in the Fifteenth. And though the theme of death certainly looms large in the Thirteenth Symphony, it is not a symphony *about* death in the way that the Fifteenth and especially the Fourteenth are. Its concerns are primarily anger, protest, and history—Ian MacDonald has characterized it as "a high-art Russian equivalent of the 'protest' songs then current in America," with Yevtushenko a "Soviet Bob Dylan."[111]

Taken as a group, Symphonies 11–13 tackle the two subjects that perhaps most preoccupied Shostakovich during this time: the conflict between conformism and protest; and the tragic cycle of history. The Thirteenth Symphony stands with its two predecessors as a powerful document of Russian history, reaching back to the *narodny* aspirations of the Eleventh Symphony (and, interestingly, opening with the same bell that had closed the Eleventh) while standing in stark and principled opposition to the Bolshevik reality of the Twelfth. The first direct plea to Russia in "Babi Yar" (Fig. 10), for instance, is reminiscent of Palace Square, with its open fifths and its harp doubling. In the second movement, that Palace Square allusion is elevated to a reference: one of Humor's many pranks is his storming of the Winter Palace. The words may be Yevtushenko's, not Shostakovich's, but it is impossible not to note the irony as the Palace, which in the Twelfth Symphony fell to Lenin's forces, now in the Thirteenth falls to a prankster—an irony perhaps heightened by the six bars immediately following this reference (from Fig. 65, b3), written in a swaggeringly bellicose style straight out of the Twelfth Symphony. Several commentators have also pointed to the fact that the Thirteenth Symphony, op. 113, was for Shostakovich not just the next symphony, but the very next work following the Twelfth, op. 112, and have noted the (deliberate?) irony by which the "Dawn of Humanity" is followed immediately by "Babi Yar." Although Shostakovich much appreciated such ironic juxtaposition, it should be borne in mind that the designation "op. 113" had originally been given to the unfinished (Ninth) quartet of 1961 or 1962. Had that quartet not been aborted, the juxtaposition between the two symphonies would not have arisen.

At the end of 1961, after twenty-five years, Shostakovich had won the battle of the Fourth Symphony. Now, at the end of 1962, he could claim another victory with the Thirteenth. Although he had been forced eventually to compromise on the text, and though performances over the next decade even with the revised text would be few and far between, his protest against Soviet anti-Semitism had been heard loud and clear. And he had emerged with impunity.

***

Three weeks after the premiere of the Thirteenth Symphony, Shostakovich would chalk up yet another victory, the long-awaited premiere on 8 January 1963 of *Katerina Izmailova*, the revised version of *Lady Macbeth*. Companies both at home and abroad clamored to stage *Katerina*, and over the next couple of years, Shostakovich supervised as many productions as he could, traveling to England, Yugoslavia, Austria, Bulgaria, and Hungary. The concerns that he had expressed to Glikman back in 1956 were still at the forefront of his mind: that Katerina, and even to an extent Sergei, should engage the audience's sympathy and that the opera's erotic aspects should not dominate. At the Stanislavsky Theater's production, for example, Shostakovich complained that Sergei was "too contemptible ... it isn't clear why Katerina would have fallen for such a nobody."[112] One apparent reversal of opinion, where he now desired a hardening rather than a softening of character, was with respect to Sonyetka. Back in 1934, he had complained to Smolich that Sonyetka should be a "simple, flirtatious girl, without any demoniacal side to her."[113] But now, in his rehearsal notes for the Kiev production, his favorite, he urged Sonyetka to be "more spiteful."[114]

The travel associated with *Katerina Izmailova*, plus his other official duties, took time away from composition. But another factor was becoming increasingly intrusive. Shostakovich's health had always been precarious; over the past forty years, visits to hospitals and sanatoria had been frequent. During his 1958 concert tour to Paris, he had experienced a loss of mobility in his right hand. In September of that year, he was in hospital for a month, from where he complained to Glikman: "I have pins and needles all the time. I can't pick up anything heavy with it. I can grip a suitcase with my fingers, but it's difficult to hang my coat on a peg, or clean my teeth."[115] He had returned to hospital for further treatment in February 1960, June 1962, and April 1963, and in November 1960 and January 1961 for the treatment of a leg fracture incurred when his legs gave way at Maxim's wedding on 22 October 1960. Visits averaged about a month in duration and were often followed up by lengthy periods of convalescence.

Not surprisingly, the compositional achievements for 1963 were slim: the *Overture on Russian and Kirghiz Folksongs* and a re-orchestration of Schumann's Cello Concerto. But his work on the score to Grigory Kozintsev's new film of *Hamlet*, released in April 1964, was yet another victory. Over the past three decades, Shostakovich's film output had necessarily been confined to Socialist Realist potboilers. The quality of the music had generally reflected his indifference to the projects. Now, working with the great film director on what was perhaps Shostakovich's favorite Shakespearean masterpiece, the result was without doubt his greatest film score.

Dealing with themes of leadership and responsibility, *Hamlet* would prove a worthy postscript to the trio of "civic" symphonies (11–13) that immediately preceded it. Symphonic in the "Eleventh Symphony" sense rather than the "Tenth Symphony," it paints and characterizes on a broad canvas. The three main characters (Hamlet, Ophelia, and the ghost) have identifiable themes that return in a variety of imaginative and probing transformations—though in the case of Ophelia, it is the sound of the harpsichord (an instrument that was making something of a revival in 1960s Russia) rather than her "dance lesson" theme or her plaintive lament that is the strongest identifier. However, as Fiona Ford points out, for Ophelia's three unaccompanied songs, Kozintsev took instead the traditional songs that had been used in the Theatre Royal, Drury Lane performances of *Hamlet* since the eighteenth century.[116] Musically, the score is in the Eleventh Symphony vein, nowhere more so than in "The Story of Horatio and the Ghost," in which eerily trilling strings and the chilling interjections of the celesta (both reminiscent of the post-massacre return of the "Palace Square" theme in the Eleventh Symphony's second movement) accompany the tuba's baleful intoning of the ghost's theme—the choice of instrument here reminding us of the tuba solo that began "Fears" (Thirteenth Symphony). The type of slashing chords that introduce the film and that often accompany Hamlet's theme would be heard later in other Shostakovich pieces dealing with the theme of civic responsibility, principally the cantata *The Execution of Stepan Razin* (1964) and the *Suite on Verses of Michelangelo* (1974).

***

The middle of 1964 saw Shostakovich's return to the quartet medium. The Ninth and Tenth Quartets (composed in May and July, respectively, and premiered together in November) were consecutive works. In many ways, the Ninth pairs up with the Thirteenth Symphony just as, for example, the Fifth Quartet had with the Tenth Symphony. Both are in five movements. In the Quartet, all five are played *attacca*; in the Symphony, it is the last three. And as Table 9.2 shows, the manner of the *attacca* connections is strikingly similar, featuring a combination of common-tone pedals (CT), thematic foreshadowing (TF; the end of one movement outlining the theme of the next), or thematic continuation (TC; the start of a movement continuing a theme from the end of the previous one).

Table 9.2
Method of Linking Movements in the Thirteenth Symphony and Ninth Quartet

Thirteenth Symphony: **1**-**2**-**3**-CT/TC-**4**-CT/TF(approx)-**5**
Ninth Quartet: **1**-CT-**2**-TF-**3**-CT/TF-**4**-CT(broken)/TF-**5**

Movement numbers are in bold.

The similarities between the two works extend to the themes themselves, with both heavily favoring narrow melodic contours, sometimes reduced to a three-note oscillation (e.g., the start of the Quartet's third movement), a two-note oscillation (e.g., the Symphony's opening bass solo or the opening violin ostinati in the Quartet's first and fourth movements), or occasionally a monotone (e.g., the opening chorus in the Symphony's fourth movement). A deeper level connection is the organizational use of the tritone, already discussed in reference to the Symphony.

In the Quartet, we hear the interval harmonically, e.g., the tritone formed by the very distinctive A-natural in the opening melody playing against the E-flat pedal, or the simultaneous sounding of two pedals (again, E-flat and A) at the end of the first movement; and melodically, e.g., the bass-line vamp (B-flat to E, the same pitches as in Humor's execution) accompanying the finale's somewhat Bartokian second theme. At the very end of the Quartet, A major jostles for attention along-side the tonic E-flat. The importance of the tritone is also connected to a use of the octatonic scale that expands upon that found in the Seventh Quartet. The fourth movement's opening melody, the accompaniment to the first theme of the finale (Fig. 67), and the second strain of the finale's second subject (Fig. 71) all possess pronounced octatonic characteristics.[117]

Like the Seventh Quartet's first movement, the Ninth's is written in a concise sonatina structure. Yet, the Ninth takes this act of "compression" one step further by partially telescoping exposition and recapitulation. At Fig. 8, while the exposition's closing theme is still playing in the viola and first violin, the tonic E-flat major along with the movement's initial oscillating figure re-establishes itself in the second violin. The first theme itself returns in the cello three bars later, yet the exposition's closing theme has still not played itself out. Especially given the almost Ustvolskayan remoteness of the themes themselves, the result is a strange layering effect, related to, yet quite unlike, the "gradually emerging" recapitulations of earlier works.

The first four movements form, in a sense, a large prelude to the finale. The dirge-like second movement inherits its first violin arioso style from the Eighth Quartet's first movement. The high-speed polka-like third movement scherzo, whose trio is a reworking of the "Cemetery" theme from the recent *Hamlet* score, leads into another slow movement, this one closer in spirit to the Eighth Quartet's fourth movement with the three lower strings intoning their melody in parallel and a slowly oscillating first violin accompaniment. And if the first four movements as a whole are preludial, this fourth movement has its own additional role as the finale's slow introduction, providing the material for its second theme (compare the start of its fourth movement with the finale, Fig. 69) and for a short snippet of its first (compare the fourth movement, Fig. 57, b8–9 with the finale, Fig. 59, b8–9).

By far the Quartet's longest movement, the finale is in sonata form with a full development that includes a "brutalizing" fugato and a recitative. Towards the end of the fourth movement, Shostakovich had introduced a strange recitative-like passage for first violin (Fig. 57). Its return here in the finale as a full-blown, unmetered recitative for cello *in alt* (Fig. 89) forms the most obvious link between the two movements. It had been almost two decades since Shostako-vich's last recitative; in terms of role (anguished stasis following a brutalizing de-velopment) and indeed gesture (the tense tremolo in the upper strings and the *sfffpp* effect just before the entrance of the solo instrument) its closest relative is the recitative from the Eighth Symphony. Yet, Shostakovich also modernizes the genre, interrupting the cello's anguished melody with a series of atonal pizzicato chords (also taken from the fourth movement). The accompanying hexachord pedal is also decidedly modernistic, though the closest comparison here might actually be Shostakovich's very first recitative, dating from 1930, from his film score, *Alone*.

Following the trauma of the fugato and recitative, the recapitulation attempts to bring the movement back to life with a somewhat gentler transformation of the first subject, now in 4/4 meter as opposed to the original 3/4 (Fig. 92). As Arthur Smith has observed, to have plunged back into the first theme in its original, highly driven state would have been unconvincingly abrupt—the "gradual gathering of momentum" that Shostakovich chose instead being the only musically logical way out.[118] As well as irreversibly altering the movement's rhythmic profile, the transformation into 4/4 allows it more easily to take in elements of both the third movement scherzo, whose presence contributes to this "re-enlivening" process, and the first movement's closing theme with which this finale will ultimately end—the first *fortissimo* ending in a Shostakovich quartet since the Second, two decades earlier.

The five-movement Ninth Quartet is a more ambitious work than the twelve-minute-long Seventh, making the level of thematic unity and the network of cyclism even more remarkable. Like the Seventh, it is in the finale that the cyclism is most fully revealed and worked out, and like the Seventh, the most momentous development of material there occurs via a fugue. In neither work is the fugue based directly on first movement material, but in both, there is a sense that the high fugal intensity "compensates" for the omission of development in their earlier, in particular, their first movements. In the Eighth Quartet, David Fanning argued that the attempted fugue in the first movement was a prelude to the realized fugue in the last.[119] That argument could be expanded and extended to the Seventh, Ninth, and for that matter, Tenth Quartets, all of which have "unfulfilled" sonatina first movements whose lack of fulfillment is subsequently dealt with, in one way or another, in the finales.

***

Shostakovich's rush to start a Tenth Quartet only six weeks after finishing the Ninth stemmed partly from his wish to overtake, in a spirit of friendly competition, the quartet output of his good friend Mieczysław Weinberg (Moisei Vainberg), who had by that time amassed nine. Shostakovich had a deep affection for both Weinberg and his music, and dedicated the Tenth Quartet to him. It is not too fanciful to suggest that the Quartet's generally muted colors and lyrical style reflect Weinberg's own peculiar strain of eloquent lyricism.

The Tenth would be the last of Shostakovich's "middle" quartets (Nos. 6–10), a group distinguishing itself from the earlier quartets by relying less on structures derived from his symphonies and more on narrative and cyclic devices. In terms of layout, the Tenth Quartet most resembles the Sixth. Both are in four movements, contrasting with the three-movement Seventh and the five-movement Eighth and Ninth. Both place the scherzo second and a slow passacaglia third, and in both, the passacaglia ground returns at the finale's climax. And in each case, the finale is the only movement that follows the preceding one *attacca*, a practice used much more extensively in the Seventh, Eighth, and Ninth Quartets. The demonic scherzo apart, the Tenth Quartet also shares the predominantly lyrical nature of the Sixth, though a comparison of the two passacaglias reveals perhaps more anguish in the later work.

If the Tenth Quartet's layout resembles the Sixth's, its eschewal of a full sonata structure in the first movement brings it closer to the Seventh or Ninth. And like those two Quartets, the Tenth ends with a cyclic return of its first movement material. That said, the Tenth Quartet is less concerned with extensive networks of cyclism than it is by the pursuit of motivic unity, a unity generated by the opening two bars (Example 9.7).

Example 9.7

As Example 9.7 shows, this opening sets up a tension between the tonic A-flat and a potential rival, E minor, and also recreates a dilemma heard in the Eleventh Symphony, namely the potential reading of the diminished fourth (A-flat) as a major third (G-sharp) and the consequent potential for an E minor/E major conflict (see Example 9.2). Yet, ironically, because the Symphony is for the most part tonally unambiguous, these harmonic ambiguities register there more strongly. Here in the Quartet, by contrast, it is more difficult to feel the "pull" of this ambiguity, since tonality itself is so vaguely established. The whole of the opening first violin solo slides into and out of briefly glimpsed tonalities. Even when A-flat looks like it is about to take hold, with the entrance of the other instruments starting at Fig. 1, it is presented in a way that sounds more like the dominant of D-flat than a tonic in its own right. In fact, A-flat only takes hold convincingly at two spots in this enigmatic five-minute *Andante*: the second half of the second subject in the recapitulation (A-flat minor) and the final twelve-bar cadential progression. All this notwithstanding, the movement contains many allusions to the opening two bars, whether it is simply the juxtaposition of incongruent harmonies (e.g., F minor and B major at Fig. 6) or implied major/minor conflicts.

The second movement scherzo is a savage, demonic affair in the style of the Tenth Symphony's scherzo. Taking up the A-flat/E minor conflict from the start of the Quartet, this movement is not only in E minor but contains a "returning of the favor," an emphasis on the octatonic scale portion that links E back to A-flat, i.e., E–F–G–A-flat. This can be heard, for example, at Fig. 23 and from Fig. 26, b11. Moreover, not only does the interval structure of the E–F–G–A-flat scale portion equate to both the first four notes of the octatonic scale and to DSCH in its scalar layout ("HCDS"), the scale itself also contains three of the four pitches (A-flat, G, and E) of the Quartet's opening (see Example 9.7).

The scherzo's second half replays themes from the first, but at even greater intensity (Example 9.8). It is set up at Fig. 31 by an ostinato accompaniment in the two violins (based on Fig. 18). Ascending from E, the ostinato in the first violin forms the aforementioned E to A-flat ("HCDS") scale portion. Descending from E, it is diatonic (E–D-sharp–C-sharp). Ten bars later, as the ostinato continues, the E Locrian theme from the start of the movement enters *in alt* in the viola and cello (Fig. 31, b11). Thus, Shostakovich creates an extraordinarily tense passage, pitting together octatonic ("HCDS"), diatonic, and modal (Locrian) elements. And if that were not enough, the second violin ostinato challenges altogether the tonal centricity of E. Its three pitches (A–B-flat–C-sharp) imply A *freygish*. The use of E here as both tonic and dominant is reminiscent of Fig. 1 in the first movement, where the purported tonic A-flat had acted similarly (see above).

Example 9.8

As the reprise progresses, the ostinato assumes an increasing prominence until, by the end, it is the sole surviving element. The close of movement is therefore dominated by the "HCDS" scale from E to A-flat. It is this very scale that then starts the third movement's passacaglia theme. Thus a suggestion of harmonic tension in the first movement becomes an actual conflict in the second, whose "resolution" occurs in the third. Like the first two movements, the third movement's tonal center is ambivalent, trying for a modally flattened E but seeming to fall back onto A minor. And though this is one of Shostakovich's more lyrical passacaglia themes (see Chapter 15), the impassioned, almost strained, use of the high cello in the movement's outer phases ties it back to the high cello's domination of the scherzo.

The finale's main rondo theme is a jaunty polka-like tune whose contour shares the tendency for narrow intervals noticed in the Ninth Quartet and Thirteenth Symphony, though Arthur Smith believes the contour to be derived more specifically from the first violin line at Fig. 44, b5–6 in the third movement.[120] The sense of relaxation in this finale comes not only from the character of the themes but also from the abandonment of the tonal/modal conflicts of the three earlier movements, though residual elements can still be found. The cyclic return of the first movement theme towards the end of the finale could be read as a reposing of those ambiguities—a psychological reopening of old wounds, so to speak. But at the very end, unlike the Seventh or Ninth Quartets, it is the finale's own theme, fragmented in a manner reminiscent of the end of the Third Quartet or Eighth Symphony, but secure in its own tonic, that wins out.

***

Back in the summer of 1960, Shostakovich had gone to Dresden for the purposes of scoring the film *Five Days, Five Nights*. What he returned with was the Eighth Quartet. In August 1964, he went on holiday to Lake Balaton in Hungary, purportedly to work on a new opera based on Mikhail Sholokov's famous novel, *The Quiet Don*. What he instead returned with was part of a setting of Yevtushenko's poem, *The Execution of Stepan Razin*, for bass solo, chorus, and orchestra.

The story of the Cossack leader Stepan Razin, quartered alive in 1671 for leading a peasant uprising against the Tsar and the ruling Boyars, had been passed down over the centuries, often embellished in typical folkloric manner. Indeed, Razin had become something of a folk hero, a Russian Robin Hood. Yevtushenko was unstinting in his portrayal of Razin's bloodthirstiness. As the hero stands before the crowd before his execution, he rues: "My sin, good people was not to hang the boyars from the towers. The sin I see in my own eyes was not to hang enough of them."[121] In the Thirteenth Symphony, Shostakovich had felt "at one with almost every word the poet had written."[122] This time, however, he felt trapped between, on the one hand, "the ethical basis of [Yevtushenko's] poetry" and its relevance to contemporary times,[123] and, on the other, the fact that "the whole idea of the piece is essentially depraved."[124] Yet, the bold, forthright score that he produced certainly betrayed no sign of moral queasiness.

Given the *verismo* naturalism of both text and score, Shostakovich had prepared himself for a rough reception. Indeed, the circumstances surrounding the December 1964 premiere had a distinct feeling of *déjà vu*. The soloist, Ivan Petrov, an odd choice given Shostakovich's opinion of him ("very stupid"),[125] showed little interest during rehearsals, failed to appear at the dress rehearsal, and was replaced at the last minute by Vitaly Gromadsky. In the event, Shostakovich need not have worried, since the expected controversy did not materialize. In fact, the cantata was awarded a State Prize, albeit belatedly, in 1968.

In setting this piece of folk history, Shostakovich turned again to what he called the *style russe*.[126] The pompous, brutal brass band introduction is reminiscent of the Thirteenth Symphony's quotation of "Akh vy seni, moi seni," with its "black" texture created from a combination of close vertical spacing in the brass and narrow melodic intervals. Meanwhile, as Jeffrey Baxter points out, both this opening and the soloist's first entrance are composed along the lines of the *byliny*, the Russian epic folksong whose typical structure Baxter characterizes as "a single melody per line in additive meter with accents at the beginning and at the cadence, particularly on the last three syllables."[127] The beginning and ending accents can be heard in the band's introduction, as can the additive meter, with phrasal elisions injecting 3/2 bars into the otherwise 4/4 context. Although the soloist's entrance does not feature the accents, the return to the same closing three-syllable cadential figure (pitch degrees 3-2-1) has a similar effect. One can also hear the narrow melodic ambitus typical of Russian folksong in both the introduction and the solo entrance, an ambitus that widens slightly with the phrasal extensions.

The chorus takes the role of the jeering, spitting crowd, a heartless mob there to enjoy a day out at the execution; a crowd spanning the gamut from prostitutes and beggars to the Tsar himself. Razin finally makes his appearance at the end of the opening procession to a wild orgy of *style russe*: folk-like oom-pah dance rhythms, and coarse whooping effects depicting the jeering of the mob—mainly octave glissandi in which each voice is given a different syllable so that the whole thing essentially sounds like noise: sopranos singing "Ay!," the altos on "Oy!," tenors on "Ukh!," and basses on "Ikh!." It is clearly related to the "Byelostok" episode in the Thirteenth Symphony, though the treatment of the whooping noises here in *Razin* is a good deal more *verismo*, less "musical" than in the Symphony. As a social phenomenon, these episodes are examples of what Caryl Emerson, in her discussion of *The Nose*, calls the "Dostoyevskian signature" of the "crowd-turned-mob": "idle curiosity that becomes voyeurism which then passes, naively and even gaily, into mass violence and torture."[128]

The crowd taunts Razin—he had tried to fight the Boyars, but only got half the job done. As the execution approaches, he tells of his lost battle, admitting to being only "half a rebel." As Malcolm MacDonald writes, "Yevtushenko's self-doubting, self-condemning Razin is very far from the cardboard revolutionary saint of conventional Soviet hagiography, and one must speculate again at Shostakovich's choice of text: did the words awake an echo of identification?"[129] Partly awed by his confession, but also stirred by an understanding of what Razin's failed fight for a good Tsar really meant, the crowd falls silent; the realization that "there are no good Tsars" stirs the first revolutionary feelings. At this point, the choir intones the soloist's melody from the beginning of the piece, but now scored in parallel fourths with the sopranos doubling the tenors at the octave and the altos doubling the basses—the debt to *Boris Godunov*, with its use of a pseudo-Russian Orthodox style to hint at revolution, could not be clearer. Again, there is the very limited melodic ambitus—a tightly woven stepwise motion around a resting tone—together with the additive metrical variations in which the addition of a beat here and a couple of beats there creates metrical fluidity—4/4, 3/4, 5/4, 3/2. And with the metrical extensions come small widenings of the melodic ambitus, as the melody creeps up the scale by an extra note or two. There is also here an unmistakable "pre-Revolutionary" allusion to the bleak, icy "Palace Square" opening of the Eleventh Symphony—heavily doubled open fifths played by muted strings *divisi*, and the occasional chilly interjection of the harp. (Incidentally, the pseudo-Orthodox scoring is not only reserved for moments of sanctimony or reflection. The entrance of the prostitutes is scored in parallel fifths, while the aforementioned whoops are written mostly in parallel fourths, though the glissandi blur any real sense of pitch.)

Following the execution, the music collapses in a typically Shostakovichian fashion, complete with tam-tam, onto a tense *pianissimo* chord cluster of two tritones (D/G-sharp and E-flat/A) in the strings. Over this cluster, the police, an emphatic but at the same time strangely ineffectual assemblage of tenors (a whiff perhaps of the ludicrous tenor police sergeant in *The Nose*), urge the crowd to celebrate, enlisting the help of cheerleading jesters (high woodwind). As a scene, this evokes the famous opening chorus of *Boris Godunov*. But unlike in *Boris*, where the crowd obeys the police officer's orders, the crowd here looks coldly and defiantly on. The Palace Square reference continues, followed by a second allusion to the Eleventh Symphony. As the text speaks of the tolling of the bell, Shostakovich's masterly combination of instruments to depict the bell in all its mighty acoustic and emotional resonance (bass clarinet, contrabassoon, timpani, tam-tam, harp, piano, pizzicato cellos, and double-basses) is reminiscent not only of the start of the coda of the Eleventh Symphony (depicting the rekindling of the revolutionary spirit),[130] but also of the monastery bell in Shostakovich's re-orchestration of *Boris Godunov*.[131]

In Yevtushenko's poem, Razin's severed head lives on. As it falls off the execution block, it cries, "not in vain...." The priest attempts to close its eyes; the head supernaturally resists. Like Nasreddin Hodja and Till Eulenspiegel, Razin gets the last laugh. The cantata's final line ("and cruelly, not hiding its triumph, the head laughed loudly at the Tsar! ...") brings us full circle to the Thirteenth Symphony's scherzo, with its mockery of Tsars.

The Execution of Stepan Razin and the score to *Hamlet* can be viewed as postscripts to Symphonies 11–13, dealing with the same issues of history and conscience, revolution and the triumph against oppressors. Enhanced throughout by its network of allusions to both the Eleventh and Thirteenth Symphonies, the end of *Razin* brings us, in a sense, full circle to the point at which the Eleventh Symphony began. The Thirteenth Symphony showed the awful consequences of the revolution conceived in the Eleventh and effected in the Twelfth. Can we perhaps read *Razin* as a plea for a new revolution, based on the fact that "there are no good Tsars"? The musicologist Henry Orlov, who two years later prepared an article to celebrate Shostakovich's sixtieth birthday, reports that the composer specifically asked him to emphasize the importance of the text describing the crowd's last-minute change of heart.[132]

***

The following year, 1965, started out ominously with a three-week stint in the hospital for suspected heart problems. Overseeing productions of *Katerina Izmailova* (including the film version) took up much of his time, and as a result, 1965 saw only two compositions—the score to the film *A Year is as Long as a Lifetime* and the *Five Romances on Texts from "Krokodil"* for bass and piano, the latter penned in just one day. *Krokodil* was an officially sanctioned satirical magazine that gave ordinary people an outlet to vent their frustrations over day-to-day matters—rudeness, bureaucracy, poor customer service, even personal problems. Shostakovich picked five letters to the editor from the edition of 30 August 1965.

Perhaps no song better exemplifies the mordant wit of the musical settings than the third, "Discretion," a pithy three-line text that Shostakovich set to the "Dies Irae" chant: "Although the hooligan Fedulov did beat me, I did not report this to our remarkable police force. I decided to restrict myself to the thrashing already received."[133]

Krokodil and the film score notwithstanding, it was the triptych of works from 1964 (the Ninth and Tenth Quartets and *The Execution of Stepan Razin*) that brought to a close what might be called "middle-period" Shostakovich—a three-decade period in which nearly all of his political battles were fought and in which most of the musical trademarks we have come to associate with him were developed. As 1966 and the Eleventh Quartet got under way, a new, palpably sparer approach to composition would emerge.

CHAPTER 10

"I LIVED ON . . . IN THE HEARTS OF MY TRUE FRIENDS" (1966–1975)

Throughout his middle period, Shostakovich had been preoccupied with concepts of cyclism and movement-linking. Although the nature of the cyclism varied from piece to piece, the most prevalent type of cyclic connection involved the recall of material from one or more previous movements at a critical, usually climactic, point in the finale. In the later middle-period works, the First Cello Concerto and the Seventh, Ninth, and Tenth Quartets, the cyclism was intensified by the subsequent interaction of the recalled material with the finale's own music, an interaction that in each case would last for the remainder of the movement, and that in the Seventh and Ninth Quartets and in the Concerto would result in the recalled material eventually gaining the upper hand. In the Eighth Quartet, the finale (a fugue on the DSCH motto) was based entirely on recalled material (the first movement's aborted stretto on DSCH), the only new material coming in the form of a countersubject, something that the first movement's stretto presentation had not allowed for.

Composed in January 1966, and premiered in May, the Eleventh Quartet was another heavily cyclic work, with its finale again consisting solely of recalled material. The result is a work perceived less as seven discrete movements than as a single movement in seven sections, an effect exacerbated by work's brevity—about eighteen minutes in total—and its *attacca* connections between each movement. Paul Dyer has compared the Quartet's macro-structure to a sonata plan: the first and second movements functioning as the two themes of an exposition; a development comprising movements three to six; and a seventh movement recapitulation in which the material from the first two "exposition" movements is recalled.[1] This move towards single-movement unity would be one of the defining features of late-period Shostakovich.

Another late-period feature of the Eleventh Quartet is its textural austerity, particularly striking after the almost symphonic density of Shostakovich's earlier quartets. Here in the Eleventh, counterpoint is almost non-existent, and about eighty percent of the work (including the entire first, second, and seventh movements) is played *mezzo piano* or lower. The Quartet also develops the tendency, found in the Thirteenth Symphony and Ninth Quartet, towards short melodic units of narrow pitch range. In those earlier works, these individual units often underwent repetition before giving way to music of a more "open" nature. The Thirteenth Symphony's opening solo (Fig. 2), for example, revolves for four bars around two pitches but then opens up in a more lyrical manner. In the Eleventh Quartet, such lyrical expansion is often lacking, giving its themes a peculiarly tight-lipped, even stunted, feel. The open lyricism of the first violin in the first movement is something of an exception, the monotonous repeated figures in the lower instruments more typical. By the end of the movement, the repeated figure is all that is left, providing a segue, *attacca*, into the second movement scherzo.

The scherzo is based almost entirely on such repeated figures. It opens with a fugato, presenting a curiously static, four-phrase subject in which the first two identical phrases form a tight circle around the tonic F (up a minor second to G-flat, down a major second to E-flat). The third and fourth phrases open the window slightly, but both end back on F. With the prevalence of this claustrophobic theme, along with the muted rhythms and attenuated dynamics, the movement emerges quite unlike any previous scherzo of Shostakovich. Even the scherzo archetypes that do remain, for example, the frequent glissandi, impinge themselves in an unusual way. Shostakovich traditionally used glissando in a scherzo to lend a heavily emphatic, sometimes ironic stamp, particularly in those *Ländler* types from the 1930s and 1940s. The Eleventh Quartet scherzo, however, has no place for earthy gestures. Here, the glissandi, by dint of their extraordinarily wide range (usually over an octave, sometimes closer to two), sound eerily disembodied. At the end of the scherzo, the material is reduced to a simple, repeated perfect fourth in the viola, providing the connection into the next movement.

Of all the Shostakovich archetypes to undergo re-examination in this Quartet, none is more striking than the Recitative that constitutes the third movement. Although the greatest concentration of recitatives in Shostakovich's output comes from the late 1930s to mid-1940s, recitative-like passages can still be found in works from the 1960s, such as the Ninth Quartet and *The Execution of Stepan Razin*. Even the start of "Fears" in the Thirteenth Symphony, with its tuba solo and timpani/low string pedal, contained the essential ingredients of a Shostakovich recitative. The recitative in the Eleventh Quartet, however, is different. The supporting harmony takes the form of an explosive tone-cluster in the three lower strings, always "resolving" onto a second cluster of C, D-flat, and D prior to each entrance of the first violin. This in itself is not unprecedented. The recitatives from the Ninth Quartet and *Razin* are also built on clusters; indeed Shostakovich's very first recitative, in the score to *Alone* (1930), was built around atonal harmony. No, the real surprise is the "melody" in the solo part, nothing more than a series of insistent repetitions, with limited variation, of a three-note figure based on the perfect fourth from the end of the scherzo. Lacking any sense of melody, the music here is pure gesture, the double-stopped presentation of the three-note figure reminiscent of the "jumping fleas" xylophone episode in *Razin*.

Although the material of the recitative is very different from that of the scherzo, the governing principle is the same: very short (usually four-bar) melodic units repeated with limited variation, with little in the way of traditional melodic growth—the obsessive, totemic repetitions becoming the *Ding an sich*. The fourth movement Etude functions similarly. The opening first violin "etude" (beginning, incidentally, with a transposed "HCDS" scale) repeats itself every four bars or so, again with small variations each time. Underneath, the other instruments repeat a short (mainly two-bar) figure, almost chant-like in its limited melodic movement. Indeed, the combination in the Quartet's inner movements of chant-like melodic fragments with obsessive repetition gives a quasi-mystical, almost Ustvolskayan air, suggesting perhaps the chanting of a mantra or the reciting of the Rosary. (Solomon Volkov, for one, has described Shostakovich's own "mumbled speech, short, nervous, stuttered phrases with repeated words."[2]) Yet, for Shostakovich, even such ascetic material was not beyond a little humor. The fifth movement presents the chant-like material as a humoresque, accompanied by an alternating two-note minor third "cuckoo" figure in the second violin that plays, unaltered, through the entire movement—an affectionate tribute, perhaps, to the Beethoven Quartet's recently deceased second violinist, Vasily Shirinsky, to whom the Eleventh Quartet is dedicated. Meanwhile, the sixth movement Elegy presents the chant material, or at least its characteristically narrow intervals, as a funeral march.

Paul Dyer's characterization of these four inner movements as a "development" of the material exposed in the first two is instructive, so long as we accept the limited sense in which the term here applies. The themes in the inner movements certainly represent transformations of those in the first two movements. But the treatment of those themes within these inner movements, with their extensive repetition and limited transformation, does not constitute development in the usual Shostakovichian sense. These movements are perhaps best characterized as "genre studies" of the earlier movements—recitative, etude, humoresque, and funeral elegy—rather than as a development of them.

The seventh movement finale—the Quartet's "recapitulation"—is based on a slow-motion replay of the Scherzo's main subject, incorporating flashbacks of first movement material (Fig. 48) as well as the "HCDS" scale figure (Fig. 45). At the end, sixteen bars of a high-C first violin pedal hang like a beam of light over the stuttering scherzo figure in the other instruments. Two bars from the end, the scherzo figure drops out, leaving the violin to fade away.

The Eleventh Quartet was premiered on 28 May 1966 at a concert that also saw the first performance of the grandiloquently titled *Preface to the Complete Collection of My Works and a Brief Reflection upon This Preface*, for bass and piano. Earlier that year, no doubt in honor of the composer's upcoming sixtieth birthday, tentative plans had been drawn up to create a new Shostakovich collected works

edition. Bemused if not actively irritated by the anniversary brouhaha, Shostakovich composed at a single sitting in March this three-minute musical parody of official honorifics. Written in a musical style not dissimilar to that of *Rayok*, the
opening "Preface" is based loosely on Pushkin's *Story of a Versifier*, while in the
subsequent "Brief Reflection" Shostakovich introduces himself, complete with an
intoning of the DSCH motif to the words "Dmitry Shostakovich," and enumerates a selection of his honors and achievements: People's Artist of the USSR; First
Secretary, Union of Composers of the RSFSR; Secretary, Union of Composers of
the USSR; and "very many other very important responsibilities and positions." A
skit it may have been, but the harmonic darkening in the run-up to the DSCH
quotation, not to mention the small quotation from the Thirteenth Symphony's
finale ("A Career"; see Chapter 9), speaks volumes.

The 28 May concert also featured Shostakovich accompanying Nesterenko in
the *Krokodil* Romances and Vishnevskaya in the *Five Satires on Verses of Sasha
Chorny*. Shostakovich's piano career had by this point ground to a halt; this was
his first public performance in over two years. Glikman attests to the composer's
nervous state in the days leading up to the concert. In *Krokodil*, Nesterenko twice
missed his entrance and, according to Glikman, Shostakovich's panic was clear to
see, the effects exacerbated by the hot and airless auditorium; heat had always been
a problem for Shostakovich.[3] Although the concert was successful, it would be the
last public performance he would ever give. Later that night, he suffered his first
heart attack.

Shostakovich approached the subject of his health with a combination of hope
and resignation. As Laurel Fay points out, he was always ready to submit himself
to new treatments and therapies, both orthodox and alternative,[4] but in his letters
to Glikman he ridicules his own wishful thinking.[5] Following the heart attack, he
spent two months in the hospital plus a further month in a sanatorium. At the
end of October, he was back in the hospital to build up further strength in his
limbs and muscles. Although under strict orders not to compose, he used his time
in the hospital to read, absorbing ideas that would manifest themselves in future
works. But any inspiration that he garnered from reading was countered by long
periods of boredom and depression—the latter not helped by the ban placed on
two of his favorite pleasures, cigarettes and alcohol.

***

Earlier that spring, Shostakovich had been able to complete his Second Cello
Concerto, which, like the First Concerto and the re-orchestration of the Schumann Concerto, was written for Rostropovich. The first orchestral work in Shostakovich's late period, the Concerto's stark, chamber-like textures are worlds away
from the "mainstream" orchestral style of works even as recent as the Thirteenth
Symphony and *The Execution of Stepan Razin*, though the First Cello Concerto
had certainly been experimenting with scaled-down textures. Like the First Concerto, the trumpets and heavy brass are absent, though there are two horns here
instead of the solitary instrument that graced the earlier work. The one section
that is expanded is the percussion, but its use both here and in other late-period

works is more intricate and chamber-like than before, de-emphasizing the "battery onslaught" and exploring instead more coloristic possibilities. Also new was the role of the solo instrument, which was more in the nature of an obbligato, less concerto-like than before. Indeed, Shostakovich wrote that this could have been "the Fourteenth Symphony with a solo cello part."[6]

That said, the sound world that most comes to mind at the start of the Second Cello Concerto is that of the First Violin Concerto. It opens, like the Violin Concerto, with an apparently wandering two-part counterpoint between the solo instrument and the orchestral cellos and basses, only this time it is the solo that begins, with the second line entering in the eighth bar. Like the opening of the Violin Concerto, the emphasis is on melody that is interval driven rather than harmonically governed. But unlike the Violin Concerto, which eventually settles into something more "middle-period" sounding, this second Cello Concerto is dominated by this unconventional melodic style. Eric Roseberry writes:

> There is little sense of structurally planned, schematic harmonic movement in a tonally ambiguous, improvisatory—even vague (though not impressionistic) harmonic field. But for its traditional melodic flow and triadic references, the pointillistic, linear elements, the concentration on intervallic cellular activity suggest the stimulus of renewed contact with Schoenberg and Webern.[7]

The very opening of the Concerto exemplifies this approach, with its descending minor second cell, x (A-flat–G), one that sounds almost like a cadential figure. Indeed, the cell is repeated in the second bar, rather in the way that Shostakovich liked to repeat cadential figures.[8] The melody presents this cell four times over its eight bars, giving it an almost totemic quality reminiscent of the Eleventh Quartet. But what does it represent? The Concerto is nominally in G minor, so that opening cell represents a Phrygian approach to the tonic, with the subsequent dips down to the low D in the next few bars possibly suggesting the dominant. Yet, G minor exists here really only at the level of suggestion. At bar 8, the cello arrives on G, but as it holds out this pedal, the orchestral cellos and basses, far from reinforcing G as the pitch center, embark on a nine-note row.

Following a tutti presentation of the opening theme in the winds (Fig. 8), scored with that contrabassoon-saturated sound familiar from both the First Violin and First Cello Concertos, the second subject enters at Fig. 11. It too is based on x, though the major key (D major) and the aching double stops give it an altogether different character. However, paralleling the first theme, the cell is presented four times over the course of the melody's first eight bars, lending a similarly insistent quality.

This insistence bleeds over into the development (Fig. 16), where the feeling of dynamic, symphonic accumulation characteristic of Shostakovich's middle-period developments is replaced by something altogether different. Certainly, the familiar thematic fragmentation is there. But rather than the restless transformations and retransformations of such fragments, Shostakovich creates a more hypnotic effect, often using simple repetitions of minimally transformed cells. Particularly striking in the early stage of the development is the grotesque transformation of x in the upper woodwinds. It is reiterated several times between Figs. 17 and 19, and in each case functions in counterpoint with another minimally transformed version of x in a different instrument, usually the solo cello. This obsessive repetition, together with the emphasis on percussive high woodwind, xylophone, and harp sonorities, replacing the brooding low string textures that have dominated up to this point, give an almost arthritic, marionette-like quality. This approach pervades into the development's later stages. Yet, despite this, and despite the fact that, unusually for a slow Shostakovich first movement, there is no marked tempo acceleration during the development (the Sixth Symphony is another exception), tension still accumulates, mainly through the ever-increasing importance of a sixteenth-note countermelody that gives the impression of a faster tempo. It should also be noted that, rightly or wrongly, performances do tend to accelerate over the course of this development.

At the peak of the development (Fig. 25), the opening theme returns in a fuller form in the strings, bassoons, and horns, a minor second higher than at the start of the movement, and harmonized in thirds. Given that the bulk of the development has not really strayed away from that first theme, the sense of return might not seem so momentous. But the fuller version together with the switch to those darker colors, not to mention the swirling high woodwinds so characteristic of Shostakovich's climactic moments, are sufficiently portentous. The orchestra is silenced by the dry thwack of the bass drum (marked *secco*, that instrument is perhaps a more suitable weapon of termination for this chamber-like score than, say, the tam-tam used for similar purposes in the corresponding moments of the Fifth or Eighth Symphonies), unleashing a short cadenza, based on x, for the cello and bass drum (Fig. 26) that eventually dissolves into the recapitulation (Fig. 28, b5). Typically for Shostakovich, the recapitulation is truncated. Untypically, the key at the very end is unclear, with D major, the key that has vied with G minor throughout the movement, appearing to gain the upper hand—a rare instance in Shostakovich of Mahlerian "progressive tonality."

The second movement scherzo is based on a ditty that was once popular amongst Odessa street merchants: "*Bubliki*! Buy my *bubliki*!"[9] The story goes that a few months prior to the Concerto's composition, playing games at a New Year's party, Shostakovich had claimed this to be his favorite tune. Presented here in the scherzo, it emerges as heavily ironic, the cello melody propelled along by the crudest of "oom-pah" rhythms in the double reeds. The cadential tag to this melody, gruffly intoned in the bassoon and contrabassoon, is based on the first movement's x cell (Fig. 40, b3–4). Lowbrow the source material may be, but Shostakovich formulates a movement that is structurally "serious"—not the usual scherzo/trio but a sonata form, complete with a short but intensifying development (Fig. 49) and a transformative recapitulation (Fig. 54). In this recap, the entire first subject area is re-characterized from its original duple-meter "oom-pah" rhythm into a wild waltz, accompanied by a grotesque trio of bassoons that attempt to derail the entire rhythmic structure, particularly from Fig. 55, where the bassoon's constantly shifting emphasis implies an alternation between 3/4 and 4/4, while the solo attempts to keep the waltz on the straight and narrow.

Like the First Cello Concerto, the Second makes use of a horn obbligato. It can be heard in the more reflective outer sections of the first movement, as well as in the scherzo's exposition and development, where it occasionally interjects that aforementioned bassoon tag. However, it is in the scherzo's recapitulation that the instrument comes into its own, playing an essential role in the recap's transformative process. At Fig. 59, a pair of horns takes over a three-note figure that had originally been heard back at Fig. 41, where it appears in the woodwinds in a simple octave doubling, and then again in the recapitulation (Fig. 56, b8, et seq.), where it is reinforced by repetition and by its presentation in the cello *in alt*, playing glissandi in parallel fifths. When the horns take it over at Fig. 59, they preserve the parallel fifths, reinforcing the more strained quality with which almost every theme in this recap has now been imbued. At Fig. 62, b4, the solo horn plays a manic version of its original material (i.e., the bassoon tag) over the cello's final presentation of the main theme, now reverted back from the waltz to the original "oom-pah" version. The coda pits first the cello against the full orchestra and then the two horns against the full orchestra—one of only two sections of tutti writing in the entire Concerto. From out of this bursts forth a thirty-two-bar-long fanfare for two horns, announcing the third movement finale. For the most part, the fanfare is scored in parallel fourths: on the one hand, a vertical application of the melodic fourths so prevalent in the scherzo; on the other, an inversion of the parallel fifths that had first initiated the horns' rise to power.

The fanfare material is then taken up by the cello cadenza. Although there had been a short cadenza in the first movement, the one here at the start of the finale is clearly the "global" cadenza for the Concerto as a whole, just as the cadenzas in the First Violin and First Cello Concertos had been. The first movement cadenza had featured interjections by the bass drum; this one plays out to the accompaniment of a continuous tambourine shake. For Shostakovich, the idea of a percussion presence in a cadenza was possibly garnered from Britten's *Cello Symphony*, which had received its world premiere in Moscow in 1964.[10] As for the skeletal rattling of the tambourine accompanying a fanfare, Shostakovich had already recently tried this in his *Hamlet* score ("Arrival of the Players").

Once the finale gets underway (Fig. 74), what emerges is an idiosyncratically structured movement, one that, as Eric Roseberry points out, "combin[es] rondo characteristics with the sonata principle" but is "not to be confused with . . . sonata rondo."[11] The rondo element can be heard in the exposition, where an alternation of the three main themes creates the structure: A–B–A–B–(Development of A+B)–C. The flute and cello "A" theme is, for this Concerto at least, both unusually lyrical and unusually stable tonally, confirming the work's G tonic in a way that the first movement never quite could. The slightly wry, march-like "B" theme (Fig. 78) provides the next step in the assertion of the percussion as a major voice in this Concerto, while the lyrical "C" theme (Fig. 91) marks a return to the first movement's secondary pitch center, D (minor, in this case).

Shortly into the "C" theme (Fig. 92), Shostakovich interjects the "marionette" woodwind idea from the first movement. Defining a development section, or at least where it starts, is not easy. Eric Roseberry places it at Fig. 91, in other words placing the entire "C" theme under the umbrella of the development rather than the exposition. Perhaps a better choice would be Fig. 95, where the "C" theme starts its own development and where the music appears to don a new momentum. Yet, other than a short modulation a few bars later, most of the ensuing development of this "C" theme, including a pseudo-cadenza version for cello and snare drum (Fig. 97), sticks rigidly to the D minor of the theme's original presentation.[12] In other words, Figs. 95 and 97 emerge more as variations of the "C" theme than as a development, a perception enhanced by the lack of the usual types of thematic interaction that one expects with Shostakovich. The center of this movement is thus even less "developmental" (in the traditional sense of the word) than its first movement counterpart had been. Its climax, the second of the Concerto's two tutti sections, is more typical: a recall of the movement's opening fanfare scored for horns and high woodwind (Fig. 99) followed by a harmonically distorted, pile-driving recall of the scherzo's *bubliki* theme (Fig. 100), the sardonicism of the original now turned decidedly nasty.

The short recapitulation presents the movement's three main themes in reverse order ("C" in the tonic G minor, "B" in C major/minor, and "A" in G minor) followed by a recall of both of the first movement's themes. In the coda (Fig. 112), a final presentation of "B," now in the tonic, gives way to the "tick-tock" whirring of percussion (woodblock, tom-tom, snare drum (both rim-click and ordinary), and xylophone), reminiscent of the coda to the Fourth Symphony's scherzo, and prescient of what would be the even longer percussion coda to the Fifteenth Symphony. Beneath this sit double basses pulsating, pizzicato, on the tonic, G, and the cello sitting on D. Two bars before the end, the percussion and basses give up, and Shostakovich presents us with what has to be the most enigmatic conclusion in the entire concerto repertoire: the cello alone finishes out the work with the D pedal (not just the dominant pedal, but the pitch that seems to have been this Concerto's secondary center), terminating abruptly with a jab, following a *crescendo* to *mezzo piano*.

The Concerto's premiere took place on 25 September 1966, Shostakovich's sixtieth birthday, in Moscow with Yevgeny Svetlanov conducting. The concert was one of the major musical events of the year. Earlier that same day, Shostakovich had been awarded both the Order of Lenin and the title "Hero of Socialist Labor." Although his dislike of official anniversary events was as waspish as it had been ten years before, he was genuinely touched by the love and affection shown to him that night by the audience—this was his first public appearance since his heart attack. Incidentally, the Concerto's premiere was originally to have been given in Leningrad with Mravinsky, but Mravinsky withdrew, apparently at the last minute, claiming that he would need until October to learn the score. Rostropovich, who had not forgotten the conductor's erratic behavior over Shostakovich's Thirteenth Symphony, refused to accept this and severed relations with Mravinsky.

How "last minute" Mravinsky's withdrawal actually was is open to debate; according to some reports, the Leningrad Philharmonic administration had simply forgotten to relay the conductor's plans to Rostropovich.[13] The Concerto's Leningrad premiere was subsequently given in November by the student orchestra at the Conservatory under Nikolai Rabinovich. As for Shostakovich, though relations with Mravinsky were eventually patched up, he would never again entrust the conductor with a first performance.

***

As previously noted, Shostakovich spent much of his two-month hospital stay that summer immersed in literature and poetry. One writer who would strike a particularly resonant chord was the Russian Symbolist poet, Alexander Blok (1880–1921). In February 1967, Shostakovich completed his setting of seven Blok poems for soprano, violin, cello, and piano. However, rather than using the set ensemble through the entire cycle, he chose instead to explore the various permutations and combinations that this particular ensemble yielded: "Ophelia's Song" (cello); "Gamayun, the Bird of Prophecy" (piano); "We Were Together" (violin), "The City Sleeps" (cello and piano); "The Tempest" (violin and piano); "Secret Signs" (violin and cello); "Music" (violin, cello, and piano).

The first vocal work of Shostakovich's late period, the *Blok* cycle would not only draw (or, more accurately, withdraw) us into a bleaker, sparer sound world—one still more rarified than the Eleventh Quartet or the Second Cello Concerto—but would to an extent redefine the very genre of the song cycle, with Shostakovich eschewing altogether the "Romance" (i.e., the traditional Russian lyrical art-song) that he had favored earlier in his career, e.g., the *Four Pushkin Romances* (1936), the *Six Romances on Words of W. Raleigh, R. Burns, and W. Shakespeare* (1942), or even the *Five Romances on Texts from "Krokodil"* (1965). Indeed, after *Krokodil*, Shostakovich never again used the title "Romance" for a song cycle,[14] in line with what would become a less lyrical, more declamatory approach to text-setting, what Dorothea Redepenning has called the "homage to the poetic word."[15] In a sense, the transformation from verbal primacy to musical primacy that Shostakovich had effected in his vocal writing in the early 1930s, evinced most obviously in the transition from *The Nose* to *Lady Macbeth*, had now been put into reverse—within the context of completely different musical styles, of course.

Indeed, it is no exaggeration to argue that such a transformation can be heard within the *Blok* cycle itself. The first song, with its continuous, lyrical cello accompaniment and its constant tugging at the primary tonality (C minor), could very easily have come out of *Lady Macbeth*—the character of Ophelia perhaps connected in Shostakovich's mind with the much stronger, though still ultimately vulnerable Katerina. Although the song's topic of "parting" had preoccupied Shostakovich for decades and would do so again in the upcoming Fourteenth Symphony and the final song cycles, its associated topic of "love" had not been dealt with overtly in Shostakovich since *Lady Macbeth*. (It had, arguably, been dealt with covertly in the form of musically encoded references to Yelena Konstantinovskaya, Galina Ustvolskaya, and Elmira Nazirova.)

The newer, more declamatory style can be heard, appropriately enough, in "Gamayun, the Bird of Prophecy." Striding piano double octaves, going through melodic twists and turns reminiscent of the low string line in the opening stages of the Tenth Symphony, declaim almost as explicitly as the voice itself the violent prophesies of Gamayun. In fact, the key (E minor), the first three notes (scale degrees 1-2-3), and to a lesser extent the insistent flat fourth scale degree (B-flat) are all reminiscent of the Tenth Symphony. Following an impressive build-up to its climax, one that in the piano reflects in microcosm the orchestral build-up of, say, the Tenth Symphony's first movement development section, the song ends in a quiet, disembodied way, as the poet contrasts the beams of love on the bird's beautiful face with the "prophetic truths" pronounced by its "blood-covered lips."[16] At the end, a long-decaying C minor chord in the piano (another example of progressive tonality) is punctuated by dry *sforzando* descending fourths (F-sharp down to C-sharp). The pedaling needed to bring this off fills the air with strange resonances. One has to go all the way back to the avant-garde First Piano Sonata to find anything comparable in Shostakovich's output.

In "Ophelia's Song," the cello had provided a continuous countermelody, equal in prominence to the voice. In "We Were Together," another love song, the violin, whose presence is featured in the text itself ("The night was disturbed, the violin sang"), is decidedly the dominant partner. As well as providing the lyrical framework for the song, it indulges in the highly untypical (for Shostakovich) activity of impressionist depictions of nature—"the quiet murmur of the streams."

As the gloom sets in over the next three songs, the theme of love disappears— the reference to a "maid's golden tresses" in "Secret Signs" the single possible exception—and the stylistic move away from the lyrical towards the declamatory becomes more decisive. It is in this portion of the cycle that those two devices so associated in Shostakovich with the themes of death and tragedy—the passacaglia and the note row—are heard. In "The City Sleeps," the poet gazes through the shimmering haze of the city night and sees in the distance the glow of dawn. Yet, the glow merely "hides the awakening of sad days," and perhaps it was the passacaglia's inbuilt theme of (tragic) history repeating itself that made it a compelling choice for Shostakovich here (see Chapter 15 for further discussion). This was in fact Shostakovich's first passacaglia in a vocal context—the passacaglia in *Lady Macbeth* had been in a non-vocal context. Likewise, the two isolated note rows in, appropriately enough, "Secret Signs" would constitute Shostakovich's first exploration, in any genre, of twelve-note writing.

The final song, "Music" (Shostakovich's own title), acts as an epilogue. It calls up images from the previous poems: the city disappearing in the mist (from "The City Sleeps," itself a recalling of the "shores ... veiled in fog" in "Ophelia's Song"); the tempest; the tears (recalling the "waves wash[ing] tears off the cliff" in "Ophelia's Song"); and the sacrifice of blood (a reference, perhaps to Gamayun's "blood-covered lips"). Yet, in the end these references all serve the song's two overriding themes—the ecstasy of life within death (another unusual Shostakovich *topos*) and the power of music. It is in a sense Shostakovich's answer to the finale of Mahler's Fourth Symphony. There, music is proclaimed in the text as the truest of heaven's delights, something that becomes a reality as the text-carrying voice finally cedes to the "pure" music of the orchestra alone. With Blok/Shostakovich, music is perhaps not so much the truest of earth's delights as the refuge from its horrors. Music gets the last say here too, as the final third of the movement is given over to the instrumental trio, though any resolution that it provides is tentative at best. At the end, the closing tonality of E-flat (presumably minor) is unsettled by the piano's fourths (A to D) punctuating the texture, a reminiscence of the closing of "Gamayun" with its F-sharp-C-sharp fourths disturbing the attempted C minor.

***

In May 1967, a year after he had graced Rostropovich with a second cello concerto, Shostakovich completed his Second Violin Concerto, a work that he dedicated, as he had the First Concerto, to David Oistrakh. The violinist believed it to have been written prematurely as a sixtieth birthday present, an error that Shostakovich "corrected" with the Violin Sonata in 1968, Oistrakh's actual sixtieth anniversary. However, as Laurel Fay notes, there is no evidence other than Oistrakh's own belief to suggest that Shostakovich had written the Concerto for this purpose.[17]

The three-movement Second Violin Concerto would turn out to be a more solo-oriented work than the Second Cello Concerto had been. Yet, there are similarities between the two, indeed between all four of Shostakovich's string concertos. In all four, subsidiary lines and countermelodies tend to be found more often in the woodwinds and horns than in the strings. And in common with both Cello Concertos, there is an absence of trumpets and heavy brass, while the horns are elevated to the role of obbligato. The single horn of the First Cello Concerto and the pair of horns in the Second have now expanded to four.

Like the Second Cello Concerto, and for that matter the First Violin Concerto, the Second Violin Concerto begins with a two-part counterpoint of the solo instrument and brooding orchestral cellos and basses. And, like the Second Cello Concerto, the bass line not only contains but reiterates over a very short period the most important seeds for the construction of the movement as a whole—in this case the intervals of a minor second and perfect fourth. The quirky, more modernistic sounding, second subject at Fig. 10 (based somewhat unusually on the subdominant, F-sharp) represents, on the surface at least, a contrast to the contemplative first subject. Yet, it is constructed from the same ingredients. The perkily wry five-note upper woodwind figure heard at the start of the second theme is dominated by the perfect fourth, while the minor second is the predominant interval both in the pizzicato accompaniment and in the violin melody, as well as in the strange, almost late-Mahlerian piccolo/solo violin duo that enters a few bars later (Fig. 11). As with the Cello Concerto, this second subject proves tonally more stable than the first.

Where this movement diverges from its Cello Concerto counterpart is in the development (Fig. 19). The difference lies not so much in what the development does—transform and contort the main exposition themes—but in how it presents itself. In the Cello Concerto, the development started, typically for a Shostakovich slow movement or *moderato*, in a restrained way, emerging almost imperceptibly from out of the exposition. In the Violin Concerto, by contrast, it takes off in a *scherzando* vein, almost as if the music were being transformed not into a development section but into a separate movement altogether. Yet, this turns out to be every bit as conducive to Shostakovich's typical brutalization techniques, more so in fact than the more "static," repetition-dependent Cello Concerto development—although like the Cello Concerto, dissonance has to take the place of brute orchestral power; the incidence of full tutti, or at least as full as the reduced instrumentation here allows for, is, as with the Cello Concerto, relatively scarce.

It is possible that Shostakovich created this *scherzando* development to compensate for the lack of a scherzo movement proper—unlike the Cello Concerto, the middle movement here would be slow. As if to prove the point, he even inserts a short quotation from the Cello Concerto's scherzo—that grotesque waltz for three bassoons, though admittedly the effect is mollified here by being scored for two bassoons and contrabassoon in an altogether less ridiculous register (Fig. 20). But this *scherzando* development demonstrates something else, something that might be viewed as complementary to his late period exploration of single-movement unity, namely the concept of movements within movements, an idea that would be expanded upon the following year in the Twelfth Quartet.

As with the Cello Concerto, the development gives way to a cadenza. In the earlier work, the cadenza held tension before the onset of the recapitulation. Here, by contrast, it falls into the recap itself, functioning essentially as the reprise of the first theme—in the double-stopping that runs through the entire cadenza, the lower voice is a modified version of the cello/bass line that had originally accompanied this first theme. Following this, the horn takes over the theme (Fig. 36), just as the woodwinds had originally (Fig. 3), though now the tonic, C-sharp, is a good deal more stable. It is here that the horn establishes itself as the work's unofficial second voice, weaving in counterpoint with the solo violin. What it was that inspired Shostakovich to write a horn obbligato in three of his four string concertos (and that is not to ignore the prominent part that it also plays in small portions of the First Violin Concerto), we do not know. At a guess, it could be said that the horn is probably the only single orchestral instrument that can begin to match the expressive range of the violin and cello, while at the same time matching, or even outdoing, their power of projection to ratchet up the tension when required. Likewise, it is perhaps not a surprise that Shostakovich found the trumpet to be the perfect official second voice for the circus antics of the First Piano Concerto.

Typically for Shostakovich, the first subject area is truncated in the recapitulation, since what had constituted the initial climax-building areas of the exposition is no longer needed. Also typically for Shostakovich in such *moderato* movements, the second subject is presented more-or-less in its entirety, though here the slower marked tempo—*Più mosso* (qtr. = 138) versus *Più mosso* (qtr. = 168) in the exposition—along with a coda that is also based on this second subject (Fig. 45) give the psychological impression of a recapitulation that is about as long as the exposition, a rare phenomenon in Shostakovich's music.

The slow second movement is neither a passacaglia nor one of Shostakovich's pseudo-passacaglias. Yet, with its more openly grieving solo line and its inexorable, triple-meter bass-line motion, there is at least a sense that it is attempting to recall, albeit as a distant memory, the passacaglia qualities of the First Violin Concerto's slow movement. Nowhere is this more apparent than at the outset, where the bass line starts on the tonic (G), climbs by semitone, leading to a cadence of sorts back to G in the ninth bar. It then continues in a new chromatic wandering, but one culminating in an even more definitive cadential jump (D to G) in bars 13–14. Although there is no repetition of the bass line here, there is a repetitive element to the violin solo; the simple G minor scale figure (1-2-3-4-3-2) heard at the very outset closes the melody at bar 14 and reopens what is now a solo violin accompaniment to the new flute theme at bar 15. The movement is a tripartite (ABA) structure, with the opening melody also opening the central "B" section as well as, initially in the "wrong" key, the final "A" section. The "B" section (Fig. 53), mostly in E minor, represents a clearing of the air, a dropping of counterpoint and countermelodies to reveal a simple violin melody soaring above the simplest of accompaniments. Linking the "B" section with the reprise of "A" is a short cadenza (a sharply "gestural" affair akin to the cello recitative in the finale of the Ninth Quartet rather than the more "organic" cadenza familiar from, say, the First Violin Concerto) followed by a strange arioso over a string tremolo.

At the end of this slow movement, the horn again makes its presence known. This time, its role is transformative, taking the movement's introspective main melody and turning it over the course of its seventeen bars into a series of refulgent D-flat major cadences. As if embarrassed by this sudden surge of confidence, the horn attempts in the last four of these bars to inject a moment of doubt with nasal stopped sonorities and a stray B-double-flat borrowed from the minor. But the cast is set. The third movement finale, which opens *attacca* with a short *adagio* featuring the violin and four muted horns barking and snarling at each other, sets off in a breezy D-flat, seemingly throwing aside all of the slow movement's introspective doubts and musings.

After the somewhat complex mix of sonata and rondo found in the Second Cello Concerto's finale, this more straightforward sonata-rondo finale (A-B-A-development/cadenza-B-A-coda) is more akin to the many variants of sonata rondo that Shostakovich had used over the previous couple of decades. For all its chromatic peppering, including at least one note row (Fig. 72, b6–8) plus several near misses, the music's tonal roots here are stronger than in the previous movements. Writing shortly after the Concerto's composition, Norman Kay, somewhat unfairly, described the movement as "one of the routine disappointments that continue to pour from a composer whose obsession about communication demands a whipped-up finale."[18] Although lighter in weight than the finale of the First Violin Concerto, and certainly less probing than the finale of the Second Cello

Concerto, this movement does work within the more serious context of the Concerto as a whole. The cadenza here, like those in the other three string concerti, is a "global" cadenza, featuring material from all three movements, though its placement within the bulk of the movement rather than as an entity that stands between, and hence outside, movements, as with the other three concerti, does somewhat diminish this role. Moreover, this cadenza is written to be played essentially *in tempo*, allying it still more specifically to the movement itself than to the Concerto as a whole.

***

Although Shostakovich's compositional style had been changing over the last year or two, he could quite easily revert back to something more "middle-period" when required. Composed in the summer of 1967 for the fiftieth anniversary of the Revolution, his symphonic poem *October* contains echoes of the Twelfth Symphony's swaggering style, not to mention a main melody whose opening intervals (1-2-min3-7) ape the start of the Tenth Symphony. The second theme was a recycling of "The Partisan" from the film *Volochayevka Days*, a quotation that had apparently been inspired by Shostakovich's visit to Mosfilm in preparation for the re-release of that film.[19] *October* is a stirring work, though, as might be expected for such an occasional piece, not tremendously profound in its musical thought. Also composed in 1967 was the *Funeral-Triumphal Prelude* dedicated to the "heroes of the Battle of Stalingrad," a work intended for tape-recorded replay at the Mamayev Hill War Memorial in Volgograd (formerly Stalingrad).

***

Shostakovich's health had stabilized somewhat during the first half of 1967. In a letter to Venyamin Basner, he disclosed that, contrary to doctor's orders, he had helped himself to a small tipple of brandy (which his wife, Irina, had hidden) and that this had helped bring the *Blok* cycle to fruition.[20] But in September, misfortune struck again when he broke his right leg, confining him to the hospital for the rest of the year. The following spring, Shostakovich relinquished his post of First Secretary of the RSFSR Composers' Union; he had first made the request back in October 1966,[21] five months after his heart attack, though he had been persuaded to continue.

Shostakovich's compositions for 1968 amounted to two: the Twelfth Quartet, completed in March, and the Violin Sonata, composed between August and October. Written as a sixtieth birthday present for David Oistrakh—the opening violin line, D-E-flat-D-flat-C-B-F-sharp, purportedly a synthesis of DSCH and "D.F." Oistrakh, i.e., D-S-(Des)-C-H-(Fis)—the three-movement Sonata makes a bleak, austere statement, though parts of the second movement scherzo recall the energy of the scherzos of the Piano Quintet or the Second Piano Trio. The bare-bones piano writing seems to have been Shostakovich's last-ditch attempt to revive his own playing, but although a private, domestic recording of the Sonata exists with Oistrakh and Shostakovich, the composer was by this time in no physical state to perform the work publicly. The outer movements, and in particular their treatment of passacaglia and note-row, are analyzed in Chapter 15.

Laid out in two movements, the Twelfth Quartet represented another move in the direction of "single-movement" unity, albeit one that, with its creation of a sonata form within a sonata form, would yield a result very different from the Eleventh Quartet. Taken by itself, the seven-minute-long first movement is in a simple sonata form, with a short development and a relatively straightforward, reverse-order recapitulation, the latter containing only a hint of "gradually emerging" ambiguity at its outset, where a rhythmic idea from the development holds out for a few bars into the start of the recap and there is a momentary confusion over time signature (Fig. 10, b5 to Fig. 11). For a formal equivalent, one has to go back over forty years to the first movement of the First Symphony, a connection seemingly emphasized by the similar "second-beat-based" waltz-like themes that make up their respective second subjects.

The twenty-minute-long second movement is split into five sections: 1) a full Shostakovich-style scherzo (i.e., with the trio returning towards the end of the scherzo reprise), one that also contains significant development of the scherzo material prior to the trio's first appearance; 2) an *Adagio* in which a chromatically wandering cello (several ten- and eleven-note rows) alternates with an almost chant-like presentation of a funeral march, complete with mysterious parallel, close-harmony, root-position triads; 3) a cadenza-style second development of the first movement material, ending with a short recall of the *Adagio* material; 4) a recapitulation of the first movement's first subject; and 5) a final section based on the second movement's opening scherzo material, one that incorporates the scherzo's moments of atonality but that also allows for an affirmation of the Quartet's D-flat major tonic. Like the first movement, the second can be viewed as a self-contained entity—essentially, a large scherzo incorporating in its middle stages the funeral march and the recalls of the first movement. But the manner in which the recalls are handled suggests an alternative reading. In section 4, the first movement material is not so much recalled (i.e., a flashback to a familiar theme but in new surroundings) as replayed, with its original tempo and textures intact—a familiar theme in familiar surroundings. If this fourth section does indeed represent the "macro recapitulation" of first movement material within the context of the Quartet as a whole, then the third section becomes the "macro development" of that material, a designation reinforced when this section is compared to the "local" first movement development. On one level, this second development functions as a cadenza for the work's dedicatee, the Beethoven Quartet's first violinist, Dmitry Tsyganov. In fact, this cadenza could be said to be the point at which the first violin takes ownership of the Quartet, a role that up until this point had been assumed by the cello. Yet, despite the fact that its treatment of the material—the typically Shostakovichian "loud" pizzicato, the chordal outbursts, and the virtuoso runs—constitutes "gestural" rather than "symphonic" development (not surprisingly for a cadenza), this second development turns out to be not only gesturally but musically more adventurous than the first movement's rather limited exploration, generating a greater build-up of tension.

In this "macro" view of the Twelfth Quartet, the entire first movement plus sections 1 and 2 of the second form the exposition, section 3 of the second movement forms the development, section 4 the recapitulation, and section 5 the coda. The two views of the Quartet's structure—the "local" and the "macro"—can happily coexist. In fact, appreciation of this extraordinary work is in part dependent upon the listener's ability to perceive two structures, the sonata form within a sonata form, simultaneously.

The Twelfth Quartet also witnesses the coming together, or at least the juxtaposition, of some of the most extreme facets of Shostakovich's writing. The most striking example is the almost dizzying throwing together of highly dissonant, chromatic music (twelve-note in the most extreme cases) alongside passages of almost banal diatonicism. At the start of the Quartet, for example, the cello's wandering, disjunct, twelve-note row snaps immediately into four bars of complete diatonicism—a didactically presented tonic D-flat major scale played in oscillating seconds, rather in the manner of an exercise. In fact, the row is designed so that its final two pitches, A-flat and D-flat, form a perfect cadence into the tonic. Inevitably, such a juxtaposition raises questions of perception. For example, is the first bar to be felt as the proverbial "air from another planet" whose strangeness immediately evaporates upon entering the second bar? Or can it indeed be felt as a long, chromatic upbeat, a hugely prolonged cadential figure? As Alan George points out, such issues directly affect interpretation. The row can be played in a "single unit," one that emphasizes its anacrusic function, or it can be played in a manner that "explore[s] the expressive possibilities inherent in the chromatic intervals of the note row."[22] Other uses of the note row are discussed in Chapter 15.

The juxtaposition of extremes is also apparent in the matter of texture. There are a few passages whose sparseness shows the influence of the Second Cello Concerto or even the Eleventh Quartet, but there is a surprisingly high incidence (surprising given the generally accepted view that "late Shostakovich" equates to thin textures) of passages whose density yields nothing to the more "symphonic" quartets of Shostakovich's middle period. In fact, the clusters formed by the manic parallel and contrary-motion scales in the scherzo portion of the second movement (the passages starting at Fig. 32, b5 and Fig. 40, b5) would not have been out of place in the Second Symphony.

***

The Twelfth Quartet and the Violin Sonata would mark Shostakovich's first real engagement with the twelve-note row—the isolated examples in the *Blok* cycle and the Second Violin Concerto notwithstanding. Shostakovich's use of twelve-note formations is discussed in Chapter 15. But what were his philosophical intentions, and how did they relate to the prevailing climate? Back in 1959, Shostakovich had noted that "not a single [dodecaphonic] work . . . has gained wide acceptance. . . . Dodecaphony not only has no future, it doesn't even have a present. It is just a 'fad' that is already passing."[23] The catalyst for this particular remark had been his apparently negative encounters with Polish and Western contemporary music at the Warsaw Autumn Festival that year. He would continue to repeat these sentiments over the next few years both at home and abroad—whether from conviction or from the need to toe the Party line, which had always viewed dodecaphony as a formalist evil. But by the late 1960s, nearly every Soviet composer of note had explored it to one degree or another—and not just the younger, radical "fringe" generation of Schnittke, Gubaidulina, Denisov, Silvestrov, and Pärt, but "establishment" figures like Shchedrin, Peiko, Salmanov, Karayev, and now Shostakovich himself. In fact, works such as Salmanov's and Karayev's Third Symphonies (1964 and 1965, respectively) came much closer to Schoenbergian serialism, i.e., serialism not just as a chromatic extension but as a structural organizer, than would anything by Shostakovich. Nevertheless, as Peter Schmelz points out, something of a double standard applied. While the young radicals continued to be castigated for their formalist dabbling, the authorities appeared to turn a blind eye where establishment composers were concerned.[24] Acknowledging the new reality, the 1968 Second Congress of the RSFSR Composers' Union passed a resolution cautiously admitting dodecaphony. With the stigma removed, Shostakovich's own rhetoric began to soften, encouraging dodecaphony as an expressive tool, though warning against its use as a compositional goal per se. It is, though, interesting to note his alleged reaction—was it serious or was it ironic?—when David Oistrakh pointed out to him the twelve-note rows in the Violin Sonata: "A serial row? No, no, not a serial row!"[25]

In his own music, dodecaphony was often associated with the theme of death; it is probably no coincidence that the work in which "death" looms the largest is also the work containing the highest occurrence of note-rows: the Fourteenth Symphony (1969). Some have argued that Shostakovich's association of dodecaphony with death stemmed from his professed view that dodecaphony was itself a moribund, lifeless system. Following this line, it could be argued that, for Shostakovich, the ultimate triumph of life and wholesome (presumably Soviet) values was demonstrated by the fact that his note-rows inevitably cede to tonal authority. In fact, the idea of employing "forbidden" styles for didactic purposes was not unknown in Soviet music—the incorporation of jazz and light music in the 1920s and 1930s, for example, being acceptable so long as its function was to expose and deride Western "immorality." But it is hard to imagine Shostakovich adopting such heavy-handed didacticism here. In any case, dodecaphony, unlike jazz in the early 1930s, had now been granted at least a modicum of official respectability. A more convincing explanation of Shostakovich's motives comes from Richard Longman:

> Shostakovich was less concerned with whether or not dodecaphony was inherently "evil" than with the convenient imagery it afforded him to express his concern with the issues of life and death. Chromaticism had always been for him—as it was for Renaissance madrigalists—the harmonic imagery of pain and tragic sentiment; twelve-tone chromaticism is simply a more extreme exploitation of this imagery, commensurate with his magnified awareness of the proximity of death.[26]

Most of the Fourteenth Symphony was composed during January and February 1969, when Shostakovich was again confined to hospital. The designating as a symphony of what is, in effect, an eleven-movement song cycle (the same number of movements, incidentally, as the *Jewish Folk Poetry* and *Michelangelo* cycles) has often been questioned. With its use of chamber forces and avoidance of symphonic forms, it contrasts with the choral Thirteenth Symphony, where symphonic structures are in operation, at least in some of the movements. Shostakovich himself was aware of the dilemma. In a letter to Glikman (1 February), he described the work as "an oratorio for soprano, bass and chamber orchestra."[27] But upon completion of the piano score a couple of weeks later, he wrote, "It cannot really be called an oratorio, since an oratorio is supposed to have a chorus . . . It shouldn't really be called a symphony either. For the first time in my life, I really do not know what to call one of my compositions."[28]

The Fourteenth Symphony presents four poets over the course of its eleven movements:

1. "De profundis" (Federico García Lorca)
2. "Malagueña" (Federico García Lorca)
3. "Lorelei" (Guillaume Apollinaire)
4. "The Suicide" from "Les Attentives" (Guillaume Apollinaire)
5. "On the Alert" from "Les Attentives" (Guillaume Apollinaire)
6. "Madame, Look!" (Guillaume Apollinaire)
7. "At the Santé Jail" (Guillaume Apollinaire)
8. "Zaporozhian Cossack's Reply to the Sultan of Constantinople (Guillaume Apollinaire)
9. "O Delvig, Delvig!" (Wilhelm Küchelbecker)
10. "The Poet's Death" (Rainer Maria Rilke)
11. "Conclusion" (Rainer Maria Rilke)

Binding this diverse set of movements is the theme of death—or more specifically, violent, unjust, or premature death: Lorelei, the angel of destruction who ultimately succumbs to her own allure; or "Madame" who laughs dementedly at her own love, "mown down by death." Ironically, all four poets had perished in unnatural circumstances.[29]

Although Shostakovich at the time emphasized the work as his secularist credo in the face of death, others have wondered whether the real theme lays elsewhere. Gerard McBurney, for example, asks if this Symphony is not primarily about oppression rather than death. As he states, in reference to "The Zaporozhian Cossack's Reply," "Shostakovich is as interested in the blighted and meaningless lives of those who are left behind or who are rotting in prison as he is in those who have actually died. They are all victims of the same oppression."[30] This is a sentiment that also turns up in the disputed *Testimony*: "It's stupid to protest death as such, but you can and must protest violent death. . . . I thought about all this when I orchestrated *Songs and Dances of Death*, and these thoughts also found reflection in the Fourteenth Symphony. I don't protest against death in it, I protest against those butchers who execute people."[31]

The Symphony's theme of death (or oppression) intersects with several other themes. Richard Longman lists four: 1) Imprisonment or Separation/Exile; 2) Destruction and Decay; 3) Creativity and Artistic Integrity; and 4) Love and Beauty. The first three had, of course, been central to Shostakovich's output for several decades; the fourth had perhaps not featured quite so heavily, at least not since *Lady Macbeth*.[32] The issue of artistic integrity had been addressed in "Regeneration" (*Four Pushkin Romances*), "Sonnet 66" (*Six Romances on Words of W. Raleigh, R. Burns, and W. Shakespeare*), and in the finale ("A Career") of the Thirteenth Symphony. "Regeneration" had also confronted the theme of destruction through its "barbarian-artist" who "scribbles meaninglessly" on a work of genius. Meanwhile, the theme of separation/exile had been heard in "Before a Long Separation" (*From Jewish Folk Poetry*), "Letter to Distant Siberia" and "Farewell" (*Four Pushkin Monologues*), and *Lady Macbeth*. And these themes would continue to resonate into the final song cycles of 1973 and 1974.

To these four subcategories could be added a fifth, the theme of squalor and degradation, both moral and physical: the smell of "salt and burning blood" in the tavern ("Malagueña");[33] the "worm-eaten couch" ("The Suicide"); a sister's incest before her brother's certain death in the trenches of battle ("On the Alert"); and the tale of the Sultan of Constantinople, "born while [his] mother was writhing in fecal spasms," "fed on filth since childhood," and "covered in wounds, sores and scabs."

In addition to these general themes and sub-themes, two specific inter-movement connections are worth pointing out. The ninth song ("O Delvig, Delvig!") is a message to Küchelbecker's poetic confrere, Delvig, and a declaration of the immortality of art. It ends with the verse, "Nor will our unions die, free, joyous and proud! But in both happiness and unhappiness will remain firm, the union of lovers of the eternal muses." The idea of the continuing union of artists in death brings the symphony full circle to its very opening line, Lorca's "A hundred ardent lovers fell into eternal sleep" ("De profundis"). As Glikman put it, "The heroes and heroines of the symphony, bound together by the power of fate, stretch out their hands to one another and form a ring of blazing fire."[34] In McBurney's view, "Now we know, or at least we can guess, who the lovers were and why they died. For Shostakovich, they weren't literally lovers as they were for Lorca, but they were friends, comrades-in-arms, fellow artists, men and women of Russia."[35] If this seems implausible, Shostakovich provides reinforcement with a musical flashback, the only such instance in the entire symphony; immediately following the "union of lovers of the eternal muses," the introduction to the next song ("The Poet's Death") quotes from the very opening of the symphony, the introduction to Lorca's "hundred ardent lovers." Richard Longman speculates further as to why the introduction to "The Poet's Death" quotes from "De Profundis," pointing out that "The Poet's Death" is the first song since the opening "De Profundis" in which death has already occurred. In the intervening songs, death is either anticipated (e.g., "On Watch") or being witnessed ("The Suicide"), or else its status is not clearly presented (e.g., "Madame, Look!").

The second inter-movement connection also stems from "De profundis." In the second verse, Lorca says of his hundred lovers that "crosses will be erected for them, so that people will not forget them." Three times during the course of the fourth song ("The Suicide"), the victim bemoans the absence of a monument: "Three lilies, three lilies on my grave where no cross stands." This suggests yet another subject of the Fourteenth Symphony, one that intersects some if not all of the aforementioned themes, namely Remembrance. We can perhaps define this theme more specifically as the erecting of monuments; not just remembrance, but the very *act* of remembrance. (In this particular instance, the image of the cross is also accompanied by a secondary pair of coincident images: Lorca's red sand and dry earth under which his lovers lay; Apollinaire's barren earth around the grave and its lilies.) Into the silence following "The Suicide's" coruscating twelve-note climax, just before the reference to the barren earth, a bell tolls (Fig. 61, b5). This bell, chiming the same pitch (B-flat), had been heard in the previous movement ("Lorelei"; Fig. 47), again following a frenetic climax (a twelve-note stretto followed by a ten-note cluster). And this is, of course, the same bell—also B-flat—that had been so pivotal in the Thirteenth Symphony. Richard Longman suggests that the connection here is "the subject of execution, inflicted by self, authority, or indirectly as is the case here [in 'Lorelei']."[36] But is it possible that Shostakovich had another connotation in mind? As "The Suicide" draws to a close, and the bell chimes again as the narrator, for the last time, invokes the lilies and the grave with no cross (Fig. 63, b4), we are reminded that in the Thirteenth Symphony, that same bell had been used to introduce the words, "There is no memorial at Babi Yar."

Adamant that vocal music should be presented in the language of the audience, Shostakovich set the texts in their Russian translations, making a few additional modifications in the process.[37] The extent and impact of these modifications vary, the most far-reaching occurring in "At the Santé Jail," where Shostakovich cuts Apollinaire's poem by half and adds a few lines of his own. Even with the excisions, "At the Santé Jail" is the longest movement in the Symphony. But Shostakovich's alterations were not only made to prevent the movement becoming too long. They also reinforce a vision of the Santé still darker and more hopeless than was Apollinaire's, a vision that was, to some extent, already built into Kudinov's translation. In Part I of Apollinaire's poem, Shostakovich adds the line, included in neither the original nor the Russian translation, "Here above me is the vault of the grave, here I died for everyone." Shostakovich clearly equates imprisonment with death, something that Apollinaire avoids, and in doing so relives the vision of entombment from "De profundis," yet another cross-movement connection. The line "here I died for everyone" seems to add a Christian reference, something reinforced later with another interpolated line, "Take from me the crown of thorns, lest it pierce my brain!." As for the imagery of the vault, this possibly stems from Kudinov's translation which, later in the poem, presents Apollinaire's

"And all the unhappy hearts beating *in* prison" as "You see how many unhappy hearts beat *under* the prison's vault!"[38]

More than Apollinaire, Shostakovich emphasizes the prisoner's isolation by removing references to certain sensory experiences: rays of sunlight through the window panes, the noise from the town, the jangling of the jailer's keys. The depiction of the prisoner writing poetry is also cut—"as though [poetry writing] were much too hopeful a thing to be doing in the kind of prison [Shostakovich] has in mind," as Gerard McBurney has put it.[39] At the very end of the poem, Apollinaire's "We are alone in my cell, Beautiful lucidity, Dear reason" ("Nous sommes seuls dans ma cellule, Belle clarté, Chère raison") becomes, in Kudinov's translation, "In the cell there are only two of us: Myself and my reason." As McBurney states: "The meaning is almost opposite. Apollinaire wanted to say that all he had to keep him for company were those wonderful things, 'la clarté,' 'la raison.' The Russian prisoner is going mad as his power of reason ("rassudok") leaves him to take up a separate existence of its own in the same cell."[40]

The Fourteenth Symphony is scored for soprano, bass, strings, and ten percussion.[41] Its unique sound world becomes apparent shortly after the opening of "De profundis." The very opening itself is quite typical for Shostakovich: its long, meandering, unaccompanied violin line, its concentration on narrow intervals oscillating around certain focal pitches, its outlining of the *Dies irae* chant (first two bars), and its tonally "self-propelling" character are all familiar traits (see Chapter 15, Example 15.20). And the cadential figure for violins and violas just prior to the entrance of the voice (Fig. 1 to Fig. 2) has a typically Shostakovichian flavor. But that cadence turns out to be the movement's first and last instance of conventionally spaced, three-part orchestral harmony. The rest of the movement (other than a couple of brief moments between Figs. 5 and 7) is couched in the simplest two-part writing; violins versus double basses; voice versus double basses; first violins and violas versus voice; and two-part double basses. The movement's bleakness is portrayed not only by the concentrated austerity of this two-part writing, but also by its focus on the double basses—Lorca's message coming literally "de profundis." These instruments are given an unusually melodic role, a fact that, ironically, only emphasizes their coldness. The omission of the cellos from this movement is a critical factor, the absence removing a major source of "warmth" from the string section and highlighting further the sonority of the basses. Shostakovich here employs a basic rule of orchestration: the wider the registral gap between instruments, the less psychoacoustic interaction there will be, and the colder and more disembodied will be the result. In the two-part violin/double bass passages, the separation averages three octaves, the absence of anything in between creating a particularly empty texture. Even in those passages where the violas double the first violins (e.g., Fig. 6), Shostakovich places them two octaves apart—again, with nothing falling in between.

At the opposite extreme to the ascetic two-part writing of "De profundis" is the dense, multi-part *divisi* to be found in several movements. In most cases, this is used as a vehicle for dissonance, for example the twelve-part split in "The Suicide"

(violins *a8*, violas *a2*, cellos *a2*) for the rising sequence of twelve-note chord clusters that appear after the words "The third one's roots lacerate my mouth" (Fig. 61,
b3–4); or the ten-part violin clusters at the end of "The Zaporozhian Cossack's
Reply." "O Delvig, Delvig!" is the exception, for here the *divisi* scoring (three solo cellos, often in close harmony) does bring out the warmth in this, the Symphony's most
tonal movement.

As in the Second Cello Concerto, the percussion is here used sparingly, in a
way that is more coloristic than orchestral, emphasizing the Symphony's chamber
quality. (The fact that the most "orchestral" of percussion instruments, the timpani, are omitted altogether is rather telling.) Certain instruments take on familiar
roles: the ethereally valedictory celesta; or the xylophone, used for grotesque
images such as the worm-eaten couch ("The Suicide") and throughout "Madame,
Look!," which at its most literal level presents a human organ laying on the
ground waiting to be mown down. And the association of the xylophone with
witchcraft might account for its use in "Lorelei." A newcomer to the Shostakovich
batteria, at least in a concert work,[42] is the vibraphone, used here twice; once at
the end of "Lorelei" as the Rhine-maiden meets her watery grave, and once in
"The Poet's Death" at the reference to "the lakes and gorges."

Shostakovich also capitalizes on the percussive possibilities of the strings, even
occasionally blurring the roles of the two families. He gives the characteristic castanet rhythms in "Malagueña" (e.g., Fig. 14) to the strings, *saltando*—only in the
movement's final bars does the castanet itself appear—while the Symphony's most
brutally percussive movement, "The Zaporozhian Cossack's Reply," contains no percussion at all. But most extraordinary of all in terms of "simulated" percussion is
the twelve-note fugato that forms the central section of "At the Santé Jail" (starting
at Fig. 91). The entire fugato is played with a pizzicato/*col legno* mixture, with only
the occasional interjection of the "real" *legno* (woodblock). The dry, skeletal effect is
described by Roy Blokker as portraying "the deep, timeless silence of imprisonment,
strings, *col legno*, and wood block marking the interminable minutes and hours with
an even, plodding rhythm."[43] Incidentally, the connection between *col legno* and the
subject of imprisonment is not new for Shostakovich; we hear it as the prisoners
make their long weary trudge through Siberia in *Lady Macbeth*.

Shostakovich's almost exclusively syllabic approach to text setting here is familiar
from previous works, and his late-period preference for a style still more declamatory than before can be witnessed, for example, in the hurtling pseudo-recitative at
the start of "Lorelei." "O Delvig, Delvig!" is the exception, with Shostakovich
reverting to the more lyrical style familiar from his middle-period "Romances."
Though the Symphony employs two voices, Shostakovich clearly prefers individual
declamation to dialogue here. Only in the final song do the two voices come
together.

The Fourteenth Symphony would represent the climax of Shostakovich's experimentation with dodecaphony. Typically for Shostakovich, twelve-note (or frequently, eleven-note) rows are used non-serially, save for the occasional inversion,
but they do generate or reflect important ideas within a given movement. For

example, the most prominent intervals in the (decorated) row that begins "De profundis" are the minor second and minor third, which turn out to be the most characteristic intervals of the ensuing vocal line. In "Malagueña," the most important interval in the first main section ("Death entered and left the tavern") is the perfect fourth, in both the vocal declamations and the diabolic, scampering violin line. Meanwhile, the malagueña-like walking bass accompaniment is a twelve-note row built mainly from ascending fourths (starting Fig. 10, b1), together with its inversion—a depiction, no doubt, of death's constant ingress and egress. In other cases, rows are built into what would be otherwise very standard diatonic commonplaces (scales, cadential jumps, etc.), thereby functioning as a mechanism to flit between seemingly incompatible tonalities. For example, the row at the start of "At the Santé Jail" climbs through five notes of a B-flat major scale (B-flat to F) followed by five notes of E minor (E to B). After the row is completed, it inverts downward through E-flat minor (B-flat to E-flat) and A major (E to A). The effect is one of disorientation (in both cases, a sudden shift to a tonal center a tritone away), yet masked behind a veneer of predictability (the more-or-less impeccable scalewise motion). Possibly Shostakovich intended the polarization of consecutive scales (i.e., the tritone jump) to signify the extreme mental shifts, possibly schizophrenic, implied by the poem's final statement, at least as presented in the Russian version, "In the cell there are only two of us: Myself and my reason." Another example of tonal/serial conflict is the xylophone solo at the start of "Madame, Look!," where a series of incompatible cadential jumps (fourths and fifths) has been serially engineered.

The Fourteenth Symphony was dedicated to Benjamin Britten; the previous year, Britten had dedicated his church parable *The Prodigal Son* to Shostakovich. The friendship between the two composers had blossomed since 1960, when Shostakovich was in the UK for the British premiere of the First Cello Concerto. He had come to view Britten as one of the greatest of all composers, and although they would meet on comparatively few occasions and communicate mainly through interpreters, Britten was the closest non-Soviet friend that Shostakovich ever had. Rostropovich characterized the friendship as one of "enormous human love and affection."[44]

Shostakovich regarded Britten's *War Requiem* in particular as one of the twentieth century's most important musical documents, and frequently commended it to his friends and fellow musicians, often describing it as "almost great."[45] His qualification would appear to have been philosophical rather than musical. As an avowed atheist convinced of the finality of death, Shostakovich was unconvinced by Britten's redemptive ending. Laurel Fay, for one, believes that the Fourteenth Symphony, with its uncompromising sense of finality, was "in a real sense . . . [Shostakovich's] creative response to the *War Requiem*."[46] Something of Britten can be heard in "Malagueña," with its treacherously high violin writing and its fast double stops, the latter flashily resonant in their use of open strings—the *Variations on a Theme of Frank Bridge* comes to mind, or the song cycle *Les illuminations*, both for string orchestra, a favorite ensemble of Britten. And the naked sound of the double basses in "De profundis," together with its associated theme of "sleep," also finds Shostakovich in Britten territory; Eric Roseberry points to "the snoring double basses" at the start of *A Midsummer Night's Dream*.[47] But it is "O Delvig, Delvig!," the emotional heart of the symphony, that brings the dedication to musical life, so to speak. As Küchelbecker calls to his beleaguered fellow poet Anton Delvig, Shostakovich, metaphorically, seems to call to his comrade-in-arms Britten; both poet and musician invoking the power and immortality of art in the face of "villains and fools." Incidentally, Shostakovich later sealed the connection by presenting Britten with a portrait of Delvig. Like Shostakovich, Britten was no stranger to ostracism; although living in a free country, his left-wing politics, pacifism, homosexuality, and distaste for what he saw as the suffocatingly quaint musical habits of his fellow English composers made him hardly the darling of the conservative Establishment.

With its paean to the immortality of art and its final affirmation, "Nor will our unions die … the union of lovers of eternal muses," "O Delvig, Delvig!" stands apart from the rest of the symphony. Levon Hakobian compares this to the orchestral interlude in *The Nose*, between Scenes 5 and 6, where Shostakovich deliberately dons a style alien to that of the rest of the work.[48] Although it deals with the characteristically Shostakovichian themes of tyranny, cruelty, and the integrity of art, this is the only poem in which death, or at least the finality of death, is rejected, something that is reflected, perhaps, in the fact that this is the Symphony's most tonally stable movement. Each stanza returns clearly to the tonic D-flat major, while the extensive chromaticism enriches rather than destabilizes; this is the only movement devoid of note-rows. The textures, too, are a far cry from the ascetic or percussive sonorities of the rest of the Symphony. The soaring, close-harmony *divisi* writing for three solo cellos (supplemented at the beginning by three violas *divisi*) could not be further removed from the barren spaces of "De profundis." In fact, Shostakovich's scoring, introducing the poetry of Wilhelm Küchelbecker, brings to mind another famous introduction to a "Wilhelm"—that of Rossini's overture to *William Tell*, a piece that would get more concrete treatment in Shostakovich's next symphony. Meanwhile, Eric Roseberry suggests that the "calm, hymnal gesture of four luminous triads that dispel the angry twelve-note 'cluster' of the previous movement could almost be taken as a salutation *à la manière de* Britten,"[49] and cites several works by the Englishman featuring "'hymnal' triadic images," including the Serenade for Tenor, Horn and Strings, *A Midsummer Night's Dream*, and *Billy Budd*. Commenting on the second stanza of "Sokrates und Alcibiades" in the *Sechs Hölderlin-Fragmente*, Roseberry states:

> [This] is a further memorable instance of a transforming "clarification" through triadic harmony. As if taking a hint from Britten, Shostakovich's later music frequently employs this expressive device of triadic "clarification." See, for example, "Night," No. 9 of the Suite on Verses of Michelangelo—a setting whose nocturnal beauty and calm suggest a response to Britten's perennial attraction towards images of sleep and darkness.[50]

Vocally, "O Delvig, Delvig!" rejects the Symphony's predominant arioso and recitative styles, taking its cue instead from the Russian "Romance" tradition—hints here of the much earlier *Four Pushkin Romances* or even the aria "Seryozha" from *Lady Macbeth*. At the start of the poem, as the name Delvig is invoked, the combination of dotted rhythm, stress, and melodic contour (based on scale degrees 6 to 5) results in exactly the same musical setting of the words "O Delvig" as had occurred on the word "Seryozha." (Is it a coincidence then that the predominant instrumental voice in "O Delvig, Delvig!" is the upper solo cello, the same instrument that had carried the "Seryozha" theme in the Eighth Quartet and would do so once again in the Fourteenth Quartet?)

At the pre-premiere performance of the Fourteenth Symphony held before an invited audience on 21 June 1969, Shostakovich spoke to the audience, explaining the philosophy behind the work. It is important to note that his final decade was generally unsullied by the cultural scandals that had dogged him for most of his life. His senior status had made him pretty much untouchable and, in any case, within the more liberal musical environment of the late 1960s, his late-period experimentation was hardly pushing the proverbial envelope. The Twelfth Quartet, for example, had been enthusiastically received—not just by audiences, but in such places as the Composers' Union and *Sovetskaya muzyka*—in the 1940s or 1950s, such a piece would likely have been condemned. Certainly, not every work in this late period was as rapturously received. But even pieces accorded a cooler reception were still spared the long knives. Perhaps as a result of this shift in his status, not to mention his increasing awareness of his own mortality, Shostakovich's speech at the pre-premiere of the Fourteenth Symphony was unusually forthright, certainly by the standards of the guarded, Party-mandated lines that he had been accustomed to mouthing in public. Alluding to one of the Symphony's sub-themes, that of artistic integrity, Shostakovich invoked the writer Ostrovsky, "who said that life is given to us only once, so we should live it honestly and handsomely in all respects and never commit base acts." He then went on to reject traditional redemptive musical portrayals of death: the "beauteous serenity" at the end of Verdi's *Otello*, the "radiant music" of *Aïda*, the "brightening" at the end of *Boris Godunov*. Even his beloved *War Requiem* by his friend and kindred spirit, Benjamin Britten, failed in this respect. For Shostakovich, the Fourteenth Symphony stood for the finality of death: "I don't see anything good about such an end to our lives and this is what I am trying to convey in this work."[51]

It was at this pre-premiere that the famous incident involving one of Shostakovich's long-time foes, Party official Pavel Apostolov, took place, an incident that ignited rumors of the Symphony's "supernatural" powers. During the performance, Apostolov became ill, stumbled out, and collapsed in the foyer. In a letter to Glikman three days later, Shostakovich wrote that Apostolov "managed to get out of the packed hall, but died a little while later."[52] Two decades on, the conductor of the performance, Rudolf Barshai, recalled events similarly: "Apostolov died almost at once."[53] *Testimony's* claim that Apostolov dropped dead "right there at the rehearsal" would appear to be somewhat exaggerated,[54] though the real mystery is the official record, which gives Apostolov's death as 19 July, almost a month after the concert.[55]

***

With further mobility problems in his hands and legs, Shostakovich spent the last couple of months of 1969 in hospital, where the hand condition that had plagued him since 1958 was finally diagnosed as a form of polio. (Recent research suggests that he was actually the victim of amyotrophic lateral sclerosis, otherwise known as motor neuron or Lou Gehrig's disease.[56]) Over the previous year, Shostakovich had taken an interest in the work of Gavriil Ilizarov, a Siberian orthopedic surgeon, but now that his condition appeared to be polio, and not an orthopedic complaint, he concluded that a visit to Ilizarov would be "of no use."[57] Three months later, he had a change of heart. In February 1970, he made the trip to Kurgan, where he subjected himself for the next three-and-a-half months to Ilizarov's regimen of exercise and physiotherapy. By March, he was speaking of the doctor as a "human genius";[58] in May, he reported improvements in his strength, mobility, and coordination, including the ability to play the piano.[59] At the end of August, Shostakovich returned for another two months to Ilizarov's clinic. During that first stint in Kurgan, he made progress on his score to Kozintsev's film *King Lear* (see Chapter 17); on his subsequent visit, he completed the Thirteenth Quartet, a work he had started a year earlier. He appeared at his most energetic when immersed in work. At the recording sessions for *King Lear* that summer, Kozintsev recalls the composer "full of energy ... run[ning] up to the conductor with ease, as if he had forgotten about his illness."[60] At other times, weakness and fatigue were all too apparent.

Cast in a single movement, the Thirteenth Quartet represents, in a sense, the culmination of Shostakovich's long preoccupation with cyclism in general, and of his more recent experiments in the art of "single-movement illusion," as practiced in the Eleventh and Twelfth Quartets, in particular. The work is in a five-part arch form (ABCBA) in which "C" is an autonomous central section, not a development of earlier material. It represents, for Shostakovich, a rare instance in which the retrogressive, or palindromic, attributes of the arch are not brought into conflict with the progressive forces of sonata form. Along with the finale of the Fifteenth Symphony, it is as pure an arch structure as Shostakovich would create. A brief, token recognition of this comes at Fig. 50, during the reprise of the B section, where the vertical accumulation of searing minor ninths, which the first time round (Fig. 17) had progressed upwards from the cello, now proceeds, palindromically, downwards from the first violin.

The Thirteenth Quartet represents a sometimes contradictory confluence of factors; the result is a work that sounds more, and at the same time, less modern than its predecessor. The Thirteenth, like the Twelfth, begins with an unaccompanied twelve-note row, but one whose first eight notes, supported by their rhythmic grouping, give away the work's tonality; the tonic (B-flat minor) function of the opening phrase answered by the leading-note (in essence, dominant) function of the second (Example 10.1). By contrast, the Twelfth Quartet's melodically disjunct and phrasally undifferentiated row is, until its last two or three pitches, quite devoid of tonal suggestion (see Chapter 15, Example 15.13).

Example 10.1

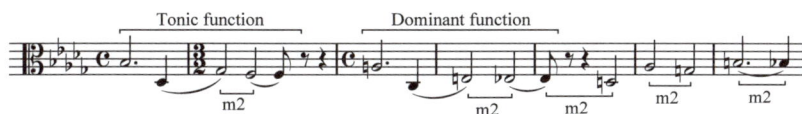

Typically, Shostakovich eschews serial development in the Schoenbergian sense. But the row does contain ingredients for more traditional motivic development, particularly the drooping minor second (bracketed "m2" in Example 10.1). Throughout the Quartet, this minor second is often to be found at the end of an upward leap (anything from a third to a seventh), as it is throughout the row shown in Example 10.1. The most striking of these comes in the Quartet's final section at Figs. 56, b7 (viola) and 57, b7 (cello), where the ascending interval is a minor sixth, producing, along with the subsequent falling minor second, the *Tristan* motif. This may, of course, be coincidental. After all, there is a far more frequent occurrence of some of the other ascending intervals that in this Quartet precede the falling minor second. But given Shostakovich's preoccupation with the *Tristan* motif at around this time—he had not only used it in the Fourteenth Symphony, but would return to it in his next two works, the Fifteenth Symphony and Fourteenth Quartet[61]—the quotation is in all likelihood not coincidental. For as Shostakovich increasingly contemplated his own death, the quotations from certain iconic works would also become more prevalent; the *Tristan* Prelude; the "Fate" motif from *Götterdämmerung* in the Fifteenth Symphony; "Dies Irae" in the Fourteenth Symphony; the row from the Berg Violin Concerto ("Dedicated to the Memory of an Angel") in the Violin Sonata; and the funeral march that is the first movement of Beethoven's *Moonlight* Sonata in the Viola Sonata. Of course, Shostakovich had already shown a predilection towards these ready-made quotations in his two Quartets from 1960: "Dies Irae" in the Eighth (conceived as his own personal requiem), and the "love-death" allusions to the *Tristan* Prelude and, possibly, the Berg Violin Concerto in the Seventh (written in memory of Nina).

If the opening row's tonal connotations and its potential for traditional motivic development mark the Thirteenth Quartet as less progressive than its predecessor, then other, mainly gestural, elements point in the opposite direction. For example, the vertical use of the aforementioned minor-second motive results in some unique sonorities. Shostakovich stacks sets of minor seconds on top of each other, but with each set registrally separated. With this strange mix of narrow and wide intervals, the effect is simultaneously dissonant and ethereal. Example 10.2 shows two versions of this aggregation, as well as a simplified version of this stack used earlier by Shostakovich in the Eleventh Quartet Recitative.

Example 10.2

Another modernist gesture is the overtly Webernesque passage (starting Fig. 19) in which a reiterating note-row accelerates, pizzicato, thrown around from one instrument to another in a burst of quick-fire pointillism. The passage also contains one iteration of the row in retrograde (Fig. 20, b4), a brief and rare concession by Shostakovich to the procedures of Second Viennese school serialism. The peculiarly hard, dry sound of pizzicato at *forte* or, as here, *fortissimo* became a favorite sonority of Shostakovich in his later years; he frequently urged his performers to play pizzicati louder than marked.[62] The effect falls short of the percussive snap-pizzicato beloved by Bartók (and indeed, used by Shostakovich himself in the finale of the Seventh Symphony), but Shostakovich was to implement his own version of percussive "noise" in this Quartet—an instruction to hit the belly of the instrument with the stick of the bow, an eerily disembodied effect found mainly in the Quartet's central section, and later as a ghostly reminiscence in the work's coda. It is probably a bit of a stretch to view this as Shostakovich's answer to Bartók; David Fanning more usefully cites the possible influence of Ustvolskaya, who had used the same effect in her Violin Sonata of 1952.[63] Either way, it joins other examples of "strings and percussion" found in Shostakovich's late period—the instrumentation of the Fourteenth Symphony, the coda of the Fifteenth, or the cello-plus-percussion cadenza of the Second Cello Concerto.

The Quartet's central section contains some of the most unusual music ever penned by Shostakovich. With its "walking" pizzicato bass line (albeit one of twelve-note construction), its swinging dotted rhythms and triplets, its bluesy triplet half-notes, and the abovementioned "percussion," this, along with the score to *Meeting on the Elbe* (see Chapter 17), would be the closest to jazz that Shostakovich ever came—certainly a far cry from the Soviet *Tea-Jazz*, essentially light dance music, found in his Suites for Jazz Orchestra from the 1930s.

The Twelfth Quartet had begun with a tonally non-suggestive note-row and ended with an affirmation of D-flat major, albeit with serial colorings popping in and out during its final bars. The Thirteenth was to invert this progress, beginning with a tonally suggestive note-row and ending on a B-flat unison, a pitch that, paradoxically, does not present itself to the listener as the Quartet's prevailing tonality. The "deception" is in the preparation. The final affirmation of B-flat minor as the work's tonic comes at Fig. 59, b11, thirty-three bars before the end. Its grip starts to loosen in the ensuing note-row, though it does attempt, rather weakly, to reassert itself at Fig. 60 for six bars. Three more rows, and whatever hold B-flat minor had has now completely evaporated, leaving the viola to muse over a four-note pattern, A–D–A–E, a pattern which, however it is viewed, functions in a world far from B-flat minor and which can provide no tonal anchorage for what happens next—the slow, final B-flat. Because of the way in which it has been pre-pared, or rather, has *not* been prepared, that B-flat hangs suspended in space. It is scored almost impossibly high for the viola, which is joined by the second violin and then the first; a grinding *crescendo* of agonizing length ending with a brutal *sffff*. In such a scoring, the B-flat seems less like a note (never mind a tonic rein-forcement) than a noise; the aural equivalent, perhaps, of a spotlight being slowly turned until it faces head-on the eyes of its victim. (The Beethoven Quartet's vio-list at the time, Fyodor Druzhinin, recalls Shostakovich's excitement on hearing Druzhinin practicing Kodály's transcription of the Bach *Chromatic Fantasy*, which includes that almost impossibly high B-flat. Shostakovich quizzed the violist on the matter. Later on, after the Beethovens were presented with the score of the new Thirteenth Quartet, it was with much excitement that Druzhinin discovered that same note at the end, something that "brought me much closer to Shostakovich."[64])

***

In June 1971, Shostakovich returned to Dr. Ilizarov for further therapy. While in Kurgan, he made a start on his Fifteenth Symphony, completing it at the Com-posers' House in Repino at the end of July. Richard Taruskin, who was present at the January 1972 premiere, writes that "The work, with its jolly quotation from Rossini in the first movement and its ravaged quotation from Wagner in the last, was puzzling, as everyone I conversed with agreed. It was not much liked, actually."[65] In a way, this enigmatic work has suffered a fate similar to that of the Sixth Symphony, with audiences unclear about its *raison d'être*, though, like the Sixth, greater familiarity over the years has enhanced its reputation.

According to Maxim Shostakovich, who conducted the premiere, his father described the first movement as a depiction of a toy shop.[66] Certainly, the opening of the development section could fit that description, with its "toy soldier" parade of trumpet, piccolo, and percussion (Figs. 15–18). But, apart from such obviously physical manifestations, the "toy shop" has often been seen as a metaphor for something more sinister—the mechanization of human feelings, possibly, or the brutal, puppet-like way in which people were manipulated under the regime. Ei-ther way, it makes for unsettled listening, especially for those expecting a more "appropriately" symphonic utterance.

The first movement's enigmatic quality also derives from the tonal quicksand upon which much of it is built. The first phrase of the extended, self-propelling opening melody is of quasi-serial construction (using ten pitches), while the mel-ody as a whole touches the tonic (with A minor emphasized over the advertised A major) only a few times during its fifty-eight-bar course. And each time the tonic is established, its preparatory upbeat is an arpeggio of A-flat major, Shostakovich using the so-called *terzgleich* ("equal third") relationship (the third of A-flat major equaling the third of A minor) to slide from under the thumb of the A-flat impostor (Example 10.3).

Example 10.3

Such nimble "escapology" rears its head again in the approach to the second subject. In the classically expected key of E major, this theme (Fig. 9) is immediately preceded (Fig. 8, b5) by strong intimations of E-flat. Tonally, the second subject begins as skittishly as the first, though a degree of stability is provided by the famous *William Tell* quotations in the trumpets starting at Fig. 12. What exactly the quotation means is again open to debate. Clearly, Shostakovich intended it, at least in part, as a bit of comedy; he was particularly adamant that the orchestra at the first rehearsal were not told about it—"I want to see their faces when they come to it."[67] But on a more serious note, Boris Tishchenko reports Maxim telling him that the *William Tell* quotation, "a father shooting above his son's head," actually expressed "Shostakovich's fears for Maxim."[68] Either way, the quotation is structurally significant. Confirming the movement's dominant key area (E major) in a way that its precursor at Fig. 9 could not, *William Tell* functions as the tonal goal of the second subject area, maybe even of the entire exposition. Moreover, Shostakovich sets the stage for the quotation with his extensive use of dactylic/anapestic rhythms in both the first and second subjects. Such "teasers" are thrown in at Fig. 8, b8, Fig. 9, b9, and Fig. 11, b3 before the quotation itself at Fig. 12. Not for the first time has Shostakovich appeared to fashion his own preliminary material around the musical attributes of a subsequently imported quotation (see, for example, the discussion of the Fifth Quartet).

Except for the distinctive "stationary ritardando" passage starting at Fig. 27 (canonic entrances of eight, then six, then five notes per bar—a reverse counterpart to the "stationary accelerando" that began the Second Symphony), the movement's development does not for the most part operate at a higher level of contrapuntal density than the exposition—an unusual move for Shostakovich, who throughout his life was generally quite traditional in this regard. Instead, what distinguishes this development is its focus on the myriad percussion sonorities that Shostakovich has made available, a resource that up to this point has been used extremely sparingly. The development opens with the aforementioned "toy soldier" snare drum and trumpet fanfare (Fig. 15), after which the xylophone takes the main melodic material with interjections from other percussion instruments. Even when the percussion instruments do take an accompanying or interjectory role, the ear is drawn to their intricacies of color, for example, the alternating tom-tom and snare drum rim click that takes place during the above-mentioned "stationary ritardando" passage. Moreover, this aspect of orchestration, set up in the development, becomes influential in the recapitulation where the percussion is far more prominent than it had been during the exposition. In fact, this sets up a pattern for the rest of the Symphony, for in each of the remaining movements the percussion gains prominence only in the latter stages.

If anything, the recapitulation is more "developmental" than the development (Fig. 36). Although based on the exposition material, there is a significant amount of thematic reordering and recombining. Indeed, there is probably not a recapitulation anywhere in Shostakovich's output that bears as little resemblance to its corresponding exposition as this one. In fact, it is only really the return of a modified first theme at Fig. 36 and a (rather vague) tonal confirmation at around Fig. 39 that even suggests "recapitulation" to the listener—which should perhaps lead one to question whether traditional sonata form terminology has much use in this movement at all.

If the opening melody of the first movement was quasi-serial in its construction, the slow movement would contain full-fledged twelve-note rows. Given the particular resonance that such rows carried for Shostakovich, it is hardly surprising that they fall into a movement saturated with funereal imagery. The movement opens with a Soviet-style brass band intoning a baleful, graveside melody in a "saturated" scoring—two trumpets in thirds, two tenor trombones in thirds an octave lower, a bass trombone and tuba in thirds an octave below that, with four horns providing the pedal. With the F minor melody filled with typically Shostakovichian pathos, the simple perfect cadence in C major at the end sounds almost deliberately banal. From out of that cadence emerges the twelve-note row in the solo cello, though the transition here from the most blatant tonality to atonality is done gradually, with the cello's first four or five notes seemingly supporting the movement's F minor tonic.

In the opening of the Twelfth Quartet, we saw how Shostakovich contrived the end of a note-row specifically to provide an appropriate transition into more tonal material—in that case, using A-flat and D-flat as the row's final pitches to announce the D-flat tonic. Here in the Symphony, he goes one step further by actually disrupting a note-row in order that its final moments can better prepare an upcoming tonic. Following three consecutive note-rows in the solo cello (Figs. 53, 54, and 55), a fourth row (Fig. 55, b7) presents, as its tenth and eleventh pitches, C and D-flat, a repeat of the fourth and sixth pitches respectively. The result, a final voice-leading of C–D-flat–A-flat, provides a more conventional approach to the return of the F minor brass chorale than would have been the case had Shostakovich stuck doggedly to the twelve-note requirement—either B–A–A-flat or A–B–A-flat.

Following the return of the brass chorale (this time diverted to a final cadence in E major) and further exploration of the dodecaphonic material, there appears a mysterious pair of almost complementary juxtaposed hexachords (Fig. 61), the first in the woodwind (C–E–G–G-sharp–B-flat–D), the second in the brass (B–D-sharp–C-sharp–E–F–A). These chords pop out seemingly from nowhere—Shostakovichian "Tristan" chords, perhaps. They provide a transition to the movement's middle section, which starts with the intoning of a funeral-march rhythm played in sixths by two flutes (Fig. 62). It is a moment of deep emotional resonance; the solo cello's trilled pedal that accompanies this flute melody recalls the violas' timeless trilling in the wastelands of the Sixth Symphony's first movement, the "flutter of lowered flags," as Nataliya Lukyanova memorably put it.[69] The dotted rhythm of the melody itself and the quiet, heavy pizzicato punctuations in the cellos and basses only reinforce this allusion to the Sixth Symphony, though the idea of a funeral march scored for flutes actually brings to mind Mahler, a composer whose influence on Shostakovich was admittedly somewhat on the wane by this point, and in particular the last song of the *Lieder eines fahrenden Gesellen*, "Die zwei Augen von meinem Schatz," though Shostakovich's austere march lacks the aching nostalgia of Mahler's. Between Figs. 62 and 69, the funeral march alternates between its presentation in the flutes and an altogether more traditional and somber presentation in the solo trombone.

The pair of hexachords that introduced this section returns at Fig. 70 to usher in the movement's climactic section. This central climax presents the funeral material in the entire brass in a blazing C major, an allusion perhaps to the "glory in death" tradition of capping minor key funeral marches with brassy major key climaxes—the *maggiore* section of the Beethoven *Eroica*, Siegfried's funeral march from *Götterdämmerung*, and the slow introduction to the finale of Shostakovich's own Fourth Symphony come to mind. In the aftermath, a replay of the two hexachords leads to a short reprise of the movement's opening chorale in E minor, now *pianissimo* in a parched *divisi* string scoring (see Chapter 6, Example 6.5b).

As the movement moves towards its close, the sonorities get still more mysterious. The three cello note-rows from Figs. 53, 54, and 55 are now replayed by, respectively, the celesta in exact inversion (Fig. 76), vibraphone in almost exact inversion (Fig. 76, b4), and solo double bass accompanied by cello harmonics (Fig. 77). The celesta, of course, had long been associated in Shostakovich's mind with images of "farewell," while the vibraphone had been used in the Fourteenth Symphony in conjunction with the idea of water or, more particularly, a watery grave. This, along with the inversion of what had been the mainly ascending cello note-rows, would perhaps imply a descent into death, something that the disembodied double bass version that eventually greets us possibly confirms. Towards the end, the brass band returns in a deeper, darker, though less saturated scoring than at the beginning. The movement comes to a halt to the sound of the funeral rhythm in the timpani. Then, two bassoons, jabbing in almost comically archaic parallel fifths, provide the transition into the scherzo.

The third movement scherzo is unique in the symphonic output of Shostakovich, coming closer to a pure humoresque than any previous example. Tonally, it is even harder to pinpoint than the first movement. At the start, the spiky twelve-note melody in the clarinet, answered by its inversion, is set against the continuing open-fifth pedals in the bassoons, creating a tantalizing pull between the modernistic and the archaic. The movement has often been compared to the Humoreske from Nielsen's Sixth Symphony. Although there is no evidence that Shostakovich was familiar with the work of the Danish composer, the similarities are remarkable. Nielsen's Humoreske is scored for chamber groupings of woodwinds, brass, and percussion, and it is these groups that dominate Shostakovich's scherzo, though the latter also makes great play of the "devilish" properties (Mahler's Fourth Symphony and Stravinsky's *L'histoire du soldat* come most readily to mind) of the solo violin. Nielsen's snide, disdainful trombone glissando "yawn" is also replicated here, most notably at Fig. 92, b6–9, where it is used to smother a quirkily harmonized version of DSCH (transposed) in the rest of the brass.

Following the quirky ending, capped with the kind of clicking percussion that had ended the Fourth Symphony's scherzo (and that will return in a much more extended form at the end of this symphony), the fourth movement finale throws us immediately back into the slow movement's somber brass sonorities. But the tone here is altogether more portentous, as Shostakovich quotes the "Fate" motif from Wagner's *Ring* cycle, or, more specifically, the motif as heard at the start of Siegfried's Funeral March, complete with the faltering "heartbeat" timpani rhythm. Following two more renditions of the motif, the first violins pick out the first three notes of the *Tristan* Prelude, which in turn becomes the upbeat to the A minor first theme of the movement's main *Allegretto*. Although Shostakovich's own theme could hardly be less Wagnerian sounding, it integrates into its somewhat winding course both the *Tristan* and the "Fate" motifs, not to mention a couple of twelve-note rows (see Chapter 15 and Examples 15.22a–c).

The finale is, to an extent, cut from the same mold as those of the Eighth and Thirteenth Symphonies. In all three cases, a superficially wistful and mild-mannered *Allegretto* cocoons moments of irony and pain. Along with the Thirteenth Quartet, this movement is as pure an arch structure as Shostakovich would ever write—A–B–C–B–A–Coda, where the "B" section is based on a re-harmonized version of the Wagner "Fate" motif (Fig. 119), and the central "C" section is a passacaglia whose ground bass apes the "Invasion" theme rhythm from the Seventh Symphony (Fig. 125). The final "A" section (Fig. 143) is in A major rather than A minor, though given the way that Shostakovich uses chromaticism here, e.g., the lowered seventh (G-natural) in the first bar, the difference is perhaps less striking than might be imagined, Shostakovich avoiding the sugary banality that such a *tièrce de Picardie* could so easily create.

In this finale, Shostakovich includes references to previous movements. But unlike that great run of "middle period" cyclic works (see Chapter 9, Table 9.1), where recalls generally took place at some centrally climactic moment of the finale, the Fifteenth Symphony's use of cyclism is, characteristically, a lot quieter, less ostentatious—recalls of the second movement hexachord pair just before the coda (Fig. 146–147), and of a snippet of the first movement's main theme in the celesta leading into the coda (Fig. 147, b10–11) and in the piccolo during the coda (Fig. 148, b8–9).

The coda itself provides one of the strangest endings in the entire symphonic repertoire. Over a multiple-*divisi* open fifth pedal (A and E) in the strings, Shostakovich replays the passacaglia bass line, split between the timpani and xylophone, accompanied by those quirky quick-fire alternations of castanet, woodblock, snare drum, and rim click familiar from the closing moments of the Second Cello Concerto or the Fourth Symphony's scherzo. This is indeed genuine "percussion ensemble" music. Meanwhile, the piccolo picks out its fragment of the first movement's main theme. Finally, after forty agonizing bars of the open fifth pedal, a four-octave C-sharp is sounded in the celesta and glockenspiel (capped with the triangle), confirming at last the Symphony's major-mode tonality. While one would ordinarily hesitate to describe the combination of glockenspiel, celesta, and triangle as "rich," the effect that this extraordinarily resonant sounding of C-sharp has on the musical landscape at this point cannot be overestimated, the pitch itself setting a stamp over the bare fifths in the strings, the metallic shimmer casting away for good the dry rattling of the wooden percussion.

It is a quirky ending to a quirky symphony. As already noted, the tonal skittishness and the chamber-like use of the percussion contribute to the Symphony's enigmatic quality. But another factor is the quotations. Certainly, this would not be the first or the last Shostakovich work to feature quotations from other composers. But nowhere in Shostakovich's concert output, except maybe the Beethoven *Kreutzer* Sonata excerpt in *Satires*, are the quotations more musically incongruous than they are here. In the case of the Rossini, it is true that Shostakovich shapes his own themes in order that the *William Tell* figure emerges as naturally as possible. But ultimately, the sheer familiarity of that quotation makes it stand out, removing the listener very briefly "out" of the Symphony, rather like the Beethoven Fifth quotation in de Falla's *The Three-Cornered Hat*. In the Wagner quotations, the sense of "otherness" is due to the sheer stylistic incongruity—other than as a convenient provider of iconic leitmotifs, Wagner was musically one of the least influential composers for Shostakovich.

Yet, incongruous as these quotations appear on the surface, one has to wonder how influential they were in Shostakovich's choice of key. Rossini's key for the *William Tell* coda was E major; Wagner's for the *Tristan* Prelude was A minor. Is it possible, then, that Shostakovich wrote the Fifteenth Symphony in A major expressly so that its first movement second subject group, in the classically expected dominant, would coincide with Rossini's key, and that its tonic-minor finale exposition would coincide with Wagner's?

***

In September 1971, Shostakovich suffered his second heart attack. He would spend the next two months in hospital plus a month in a sanatorium. The ensuing compositional hiatus—excluding a transcription of Gaetano Braga's once popular 1861 song *Leggenda Valacca* (Angel's Serenade), the song that had inspired one of Shostakovich's favorite stories, Chekhov's *The Black Monk*—would last until March 1973, the longest in Shostakovich's career. In the intervening year, 1972, he supervised the Moscow and Leningrad premieres of the Fifteenth Symphony and made trips to Germany, England (twice), Ireland, and Azerbaijan. With his physical strength and mobility on the decline, the foreign travel, his first in several years, was extremely arduous. Much of the time between trips was spent simply recuperating. In December, Shostakovich was back in hospital, ostensibly to treat a case of kidney stones. But while in treatment, a cyst was discovered on his left lung. He spent the next two months receiving radiation.[70]

The barren spell finally broke the following spring. Between March and April 1973, Shostakovich penned the Fourteenth Quartet, the first of a group of six works representing his final thoughts on music, life, and death—works written in remarkably quick succession, given both the composer's physical state and his insistence on maintaining as much of his official schedule as his health would allow.

In many ways, the Fourteenth Quartet retrenches from the general trends of Shostakovich's late period, perhaps because this was his first re-engagement with composition in almost two years; in that sense, the Quartet's role could be compared to that of the First Quartet following the traumas of 1936-1937, or the Sixth Quartet following Shostakovich's personal crises of the mid-1950s. Other than one very brief moment of eleven- and twelve-note pointillism in the finale (Fig. 69), the Fourteenth largely backs away from the modernistic exploits of the two previous quartets. Its tonal moorings are relatively strong, and, other than the fact that the work's sonority is overall a little sparer and less "orchestral," most of it could pass off as a Shostakovich quartet from the 1940s or 1950s.

With its one-note viola vamp and its deliberately archaic melody, the start of the first movement has a simplicity reminiscent of the Sixth Quartet's opening, though the tune here—a rather academic sequencing of a one-bar eighteenth-century melodic archetype, colored in its fourth bar by a typically Shostakovichian cadential figure peppered with flattened tones—is perhaps drier and less memorable than its Sixth Quartet counterpart, at least at the outset. Yet, as with so many of those earlier quartets, the initial, deceptively Haydnesque melody accumulates chromatic density over the course of its exposition. Meanwhile, the second theme, with its Mahlerian *Ländler* gestures, especially the sardonic pointing of the motion between the first and second beats of the bar, takes us back to the First Quartet, whose first movement's second subject has a similar bearing.

Structurally, this first movement is similar to that of the Twelfth Quartet, a sonata form with reverse recapitulation, and shows a briefly rekindled interest in the traditional role of the first-movement development in a string quartet. Indeed, of all the quartets written since the Sixth (1956), only the Twelfth had been in possession of a first-movement development, and that was an unusually brief example, probably because of the presence of a second, more extensive development of the same material in the following movement. Even if lacking the contrapuntal complexity of the great developments of, say, the Third or Fifth Quartets, the development here in the Fourteenth fulfills the essential criteria of exploration and of shedding new light on old material. For example, the appearance in the viola of a dactylic ostinato accompanying a presentation of the first theme at the start of the development at Fig. 17—essentially a "rhythmic" version of the one-note viola part that accompanied the same theme at the start of the movement—does not

initially appear to contribute much in the way of developmental tension. Yet, that
ostinato by its very immutability and implacability soon creates tension against the
now increasingly chromatic presentation of the cello theme. The climax (Figs. 23–25)
sees yet another one-note ostinato, more animated than before, whose rhythm quotes
directly the opening "Fate" motto of Tchaikovsky's Fourth Symphony. Ultimately,
the presence of this development contributes to a restoration of first-movement
weight and authority, something that had been steadily eroding in the predominantly
finale-oriented quartets of the 1960s.

As if to emphasize this renewed look at the first-movement development, the
structure goes on to provide a new take on the "gradually emerging" recapitulation, that Shostakovich trademark all but abandoned since the mid-1950s. The
second subject reprise, in the key of A-flat, retains elements of the development,
particularly the slurred-pair ostinato figure appearing from Fig. 29. It then fades
out to reveal a viola cadenza on this second theme, fashioned with chordal flourishes somewhat in the style of unaccompanied Bach, a passage that Shostakovich
referred to as his "chaconne."[71] Only in the ensuing first subject reprise (Fig. 33,
b3) does the tonic return, albeit in the minor—the full F-sharp major tonality is
restored at Fig. 35. Yet, this first theme reprise, and even the coda, is unable to
shake off the development's influence; comparing Fig. 33, b3 with the movement's
opening, we see that the dotted rhythms of the earlier presentation are now
replaced by the development section's defining dactylic rhythm.

The slow, D minor, ternary-form second movement opens with the first violin
intoning the *Tristan* quotation (D–B-flat–A) that had played such an important
role in the Fifteenth Symphony and the Thirteenth Quartet. The reference sets
the mood for the movement's bleak, austere first section, most of which is presented as a duet for first violin and cello. Both the mood and the texture warm-up
for the A major middle section (Fig. 52, b2), where a second allusion to the Fifteenth Symphony can be heard in the form of a persistent three-note accompanimental pizzicato figure, one whose rhythmic profile apes that of the pizzicato
figure accompanying the main melody of the Symphony's finale (Fig. 113).

The emotional core not just of this middle section but of the movement as a
whole comes at Fig. 53 with a doleful melody that is not only highly impassioned in its own right, but seems also to allude to the funereal brass incantations
in the Fifteenth Symphony's slow movement (Example 10.4). In fact, this melody
represents the emotional core of the Quartet as a whole. It is foreshadowed in
the last moments of the first movement (Fig. 40) and also gets the last word at
the end of the finale (Fig. 93). Like the astringent neo-classicism of the first
movement, the aching romanticism of this theme reinforces the Fourteenth
Quartet's old-fashioned, retrospective cut. Shostakovich referred to it as "my Italian bit,"[72] though with its use of a combination mode in which the bottom half
of A *freygish* (A–B-flat–C-sharp–D–E) is grafted onto the top half of an oscillating A minor scale (the natural form, F–G, in the melody and the melodic variant, F-sharp–G-sharp, in the accompaniment), it possibly sounds more Jewish in
inflection.

Example 10.4

The third movement finale demonstrates the type of cyclism familiar from Shostakovich's "middle period" quartets. Towards the development's climax is an extraordinary passage, in which two-note fragments are thrown wildly around the quartet from instrument to instrument (Fig. 69). The effect is almost pointillistic, especially given the almost serial nature of the pitches (eleven- and twelve-note rows). At Fig. 71, the eighth-note pairs break into triplets, yielding a fragmented version of the first movement's second theme. And at Fig. 72, it breaks into sixteenth notes, yielding a few bars later a fragmented version of the second movement's main theme. The placement of these recalls towards the climax of the development is in line with Shostakovich's "middle-period" practice, though the fragmented, pointillistic treatment makes the recalled melodies less obvious to the ear.

The finale's closing minutes are given over almost entirely to second movement material. But these final moments are not merely flashbacks. Rather, they offer closure to the second movement material, a closure that had not occurred in the second movement itself. There, there had been no tonic (D minor) resolution of the main theme. But here in the finale's coda, that theme returns in D minor (Fig. 86), after which the slow movement's middle theme returns in the Quartet's tonic, F-sharp major (Fig. 89). The Quartet ends, *morendo*, with the "Italian bit," achingly stretched out. In other words, the first objective of the finale's coda is to close out the second movement tonally (D minor) and thematically before finally, and still with second movement material, closing out itself. Structurally, then, though the Fourteenth Quartet does not strive for single-movement unity in the way that the Eleventh, Fifteenth, and especially the Thirteenth do, it does share with the Twelfth Quartet the idea of tiding over unfinished business from one movement to a subsequent movement.

The Fourteenth was dedicated to the Beethoven Quartet's cellist, Sergei Shirinsky. This manifests itself in a number of ways, for example, the placing of the cello at the top of the texture in the aforementioned "Italian" melody, a placement that comes up again in the work's final moments—the *morendo* F-sharp major chord scored with the viola at the bottom, the two violins in the middle, and the cello at the top, the placing of the solo cello *in alt* also having been a feature of the Fifteenth Symphony. More specifically, the Quartet offered its dedicatee a melodic encryption along the lines of the Tenth Symphony's "Elmira," as well as a quotation. Bars 2–7 of the finale's main theme—D-sharp–E–D-natural–E–G–A—contain a musical encryption of the letters that make up "Seryozha," the affectionate form of "Sergei."[73] Later in the finale (Fig. 75), Shostakovich inserts a quotation from the famous "Seryozha" aria from *Lady Macbeth* ("Seryozha! My dearest!"), giving it to the cello—the same instrument that had played this quotation back in the Eighth Quartet. Given that Shirinsky had also been the cellist at the Eighth's premiere, we must wonder whether the choice of instrument in that earlier quotation represented a similar pun on Shostakovich's part.

Discussing the first movement of the Fifth Quartet, it was suggested that the Ustvolskaya quotation, which appears at the development's climax, may have influenced Shostakovich as he went about fashioning his earlier exposition material. Here in the Fourteenth, one is likewise struck by a similarity between the imported "Seryozha" theme and several of the Quartet's own themes; in particular, the main theme of the finale and the pivotal "Italian bit" that appears in all three movements. Did Shostakovich have in mind the "Seryozha" theme while composing the rest of the Quartet? Or is this connection merely coincidental? After all, such narrow, oscillating figures had been characteristic of Shostakovich's writing for at least a decade.

***

In the summer of 1973, Shostakovich made trips to Denmark and the USA,[74] where he received an honorary doctorate from Northwestern University. In America, doctors confirmed what he had feared all along—that the decline in his health was unstoppable. Upon his return home, he went to the Baltic Sea spa town of Pärnu in Estonia, where in the week between 31 July and 7 August, he wrote his *Six Poems of Marina Tsvetayeva*: "My Poems"; Whence All This Tenderness?"; "Hamlet's Dialogue with his Conscience"; "The Poet and the Tsar"; "No, the Drum Did Beat"; and "To Anna Akhmatova." Tsvetayeva's stormy and mostly tragic life had ended with her suicide in 1941 at the age of 48, but it was not until the 1960s that her works began to be circulated in the Soviet Union. Her terse, high-strung, bitter but perceptive poetry resonated with Shostakovich. The choice of verses reflected familiar Shostakovichian themes—creativity ("My Poems"), conscience ("Hamlet's Dialogue"), the hypocrisy of official honors ("No, the Drum Did Beat"), and the conflict between ruler and artist (the last three songs)—as well as the less frequently visited theme of love ("Whence All This Tenderness" and "Hamlet's Dialogue"). Shostakovich had traditionally favored soprano or bass voices for his song cycles, but in specifying a contralto here, he had apparently wanted to emulate the voice of Tsvetayeva herself: "thick, raspy, powerful, shrouded in the 'bitterness of homegrown tobacco,' a voice that had 'smoked, smoked, and wept,'" as Sofia Khentova put it.[75] Yet, though hardly optimistic in the traditional sense, the *Tsvetayeva* cycle does step back from the abyss that Shostakovich had so brutally confronted in the Fourteenth Symphony. As Malcolm MacDonald writes, "though the Tsvetayeva and Michelangelo cycles are only half turned again to the outside world, one receives the impression of Shostakovich striving finally to sort out and identify the essential issues and attitudes which will help him approach death, rather than railing against it."[76]

The cycle opens ("My Poems") with the young Tsevetayeva introducing herself and contemplating a better future for her work: "Scattered in the dust of bookshops (where no one has ever bought them!), my verses, like vintage wines, will have their time!"[77] As if to emphasize Tsvetayeva's sense of her own impenetrability, Shostakovich writes in that most psychologically intractable of keys, E-flat minor—the key, incidentally, of his very next work, the Fifteenth Quartet, and also the key in which his previous song cycle (*Alexander Blok*) had ended. And the song itself is based upon yet another icon of impenetrability, the twelve-note row heard right at the outset in the piano. Yet, the structure of the row itself is perhaps more reflective of the more resigned, less uncompromising attitude towards death that Shostakovich shows in this cycle. For unlike the row that began "Secret Signs" (*Blok*), where the order of pitches gave no sense, until the end, of the song's B minor tonality, this one is about as tonal as a twelve-note row can get, the first seven notes in particular pointing very strongly towards E-flat minor.

As Caryl Emerson notes, Shostakovich, writing three decades after Tsvetayeva's death, was able to change at will the perspectives of time for his own expressive purposes. Referring to the incongruous use of a chesty contralto to recite an essentially optimistic verse (i.e., "My Poems") by a woman barely out of her teens, Emerson notes that this poem had become something of a calling-card for Tsvetayeva later in life—she would quote it when asked about her fate as a poet. Shostakovich here transmits the poem seemingly with Tsvetayeva's later perspective, with "a voice that had already experienced that later fate."[78] Something similar could be said about the final poem, "To Anna Akhmatova," Shostakovich imposing his own perspective of Akhmatova the national icon on Tsvetayeva's poem, penned in 1916 well before Akhmatova had achieved such status. As Emerson puts it, "These poems from the 1910s [i.e., "My Poems" and "To Anna Akhmatova"] are early promises—promises remembered, made good, and performed by their aged poets."[79]

"Whence All This Tenderness?" was dedicated to Osip Mandelshtam, the poet with whom Tsvetayeva had briefly been involved. Although the tempestuous Tsvetayeva remained married to her husband, a man she truly loved, she would have several affairs during the course of her life, all of them ending in disappointment. Mandelshtam was no exception. In the poem, she asks, "Whence all this tenderness? These curls are not the first I ever stroked, and I've known lips darker than yours." The unsettled nature of the poem, indeed of Tsvetayeva's love in general, always searching, never quite finding, is perhaps reflected in the song with its sequences of undulating fourths in the piano, hinting at one key after another but not really belonging to any key. Even the one solid tonal center in this piece, A major, is presented in a provisional manner. The last A major harmony (A/C-sharp dyad) is struck in the piano four bars before the end. With the pedal down over the final four bars, that harmony gradually recedes from the listener's consciousness, giving way to that restless undulating figure, whose tones accumulate over that same pedal and shroud the end in mystery.

If "Whence All This Tenderness?" is about the disappointment of love, "Hamlet's Dialogue with his Conscience" ruminates over the dead Ophelia, languishing in the mud at the bottom of the river. It is more declamatory, as Shostakovich's works dealing with the theme of conscience tended to be. Yet, it is as tonally unsettled as "Whence All This Tenderness?," with its harmonies constantly searching for, but never achieving, resolution, at least not until the end. Still more declamatory is "Poet and Tsar," with its twelve-note ground bass supporting a series of stentorian major dyads (see Chapter 15). Not for the first time in Shostakovich's music, Pushkin is presented as the exemplar for the relationship between artist and ruler. Tsvetayeva's text here ("Rebuking the author and snipping his manuscript, The beastly butcher of Polish land") would appear to recall Pushkin's own "barbarian artist" who "blackens over a picture of genius," words tellingly set by Shostakovich in late 1936 in his *Four Pushkin Romances*.

As a man who had himself had his fill of "celebrations of honor," Shostakovich often quipped that his friend Sollertinsky's funeral had been adorned with so much honor there was barely enough room for his family. "No, the Drum Did Beat" continues the theme of Pushkin and the monarch with its depiction of the poet's funeral, apparently a hushed up, by-invitation-only affair, with its military trappings (Shostakovich playing up Tsvetayeva's own percussively martial rhythms, e.g., "Net, bil baraban"), its impenetrable ring of police surrounding the coffin: "It's such an honor, that even the closest friends are left out.... So homage-filled, homage-filled, homage-filled, damned too much homage!" At the end, Tsvetayeva quotes the Tsar's own description of Pushkin—"the wisest man in all of Russia." This provides an ironic conclusion to the poem's searing indictment of official hypocrisy. Yet, as Emerson notes, with this line, the Tsar is also seen to wrest dignity from the hands of the "inflated Gogolian frauds" (i.e., the police) who have thus far dominated the proceedings.[80]

Shostakovich sets Tsvetayeva's poems in chronological order,[81] except for the final song, which goes back to her early work. This reinforces the work's sense of biographical cyclism in much the same way as the positioning of the self-quotations had reinforced the autobiographical cyclism of the Eighth Quartet (i.e., chronological order over the first three movements and reverse chronological order over the last two). And the sense of cyclism is further reinforced by the internal thematic connections. The two outer songs address poets (Tsvetayeva herself and Anna Akhmatova) while the four central songs are about poets (Mandelshtam and Pushkin) or a Literary creation (Hamlet). And within those central songs are additional chains of thematic continuity. "Whence Such Tenderness?" and "Hamlet's Dialogue with his Conscience" are connected by the theme of love, or more specifically, broken love, while "The Poet and the Tsar" and "No, the Drum Did Beat" together form a mini-drama on the career, and on the memory of the career, of Pushkin. And while the final song ("To Anna Akhmatova") links the cycle back to the first song ("My Poems"), it at the same time inherits the theme of the conflict between artist and ruler that is at the core of the two Pushkin songs.

The *Tsvetayeva* cycle was premiered in November 1973. Two months later, Shostakovich created an orchestral version, which was first performed in June 1974. Scored for contralto and small orchestra, textures are predictably spare in Shostakovich's typical late-period style. One item of familiarity, though, is the use of the bell in the final movement. In both the Thirteenth and Fourteenth Symphonies, the bell had acted as the symbol of remembrance, and would appear to do so here too, as Shostakovich remembers Akhmatova.

***

If the *Tsvetayeva* cycle, like so many other works of late Shostakovich, dwelt on the theme of conscience, it was ironic that one of the hardest trials of conscience Shostakovich would ever have to face would come after the ink on the song cycle had barely dried. On 21 August, three weeks after the completion of the cycle, the nuclear physicist Andrei Sakharov gave a press conference to western journalists, where he gave his frank views on the directions the Soviet Union was taking.[82] One of the official responses to this "outrage" came in the form of a letter ("He Disgraces the Calling of Citizen") published in *Pravda* on 3 September. Signed by twelve musicians, including Shostakovich, Khachaturian, Kabalevsky, and Khrennikov, the letter expressed its support for the USSR Academy of Science's condemnation of Sakharov.[83] To a younger generation that had sometimes been exasperated by Shostakovich's apparent inability to "speak out," this hit a new low—how could a man who had himself been on the sharp end of such denunciations so cravenly have joined the baying mob? The resulting snub from some of his younger colleagues was almost as hurtful, though of course for entirely different reasons, as the humiliation that he had undergone following the 1948 anti-formalism purges. At the same time, though, many of those close to Shostakovich understood the extreme pressure that the physically vulnerable composer had been placed under. Although his own safety may not have been in jeopardy by that point, there was still, to paraphrase Yevtushenko's *A Career*, "his family to consider." Rostropovich, amongst others, reports that Shostakovich suffered extreme guilt over the signing.[84] What is somewhat puzzling is Irina Shostakovich's recollection of events. Like many others close to the composer, Irina has told of the lengths to which Shostakovich went in order to avoid signing such official documents; on one occasion, the two of them spent an entire day at the cinema "seeing one old film after another," hoping to avoid a certain official—unsuccessfully as it would turn out, since the official did indeed show up after the couple had returned home late at night.[85] But with regard to the Sakharov denunciation, Irina claims not that Shostakovich signed the letter under pressure but that, in fact, he did not see it or sign it at all:

> That day I answered the numerous calls from the *Pravda* office, saying that Dmitry was out, then that he was at the dacha, and when I was told that they were sending a car there, we simply left home and stayed out all evening when the paper had gone to press. Nevertheless Shostakovich's name appeared among the signatures. A short while ago we asked to see the original of that letter, but the *Pravda* people refused to show

it to us, conceding, however, that "such was the way things were done then." I know they were. The same was done with the letter in defense of Mikis Theodorakis—at the time Dmitry Shostakovich was away in hospital. Trying to dispute the signature after the event was altogether futile.[86]

***

Although 1974 brought no better health than the previous year, Shostakovich was now starting to come to terms with his condition. Emotionally more harrowing was the emigration in May of two of his dearest friends and musical colleagues, Rostropovich and Vishnevskaya. Since Rostropovich's famous 1970 letter in support of the dissident Solzhenitsyn, the couple had become *personae non gratae* and had been stripped almost entirely of their musical life. Upon receiving the news of their emigration, a tearful Shostakovich lamented, "In whose hands are you leaving me to die?"[87] Was this possibly a subconscious or even a conscious reference to the Musorgskian line, "To whom are you abandoning us?," a line that had been co-opted by Shostakovich himself in *Lady Macbeth*? Indeed, his last request to the couple before their departure was that, once in the West, they record *Lady Macbeth* in the original version, a request that they would indeed honor four years later in London.

For Shostakovich, who had already been unwittingly embroiled in the Sakharov scandal, the fate of the Rostropoviches only reinforced his continuing distrust of a repressive and hypocritical Soviet government. That January, for example, he had bemoaned the upcoming centenary celebration of Meyerhold's birth: "Do you think they will mention his arrest, or announce that he was an innocent victim of Stalin's bloodlust, or refer to the tragedy of his death? Will anything be said about the brutal murder of his wife, Zinayda Raikh? Of course not. They will go on about what a good director he was."[88] Shostakovich's prediction would prove depressingly accurate.

On a happier note, September 1974 saw the first performance in Russia in forty-four years of *The Nose*. As so often in those final years, Shostakovich's immersion in rehearsals seemed to give him back some of his old vitality. More than that, Boris Pokrovsky's outstandingly successful Moscow Chamber Theater production reconfirmed for Shostakovich his original faith in the opera.

***

Composed mainly during a two-week stay in hospital in May 1974, Shostakovich's Fifteenth Quartet could perhaps be said to continue where the Thirteenth left off. Re-embracing the type of modernist tendencies that the Fourteenth Quartet largely eschewed—including suggestions of *Klangfarbenmelodie* and the occasional note-row—it also continued Shostakovich's late-quartet exploration of the possibilities of single-movement unity, an exercise that had also bypassed the Fourteenth. Written in six movements without break, the Fifteenth Quartet presents a suite of genre stereotypes (Elegy, Serenade, Intermezzo, Nocturne, Funeral March, Epilogue) all subsumed under the iron-fisted rule of an unwavering *Adagio*. The metronome marking, quarter = 80, applies to five of the six movements. Only in the Funeral March and in the Epilogue's four flashbacks to the Funeral March does the marked tempo change, dropping to quarter = 60. This concept of a modular tempo was also found in the single-movement Thirteenth Quartet, where the faster central section was designed in a *doppio movimento* relationship to the slow outer parts, ensuring a constant pulse throughout.

The use of a single key, E-flat minor, for all six movements achieves simultaneously two, ostensibly contradictory, aims. On the one hand, by imitating the typical tonal layout of the Baroque suite (i.e., all movements in the same key), it reinforces the suspicion that this quartet is more an assemblage of set-piece movements than something conceived organically or "symphonically." On the other hand, it helps drive the fact that, as Richard Burke argues in Chapter 16, the Fifteenth is not really a six-movement quartet, but a single-movement work in six sections.

With its slow tempo and fugal texture, the work's opening reminds us of the Eighth Quartet. Even the Eighth Quartet's "wrong" fourth entrance is replicated here: entrances on D, A, D, G in the Eighth; E-flat, B-flat, E-flat, F in the Fifteenth. That is where the similarity ends, however. In the Eighth Quartet, the voices enter in quick succession (stretto), creating a compact build-up of the four-part texture. In particular, the spacing between the second entrance (viola) and the third (second violin) is particularly short—notable, because in a four-voice fugal exposition the third voice is the one most likely to be delayed. By contrast, the Fifteenth Quartet's threadbare subject presents five pitches spread over seven bars—it is three-and-a-half bars before it even moves off the first note—resulting in a much slower piling up of texture. The delay of the third voice results in twenty-one bars, in slow tempo, of spare, two-part texture. And the spareness is not just textural. Whereas the Eighth plunges us immediately into a chromatically rich and unsettled world that is driven at least in part by the harmonic ambiguity of DSCH, the opening of the Fifteenth puts up severe resistance to any chromatic inroads, the fugue moving strictly diatonically—the Quartet's first chromaticism does not appear until the eighth bar of the second theme (Fig. 6, b8), almost four minutes into the movement. In fact, the fugue's rigid use of the natural minor scale, with its emphasis on the motion from the sub-tonic D-flat to the tonic E-flat, gives a modal (Aeolian) character. That, together with the subject's conjunct melodic motion and the constant returning to the initial E-flat during its seven-bar course (a "resting tone," so to speak), gives an almost chant-like impression.

Given the Quartet's single-minded, unrelieved gloom ("play it so that flies drop dead in mid-air, and the audience starts leaving the hall from sheer boredom," Shostakovich once told Druzhinin[89]) and a mode of communication that is the very opposite of "open-hearted," many have suggested that Shostakovich may in part have chosen E-flat minor, one of the least resonant keys for strings, expressly for its peculiarly choked, gray sound. This becomes significant when considering the C major second theme (Fig. 6); the "release" that Shostakovich provides here is not only tonal (the simple purity of C major after the tortuousness of E-flat minor) but also timbral, by dint of the opening up of the string sound itself— literally, in the case of the accompanying viola and cello open-C pedals. As Jonathan Drury argues, the fact that some of the obvious contrasts that would normally be taken for granted in a multi-movement work (in particular, tempo and key) are absent in this Quartet makes the subtle contrasts, such as the juxtaposition of string timbre in C major versus that in E-flat minor, that much more telling.[90]

The relationship between this and the remaining movements is discussed in Chapter 16. One point worth making here, though, concerns the use of the *Tristan* motive to launch a melody (Fig. 32 in the second movement "Serenade"). The preoccupation with *Tristan* in Shostakovich's late works may indeed reflect, to a greater or lesser degree, Wagnerian ideas of "love-death." But it is also a product of a more general predilection, already noted with the Thirteenth Quartet, for patterns based on a rising leap followed by a descending minor (occasionally major) second. Richard Longman, for one, has described "this persistent crushing of intervals by a semitone" as "perhaps the most significant characteristic of Shostakovich's tragic expression."[91] Longman takes as perhaps the most extreme example of this practice the second theme in the Fifteenth Quartet's first movement where, following the initial phrase of strictly diatonic C major, the music continues (Fig. 7) by flattening, one by one, every note of the C major scale. "Thus," as Longman puts it, "the second section depresses the tone set by the first."[92]

Because of the sudden death of the Beethoven Quartet's cellist Sergei Shirinsky, the Fifteenth received its November 1974 Leningrad premiere with the Taneyev Quartet. It would be the only quartet other than the First (premiered by the Glazunovs) not to be premiered by the Beethovens, though the latter group would give the first Moscow performance in January 1975.

∗∗∗

In July 1974, only two months after the completion of the Fifteenth Quartet, Shostakovich composed what, along with the Fourteenth Symphony, would be his most monumental song cycle, the *Suite on Verses of Michelangelo*, ostensibly in preparation for the five hundredth anniversary of Michelangelo's birth in 1975. Like the Fourteenth Symphony, this cycle comprises eleven movements:

Shostakovich's title	Original source
1) Truth	Sonnet 3 to Pope Julius II
2) Morning	Sonnet 20
3) Love	Sonnet 25
4) Parting	Madrigal "Com'arò dunque ardire"
5) Anger	Sonnet 4 on Rome in the Pontificate of Julius II
6) Dante	Sonnet 1 on Dante Alighieri
7) To the Exile	Sonnet 2 on Dante Alighieri
8) Creativity	Sonnet 61 on the death of Vittoria Colonna
9) Night	An appreciation of Michelangelo's "Night" by Giovan Strozzi followed by Michelangelo's response
10) Death	Sonnet 69
11) Immortality	Epitaph for Cecchino Bracci Fiorentino – Epigrams 14 and 12

Unlike the *Blok* and *Tsvetayeva* cycles, where Shostakovich's declamatory late-period style was tempered, in certain poems at least, by a more lyrical style, the *Michelangelo* cycle was almost uncompromising in the spareness and ruggedness of its writing, both pianistic and vocal. The first song, "Truth," could hardly be more representative. It opens with five bars of craggy two-part counterpoint in the piano—Dorothea Redepenning has described it as "a kind of archaic heterophony," a perhaps deliberate attempt to create an atmosphere of "early music" for these Michelangelo settings.[93] Although the left hand follows a mainly scalar outline and though the counterpoint throws up the occasional dyad or triad (D-flat major in bar 2, C major in bar 3), the music is, for the most part, without tonal center, although A minor would appear to be the final destination. In bar 6, the piano is reduced to a single line, outlining a pair of rising fourths (B–E–A). The importance of this is two-fold. Firstly, the rising fourth interval, often appearing in consecutive pairs (as here) or in non-consecutive pairs (as in the opening of the sixth song, "Dante"—D–G–C-sharp–F-sharp), would become one of the defining compositional germs of the cycle as a whole.[94] Secondly, the reduction to a single line in preparation for the entrance of the voice a bar later prepares us for the absolute simplicity with which Shostakovich will accompany the voice, allowing counterpoint only during the song's short piano interludes. (These first seven bars, identical to the first seven bars of the tenth song, "Death," can be seen in Chapter 15, Example 15.12.)

The sonnet's plea for truth is made via an indictment of Pope Julius II, a man who, Michelangelo tells us, heeded and rewarded liars and gossips. It is a poem spoken in anger, and Shostakovich sets it in that spirit. In fact, the subject of "truth" had frequently brought forth flashes of anger from Shostakovich, whether or not such anger was built into the original text. The poem "Babi Yar," for example, though unequivocal in its condemnation of anti-Semitism, had been conceived by Yevtushenko not as an accusation but as an appeal, a plea to the higher conscience of the Russian people to put an end to this scourge. It was only in Shostakovich's angry, hard-edged setting that Yevtushenko's impassioned plea turned into a document of accusation.

The next three songs, "Morning," "Love," and "Parting," form a group based on the theme of love, a *topos* that Shostakovich had tended to avoid in the great song cycles of his middle period. It is almost as if the traumatic experience of *Lady Macbeth* had frightened him off the subject for the next few decades—post-1936, we see reference to it only in coded form in non-vocal works: the Ustvolskaya quotation in the Fifth Quartet, the Nazirova "code" in the Tenth Symphony, and, as recent research has suggested, references to Yelena Konstantinovskaya in the Fifth Symphony. But if "love" went underground, so to speak, during Shostakovich's middle period, it would re-emerge with renewed purpose towards the end of his life. Four of the five late-period song cycles (including the Fourteenth Symphony) feature "love" as a poetic *topos*. In some cases, "love" intersects with other characteristically Shostakovichian topics. "Ophelia's Song" from the *Alexander Blok* cycle and "Hamlet's Dialogue with his Conscience" from the *Marina Tsvetayeva* cycle certainly have additional connotations: "parting" or "separation" in the former case, and "conscience" in the latter. And in the Fourteenth Symphony, the fate of love is a decidedly violent one. But amid all the late-period gloom, there are cases of more straightforward love. "We Were Together" from the *Blok* cycle and "Whence Such Tenderness" from *Marina Tsvetayeva* may both be tinged with nostalgia, even regret, but their overriding theme is that of romantic love. And the same would be true for the three love songs here in the *Michelangelo* suite.

Shostakovich provided Michelangelo's verses with titles of his own, titles that seem to have been created not just to reflect his interpretation of Michelangelo's individual poems but to promote the trajectory of certain groups of songs and of the cycle as a whole. In the case of the "love" triptych, three otherwise unconnected poems are now linked by Shostakovich, and by the simple act of titling are set into an organic relationship with one another, a journey of love—youthful love (or maybe simply lust), mature love, and finally love that is threatened by separation and death. In the first poem, for example, neither Michelangelo's original nor Abram Efros' Russian translation contains the word "morning" or even an allusion to the concept of morning. But Shostakovich would have appeared to have chosen the title in response to what are very clearly adolescent images of love, images in which items of clothing are anthropomorphized and given the power of erotic feeling.

> How enjoyable it is when flowers,
> Gaily twining along her golden plaits,
> Touch each other in eager rivalry
> As if each one wanted to kiss her sweet head.
>
> And how pleasant for the dress
> To cling tightly round her waist,
> Then billow like a wave.
> And how comforting for the golden net to embrace her throat.
>
> Still more tenderly the braid of splendid ribbon,
> Shining in its patterned embroidery,
> Closes round the young breasts;
>
> And the pure belt, twining round her waist,
> Appears to be whispering: "I shall not part from you . . ."
> Oh, how much there is to do here for my hands![95]

The adolescence of these images is reflected in the music itself. The first two stanzas, with their emphasis on monotone, have a palpitating, almost hyperventilating recitative quality about them. However, in the third stanza, the harmony becomes almost gushingly sentimental, recalling, albeit very briefly, the style of the old Russian romance.

In contrast to "Morning," with its very simple and idealistic viewpoint, the second song of the triptych, "Love," presents an altogether more mature, multi-faceted view of the subject. It is a more reflective poem, one that muses on eroticism, but one that takes on a more spiritual aspect and also confronts the battle that so often exists in love, the battle between truth and self-delusion. The breathless recitative is now gone and the delivery is more contemplative, though Shostakovich's strangely mercurial quicksand introduction returns at the end of each stanza. Meanwhile, the third song, the indelibly sad "Parting," returns us to more familiar Shostakovichian territory. In fact, even its sub-theme, the preservation of the memory of love following a separation (whether due to death or otherwise), is a familiar one—the song's final line, "But so that fate shall not drive my devotion from your memory I shall leave my heart with you," bringing to mind the song "What Does My Name Mean to You?" from the *Four Pushkin Monologues*.

The three love songs are certainly not as brutally atonal as "Truth." Yet, tonality can sometimes be hard to pin down—even "Parting," the most tonal of the three with mainly triadic block-chord motion, moves almost rudderless from one implied tonality to another. And while all three songs have their moments of tenderness, the rhetorical tone is always there—in the background in "Morning," but more to the forefront in "Love" and "Parting," the latter presented in a declamatory recitative-like manner, with much of its text pronounced on a monotone. Indeed, the opening chord of "Parting" is the same third-inversion dominant seventh that had launched the Second Quartet's Recitative, a connection that registers even more strongly in the orchestral version, where this song is scored only for strings.

Following this "love" interlude, the fifth song, "Anger," resumes the tirade against Julius II, though the diatribe is now framed in more overtly religious terms, with Michelangelo declaring how the shenanigans of Rome are an affront to Christ ("Let him not descend into our neighbouring villages, or again his blood will splash to the stars"), the hammered chords in the piano providing a more direct brutality here than the starkly angular counterpoint in "Truth." Whatever the limitations of Efros' translation, one line here that might for Shostakovich have hit even closer to home in the translation is Michelangelo's "The roads are closed to all piety," translated by Efros as "and we are keeping mercy under lock and key." "Truth" and "Anger," then, could be said to bookend a mini-cycle of five songs within the context of the larger cycle. Yet, it should be noted that the emphasis in "Anger" on declamatory monotone, in both the voice and the piano, also makes it a logical successor to "Parting," a song that had already shown a move away from the more lyrical style of the other two love songs. In other words, though "Parting" is clearly a song of closure in its own right, it is also a transition—one that reintegrates the "love" interlude back into the main cycle.

Dante, his exile from his native Florence, and his treatment at the hands of the ungrateful mob form the subject of the sixth and seventh songs ("Dante" and "To the Exile"). The declamatory tone is consistent throughout the two songs, with the opening of "Dante" reminiscent rhythmically of the stentorian horn call that had ushered in the passacaglia of the First Violin Concerto. In "To the Exile," meanwhile, the piano's brutal pounding provides a highly graphic representation of the line "and the door that even heaven did not close, Dante's homeland slammed shut with malice." Declamatory vocal line and percussive accompaniment reach their peak in the eighth song, "Creativity," Michelangelo's paean to God the "divine blacksmith" who shapes out human life with his hammer. Here, even the softer passages are devoid of lyricism. Creation is a rough-hewn process, for God, for Michelangelo, and for Shostakovich—the whiplash A-sharp/C-sharp dyad at the start of the song and the A-sharp/E dyads at the end reminding us perhaps of the equally savage B-flat/D-flat dyads at the start of the Tenth Symphony's scherzo.

The ninth song, "Night," is a short dialogue between Michelangelo the sculptor and the poet Giovan Battista Strozzi. In the first stanza, Strozzi praises Michelangelo's statue of "Night," urging him to "awaken" the night that has been fashioned by an angel out of stone. In the second, Michelangelo replies that he would indeed rather be that stone, unable to see or hear the ruin and shame in the world that surrounds it. The vocal line here is based on the same quotation from Galina Ustvolskaya's Clarinet Trio that Shostakovich had used in the outer movements of the Fifth Quartet, and it is surely pertinent to wonder, as Louis Blois does in Chapter 19, whether Michelangelo's rejection of Strozzi may have brought to Shostakovich's mind Ustvolskaya's rejection of him. In the Quartet, composed in 1952 at the height of his infatuation with her, the quotations are by turns passionate and turbulent, coy and withdrawn, and, in the aftermath of the finale's development, somewhat shell-shocked. Here in "Night," the quotation is, as Blois puts it, "resigned and darkly melancholic." Between Strozzi's plea and Michelangelo's reply Shostakovich inserts another self-quotation, three bars of, appropriately enough, the "Death of a Poet" from the Fourteenth Symphony (Figs. 128 and 132 in the Symphony), identical in key and, in the orchestral version of the cycle, in scoring.

The placement of "Night" gives it a transitional status. Its reference in the first half to the hammering out of life and worldly phenomena by divine hand links it back to "Creativity," while the reluctance of the sculptor in the second half to embrace life looks forward to the tenth song, "Death." In many ways the "official" conclusion to the cycle, "Death" returns us back to where we began, with an attack on a world in which "evil triumphs over honesty." The opening seven bars are an exact replica of the opening of the first song, "Truth," but now, the poet is not so much angry as weary; in this dark world, his soul begs for death. For the terminally ill Shostakovich, an atheist resolutely opposed to any concept of afterlife, Michelangelo's final question must have held particular significance: why put trust in eternal salvation when death holds us for ever? The inevitability and implacable progress of death is reflected, rather typically for Shostakovich, in a passacaglia based loosely on the stepwise lines of the song's opening (see Chapter 15 for analysis). The cyclic aspect of this song is reinforced not only with these first seven bars, but by the fact that C-sharp, the pitch that for a brief moment threatened to establish itself as a key at the start of the cycle (there spelled D-flat, see above), becomes the pitch center for the passacaglia as well as for the song's closing section, where it appears as a pedal underneath yet another replay, this time *pianissimo*, of those opening seven bars. As the now-familiar tortuous two-part counterpoint goes once again through its flirt-and-escape routine, C-sharp exerts its death grip.

With this, the text has come full circle thematically, the music has come full circle thematically, and the poet finally has uttered his wish for death. Meanwhile the key vaguely promised at the start of the cycle has finally come through. Textually, thematically, and tonally, the Michelangelo Suite, a cycle of anger, defiance, weariness, and death (with, of course, an interlude for love) has reached its conclusion. Except, that is, for the small matter of the eleventh song, "Immortality." With its cheekily banal opening melody in F-sharp major, appropriated from Shostakovich's abandoned mini-opera from his early teenage years, *The Gypsies*, "Immortality," thumbs its nose at the preceding gloom: "I'm not dead; I merely changed my address," as Michelangelo put it. Even outside the context of the cycle, the song seems highly ironic—a poem dedicated to timelessness set to music that is almost mechanistic, with its metronome-like rhythms and "musical box"-type melodies. But considered in context, it is even more problematic, since the previous song, "Death," had seemed so final not just for the obvious textual reasons but also because of those cyclic aspects—the final return of the cycle's opening music, now sealed by the long-promised pitch center of C-sharp. "Immortality," then, rather like the final scene of Mozart's *Don Giovanni*, seems to stand somewhat apart—an epilogue to a song cycle that has already had its conclusion rather than the conclusion itself.

For Shostakovich the atheist, immortality was about the eternal survival not of the soul but of artistic creation—"I lived on in the hearts of my true friends," as Michelangelo put it. And if the cycle is viewed ultimately as a paean to life as revealed through creativity rather than as a more conventional reflection of life and death—and it can of course be viewed as both—then "Immortality," with its quotation of early Shostakovich, far from being an awkward misfit, becomes indeed a logical cyclic conclusion—the cycle now redefined as the entire span of Shostakovich's life, from *The Gypsies* at one end to the *Michelangelo* Suite at the other, rather than simply the *Michelangelo* Suite itself. In this reading, the C-sharp destination of the first ten songs can be viewed as the long dominant preparation to the F-sharp of the final song. In the coda to "Immortality," Shostakovich brings back the accompanying harmony to the opening melody but not the melody itself, something that is perhaps tempting to view as a musical corollary of immortality—the mortal coil may have been shaken off, but the inner soul lives on.

The orchestral version of the song cycle (the date of which is somewhat uncertain) provides its own perspectives,[96] though accompanimental textures are still kept spare, allowing for maximum intelligibility of the text. The two-part counterpoint that opens both "Truth" and "Death" is given to two trumpets, exacerbating, as Redepenning observes,[97] the atmosphere of "early music," though at the same time attenuating the craggy percussiveness of the piano's distinctive attacks. When the passage returns at the end of "Death," the trumpets are muted, sounding remote and desolate against the long bass pedal. The gloom of Shostakovich's many low-register statements is made still more lugubrious in their new settings for cellos and double basses, or occasionally more disembodied in the solo double bass, as at the end of "Morning." Meanwhile, the hammer-blow chords in "Creativity" gain in their austere power, and with their very similar orchestration remind us of the whiplash chords that had opened the *Hamlet* film score—creativity and conscience perhaps two sides of the same coin. (Shostakovich himself acknowledged the connection between the two.[98]) Typically for a valedictory statement, Shostakovich gives the celesta prominence in "Immortality," though as the coda fades away with its repeated F-sharp major chords, it is the harp not the celesta that gets the final word.

***

Shostakovich's remarkable summer of composition would come to a close with the *Four Verses of Captain Lebyadkin*, completed in August 1974. One of the Mahlerian heirlooms that Shostakovich had inherited was the ability to combine or juxtapose the lofty with the crude, and no better example of that can be found than the juxtaposition of the two song cycles, the one dedicated to the great moral humanist Michelangelo, the other to the crude, drunken buffoon that was Captain Ignaty Lebyadkin, a particularly odious character from Dostoyevsky's *The Devils* (or *The Possessed*). Lebyadkin fancied himself as a revolutionary. Shostakovich, who took the coarsely belligerent, envious poems penned by Lebyadkin himself, interspersing them with other sections of Dostoyevsky's text, thought of Lebyadkin not just as a buffoon whose idea of revolution was all mouth and no trousers, but as something more sinister.[99] Musically, the cycle is written in the crudest style, Lebyadkin's verbal filth grunted and spat out—it might be described as a more dissonant, more venomous take on the *Krokodil* Romances.

***

That Shostakovich had not quite given up on a cure for his condition was demonstrated by his visits in the spring of 1975 to a faith healer. As Glikman reports it, through a process of the laying-on of hands, the woman (dubbed "a witch" by Shostakovich) induced healing burns on the skin.[100] On 10 May, Shostakovich made what would be his last public appearance, at the premiere of the *Lebyadkin* cycle. He spent most of July in hospital following a scare involving his heart at the beginning of the month. Glikman recalls a phone conversation on 29 July; the composer's voice was "dull, as if covered in some kind of shroud."[101] Shostakovich was released on 1 August but was readmitted a few days later; a coughing fit, resulting from choking on a piece of fruit, had aggravated the heart condition. While he was hospitalized, doctors discovered a spreading of the lung cancer that had first shown up in 1972. It was this, and not the heart condition, that proved fatal. On the evening of 9 August, Dmitry Shostakovich passed away as a result of suffocation caused by the spread of the cancer into the artery connecting the heart and lungs.

The first that the world knew of Shostakovich's death was an announcement made at the Tanglewood Music Festival in Massachusetts, where Rostropovich was due to perform the Second Cello Concerto. The official announcement in the Soviet Union had to be delayed by two days because of the need to secure Brezhnev's approval for the wording of the official obituary. At the funeral, held on 14 August in the Great Hall of the Moscow Conservatory, Shostakovich's body lay "in state" while, to the accompaniment of pre-recorded music, the public processed around the coffin. Khrennikov spoke, as did Vasily Kukharsky from the

Ministry of Culture and Rodion Shchedrin, Shostakovich's successor at the RSFSR Composers' Union. A worker from Leningrad paid tribute on behalf of that city's working class. All mouthed the required platitudes. Then to the cemetery at Novodevichy, where there were more speeches—this time Georgian composer and Minister of Culture Otar Taktakishvili and Leningrad composer Andrei Petrov. On a cold and rainy late afternoon, Shostakovich's body was laid to rest.

***

On 25 September 1975, Shostakovich would have turned sixty-nine. His birthday was marked by a performance at his home before an invited audience of his Viola Sonata, his final composition, written in the late spring and completed while he had been in the hospital in July—the work's dedicatee Fyodor Druzhinin had picked up the corrected parts only three days before the composer's death.

The recent discovery of a sketch of the Sonata notated in the bass clef has led the archivist Manashir Yakubov to surmise that the work was originally conceived not for the viola, but for the cello. The sketch also helps explain a rather cryptic comment that Shostakovich had made to Rostropovich upon the latter's departure from the Soviet Union in 1974: "If you receive an anonymous packet when you are abroad, don't throw it out; who knows, it might have an interesting composition inside."[102] Given that it would have been practically impossible for Shostakovich to have dedicated a new work to the "disgraced" Rostropovich, it would appear that rather than dedicating the Sonata to another cellist, or omitting a dedication altogether, he had decided to transfer the work to the viola and dedicate it to Druzhinin, an artist he had come to admire greatly.

The Viola Sonata is one of Shostakovich's most darkly austere pieces. It is, of course, tempting to "read" things into a composer's valedictory work, but in Shostakovich's case, he seems to have left behind so many clues that it is hard to avoid the conclusion that the Viola Sonata really was a conscious summing up of his life. The first clue comes with the almost bell-like tolling of the notes D–E-flat–C (i.e., an incomplete version of the DSCH motif) in the piano, first heard at Fig. 3 and then at various points throughout the first movement. The second movement scherzo is based almost entirely on music from Shostakovich's unfinished opera *The Gamblers* (1942)—the first 73 bars correspond to the Overture, while other sections are taken from later in the opera. But it was in the third movement finale that Shostakovich, in an unusually systematic way, set down his legacy.

Over the course of these chapters, we have discussed those composers who were particularly influential for Shostakovich. In many cases, he acknowledged the influence in a specific way, often with quotations that in some philosophical or dramaturgical way connected with the music at hand: *Boris Godunov* quoted in *Lady Macbeth*; *Das Lied von der Erde* quoted in the Tenth Symphony and alluded to in the Fifth Quartet; the Berg Violin Concerto quoted in the Violin Sonata and alluded to in the Seventh Quartet; or even the wholesale assumption of the Twenty-Four Prelude and Fugue genre. But one major compositional force in Shostakovich's life that had received less of this type of "recognition" was Beethoven. Of course, there was the inevitable snippet of the *Kreutzer* Sonata in the final song of *Satires* ("Kreutzer Sonata"), and at the start of 1975, Shostakovich had made an orchestration of Beethoven's little ditty "Song of Mephistopheles in Auerbach's Cellar" ("Song of the Flea"). But now, in the Viola Sonata, he would repay the debt properly, basing the finale on the first movement of Beethoven's *Moonlight* Sonata. Shostakovich specifically told Druzhinin: "the finale is an adagio in memory of Beethoven; but don't let that inhibit you. The music is bright, bright and clear."[103] Indeed, for a "bright and clear" memorial to Beethoven composed by a man who knew that his own days were numbered, the *Moonlight* Sonata was a particularly apt choice, with its combination of, on the one hand, its funeral-march rhythms and intonations and, on the other, that peculiar harmonic luminescence that had earned the Sonata its nickname in the first place. In Shostakovich's hands, the music flows more tentatively, as Beethoven's continuously rippling triplet accompaniment is turned into an eighth-note figure, with the occasional agogic pause. Yet, from out of this darkly tenuous reinterpretation emerges the occasional flash of Beethoven's harmonies, creating a particularly haunting mixture of late-Shostakovichian gloom and late-classical luminescence.

Just over a third of the way into this fifteen-minute movement, something extraordinary happens. Between bars 66 and 90, Shostakovich incorporates short (a few notes long) excerpts from each of his symphonies, except, apparently, the Eleventh—in most cases from their respective opening themes. In the midst of a memorial to one great composer, the life story of another flashes by. Unlike Shostakovich's many previous quotations and self-quotations, most of which had stood in relief from the surrounding music, these excerpts are incorporated seamlessly into the viola or the piano line. So seamlessly, in fact, that they were only discovered three decades later, in 2006.[104]

Following a cadenza and a return to the *Moonlight* theme is a short quotation from Strauss' *Don Quixote*, from that transcendental moment when the soul leaves the hero's body—perhaps another sign that the work was originally conceived for cello. Finally the movement comes to rest in a deep, rapt peace. If C major was for Shostakovich the signifier of new beginnings—the First Quartet or the first of the Twenty-Four Preludes and Fugues—it was also the key in which his music, indeed his life, would come to an end.

With sisters Mariya (l) and Zoya (r) (1913).

With cat (early-mid 1920s).

With Nina Varzar and Ivan Sollertinsky (1932).

Performing his First Piano Concerto (mid to late 1930s).

Pencil sketch by G. Effros (1933).

With Yevgeny Mravinsky (1937).

Cartoon by the 'Kukryniksy' group (1942).

With his son, Maxim (early 1960s).

Aboard the Leningrad-Moscow 'Strela' ('Arrow') (1965).

With Mstislav Rostropovich, Galina Vishnevskaya, and David Oistrakh (1967).

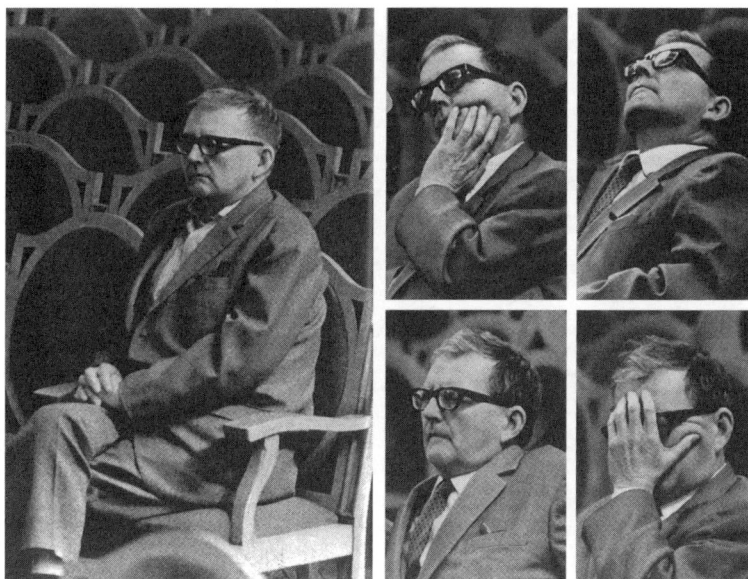

At rehearsal (early 1970s).

With Irina (early 1970s).

With cat (1973).

Commemorative stamp (issued 1976).

PART III

ANALYZING SHOSTAKOVICH

CHAPTER 11

SHOSTAKOVICH THE DRAMATIST: *THE NOSE* AND *THE LADY MACBETH OF THE MTSENSK DISTRICT*[1]

James Morgan

The musicologist Carl Dahlhaus locates the drama of opera in what he calls "the configuration of character and affect."[2] It is not the external events on stage—the plot—but the relationships between the characters that provide the tension. Furthermore, opera is for Dahlhaus relentlessly synchronic; it unfolds in a permanently present tense. Dahlhaus's ideas recall Mikhail Bakhtin's conception of the polyphonic novel, where the synchronic play of multiple voices takes precedence over the teleological movement of the plot.[3] From a different perspective, Herbert Lindenberger has also compared opera to the polyphonic novel, claiming a common "propensity towards extravagant utterance [and] an appetite to absorb and even swallow up other genres."[4] Although opera is no more a novel than it is a drama, I conceive of it as a configuration of dialogues, to use Bakhtin's term, between music, text, and performance that arise both within an opera and, in a sense, outside it, in the genres and media that it swallows.

While these dialogues occur in any opera, they loom even larger in the context of an operatic adaptation. An adaptation is a reinterpretation, a recasting of another's work, and as Caryl Emerson has argued, it is where "coauthorship is ... celebrated ... and dialogue among versions is inevitably explicit."[5] From this point of view, the frequently invoked criterion of fidelity to a source text becomes an empty category. It is interesting only inasmuch as it provides easily accessible material with which to engage the dialogue between a source text and its adaptations, both of which retain an independent voice in the listener's apprehension of the opera.

The Nose

Shostakovich's first opera, *The Nose*, based on Gogol's short story of the same title, presents a striking example of adaptation.[6] It engages in dialogue with its basic source text, yet it also draws from a whole series of Gogol's works as well as Dostoyevsky's *The Brothers Karamazov*.[7] The music, too, is a product of mixed parentage. *The Nose*, with its strikingly modernist score, fits comfortably in the tradition of post-Wagnerian, through-composed operas: several critics have stressed connections between *The Nose* and Western Modernism, most notably Alban Berg's *Wozzeck*. Other elements, however, including Gogol's specifically Russian source text, the opera's Meyerholdian production, and its musical and textual allusions to earlier Russian operas, link *The Nose* with both the Soviet 1920s and Shostakovich's native Russian tradition. In this context, Musorgsky rather than Wagner is Shostakovich's operatic predecessor.[8] All of these elements lend their voices to the rich polyphony of Shostakovich's chaotic opera.

In the analysis that follows, I isolate as much as possible musical voices from literary and performative ones in order to see clearly their dialogic play and transforming power. In a sense, an opera represents a series of interlocking transformations. First, the librettist (often the composer) adapts a source text into a workable libretto, thus setting the two in dialogue. The composer in turn transforms the libretto into opera: the tension of text and music that makes its own comment on the source text. The opera undergoes a further transformation when staged or recorded. Within this network of adaptation and transformation, I address three dialogues: between source text and libretto, between source text and opera, and between opera and performance. A fourth dialogue, that between libretto and music, lurks behind the other three and will figure to varying degrees in each of the sections that follow.

Source Text and Libretto—From "The Nose" to *The Nose*

Shostakovich began his first opera under the influence of the musicologists Ivan Sollertinsky and Boris Asafyev, the second of whom was close to the stage director Vsevolod Meyerhold. Asafyev conceived of opera as a "theatrical symphony," in which the score was constructed in accordance with the specific demands of the stage. He saw Meyerhold's innovative theater as the optimum breeding ground for this theatricalized opera, and arranged for Shostakovich to take a job there. Meyerhold in turn let Shostakovich live and work in his apartment in Moscow, where the composer wrote a good deal of *The Nose*.[9] Asafyev himself was concerned with the difficulty of merging theater and serious music. In a letter to Meyerhold about the latter's production of Griboyedov's *Woe from Wit*, he theorized:

In the theater, music, as far as the public is concerned, is only a lulling background or an annoying accompaniment that gets in the way of "what the words mean." And that's the whole problem. Music as a living impulse, music included in a dramatic production as an integral element in the dialogue—that, alas, no one understands.... Of course it could be made totally understandable only in a situation where the actor was also a real musician/improviser and actually found the stimulus for his lines in the music. It's possible.[10]

Shostakovich in his own way met Asafyev's challenge to turn singers into actors and to make music an integral element of the dialogue, claiming, "I have symphonized Gogol's text not in the form of absolute or pure symphony, but as a theatrical symphony, a good example of which is Meyerhold's production of *The Inspector General*."[11] Meyerhold's innovative methods do play a significant role in Shostakovich's opera. These techniques include the compilation of text from a variety of relevant sources, complex and extreme variations in tempo, extensive choreography of crowd scenes, and pantomime.[12] In this section, I will address the process by which Shostakovich and his collaborators assembled their libretto. Below, I will focus on pantomime and the role of the orchestra.

In *The Nose*, as with most operas based on literary sources, changes in Gogol's story occur not only in the musicalization of the text and narration but also within the text itself. The plot of "The Nose" is, admittedly, anecdotal—no characters develop and, despite a good deal of frenetic activity, not much really happens. The Soviet critic V. M. Bogdanov-Berezovsky considered it unsuitable for operatic adaptation,[13] while David Drew commented "Given the Gogol material, *The Nose* has no business to be longer than *Mavra* [Stravinsky's one-act opera based on Pushkin's narrative poem 'Little House in Kolomna']."[14] Conversely, Caryl Emerson found the text particularly suited to Shostakovich's style: "Gogol's story is a gift for modernist opera: its narrator is never in control of his text, and at crucial moments a fog descends, 'no one knows what happened next'."[15] In the end, Shostakovich compiled his libretto not only from "The Nose" but also from a selection of other works by Gogol, most notably *The Marriage*.[16] In *The Nose*, the composer and his collaborators wove a tapestry of Gogol's words, draping it over the story's anecdotal plot and augmenting it with the excerpt from Dostoyevsky.[17]

The basic plot—a petty bureaucrat awakes one morning to find his nose missing, rushes around Petersburg in search of it, and wakes up another day to find it firmly back in place—and the major sub-plot—the petty bureaucrat's drunken barber awakes to find a severed nose in his morning bread and because of it has a run-in with the police—remain substantially unchanged in the transition from story to opera. However, several scenes and characters are expanded. Shostakovich based the long scene at the posting inn where the nose is captured (Act III, Scene 7, no. 12) on a single sentence in Gogol's story, and developed an extended crowd scene (Act III, Intermezzo, no. 14), in which the residents of Petersburg search for the walking, talking nose, from a series of Gogolian cues.[18] He also added dialogue in the scene between Kovalyov and the Podtochinas at the end of the opera

(Epilogue, Scene 10, no. 16), invented the character Yaryzhkin, with whom Kovalyov writes his letter to Podtochina in the split-stage letter-reading quartet (Act III,
Scene 8, no. 13), and expanded several roles, including Podtochina's daughter,
who in the story is mentioned throughout but appears only for an instant at the
end, and Ivan, Kovalyov's servant. These characters come in large measure from
Gogol's play, *The Marriage*.

There are also cuts. Along with masses of dilatory Gogolian detail, Shostakovich
omitted Kovalyov's two trips to a café where he first mourns the loss of his nose
and later rejoices in its return. However, in order to retain the framing function of
the café scenes, Shostakovich replaced them with a bit of dialogue, taken from
Chapter 1 of "The Nose," concerning the barber's fetid hands (Act I, Introduction, no. 1; Epilogue, Scene 9, no. 15). He also removed Kovalyov's first glimpse
of the nose outside the cathedral and his unpleasant visit with the police commis-
sioner, who tells him that decent people do not lose track of their noses.

Shostakovich also adapted the majority of Gogol's narration, with the orchestra
taking over part of that function. In addition, he condensed chunks of narrative,
making adjustments in the person and tense of verb forms, and transferred them
into the mouths of characters. This is especially effective with free indirect discourse, in which the narrator conveys a character's emotions or apprehension of
events. In Act I, Scene 1, for instance, Ivan Yakovlevich rues his wife's impatience
with his whims. In Gogol's story, the narrator tells his reader, "That is, Ivan
Yakovlevich would have liked to have both one and the other, but he knew that it
was entirely impossible to demand two things at once, since Praskovya Osipovna
really didn't like such whims."[19] In the opera, after making clear that he will eat
bread and not drink coffee, the barber intones, "That is, I feel like having both
one and the other, but it's entirely impossible to demand two things at once. Praskovya Osipovna doesn't like such whims."[20] This method of transferring free,
indirect discourse to dialogue theatricalizes the thoughts of characters, shifting
them from story to stage. In addition, the shift in tense from the narrative past to
the operatic present speaks on a textual level to what Dahlhaus calls "the predomi-
nance of the present" in music.[21] Shostakovich continued this practice throughout
the opera.

Among the most interesting of Shostakovich's additions is his expansion of the
role of Ivan, Kovalyov's servant. Ivan, who makes only a brief appearance in
Gogol's tale, has a major role in the opera. Shostakovich developed this role, at
least in part, from the servant characters in Gogol's plays. In the tale, Ivan first
appears when Kovalyov comes home after searching for his nose: he sits silently on
the couch, spitting at the ceiling. Kovalyov abuses him and begins to lament his
loss. Ivan shows up again when Kovalyov sends him for the doctor, and once more
when the nose reappears on his master's face. Only in this last scene does the servant have anything to say, and it is only one line. In the opera, by contrast, Ivan
provides an important foil for Kovalyov. When Kovalyov first finds his nose missing (Act I, Scene 3, no. 5), he asks his man to fetch a series of items and then
requests a pinch to make sure he is not dreaming. Ivan fulfills this latter task with

glee. Later in this scene, when Kovalyov decides to go out, Ivan asks him where he is going. This interaction between master and servant recalls the first scene of Gogol's play, *The Marriage*, where the protagonist Podkolesin spars with his clever and put-upon servant Stepan, as well as Khlestakov's relationship with his servant Osip in *The Inspector General*.

Shostakovich further expanded Ivan's role in Act II, Scene 6, No. 11. Here he sings a folk tune accompanied only by a balalaika and, at the end, by the wavering, metallic sound of the flexatone. His words come from Smerdyakov's song in *The Brothers Karamazov*, the only extended interpolation from a wholly non-Gogolian source.

> With invincible force I am bound to my dear,
> Lord have mercy on her and on me!
> What do I care for royal wealth if but my dear one be in health!
> Lord have mercy on her and on me![22]

The text's central concerns are sexual desire and erotic love, and contrast with the ironic, liturgical refrain "Lord have mercy" (*Gospodi pomilui*). It is also an ironic comment on Kovalyov's truant nose, whose absence contrasts with the "invincible force" with which Ivan is attached to his "dear one." Furthermore, the song itself provides an ironic counterpoint to Kovalyov's pathetic arioso, immediately following, in which he laments his incalculable loss.

The words to Kovalyov's arioso, unlike those in Ivan's song, are taken almost verbatim from the free, indirect discourse of Gogol's narration. Kovalyov's disjointed vocal line contrasts with the stanzaic form of Ivan's tune, just as the text, no less disjointed than the music, contrasts with the simplicity of Ivan's bawdy sentiments. Like Ivan, however, Kovalyov, pining for his nose, invokes God. While I will resist the temptation to make more than a syntagmatic link between Ivan's beloved and Kovalyov's nose, the absurd connection between the objects of their musical effusions remains. These scenes, with the interaction and absurd parallel between master and servant, are absent in Gogol and bear the complicating, rather than simplifying, imprint of Shostakovich's adaptation. (Andrew Wachtel has proposed a more strictly operatic source for Shostakovich's enlargement of a servant's role, namely the Italian *opera buffa*, exemplified by Paisello's or Rossini's *The Barber of Seville* or Mozart's *The Marriage of Figaro*.[23])

A further example not only of Shostakovich's innovation but also of his role as interpreter of Gogol's works involves his treatment of Kovalyov's preoccupation with marriage, and the strong subtextual presence in the opera of Gogol's play *The Marriage*. "The Nose" foregrounds the themes of marriage and sex, but *The Nose*, especially where its libretto relies on *The Marriage*, raises them to the level of obsession. Shostakovich may have drawn on this source so heavily because it was the source text for Musorgsky's early experiment with *Literatur-Oper*. However, it is equally possible that Shostakovich had his own interest in the subject. A preoccupation with sex was by no means odd for an artist of the 1920s in the Soviet

Union, a decade in which attention, whether explicit or allusive, to physiological
details of human life was common. Reviewing the first production in 1930, M.
Yankovsky noted cryptically: "The composer was undoubtedly attracted by the
sexual state of affairs which in fact led Gogol to write 'The Nose'."[24] Yankovsky
does not divulge what exactly constitutes for him Gogol's "sexual state of affairs,"
though he was perhaps pointing to the ribald association of noses with male geni-
tals, common at least since, if not earlier than, Laurence Sterne's *Tristram Shandy*.
As with many of the opera's more prurient elements, this association is most clear
in an excerpt that Shostakovich takes not from "The Nose," but from *The Marriage*. Here, the prospective bride, Agafiya Tikhonovna, is quizzing the match-
maker, Fekla Ivanovna, about one of her many suitors.

> AGAFIYA TIKHONOVNA: What kind of hair does he have?
> FEKLA IVANOVNA: Nice hair.
> AGAFIYA TIKHONOVNA: And his nose?
> FEKLA IVANOVNA: Eh—and his nose is nice too. Everything is in its place.[25]

Significantly, Shostakovich adds a similar exchange to his libretto. When the doctor
is examining the now noseless Kovalyov, he asks his patient about other parts of his
body (Act II, Scene 6, no. 11).

> DOCTOR: And you do have everything you should in its place, eh?
> KOVALYOV: And what business is it of yours what I've got?![26]

With this interpolation, Shostakovich clearly indicates that in his reading of "The
Nose," a nose is not simply a nose.

References to *The Marriage* abound throughout the opera. I have already discussed the relationship between Ivan and Kovalyov, which Shostakovich derived in
part from the relationship between Podkolesin and Stepan. Another important resonance occurs in the scene at the Petersburg posting inn (Act III, Scene 7,
no. 12). In one of the several mini-scenes that accumulate to form the larger picture, a group of police officers surrounds a woman selling bagels—fresh, fleshy
bread—and proceeds to grope her. (This association between bread and flesh—
here implicit—was more explicit at the beginning of the opera, when the barber
Ivan Yakovlevich, immediately before finding Kovalyov's nose, cuts open his bread
and describes it as "fleshy."[27]) One of the officers mocks her with the "polite"
request, "Permit me to be curious," a line from *The Marriage*.[28] Bogdanov-Berezovsky found in this scene "the kernel of the same pathological sadism which fills
whole scenes in Shostakovich's next opera.... it is simply a sexual episode which
the author plays up for the sake of his own personal satisfaction ... a dangerous
tendency towards rude naturalism and physiology in Shostakovich's music."[29] He
goes on to compare this scene of sexual violence to the one in *Lady Macbeth* where
the workmen fondle Katerina's cook and taunt her with similar words. This is
indeed an apt comparison between two operas that on many levels are vastly

different. Bogdanov-Berezovsky overlooks the allusion to *The Marriage*, perhaps wishing to place the responsibility for this sexual content squarely on Shostakovich's shoulders. Yet, whatever "personal satisfaction" is inherent in this "dangerous tendency towards rude naturalism," Shostakovich has clearly incorporated some of the knottier twists of Gogol's own sexual labyrinth.

The most important of these twists is Kovalyov's preoccupation with marriage, an obsession that drives many of Gogol's protagonists. For Kovalyov, and most likely for Gogol, a woman's desire for marriage is more or less equivalent with the expression, as far as it is allowed in respectable society, of female sexuality. In matchmaking, female desire, always a dangerous force, allies itself with the rapacity of mothers who wish to marry their daughters off to well-placed suitors. Marriage, therefore, represents a double trap of menacing feminine appetites. In Gogol's story, Kovalyov is courting the daughter of a certain Podtochina. After his nose disappears, he decides at one point that Podtochina, hoping to force him into marriage with her daughter, has arranged for its removal by magic. He broods over this accusation for a while and, in a later scene, sends her a letter threatening legal action if his nose is not returned to its proper place. Her confused and slightly indignant reply to his incomprehensible letter convinces him that she is not responsible for his misfortune.

In the opera, Shostakovich simultaneously compressed these events into a single scene (Act III, Scene 8, no. 13) and expanded them to include not only Podtochina and Kovalyov but also Podtochina's daughter and Kovalyov's friend, Yaryzhkin, both of whom are absent in Gogol's story. Kovalyov complains to Yaryzhkin of Podtochina's treachery, and it is Yaryzhkin who suggests that he write a letter. When they send the letter to Podtochina, the stage splits to reveal the lady's apartment. Here, the daughter is telling fortunes, hoping the cards will reveal the identity of her future husband. Podtochina thinks it will be Kovalyov, but the daughter doesn't believe her. Upon receiving the letter, Podtochina scribbles a reply and sends it off. The two ladies, in a duet, proceed to read Kovalyov's absurd accusation. The duet soon expands into a quartet when Kovalyov and Yaryzhkin receive and read her reply. When the letters are finished, Podtochina's apartment disappears, and the two men agree that the lady is innocent.

Among the most notable features of this scene is the addition of Podtochina's daughter and the lines she sings. Her initial lines, concerning her fortune telling, follow almost exactly those of Agafiya Tikhonovna in *The Marriage*. This prospective bride, the daughter of a merchant, is desperately searching for a well-placed husband, preferably one from the gentry. The fortune-telling scene from *The Marriage*, which a Russian audience would recognize immediately, thus connects Podtochina's daughter with Agafiya Tikhonovna, whose fiancé, Podkolesin (Mr. Under-the-Wheels), gets cold feet ten minutes before his wedding, jumps out of a window and runs away. This fate, that is, the frustration of female sexuality as expressed through the desire to marry, is echoed by Kovalyov's ultimate decision, after his nose has been restored to its proper place, not to marry Podtochina's daughter. This marks a further "sexual" similarity with *Lady Macbeth*: the active sexual longing, and the ultimate rejection, experienced by female characters. The

speech of Podtochina's daughter, reflecting the barely repressed Agafiya Tikhonovna, might not match the explicit sexuality of Katerina's aria, but her sexual
longing is palpable.[30]

The presence of these issues—the interaction between master and servant, and
Kovalyov's preoccupation with marriage—in Shostakovich's adaptation invites several conclusions. First, the libretto forms a dialogic relationship with its source
text. Hardly a strict adaptation, the opera presents the story of Kovalyov's missing
nose in a radically new form, incorporating elements from other works of Gogol
to comment and enlarge upon its events and dialogues. Second, far from simplifying Gogol's story in order to fit it into the confining limits of a libretto, Shostakovich has complicated it, enlarging upon issues that are secondary in Gogol's text.
Finally, the introduction of music into the already complex polyphony of voices
only further complicates the opera's drama.

Source Text and Opera: Shostakovich's Gogol and Berg's Büchner

Since the premiere of *The Nose* in 1930, critics have debated the presence of
parallels between it and Alban Berg's *Wozzeck*. Inasmuch as Berg represented for
the nascent Stalinist criticism of the late 1920s a synecdoche for decadent Western
modernism, these debates also contain an ominous political subtext that precludes
any straightforward analysis of Shostakovich's remarks on the issue. For this reason, I will compare the relationships these two operas have with their source texts.
Although I will argue that parallels between the operas themselves are minimal,
such a comparison provides crucial insight into the process of adaptation and
reveals several salient aspects of Shostakovich's adaptation of Gogol's story.

Shostakovich was well aware of recent operas from Berlin, many of which
appeared in Leningrad between 1926 and 1930.[31] He saw *Wozzeck*, unarguably the
most influential of this crop, all eight or nine times it was given there. Nevertheless,
in *Testimony*, the composer's disputed memoirs, he denied that *Wozzeck* had any
direct influence on either of his operas,[32] a denial repeated in another interview from
the early 1970s: "In conversation, D.D. Shostakovich confirmed that *The Nose's* connection with *Wozzeck* is exaggerated. I will hardly err if I say that such a 'confirmation' can be understood as a full rejection by the composer of a connection between
The Nose and A. Berg's opera."[33] David Drew shares this opinion. "True, [*The Nose*]
begins with an army officer being shaved. But one shave doesn't make a *Wozzeck*,
and if Berg's opera has left any mark on the music, it is the merest nick."[34]

Despite these protestations, to which I would add the unbridgeable gulf in tone
that separates *The Nose* from *Wozzeck*, many have argued that there is indeed a
close link. Both operas concern heroes who get into trouble with the bureaucracy
and both have a similar structure: a series of short, seemingly disconnected scenes.
The first argument may be true, but it ignores the fact that both heroes suffer,
both in the source texts and in the operas, from a good deal more than bureaucracy. The second argument is superficial. *Wozzeck* is very tightly structured: each
of the three acts contains five scenes, each based in turn on a given musical form

or element. The first act introduces five characters in succession. The second, containing the main dramatic action, is structured as a "symphony," and the third presents a series of inventions, each on a single musical element.[35] *The Nose*, on the other hand, has a fairly symmetrical, circular structure. The recurring dialogue between Kovalyov and the barber serves to frame the piece, while Kovalyov's lament at the newspaper office forms the center. The other scenes radiate around this central scene of Kovalyov's discomfiture.[36] Thus, there is little thematic or structural connection between the operas.

On a different level, Carolyn Roberts Finlay sees a close connection between the two composers' attitudes towards the process of operatic adaptation:

> Berg has said that his only thought was to form "the music in such a way that it is always conscious of its duty to serve the drama," and Shostakovich echoed these sentiments: "the music in [*The Nose*] does not play a self-sufficient role. Here, the emphasis is on serving the text."[37]

This connection is certainly not unique to these two composers; it merely links them to a larger tradition, both Western and Russian, one that emphasizes the importance of operatic text vis-à-vis music. Furthermore, the comparison is misleading: Berg and Shostakovich were not claiming the same thing. Although Berg promised to serve the drama, it was not so much the text he hoped to serve, but the drama, the conflict inherent in the nearly static configuration of characters.[38] On the other hand, Shostakovich promised to focus on the language of the libretto itself.

In his approach to vocal setting, Shostakovich followed Musorgsky, who strove for a "normative recitative" that would mimic human speech.[39] Accordingly, Shostakovich wrote the vocal music of *The Nose* so that the words are, for operatic discourse, unusually audible. Unlike Musorgsky, however, Shostakovich often subverts normal speech patterns by placing stress on odd syllables and forcing singers to reach the outside limits of their ranges, usually the upper. This practice makes characters—or, as many critics would say, caricatures—such as the police sergeant or Kovalyov seem even more absurd than they already are. Alla Bretanitskaya identifies this practice as Shostakovich's exploitation of "recitative with alogical stress"—the stress in a sentence coming on the "wrong" word or syllable. She cites the barber's request for hot bread (Act I, Scene 1, no. 2). Here he sings an improbably high (and thus stressed) A-flat on the first, unstressed syllable of the word "hot" (*goryachogo*) and descends an octave and a half (to a D) for the second, stressed syllable (Example 11.1). As Bretanitskaya remarks, "The displacement of the libretto's accent often combines with the use of the 'critical point' of the singer's range."[40]

Example 11.1

To return to Berg and Shostakovich, many of the similarities and contrasts between their operas stem from similarities and contrasts in the source texts themselves. It is significant that Woyzeck (about 1837) and "The Nose" (written 1833–1834; first published 1836, final edition 1842) were written at nearly the same time, that is, eighty to ninety years before their operatic adaptations: *Wozzeck* (1917–1921; premiere in Berlin 1925) and *The Nose* (1927–1928; premiere in Leningrad 1930). That no one could conceive of an operatic version of these works until the twentieth century alone motivates a comparison.[41] Büchner's slim literary output—three short plays and a brief novel—is notable for its unsentimental sense of despair and its depiction of a frighteningly dreary and strikingly modern world. In a sense, Büchner is an interesting analogue to Gogol, who, for all his humor, often renders a similarly modern—that is, anachronistic—absurdity. Furthermore, Büchner was not fully appreciated until the beginning of the twentieth century, and though Gogol was celebrated during his lifetime, his works suffered at the hands of contemporary critics who saw in them only the "naturalism" they wanted. Like the reputations of many nineteenth-century literary figures, Gogol's image underwent a radical transformation in the twentieth century, especially in the 1920s, and it is this "revised" Gogol that Shostakovich celebrates. Gogol's works served as the source text for many nineteenth-century Russian operas, but as Emerson has remarked, "an operatic embodiment of the grotesque, surreal aspect of Gogol required a twentieth-century musical syntax and—quite possibly—the aesthetics of film."[42]

Both writers were, at least in part, concerned with the minutiae of life, the limitations of the body and its functions, and the vulgarity and inhumanity of society. Compare for instance Woyzeck's inability to refrain from urination with the mysterious disappearance of Kovalyov's nose. In Woyzeck's case, the Doctor is convinced that the muscle involved in urination is subject to the will, that is, the truly free man need not excrete any waste,[43] whereas the doctor in "The Nose" assures Kovalyov that he will be much better off if he lives without his nose than if he has it reattached. Both examples are satire, parodies of self-satisfied, arrogant but ultimately ignorant doctors. More important, however, both urination and noses, regardless of one's take on the psychological resonance of the nose, are inescapable and somehow shameful or ridiculous parts of human existence. Just as any person who urinates is not fully free, any person who has a nose is slightly absurd. Conversely, any person who does not urinate is dead, just as a person without a nose is, in Kovalyov's words, "the devil knows what."

Woyzeck's and Kovalyov's stubborn, if slightly ridiculous, affirmations of their humanity find further resonance in a second intriguing parallel between these texts. Ivan Yakovlevich, the barber, discovers Kovalyov's nose in his bread on March 25, the Feast of the Annunciation, which celebrates Gabriel's announcement to Mary that she is to give birth to the incarnation of God. It is, as Ann Shukman points out, the "supreme sublimation of sexuality."[44] More generally, however, as the celebration of one body's improbable divinity, it is the renunciation of the body's naturally human functions. Oddly enough, this particular holiday also pertains to Woyzeck, whose only knowledge of his identity comes from a piece of paper that has his name, his rank, and his birthday, the last listed as the Feast of the Annunciation.[45] This birth date is an ironic comment on the most decidedly human Woyzeck, born on such a divine day. In Gogol's story, this is the day Kovalyov chases his nose, the proof of his humanity, into the nearly empty Kazan Cathedral, where, on a high holiday, "Few worshipers were inside the church; they all stood just by the exit, near the door."[46] The reference to this holiday is absent in both operas, where the date is never mentioned. Shostakovich, however, does not fully obscure the allusion to religion. He places the scene of Kovalyov's confrontation with his nose in the cathedral. In doing so, he was following Gogol's original intention, as tsarist censorship had forced the author to move this scene to the department store *Gostinyi dvor.*[47]

As the cathedral scene (Act I, Scene 4, no. 7) begins, a choir sings a beautiful wordless hymn while the orchestra provides a gentle accompaniment. The choir becomes, in effect, an extension of the orchestra in its role as accompanist to the action and dialogue on stage. Unencumbered by text, the music amplifies the irony and pathos implicit in Kovalyov's confrontation with his nose and its setting in a cathedral. It loses, if only for the duration of the scene, the frenetic forward motion of the preceding galop, and sinks into unhurried contemplation. There is a religiosity here that, whether genuine or ironic, provides an independent counterpoint to Kovalyov's absurd demand that his nose know its proper place. The orchestra and choir, especially the soaring soprano line, repeatedly break through the preposterous dialogue and form independent voices in the polyphony. These voices play roles that are either absent in Gogol or fulfilled by the narrator. Thus, Shostakovich's cathedral scene is more elaborate than Gogol's and lends further credence to the contention that opera, rather than simplifying its source texts, tends to complicate them.

Opera and Performance: Shostakovich's Orchestra

If in Shostakovich's cathedral scene the orchestra and choir have distinct musical voices that take on the function of a verbal narrator, then one can posit that the opera is in fact a sort of narrative. In a sense, this is true of any opera. Gary Schmidgall has observed that in *Wozzeck*, the music "does not 'parallel' the text but develops apart from the vocal line and leads an expressive life of its own while never departing from the dramatic action. Berg's music inhabits and makes us constantly aware of the language within Büchner's language."[48] If Berg's music indeed reveals a second layer of language in Büchner's drama, he has in essence added a narrator; in the change of medium—drama to opera, or more generally, text to music—he has transformed the drama into a sort of narrative.

"The Nose," however, is already a narrative. Gogol's narrator does his best to maintain a straightforward narration, but he is overwhelmed by his absurdly complicated story and breaks off inexplicably at crucial moments. Although he is clearly not in control of his story and often loses control of his telling, the narrator

is a salient feature of Gogol's text. "The Nose," therefore, does not require a transformation from drama to narrative to accompany the transition from text to
music. Rather, Shostakovich shifted the narrator's duties from Gogol's verbal text
to his musical one, inevitably altering them in the process. However, in his explanation of the connection between Gogol's narration and his score, he failed to distinguish between Gogol and the narrator of "The Nose":

> The music in this spectacle does not play a self-sufficient role. Here the emphasis is
> on its service to the text. I will add that the music does not carry an intentionally
> "parodistic" coloring. Despite the comedy of the events on stage, the music is not
> comic. I consider this correct, since Gogol relates all comic events in a serious tone.
> In this lies the strength and merit of Gogol's humor. He is not "witty." The music
> also tries not to be "witty."[49]

As with much of Shostakovich's auto-commentary, these remarks seem either woe-
fully uninsightful or willfully obfuscating.[50] The score is in fact full of musical jokes
and witty sound effects; it is indeed as comic as the events on stage. Besides this, it
asserts its own reading of the events and has an independent voice in the dialogue of
the opera. This assured operatic narrator is quite distinct from Gogol's touchingly
confused storyteller. And despite the music's interdependence with the text, it functions much like music in other operas. As Joseph Kerman puts it,

> Music, with its special unifying capacities, can, first of all, assert a unique mood over
> an entire train of action, can as it were define a field in which a certain range of
> action and cognate feeling, and only that range, is possible.... Second, music can
> indeed "advance an action" in the sense of interpreting action or conveying the char-
> acter's apprehension of it.[51]

Although an opera's music includes both the orchestra's accompaniment and the
characters' singing, I wish to emphasize here the role of the orchestra. Insofar as the
orchestra in *The Nose* fulfills the functions Kerman enumerates—setting the mood and
advancing the action—I want to suggest that it adds another voice to the dialogue on
the stage. In the absence of verbal narration, the orchestra takes on a certain narrative
function.[52] It is not just accompaniment to the sung and spoken texts, but also the filter, no more objective than a verbal narrator, through which the audience perceives the
events and dialogue of the opera. (Compare, for instance, Wagner's idea that the role
of the chorus in Greek tragedy was transferred to the orchestra in opera.[53])

An example of the orchestra's independent narrative voice occurs in Act I. In
the opening scene, the barber's wife, disgusted by the severed nose in her husband's bread, ejects him from their house and threatens to denounce him to the
authorities. Frightened, the barber envisions a police sergeant looming menacingly
in front of him. The orchestra responds to this specter with a triumphant polonaise. Galina Grigoryeva has identified this tune as a parodic deformation of
"Resound, Thunder of Victory," an eighteenth-century polonaise that Tchaikovsky
used in *The Queen of Spades* to accompany Catherine the Great's entrance at a

ball.[54] The barber associates the image of the sergeant with the trappings of power, expressed here, parodically, by the music of royalty; the orchestra employs a musical equivalent of free, indirect discourse, conveying the barber's thoughts and emotions without the addition of text.

In the following scene, Ivan runs along an embankment and tosses the nose into a canal. The sergeant appears and, in an extremely high tenor accompanied by frenetic tremolo from a battery of domras (a sister to the balalaika), demands that the agitated barber account for himself. Both the balalaika accompaniment and the high tenor line comment ironically on the sergeant's self-importance. His ridiculous voice strikes the audience as absurd just as it strikes fear in Ivan Yakovlevich, while the orchestra's accompaniment identifies him with the domra, clearly marking him as a native Russian and an unsophisticated boor. The orchestra's presentation of the sergeant contrasts with, and indeed contradicts, Ivan Yakovlevich's apprehension of him. This disparity in associations vividly demonstrates the narrating function of the orchestra. The barber associates the police sergeant with power, and the orchestra conveys this association with an operatic form of free indirect discourse. When the police sergeant appears in person, however, the orchestra-narrator conveys its own opinion and exposes him as the self-important buffoon he is.[55]

Beyond exploiting the orchestra's independent narrative voice, Shostakovich further expanded the orchestra's role with the entr'actes, giving them a weight and significance equal to that of the characters' music. In the course of a fairly short opera—approximately an hour and three-quarters—the orchestra plays extended passages by itself on at least seven occasions.[56] There are also two mass crowd scenes (Act III, Scene 7, no. 12 and Act III, Intermezzo, no. 14) at the climax of which human voices are reduced to rhythmic ostinati, in essence an extension of the orchestra.

Short passages for solo or small groups of instruments dominate the score; one solo or group passage follows hard upon the previous one, as if in heated conversation. This practice follows the vocal writing; as the Soviet musicologist Valentina Rubtsova has pointed out, the libretto almost entirely excludes long monologues in favor of "more or less extended rejoinders."[57] The orchestration, again following the vocal writing, tends to favor registral extremity. Piccolo and bass clarinet, for instance, receive a lot of attention. These observations lead to a paradox: if the role of the orchestra is increased, given the frequency of its "solo" role in entr'actes, it is simultaneously decreased, at least in the traditional sense, with the relatively infrequent appearance of full ensemble writing.

To place Shostakovich's use of his orchestra in context, I should note that the operatic orchestra is rarely allowed a self-sufficient role. W. H. Auden, who as well as anyone can serve as the spokesman for the conventions of the "golden age" of opera, provides a useful—if perhaps excessively categorical—definition of the orchestra's role:

In opera the orchestra is addressed to the singers, not to the audience. An opera-lover will put up with and even enjoy an orchestral interlude on the condition that he knows the singers cannot sing just now because they are tired or the scene-shifters are at work, but any use of the orchestra by itself which is not filling in time is, for him, wasting it.[58]

Seen this way, orchestral music in opera plays an obscuring, dilatory role, and, much like film music, is unsuccessful if it calls too much attention to itself. For Auden, then, *The Nose*, with its frequent orchestral interpolations, would not be a very satisfying opera. Yet, these orchestral sections are not merely to cover scene shifts or resting singers. Shostakovich's frequent entr'actes provide an opportunity for pantomime. An example is Ivan Yakovlevich's mad dash along the embankment and the ensuing percussion interlude (Act I, Scene 2, no. 3 and entr'acte, no. 4). The barber runs out onto the embankment, hoping to toss the severed nose into the canal. His flight is accompanied by the constant beat of the bass drum and an ever-expanding canon for strings. At its culmination, this canon consists of fifteen separate voices, "ultrapolyphony" comparable to that in Shostakovich's contemporaneous Second Symphony. Larisa Bubennikova observes that "the gloomy theme of the canon, growing voice by voice, engenders the effect of increasing tension and accompanies the scene of Ivan Yakovlevich's mad flight."[59] This cancerous polyphony acts on a narrative level as another example of free, indirect discourse that conveys the barber's state of mind without text. This device is foreign to opera as Auden conceives it, where Ivan's emotions would emerge in an aria, and the orchestra would play a supporting role, accompanying and commenting upon the singer's music and words. By contrast, *The Nose* here relies entirely upon the orchestra to convey Ivan's increasing obsession with the nose.[60]

After Ivan's ill-fated interview with the police sergeant, the orchestra launches into an innovative entr'acte scored for nine unpitched percussion instruments. On a recording, it quickly grows tiresome, yet this entr'acte is not simply a display of rhythmic inventiveness. Shostakovich, exploiting after Meyerhold and others the theatrical technique of pantomime, combined this clamorous interlude with a chase scene reminiscent of, if not borrowed from, the new art of cinema. In Bubennikova's distillation, the events that the percussion entr'acte accompanies are as follows:

> On one of the many bridges in St. Petersburg the police sergeant and Ivan Yakovlevich freeze facing one another. The only audible sound is the barber's heavy heartbeat, represented by the bass drum. In a burst of despair the unfortunate [barber] with one motion tosses the sergeant into the water. The latter, floundering, piercingly blows his police whistle; ten hearty policemen appear. They save their captain and set off in pursuit of the fleeing Ivan Yakovlevich.... Under the clamor and crash of the drums the policemen follow the barber at a jog and catch up with him. With this the vision cuts off. Everything vanishes in absolute darkness.[61]

As Bubennikova observes, the pantomime deepens the scene's theatrical potential, allowing the economical exposition of plot material. (This action is absent in Gogol's story, where a mist envelops the police inspector and the hapless barber immediately after their interview.) The scene also highlights the orchestra's, or rather, a small ensemble's equal role alongside the words, music, and action of the characters on stage. The percussive effects interact closely with the events on stage—the beating heart, the running cops, warning shots—and the whole scene resembles a silent movie.[62] This cinematic aesthetic runs throughout the opera, and it is interesting to note Shostakovich's former experience as a pianist for silent movies—one can imagine similarities between this percussion interlude, as an accompaniment for pantomime, and Shostakovich's notoriously quirky accompaniments to motion pictures.

The other orchestral entr'actes play a similar role. Both Kovalyov and the police sergeant spend a fair amount of time on stage not singing, but in pantomime accompanied by the orchestra. The music may convey their excitement, as in their respective galops (for Kovalyov, Act I, Galop, no. 6; for the police sergeant, Act III, Scene 7, no. 12), or it may convey Kovalyov's contemplation of his missing nose, as in the entr'acte after his visit to the newspaper office (Act II, entr'acte, no. 10). Regardless, the orchestra in these scenes has unusual narrative independence. Similarly, the crowd scenes in the posting inn and on the streets of Petersburg (Act III, Scene 7, no. 12 and Intermezzo, no. 14) resemble at their apogee a sort of pantomime with voices. As noted above, the voices here blend into the texture of the orchestra, functioning, as it were, as an extension of Shostakovich's percussion or string sections. Here, as in the percussion interlude, the staging is highly cinematic, a series of "quick-cut" vignettes that introduce a character or group of characters for a moment before moving on to the next. This technique transposes to the operatic stage Gogol's manner of presenting crowd scenes as a series of quickly sketched and loosely connected verbal portraits. By exploiting techniques and concepts borrowed from Meyerhold's theater, the new art of cinema, and Asafyev's theory of symphonized theater, Shostakovich created an orchestral narrator with a radically independent voice.

The preceding discussion suggests that *The Nose*, as a twentieth-century extrapolation of operatic form, tends, in Lindenberger's phrase, "to swallow up other genres."[63] In it are literary elements of drama and narrative, performative elements such as pantomime and film, and musical elements of symphony (i.e., Brentanitskaya's detection of the opera's "sonata form" and as well as Asafyev's notion of a "theatrical symphony"), highly atrophied chamber music, as well as more traditional operatic styles. Ultimately the work emerges as a hybrid genre, in its mixing not only of text, music, and theater but also of genres specific to all three. In this sense it exemplifies the array of tensions—between text and music, drama and narrative, theatricality and musicality—that characterizes opera as an art.

The Lady Macbeth of the Mtsensk District

In 1944, Boris Asafyev described the second decade of the twentieth century as marking the end of the "heroic period" of Russian opera. Singling out Rimsky-Korsakov's final opera, *Le coq d'or* (1906-1907, premiere 1909) as the first indication of this decline, he remarked that its "sarcasm … is notable because even romantic love, the usual stimulus of operatic action, undergoes ironic debunking." This downgrading of the romantic love that, according to Asafyev, had provided Russian composers with a source of human emotion, fidelity, and lyricism that they could shape into "images of self-sacrifice (*samopozhertvovaniye*) and even tragic self-renunciation (*samootrecheniye*)" represented a crisis in Russian opera, a crisis that reached its nadir with Shostakovich's "musical theater without ethics: *The Nose* and *Lady Macbeth*." For Asafyev, the status of romantic love is connected to the status of women, to the frequency of "beautiful images of selfless (*samootverzhennye*) women and maidens in Russian opera." Conversely, a female character who values her self (*samo*) would signal a decline in the ethics of Russian opera, presumably because such a character would act according to her own, inevitably lustful, desires rather than subordinate them to her lover's heroic quest. Tracing the development of Russian opera from Rimsky-Korsakov to Shostakovich, Asafyev sees "the transformation of the Russian woman's feelings of love into sensual poison," a transformation that finds its culmination in the character of Katerina Izmailova.[64]

Eight years earlier, Asafyev had written another article about *Lady Macbeth*, this one in the aftermath of the attacks in *Pravda*. Here, he had detected "an indubitable attempt … to overcome the nightmare of the past in the creation of a new image of woman," an attempt that failed, says Asafyev, because "overcoming the nightmare of violence by means of a naturalistic display of violence is a method foreign to Soviet artistic creation."[65] Anyone familiar with Soviet literature of the 1920s would dismiss this notion, but Asafyev's identification of a "new image of woman" in opera, a woman who would choose violence over meekness, selfishness over self-sacrifice, and revenge over "tragic self-renunciation" is compelling, even if Asafyev himself might not wish to connect his two readings. More recently, Lev Anninsky has made a similar point: "In place of a woman who suffers her passions patiently, poeticized by the century-long development of Russian opera, [*Lady Macbeth*] brings to the foreground a rebellious and willful nature."[66] Solomon Volkov went further, proclaiming the opera "a feminist apotheosis" and speculating that its "strongly feminist statement" was among the reasons for *Pravda's* denunciation.[67] The character of Katerina represents a refreshing shift from the parade of female victims that opera tends to present.[68] Even the sexually dangerous Carmen and the warrior Brünnhilde eventually succumb to some form of masculine violence. But Katerina never gives in, murdering the men who threaten her, choosing her own lover, and punishing his desertion by means of another murder and suicide. In the following pages, I will consider to what degree Katerina represents a "new" or even feminist portrait, arguing that she shares characteristics with traditional Russian heroines, the New Soviet Woman, and even femmes fatales more familiar to consumers of American pulp fiction and film noir.

The prototype for this "new image of woman" emerged from the pen of Nikolai Leskov, who in 1864, the year he wrote his novella *The Lady Macbeth of the Mtsensk District*, was particularly concerned with the women's liberation movement in Russia. He conceived of the story as the first in a series of twelve "sketches of typical characters, female only, of our locality."[69] Although one might question whether a multiple murderer is truly a "typical character," Leskov does attempt to ground the story in a recognizable reality: the merchant milieu of rural Russia. Leskov held the view that dramatic and even tragic conflict exists even in the unpoetic world of Russia's peasants and merchants.[70] To demonstrate this, he dubbed Katerina L'vovna a "Lady Macbeth," and attempted to raise her squalid story to the level of tragedy. The focus on the merchant class invites comparison with Alexander Ostrovsky's play, *The Storm* (*Groza*), in which another Katerina has an adulterous affair and commits suicide, although not murder.

Like Leskov, Shostakovich conceived of his *Lady Macbeth* as part of a series of works about Russian women.[71] Although he saw Leskov's story as "a most truthful and tragic portrait of the fate of a talented, clever, and exceptional woman perishing in the nightmarish conditions of prerevolutionary Russia,"[72] he also declared "Leskov was unable to interpret correctly the events taking place in his story. My role as a Soviet composer consists in retaining the power of Leskov's narrative while using a critical approach to explain these events from our Soviet point of view."[73] This "Soviet point of view" is paraphrased by Anninsky: "In his story, Leskov drags out the old morality and judges like a humanist; the eyes and ears of a Soviet composer were required to do what Leskov was unable to: to see beyond the external crimes of the heroine and to show the true murderer—the autocratic regime."[74]

Whatever the sincerity of Shostakovich's remarks, he did make significant changes to the story in order to soften Katerina: her father-in-law actively torments her, even before her affair with the steward, Sergei; she initiates her husband's murder but does not strike the fatal blow; and, most important, she does not murder a child, which in Leskov's story leads to her capture and punishment. (As Shostakovich noted somewhat impishly, "The killing of a child, however it might be explained, always creates a negative impression."[75]) And it is Katerina alone who expresses remorse. As for the victims of her violence, they are made to seem even less redeemable than she is. Shostakovich recasts the story in a strongly satirical vein, reserving any lyric pathos for the "talented, clever, and exceptional" heroine, rendering her the only human character amid the expressionistic caricatures that surround her.

Of course, the glorification of a murderer who claims for herself the role of victim should elicit at least some degree of ethical queasiness. Richard Taruskin argues that the opera's justification of Katerina is morally equivalent to a justification of the terror and class-based murder that characterized Stalin's regime. As an apotheosis of Stalinist oppression played out in joyless, violent sex and brutal murder, Shostakovich's opera deserved (and deserves) in Taruskin's view to be suppressed, if not for the reasons enumerated in the famous *Pravda* article.[76] Yet, ironically, although murder and suicide are still often presented—or even celebrated—as a woman's only recourse amid the violence of a patriarchal world (compare the 1991 film *Thelma and Louise*), such a renunciation of life seems only to reinstate the victimization that opera has always purveyed, undercutting the image of a powerful heroine.

Lady Macbeth's unresolved tension between powerful heroine and oppressed victim has prompted a varied response. *Pravda* famously denounced the opera's "Muddle Instead of Music," specifically condemning its sexual content: "The music quacks, grunts, and growls … in order to express the amatory scenes as naturalistically as possible. And "love" is smeared all over the opera in this vulgar manner. The merchant's double bed occupies the central position on the stage. On it all problems are solved."[77] The bed may indeed have dominated the stage in the production that Stalin saw, but it is clearly an exaggeration to call it the solution to all problems, given that only two of the nine scenes take place in Katerina's bedroom. However, taking this exaggeration as a productive misreading does at least point to the pervasive atmosphere of sexual violence (rather than sex itself) in the opera.

Taruskin compares the Katerinas of Leskov and Shostakovich with the heroine of Ostrovsky's *The Storm*. He notes, as have several commentators before him, that Shostakovich overlaid elements of *The Storm* onto his opera, most notably the scene, absent in Leskov's novella, in which Zinovy says farewell to his wife and Boris extracts from her an oath to be faithful. Leskov himself was aware of the connection between the two Katerinas, and conceived of his at least in part as a polemic against the notion of an almost saintly merchant woman who, saddled with an ineffectual husband and tortured by her oppressive mother-in-law, kills herself after she breaks that vow of fidelity.[78] Shostakovich's theatrical adaptation of Leskov, then, inevitably drags *The Storm* along as a built-in subtext. And as Anninsky demonstrates, Ostrovsky's Katerina nearly always overshadows Leskov's darker portrait. Recounting his reaction to Andrei Goncharov's late 1970s theatrical adaptation of Leskov's story at Moscow's Mayakovsky Theater, in which Sergei murdered the child and Katerina crossed herself between killing Sonyetka and committing suicide, Anninsky concludes: "Alas, I thought, a Russian person can not bear the thought of a criminal female soul … [we need to] save our last spiritual stronghold: the radiant, loving, guiltless and priceless female soul."[79] In Anninsky's reading, Shostakovich is not providing a feminist revaluation of Katerina so much as he is beginning the process of reintegrating her into the traditional pantheon of Russian heroines.[80]

As Hugh MacLean argues, however, even Leskov's Katerina evokes sympathy from the reader. Her situation really is oppressive, and her two victims were "obstacles" to her love with Sergei: "the story evokes … powerful, presocial emotions, forcing us not only to condone but vicariously to share in two murders."[81] The reader feels the same attraction to, even identification with, Katerina and Sergei as one does with the adulterous and murderous couples in novels such as James Cain's *The Postman Always Rings Twice* (1934) or *Double Indemnity* (1936), both of which were adapted into movies. Yet, we cease to identify with Leskov's Katerina when she, pregnant with Sergei's child, murders her young nephew with her firm bosom, upending the notion of maternal behavior by using the source of sustenance as a murder weapon. (In another interesting connection to *Double Indemnity*, the femme fatale in Cain's novel, Phyllis, is revealed at the end to be a serial killer of children. And, like Shostakovich, Billy Wilder in his film adaptation of *Double Indemnity* drops all reference to Phyllis' murder of children, even if he is not particularly interested in rehabilitating her.) But even if Shostakovich has whitewashed his heroine and we are willing to understand this whitewashing less as an ideological justification of murder (Taruskin) than a chivalrous (or quasi-feminist) reassignment of blame (Anninsky), the opera suffers from the same type of contradiction as Leskov's story. By constructing inhumanly oppressive surroundings for their heroines, both force her to assert her humanity, her desire for freedom and love, by means of adultery and then murder—two crimes that in popular consciousness are inextricably linked (think of Vronsky standing over Anna Karenina after their sexual encounter the way a murderer stands over his victim) and that point, ultimately, to their perpetrator's loss of humanity. As a product of her environment, Katerina is ultimately deprived of her own personality, reduced to the sum of the social pathology around her.

A comparison of Shostakovich and Alexander Preis' libretto with Leskov's story will demonstrate that in the first two acts, Shostakovich's heroine, at both a textual and musical level, is a stronger character than Leskov's even as her situation is more pathetic. Her plight is so unbearable that it becomes, in Shostakovich's interpretation, a more understandable spur to her criminal actions. In the third act, Katerina largely disappears, only to reappear in the fourth as a more conventionally tragic operatic heroine. These distinctions follow from what Anninsky calls Shostakovich's "ethical conception" of the opera and control the changes inherent in the process of transforming a story into an opera. Opera, as a staged narrative, sung rather than spoken, slows down the progress of the adapted plot and makes external (at least to the audience) the internal thoughts and emotions of the characters. Opera requires the librettist adapting an existing text both to compress and to expand. By compression, I mean the reduction of expository material, the tightening of dialogue, and the omission of characters and plot points that do not "fit," whether due to time constraints—it takes a lot longer to sing than to speak—or to ideological conception. And by expansion I mean the invention of new characters and plot points consistent with the composer's and librettist's view of the work (for example, *The Nose*'s importation of material from other sources), and the production of text for arias through which the characters can reveal themselves. According to Dahlhaus, arias are what most distinguish opera from drama (or in the case of *Lady Macbeth*, from the source text), specifically by suspending the forward movement of the plot, which in traditional opera is carried by recitative. Arias take opera outside temporality.[82]

In *Lady Macbeth*, we can take this idea even further by noting, as does Emerson, that Leskov's story achieves its terrifying effect precisely because of the detachment of the narration: except for the stylized dream sequences, we never see inside Katerina's head, are never privy to her thoughts.[83] In the shift to opera, however, Katerina must open up and reveal herself to the audience. The operatic Katerina is inevitably more human than her prototype, since by providing her with lyrical arias, Shostakovich provides us with a window into her internal life. In her first aria, for example, the beautiful, aching music about her boredom and depression gives way to slightly discordant, even angry tones as she identifies herself as the wife of Zinovy Izmailov. The music rises in volume and pitch to a climax on his last name, after which she relaxes back into a folk-inflected contemplation of the activity around her.

Shostakovich, however, has not allowed us such access to the interior lives of any of the other characters, who remain expressionistic caricatures. As Geoffrey Norris points out, "When lyrical music is allotted to other characters, it is tinged with insincerity,"[84] and as Taruskin has stated, Shostakovich "accompan[ies] the singing ... and the movements of all figures except Katerina with trudging or galoping ostinatos—inflexible rigorous rhythmic pulsations that characterize them one and all as soulless, insensate automatons, comic-book creatures, incapable of experiencing or inspiring an emotional response of any kind.... It is sheer dehumanization."[85] Taruskin's tendentiousness aside, this contrast of treatment becomes apparent immediately after Katerina's first aria, when Boris enters looking for mushrooms. The relaxed flow of Katerina's music gives way to an ominous pulse of the bass drum and low strings. The solo bassoon bounces along almost comically, recalling the much faster music accompanying the barber Ivan Yakovlevich's trip across Petersburg in *The Nose*. Boris' singing never gains the dignity of melody, just as his emotional range is limited to hunger and his abiding anger at Katerina. By concentrating all the lyric pathos in Katerina, the opera explicitly separates her from the world around her, rendering her music "an aria from a different opera," as the Russian idiom goes. Recalling Dahlhaus' point about the distinctive temporality of aria, it emerges that Katerina alone is outside time, that in slowing down the opera's otherwise frenetic pace, she struggles against the forward progress of the plot. We can see this struggle throughout the opera and the story: in her boredom she hearkens back to her youthful days of freedom; she murders Boris and Zinovy—representatives of the repressive patriarchal and temporal order—to prolong her affair with Sergei; and she commits her final murder-suicide to reverse Sergei's hostile boredom and abandonment. Interestingly enough, this temporal displacement has an explicit role in the source text, where Leskov contrasts Katerina and Sergei's pastoral idyll under an apple tree with Zinovy's enormous silver watch, ticking ominously as it hangs from the marital bed.

Katerina's disconnection from the world surrounding her, however, goes beyond this strictly musical dimension of temporality. The operatic Katerina lives in a world of sexualized violence that is largely muted in Leskov's story. Shostakovich intensifies the dangerous interplay of female sexuality and male impotence, and presents all sexual relationships as the product or cause of violence. Like a femme fatale in a 1930s film noir, Katerina, with her monstrous sexuality and penchant for murder, signals the instability of the culture that produced her: male fears of sexual and political overthrow.[86] What is more, Shostakovich overlays Katerina's character with elements of a quasi-feminist revolt against male tyranny. In the end, this sympathetic portrait of a female criminal suggests a relevance to debates about the role of women in Soviet society in the late 1920s and early 1930s.

In both story and opera, the set up is similar. Katerina is a merchant's wife, childless and bored, who regrets her decision to marry. Her father-in-law Boris and her husband Zinovy constantly reproach her for not providing an heir. In Leskov, these reproaches derive from understandable emotions. "Childlessness distressed Zinovy Borisich very much … and greatly saddened the old man Boris Timofeyich and even Katerina L'vovna herself."[87] The reproaches are presented as a fact of life, outside of any specific context. We never see her respond to them, so they become another reminder of her unenviable position, "the unrelieved monotony of the merchant's tall house, with its high fence and loose watchdogs."[88] In contrast, the opera necessarily has Boris utter these reproaches on stage, but gives him no mitigating emotions—his deepest sadness is connected to the lack of any heir to their accumulated capital. What is more, Katerina responds to him, and her response immediately puts sex, or more precisely impotence, at center stage: "Zinovy is unable to put a child in my womb."[89] Boris' rejoinder is even more explicitly sexual, as he insists that her failure to get pregnant is her fault because she is a "cold fish," but that at the same time, she would like to have an affair in order to mock her husband. In this operatic context, the high fences and watchdogs, which in Leskov merely signified boredom, now become precautions against Katerina's paradoxical and dangerous sexuality.

Boris further displays his obsession with adultery later in Scene 1, when it comes time for Zinovy to depart on business. In an episode that Shostakovich imported from Ostrovsky's *The Storm*, Katerina's father-in-law forces her to make an oath to remain faithful to her husband. The music and the libretto emphasize Zinovy's weakness.[90] He calls his father "papa," lets Boris bully him and his wife, and speaks to Katerina through his father. Zinovy's farewell to Katerina sweeps upwards with apparent passion but is so brief as to be ridiculous. What is more, he immediately undercuts it by asking his father to ensure her continued obedience. This Boris does by insisting she vow her fidelity, his abrupt shouts of "An oath!" echoed by a grunting trombone that prefigures that instrument's famous "pornophonic" glissandi that accompany Sergei's climax in Scene 3. The presence of this sexualized trombone suggests that Boris' obsession with Katerina's inevitable infidelity stems from his own unsavory desire for her, which he expresses explicitly in Scene 4, just before he discovers that Sergei has beaten him to it. Here, his description of Katerina as "hot-blooded"[91] contradicts his remark in Scene 1 that she is "as cold as a fish."[92]

Following the trombone thrusts, Boris temporarily turns his attention away from Katerina. In the ensuing conversation between father and son, an ironic lyricism pervades as Boris, butchering some random French phrases ("S'il vous plaît, rendez vous. Sauce provençale …"), gently reminds Zinovy that young wives tend to stray. His remark that "Young wives are all the same" appears to be nothing more than a standard put-down of women, made by a coarse and ignorant man.[93] But as Alla Bogdanova points out, this line is a reference to Anton Chekhov's story "In the Post Office."[94] And so, armed with a Chekhov quotation and some butchered French, Boris would appear to be making reference to Katerina's "European" standards of behavior, behavior that he might even interpret as "operatic" or "literary." But since Boris' reference to Chekhov is anachronistic and his personality would seem to rule out reading novels or going to the theater, it is the opera itself, rather than the character of Boris, which explicitly sets up the expectation that Katerina will indeed behave like an operatic or literary heroine, even if she herself is illiterate.[95]

This father-son interlude comes to an abrupt halt with Boris' renewed demand, sung harshly and without accompaniment, that Katerina take the oath. Like its prototype in *The Storm*, the episode establishes adultery and betrayal as a main theme of the opera. Shostakovich departs from *The Storm*, however, in that Ostrovsky's Katerina has just admitted her illicit infatuation to her sister-in-law, who subsequently does everything she can to put the two lovers together. This Katerina is aware of her vulnerability and insists that her husband accept her oath; that he will not in essence seals her tragic fate. However, for Shostakovich's Katerina, the oath seems to set the opera's plot in motion, even to suggest to her the possibility of adultery and other such "literary" behavior.

Katerina's "literary" qualities and Zinovy's impotence again arise towards the end of Scene 5, in the argument that leads up to the second murder. The text draws on Leskov's original, where, in Chapter 7, Zinovy returns from his trip to confront Katerina about the rumors he has heard about her affair. The libretto, however, adds new elements to their characterization. Katerina and Zinovy's discussion begins as a dialogue, but as it reaches its climax, Shostakovich exploits the possibility of two voices singing at once, straining for dominance. Katerina sings:

> I don't like it when people speak insolently to me. Explain to me which "amours" you're talking about? You know absolutely nothing and I know everything. I will not allow you or anyone else to speak to me about my "amours." You have no right to judge me, Don't touch me, you disgusting, pathetic man, I can't even call you a husband. You're simply a stump, a blockhead, feeble, weak, like a cold fish. You disgust me, you pathetic tradesman.[96]

Zinovy responds:

> Look here, Katerina, you've become awfully (*bol'no*; lit. painfully) voluble; you speak as though you were writing; What is this? Why do you have such impudent manners? … Just you wait, Katerina, I will find out everything and punish you, I will whip you cruelly, painfully (*bol'no*), painfully, painfully, painfully, painfully. I am your husband before God and the Tsar. I am responsible for the honor of my family. Tell me the truth![97]

Katerina's rejection of Zinovy's insolent talk does not occur in Leskov. Nor do her insults, which recall Boris' reproaches of her ("cold fish") in Scene 1 and suggest that his behavior has rubbed off on her—now that she is in a dominant position, she intends to make the most of it. In the story, Katerina registers this shift in her attitude towards her husband by saying "Your Katerina Lvovna isn't very (*bol'no*) frightened," which is enough for Zinovy to respond, "Somehow you've become awfully (*bol'no*) voluble here."[98] This phrase, "bol'no rechista stala" ("have become awfully voluble"), is one of the opera's few direct borrowings from the source text, and Shostakovich, perhaps picking up on the way Zinovy echoes Katerina's use of the epithet *bol'no*, has him echo it compulsively in his threat to beat her. This threat is also absent in Leskov, but provides another interesting parallel to Ostrovsky, where the weak, cuckolded husband, Tikhon, whose name derives from the word for "quiet," tells an acquaintance that, "True, I did give her a little whipping [after Katerina confessed her adultery to him], but only because mama made me."[99] Also absent in Leskov is the reference to the literary quality of Katerina's speech, and Zinovy's invocation of God and Tsar as the source of his power over her—in the story he states only that "No one has taken away my power over you and no one can take it away."[100] Taken together, these changes again point to a more oppressive and violent atmosphere in Katerina's world, in which both divine and secular powers conspire to defeat her. They also suggest a more self-consciously feminist Katerina, who has come to reject the judgment of society and the authority of her husband. The newly literary aspect of this diatribe suggests a social consciousness that one would not expect in an illiterate merchant's wife, and her rejection of her impotent husband becomes a rebellion against the church and autocracy. The simple-minded protagonist of a horror story has found herself in the center of a feminist revolt.

Katerina's feminist consciousness, if we can call it that, emerges most explicitly in Scene 2 (corresponding to the second chapter of Leskov's tale), where she encounters a group of workers harassing the cook Aksinya. In both works, the scene shows the atmosphere of the Izmailov work yard and gives Katerina and Sergei an opportunity to become acquainted. In Leskov, the tone is light: it is a "sunny and brisk" day and Katerina is attracted by the sound of "such merry laughter in the gallery."[101] The workers are teasing Aksinya by weighing her, and although she is fighting back, her "cursing is mostly in jest." Katerina responds in a "humorous tone of voice," asking the workers to weigh her too. She vaunts her strength and accepts Sergei's challenge to arm-wrestle. He hurts her by pressing on her ring, so she pushes him away. He ups the ante by offering to wrestle. Before she can react, he embraces her and "seats her gently on an overturned barrel."[102] The chapter ends with Aksinya telling Katerina about Sergei's bad reputation.

Although Shostakovich and Preis retained the basic elements of this scene, they altered the tone radically and added elements that change Katerina's characterization. It is one of the most frenetic scenes in an opera full of frenetic scenes, beginning with the cook's insistent shrieks and galloping, percussion-heavy music, Instead of weighing the cook, the workers are pinching and fondling her. Each of her assailants sings about—and pinches—a different body part: her breasts, her nose, her leg, her arms, her face. She protests throughout her ordeal, screaming ("It hurts! Keep your hands off, you shameless devil, hands off!")[103] and fighting back, especially with Sergei, who is her chief tormenter. In the end, she complains, "My breast is covered with bruises! ... He's torn my skirt to pieces."[104] As he has throughout the opera, Shostakovich has intensified and made explicit the current of sexual violence that the story merely hints at. And by putting Sergei in the center of the scene with Aksinya, the opera makes amply clear that his treatment of women is in no way preferable to that of Boris and Zinovy.

The operatic Sergei further indulges his violence towards women in his wrestling match with Katerina. As in the story, Sergei squeezes Katerina's ring into her hand, hurting her and prompting her to push him away. The opera, however, intensifies the moment by having him suggest that her wedding ring, and by extension her marriage, is suffocating her. He is undoubtedly correct, but Katerina's response, "It hurts! Let go!" (*Bol'no! Pusti!*),[105] recalls Aksinya's screeching and links the two women as victims of Sergei's violence. Finally, Sergei and Katerina's wrestling match ends not with a stolen embrace and a gentle release, but with a violent tumble on the ground, where the vigilant Boris discovers the future lovers. By emphasizing the misery of Katerina's marriage, which includes Boris' harassment, and presenting the violent Sergei as her only alternative, the opera paints a much starker picture than the story of Katerina's unendurable predicament.

The most conspicuous addition to this scene, however, is Katerina's vehement response to Sergei's violence against Aksinya. When Katerina enters, the music comes to an abrupt halt as she orders Sergei to release the cook:

KATERINA: So you enjoy mocking a woman?
SERGEI: Who else can we make fun of?
KATERINA: So a woman's only there for you to make fun of, is she?
SERGEI: What other reason is there?
…

KATERINA: You men certainly think a lot of yourselves; do you think you're the only ones who are strong and brave, the only ones with any wisdom? Haven't you heard about the times when women kept the whole family from starving? And how in wartime women gave the enemy a beating? There have been times when women sacrificed their lives for their husbands or sweethearts. But this means nothing to you. Well, I'll give you a good thrashing to show you what a woman's good for.[106]

Just as Zinovy wonders at Katerina's new rhetorical skills, audiences may well ask where an illiterate merchant's wife would have learned this feminist ideology and the calm assurance to deliver it to a group of workers. Marina Tcherkashina holds that this arioso "glorifies a selflessness of which a woman so much despised in her life is nevertheless capable,"[107] thus re-inscribing Katerina into the roster of traditionally selfless Russian heroines. It is not clear, however, why a woman with such an exalted notion of feminine valor would descend to adultery and murder. I would venture to suggest that just as Shostakovich added elements of Ostrovsky's Katerina to Leskov's, here he has included echoes of several varieties of Russian feminism. As Emerson has noted, Shostakovich picks up on the traditional Russian theme of a woman's lot, including such models as the Decembrist wives.[108] These women, who followed their exiled husbands to Siberia after the Decembrist revolt in 1825, might be what Katerina has in mind when she invokes women who "sacrifice their lives for their husbands." The image of women giving "the enemy a beating," however, suggests the Russian Civil War, in which women did have an active role in the Red Army.[109] And her threat to give Sergei a "good thrashing" certainly does not accord with the meek creature who usually endures a woman's lot. On the contrary, it recalls the often violent battle of the sexes found in Fyodor Gladkov's *Cement* (1925). Gladkov's novel was the source of the literary prototype of the New Soviet Woman, Dasha Chumalova, who transformed herself from a docile wife and mother into a model communist: independent, sexually liberated, and never without her red headscarf. Katerina is not in the same category, to be sure, but her own sexual assertiveness does present a similar challenge to the sexually violent, male-dominated world around her. In the context of the early 1930s, when the model image of Soviet women was shifting from the openly feminist New Soviet Woman back to the more traditional wife and mother, Katerina's revolt, even if nominally against a representative of the old order, could be threatening enough to warrant banishment.

The Katerina discussed thus far is that of the opera's first two acts, which end with her triumphant announcement to Sergei that he is now her husband. As her triumph disintegrates, however, she becomes a much more conventional operatic heroine. The third act presents a fearful Katerina who surrenders to the police without a struggle; the fourth depicts her utter defeat and degradation, culminating in her final crime.

In the third act, Katerina largely disappears, making way for satiric portrayals of the shabby peasant who discovers Zinovy's body, the police force who are delighted to have a pretext for crashing Katerina's wedding party, and the village priest who blithely leads the drunken mob of wedding guests in song. Nothing in this act bears much relation to Leskov's text, in which the townspeople witness Katerina's third murder and drag her off to the authorities. For Taruskin, this alteration "reserve[s] the moral high ground for the heroine"[110] who, unsullied by the murder of the child and meek in her submission to the authorities, still stands tall against the vulgar and immoral backdrop of her surroundings. It also requires that Sergei and Katerina become exceptionally stupid, since the discovery of their crime now hinges on their failure to bury Zinovy, something the cunning Katerina of the first two acts—or, for that matter, Leskov's Katerina—would never omit.

Katerina's brief appearances in Act III revolve around Zinovy's body. At the beginning of Scene 6, Sergei chases her away from the cellar in which he has incautiously stowed Zinovy's rotting corpse. Later, during their wedding celebration, she notices that the lock has been broken and realizes too late the need to flee. In neither case does Shostakovich allow her any extended music. Having committed her murders, she is now powerless against the forward movement of the plot. Indeed she sets the plot in motion, since her obsession with the cellar leads the shabby peasant to his discovery. Furthermore, her failure to resist the police in Scene 8 suggests that she is no longer even inclined to fight the forward momentum of time as she did in the first half of the opera.

As if to make up for Katerina's absence, the act's relentless satire upends the opera's usual distribution of music, providing extended passages for the shabby peasant, the police brigade, and the priest, figures who are essentially marginal to the story. Like arias, these scenes slow down the progression of the plot—one almost gets the sense that Shostakovich felt the need to pad out the second half of his opera, which clocks in at about an hour. Unlike arias, however, they reveal nothing but the empty vulgarity—the *poshlost'*—of the characters who sing them. In the end, these scenes play as not much more than plot devices: the shabby peasant must find the body so the police can arrest Katerina and Sergei at their moment of triumph. Their emotional content is limited to soulless alcoholism, provincial boredom, and open resentment of Katerina's sudden success.

In his song, which Taruskin calls "the most brazen piece of bordello trash ever authored by a 'serious' composer,"[111] the shabby peasant celebrates the joys of alcoholism. Against a boisterous galop, he lists his drunken family members and brags about his capacity for vodka, employing hiccups as a comic refrain. He contrasts his poverty and lack of alcohol with Sergei's new-found status as a rich woman's husband and wonders why he deserves any less. For Shostakovich, this envy explains why the peasant runs off to the police to report Zinovy's decomposing corpse, as though the corpse itself provided no compelling reason. According to Galina Vishnevskaya, the composer said "That bastard ran to the police, overjoyed that he could inform on her.... That's a hymn to all informers!"[112] From the composer's point of view, the shabby peasant's actions were even less excusable than Katerina's murders.

The police brigade, which recalls the absurd police officers in *The Nose*, fares no better. The self-aggrandizing sergeant leads his force in a pseudo-dignified call-and-response chorale, in which he defends their bribe-taking and characterizes policemen as selfless public servants defending society against nihilists. The music itself has a satirical grandeur, the stately pace undercut by the absurd words and the lugubrious grunts and groans from the chorus. The sergeant sings: "The sun and the moon take turns, Even the stars shine only at night. But a policeman is always at his post, Come rain or shine, drought or fog."[113] This contrast with the natural world recalls the way Katerina catalogues the sex lives of various animals to convey her own boredom at the beginning of the opera. The echo suggests that provincial boredom affects the entire society, but it also points to a link between Katerina's escape from that boredom by adultery and murder and the police force's own gleeful violence against the absurd school teacher and, later, against Sergei. Shostakovich would probably reject this comparison, however, since for him their motivation for pursuing Katerina is as underhanded as that of the shabby peasant. That she actually committed two murders is only a pretext for them to get back at her for excluding them from her guest list. Their reaction to the news of the murder is laughter and a jubilant exclamation of "What a godsend!"[114]

The cumulative effect of this third act, which culminates with the unedifying spectacle of the village priest lulling the wedding guests to a drunken sleep and speculating about Sergei and Katerina's sexual habits, is to depict through comedy the absolute degradation of the society—and its figures of authority—around Katerina. Shostakovich's satire is perhaps too effective, too belittling of the figures that oppress his heroine. The joyless slapstick that accompanies them undercuts the opera's goal of promoting Katerina as a victim. As Caryl Emerson has argued, "we cannot take [Katerina's] environment seriously enough to believe that it has victimized her."[115] On the other hand, certain aspects of Shostakovich's satiric world—the power of informers and the gleeful brutality of the police—would have been, to Shostakovich's audience, chilling reminders of the Stalinist nightmare. The very absurdity of these characters reflected all too accurately the absurdity of their real-life counterparts as well as their actual power to oppress. Regardless of the environment in which he places her, however, Shostakovich denies Katerina the opportunity to grapple with the seriousness of her own crimes as say, Dostoyevsky allows Raskolnikov to do in *Crime and Punishment*. By doing so he denies her the freedom that makes our identification with Raskolnikov so devastating. (In fact, Emerson argues persuasively that Shostakovich's portrayal of Katerina is in no way "Dostoyevskian."[116]) Shostakovich's indirect justification of Katerina in Act III by means of a denunciation of the society around her is both ineffective and ethically dubious, even if the satiric picture of the society around her is genuinely terrifying.

In contrast, the fourth act plays it straight, focusing on Katerina, who gets two extended solo passages, and her new position of disgrace among the convicts. The music loses its satirical edge as Katerina's punishment brings degradation, a certain self-awareness, and the final catastrophe. Shostakovich preserves all the significant events of Leskov's text while streamlining the proceedings, thus producing a most effective and efficient thirty minutes of musical drama. The libretto compresses the action to a single night in a single location, eliminates Katerina's second rival and her beating on Sergei's orders, and adds new characters: the old convict who offers the only words of kindness in the act (perhaps in the entire opera), the woman convict who torments Katerina, and their attendant choruses.

At the beginning of Act IV, Katerina is bribing the sentry for time with Sergei. Her music mostly hangs on a single note, conveying her physical and emotional exhaustion. Her tone changes (though the agitated viola accompaniment does not) as soon as she reaches Sergei, becoming more lyrical as she tells him, "Everything is forgotten as soon as you're with me."[117] Sergei, perhaps echoing the audience's reaction, catches her out on this "forgetting" and reminds her of her sin. For the self-centered Sergei, however, her sin is not the murders but making him a convict. Sergei's rejection is the first step on Katerina's path to self-awareness, since hitherto his presence had allowed her to forget her sin. Even so, in this aria she focuses not on her guilt, but on the difficulty of adjusting to the life of a convict and on Sergei's rejection.

In the bravura scene that follows, Katerina suffers further degradation when Sergei pretends to reconcile with her, taking her wool stockings in order to seduce Sonyetka. As in the previous scene, Shostakovich rapidly shifts the tone of the music as the scene develops: Sonyetka's vulgarity alternates with Sergei's parody of a Tchaikovskian romantic tenor. Katerina again grows lyrical as she basks in Sergei's attentions, but becomes desperate when she understands his betrayal. The chorus of women convicts then picks up the thread, mocking and grabbing at Katerina much the way the workmen tormented Aksinya in Scene 2. Rescued by the sentry, Katerina breaks free to deliver her final arioso, in which she recognizes the depths of her degradation and her own evil. Comparing her conscience to the frightening waves on a black lake, she sings slowly over an ominous rumbling in the orchestra, compulsively repeating the words "huge," "black," and "waves." After this haunting passage, she falls silent for the rest of the opera, expressing her final rage by murder and suicide. This violence brings us back to the Katerina of the first half of the opera, who had destroyed everything that made her life intolerable. But by the end of Act IV, she seems to recognize that she herself is at the root of the horror around her. Emerson suggests that Katerina's suicide "appears to be more self-punishment than revenge against her lover and rival."[118] That she does kill Sonyetka, however, suggests that revenge is at least as important as self-annihilation. For Asafyev, already decrying the lack of selflessness in contemporary Soviet opera, such a thoroughly modernist deformation of selflessness (i.e., one that involved suicide) could hardly have been a comfort.

In the first two acts, Shostakovich's Katerina is both a new and an old heroine. Although no one who had seen *Salome* or countless other operas could be surprised by a sexually voracious operatic heroine, Katerina was a novel figure for Russian opera. On the other hand, she clearly shares features with traditional Russian heroines, with Ostrovsky's Katerina as a prototype. Although her portrayal shifts significantly in the second half of the opera, she is at her most vivid—and attracts the most attention from critics and audiences—in her triumphant rampage against the figures of male authority in her family. In this guise, a pre-revolutionary heroine updated for a revolutionary age, Katerina, perhaps inevitably, reflects as much the period of the opera's composition as she does the nominal setting of the opera. As such, she can be, as Taruskin sees it, an emblem of a murderous new regime or, as I would argue, a Russian version of the femme fatale who represents the unbearable contradictions in a society in transition.

CHAPTER 12

SHOSTAKOVICH AND *WOZZECK'S* SECRET: TOWARD THE FORMATION OF A "SHOSTAKOVICH MODE"

David Haas

It was a confident, accomplished, famous, and still fairly young Dmitry Shostakovich who came to Moscow in February 1935 as a delegate from Leningrad to the first ever All-Union Conference on Soviet Symphonism. If the published transcripts in *Sovetskaya muzyka* are any indication, this was a conference dominated not by composers but by music critics and arts pundits. Nevertheless, Shostakovich did speak and a summary of his possibly impromptu reaction to the conference made it into print. While much of his gently ironic speech targets the unbearable pompous of his immediate predecessors at the microphone, at least two points reveal something of his own musical interests. The first, which is not my concern here and belongs more properly to the often vitriolic debates over the life and opinions of Shostakovich, was a plea that Soviet composers not forget that sometimes it is their task merely to entertain an audience.[1] The second was to urge the Composers' Union to do more to acquaint Soviet composers with Western European trends: "Perhaps there would be no sense in giving frequent performances of the music [of Western composers] and overloading our concert programs with them; however, in my opinion, the Union of Soviet Composers should organize seminars for the study of such prominent composers as Alban Berg, Weill, and others."[2]

Outside Russia, the situation in the 1930s was not much different with respect to Berg seminars. However, since the Second World War, there have been Berg seminars and conferences aplenty, though far fewer Shostakovich seminars and, to my knowledge, no seminars anywhere in which Berg's relevance to Russian music and to Shostakovich has been scrutinized.[3] The segregation of Shostakovich and Berg studies is nowhere more apparent than in the analytical approaches routinely brought to bear on their music. This can be illustrated by the following four examples. Least interesting analytically is Example 12.1, a bit of wrong-note high-jinks from the opening of Shostakovich's First Piano Concerto (1933).

Example 12.1

One could label the opening C scale as a deviation into the major mode and call the troublesome D-flat scale a fleeting tonicization of the Neapolitan supertonic, followed by the expected dominant G, resolving to tonic C in the (presumably) minor mode in bar 3. But to insist on a rationale that is consistent with nineteenth-century norms is to risk overlooking a more immediate stylistic context and the likelihood that Shostakovich is here responding to the polytonal forays of Ravel, Milhaud, Bartók and—in the opinion of many a contemporary—of Stravinsky and Berg as well. Moreover, as we will see, that combination of a scale rising from a half-step (or descending to it, as in the Concerto) together with a segment of whole-step motion will recur frequently in the works that follow the Concerto.

Since Example 12.2, the opening bars of the "Rondo marziale" in Act I of *Wozzeck*, is by Alban Berg of the Second Viennese School, it is not to be dismissed as mere horseplay, or as C major with wrong notes, or as bitonality, even though Berg himself cited it as an example of "so-called 'polytonality' . . . with [a] 'false bass.'"[4]

Example 12.2

There is no thorough analysis of this passage in any of the English-language monographs on Berg and no analyst who has substantiated either Berg's polytonal or a pitch-class set atonal reading. However, subsets extractable from the passage, e.g., the white-note diatonic collection and "whole-tone-plus-one" pitch class sets,[5] play a vital role in the analysis of other passages that have sparked considerable theoretic commentary.

Example 12.3 is from the first movement of Shostakovich's Fourth Symphony (1936), a passage that most writers accept as the beginning of the second theme group. Even though Shostakovich had restored key signatures in three important instrumental works preceding it (the First Piano Concerto, Cello Sonata, and Twenty-Four Piano Preludes, op. 34), the Fourth has none attached to any of its three movements. Nevertheless, the all-but-unchallenged assumption that Shostakovich should be approached as a tonal composer has led the six authors of extended analytical essays to assign this thematic statement both a tonic pitch and, as an extrapolation, a Western European mode. The rival theories to date are: 1) that the passage is in A major (Pauline Fairclough);[6] 2) that it is in E minor (Karen Kopp);[7] 3) that it is in "E minor, mov[ing] quickly away" (Joseph Darby);[8] 4) that it is in E minor but with a Dorian (raised) sixth and a flattened second; or else, A major, then modulation (Marina Sabinina);[9] 5) that it involves either "a mixed mode Aeolian inflection" or a "Dorian E" (Eric Roseberry);[10] or 6) that it gives an A major melody over an accompaniment implying E minor (Richard Longman).[11]

Example 12.3

Example 12.4 shows the passacaglia theme from Act II of *Lady Macbeth of the Mtsensk District*, a passage that has elicited considerable analytical attention from Soviet authors.

Example 12.4

In 1946, Alexander Dolzhansky used this passage to launch a decades-long search for a special mode (*lad*) unique to Shostakovich.[12] In her lucid comparative study, Ellon Carpenter created a table juxtaposing two seven-note, five eight-note, and five nine-note attempts by Dolzhansky and other Soviet theorists to fix and label the "Shostakovich mode."[13] I have not reproduced it here, because each version is conditioned by a particular set of analytical priorities and a particular methodology within the daunting field of twentieth-century Russian modal theory. Moreover, I do not agree with Dolzhansky's unsubstantiated decision to base his theory of the "Shostakovich mode" on this passacaglia theme.

Turning instead from an isolated symphonic interlude in the opera to the Twenty-Four Piano Preludes, op. 34, and to the Fourth and Fifth Symphonies, another pitch collection (Example 12.5) appears with far greater frequency, one similar to Dolzhansky's, but with the B-flat from the *Lady Macbeth* passage now replaced by B-natural.

Example 12.5

Example 12.6 shows the mode, based on C-sharp, as it appears toward the end of the F-sharp minor Prelude. In fact, the aforementioned troublesome example from the Fourth Symphony (Example 12.3) also turns out to be based on the mode (again based on C-sharp).

Example 12.6

Table 12.1 lists twenty passages, all taken from the Preludes, op. 34, containing examples of this "Shostakovich mode" at various transpositions. In all but one case (the opening of Prelude No. 6), the passages are taken from the interiors of the preludes, after the assigned tonic has been established to some degree. Most of the passages show linear (scalar) usage in at least one hand, and most highlight three salient aspects of the collection: 1) a five-pitch whole tone segment, 2) an ascending quasi-Phrygian minor second, and 3) two interlocking minor triads.

On the basis of Carpenter's research, it seems that no Russian theorist has proposed a seven-pitch scale identical to the one that I claim to find in the Preludes. Nevertheless, the seven pitches of my scale do appear in six of the eight- and nine-note

Table 12.1
Partial Listing of Appearances of Seven-Note "Shostakovich Mode" from the Preludes, op. 34

Prelude	Location, Hand	Starting Pitch in Prime Form
1 in C	14–17, left	D
3 in G	6–8, left	B
3 in G	16–18, left	E
3 in G	29–32, both	C-sharp
5 in D	2–4, left	C-sharp
5 in D	6–7, both	B
5 in D	16, both	B
5 in D	17, both	A
6 in B min	1–4 (beat 1), right	F-sharp
6 in B min	6–12, right	B
7 in A	15–16, right	A
7 in A	8–17, left (bass "Urlinie" only)	A
8 in F-sharp min	14–15, right	B
8 in F-sharp min	39–40, right	C-sharp
9 in E	36–40, both	C-sharp
10 in C-sharp min	22 (beat 2)–25 (beat 1) both	F-sharp
10 in C-sharp min	58–62, both	G-sharp
12 in G-sharp min	5 (beats 2¾ to 4), right	B
12 in G-sharp min	21, both	B
15 in D-flat	23–25 (beat 2), left	B

min = minor.

variants presented in Carpenter's comparative study.[14] There may be an easy explanation for the exclusion of my variant. In contradistinction to such exotic creatures as the "Aeolian double-lowered melodic mode," "double-lowered Phrygian," and "Alexandrian decachord," the seven-note collection (sometimes dubbed the "acoustic collection") in my examples is also identical in pitch content to the ordinary ascending melodic minor scale.[15]

The preponderance of this seven-pitch collection in instrumental works composed after the completion of *Lady Macbeth*, that is, after 1932, coincides with Shostakovich's decision to employ key signatures again. Key signatures return already in the Twenty-four Piano Preludes (completed March 1933). Beginning with the First Prelude in C, the set traverses all the keys, arranged in the circle of fifths order employed by Chopin and Scriabin, but with considerably freer internal modulatory schemes. When the transposition levels of my seven-pitch mode are matched against the scales suggested by Shostakovich's key signatures, an interesting pattern emerges: in most cases, the seven-pitch mode produces alterations to three, four, or more pitches of the given Prelude's assigned diatonic key. Thus, one might conclude that its function is not to stabilize the tonic of the work but to modulate away from it, perhaps to the extent of temporarily tonicizing another pitch. Whatever the specific harmonic interpretation, the mere presence of so many accidentals that challenge a prelude's assigned key suggests that we may have something of a hybrid, an interaction of at least two different mode formations.

The remarkable versatility of this seven-note collection can be traced to aspects of its intervallic structure. Removed from specific historical and stylistic contexts, it can be seen as a modification of the diatonic collection, e.g., a D scale with F-sharp chromatically altered to F-natural. Yet this alteration results in only two significant changes to the interval vector: one perfect fourth from the diatonic collection (C-sharp to F-sharp) is collapsed into a major third (C-sharp to F) and another (F-sharp to B) is expanded out to make a second tritone (F to B). All the other intervals, including the five major seconds, remain the same (see Table 12.2). There is practically no loss at all in its ability to interface with multiple transpositions of the diatonic collections, in other words, with multiple keys.

Table 12.2
Interval Vector Comparison between Major Scale and the "Shostakovich Mode"[16]

Set No.	Prime Form of Set	Interval Vector
7–35 (Diatonic major scale)	C-sharp, D, E, F-sharp, G, A, B	[254361]
7–34 ("Shostakovich mode")	C-sharp, D, E, F, G, A, B	[254442]

My conjectured "Shostakovich mode" possesses two further interfacing capabilities, not present in the diatonic collection. It encompasses five of the six pitches of the whole-tone scale, as well as six of the eight pitches of an octatonic scale. Example 12.7 shows the "Shostakovich mode" based on C-sharp. (The pitch "B" is shown twice to clarify its role in both the octatonic and the whole-tone portions of this mode.)

Example 12.7

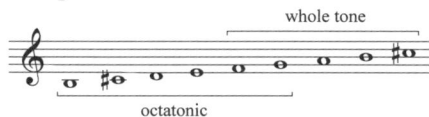

When one seven-pitch scale formation can so effectively mimic and interface with various diatonic realms and with two symmetrical scales, when it possesses not one but two tritones, then it is inevitably prone to foster considerable tonal ambiguity. Without pitch emphasis or pitch repetition, or various tonic-establishing gestures from the common-practice period, this collection will not fulfill the minimum conditions for tonal centricity. Although each appearance of the "Shostakovich mode" in Table 12.1 was given a designated "starting pitch," it must be stressed that the mode itself has no tonic. Rather, the mode is an incursion introduced as a vehicle for traveling to and from or between tonalities, or in order to question the prevailing tonality. It is analogous to what Schoenberg termed "vagrant sonorities,"[17] which also have no home key, but which are used in relation to keys with tonics. Because of its inherent lack of tonic-reinforcing gestures, this seven-note collection is, *per se*, atonal, regardless of the tonal environment in which it is placed.

Is Shostakovich then an atonal composer? Does he create pockets of atonality whenever he introduces this collection? To make either claim would be to reject virtually all Russian and non-Russian analysis of his music. And they would be false claims, since Shostakovich was not at all sparing in his use of tonic-reinforcing gestures. It is instead more accurate to conceive of Shostakovich's harmonic and modal practice not as functionally tonal or atonal but as a continuum extending from absolute tonal clarity to the irresolvable ambiguities that result from monophonic passages based on nondiatonic or hybrid modes in which no traditional devices of tonic marking appear.

It is not my intention here to analyze Shostakovich's harmonic practice in terms of scales and scale fragments derived from pure or altered Western or Eastern Church modes or Eastern European folk modes. Instead, I propose that we treat the set of seven pitches merely as an independent referential collection interacting with the conventional diatonic modes suggested by key signatures and cadences— just as most theorists would do with respect to Berg's music. In any case, the examples above from the Fourth Symphony and the Preludes should be sufficiently far enough removed from common-practice employment to rule out any attempt to explain away these and other passages as odd and seemingly random modulations to distant minor keys.

If one believes more in stylistic "evolutionism" than in mode or pitch-class set "creationism," then the logical next step after collecting examples of the seven-pitch scale is to seek out significant historical precedents. In my case, the search did not begin with Berg. I first sought out earlier tonal precedents from Western Europe and Russia, passages that presented the entire scale rising up from a quasi-Phrygian minor second interval and that gave this minor second some equally striking metrical emphasis. The search led me to consider a long list of works, usually in minor keys. Among those that were certainly known to Shostakovich were: Beethoven's Third Piano Concerto (outer movements),[18] Chopin's A-flat Polonaise,[19] Musorgsky's *Pictures at an Exhibition*,[20] Tchaikovsky's Fourth Symphony,[21] and the Letter Scene from *Eugene Onegin*.[22] It is important to emphasize that these works were considered merely for their anomalous use of the pitch collection within the context of nineteenth-century tonality, and not as precedents of 1920s bitonality or any proposed Shostakovich mode.

The decision to crack open the score of Berg's *Wozzeck* (as well as the half dozen or so monographs analyzing his music) to seek out a different sort of precedent was motivated by the passage from Shostakovich's Fourth Symphony presented in Example 12.3. How was it possible that Shostakovich could compose a 26-measure passage using only the seven pitches of the D minor (ascending melodic) scale, and yet not a single analyst would hear it in D minor? At this stage, it is useful to recall Allen Forte's 50-page essay on the so-called "D minor Inter-lude" from *Wozzeck*, Act III, in which he claims that a reading based on atonal pitch-class sets is analytically more defensible than the more conventional reading using the chord grammar of extended tonality. Forte concludes that "the atonal structure exhibits qualities that render it far superior to a conventional and—I believe—essentially arbitrary tonal framework. On the basis of a single analytical desideratum alone, namely completeness, the atonal interpretation must be regarded as preferable."[23] I was then reminded of the sentimental attachment of the Second Viennese School to the important tonality of D minor, which is truly central and uniquely so to the Austro-Germanic mainstream. Prominent already in various movements and works by Bruckner and Mahler, and crucial to Strauss's *Elektra*, it is also the tonality of Schoenberg's *Verklärte Nacht* and First String Quartet, Berg's *Lied*, op. 2, No. 1, and implicit in the first hexachord of the tone row of his concert aria *Der Wein* (D, E, F, G, A, B-flat).

The chances of a significant influence from *Wozzeck* are increased by the exter-nal evidence. I have already noted Shostakovich's outspoken advocacy of Berg as late as 1935. Fifteen years ago, Maxim Shostakovich informed me that his father "adored *Wozzeck* and always kept the score at the piano." It is also necessary to bear in mind the sensation that occurred in 1927 when Berg and *Wozzeck* came to Leningrad in time for a production at the Malyi Opera, which opened on June 11. Berg would never forget the thrill of seeing his surname in Cyrillic emblaz-oned on the affiches throughout the city. (He was also destined to become some-what of a matinee idol once it was noted that he bore a striking resemblance to Oscar Wilde.) Shostakovich met Berg at a reception and made a sufficient impres-sion on him to induce Berg to send him a congratulatory note after a performance of the First Symphony in 1928.

The *Wozzeck* production drew favorable attention from all the influential critics. Boris Asafyev, ever the tireless champion of new trends, could normally be counted on to identify how a piece reflected the contemporary world. Yet in his essay for the special *Wozzeck* issue of *Novaya muzyka*, a modern music bimonthly published in Leningrad, his focus was on the opera's traditional aspects. He even questioned whether there really was significant innovation: "Strictly speaking, Berg's music in *Wozzeck* is not original with respect to any particular novelty in the material or 'radical' treatment of it. Rather the finest attainments from the nineteenth-century music dramas of Germany and Italy are transmitted through the prism of Schönberg's methods, albeit with an extraction of certain traits of sa-lon lyricism and the romance in the final phase."[24] This emphasis on the opera's traditional aspects also comes across in the essay by Vladimir Dranishnikov, the conductor of the production, who took on the task of providing the Russian audi-ence with the now familiar scene-by-scene listing of traditional forms employed by Berg.[25]

One does not have to go very far in the Berg literature to learn of the existence of a structurally important six-note collection consisting of the pitches G, D, B, F, A, and C-sharp, which can be reordered into a scale—C-sharp, D, F, G, A, and B.

Berg himself had already identified it in a lecture he wrote in 1929 for a Dresden performance of *Wozzeck*.[26] George Perle calls it "the principal referential chord of the work as a whole."[27] Add one pitch to it—E—and we create the seven-note collection under consideration. But is the identity of pitch content significant? How certain can we be that Shostakovich needed *Wozzeck* to remind him of the compositional potential of the melodic minor scale? And, finally, why does Shostakovich's music of the 1930s sound nothing like the *Wozzeck* as conceptualized in sophisticated recent Anglo-American pitch-class analysis?

It should be understood that the *Wozzeck* of late twentieth-century theorists is not the *Wozzeck* presented in both popular and scholarly publications of the 1920s. Not only in the Soviet Union, but also in Austria and Germany, the interpretive priorities—or rather *strategies*—were simply different, because they had to be. Any mention of its being an "atonal masterpiece" in the advance publicity, the more substantive essays, or the favorable reviews would have done little to win converts, at least not after 1924, when a sharply critical essay by Emil Petschnig, stigmatizing the whole idea of atonal opera, appeared in the German journal *Die Musik*, under the title "Atonales Opernschaffen" [Creating Atonal Opera].[28] Instead of foregrounding the unconventional harmonic vocabulary, *Wozzeck's* champions of the 1920s focused on its countless allusions to more familiar styles, repertoires, genres, and on Berg's respect for time-honored compositional principles. And while Schoenberg's influence was acknowledged, so too were the influences from Wagner and Bizet, Debussy, cafe music, military bands, folk songs, and tonality itself, in the lushly scored D minor Interlude of Act III.

This bridge-building strategy is nowhere more evident than in the lecture that Berg wrote in anticipation of a 1929 production of *Wozzeck* in the North German provincial town of Oldenburg. Among other concerns, the composer identifies that of differentiating stylistically between art music and folk music, while preserving his "so-called atonal harmony." The secret of the pseudo-folk style he devised was harmonic simplicity:

> I took great care to ensure that everything to do with folk music in the opera (including the atonal harmonies) has an easily understood simplicity. Thus, for example, these sections favour symmetrically built periods and phrase structure, *harmonies that are based on thirds (or, more especially, fourths), and melodic patterns in which an important role is played by the whole tone scale and the perfect fourth*, as opposed to the diminished and augmented intervals which otherwise dominate the atonal music of the Viennese school.[29] [Italics added]

Berg's success in this regard has been substantiated by later theorists, whether those who describe the harmonic vocabulary in prose, applying such labels as quasi-whole tone, polytonal, bitonal, etc., or those who extract pitch-class sets showing a preponderance of interval classes 2, 4, and 5, i.e., major seconds, major thirds, and perfect fourths.

The most important of the pitch-class sets must certainly be the "quasi-cadential chord" that was mentioned by Berg and demonstrated by the orchestra during the

Oldenburg lecture. Berg explained its compositional function in the opera by making an analogy with tonal practice:

> The point in a tonal composition at which the return to and establishment of the main key is made clear, so that it is recognizable to the eyes and ears of even the layman, must also be the point at which the harmonic circle closes in an atonal work. This sense of closure was first of all ensured by having each act of the opera steer towards one and the same closing chord, a chord that acted in the manner of a cadence and that was dwelled on as if on a tonic.[30]

In fact, this closing figure contains not one chord but two, locked in perpetual oscillation at the ends of Acts I and III, over two (G, D) of the three (G, D, A) pitches common to both chords, as shown in Example 12.8. Of these chords, the second (G–D–B–F–A–C-sharp) corresponds to Perle's "principal referential chord" cited above. Add an E, and we have verticalized the seven pitches of the D melodic minor scale.

Example 12.8

This raises an obvious question: Given the significance of this collection, why does more of *Wozzeck* not sound like or suggest a D minor tonality? The answer is simple. Like Shostakovich's seven-pitch scalar formation, Berg's hexachord with its five-pitch whole-tone fragment and two tritones cannot establish D as tonic without tonic-reinforcing gestures. These gestures are certainly present in the D minor Interlude of Act III but they are withheld elsewhere. On the other hand, a mere reordering of the six pitches from stacked thirds into the stepwise string F–G–A–B–C-sharp–D makes countless tonal or pseudo-tonal melodic phrases possible. As a result, Berg is able to compose numerous passages on the fringes of tonality, apparently reveling in paradoxical situations, which for George Perle exemplify tonic functionality without diatonicism, and diatonicism without a tonic.[31]

We can now turn to the second problem, namely the disparity between the musical styles of Shostakovich and Berg. Some of this can be explained by factors of time and place. Berg was a student of Schoenberg, the author of a *Harmonielehre*, which, for all of its fulminations against other theory textbooks, was a product of common-practice Austro-Germanic instrumental music and musical thought. *Wozzeck* would be unthinkable without the achievements and values of that tradition: its genres, musical forms, contrapuntal technique, and textures of four or more voices.

Shostakovich, too, was a beneficiary of Western European training. And his teacher's teacher, Rimsky-Korsakov, was the author of a textbook on tonal harmony. But by the time of the *Wozzeck* premiere, Shostakovich had already severed ties with his composition teacher Maximilian Shteinberg, on account of irreconcilable aesthetic differences.[32] A number of Leningrad musicians including Boris Asafyev had by then assumed that he was moving closer to the controversial aesthetic and style of the junior theory and composition faculty at the Leningrad Conservatory led by Vladimir Shcherbachov and fully endorsed by Asafyev.[33] From a curricular standpoint, the most striking innovation of the so-called "Shcherbachov School" was the addition of a course on melody to the core curriculum for young composers, taught by Pyotr Ryazanov. Inspired in part by a recent Russian translation of Ernst Kurth's *Grundlagen des linearen Kontrapunkts*, and in part by his own research into the melodic structure of indigenous folksong, Ryazanov designed a course in which melody was no longer part of a large system of musical thought, but was approached in its own right as a complex synthesis of factors of pitch, interval, meter, stability, instability, and developmental procedures. The intense scrutiny of the melodic line by Ryazanov and others of the Shcherbachov faction, including their composition students, eventually led to a trend of composition in Leningrad known as "linearism." If Ryazanov's primary concern lay with the analysis of the melodic line, Shcherbachov himself insisted that his composition students demonstrate both an awareness and an aptitude for the composition of long lines. Mikhail Chulaki recalled the challenge of composing "slow, predominately instrumental arias of [broad] melodic respiration. In completing the assignment, the student learned to construct an expressive melody with one culmination and a subsequent descent. No 'quadratics,' no full cadences—all was to be done with the utmost plasticity."[34]

By 1927, fruits of this new interest in the creative potential of the melodic line had reached the concert hall. On 14 December 1927, Vladimir Dranishnikov and the Leningrad Philharmonic gave the world premiere of Shcherbachov's Second Symphony based on the apocalyptic poetry of Alexander Blok, in which linear composition was explored within a late-Romantic harmonic idiom. In the same year, both Moscow and Leningrad heard the more brazenly modernistic Septet of Shcherbachov's pupil Popov, featuring a more overtly polystylistic interaction of diatonic, chromatic, and freely dissonant pitch languages.[35]

Although Shostakovich never studied under Ryazanov or Shcherbachov, he was known to solicit their opinions.[36] Furthermore, his dedication of the Scherzo for Orchestra, op. 7, to Ryazanov suggests something more than a casual acquaintance. Shostakovich's immediate response to the linear style of Leningrad is evident in his compositions of the late 1920s: the *Aphorisms* for Piano, the Second and Third Symphonies, and the opera *The Nose*. But similar textures consisting of one highly detailed expansive melodic line placed over a less ornate secondary voice, or an ostinato figure, or a pedal point, or nothing at all also occupy long stretches of the Preludes, op. 34, the Cello Sonata, the Fourth and Fifth Symphonies, and many other works from the 1930s and later.

If texture is clearly not the basis for my claim of a significant Bergian influence, what other overriding factors are there? By way of a conclusion, I will comment on the three that I consider significant for Shostakovich's compositions from 1932 up through the alleged work of rehabilitation, the Fifth Symphony of 1937. The first is his marked use of the great Austro-Germanic key of D minor as filtered through the late Romantic and post-tonal works of Strauss, Schoenberg, and Berg. D minor appears as the tonic or as an important secondary key in four major instrumental works of the early to mid-1930s: the passacaglia from *Lady Macbeth* (here, C-sharp rather than D is tonicized, even though the pitch content suggests D minor); the Cello Sonata in D minor (1934); the Fourth Symphony (wherein D minor pitch content is significant in both outer movements and D minor is the tonality for the middle movement); and finally, the Fifth Symphony in D minor.

The second trait is the technique of using the thirds, fourths, and whole-tone subsets of the acoustic collection without establishing either an unambiguous tonic or tonic functionality of the other pitches. Berg claimed to have developed the technique in order to produce a primitive dialect of atonality suitable for the compositions of military marches and folksongs, in other words, to serve particular aesthetic ends in *Wozzeck* (see italicized portion of the above quotation). Shostakovich was reprimanded in 1936 for presuming that he also was entitled to a comparable degree of aesthetic autonomy. Paradoxically, his employment of surface gestures that Berg considered primitive, namely, ostinati based on ascending fourths, tertian harmonization, and diatonic or quasi-diatonic melody, was sufficient to restore his reputation as Soviet artist even when—and this is the point—those simple surface gestures are contradicted by disorienting ambiguities of affect and key. In this light, Esti Sheinberg is to be commended for giving serious consideration to how the layering and interpenetration of harmonic languages (e.g., a tonal layer and a layer based on relationships of seconds) can contribute to the achievement of irony and parody, no less than the gestural distortion of marches, dances, and popular styles.[37]

The final trait might fairly be called *the* secret or at least *a* secret of *Wozzeck*: namely the pitch content of the hexachord used to close the first scene and all three acts, with significance also for the D minor Interlude. This hexachord consisting of pitches C-sharp, D, F, G, A, and B is equally at home and capable of interfacing with minor key, modal, whole-tone, and atonal contexts or remaining on the borders between. When the E is added and the collection appears, at this or another transposition level, in Shostakovich's pared down textures, it becomes yet more adaptable and more elusive, especially when it is placed in contexts that emphasize different intervallic properties.

The last three examples are taken from the Fifth Symphony. My analysis of the opening ten bars shows successive presentations of the collection at three different transposition levels (Example 12.9). All but one pitch in the introduction (D-sharp, circled in bars 2 and 3) can be explained in this way. And in the ensuing first theme, only one pitch does not fit into the respective collections (D, circled in bar 10), while in the accompanimental vamp, only three additional pitches do not fit (B, A, and E, circled in bars 10 and 11).

Example 12.9

In Example 12.10, from the third movement, the collection makes possible a juxtaposition of the movement's dominant (C-sharp) to its tonic (F-sharp minor), using D-minor scalar material that anticipates the finale. In effect, this passage represents a bridge of sorts between two movements that contrast in so many respects.

Example 12.10

Most surprising of all, perhaps, are the final moments of the Symphony, a massive thirty-five bar prolongation of the tonic D major chord (Fig. 131). The chord itself (D–F-sharp–A) accounts for the lion's share of these thirty-five bars. In fact, only four other harmonies appear: the minor subdominant chord (D–G–B-flat) clashing with the ongoing dominant pedal A; the chord D–A–C; and two dyads created incidentally as a result of passing and neighbor notes in the melodic line, A–E and E–G (plus the ongoing dominant pedal). Thus, the pitches in these closing thirty-five bars are: D–E–F-sharp–G–A–B-flat–C-natural. Although the key signature indicates D major, and though these final bars could not be more dissimilar in theme, dissonance level, and affect, this pitch content (which amounts to the "Shostakovich mode" based on F-sharp) is identical to mm. 3–4 of the first movement (see Example 12.9). I seriously doubt that this is a coincidence. What may well be a coincidence, but is too striking to pass over, is yet another bridge from Shostakovich's Fifth to a work by Berg, who by the time of his death in 1935 had become *persona non grata* for the Soviet musical establishment. This time it is to Berg's dodecaphonic Violin Concerto of 1935. The first seven pitches of the prime form of the Concerto's famous row are G–B-flat–D–F-sharp–A–C–E. Reorder the row so as to change its implied triads to a scalar formation and we have all the pitches Shostakovich needed to counterfeit a D major triumph and bring his Symphony to an end—simultaneously—in both a private mode and a public key.[38]

SHOSTAKOVICH'S "TRADEMARK" FORM: THE ARCH-SONATA IN THE FIRST MOVEMENT OF THE FIFTH SYMPHONY

Michael Mishra

Unable, for obvious reasons, to discuss publicly the political machinations that had led to the withdrawal of the Fourth Symphony, Shostakovich typically deflected questions, criticizing the work itself, in particular its sprawling dimensions, or "grandiosomania." Knowing what we now do about the circumstances of the withdrawal,[1] we can understand the tactic to have been, in part at least, a convenient and politically safe way to save face. Yet, buried within Shostakovich's comments for public consumption was maybe a kernel of truth. For whatever it was that the Fifth Symphony ultimately represented, and no matter the extent to which it in other respects ignored the Party's "advice," no one could deny its rejection of the earlier symphony's structural and tonal maximalism.

Introductory Ritornello

This new economy of means is apparent right from the outset, and is easily revealed by comparing the Fifth Symphony's introduction with those of its predecessors. The Second Symphony, for example, opens with four minutes of subterranean "ultrapolyphony," where the goal is clearly the accumulation of texture and not the establishment of symphonic momentum. Symphonic momentum is not much in evidence at the start of the Third Symphony either—a ramble of uncertain direction for one, then two clarinets. A sketch for an aborted Fourth Symphony (1934) shows another meandering opening—this time for solo viola—that makes one wonder whether Shostakovich may have had in mind the viola opening to Mahler's Tenth Symphony.[2] Certainly, nobody could accuse the opening of the actual Fourth Symphony of lacking purpose, but the opening of the Fifth achieves a comparable expository force through less ostentatious means. Unlike the Fourth, where the "grandiosomanic" orchestral palette is laid out at the start, the austere opening of the Fifth, with its simple, two-part dialogue between low and high strings, is as terse as it is dramatic. Like the Fourth, it establishes tonality within a few bars, but does so in a more Classical manner, using, as Classical period music so often does, a dominant preparation of the forthcoming tonic (bars 4 and 5). By contrast, the opening of the Fourth projects its tonality "by assertion" (as Theodor Adorno might have put it). There, the scalar outline of the first five bars prepares only very obliquely the C minor tonic so immediately and emphatically asserted in bar 6.

The turbulence of the Fifth Symphony's introduction (see Chapter 12, Example 12.9) is fueled by several ingredients: an opening gesture emphasizing the unstable ascending minor sixth (with all its *Tristan* associations); the canonic texture pitting low strings against high; the superimposition in the third bar of rising D major and falling D minor; and the tense, French Overture style double-dotted rhythm—indeed, Eric Roseberry points to a connection between this opening and that famously disruptive passage in the finale of Beethoven's Seventh Symphony (bar 129, et seq.), where one minor sixth answers another, high strings against low, in a similar dotted rhythm.[3] But the economy of Shostakovich's introduction is every bit as striking as its forcefulness. In just four bars, it sets up several important features of the movement and of the Symphony as a whole. At the same time, these four bars effect a self-dissipating transition from the tense angularity of the opening to the calmer waters of the movement's first subject. The opening minor sixth contracts to a perfect fifth, then a minor third, and finally to conjunct scalar motion. The clash between D major and D minor is resolved as the contrary lines converge in the next bar onto a single pitch, the dominant, A. By the end of the fourth bar, those tense, disjunct, marcato double-dotted rhythms have transformed into a legato single-dotted figure articulating tonally stable rising fourths (V-i in D minor), and the transition is complete.

First Subject

The gradual, transitional manner of the Fifth Symphony's introduction sets the tone for much of the rest of the movement. The Fourth and Fifth Symphonies are both distinguished by their early establishment of key, especially in comparison with their predecessors. But that is where the similarity ends. Eleven bars into the Fourth, the tonality, which had been established in bar 6 "by assertion," abruptly changes. By contrast, the first subject of the Fifth glides in and out of D minor just as seamlessly as the theme itself had emerged from the introductory material.[4] Shostakovich effects this through a process of gradual chromatic alteration: the first bar (Fig. 1; see Example 12.9) is completely diatonic, the second introduces the Neapolitan degree, creating a Phrygian approach to the tonic (E-flat to D). The introduction of more flattened pitches over the next few bars continues the process of gradual chromatic alteration and leads ultimately into a restatement of the introductory material, now in C minor, at Fig. 2, b2.

Such seamless, melodically driven modulation would become highly characteristic of Shostakovich. Also characteristic is the way in which the tonic, D minor, makes its presence felt intermittently during the course of the first subject group's three strains. The second strain (Fig. 3), although as tonally fluid as the first, does briefly return to D minor at its climax (Fig. 4, b2) before once again moving away. The short third strain at Fig. 5, b2 is in D minor, and becomes the transition to the extended restatement of the introductory material at Fig. 6. Thus, we have a first subject group, which, on the one hand, is in a constant state of tonal flux, yet which returns to its tonic at pivotal moments. The cohesiveness of this group is at least partly attributable to this overarching, if loosely held, tonal structure.

The other unifying factor is the introductory material, which in the first half of the exposition functions as a ritornello. It appears after the first subject's first strain (Fig. 2, b2), a fragment of it appears after the second strain (Fig. 5), and it returns in an expanded form after the third strain (Fig. 6) where it becomes the transition to the second subject. Not only does this ritornello connect the various strains of the first subject, but certain parts of the first subject are themselves also derived from it. The descending scalar pattern from the ritornello's third bar, for example, can be found embedded in all three strains of the first subject (Fig. 1, b4; Fig. 3, b2; and Fig. 5, b3).

The transition to the second subject (Fig. 6) is almost a mini-development. It contains glimpses of at least two tension-building devices that will be used later in the real development section and that, indeed, tend to define Shostakovich's developments in general: the contrapuntal playing of themes against either themselves or other themes (e.g., the ritornello used in counterpoint against a snippet of the first subject at Fig. 6), and the use of registral extremes. The climax of this transition contains one of the most definitive presentations of tonality since the start of the first subject. On one level, this statement of C major (Fig. 7, b3) appears to bring a note of optimism. The entrance of the trumpets here (their first appearance in the work) lends an almost baroque-like festiveness to this cadence. However, the easy assertion of trumpets and of C major becomes gradually overshadowed by the ascending, increasingly strained cello tessitura—a sonority that becomes a crucial factor at the slow movement's climax—and the extraordinarily piercing timbre (first violins, flutes, and E-flat clarinet) of the high inverted pedal. The effect owes much to another composer who specialized in orchestrating otherwise consonant, major key passages in an ironic or anguished way, namely Mahler.

Following this emotionally ambiguous C major flourish, the opening ritornello is restated in D minor (Fig. 8, b2), thus creating a return to the tonic at about the most unlikely point in a sonata-type movement—just before the second subject. This return in a sense "unwinds" all of the tonal exploration that has taken place thus far, and creates out of this first subject group a miniature cyclic entity—cyclic in the most literal sense of music that returns full-circle (both tonally and thematically) to where it began. As a result, Shostakovich redefines the whole concept of "transition," because the actual preparation for the second tonal area now takes place at the last minute. A mere three bars before the new theme's arrival, Shostakovich makes a simple one-note alteration to the ritornello material. Like the proverbial rabbit out of the hat, D minor is instantly transformed to E-flat minor. Yet, although this new key seems, at the local level, to have been rather hastily prepared, it can be viewed as a longer-term structural elevation of the pitch E-flat, first heard as a brief but striking chromatic inflection in the first theme (Fig. 1, b2). This Beethovenian technique of tonal planning, where a "surprise" note in an otherwise diatonic melody is elevated later on to become a tonal center in its own right, would be used frequently by Shostakovich in the years to come.

Second Subject

The second subject (Fig. 9) brings about a simplification of texture: a slow, soaring melody in the first violins (identified by Lev Mazel as an allusion to the Habanera from Bizet's *Carmen*—see Chapter 1), whose rhythmic shape is an augmentation of the movement's introductory motive, and whose melodic contour, although not exactly related, reflects the introduction's wide leaps; and a homophonic, dactylic accompaniment in the other strings (a reversal of the anapestic motive first heard in bar 4), with the occasional harp chord (its first appearance in the work) marking some of the harmonic changes. Yet, in its way, this second subject turns out to be every bit as unsettled as the first. Many of the chords underlining this melody, which starts in E-flat minor and ends in E major (Fig. 11, b3), contain added tones or are formed on altered scale degrees.[5] Just as important as the chords themselves is Shostakovich's manipulation of harmonic rhythm. While the actual melody is quite regular in its rhythmic construction, the underlying harmonic rhythm constantly fluctuates, creating a subtext of agitation beneath the theme's surface coolness. At Fig. 10, for example, the listener is lulled by three bars of unchanging harmony, only to be thrown immediately into six different chords in as many beats—a sudden twelve-fold increase in harmonic rhythm. Moreover, the six changing chords all occur under the umbrella of a single unchanging melodic pitch in the first violins, highlighting the conflict between a seemingly timeless melody and its agitated accompaniment.

Yet another type of tension can be felt right at the start of the second subject, in the form of the strange rhythmic jolt at Fig. 9, where the new melody appears to enter two beats early, as if the result of a bad edit. Shostakovich starts the accompaniment midway through the previous bar, where he indicates an approximate doubling of the tempo. The jolt occurs because the rhythmic structure of the new melody is designed to require six beats of introductory vamp (which it subsequently gets at Fig. 15 and again at Fig. 39), rather than the four beats that it gets here.

Different though they are to each other, both the first and second subjects of this exposition share a similar approach to melodic writing—long-limbed and exploratory. Here, melody is as likely to drive harmony as vice-versa. Richard

Longman rather fittingly invokes that other exponent of the seemingly self-propelling melody, Berlioz:

> Shostakovich seldom ... expresses himself in the manner of a conventional melodist, with balanced phrases and harmonic periodicity, a feature for which the most appropriate historical precedent is found in Berlioz, who developed a highly idiosyncratic, asymmetrical linear style, but for whom the foundational pull of the cadence still dominated the linear conception. The literary technique, whereby the flow of writing indicates a psychological "stream of consciousness," finds its counterpart in Berlioz's desire to correlate the behaviour of thematic ideas, in their linear "exposition" and "development," with a pre-conceived and possibly programmatic expressive scheme. Something similar can often be found in Shostakovich's compositional process.[6]

Development

Most commentators place the start of the development at Fig. 17, where the music breaks suddenly into a faster tempo and a new texture. It is here that the inexorable build-up to the movement's climax begins. However, there is a case for placing the development's beginning at Fig. 15,[7] notwithstanding the fact that the passage between Fig. 15 and Fig. 17, a restatement of the second subject in the violas, bears more resemblance to what has been rather than to what is coming. Viewing the form dynamically (i.e., in terms of musical function) rather than statically (i.e., marking off sections based on surface resemblances and differences), it is at Fig. 15 that the music first suggests its new, ominous course. The awkward major seventh drop between the melody's third and fourth notes (Figs. 15, b4–5), replacing the lyrical minor seventh in the original version (Fig. 9, b3–4), provides a sinister twist here. And not only is the accompanying harmony generally more dissonant than before, but the scoring in divided cellos and divided basses is murkier and more threatening than the simpler, more transparent spacing earlier.

However, the largest difference at Fig. 15 is the replacement of violins with violas for the melody itself. From the theoretical standpoint, the violas here go about as high, relative to their highest open string, as the violins had done, relative to theirs. In practice, however, this is more difficult terrain for the violas. Not only is intonation in this region more problematic—sometimes even with top rank orchestras—but the sound itself has a sense of strain, a somewhat pinched quality compared to the violin. Yet, Shostakovich uses this "failing" to musical advantage, for his switching to the violas at Fig. 15 heightens the sense of imminent danger for both performer and listener. Something similar happens at the same point in the Eighth Symphony, the development of which also starts with the recall of an exposition theme, this time the work's introduction. In its original presentation at the start of the Eighth, this theme is given commandingly by the cellos and double basses. At the start of the development (Fig. 17), Shostakovich scores it hauntingly for four flutes in unison in their very lowest register, once again deliberately exploiting a weak register to enhance the sense of frailty and impending disaster. Mahler's influence once again looms large.

If Fig. 15 marks the psychological start of the development, Fig. 17 provides the first move towards the movement's *Allegro*. At Fig. 17, b3, the first subject returns, in F Phrygian, scored for four horns in their pedal register, accompanied by ("pitted against" might be more accurate) the anapest from Fig. 12—the first glimpse of what is to be one of the defining features of this development, indeed of Shostakovich's development sections in general, namely the presentation of earlier themes in direct counterpoint with each other, replete with all the usual baroque techniques: augmentation, diminution, inversion, fragmentation, and stretto.

The sense of increased activity at Fig. 17 derives more from the change to a percussive texture (pizzicato cellos/basses and piano) than from Shostakovich's small tempo increase (quarter = 84 to quarter = 92). But the control of the ensuing *accelerando* is one of the most remarkable aspects of the movement. There are two simultaneous and seemingly contradictory factors at work. On the one hand, the *accelerando* itself occurs very gradually over forty-two bars (Fig. 18, b4 to Fig. 25, b4),[8] giving an almost Sibelius-like sense of slow, organic change. Yet the transition from the exposition's *Moderato* to the development's central *Allegro* actually feels quite concise. How can these two apparently contradictory impressions be reconciled? The fact that, for example, Fig. 19 feels significantly faster than Fig. 17 actually has less to do with the *accelerando* (a modest push from quarter = 92 to quarter = 104) than with the melody's rhythmic diminution at Fig. 19. Fig. 18 represents an intermediate step, with the melody in the original note values in the trumpets pitted against the rhythmic diminution in the horns. However, while the pacing of the melody at Fig. 19 has indeed doubled, the underlying anapestic accompaniment, the rhythmic values of which have not altered, has accelerated only as much as the overall pulse has (i.e., 92 to 104). And so Shostakovich creates an *accelerando* that works simultaneously on two temporal planes. As the development progresses, a similar process takes place with the anapestic accompanimental figure, as it eventually becomes superseded by *its* diminution. At Fig. 19, b5, a dactyl (an anapest in reverse) at double speed forms part of the woodwind quotation of the movement's introductory theme. Over the next eight bars, the original and double-speed versions appear in counterpoint with each other. Finally, at Fig. 21, b3, the originally paced anapest disappears altogether. By Fig. 24, the fast dactyl is the predominant accompanimental figure, and remains so until Fig. 32.

The *accelerando* is suddenly thwarted by the arrival of the first subject in a militaristic guise (Fig. 27). Both the scoring for three trumpets and the use of the bright Lydian mode give this march a steely incisiveness. As David Fanning notes, this point also represents the culmination of a long process of tonal ascent, i.e., from D minor/Phrygian (1st theme), via E-flat minor (2nd theme), to F Phrygian (start of development), and F Lydian (here at Fig. 27). As Fanning writes, the move from F Phrygian to F Lydian "both continues and frustrates the overall sensation of ascent (raising of second, third, fourth, sixth, and seventh degrees, combined with immobility of 'tonic')."[9] This tonal "frustration" is reinforced by Shostakovich's control of tempo. Following the *poco stringendo* at Fig. 26, b7, the brakes are then suddenly applied two bars later for the start of the march (*poco sostenuto*)—an instruction that is often ignored in performance, thus negating the feeling of a reactive force, of a new, slower tempo crushing the old one into submission.

The point of maximum dissonance in this development is reached at Fig. 30 with a clash between the exposition's two principal key centers—an E-flat minor (or more, specifically, E-flat Phrygian) scale in the horns and trumpets superimposed over D minor triads in the rest of the orchestra. Fanning has compared this moment to the famous "Schreckensfanfare" that opens the finale of Beethoven's Ninth Symphony. As Fanning points out, each represents an emotional crisis point, and each consists of a superimposition of the two principal tonal areas of the respective first movements.[10] Given that Fig. 30 is the point at which the aforementioned tonal ascent is finally halted, it is tempting to extend the Beethoven Ninth analogy. Could Shostakovich possibly have had in mind here the text associated with Beethoven's "Schreckensfanfare": "O Freunde! Nicht diese Töne"—an acknowledgement that enough is enough?

If the crisis at Fig. 30 represents the climax of the conflict between the exposition's two main tonal areas, it is also the culmination of a more local process involving the creation of bitonality through ostinato. There is a progression of dissonance starting at Fig. 27, where the melody in F Lydian plays over a tonic-dominant ostinato (providing, incidentally, the first clear tonal center since the start of the development). The harmonic tension increases at Fig. 28, b2 (melody in A Phrygian, ostinato still in F), and intensifies still further, as the note A emerges as its own ostinato, becoming part of the D minor ostinato finally to clash with the trumpets' high B-flat at Fig. 30. In fact, this creation of dissonance through ostinato continues beyond Fig. 30. However, in terms purely of harmonic dissonance, the great clash at Fig. 30 represents the culmination of this process. Neither the subsequent chromatic descent over the D minor ostinato (Fig. 31) nor the clash between B-flat minor and the D pedal (Fig. 31, b4–5) quite matches the dissonant intensity of Fig. 30. Fig. 30, then, represents a convergence of no fewer than three independent factors: the clash between the exposition's two principal tonal areas; the halting and subsequent reversal of the movement's overall tonal ascent; and the climax of a progression of dissonance created by a characteristic use of ostinato.

This crisis point is manifested not just harmonically, but also timbrally and registrally, demonstrating a much underrated aspect of Shostakovich's composition, namely the ability to use orchestration for structural purposes. At Fig. 30, the trumpets' high C (sounding B-flat) is their highest note in the movement, and causes this already dissonant moment to sound particularly strident. It is also notable that Shostakovich uses the cymbals particularly sparingly during this movement, reserving them only for the most significant structural points. Other than one crash at the start of the "military" episode (Fig. 27), and three crashes

introducing and subsequently punctuating the first theme's restatement as the recapitulation begins to emerge (Fig. 36 et seq.), the only appearance of the cymbals
in the movement is here at Fig. 30.

Of course, harmony is not the only generator of musical tension. Between Figs. 31
and 32, the *poco stringendo* indication, the switch from a lighter ostinato (xylophone) to a heavier one (timpani and snare drum), and the quickly descending
chromatic line all combine to create an almost unstoppable momentum. This
intensification occurs despite the mollifying of dissonance following Fig. 30. The
two bars before Fig. 32 witness the proverbial clash between the immovable object
(the rhythmic inertia of the syncopated closing theme motive—from Fig. 13—in
augmentation) and the irresistible force (the frenetic percussion).

Although the development up to this point has drawn from each of the movement's main themes, it has been the transformations of the first subject that have
resonated the most strongly. The few definable tonal centers in this development
are all associated with first-subject transformations—F Phrygian (Fig. 17), F
Lydian (Fig. 27), D minor/E-flat Phrygian (Fig. 30). And these particular transformations stand out orchestrally with their percussive reinforcement: piano and pizzicato low strings (Fig. 17); snare drum and timpani (Fig. 27); xylophone and
cymbals (Fig. 30). At Fig. 32, however, the emphasis shifts away from the first
subject and onto the introduction and second subject material. And the creating
of tension by what one might term "vertical" means (a few strong tonal centers reinforced by heavy percussion) is now replaced by a more horizontal accumulation.
The accompaniment at Fig. 32 is a stretto working of the movement's canonic
introduction, while the brass and double basses intone a canonic version of the
movement's second subject. Given that the second subject is itself a rhythmic augmentation of the introduction, the effect is essentially that of a cantus firmus supporting contrapuntal variations of itself.

Recapitulation

The start of the recapitulation is traditionally a defining moment in a sonata
form movement. This is no less so with Shostakovich, yet in this movement,
authors differ in their placement of the recapitulation's point of arrival.

Several commentators (e.g., Jacques Wildberger and Hugh Ottaway)[11] place the
recapitulation at Fig. 36, the *largamente* re-establishment of the first subject in an
orchestral unison. It is here that the music is, in the words of David Fanning,
"called to order by the authoritarian recitative, which proclaims the opening of
the recapitulation."[12] Following the development's contrapuntally "brutalized" thematic treatment, the unison appearance at Fig. 36 of the first subject in a straightforward, "unbrutalized" form indeed represents the thematic point of resolution.
And although this appearance omits the theme's opening, and corresponds only to
its second and third strains, our perception of thematic resolution remains intact.
Fig. 36 is also the point at which the brakes are imposed, and the basic slow-to-
moderate pulse of the movement re-established; and it is at Fig. 36 that the D

minor tonic returns. There is even, as one might traditionally expect at this juncture, a sort of dominant preparation (cf. bars 4 and 5). In the four bars preceding Fig. 36, the strings and woodwinds reiterate a high inverted dominant pedal, while the brass harmonically align themselves in preparation for the big cadence at Fig. 36.

However, the above interpretation fails to account for the unresolved tension not only at Fig. 36, but through the entire passage between Figs. 36 and 38, b3, i.e., through the entire restatement of the first theme (Example 13.1 shows a harmonic reduction of this passage). In the first place, the cadence at Fig. 36 does not fully convince, despite four bars of dominant preparation. The hollow chord of arrival, a bare fifth (D and A), is partly responsible, but so is the dominant preparation itself, which is based not on dominant but on second inversion tonic harmony, or, at least, two notes of it (A and D). Despite its spectacular timpani entrance and "authoritarian" posture, Fig. 36 is not so much a cadence as a mere switching of a "second inversion" dyad (A and D) into a "root position" dyad (D and A). Although the restatement of the first theme that emerges from Fig. 36 goes some way towards tonal reinforcement, the next cadence at Fig. 36, b4 is even less authoritative. The chord of departure is reduced to one note, the timpani A, removing any second inversion connotation. But this time, the instability results from the added-seventh chord of arrival (D, A, C, with the seventh in the bass). This instability is enhanced rhythmically by the insertion of an extra beat. (One expects the melody at Fig. 37 to start one beat earlier, as it does in the exposition. As a result, Fig. 37 is altered to 5/4 time so that the melody has an extra beat to catch up with itself.)

Example 13.1

Unlike these weak cadences, the progression between Fig. 38 and 38, b3 establishes the dominant of D convincingly. The bass line, with its strong tendential pull (B, B-flat, A) creates a Phrygian-style cadence which collapses, *con tutta forza*, onto an imposing six-bar dominant pedal (using the work's anapest motive), over which is intoned the movement's introductory theme in the brass. The tonal collapse at Fig. 38, b3 is reinforced orchestrally by the use of the tam-tam, an instrument used only twice in this Symphony, and one historically associated with moments of collapse or even shipwreck (e.g., Strauss' *Ein Heldenleben* or Rimsky-Korsakov's *Scheherazade*). The dominant pedal then resolves at Fig. 39 for the return of the second subject in D major. As a result, several authors (Joseph Huband,[13] Bill Stanley,[14] and Tim Souster[15]) consider Fig. 39, with its fuller tonal resolution, to represent the starting point of the recapitulation.

In an attempt to reconcile this problem of placement, several commentators (e.g., Eric Roseberry,[16] Hugh Ottaway,[17] and Richard Longman[18]) refer to a development/recapitulation overlap spanning Figs. 36 to 39. Discussing a similar dilemma in the Tenth Symphony's first movement, David Fanning acknowledges that "recapitulation is not suddenly registered, but gradually impinges on the consciousness of the listener."[19] Although the Fifth cannot match the Tenth in the imperceptibility of its transitions—the beginning and end of the overlap phase (Figs. 36 and 38, b3) are marked with grand rhetorical gestures, the likes of which are not found in the Tenth—the concept of a recapitulation that is revealed only in stages very much applies here too. Here and elsewhere in this volume, I have coined (based on Fanning's observation) the term "gradually emerging recapitulation" to describe this process. Although Shostakovich was not the first to explore this idea—the finale of Dvorak's Ninth Symphony provides an interesting parallel[20]—it would become a defining aspect of his symphonic and chamber composition for at least the next couple of decades. (Incidentally, Karen Kopp places the recapitulation back at Fig. 32.[21] Although Fig. 32 does indeed restate the movement's introduction in a canonic presentation and might on paper appear recapitulatory, there is little resolution here; much as in a baroque fugue, the stretto presentation generates rather than dissipates tension.)

Finally, in considering this issue, we should not underestimate the power of performance to affect our perception of how exactly the recapitulation emerges. In the second of André Previn's two recordings, for example, both the very substantial *ritardando* in the dominant preparation before Fig. 36 and the stately rendition of the ensuing *largamente* suggest Fig. 36 as the start of the recap.[22] By contrast, Neeme Järvi's recording preserves more of the developmental momentum through the disputed territory, finally reaching its climax at Fig. 38, b3.[23]

Reprise of Second Subject

The crushing anapests at Fig. 38, b3 resolve onto a faster, gentler version of the same rhythm at Fig. 39, setting the stage for the reprise of the second subject, now presented in D major as a one-bar canon between flute and horn. Ian MacDonald has characterized the reprise—with the copy-cat horn slavishly following the flute—as an example of Shostakovichian lampoonery.[24] Musical mimicry seemingly connoting slavish stupidity was a common enough feature in Shostakovich—the oboe/bassoon variation (Fig. 25) of the Seventh Symphony's march theme comes to mind, with the bassoon dutifully mimicking, in full, the oboe's every banal utterance. Yet, there, the humor stems not just from the mimicry but also from the blatant hijacking of symphonic progress, something that is not in evidence here in the Fifth Symphony's flute/horn duo. Indeed, the second subject reprise here appears to represent a genuine attempt at resolution after the development's brutality and is perhaps the Symphony's one true moment of sunshine, a place where tragedy and irony are kept, temporarily, at bay. It is not just the change to D major from the exposition's tense E-flat minor. The simple canonic presentation here causes the melodic activity to occur at twice the rate as in the exposition, thus taking some of the stress off the melody's long lines; the motion is now lighter, the air easier. A comparison also reveals less agitation in both the harmony and the harmonic rhythm here compared to the exposition. The little rhythmic disorientation—the "bad edit"—from Fig. 9 is also gone; the theme now comes in on the "right" beat. Finally, this reprise could be said to represent the resolution, in canonic form, of the tension-building stretto on this same theme at Fig. 32. In fact, Eric Roseberry has suggested that this reprise of the second theme represents also an allusion to its roots, i.e., the movement's canonic introductory theme.[25]

Towards the end of this reprise (Fig. 41, b2), the clarinet throws in a reminiscence of the third strain from the first subject group (cf. Fig. 5, b2). It emerges naturally from out of the second subject melody, floating above the continuing second subject accompaniment, and creates yet another level of resolution as first and second subjects become temporarily one. This is perhaps a continuity of a process first seen in the Fourth Symphony's first movement where, at the point of recapitulation, the second subject is made to behave as if it were the first subject (see "Comparison of First Movement with Earlier Models," below). Here in the Fifth Symphony, the thematic simile has become a metaphor, so to speak. The treatment of the inverted second theme at Fig. 42 is also somewhat resolved, with its accompanimental figures lacking the lurching "hairpins" of its exposition counterpart (Fig. 12). The melody is given to a solo bassoon, as opposed to the violas in the exposition. As Eric Roseberry points out, Shostakovich frequently used the bassoon for the purposes of "recharacterizing" a theme in his recapitulations,[26] although in this case the reprised melody is preserved in its original form.

Coda

After the glimmer of hope of the second subject reprise, the coda reasserts the air of tragic tension. It begins with an inversion of the first subject's first strain in E Phrygian (Fig. 44, b2), followed by a reprise of its third strain in D minor (Fig. 45, b2); both are accompanied by the movement's introductory vamp. Why did Shostakovich create an inversion for this, the only appearance of the first strain in the recapitulation? Perhaps it is because it was this first strain that received the most brutalized treatment during the development section—in particular, the transformation for four horns at Fig. 17, b3, the grotesque march for three trumpets at Fig. 27, and the crisis point at Fig. 30. That it never again appears in its original form suggests perhaps that it had been literally "killed off" in the mind of the composer. The use of inversion here creates the effect of a theme rising from the ashes of past catastrophe into the rarefied air from which it originally came, returning us full circle. This gives way to the rising first subject third strain (where the piccolo's sound literally rises from out of the flute's), and finally to the ascending chromatic scales in the celesta that bring the movement to a close. (Incidentally, a transformation of this "inverted" flute melody is heard in the slow movement as a low second flute countermelody to the movement's second theme—Fig. 80.)

The transition to D minor at Fig. 45, b2 is done via a dominant-to-tonic "calling to order" in the trumpets and timpani. The bright, pealing cadences of C major that had marked the trumpets' first appearance in the movement (Fig. 7, b3) have here been transformed into a D minor deathwatch. Shostakovich effects not just a darkening of tonality, but also a darkening of tone, using the lower register of the trumpets to create a more sinister timbre. The unison scoring (as opposed to the two-part harmony at Fig. 7, b3) creates an additional "dirtying" of the tone, caused by the inevitable problems of pitch when two trumpets play in unison, *pianissimo*, in their lower register.

The use of the celesta at the very end, its only appearance in the movement, recalls the close of the Fourth Symphony. Shostakovich went on to use the celesta to conclude both the Thirteenth and the Fifteenth Symphonies. In all four examples, the instrument provides a glint of light over a long decaying string chord, and plays an important role in establishing the closing tonalities of the respective movements: here in the Fifth and at the end of the Thirteenth Symphony, it provides a chromatically inflected figuration that at the same time supports the tonic; at the end of the Fifteenth Symphony, the celesta provides the long-awaited defining C-sharp over a dyad of A and E; and at the end of the Fourth Symphony, having spun around the tonic triad (C minor) for seventy-six bars, the celesta's final two notes (A and D) ensure that the work ends in a shroud of tonal uncertainty.

Comparison of the First Movement with Earlier Models

The idea of a gradually emerging recapitulation and the associated development of a combined sonata/arch form constituted Shostakovich's most significant innovation in the realm of symphonic thought, one that would be revisited in the Eighth Symphony and achieve its supreme mastery in the Tenth. Yet, it was not formulated overnight. The First Symphony and, in particular, the Cello Sonata and Fourth Symphony played an essential part in its formulation (Table 13.1). In tracing its evolution, we may consider four aspects that help define this unique form: 1) the manner in which the development section heightens tension; 2) disorientation at the point of recapitulation; 3) thematic transformation in the recapitulation; and 4) the fact that the "fully emerged" recapitulation occurs with the second subject theme, and the implications of this for a palindromic or arch-like structure.

Development

Although Shostakovich's First Symphony was rightly praised for its skill and originality, one of the tell-tale signs of its composer's creative immaturity came with the first movement's short development section. Although providing variety

Table 13.1

Overviews of Form in the First Movements of Shostakovich's Symphony No. 1, Cello Sonata, Symphony No. 4, and Symphony No. 5

	Exposition ⟶ Development ⟶ Recapitulation	
Synphony No. 1	Intro →T1→T2	T2→T1→Intro
Cello Sonata	T1→T2	T2→T1
Symphony No. 4	Intro→T1→T1a→T2	Intro→T2→T1a→T1
Symphony No. 5	Intro→T1→T2	T1→T2→T1
		(Fig. 36)

Intro = introductory theme, T1 = 1st theme, T2 = 2nd theme.

and giving a glimpse of Shostakovich's future techniques of thematic combination, it did comparatively little to further symphonic tension beyond what was already established in the exposition. A step forward would come with the first movement of the Cello Sonata. Here, the development does stand out from the other sections, if only by its intensification of rhythm. The process starts with the introduction of a propulsive anapest figure in the piano at the end of the exposition (bar 107), continued by the cello, pizzicato (bar 111). Absent for most of the exposition and recapitulation, this anapest is found in almost every bar of the development, infusing that section with an urgency not felt earlier in the movement. Interestingly, a similar anapest is used early in the development in the Fifth Symphony, launching the *più mosso* at Fig. 17. Unlike the Sonata, the anapest in the Symphony was an important feature from the outset, but it becomes particularly insistent at Fig. 17, due to the faster tempo and to the new, percussive texture (pizzicato cellos/basses and piano). Is it coincidental that this scoring is almost identical to the piano and cello pizzicato at end of the Cello Sonata's exposition?

Increased urgency is even more apparent in the comparatively short development of the Fourth Symphony's first movement. This is in part due to the more continuous nature of this section compared to the more disjointed exposition. The climactic fugato (Fig. 63) may be more impressive for its visceral impact than for its tonal argument, but its whirlwind creates a cumulative momentum found neither in Shostakovich's earlier developments nor, for that matter, in his earlier fugal writing, e.g., the fugati in the Second and Third Symphonies. The development's climax (starting at Fig. 75) is prophetic of the Fifth Symphony's development, with its pounding percussion dactyls (cf. Fifth Symphony, Fig. 27) and its canonic thematic presentation. For an example of the latter, compare Figs. 75–77 in the Fourth with Fig. 32 in the Fifth. In each case, the development's climax is reached via a canon in the brass of a rhythmically augmented exposition theme— the first subject in the Fourth, the second subject in the Fifth.

Where the Fifth Symphony represents an advance over the Fourth is in its superior maintaining of tension between the development's climax and the start of the recapitulation. Here, the Fourth is literally eaten up by its own fury. The apoplectic spasms at Fig. 78, b8 lead almost to disintegration, while the various attempts to regain momentum via the first theme end in frustration (Figs. 79–84). A moment's hope is provided by a waltz-like transformation of the second subject (Fig. 84), but by Fig. 90, the flame is completely burned out.

This entire section is, in a way, representative of the dilemma of the Fourth Symphony. The gradual sapping of momentum is actually rather dramatic and effective in its own terms. But as a preparation for a recap that will itself represent a winding down of musical activity, it is problematic. Shostakovich attempts to reaffirm a sense of purpose to the upcoming recapitulation with a sequence of ever-louder, ever more dissonant chords in the brass and percussion, culminating in a blood-curdling twelve-note cluster, *fffff*, perhaps the ultimate "Schreckens-fanfare" (Figs. 90–91). Next to this twelve-note monstrosity, the Fifth Symphony's crisis chord at Fig. 30 seems relatively tame. Yet, because of the longer-term preparation of its dissonance, it is the latter that makes the more tumultuous impression. Once again, a device used "by assertion" in the Fourth Symphony is, in the Fifth, sublimated in a way both subtler and more powerful. Michael Steinberg compares the relationship between the Fifth Symphony and the Fourth with that between Beethoven's *Leonore III* and *Leonore II* Overtures:

> No. 2 is more daring, the more original; No. 3 is the more controlled, the more classical, and the more dramatic and exciting for it. We may return more often to No. 3, but we also need the stubborn and maverick individuality of the other. Without it we cannot know Beethoven, and without the experience of working his way through the problems of the Second *Leonore* Overture he could not have achieved the Third.[27]

Disorientation and the "Gradually Emerging" Recapitulation

As previously noted, the phenomenon of the "gradually emerging" recapitulation had its roots in earlier music. To the aforementioned finale of Dvorak's Ninth Symphony, one could add the outer movements of Schumann's Fourth, the finales of some of the Bruckner symphonies, and perhaps most pertinent of all, the first movement of Tchaikovsky's Sixth. In terms of Shostakovich's output, once again, the first movements of the First Symphony, Cello Sonata, and Fourth Symphonies would turn out to be staging posts in the formulation of this phenomenon. In the First Symphony, the recapitulation starts with a straightforward restatement of the movement's second subject (Fig. 32), the first stage in a recap that will present the three main exposition themes in reverse order. Likewise, the recapitulation of the Fourth begins with the second subject and presents its two themes in reverse order. But there is a significant difference. In the Fourth Symphony, following a modified reprise of the short introductory material (Fig. 92), Shostakovich lands onto the ostinato C minor chords, which, at the start of the movement, set the stage for the first subject (compare Fig. 93 with Fig. 1). For one bar, there is a full sense of recapitulatory force as tonal and thematic elements align. What we do not know, until the following bar, is that this C minor ostinato is to accompany not the reprise of the first subject, but a rhythmically altered version of the second. The second subject reprise in the First Symphony was straightforward (Fig. 32), untransformed, and presented in its own familiar surroundings. But in the Fourth Symphony, Shostakovich has created a temporary disorientation, dressing up the second subject so as to appear like the first. (It is perhaps a tribute to this movement's underestimated thematic unity that the listener is easily duped into believing that what is actually taking place is a recapitulation of a somewhat altered first theme.)

With this disorientation, Shostakovich in the Fourth Symphony provides an aural corollary to the Gestalt theory of "closure." Generally used in the field of visual perception, this theory states that an object can still be perceived as such even if certain visual cues are missing from its representation. (For example, a picture of a triangle in which a small part of one side or a corner is missing will still be perceived as a triangle.) Here, at the point of recapitulation, Shostakovich provides all but one of the expected first subject "cues": the introductory woodwind material, the re-establishment of the original tempo, the unequivocal return to C minor (particularly striking within the context of a movement with very little tonal stability), the hammering ostinato in the low-middle strings, and the scoring of the ensuing theme for two trumpets and two trombones (although omitting the violins). The only missing cue is the theme itself, which has been replaced by a variant of the second subject. Yet, even without this seemingly crucial element, the recapitulatory force of this moment remains resoundingly intact.

All of this brings us back to the question of how sonata form is primarily perceived: tonally or thematically? This example from the Fourth Symphony forces us to evaluate which aspects of composition (aural cues) are critical to our perception of recapitulation. Here, at least, melody would not seem to be uppermost, for we easily accept the concept of a return to recapitulation despite the absence of a first theme. In the Fifth Symphony, Shostakovich proves a similar point, though by the opposite route. In that context, the return of the first theme at Fig. 36, even with a tentative tonic, is not enough to suggest a fully convincing recapitulation. Thus, the gradually emerging recapitulation of the Fifth is related to the thematic disorientation described in the Fourth. In each case, our perception of recapitulation depends ultimately on the strength of tonal rather than thematic establishment.

Disorientation, albeit of a more traditional type, can also be found in the first movement of the Cello Sonata. Like the First and Fourth Symphonies, the Sonata's recap starts with the second subject and works backwards. However, the tonic (major) is not established until the cello's presentation of this second theme, the initial piano presentation having begun in the submediant, B-flat. This disorientation is particularly apparent since in the exposition both presentations had been in the same key (B major).

Thematic Transformation

As we have seen, the ambiguity at the start of the Fourth Symphony's recapitulation stems not from the fact that the second subject is presented first, but from the fact that it is dressed up so as to make it resemble the first subject. In fact, each theme in this reprise is significantly transformed compared to the exposition. For example, the solo violin at Fig. 101, in 4/4 time and with a simple homophonic pizzicato accompaniment, represents both a textural resolution of the formerly contrapuntal presentation, and a rhythmic stabilization of the original mixed meters (cf. Fig. 7, b3). Similarly, the movement's first theme is transformed into a slow-motion replay for bassoon (Fig. 103).[28]

Such thematic transformation is also present in the first movement of the Cello Sonata. There, the end of the development leads into what is initially a straightforward reprise of the second subject (bar 171), albeit with the aforementioned tonal disorientation. However, the impassioned second half of this theme, which had constituted the exposition's climax (bar 95), is never restated. Instead, the theme disappears into a fermata from which emerges, in the tonic, the first theme in a macabre, slow-motion replay (quarter = 50 as compared to 138 in the exposition). The once flowing piano arpeggios are now reduced to a series of brittle chords, while the sonority of the cello itself assumes an uncharacteristic pallor (bar 196). Both the denial of the second subject's climax and the ghostly transformation of the first subject cause the hitherto lyrical movement to turn quickly and unexpectedly sour.

Thus, we find extensive thematic transformation in the first movement recapitulations of the Cello Sonata, the Fourth and Fifth Symphonies, not to mention the Eighth and Tenth. Within the context of the symphonies, the transformations are perhaps not surprising, created as the inevitable response to the brutality of the respective development sections. However, this cannot be said about the Cello Sonata. Yes, the Sonata's development, in common with those in the symphonies, introduces a new urgency, as discussed above. But at the same time, it does not partake in the brutalization and subsequent devastation that we find in the symphonies. In other words, there is nothing in that development that portends the movement's subsequent thematic emasculation. So, in the context of Shostakovich's evolution as a symphonist, we can see that the act of thematic transformation, which in the Cello Sonata carries a certain shock value, becomes in the later works a more fully integrated structural response.

If the Fifth Symphony consequently possesses a higher level of symphonic integration than either the Fourth or the Cello Sonata, it is in part because of the greater subtlety of its transformations. In the Fifth, they involve for the most part changes in harmonic rhythm, rhythmic emphasis, and texture. Even the most radical transformation, the inversion of the first theme in the coda (Fig. 44, b2), is integrated naturally into the coda's predominantly rising figurations. Compare this to the more drastic transformations in the two earlier works; the grotesque timbral changes, the dramatic fermatas, and the tempo manipulations. The transformations in the Fifth register as strongly, without impeding the larger progress of the movement.

Arch Form

Writers frequently refer to the arch-like or cyclic quality of the Fifth Symphony's first movement. Arch form is usually associated with thematic palindrome, and to an extent this is what happens here; the "fully emerged" recapitulation begins with the second subject (Fig. 39), while first subject material is kept until later, essentially forming the movement's coda. Yet, partly because the first subject does appear at Fig. 36 (i.e., where the recap starts to make its presence known) and partly because there is greater integration and more cross-referencing between the themes themselves, the palindrome here emerges as more general, less strict than in the earlier works, particularly the First Symphony. For example, as we have seen, the reprise of the second subject also contains a strain of the first (Fig. 41, b2), while the introductory theme not only introduces the second theme reprise (Fig. 38, b4) but also underpins the entire coda. In the First Symphony, the themes are more discrete, with less bleed-through, and the symmetry of the arch structure emerges with no competing forces. The Fifth, on the other hand, mingles to a more profound degree the palindromic, retrogressive demands of arch form with the progressive demands of the sonata principle, producing a creative tension not felt in the earlier work.

Structural Connections with Other Movements

No analysis would be complete without discussion of the ways in which this first movement projects itself onto the rest of the work. Most obvious are the inter-movement motivic relationships, a hallmark of Shostakovich. However, just as important is the longer-term playing out of the short and medium term cyclic attributes noted in the discussion of the first movement. A brief discussion of these two features follows. A more general stylistic discussion of the Symphony's second, third, and fourth movements can be found in Chapter 6; the discussion below will focus only on those aspects that specifically relate back to the Symphony's first movement.

In some ways, the second movement scherzo functions as a response to the unresolved tensions of the first movement, and it is no surprise to find that the two movements share certain characteristics. Unlike the contrapuntal opening of the first movement, the scherzo begins with a simple monodic declamation. However, both launch with the sonority of unaccompanied cellos and basses, and both contain a degree of tonal ambiguity. In the scherzo, it is not until the melody at Fig. 49 that the tonic, A minor, is really established. Up to this point, C major is also a candidate (this despite the A minor scale in the fifth and sixth bars). As discussed above, the first movement's introduction also functions as a ritornello, sometimes accompanying, sometimes linking the various thematic strains. While the scherzo's opening is not woven into the subsequent fabric to anything like the same degree, we can, for example, find its first four bars functioning as the bass line to the melody at Fig. 51—its next four bars become the melody itself.

On a local level, the first theme (Fig. 49; Example 13.2a) is an outgrowth of the movement's opening three pitches (E–D–C). But it is also connected to the first movement's first subject, with its descending scalar motion from dominant to tonic (Example 13.2b). Of course, the scalar descending fifth is such a commonplace in Western music that its appearance at the start of these two melo-dies may be more coincidence than connection. Yet the link is reinforced by two other features. The first is the rhythmic profile of the first three notes: in both cases, one long note followed by two short. The second, and perhaps more impor-tant, is the emphasis placed on the supertonic degree. In the first movement, this was achieved through chromatic coloration. Here in the scherzo, the supertonic is emphasized with a trill (Fig. 49, b2). In each case, the supertonic enjoys the natu-ral stress of being placed on the first beat of the bar.

Example 13.2a

Example 13.2b

These respective first themes, then, with their different ways of stressing the sec-ond degree of the scale, seem to represent two sides of the same musical coin. Moreover, just as the Neapolitan relationship would assume a larger structural role in the first movement, the "trill motive,"[29] in a much less ambitious way, takes on its own life in the scherzo, e.g., the sequence at Fig. 53, b8, et seq. (While one can become too eager in the search for thematic allusions, it is difficult not to hear in this "trill motive" a reference to the scherzo of Mahler's Sixth Symphony (bar 16–17, et al.), another *Ländler*-type movement.)

The trill thus replaces the Neapolitan coloration as the means of melodic super-tonic emphasis. However, the Neapolitan tonal relationship is present in this scherzo, just as it had been in the first movement, namely in the surprise modula-tion to C-sharp minor in the scherzo's reprise (Fig. 69) of a theme which, the first time around, is presented in C minor (Fig. 53). This modulation is in fact the sole compositional difference, other than re-orchestration, between the A and A' sec-tions of this otherwise classically arranged (scherzo-trio-scherzo-coda) movement. To an even greater degree than in the first movement, Shostakovich prepares this modulation literally at the last moment (F-sharp replaces F-natural one eighth note before the start of the theme). The subsequent return to C minor for the sec-ond half of the theme (Fig. 70, b9) is carried out with equal speed. The effect is to put this "raised" passage almost in quotation marks. Shostakovich makes the point orchestrally too. The theme, in the horns at Figs. 54, 56, and 72 (all in C minor), is temporarily shifted to the brighter trumpets for its one appearance in C-sharp minor at Fig. 70.

A further motivic connection to the first movement can be found in the two transformations of a rising minor ninth motive—compare the second movement (Fig. 53, b4; Example 13.3a) with the first movement (Fig. 1, b3; Example 13.3b). In addition to the melodic contour, there is a similar rhythmic profile: a long note (or several repeated shorter notes) at the bottom of the run, followed by a faster ascent.

Example 13.3a

Example 13.3b

Although the finale is not related formally to the first movement,[30] important cross-references exist. The first movement's approach to tension-building through tonal ascent is, in part, replicated. In the finale, following the D minor opening, the next major structural point, the return of the opening theme (Fig. 104), is cast in E-flat minor, a relationship exactly paralleling that between the opening movement's first and second subjects. In fact, the ascent here in the finale continues on to E minor four bars later.

The first movement and the finale both contain passages that might be described as a "rush to disaster." In the first movement, this occurs at Fig. 31, immediately after the "crisis chord" at Fig. 30. Most of the orchestra hurtles downwards, *poco stringendo*, leading to the tragic stretto presentation of the introductory and second subject material in the brass (Fig. 32). In the finale, a similar descent occurs (Fig. 110, b11), leading to a bitonal stretto presentation of the movement's opening material in the brass. In fact, the descents themselves are similarly constructed. In the first movement, the descent occurs in parallel sixths; in the finale mainly in first inversion chords, i.e., chords in which the sixth is the defining interval. Both descents end on a dissonance; the first movement's on a grinding chord of B-flat minor over a D pedal; the finale's on a diminished seventh chord built on D. In the first movement, the tension is heightened by the presence of a pounding ostinato, in the finale by a screaming high pedal. Both the ostinato and the pedal act as a linear constant, albeit a highly energized one, from which the descending scale pulls away.

The fourth movement coda begins with reminders of two previous passages in the Symphony. The growling unison pedal for four horns (Fig. 121, b4) reminds us of the start of the first movement's brutalizing development (Fig. 17, b3), while the melody in the clarinets and bassoons is reminiscent of the scoring of the slow movement's first theme as it appears at the outset of its tragic build-up (Fig. 87). These two orchestrational reminiscences of the Symphony's tragic past—or, more specifically, reminiscences of passages that *inaugurate* motion towards two of the Symphony's tragic peaks—plus the portentous murmurings of distant percussion set the tone of this coda. Following immediately on the heels of the Pushkin quotation, with its "Visions of original, pure days," these grim reminders of the past are particularly striking.

In the Symphony's D major peroration, there are two final reminders of the first movement's influence. The clash at Fig. 133 between the subdominant minor dyad (G and B-flat) in the trumpets and trombones against the tonic-based bare fifth dyad (D and A) in the rest of the orchestra provides the one moment of harmonic stress in this otherwise purely tonic-dominant environment (Example 13.4a). But it also provides a reminder of the very opening of the Symphony (Example 13.4b): its turbulent melodic leap, D to B-flat, here rendered as a harmonic discord. In both cases, the B-flat resolves downwards to A.

Example 13.4a

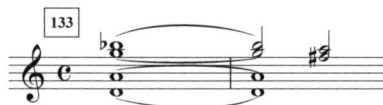

Example 13.4b

The second reminiscence of the Symphony's opening is an augmentation at Fig. 134 of the anapest rhythm from bar 4 of the first movement. This rhythm proves to be one of the Symphony's most durable elements, appearing in a variety of transformations throughout the work. This final manifestation at Fig. 134 is almost a tribute to its durability: carrying on its shoulders a set of weighty D major tonic chords, it appears almost as an act of defiance in the face of all the odds.

In any of the usual senses of the word, Shostakovich's Fifth Symphony would probably not be considered a cyclic work. There is neither wholesale cross-referencing of themes between movements (as there is, for example, in the Eleventh or

Twelfth Symphonies), nor is there an *idée fixe* that carries over the course of the entire work (as in the Eighth Quartet). But in the most linguistically pure sense—that in which "cyclic" is the adjective of "cycle"—the Fifth Symphony does contain several important manifestations. In the short term, the first movement's first subject group can be seen as both tonally and thematically cyclic. Where typically, in a sonata style movement, one expects a "progressive" approach to modulation between first and second subject, there is here a "cyclic" return both to the movement's tonic and to its introductory material just moments before the entrance of the second theme. Likewise, in the medium term, the entire first movement, with its arch-like construction, is also cyclic: a symphonic journey that ends where it began. By the end of the Symphony, we have experienced the cyclic projection of the work as a whole, with its "verticalization" of the Symphony's opening melodic minor sixth (Fig. 133) and the final protracted assertion of its most important rhythmic germ, the three-note anapest (Fig. 134). Within this framework of short-, medium-, and long-term cyclism can be found the many other cross-movement references: the frequent appearance of the anapest; descending scalar figures that stress, in one way or another, the supertonic degree; the use of the Phrygian mode and Phrygian-type approaches to important cadences; canonic deployment of themes in the brass before major climaxes in the outer movements, followed by the use of the tam-tam to signify collapse; the use of the celesta to close the two slower movements, etc.

In the nineteenth century, the use of cyclism was often tied in with a work's extramusical elements. Shostakovich too was influenced by that tradition. In the Eleventh Symphony, the bleak references in the second and fourth movements to the opening "Palace Square" material have an obviously programmatic function, while the recurrence of the composer's own DSCH monogram in the Eighth Quartet emphasizes the autobiographical nature of that work. In the Fifth Symphony, the cyclism exists on a more subtextual level, yet one that ultimately gives added meaning to the finale's Pushkin quotations and its cyclic "visions of original, pure days."

Table 13.2
Shostakovich Symphony No. 5, First Movement: Overview of Form

	Fig.	Initial Key
Exposition		
Introduction—ritornello theme		D min
Theme 1: 1st strain	1	D min/Phrygian
Ritornello	2, b2	C min
2nd strain	3	A min
3rd strain	5, b2	D min
Ritornello	6	D min
Theme 2	9	E-flat min
Closing theme	13	B-flat min

(Continued)

Table 13.2 (*continued*)

	Fig.	Initial Key
Development		
Section 1: based on theme 2	15	B min
Section 2: based mostly on theme 1	17	F Phrygian
Section 3: based on theme 1	27	F Lydian
Section 4: based on introduction/theme 2	32	B-flat min
Section 5: transformed recap of theme 1	36	D min
		joint development/recap area, or "gradually emerging" recapitulation
Recapitulation and Coda		
Theme 1	36	D min
Theme 2	39	D maj
Closing theme	43	A min
Theme 1 (Coda)	44	E Phrygian - D min

min = minor; maj = major.

CHAPTER 14

TWENTY-FOUR PRELUDES AND FUGUES, OP. 87: STRUCTURAL MODEL AND MANIPULATION

Andrew Grobengieser

Many studies of recent years have recognized the need to uncover the meaning of an often overused concept: that of *genre*. Jeffrey Kallberg, for example, suggests that many studies seek to define a genre "according to those characteristics shared by all of its members, mistakenly assuming that shared characteristics inevitably form part of any definition."[1] A system of classification that groups by similarities alone ignores attributes such as history, function, interpretation, and communicability from composer to listener.

Musical analysis, in and of itself, sits somewhat at odds with the study of genre; the former often uses the latter as a means to a predetermined end, searching for shared characteristics above any associations of historical function or reception. Such generic categorization is an inherent and necessary part of any analytical system and, with its establishment of "norms," enables us to converse efficiently about music. But it can threaten to explain away idiosyncrasies as "deviations" rather than as necessary elements of a unique musical composition. Essentially, we are presented with the problem of "prescriptive" versus "descriptive" analysis. The former assumes a mold into which music is poured; the latter acknowledges the composition as an individual, detailed realization of underlying principles. Analysis is at its most effective when it can balance generalization, a tool necessary for the distillation of fundamental principles, with specificity, which gives us a reason for analyzing a given musical composition in the first place.

As we attempt to determine why genre plays such a delicate role in analysis, we can see that specific works have had a role in "defining" the genres to which they belong. Let us take, for example, the contrapuntal keyboard music of the late Baroque, and perhaps its pinnacle work, J. S. Bach's *Well-Tempered Clavier*. The preludes and fugues amassed in this collection are both a virtual treatise in tonal counterpoint and a distinct representation of the concept of a prelude/fugue cycle. This is to say that while the individual preludes and fugues stand as definitive examples of Bach's contrapuntal style, they just as importantly constitute parts of a whole and, as such, have served to define the prelude/fugue cycle in terms of overall layout and philosophy. Genre association may occur at different levels within the same work: at the first level, the notion of the "prelude" or the "fugue"; secondly, the way in which a prelude/fugue pair may exist as a unit; and at the highest level, the concept of the prelude/fugue cycle as evidenced by the inclusion and equal representation of all major and minor keys and the consistency of compositional language. And the *Well-Tempered Clavier* is arguably the work from which we derive all of these genre-related associations.

Though born of a vastly different compositional universe, Shostakovich's Twenty-four Preludes and Fugues, op. 87, invites similar assumptions about genre. Two centuries after the *Well-Tempered Clavier*, Shostakovich constructed a work of comparable magnitude that further explored the challenges of the prelude/fugue cycle. Viewed in light of our genre discussion, questions abound. What is the function of a prelude in the context of a twentieth-century work? What principles underlie the construction of a Shostakovich fugue? Do these observations suggest the existence of a conceptual model that underlies the prelude or fugue? And can we learn anything about the process by which such a model is transformed (regardless of Shostakovich's own cognition of it) into a unique result?

Shostakovich fully realized his debt to Bach.[2] At the very outset, in the Prelude No. 1 in C, he presents a five-note tonic triad (Example 14.1b) that is nothing more than a simultaneous sounding of the first five notes of Bach's C major Prelude from *Well-Tempered Clavier I*, identical in register and doubling (Example 14.1a); no tribute could be simpler. Another reference may be heard in the broken chords and scales of Prelude No. 10 in C-sharp minor (Example 14.2b), which echo the texture of the E-flat major Prelude from *Well-Tempered Clavier I* (Example 14.2a).

Example 14.1a

Example 14.1b

Example 14.2a

Example 14.2b

Such comparisons might constitute a first step in determining the influences acting upon Shostakovich. Yet, one would also have to consider the prelude and/or fugue repertoire post-Bach. Twentieth-century examples include Hindemith's *Ludus Tonalis* (1942) or even Shostakovich's own Twenty-four Preludes, op. 34 (1933). This in turn raises a new question: what properties does a fugue without traditional tonal orientation share with a fugue composed during the first half of the eighteenth century? Devising a meaningful analytical method poses a challenge.

This study is designed to take a step in that direction. However, rather than using analytical comparisons with other works, it is, in a way, self-referential. By looking at the entire set and observing the degree to which Shostakovich's language is consistent from one prelude/fugue pair to the next, an underlying structural model may be revealed – "structure" here incorporating form, tonality (or its absence), development, and other principles of organization – a model from which individual prelude/fugue pairs are generated. As previously discussed, such a paradigm has both benefits and drawbacks. On the positive side, it allows for logical discussion of formal elements and satisfies the need for a frame of reference. Conversely, a model too narrow in scope cannot account for "exceptions" and denies the individuality of one work as distinguished from the whole. Therefore, there has to be another part of the equation. By applying a paradigm to the individual pieces and observing the connections and relationships that result, it is possible to observe "manipulation" of the model. Manipulation is the process by which the model undergoes transformation and becomes the actual work. It may manifest itself as a developmental scheme, a relationship between pitches or tonalities, or any other compositional device. The underlying idea is that the music is generated in a fairly consistent way by the manipulation of elements unique to each prelude/fugue pair.

The subsequent discussion is laid out so as to correspond with the dual approaches of model and manipulation. Firstly, the compositional language of the set will be considered, and both the traditional and non-traditional elements in Shostakovich's conception of tonality and counterpoint discussed. Then, the premise of model will be established by examining the entire set from a surface level, defining the important parameters, and drawing up meaningful generalizations that will ultimately serve as basis for comparison. Finally, the analytical process will be reversed: with a detailed examination of two prelude/fugue pairs (Nos. 3 and 8), we will observe how, through some specific form of manipulation, the individual work is realized.

Compositional Language

One of the most distinctive properties of Shostakovich's op. 87 is its diversity. The individual preludes and fugues are as unique in character as any of his works, programmatic or not. They range from the serious to the light-hearted, from the improvisational to the thoroughly academic. The preludes, in particular, prove to be a vehicle for great variety. They may take the form of etudes, such as Nos. 2 or 21; or dance-like pieces, for instance Nos. 11 and 15. Shostakovich effectively borrows elements from other musical styles and settings, whether rhythmic, textural, or otherwise, and uses them as seeds from which the character of the prelude is defined. Witness the gentle sarabande rhythm of No. 1, the chant-like unison recitatives of Nos. 3 and 9, or the weighty passacaglia subject of No. 12. Even in this supposedly non-programmatic work, one may find Shostakovich parodying the very elements that give the music its character: hence the biting sarcasm that transforms Prelude No. 8 from an innocent dance into a comedy of false starts and ambiguous chromaticism. Though necessarily more limited by the constraints of the genre, the fugues also exhibit a great deal of diversity. In the *Well-Tempered Clavier*, preludes (by their very name) serve more or less to set up the more "academic" fugues that follow. In the Shostakovich, however, the preludes themselves are of sufficient weight and complexity that their corresponding fugues take on the added responsibility of having to complete or comment upon music already heard. This makes the prelude, in every regard, a tough act to follow.

So what holds the set together in terms of language? What are the elements that give it a unity of expression that is uniquely Shostakovich's? The answers to these questions go beyond, but do not exclude, the analytical basics: tonality, form, texture, design, and the like. A comprehensive study of these elements and their transformations will provide a syntax from which to work.

Tonality

Shostakovich's music ranges from tonal conservatism to free dissonance. Yet, even in highly dissonant situations, his method is mostly geared toward tonal ears, but replacing expectations of harmonic progression and key with those of relative intervallic tension and resolution. No longer does the *harmonic* relationship have to be the governing factor in a cadence; even the singular resolution of a tendency tone is an option. Though some may view this as a weaker system of tonal organization, it is in fact an expanded one.

Regardless of the degree to which tonality (in the traditional sense) has been obscured, Shostakovich's treatment of dissonance through intervallic tension and release orients the tonal listener to a state of perception where consonance and dissonance are integrally linked to both the vertical and linear aspects of counterpoint. To observe the universality of this type of language, let us compare two contrasting fugue subjects, those of No. 22 in G minor and No. 15 in D-flat. The former (Example 14.3) is purely diatonic, and although it lacks the leading tone F-sharp, it is thoroughly tonal in effect; the line sets up expectations and resolves them. The minor-sixth leap up to E-flat and subsequent descent to D is an expressive gesture that would not have been out of place in a Baroque fugue subject (the three-note combination of scale degrees 1, 5, and ♭6, in any order, is a favorite of Shostakovich and is encountered frequently throughout op. 87); the B-flat–C–B-flat neighbor-tone motion spanning bars 3–5 also fulfills expectations.

Example 14.3

Upon the return of this subject in the tonic at bar 15, i.e., the exposition's third statement, this pure diatonicism is reaffirmed by the harmony created by the subject together with its accompanying countersubjects; though this later passage is still lacking a leading tone, its tonality remains without question.

Now, let us observe a distinct contrast: the subject of the D-flat Fugue is an eleven-note chromatic "wedge" with D-flat as its axis (Example 14.4). There exist no expectations of tonal resolution of the pitches; the only real expectation is that the wedge continues to expand. However, when the subject re-enters at the tonic pitch level in bar 19, the countersubjects are constructed in a manner consistent with those of the G minor Fugue; namely, the vertical intervallic structures are primarily triadic. Though these are hardly functional chords within a key, the sonorities are familiar. Consonance is preserved as a fundamental truth. Though the subjects of the two fugues are geared towards different aural effects and expectations, they are both able to be incorporated into the same system. Questioning whether or not that system is to be construed as a *tonality* may be missing the mark; Shostakovich creates a mode of listening that incorporates diatonicism and chromaticism equally, and intervallic counterpoint is the arbiter.

Example 14.4

A major feature of Shostakovich's expanded tonal language is his consistent rejection of the seventh scale degree as a leading tone to the tonic, e.g., in the G minor Fugue we just observed. This perhaps serves as the first step in getting the ear to focus more on the intervallic relationships and counterpoint than on tonal expectations. What is required, then, is a broader definition of the term "leading tone." Any pitch that sets up an expectation, whether in context or not, is a leading tone. It may be part of an isolated sonority, or part of a much larger linear scheme. It follows, then, that if Shostakovich wants to achieve a resolute cadence without the 7–8 leading tone, he must do so either through linear motion, or by establishing a context in which specific pitches fulfill expectations. Though purely linear aspects will be discussed later, our exploration of tonality would not be complete without some mention of them here. Example 14.5 is from the end of Prelude No. 7 in A major. The cadential arrival of the tonic is achieved through entirely linear motion; the C-flat–G-flat dyad compresses to D-flat–F before finally converging in bar 23 on E, the fifth of the tonic A. This sort of linear cadence will be observed frequently throughout our study. These mannerisms are as much a part of Shostakovich's language as are his notions of intervallic logic and progression; they represent an aesthetic of tonality freed from many of its traditional confines.

Example 14.5

Modality

The removal, or at least de-emphasis, of functional leading tones often replaces the stability of the diatonic major/minor framework with a sense of modality generated by an equalization among scale degrees. Linear motion can serve either to highlight a specific modal reference or to effectively obscure any sense of centricity around a particular mode, major/minor or otherwise. Naturally, modal connections cannot be made in highly chromatic passages; only when Shostakovich stays with a particular system of diatonic pitches (whether they be diatonic to the overriding key or not)[3] can modal perception occur. Although many of the works in the set are geared more towards linear chromaticism than diatonicism, the modal aspect of a great number of others is too significant to be ignored. In fact, the "floating" quality of the less chromatic pieces can be attributed to an almost pandiatonic treatment of the musical material in some instances; again, the emancipation of tendency tones has a direct effect upon perception.

Modality manifests itself in a number of ways throughout op. 87. Strict modal preservation is perhaps no more obvious than in the Fugue No. 1 in C major. This fugue does not incorporate a single chromatic tone; it is played entirely upon the white notes of the keyboard. The subject is tonally logical; a typical fugal exposition is expected. But the first hint that this fugue will be unique comes with the answer at the dominant. The subject's opening fifth, C-G, would seem to require a tonally adjusted G-C in the answer—not an outrageous assumption even for Shostakovich, who, as we will see later, employs tonal answers with marked consistency. But instead, we are presented with a real dominant answer beginning with G-D. Though the subject itself contains no leading tone, the countersubject here employs F-natural rather than F-sharp, giving this real dominant answer phase a Mixolydian coloring. At this point, the plan of the fugue is laid out: all subsequent entries open with the "real" fifth, regardless of pitch level, yet white-note modality is preserved throughout. The middle entry on E at bar 40 sounds in the Phrygian mode, while its answer on B (bar 48) appears in the Locrian; the middle entry on A (bar 58) sounds in the Aeolian mode and its answer on D (bar 66) is in the Dorian. The subject's final appearance on F (bar 87) is the Lydian mode.

In addition to generating modality through pandiatonic preservation, Shostakovich sometimes creates themes that are themselves modally inflected. The theme of Prelude No. 18 in F minor (Example 14.6) is a ponderous statement in the natural minor (Aeolian) mode. In particular, it reflects the weight of the unraised sixth and seventh scale degrees, D-flat and E-flat. The line is an attempt to push them upwards toward the tonic, but their innate gravity pulls them back down and causes the melody to sink even lower. Replacing the E-flat with a leading tone E-natural would defeat the purpose of this theme, which is the exploitation of these modal degrees and their tendencies.

Example 14.6

Another modally inflected theme is the subject of Fugue No. 19 in E-flat (Example 14.7). The repeated emphasis of F-flat creates a "Jewish" (*freygish*) element—♭2 within an otherwise major-mode framework.

Example 14.7

Linear Aspects

Perhaps the most defining element of op. 87 is that of its linear construction; after all, is not the mark of any good contrapuntist the ability to control the vertical by way of the horizontal? So much of what we have already seen of Shostakovich's tonal language is inextricably linked to the linear context in which it occurs. It is impossible to speak, for instance, of non-traditional cadences without mention of the horizontal motions that generate them. While the contrapuntal elements of the fugue may seem obvious, it is worth pointing out that a similar system of linear organization may be witnessed in the preludes. The way in which Shostakovich creates dramatic motion in this extended tonal system results from the interactive motions of all individual voices, sometimes expanding or compressing the texture, at other times smoothly guiding the contrapuntal fabric into ambiguous or striking harmonic areas. Regardless of the net effect, harmonic motion is achieved through the linear motions of the component voices, which may work either as a group or as separate forces. Yet rarely does Shostakovich let his individual voices run their course without any concern for verticality. Even in highly chromatic counterpoint, many individual vertical "snapshots" produce highly consonant sonorities.

One of the most frequent manifestations of linear motion is that of textural expansion or compression. This is a spatially oriented process in which a polyphonic texture either pushes its extremes outward or pulls them inward, resulting in a change of ambitus and usually delineating a structural event. Such expansions and compressions are most obvious when they involve chromatic motion in the outer voices. A chromatic linear expansion in an otherwise diatonic context will highlight itself as a significant event and in all likelihood will be the gateway to a modulation. For example, the chromatic motion in measure 12 of the Prelude No. 1 in C (Example 14.8) allows Shostakovich to move from C major to what sounds like E-flat in measure 13. The expansion, in this case, has two stages: the dissonance on beat 2 of measure 12 signals the change, and the outward motion then continues to the E-flat chord on the following downbeat. (Conversely, linear compression may be observed in measure 30 of the same Prelude, where a diatonic ninth chord on D caves inward to become a supertonic seventh chord that precedes a flat-key tonality.)

Example 14.8

Something similar to Example 14.8 can be found in the Prelude No. 16 in B-flat minor, which is based upon a repeating 20-bar harmonic progression in which the eighth and ninth bars consistently employ a D major sonority. Shostakovich's initial presentation of this striking change is made clear by a linear expansion in the outer voices. Though this motion is somewhat obscured in later repetitions, its presentation here as a simple registral expansion serves as the voice-leading paradigm from which the later passages are generated.

In the previous examples, Shostakovich used linear expansion/compression to move between contrasting tonal sonorities within an overriding diatonicism. However, he is able to utilize similar principles when pivoting between larger-scale tonalities. All of the harmonic motions in the first thirty measures of Fugue No. 17 in A-flat are closely related to the central tonality; at measure 31, however, a sudden move to B major (Example 14.9) begins a section of the fugue in which subjects enter on foreign scale degrees. Though the harmonic change itself is striking, and seemingly unprepared, the voice-leading is remarkably smooth. As the last beat of bar 30 moves into the first beat of bar 31, E-flat is respelled as D-sharp and the moving pitches C and G resolve by half-step to B and F-sharp. One of the fugue's most important structural events is thus seamlessly connected through linear motion.

Example 14.9

Shostakovich takes linear modulation to its extreme in the Prelude No. 23 in F. Nearly every bar of this relatively short prelude (thirty-one measures) contains a harmonic twist of some sort. Here, linear modulations, chromatic expansions, and functional diatonicism combine to create a journey through fifteen to twenty different keys. Though the frequent harmonic changes may seem erratic to the tonal listener, they nevertheless invite a mode of perception that reconciles harmonic progression with linear concerns by way of chromatic voice-leading. Such linear modulation can be found, for example, in bars 1–2, 7, 16–17, and 20–21.

With foreign tonalities sliding into and out of each other in such a consistently smooth manner, it is all the more striking when, on occasion, a smooth connection is eschewed in favor of an abrupt change. A brilliant passage in the Fugue No. 3 in G contains a prolongation of E-flat in bars 57–60; repetition of the fugue's head motive is followed by a driving chain of thirds through bar 60. Without any harmonic or linear preparation, however, the downbeat of bar 61 brings a tonic entry of the subject in stretto (Example 14.10). Since this type of disjunct writing is rare in op. 87, it has a unique effect. Abrupt harmonic changes are nothing new, but rather than smoothing this one over with linear motion, Shostakovich maintains the abruptness as a device in its own right.

Example 14.10

Model and Manipulation

As discussed earlier, "model" is not solely a form; it is not solely a process. Furthermore, the individual composition exists only once the model is subjected to "manipulation," a process unique to each prelude and fugue pair. The consistency in manipulation, more than anything else, is what links the two together. Our exploration of model, then, is effective only to the degree to which it clarifies and provides meaning to the process of manipulation.

Prelude

The preludes of op. 87, as we have briefly observed, exhibit a variety of characteristic textures and moods. One aspect that nearly all of them share, however, is a narrative, discursive quality. The Shostakovich prelude operates much like a nineteenth-century character piece, in that a relatively small amount of musical material is taken on a developmental path not unlike a dramatic storyline. Rather than presenting and contrasting large blocks of thematic material, the preludes subject a small motive, melody, or progression to a series of unfoldings, each of which plays an integral part in the larger scheme that constitutes the basis for the prelude's form.

In many regards, the preludes of the *Well-Tempered Clavier* share a similar premise: the unfolding of a rhythmic or melodic motive. But where Bach's preludes often operate within some identifiable hierarchy of traditional form, those of Shostakovich have their form governed by the unfoldings themselves, not by harmonic structure or design. The unfolding process occurs in stages; we will term it a method of "developing variation." Such development through repetition mandates at least a certain number of occurrences of the source material, and so it is not surprising that preludes in strict AB (binary) or ABA (rounded binary/ternary) form are rare. Nos. 2, 15, and 17 constitute the exceptions. All the other preludes contain at least three points of return marking the beginning of each new unfolding, thus creating formal divisions that supersede, but do not exclude, those based strictly on harmonic structure.

Three primary manifestations of the developing-variation process are exhibited in op. 87. Though the distinctions between them may be blurred at times, they account for nearly all of the identifiable formal structures within the preludes. The first (and least common) of these is the prelude based on the varied repetition of just one source motive, theme, or progression. It may be visualized as such:

A1 - A2 - A3 - A4 - etc.

In its simplest form, this structure resembles nothing more than a set of continuous variations, and is, perhaps not surprisingly, most clearly observed in the passacaglias of Prelude Nos. 12 and 16. The developmental process, in this case, is represented by the progress of the variations themselves, rather than as a shaping element within each individual statement. For instance, in Prelude No. 16, a twenty-bar theme is gradually subjected to diminutions: first eighth-notes, then eighth-note triplets, then sixteenth notes. The final statement is an extended reflection on the first and serves to wind the rhythmic energy down. Since each variation exhibits its own consistency of tone, the dramatic development through the prelude is simply played out by the way in which one variation turns into the next.

In the second category, the developing variations take the form of statement/departure; the "statement" represents the source material, while the "departure" is a developmental path that immediately follows. Additionally, each departure is given meaning as the prelude unfolds through subsequent returns of the statement. A graphic representation is more difficult here, but in its most intuitive form would appear as such:

A1-------departure--A2-------departure--A3-------departure-etc.

The departures may comprise motivic breakdown or transformation, thematic sequencing, ambiguous tonality (at least, relative to the stability of the statement), or any combination of these elements. It is sometimes difficult to pinpoint exactly where they take effect; but this is not a problem, since these departures represent a process rather than delineate sections. Numerous preludes throughout the set exhibit this structural type; it has an inherently narrative quality that allows Shostakovich a high degree of latitude in realizing the developmental process.

Prelude No. 22 in G minor is a highly lyrical piece whose melody is represented by an extended chain of eighth-note dyads. This ever-moving melodic line is set off by a relatively static quarter-note accompaniment figure. The presence of G minor as a stable tonic, combined with the diatonicism of the eighth-note line, is thus the governing factor in perceiving the "points of return" throughout the Prelude. The drama is created by the way in which the initial stability transforms itself into instability following each arrival of this statement. Significant points of return may be observed at measures 20 and 45, and perhaps even at measure 72, where subdominant harmony is made to sound stable by virtue of context. Each of these arrivals follows a passage in which harmonic references become clouded; the arrivals themselves clear the tension and pave the way for the next stage in development. In the initial statement, the move from the curious G-flat back to G-natural in measure (m.)8 sets forth the kernel of development that will gradually come to fruition. G minor moves to a neighboring subdominant in m. 12, and from there slides into a foreign B major at m. 16. The first significant return at m. 20 sets up a more extended departure that introduces foreign pitches over tonic pedal (D-flat in m. 23, A-flat in m. 24), returns to diatonicism by m. 31, inverts the texture at m. 34, and finally moves to C minor and B major sonorities that are analogous to those that ended the first departure. Measure 45 marks the next point of return and the beginning of the third statement. The chromatic half-step to G-flat in m. 50 echoes that of the first statement, but here G-flat is prolonged for thirteen bars; instead of returning directly to the tonic G minor, the harmonic path grows more obscure. The relative stability of subdominant harmony at m. 72 marks the textural return; the harmonic return is delayed until approximately m. 77, where the bass register functions as motivic link to the fugue (Example 14.11).

Example 14.11 - harmonic/formal scheme of Prelude No. 22

A1					A2			A3		A4
measure: 1	(5)	(8)	(12)	(16)	20	(37)	(39)	45	(50)	72
g	G♭	g	c	B	g	c	B	g	G♭	C (G♭ - g)

The third major category of prelude structure is a logical extension of the second: what we previously called a "departure" now stands on its own as an identifiable second statement, one that exists in contrast to the primary statement. The two statements are nearly equal in significance to the design of the piece. They often serve as complements of one another, or exist in a call-answer relationship. A graphic description might be as such:

A1-B1-A2-B2-A3-B3-etc.

A variety of developmental processes is possible. A1 may develop into A2 and A3 without any recourse to B material; A and B may be different strata of a dual texture; or all statements may be linked by one overriding process.

Prelude No. 11 in B is a particularly distinctive realization of this third type. Its merry, dance-like character almost trivializes the underlying contrast of its two constituent themes and the way in which this contrast is played out during the course of the piece. The A material is basically comprised of a leaping diatonic melody (mm. 1–4) whose motivic cells are then sequenced (mm. 4–8) and placed over a staccato bass line (mm. 9–14). A brief transition sets up the B material (m. 18ff.), which is harmonically polarized from A by the distance of a tritone (F major). The B material is highly chromatic, but takes motivic references from A. And so, while the B material stands on its own as a thematic and harmonic entity, its character is derived from pre-existing motivic cells. A retransition in mm. 30–35 leads to the tonic return of A, altered in register from its previous occurrence. The last portion of this A section is displaced up a half-step to C major (mm. 46–48), a harmonic change that, although curious, points toward an even more important event: the transposition of the B section to the tonic B major at measure 55. What we have is a miniature sonata form without a development; the initial harmonic contrast between the A and B sections is resolved by having the B section return in the tonic key. This is but one of many ways in which Shostakovich realizes the bithematic prelude model. Others may be more variation-based, or, as we will later see in the G major Prelude, may take a stratified approach, wherein A and B represent individual textural layers that eventually interact with one another (Example 14.12).

Example 14.12 - harmonic/formal scheme of Prelude No. 11

	A	B	A1	B1	coda (B)	
measure:	1	18	35	55	65	70
	B major	F major	B major	B major		

It should be clear by now that trying to establish a rigid formal paradigm for preludes is problematic and, ultimately, damaging. Uncovering the model, however, is not: Shostakovich creates form by the process of developing variation. Our three categories serve to illustrate three degrees to which unfolding may occur. The developmental process within each prelude, regardless of category, sets up important relationships concerning pitch, harmony, motive, and rhythm that may factor significantly in the realization of the corresponding fugue.

Fugue

The fugues of op. 87 are based on many of the same conventions as fugues of two centuries earlier: tonic/dominant tonal relationships in the exposition, identifiable, recurring countersubjects, invertible counterpoint, middle entries, stretto, etc. The tonic/dominant relationship is present almost as a guiding truth, anchoring fugal expositions regardless of a subject's actual tonal profile. Shostakovich consistently employs tonal answers when compositional circumstances would call for them, i.e., when the fugue's subject modulates or hovers about the fifth scale degree. Though his recognition of tonal imitation as an important aesthetic may seem at odds with his extended harmonic language, it nonetheless shows an effort to recognize and uphold the quasi-academic quality of fugal construction. It may even suggest that there are certain fugal conventions that no compositional language, no matter how unique, may deny; for Shostakovich, tonal imitation is one of them.

Expositions tend to be the most standardized of the fugue sections. Regardless of style, it is the exposition that outlines the relationship between subject and answer and establishes tonal orientation. Shostakovich's expositions indeed fulfill these functions; however, the layout of material beyond the exposition represents a consistent effort towards maintaining that subject/answer principle as a major force of fugal organization. A remarkable pattern emerges: the scheme of middle entries is realized in the form of ordered pairs, each of which maintains the tonic/dominant polarity that was first witnessed in the exposition. For example, an entry on the submediant will be immediately followed by an answer at the mediant, i.e., that submediant's "dominant." Additionally, this new answer will usually preserve the quality of the original answer in terms of real or tonal imitation. Occasionally, the tonic and dominant roles will be reversed, but the pairing remains by fifth. Rarely does one entry stand alone without a paired answer. And when this regularity is interrupted – when an entry stands alone, for instance – it usually constitutes part of an important harmonic or structural principle unique to the manipulation of that particular fugue.

Not only does Shostakovich use paired middle entries to begin the body of a fugue, the pitch levels of the first of these entries are amazingly consistent. Fugues in minor keys nearly always have the first pair relative to the mediant (III), the second pair the submediant (VI); those in major keys begin the first entry at the submediant (vi), the second pair usually tonic (I), dominant (V), or supertonic (ii). Though the patterns are nowhere near standardized (especially in major) and usually break down after the second pair, the initial consistency cannot be ignored. Deviation from such paradigms is an essential part of the manipulation process and, as we will see, results from the exploitation of elements emphasized by the prelude/fugue pair as a unit. Table 14.1 shows the similarities between pitch levels of the initial middle entries in all twenty-four fugues. In order to show overriding similarities, this chart omits a single tonic-dominant pairing just after the expositions of Fugues 6, 10, and 24, as well as an unpaired middle-entry in Fugue No. 3. Pairs listed in italics are those that do not conform to the paradigm of tonic/dominant polarity.

Beyond these middle entries, there are a number of structural differences across the set. But most of the fugues lead to at least one major arrival point that articulates an important structural moment. This arrival is usually preceded by a preparatory area (perhaps a dominant pedal), and involves 1) a reduction of texture to one voice, 2) tonic entry of the subject, and/or 3) stretto treatment of the subject. The combination of these factors marks this moment as a recapitulation, a point at which the listener can easily grasp the importance of the returning material. The compositional problems that constitute the unique manipulation process may or may not have been worked out by this time, but the arrival is nonetheless significant in the formal scheme.

The models discussed thus far deal with the prelude and fugue as separate entities; but the notion of prelude/fugue correlation is essential if we wish to comprehend how Shostakovich controls the musical processes set forth in each piece. Connections may be observed as surface links, such as the introduction of the fugue subject in the final bars of Prelude No. 12 in G-sharp minor. But the relationships that exist below the surface are at the very heart of the manipulation process. We will next examine manipulation as manifested in two individual prelude/fugue pairs. Although the system of analysis used is in many ways

Table 14.1
Pitch-Level Relationships of First Two Middle-Entry Pairs

Major-Key Fugues

No.	Key	Pair 1 – scale degree (mode)		Pair 2 – scale degree (mode)	
		Subject	Answer	Subject	Answer
1	C	3 (Phrygian)	V of 3 (Locrian)	V of 2 (Aeolian)	2 (Dorian)
3	G	2 (min)	V of 2 (min)	V of ♭6 (maj)	♭6 (maj)
5	D	6 (min)	V of 6 (min)	1 (maj)	V of 1 (maj)
7	A	6 (min)	V of 6 (min)	1 (maj)	V of 1 (maj)
9	E	6 (min)	V of 6 (min)	V of 1 (maj)	1 (maj)
11	B	6 (min)	V of 6 (min)	V of 5 (maj)	5 (maj)
13	F-sharp	6 (min)	V of 6 (min)	5 (maj)	V of 5 (maj)
15	D-flat	6 (min)	V of 6 (min)	V of 5 (maj)	5 (maj)
17	A-flat	6 (min)	V of 6 (min)	♯2 *(maj)*	7 *(maj)*
19	E-flat	6 (min)	V of 6 (min)	V of 5 (min)	5 (maj)
21	B-flat*	3 *(min)*	5 *(maj)*	7 *(min)*	2 *(maj)*
		All pairings in this fugue are mediant relationships, even in the exposition.			
23	F	6 (min)	V of 6 (min)	♭6 (maj)	V of ♭6 (maj)

Minor-Key Fugues

No.	Key	Pair 1 – scale degree (mode)		Pair 2 – scale degree (mode)	
		Subject	Answer	Subject	Answer
2	a	3 (maj)	V of 3 (maj)	♯6 *(min)*	♯2 *(min)*
4	e	3 (maj)	V of 3 (maj)	V of ♭2 (maj)	♭2 (maj)
		additionally, following the second exposition, in the dominant, of double fugue:			
		3 (min)	V of 3 (min)	♭2 (min)	V of ♭2 (min)
6	b	3 (maj)	V of 3 (maj)	6 (min)	V of 6 (min)
8	f-sharp	♭4 (min)	V of ♭4 (min)	V of 6 (min)	6 (min)
10	c-sharp	3 (maj)	V of 3 (maj)	6 (maj)	V of 6 (maj)
12	g-sharp	3 (maj)	V of 3 (maj)	1 (maj)	V of 1 (maj)
14	e-flat	3 (maj)	V of 3 (maj)	V of ♯5 (min)	♯5 (min)
16	b-flat	3 (maj)	V of 3 (maj)	V of 2 (maj)	2 (min)
18	f	3 (maj)	V of 3 (maj)	V of ♭2 (maj)	♭2 (maj)
20	c	3 (maj)	V of 3 (maj)	V of ♭2 (maj)	♭2 (maj)
22	g	3 (maj)	V of 3 (maj)	V of ♭2 (maj)	♭2 (maj)
24	d	3 (maj)	V of 3 (maj)	V of ♭2 (maj)	♭2 (maj)

min = minor; maj = major.

conventional, it is nonetheless geared towards articulating the way in which generative elements become the catalysts in a transition from abstract model to fully-realized work.

Prelude and Fugue No. 3 in G

Prelude

Where the first two preludes of op. 87 are reminiscent of Baroque textures –
the sarabande of No. 1 in C major and the arpeggiated compound melodies of
No. 2 in A minor—the G major Prelude represents the first truly original textural
idea in the set, a juxtaposition of two thematic ideas, contrasting in motivic character and content. What we will see over the course of this prelude is a structural
plan that is delineated by the interaction and development of these two layers.
First, however, it will be necessary to identify the content and significance of the
dual-layer texture in terms of its relationship to the prelude model, or more specifically, the principle of developing variation.

The opening seven bars (Example 14.13) set the tone of the piece with its dark,
ponderous, chant-like melody in the low register of the piano. Though the official
key is G major, it is far from being in place as an explicit harmonic reference
within this first phrase. In fact, the tonality initially tends to gravitate downwards
towards the relative E minor. The modal ambiguity of this mediant relationship is
heightened by the sonorous arrival of C major, submediant to E minor, in measure
7. We will distinguish this opening material as layer "A" of a dual-layer texture.

Example 14.13

This opening melody is characterized by a set of "middleground" descending third
progressions (measures 1–2, 3–4, 4–5, 5–6), as well as the larger descending third
motion in the top voice from measures 1–7. If this melody represents a layer, or
stratum, of the musical texture, the treble-register eighth notes that follow it constitute a contrasting layer. The arrival of C major harmony in measure 7 marks a point
at which the first stratum ends (or rests temporarily) and the second begins.
Example 14.14 shows layer "B" in its initial, thematic, form. The overall contour of
B greatly resembles that of A, especially in its use of the "middleground" third (measures 8–9, the first half of 10, and the second half of 10 into the first beat of 11).

Example 14.14

Note that the basic melodic line in measure 11 does not continue in the expected stepwise pattern. Instead of an explicit G on the downbeat of measure 12, an open fifth, E-B, implies the missing G as the third of an E minor sonority. We shall see that the descending third at the end of the treble-register B motive, frustrated here, becomes increasingly important in subsequent statements.

Up to this point, the two motive-layers are consistently separated by register: layer A utilizes the bass register and arrives at the C major sonority; and layer B provides contrast in the upper register. However, at measure 12, the B motive is transferred into the bass, where it begins again at the E pitch level. This bass-register "tail" to the B motive is still part of the second stratum because of its motivic origin. The true A stratum is regained in the passage from measures 15–17, where the beginning of motive A is presented in diminution on F-sharp. This two-bar link enables the proper registers to be regained and allows the tonality to move back up to G major. Measure 17, then, marks the true beginning of the second statement as dictated by our method of developing variation.

What we observe in these first sixteen measures is a contrast between two thematic strata, each with its own character and structural function. Their interaction is most clearly seen at the point where the first layer arrives at a chord which is prolonged beneath the second layer; in the case of this first section of the prelude, the arrival of C major at measure 7 provides a harmonic underpinning which provides an aural context for the B motive. In other words, B will be heard in the context of A, but not vice versa. The modality of the A subject (the G major/E minor ambiguity) and the significance of the subdominant C major harmony (linked by descending mediants) announce themselves as structural concerns early on. Example 14.15 illustrates the harmonic and motivic content of the opening statements:

Example 14.15 - formal structure, mm. 1-17

Measure:	1	7	8	12	15	17
Layer:	A		B		link	A(1)
Motive:	A		B	(B)		from A
Harmony:	G/e	C------------------------------e			(F$^\sharp$)	G

Our discussion of the prelude model noted that subsequent statements of developed material contain significant alterations as part of an underlying process. The restatement of A at measure 17 is accompanied by an inner-voice pedal tone D. But more important than this textural thickening is the introduction of chromatic pitches – for the first time in this prelude. The A-sharp in measure 19 and the F-natural in the subsequent measure are aurally striking because they are non-diatonic and because they represent deviations from a familiar theme. The second part of the A theme becomes altered in other ways: measures 20 and 21 represent measures 3 and 4, now at a lower pitch level; the material from measures 5 through 7 is noticeably absent, replaced by a stepwise ascent that preserves the previously introduced F-natural. The harmonic arrival that was represented by C major in the first statement is now B-flat major (♭III) at the downbeat of measure 23. The function of the A repetition, then, is to gradually weaken G major by introducing foreign pitches, and to set up the arrival of B-flat major as mode-mixture harmony.

The B layer that is regained in measure 23 is not as easily explained as the preceding A. It is not entirely analogous to the original B theme at measure 8 because it cannot be placed into the harmonic context of the prolonged chord, B-flat major. In fact, the F-sharp of measure 24 and the C-sharp and B-natural of measure 26 imply D major (with one alteration, the high B-flat) bitonally superimposed over the underlying B-flat. The fact that the initial B motive began on the fifth scale degree of a significant harmony (G in C major) supports a similar analysis here (A as the fifth of D major). But since this melody is neither wholly in D nor in B-flat, the validity of interpreting layer B in the context of layer A is thrown into jeopardy. Heightening the tonal ambiguity is the registral transfer of the B motive to the bass in measure 27. Perhaps the most likely justification for its origin on C-natural lies in its eventual destination. Whereas the corresponding "tail" in measures 12 through 14 made a diatonic, stepwise descent (E-D-C-B-A-G) to the F-sharp of measure 15, the descent in this case (C–B-flat–A–G–F-sharp–E) preserves the bitonality of the preceding bars and ends with a similar half-step resolution to E-flat.

The arrival on E-flat in measure 30 corresponds formally to the link of measures 15–17, but has a significantly different function. Whereas the earlier link on F-sharp purely bridged the gap between E minor and G major, this new link is actually treated as a structural arrival on ♭VI, a mode mixture harmony related to the previous ♭III. Measures 30–36 prolong E-flat major, extending melodic fragments of the diminished A motive to arrive at a higher register for the next statement of the A layer. Example 14.16 illustrates the layout of this second statement of layers A and B:

Example 14.16 - formal structure, mm. 17-37

Measure:	17			23	27	30	37
Layer:	A(1)			B(1)		(link)	A(2)+B(2)
Motive:	A			B	(B)	from A	A+B
Harmony:	G	(weakened)		B♭ (+D)	?	E♭	G
				(♭III)		(♭VI)	

The most significant arrival point within the prelude is represented by the repetition at measure 37, for here both layers are reconciled. Motive A is now heard in the tonic in the uppermost voice (along with droning pedal tones G and D) while the bass sounds a tonic-level motive B. The stratification within the first two statements has reached its final stage, in which both layers are brought together simultaneously. Since the layers are not heard consecutively in this final statement, their brevity when combined necessitates additional material to provide this climax with a weight equal to that of the previous sections. Indeed, at the end of measure 39, the expected progression is interrupted; the thematic block begins anew in measure 40, prolonging the texture for another four measures.

We noted earlier how the basic melodic line at the end of the B motive is frustrated in its first occurrence at measures 11–12. The tendency for this line to keep moving down by step becomes an important factor in the construction of the final section of this prelude. The interruption at measures 39–40 of the final A/B block coincides with the end of the bass B motive; instead of a resolution to C on the downbeat of measure 40, which would have been contrapuntally satisfying, a frustration similar to the one in 11–12 is the catalyst for the subsequent thematic repetition. The second time around, however (mm. 42–43), the resolution to C does occur, and prompts further spinning-out of the last part of the motive. The mordent-like sixteenth-note figure is now heard on C, and the ensuing bass descent continues on in the expected manner, finally "resolving" to the curious F-natural that ends the prelude.

The most justifiable argument for the F natural at measure 44 is a contrapuntal one, in recognizing the significance of linear expectations; the stepwise descending third (or at least its expectation) characterizes the end of the B motive throughout the prelude. In many ways, the resolution is never completely satisfied; at measure 11, only implied; at measure 27, given explicitly but tonally ambiguous; at measure 40, interrupted; and at measures 43 and 44, resolved consecutively, but in a manner that goes a "step too far" and lands on the F-natural. The passage from measures 44 through 48, while existing as a surface link to the fugue, also serves as a reminder of the power of contrapuntal tendencies. For while the descent at the end of the B motive finally rested on F-natural, the upper register's echo of the B motive descends chromatically in measures 46–48 (B–B-flat–A–A-flat) and gets its final resolution to G with the first note of the fugue. On a motivic level, then, the descending third has become an important construct. We observed the various middleground thirds that characterized the A motive and its transformation into B. Clearly, the third-descent that is set up at the end of B has its motivic origins in A.

If we take a step back to look at overall structural concerns within the G major Prelude, our developing-variation model is supplemented with additional factors. Of the three main sections, the first two represent a diverging of the two thematic strata, and the third represents their coming together. This very process, then, provides the foundation upon which the dramatic course of the prelude is played out. The way in which the component layers differ from one statement to the next constitutes the developmental scheme. Observe the following structural diagram (Example 14.17).

Example 14.17 - G major Prelude, formal structure

SECTION:	A	B		A1	B1		*	A2+B2	trans
HARMONY:	G/e	C	e	G/e	B♭	?	E♭	G	+F
MEASURE:	1	8	12	17	23	27	30	37	44

Major harmonic arrivals other than tonic restatements are the prolonged harmonies underneath the first two B layers – C major (IV) at measure 8 and B-flat major (♭III) at m. 23 – and the "link" section's emphasis of E-flat major (♭VI) at m. 30. These, along with the ♭VII bass in the transition to the fugue, are the only truly harmonic events (other than tonic returns) in the entire prelude. The first "developed variation," A1/B1, introduces mode-mixture pitches and chords in place of the pure diatonicism of the first section. The use of such chords as points of tonal arrival constitutes the prelude's most significant harmonic events, and will have great bearing on the subsequent fugue.

This prelude's duo-thematic quality presents an intriguing realization of the prelude model in that it operates at levels other than the simple variation and development of a single thematic source; instead, relationships between the two thematic layers contribute to the developmental process in addition to providing foreground contrast.

Fugue

An overview of the op. 87 fugues revealed several structural consistencies: standard expositions, tonal imitation, paired middle entries, and stretto recapitulation. However, the individual manifestations of these elements are better put into context if the fugues are viewed with respect to their corresponding preludes. If a certain property of a fugue can be clarified or justified by a relationship to its prelude, then such an observation is a worthy one. In terms of harmonic design, the G major Fugue can be seen to be a logical outgrowth of the prelude.

Though many of the transitions from prelude to fugue are marked *attacca*, this is the only one in which a melodic line is actually completed by the arrival of a fugue—the subject's first pitch, G, is the goal of the descending chromatic line in the final bars of the prelude. The subject itself is a flighty one; the opening upward sweep of a seventh is answered by a narrowing of register, followed by another ascending seventh and gradual scalar descent. Example 14.18 illustrates how the subject makes use of the scalar third that was an essential motivic element in the prelude:

Example 14.18

The three-voice exposition follows a strict tonic-dominant-tonic plan, the dominant answer being real. Shostakovich introduces two countersubjects. The first, entering in measure 5, complements the subject in hocket fashion before adding rhythmic intensity in the form of sixteenth-note dyads. The end of this countersubject echoes the opening scalar motive of the subject, as if it were a false entry. The second of the countersubjects enters in measure 11 and provides a purely metrical counterpart to the rest of the texture. Following the exposition proper, a two-voice episode from measures 16 through 21 treats the subject's initial motive in imitation.

An essential part of our fugue model was the concept of paired middle entries and their relationship to the overall compositional design. The first two entries in the body of this fugue are at the pitch levels of A (m. 22) and E (m. 26). Though both of these are tonally altered to sound in the natural minor mode, they nonetheless exist at the distance of a perfect fifth and at the same temporal interval as the original subject and answer. Measures 31–34 present an episode identical to the one in measures 16–19, albeit transposed and contrapuntally inverted. Their function is to set up a subject entry on C (IV) in measure 35. In the typical scheme of Shostakovich fugues, this entry would be paired with one at the distance of a fifth above or below; however, this one stands completely alone, a significant event considering the overall infrequency of such a phenomenon in the entire set of fugues. The formal scheme of the fugue, up to this crucial point, is illustrated in Example 14.19:

Example 14.19 - formal structure, mm. 1-39

SECTION:	Exposition			Episode	Entries		Episode	Entry
PITCH LEVEL:	I	V	I		a (ii) + e (vi)		C (IV)	C
MEASURE:	1	5	11	16	22	26	31	35

Following the lone entry on the subdominant, another contrapuntally identical episode spans measures 40–43, lowering the C major tonality by whole-step to B-flat major at measure 44. This striking harmonic change signals another important event within the body of the fugue: the introduction of mode-mixture key areas.

The subject entry on B-flat is logically paired with one on E-flat four bars later. Viewed in a tonic-dominant relationship, E-flat (♭VI) becomes the referential tonic; B-flat precedes it as the dominant.

An episode beginning in measure 53 employs the same contrapuntal arrangement as earlier episodes, sequentially extending the opening scale motive through the end of measure 60. Measure 61, however, suddenly interrupts the texture with a tonic-level recapitulation of the subject. Tonic stretto ensues a half-measure later. The direct intrusion of G major into the flat-key tonality marks this moment as a structural dividing point. Example 14.20 continues the formal diagram:

Example 14.20 - formal structure, mm. 40-69

SECTION:	Episode	Entries		Episode	Recap 1	
PITCH LEVEL:		Bb (♭III) + E♭ (♭VI)			G (stretto) + D	
MEASURE:	40	44	48	53	61	65

As the diagram shows, the temporary recapitulation at measure 61 has a stretto answer in the dominant at measure 65. The half-measure interval at which the stretto occurs in this passage causes an "offset" episode in the second half of measure 70. Although the direct return to diatonicism introduced in measure 61 is significant, it does not last; at measure 75, stretto entries on F major (♭VII) indicate that the true recapitulation has not yet occurred. The F major entry is answered at the distance of a fifth below when B-flat major makes its appearance in measure 79. Again, we have a significant middle entry pair on mode-mixture pitch levels, ♭VII and ♭III. An episodic extension of the scalar motive (mm. 83–87) reintroduces G major and prepares the true recapitulation, which arrives in triple stretto at measure 88. Example 14.21 illustrates the final section of the fugue:

Example 14.21 - formal structure, mm. 70-end

SECTION:	Episode	Entries		Episode	Recap 2	coda
PITCH LEVEL:		F (♭VII) + B♭ (♭III)			G	A♭/E♭ - G
		(stretto)			(triple stretto)	
MEASURE:	70	75	79	83	88	94

The energy of the triple-stretto tonic subject winds down in the form of a coda, placing a rhythmically augmented subject on E-flat (♭VI) above a temporary Neapolitan (♭II) root. A direct motion to G in the bass of measure 97 is followed two measures later by the tonic resolution of the upper voices and a statement of the tail of the subject.

In this fugue we can see all of the devices that were discussed as part of the fugal model: re-use of contrapuntal textures (episodes, countersubjects); traditional exposition; paired middle entries; and a hierarchy of subject recapitulations. But the significance of fugal manipulation in this case lies in the harmonic relationships set forth by the middle-entry pitch levels. Three specific events mark themselves as important: 1) the unpaired entry on C major at measure 35; 2) the mode-mixture entries of B-flat and E-flat (♭VI) at measure 44; and 3) the similar entries of F and B-flat (♭III) at measure 75. All other aspects of the fugue can be explained as purely diatonic or structurally formalized. Looking back to the harmonic arrivals that emerged in the prelude, we can observe a striking correspondence: the "A" stratum found points of rest on C major (IV), B-flat major (♭III), and E-flat major (♭VI). The first of these perhaps justifies the curiously unpaired C major middle entry. The fact that the only foreign keys hinted at in the prelude and the fugue are mode-mixture keys cannot be disputed.

The G major Fugue, then, is in many ways a realization of the properties established through the prelude's developing variations. Though we are able to note motivic similarities between the prelude and fugue—the appearance of the scalar third—the most striking corroboration is to be found in harmonic structure. It is important to keep in mind that our goal in discussing the individual manipulations of the pieces is not solely to search out feasible prelude/fugue connections. Rather, meaningful analysis will point out such relationships when they have bearing on the transition from abstracted model to unique work.

Prelude and Fugue No. 8 in F-Sharp Minor

Prelude

In our initial discussion of the op. 87 preludes, we were able to justify their existence as "character pieces," noting the diversity of thematic substance across the set and the tight motivic unity within individual preludes. The F-sharp minor Prelude stands as a perfect example of how Shostakovich's stylistic tendencies may owe to a pre-existent source—in this case, the folk dance. Shostakovich held folk music (especially Jewish) in high regard; the strong melodic gestures and repetitive staccato accompaniment lend such a strong dance-like character to the work that it transcends its role as mere "prelude" (within the context of the set) to stand as a thoroughly unique composition and a decisively personal statement on the part of Shostakovich.

Because of the continuity of the dance-like accompaniment figurations, the developing-variation process in this prelude is exhibited strictly through melodic returns rather than points of textural arrival or repetition. Furthermore, the melodic construction does not exhibit any regularity of phrase structure. Instead of relying on standard antecedent/consequent phrase logic, the melody is spun out through the stringing-together of short motivic ideas, developed and expanded in each variation. These motivic "cells" can be characterized by rhythm, contour, intervallic content, or combinations thereof. The transformations of these elements from one occurrence to the next provide a formal logic governed by process; it is in this regard that we shall see striking relationships to fugal construction.

The opening of the prelude sets up the texture with an ostinato accompaniment figure that is joined by the melody two bars later. The initial melodic motive, which we will call *a*, is characterized by an anapest rhythm on a single pitch; the returns of this motive later in the prelude thus become easily recognizable as signaling new variations (Example 14.22).

Example 14.22 - motive a*, mm. 3-4*

The next significant motive in this opening statement occurs in measures 6 and 7. The meandering nature of this legato scalar fragment (utilizing the natural sixth and seventh scale degrees) lends a modal flavor to what had been solid tonic harmony in the opening measures. This motive *b*, then, provides a distinctly different character to that of *a*, in both rhythmic and tonal content (Example 14.23).

Example 14.23 - motive b*, mm. 6-7*

Motive *b* is echoed in the eighth and ninth measures, heightening the phrasal ambiguity already created by the elision between measures 5 and 6. The tonal direction thus far has been static; other than the slight change in ostinato accompaniment at measure 6, F-sharp minor has been prolonged. This lack of tonal progression is what allows the melodic element to come to the forefront as the most crucial determinant of formal logic and design. In fact, tonal structure is not a very significant factor in the construction of this prelude.

The initial melody continues to spin itself out, introducing significant chromaticism at measure 10. Scalar diatonicism is replaced with semitone motion that still hovers about the upper portion of the F-sharp minor scale. The note-to-note intervallic distribution groups itself into "iambic primes," sixteenth-note dyads, with each weak-beat sixteenth anticipating the pitch of the following strong beat. The chromaticism of this line merits our labeling it a third distinct motive, *c* (Example 14.24).

Example 14.24

Measure 12 returns to diatonicism with a motive derived from *b*, but more rhythmically active. At measure 14, the only harmonic change within the entire thematic statement occurs in the accompaniment figure, which moves down by whole-step to the subtonic, E major. Above it, an ascending melodic link, based on measures 4–5 quickly prepares the first return of the opening motive. The move to E major, then, is significant only in that it winds off the first section of the prelude; primary interest lies in the motivic cells that have already been introduced. Example 14.25 maps the prelude's opening statement:

Example 14.25 - formal structure, mm. 1-16

MOTIVE:		a	link	b	(b)		c	(like b)	link
HARMONY:	f♯								E (♮VII)
MEASURE:	1		3	5	6	8	10	12	14

The return of the staccato *a* motive at measure 17 announces itself as the beginning of the first variation. Rather than moving directly into the *b* motive (or some version of it), the melody takes up an inverted imitation of the accompaniment pattern, combining short articulations and comedic grace-note figures. This motive *d*, as we will call it,[4] is more characteristically dance-like than any of the previous motives (Example 14.26).

Example 14.26

Not all of motive *d* is new; the sixteenth-note tail figure on its fourth beat (B-flat–A–A–G-sharp) is a clear reference to the chromatic dyads of motive *c*. In this context, B-flat serves as an upper neighbor to the consonant A, and Shostakovich's spelling, i.e., B-flat rather than A-sharp, reflects this relationship. We will encounter the special relationship of the minor third and its half-step upper neighbor in both the prelude and fugue.

Motive *d* repeats in measures 21 and 22, but is altered to fit into a dominant-harmony context. As a result, the four-bar passage from 19 to 22 is the most logical—by conventional norms—that we have heard in terms of harmonic rhythm and phrase structure: a two-measure motive heard in the tonic, then in the dominant. But this regularity does not last; the sixteenth-note tail to motive *d* in measure 22 spins itself out into an entirely ambiguous passage that exploits the pitch-class relationships first heard in motive *c*. Measures 23–26 each contain the upper/lower chromatic neighbor idea in some form. The pitch series is even to be found in the accompaniment: the syncopations bridging measure 25 to 26 contain a B-flat–A–G-sharp double-neighbor motion.

The ambiguity of the passage beginning at measure 23 is partly due to the change of function in the left hand from accompanimental figuration to free counterpoint. But it is in this passage that a number of crucial relationships emerge. The half-step sixteenths in the transformations of motive *c* in measure 26 suddenly leap down by perfect fourth in measure 27; this new m2-P4 pitch series repeats in the very next measure. In the meantime, the syncopated left hand rhythmically augments a transposition of these pitches. Thus, the semitone that was originally introduced in the *c* motive has grown to generate a new, pitch-oriented motive, which we will call *x* (Example 14.27):

Example 14.27

The descending perfect fourth from *x* permeates much of the remainder of the prelude's middle section: lower voice, mm. 29 and 32–34; upper voice, mm. 33–35. Transformations of *c*, *d*, and *x*, all of which contain the sixteenth-note semitone dyads, serve as motivic anchors in a tonally ambiguous environment. The first thematic variation, then, represents a journey from stability to instability in two ways: the harmonic transition from tonic/dominant polarization to non-centricity, and the transformations of familiar motives into new ones. The presence, lack, or reordering of motives from the first statement into the second is mostly governed by the process that transforms the semitones from *c* into the recognizable pitch set that comprises *x*. The middle section might be illustrated as such (Example 14.28):

Example 14.28 - formal structure, mm. 17-36

MOTIVE:	a	d (incl. c)	(d)	c (incl. b)		c->x	d	c(x)	
HARMONY:	f♯	f♯	C♯(V)	(f♯) ambig.				f♯/D	B
MEASURE:	17	19	21	23		27	29	32	36

The final thematic group begins with the return of *a* at the end of measure 36. Instead of an exact tonic return in F-sharp minor, however, the prevailing harmony here is that of the major subdominant, B major. Though the change of mode and key center for the final variation is aurally striking, the return of accompanimental figuration and the *a* motive is still identifiable as a structural landmark. Our chromatic half-steps from motive *c* recur in measures 38 and 39. Their goal here, however, is another motivic transformation: the sixteenth-note patterns of measures 40 and 41 represent an intervallic relationship already encountered in the corresponding section of the first variation, at m. 20. Examples 14.29a and 14.29b illustrate both manifestations of the minor third/upper chromatic neighbor relationship:

Example 14.29a - m. 20

Example 14.29b - m. 40

Since the motivic transformation at measure 40 is not entirely new, we will not assign it special status as an individual motive. But we can see that it occurs in the same relative location as motive *d* in the first variation. The melody continues to spin out into a melodic link (without motivic association) in measures 42–45; the last part of this link, however, resembles the link that tied the original *a* motive to *b* in measure 5. As expected, the *b* motive returns here; we are witnessing, in this final variation, a reconciliation and combination of the two previous thematic groups. However, a significant change has occurred in this last statement of *b* at measure 46; the second eighth note of the left-hand accompaniment has now become G-natural. The special significance of this transformation is that the new accompaniment pattern is an exact statement of the intervals comprising our *x* motive: minor second, followed by descending perfect fourth (Example 14.30):

Example 14.30 - m. 46, L.H. x motive

The remaining material in the final section of the prelude serves as a recapitulation of the important motivic transformations. Motive *c* at measures 50–51 turns into motive *x* at measures 51–52, just as it did at measure 27. The accompaniment figuration against the *x* motive is a blatant recurrence of the minor third/upper chromatic neighbor pitch set, which we did not label as a motive but to which we assigned significant intervallic status. The prelude winds down with tonic statements of the *d* motive (which were absent from their expected location earlier in the variation) and finally breaks down into sixteenth-note murmurs of the prelude's most important interval, the minor second. Again, this minor second illustrates the special nature of B-flat as upper neighbor to the minor third scale degree, A. Example 14.31 illustrates the prelude's final section:

Example 14.31 - formal structure, mm. 36-end

MOTIVE:	a	(from c)	(from c)	link	b	c	x	d	fragments
HARMONY:	B (IV)				f#(with ♭2 and ♭4)				
MEASURE:	36	38	40	42	46	50	52	56	59-63

We can see that the prelude's final variation recaps all the original motives in much the same order; however, it also incorporates the important motivic transformations that first appeared in the middle variation. Perhaps the most accurate summary of the developmental logic in this prelude lies in the emergence of: 1) G-natural as upper chromatic neighbor to the tonic F-sharp, lending a sense of Phrygian modality; 2) B-flat as upper chromatic neighbor to the minor third scale degree, A; and 3) the *x* motive, which takes on its own identity by the end of the prelude. The first two of these, the pitches G and B-flat, constitute the most distinct differences between the prelude's first and last sections. The process underlying the prelude manipulation in this case is one of motivic transformation incorporating distinct pitch-class and intervallic relationships; similar principles will govern the construction of the Fugue.

Fugue

No discussion of the F-sharp minor Fugue may begin without analysis of its most crucial element, the subject; for Shostakovich created a melody whose pitch relationships do not strongly convey the tonic key, and whose inner turmoil provides the basis for the dramatic undercurrent of the entire fugue. The opening motive's emphasis of the third and fourth scale degrees downplays the significance of the F-sharp tonic, which arrives on an offbeat (Example 14.32a). Note that the initial anapest rhythm, crisply articulated in the prelude, is here transformed to become the opening gesture of a yearning, ponderous melody, unsure of its origin or destination but passionate nonetheless. The opening motive is repeated to set up an expectation of contrast. The contrast comes in the form of a short "sigh" (Example 14.32b) composed of the exact pitches of the prelude's motive *x*. The pull of the E-flat down to the D, while maintaining dramatic intensity, does nothing to clarify tonality. The subject exists in a realm of pure melody, drawing tension and release from a purely intervallic standpoint, with little recourse to harmonic structure. It is then rounded off by a single statement of the opening motive; the entire subject stands as a miniature ABA' form.

Example 14.32a

Example 14.32b

The purely melody-oriented nature of the subject, together with its lack of centricity around F-sharp, will have great impact on contrapuntal relationships, especially those that are based on the fundamentality of tonic/dominant polarity. If a subject does not "represent" the tonic, then how can its answer "represent" the dominant? Addressing this question from a harmonic framework is actually a misguided approach; we would do better to take counterpoint as our sole concern. When the second voice enters at the distance of a perfect fifth in measure 10, we do not hear C-sharp minor answering F-sharp minor. Rather, we focus on the intervallic relationships between the answer's melody and the countersubject (Example 14.33):

Example 14.33

Most of the countersubject is a scalar descent through a Locrian-mode fifth (G–F-sharp–E–D–C-sharp). The G-natural and D-natural distort any sense of C-sharp as dominant, but the overall linear progression of parallel sixths and thirds that result between the two voices lends intervallic logic. Already, we can observe the power of the descending half-step—which announced itself in the prelude—in the "resolutions" of G-natural to F-sharp in measure 11, D to C-sharp in measure 12, B-flat to A in measure 14, and A to G-sharp in measure 16. The "sigh" motive first heard in measure 5 of the subject develops into a series of downward-resolving tendency tones.

The last subject entry of the exposition, while technically at the tonic pitch level, is accompanied by the first countersubject in transposed form and a second countersubject beginning on foreign C-natural (Example 14.34). While the complete three-voice texture does not operate within F-sharp minor, it exhibits a great deal of intervallic parallelism and thus remains highly comprehensible.

Example 14.34

The end of the exposition proper is followed by a four-bar episode from measures 30–33; its function is to "harmonically" prepare the first of the middle entries, which occurs at the pitch level of B-flat minor in measure 34. The rapid transition to this foreign area (technically ♭iv) is certainly eased by the abundance of chromaticism in the exposition. Furthermore, the significance of B-flat in the context of F-sharp minor is not entirely new, for we saw its emergence within the prelude. The entry found in measure 43 can be seen to be the "dominant" pairing (F minor) of B-flat. Shostakovich's consistency of pairing by fifth continues with the next two entries: A minor (iii) at m. 56 and D minor (vi) at m. 65. Each of these middle entries is accompanied by exact statements of the two countersubjects in invertible counterpoint. Example 14.35 is a structural illustration of the fugue thus far, including the exposition and first two pairs of middle entries. "Pitch level" is strictly a technical label describing the pitch class and quality of entries, rather than the key areas that may be aurally implied:

Example 14.35 - formal structure, mm. 1-73

SECTION:	Exposition			Episode	Entry pair 1		Episode	Entry pair 2	
PITCH LEVEL:	f♯	c♯	f♯		b♭	f		a	d
MEASURE:	1	10	21	30	34	43	52	56	64

A pseudo-entry in the bass register at measure 78 acts as a dominant pedal point restoring F-sharp minor as a legitimate tonal center. Though the statement begins as an intervallically-altered subject, it changes in measures 84–86 to emphasize pitches B-flat, A, and F-sharp, which comprise the minor third/upper neighbor pitch cell that got special attention in the prelude. We will shortly see that this particular instance is a foreshadowing of the subject's final transformation.

As in many of Shostakovich's fugues, the arrival of the dominant signals a change in texture: stretto entries of the subject. This particular stretto, however, is between F-sharp minor (tonic) and D-sharp minor, and has its own pairing at the distance of a perfect fifth below, B minor/G-sharp minor, at measures 97 and 98. In each case, the stretto breaks down quickly into typical subject/countersubject texture. However, at measure 108, two subjects on E minor and G minor enter one beat apart and continue to full fruition. The significance of this first complete stretto is highlighted by an intervallic transformation within the subjects themselves. The first whole-step of each subject has become a half-step; the first complete motive, then, is precisely the minor third/upper neighbor pitch collection that emerged in the prelude and that was hinted at in measures 84–86 of the fugue (Example 14.36).

Example 14.36

The final section of the fugue uses only the new version of the subject. A false entry in the bass register at measure 124 is altered to act as a return of the tonic. Above it, parallel thirds emphasize the upper chromatic neighbors to pitches

F-sharp and A. At measure 128, the ultimate version of the subject recapitulates in the tonic; it is here that the minor third scale degree is most clearly juxtaposed against its upper neighbor, B-flat, and in much the same way as the prelude's final motivic transformation. In the last two bars of the fugue, B-flat becomes reinterpreted as a consonant Picardy A-sharp. The continuation of our structural illustration, then, is as follows:

Example 14.37 - formal structure, mm. 74-end

SECTION:	Episode	Pedal	Recap 1	(Stretto pairing)	Stretto	Recap 2
PITCH LEVEL:		C♯	f♯/d♯	b/g♯	e/g (alt.)	f♯/F♯
MEASURE:	74	78	86	97	108	128

Perhaps the most defining element of the F-sharp minor Fugue, other than its special subject, is the way in which the semitone is used to provide both immediate comprehensibility and large-scale process. On the one hand, harmonic ambiguity in the complete three-voice texture is counterbalanced with intervallic tension and release guided by the descending semitone. At the same time, the transformation of the subject's opening motive from major second to minor second—and the resulting pitch collection—provides a structural logic that is clearly paralleled in the prelude.[5] In many ways, the F-sharp minor Fugue is one of the most monumental of the set in terms of small- and large-scale correspondence with its accompanying prelude.

CHAPTER 15

SHOSTAKOVICH, THE PASSACAGLIA, AND SERIALISM

Lyn Henderson

Shostakovich and the Passacaglia: Breaking New Ground?[1]

Shostakovich revered Bach's music, and in 1950–1951 he commemorated the bicentenary of his hero's death with a set of twenty-four preludes and fugues in which not only the sheer scale of his tribute, but also the unhesitating conditioning of his own style by that of the eighteenth-century master, uncovered just how profound was his veneration. Time traveling was, of course, nothing new in Russian music, as Tchaikovsky's rococo stylizations or Stravinsky's neoclassicism suffice to show. But what is so remarkable about Shostakovich's 1950 tribute is the range and assurance displayed in the work, composed within a period of less than five months.

Yet should this range and assurance seem so surprising? In fact, one baroque form, the passacaglia, had intermittently drawn Shostakovich over the preceding twenty years or so. He was not alone in this interest; there was a widespread revival of the form in the second quarter of the twentieth century. But while Shostakovich's passacaglias of this period are especially revealing in charting his progress towards the neo-baroque synthesis accomplished in the great 1950 collection, this is only half the tale, for during the following quarter century he would take the form in a direction that could never have been predicted from what had gone before, and that would culminate in twin peaks of achievement, the finale of the Violin Sonata of 1968 and the penultimate setting, "Death," of what is perhaps his greatest song cycle, the *Suite on Verses of Michelangelo Buonarroti* (1974).

The first intimation of passacaglia in Shostakovich's music had appeared in the modernist Second Symphony (1927)—five statements of a three-bar ground (Fig. 5).[2] Yet, because of the music's implacable atonality, the ground is denied any

function as the harmonic determinant of the freer wind parts. Manifestly, this
deprives the passage of true passacaglia status, but in the works that followed, a
triad-based syntax rapidly became more assertive, tonality stronger, and such stylization feasible. Five years on, this became evident in his opera *Lady Macbeth of the
Mtsensk District* (1932), Shostakovich clearly deciding that the unremitting tread
of a baroque idiom would be peculiarly apt for projecting the inexorably unfolding repercussions of Katerina's sexual passion. In this opera, marks of the baroque
appear almost exclusively at moments when this drive is operative,[3] with the
opera's dramatic crux (the heroine's murder of her father-in-law) prompting Shostakovich's first authentic passacaglia (if we do not include a forty-second-long
example in *New Babylon.*)

Even the most cursory comparison of the opera's brooding tonal ground (Act
II, entr'acte) with the Second Symphony's atonal weave suffices to uncover the stylistic shift. In the opening of the entr'acte, prior to the start of the ground, a D
melodic minor stepwise ascent in bars 3-5 prefigures the ground's own course, but
bar 7's emphatic C-sharp minor triad presents a new tonal area. From there, a type
of C-sharp minor with a scattering of modally flattened inflections is confirmed as
the passacaglia's home key (Example 15.1).[4]

Example 15.1

The ground is given twelve statements, and though the free parts rarely coalesce
into pure triads and their progress might on occasion seem willful, they generally
defer to the ground's harmonic conditioning, with the pervasive dotted rhythms
making baroque affinities clearer. This passacaglia powerfully demonstrated Shostakovich's awareness of the form's dramatic potential, but its use, until his later
years, would be confined to purely instrumental contexts.

In fact, it is not until the 1940s that the passacaglia becomes really established
as a fundamental element in Shostakovich's music. The first of the three examples
from this decade constitutes the penultimate movement of the Eighth Symphony
(1943, Example 15.2).[5] The one-bar rhythmic matrix stamped upon the first six
bars of this nine-bar ground supplies an instant baroque resonance, though this is
countered by the shift in bars 5 and 6 from tonic G-sharp minor into a distant C
major, a move that quietly asserts the key of the finale to come, where a measure
of relief will be found from this movement's anguish. This short-term tonal digression would have posed a problem to a composer intent upon a consistent triadic
structure, and it is no surprise that the ground initially exercises appreciably less
harmonic control than had that of *Lady Macbeth*, the mainly semitonal movement
of the free melodies generating here an almost perpetual harmonic drift that only

intermittently crystallizes into short-lived triadic formations. But this is a "context" passacaglia designed as a stage within a broader unfolding experience, and as its end approaches this tonal opposition is set center-stage in the upper parts' defiant rotation around a G-sharp minor triad for almost six bars—an uncompromising last affirmation of this movement's tonic against the pull of the rival key so implacably asserted in the ground's fifth and sixth bars. But then G-sharp minor yields—for on its next statement the ground will finally halt on its closing F-double sharp, which is now reinterpreted as a G dominant, thus creating the hinge on which the music may be gently turned into the finale's brighter C major.

Example 15.2

A persistent tonal tension such as is present in the Eighth Symphony, and which is also finally resolved, is even more prominent in Shostakovich's next passacaglia, the B-flat minor third movement of the Second Piano Trio (1944, Example 15.3). But otherwise the nature of the musical constant could hardly be farther removed from that of the earlier work, for this time it is an eight-bar structure of stentorian dotted whole-note piano chords, given six doggedly unvaried statements. But though it begins with the most tonal of tonic-to-dominant progressions, the third chord is a less stable C major second inversion, after which the remaining chords are generated as much by the stepwise, mainly semitonal, movement of the three parts in the piano right hand as by the orientation of the bass, recalling the harmonic method in the earlier part of the Eighth Symphony's passacaglia.

Example 15.3

Such a totally specified and rigidly unchanging "realization" was unprecedented in baroque practice, but what, with regard to a liaison with the baroque, is most significant here is the two strings' contributions. The stark assertiveness of the piano chords was likely to rein in any serious bid for harmonic independence from these players. In fact, their lines show a radical shift towards a baroque melodic idiom and a respect for the harmony; moreover, the cello enters in imitation of the violin, exactly as might a second instrument in a baroque trio sonata, then shadows its companion in a strict canon that persists for almost half the movement. Even beyond this, the music remains in character single-minded, the movement displaying no sectional divisions such as are exhibited in the Eighth Symphony's passacaglia. Imitation based upon the opening phrase is also a feature of the movement's closing stages.

Yet while this movement has shown a drastic shift melodically towards a baroque manner, in tonal behavior it has taken a very different direction. Like the Eighth Symphony's passacaglia, it is a "context" movement. But where the foretelling of the key to come in that ground's fifth and sixth bars had been merely insidiously insistent, the Trio's ground strives remorselessly to regain the Trio's tonic E, each time coming agonizingly close to its goal by concluding on a limpid B/D dyad, each time thwarted by the F which gently edges the dyad a semitone downward, thus yet again restoring the movement's B-flat minor tonic—that is, until the final rotation, where the B of the B/D dyad is sifted out, dwelt upon, then begins to pulse in eighth notes, is quickly companioned by a G-sharp, an E is added, and the Trio's long-sought tonic is reached. But despite its new major mode, the finale proves to be a tense *danse macabre*, and though the ground's B-flat minor resumption in the coda gives way to an E major close, this offers little comfort.

While creating key linkage with the Trio's overall tonic E, the tritonal polarity of this harmonic ground stamps the movement with a tonal dualism totally alien to the historical model. The characteristics displayed in the third movement of the First Violin Concerto (1948) are therefore as unexpected as they are decisive, for here the F minor passacaglia rejects any key linkage with the rest of the work and displays a tonal single-mindedness as absolute as any baroque predecessor (though with its emphasis on G-flat providing a Neapolitan coloring). The crisp phrases of the robust seventeen-bar ground, with prevalent intervals of fourths and fifths acting as strong harmonic indicators, bring it far closer to baroque precedents than the bass part of the Trio's ground; throughout the movement the harmony is mainly triadic and never significantly at odds with the ground. With the soloist's entry (statement 3) a canon begins, for the violin's sweetly lyrical line is taken up exactly by bassoons and English horn in statement 4, while the violin's extension of its cantilena here is in turn rerun exactly by the lower strings throughout the fifth statement.

As a self-contained tonal event in a single key, with a mainly triadic harmonic vocabulary and syntax, an unabashedly diatonic flow of highly expressive cantilena, and a spacious canon that spans three of the ground's nine statements, this passacaglia was Shostakovich's surest repossession of the baroque to date. Yet perhaps the most crucial condition established here concerns harmonic movement. That of the Eighth Symphony had merely drifted, that of the Second Piano Trio had initially moved decisively, but with monumental slowness and a slackening of impetus once the tonic-dominant move was passed. But in the Concerto's passacaglia, there is throughout that purposeful tread that is an essential property of baroque style, however measured its pace. The final condition for the consummation of Shostakovich's stylistic liaison with the baroque was now firmly in place.

As noted earlier, the Twenty-Four Preludes and Fugues, op. 87, was the crowning point in Shostakovich's rediscovery of the baroque. Many individual movements show a felicitous response to eighteenth-century models; though rarely approaching pastiche, they nonetheless reveal baroque traits in plenty. The B minor prelude's heavily dotted rhythms hint at the French overture and Bach's citing of it in his D major fugue (WTC, Book 1), while the C-sharp minor prelude resembles Bach's E-flat major prelude (WTC, Book 1) in its busy thematic patterning (see Chapter 14, Examples 14.2a and 14.2b). The baroque suite's dance movements prompt a variety of stylizations; the C major prelude echoes the rhythms of the sarabande, the D major recalls the minuet in general character and the B major evokes a gavotte. Sometimes the baroque fugue's formal disciplines seem to rein in the harmonic idiom close to baroque boundaries; the B-flat minor fugue shows an absolute diatonicism with intricate ricercar rhythms, the E major's subject is strongly tonal—its ensuing deployment mainly diatonic with strict canon—whereas the G major (like a French gigue in its meter and rhythmic structure) is almost entirely diatonic and the E-flat minor submits unconditionally to baroque syntax. This list is not exhaustive.

In the G-sharp minor Twelfth Prelude, the ground's ten tonally enclosed statements are the constant harmonic determinant. The related free parts enter in turn (bars 13 and 25, respectively), the second free part closely imitating the first in both pitch and rhythm for its first seven bars. Shostakovich broadens his harmonic language beyond that of the Violin Concerto, because dissonance may be prolonged by step to another dissonance, e.g., bars 43–44. In striking contrast to the outer flanks of this ternary structure, the central section's cantilena (bars 49–94) resembles a baroque aria. Yet, the third section's opening (ground bass entry at bar 95, pre-empted by the right hand at bar 94) is marked by canon, and the whole piece projects far more faithfully than the Concerto's passacaglia one crucial feature of the baroque model in that texturally it is more consistently linear. In fact, the Twelfth Prelude is the peak of Shostakovich's regeneration of passacaglia in terms of the baroque.[6] Now he would seek a radically new orientation.

The emergence in the Violin Concerto and Twelfth Prelude of grounds with several well-defined phrases giving them a more autonomous identity is just one indicator of a burgeoning melodic tendency in Shostakovich's passacaglias. True, the ground itself initially regresses to the purely functional in the Sixth Quartet's third movement (1956, Example 15.4, line b), and this passacaglia's opening stretch, with the upper three strings entering in turn with a rising fourth plus an extension built mainly from quarter notes and eighth-note pairs, suggests a fugal model. Yet these melodies, for all their similarities, are not identical. Rather, with their wide spacing in time, they initiate a gentle and unbroken process of thematic evolution that culminates very naturally in the mini-cantilena at the movement's heart, where an exquisite and profoundly affecting melody steals in above whispered triads as continuation of this spacious evolutionary process (Fig. 59). But though, in contrast with the central section of the Twelfth Prelude, the ground itself retreats, its ghost lingers in augmented notes, gently guiding the music's course and foreshadowing the true ground's return at Fig. 60. Here, a unique touch: as the ground re-enters, the solitary free part (Example 15.4, line a) turns out to be a decorated version of the ground itself, the most literal integration of functional ground and deeply expressive melody in all Shostakovich's passacaglias. And in another inter-movement coupling, B-flat minor's climactic return in the finale signals also the ground's resumption, this time in canon (Fig. 80).

Example 15.4

This heightened emphasis on lyrical melody was soon to be strengthened by a new influence. Shostakovich first met Benjamin Britten in September 1960. For the latter, the passacaglia had also been a significant preoccupation, and one in which the ground's nature had long been enlarged to encompass a lyrical dimension enabling it to function as melody in its own right (in, say, "Death, be not proud," the last of the *Holy Sonnets of John Donne* (1945)). A single example stands out among Shostakovich's passacaglias that may have been nurtured under Britten's sun: that of the third movement of the Tenth Quartet (1964). With Shostakovich's well-known admiration of the *War Requiem* (1961), a work he got to know in the summer of 1963, one possible forebear is that work's "Agnus Dei"— an intense movement that is essentially a duet between the ground and the solo tenor line, the remaining parts acting chiefly as harmonic fillers. Such a description could equally fit Shostakovich's Tenth Quartet passacaglia, two parts (the nine-bar ground and the first violin's more spacious free part, likewise with predominantly stepwise movement) driving the music forward in continuous counterpoint, the remaining parts serving a purely harmonic function.

This was unprecedented in Shostakovich. Equally novel is another trait sometimes favored by Britten, namely the ground's treble placing at the outset.[7] But most striking of all is the ground itself, for this is now uncompromisingly a fully formed melody of great expressive power, and though the harmony is triadic, metrical shifts dislocate the steady measured tread typical of the baroque model. Above this the first violin spins an increasingly independent cantilena whose mainly stepwise movement nevertheless ensures that the sometimes astringent norm of dissonance never sounds willful. The ground's authority is loosened in its final statements, where it is subjected increasingly to modifications in interval and rhythm, with at times only its general contour remaining, before being finally dissolved. Indeed, this passacaglia will prove to be a transitional case: both curator of the past and harbinger of the future.

Although the Tenth Quartet's passacaglia never for one moment sounds like Britten, it is difficult to believe that it would have come out quite the way it did, but for the presence of the English composer. And in a general broadening of Shostakovich's creative perspective, his passacaglias seem now to a degree to shadow Britten's own course, as evidenced by the *Seven Poems of Alexander Blok* (1967), which contain Shostakovich's first examples both of vocal passacaglia and 12-note music. And in the first movement of the Violin Sonata (1968), Shostakovich united passacaglia and serialism by constructing the ground itself as a 12-note series, just as Britten had done in the final scene of *The Turn of the Screw* (1954), an opera that Shostakovich had seen during his 1962 visit to the Edinburgh Festival.[8] Shostakovich's eight-bar ground is a widely arching, mainly ascending, and patently "melodic" note-row plus a free bar, answered by its exact inversion (Example 15.17). It will receive three unbroken statements and a partial, rhythmically changed fourth (Fig. 3) before relinquishing its hold.

But it is the Sonata's great finale that is the more fascinating. Here again passacaglia and note-row meet, though the latter is now mainly a decorative element within a structure that also incorporates a variety of historical precedents. The ground here (shown in both Examples 15.5b and 15.7) frequently functions more as a cantus firmus in that its only constant is its string of pitch classes. At times its melodic integrity is compromised by octave transpositions; at times the ground is transposed. But most novel of all is Shostakovich's readiness to make radical adjustments to the rhythmic structure, undermining the implacable pacing of a conventional passacaglia. After its eight-bar introduction, the movement divides into three distinct sections plus a coda. The first section comprises the theme, plus variations 1–8 (Figs. 59–68, b12: all G-based), the second variations 9–15 (Figs. 69–75, b18: statements in a variety of keys). There follows a six-bar allusion to the movement's introduction before the third section, variations 16 and 17 (Figs. 77–79: both G-based). This third section incorporates material from earlier in the movement, and the coda extends this process, also drawing in a portion of the first movement.

Even in the nineteenth century, Russian musicians were more aware of the deeper recesses of Western music than we might expect, in view of their relatively late entry into the European musical mainstream,[9] and this passacaglia seems to bear out such familiarity, for the variations of the first section include an element which could have been suggested by sixteenth-century *cantus firmus* treatment. Although variation 2 (Fig. 60) for solo piano stretches Renaissance syntax, it displays all the textural "purity" of a polyphonic style. More pointedly, during its first three bars the left-hand free part is designed with three-beat groupings, in rhythmic counterpoint to the right-hand *cantus firmus*. Even more significantly, a line built from repetitions (exact or close) of a brief melodic idea—in much the same way as mid-sixteenth-century English keyboard composers counterpointed a *cantus firmus* (see, for instance, Nicholas Carleton's *Gloria tibi Trinitas* shown in Example 15.5a[10])—underpins more than half of variation 3 (Fig. 62; Example 15.5b) and resurges in variation 5 (Fig. 64) before eventually giving way to a free, unbroken torrent of sixteenth notes.

Example 15.5a

Example 15.5b

Example 15.5b continued.

Ground contd.

These variations provide whiffs of historical styles, rather than pastiche, and there are more to come—for instance, a baroque chorale in variation 7 (Fig. 66; Example 15.6), though here the ground, in the piano right hand, is disrupted by a twelve-note row's magisterially extended cadence into C before resuming its prescribed course.

Example 15.6

66   a tempo

Partial ground

Twelve-note row

a tempo (poco meno)

The stylistic backdrop has now moved to the eighteenth century with hints of "character" variations—a baroque gigue in the *moto perpetuo* quarter note triplets of variation 11 (Fig. 71), even perhaps echoes of a typical allemande texture in the busy dueting sixteenth note lines above the cantus firmus in variation 12 (Fig. 72). And if this seems fanciful, there can be little doubting the baroque resonances in the unaccompanied violin variation, no. 15 (Fig. 75).

Yet the most significant resonance will be from Shostakovich's own century. That feline entry of a twelve-note row as an appendage to the cadence in variation 7 (Example 15.6) is scant preparation for the role such series will shortly play. In variation 9 (Fig. 69), a thirty-six-note melody constructed from three successive note-rows combines with the ground to make a double theme that will be the basis for the movement's second section (Example 15.7).

Example 15.7

Again a historical precedent (now nineteenth century) might be suspected, this time the variation finale of Beethoven's *Eroica* Symphony, where a melody likewise joins the "passacaglia" bass to provide a double theme. But the two cases differ in what follows, for while Shostakovich's note-row theme becomes the main subject for variation, his double theme principle is preserved throughout the section; Beethoven, by contrast, metes out variation treatment to both themes within a much freer structure, and they are treated both in association and singly.

Having introduced the double theme, Shostakovich reruns it in variation 10 (Fig. 70), but with a new metrical filling that suggests a dance. This second hearing is wisely judged, because from this point the aural definition of the note-row theme becomes clouded and even disappears, as when the "gigue" and "allemande" variations (nos. 11 and 12) decorate its contour. In variation 13 (Fig. 73; Example 15.8), the roles of the 29-note ground and the 36-note triple-row are largely switched. The 36-note melody forms the keyboard bass, whereas most of the ground (notes 8–29) is played in the violin. In the first three bars of this variation, the role-reversal is somewhat blurred: the first four notes of the ground appear as alternate pitches in the keyboard bass (circled in Example 15.8), while the violin plays a "decorated" version of the first row. Regardless of placement, each of the ground's notes has at least one repetition: the first three are echoed by the keyboard treble (the first notes of bars 1–3), and the first four appear also in bars 1–3 of the violin's "decorated" note-row. The ground's fifth and sixth notes in the piano treble (E-flat and A-flat; bars 3–4) are self-echoed in more assertive fashion in bar 5 (D-sharp and G-sharp), whereas the seventh, found initially in the violin's final semiquaver of bar 5, is then shared by all parts in bar 6. The ground's notes 8–29 are all self-echoed in the violin except the G-natural (note 22), which is duplicated by piano treble. And there is a further intriguing feature. The variations in the movement's outer sections are G-based, but the first five of the seven variations that form this central section are respectively on G-sharp, A, F, C-sharp, and B-flat. A curious succession—except that it mirrors in retrograde the intervallic relationships between the first five notes of the note-row. Fortuitous? Surely not.

The recurrence of the movement's introduction signals entry into the Sonata's final stages. The ground's penultimate appearance in variation 16 (Fig. 77), G-based once more, is made without its recent partner, the 36-note melody. Next, the first note-row has its turn (Fig. 78), then in the final variation (Fig. 78, b6), ground and note-rows are rerun, their parts now inverted. The eighth-note figuration of Example 15.5b returns and comes into its own to explore a relationship with the note-row theme. But then, very briefly, before the coda is heralded by the return of a portion of the first movement, a further note-row rises in the violin, its first half lifted literally from the most famous row of all: that of the Berg Violin Concerto (Example 15.9). So *that*, it seems, was the seed from which bits of this movement have grown, and which has conditioned others, for it is the provider (transposed) of the first four notes of the movement's note-row melody,[11] and therefore of part of the key structure of the movement's second section. It also seems to have determined how the ground itself should begin, and may have conditioned the opening of that eighth-note figuration which has discovered a fuller potential in the movement's final section.[12]

Example 15.8

Example 15.9

After this, Shostakovich's final instrumental passacaglia, in the fourth movement of the Fifteenth Symphony (1971), sounds strangely old-fashioned, with
its fourteen-bar unvaried ground and free parts that equally scrupulously recognize baroque practice. Yet, although this passacaglia looks back thirty years to
the "march" theme from the Seventh Symphony (see Chapter 6, Example 6.2),
its first eight bars plus two beats are also a 12-note row (with one extra
pitch), and thus provide a second instrumental example of these procedures'
fusion.

The three remaining examples of passacaglia occur within song cycles, and
although one predates the Violin Sonata and Fifteenth Symphony, they will be
considered together, for although to some extent they shadow the instrumental
cases in their substitution of baroque stylization with a more personal idiom, their
individual qualities are fashioned by the words, with novel and far-reaching
consequences.

"The City Sleeps," from *Seven Poems of Alexander Blok* (1967), is a gloom-ridden
nocturne. Alone, the poet muses on the city "shrouded in mist," observes the reflections of dawn "in the distance, across the Neva," then ponders painful memories.
Even before a note has been sung, the ground itself (Example 15.10) seems to ad-
umbrate his shifting moods: passive reflection (for any sense of purpose generated
by the initial rising fourths and dotted rhythms is lost in the ensuing quarter-note
drift), the intrusion of irrepressible thoughts (the twist towards a seeming B minor),
then a deepening dejection (the B–C oscillation that follows this tritonal wrench,
and the prolongation of the final C as substitute for the ground's initial F as the
restatement begins in bar 10).

The song is structured upon three unbroken statements of this ground separated
from a fourth, slightly adjusted statement by twelve new, though related, bars. If
this interpolation recalls the similar procedure in the passacaglia of the Sixth
Quartet, the Second Piano Trio's ground-plus-immutable-superstructure is paralleled in the equally unchanging role of the cello, whose inevitable "slurring"

during double stopping heightens the first stanza's mood of bleak desolation, just as its chromaticism reinforces the tonal tension within the ground.

Example 15.10

With the second stanza (and the free section), the poet shifts from the reflective to the confessional. Against the cello's chugging eighth notes, the vocal line becomes active, with the approaching dawn caught, perhaps, in the broad sweep of a rising broken chord that falls away in a gentle stepwise descent (Fig. 19). But despite the expressive peak of a rise to E-flat (Fig. 20, b2), "the awakening of sad days" brings only renewed melancholy, and the vocal part, drained once more of energy, is drawn again to cross-rhythms, with a weary semitonal inflection (Fig. 20, b3), to close into the languor of repeated tonics. For nothing has changed, and the ground's impassive restatement can only mirror the poet's lingering anguish.

Alexander Pushkin "enjoyed" one extraordinary privilege. In tacit recognition of the power that his words wielded with an adoring public, Tsar Nicholas I took upon himself personally to censor his works, and this provided the early twentieth century poet, Marina Tsvetayeva, with the subject for her scathing "Poet and Tsar," which became the first of a pair of poems concerned with Pushkin used by Shostakovich in his *Six Poems of Marina Tsvetayeva* (1973). Shostakovich's setting of this bitterly satirical lyric results in perhaps the most eccentric of his passacaglias, for he makes his treatment of the ground itself a musical metaphor of the process of literary mutilation that is the subject of the text, reshuffling its constituent chords until its very identity is finally destroyed. Patently, such a draconian process would have produced musical incoherence within a tonal context: hence Shostakovich's choice of a 12-note ground, his first in a vocal context. With a pomposity that mimics the Tsar's imperial self-assurance, the ground's *fortissimo* first statement (Example 15.11) supports a trail of twelve majestic whole note dyads, the vocal part always consonant with the unchanging major third sonorities as the poet scrutinizes a "hallful" of statues.

Example 15.11

Moderato ♩= 144 *ff*

Po- tu - sto - ron - nim   za - lom   tsa - rei...

ff ① ② ③ ④ ⑤ ⑥ ⑦

In this other-world room of the tsars...

ff

Kto ne- pre- klon- nyi   mra - mor- nyi   sei ?

⑧ ⑨ ⑩ ⑪ ⑫

Who is this unbending marble?

With the poet's curiosity roused by one of these statues ("Who is this unbend-ing marble?"), and with the royal identification being made, eighth note figuration begins to disturb the seemingly monolithic stability as "the pitiful gendarme [Nicholas] of Pushkinian fame" embarks on his corrective agenda; unceremoni-ously, Shostakovich thrusts chord 3 between chords 9 and 10 of the ground's sec-ond statement, and attacks the ground's other crucial attribute, subverting its isometric, purposeful tread with dotted whole notes and half notes. Small wonder that, for their part, the eighth-note rhythms are promptly goaded into yet more disruptive sixteenth notes. By now, Nicholas's destructive temper knows no bounds. Complete derangement seems imminent as he shakes the ground's third statement into dreadful disorder, with pitches 5 to 12 re-grouped as 8-9-5-12-10-6-11-7, with yet more metric and rhythmic alteration, the Tsar "who found fault with the author, cut to pieces his manuscript" now even inserting a piece of mate-rial of his own (bar 29, second half). By the end, his indignation overleaps itself, and if the postlude's three unrelated note-rows of *fortissimo, moto perpetuo* eighth notes denote rampant fury, then their final disintegration into a free chromatic descent must surely signify that Nicholas has bellowed himself witless!

In the year before his death, Shostakovich composed his final passacaglia as the forceful penultimate setting, "Death," in a second commemorative work, *Suite on*

Verses of Michelangelo Buonarroti for bass and piano (1974), saluting a genius in anticipation of the 500th anniversary of Michelangelo's birth in March 1975. The choice of passacaglia seems to associate the inevitability of the form's constant unfolding with the inescapable progress through life to death, in a manner similar to Shostakovich's first true passacaglia in *Lady Macbeth*. But the weary premonitions of age are very different from the obsessive passions of youth, and the old painter's gloomy reflections are underpinned by a ground of unstable metrical structure; thus, like that of the Violin Sonata's third movement, it is given *cantus firmus* as much as conventional passacaglia treatment.

The opposing forces of damnation and redemption are the very nub of this poem, and from the outset (Example 15.12), a matching dualism permeates the music. Satan ranges (literally) through the introduction's first five bars, with the *diabolus in musica* present not only horizontally and vertically but also as boundaries of phrases or phrase segments (see ⊗ in Example 15.12); by contrast, bars 6–9 breathe a diatonic purity, reinforced by the preponderance of "perfect" fourths. This opposition is extended into the ground itself (bar 10), whose first four pitches repeat the intervallic structure of bars 1–2, left hand, with the following three pitches repeating the structure a tritone above the opening three. The descent from A-sharp then asserts a more diatonic stability whose "secure" character will be confirmed in the ground's fourth rotation, where it will underpin the healing diatonic "redemption chords." Both the introduction's treble and the ground itself are 11-note rows, with the latter repeating D-sharp.

The mainly eighth-note vocal part is syllabic, with short, arioso-style phrases. But their apparently functional character is deceptively illuminating, as Example 15.12 reveals; while the vagaries of life, with its manifold temptations, are allotted twisting, stepwise movement, "death" (bar 10) is presented in the stillness of the monotone; its hour is close but still unknown—yet it is surely glimpsed in the fateful pendulum of oscillating fourths (bar 11). As the old man meditates on life, an octave leap (bars 12–13) suggests a momentary surge of energy, but his line relapses into monotone as he regrets the passage of fleshly pleasures (bars 15–16).

Across a three-bar break in the ground, the piano marks out the rhythms of a funeral march. But the ground's fourth rotation discovers the other side of Christian destiny, its end now supporting the "redemption chords": five triads, four "unblemished and pure," the fifth bringing a touch of dissonance as, with mainly stepwise upper parts, the music eases into the second free, this time consonant, passage ("When, O Lord, will come that which Thy faithful await?"). Beckoned by this heavenly image, funeral march rhythms return to encircle the fifth rotation (bars 38–42), and though "faith weakens in delayings," the resumed "redemption chords" (bar 41) are a solace. The old man is amazed at God's salvation and, echoing the brief resurgence of life, an octave leap now signals the confrontation with death (bars 46–47), giving way to a broken descent to F-sharp. Finally the piano reruns its prelude as postlude. But all is now underpinned by a pedal C-sharp (Example 15.12, insert, Shostakovich's notation enharmonically respelled to reflect the new tonal environment) whose presence "miraculously" transforms the desolate, tritone-filled opening two bars into a benign cadence on C-sharp, then mitigates the bleakness of what follows to end in a kind of peace.

Example 15.12

This somber final song also prompts a final question. By the time of its composition, Shostakovich was a man wracked by ill-health, and it is surely not too fanciful to extend the image of the ground's weary progress as an analogue, not just of the poet's inescapable path through life to death, but that of the ailing composer himself. Was he haunted by thoughts of his own mortality? And was this, his final passacaglia, really his personal requiem?

Shostakovich and Serialism: the Case of the Disappearing Note-Row

Now that four decades have passed since Shostakovich's first excursions into serial technique, a perspective has unfolded deep enough to permit a more secure assessment of his aims and methods in this field. Five writers in particular have already contributed their findings. Hans Keller, discussing the Twelfth Quartet, notes the commanding and prophetic presence of the fourth and semitone in the opening note-row, and the particular role of the tonic's and dominant's Neapolitan in many rows in foreshadowing the movement's harmonic course.[13] But the prime purpose is to assert a debt to Schoenberg's First Chamber Symphony in the overall structure of the piece. Eric Roseberry refutes this claim, but finds "illuminating parallels" between the works.[14] Roseberry explores structural, stylistic, motivic, and thematic links between Shostakovich's last five quartets; he identifies mediant relationships of key between them, and similarities of tempo.

Jacques Wildberger has defined the partial, idiosyncratic role of serialism in the Fourteenth Symphony and the Thirteenth Quartet.[15] He finds that a single note-row is not a work's controlling factor and that several unrelated note-rows with various functions might co-exist. They are able to suggest a key through their pitch contours, but can also be the means of its estrangement or even abolition. Shostakovich usually shunned retrograde and retrograde-inversion, thus retaining a row's original melodic contours. Focusing especially on the Fifteenth Symphony, Peter Child applauds the "technical finesse" with which Shostakovich combines atonal method with diatonic, tonal technique by means of parallels between the intervallic content of their voice-leading structures.[16] Finally, Peter J. Schmelz places Shostakovich firmly within the context of the Soviet Union of the time, where many composers were experimenting with serialism.[17] He finds that of these, it was the younger, more rebellious composers such as Volkonsky, Pärt, and Schnittke who wielded the most influence on Shostakovich though, ironically, establishment figures like Salmanov and Karayev had gone further in incorporating the tools of 12-note music into their techniques.[18]

Shostakovich was never to grant serialism Schoenberg's all-embracing control, where the single note-row exerted absolute power throughout a movement or entire work. He might use many unrelated note-rows, but always they remained an adjunct to his existing style. Indeed, his chipping away of the very tenets of 12-note music that were the guardians of equal pitch status would ultimately lead to the destruction of the note-row as such.[19]

Shostakovich's first experiment with serialism was in the *Seven Poems of Alexander Blok* (1967). In the sixth movement ("Secret Signs"), two unrelated, thematic note-rows demonstrated a highly individual approach, as did the two rather similar note-rows of the Second Violin Concerto's third movement (1967). But it was the Twelfth Quartet (1968) that marked the first inclusion of note-rows as a fundamental, substantial component in Shostakovich's work. The first movement contains at least eight different note-rows, each of them a single-instrument entity with no role as the harmonic determinant. The note-rows fall into two clear family groups, defined by their contrasting rhythmic characters. Those of the first are simply a stubborn trail of eighth notes, whose lack of rhythmic interest is bound to focus attention upon the pitch structure. One such note-row introduces the movement in the cello, a row so ordered as progressively to foreshadow the D-flat tonic (Example 15.13).

Example 15.13

Likewise, the second note-row momentarily disturbs the prevailing D-flat in the center of Fig. 2, b3, only to highlight its immediate re-emergence, while at Fig. 3, b6, the even greater disruption to that key leads firmly to A-flat for the second theme. Throughout the movement, these isometric note-rows operate within the tonal parameter.

In striking contrast, the two note-rows that form the second theme (Fig. 4) are given a rhythmic structure that renders them explicitly thematic. Their pitches are so arranged as to intimate an A-flat identity, confirmed in the second row by an A-flat/E-flat double pedal. This second note-row contains a mordent in its two opening pitches, and though this is a permissible license in orthodox serial technique, it is one upon which Shostakovich will build in his gradual loosening of the bonds of 12-note serialism (Example 15.14). Prophetic, too, of his revisionist intentions is the addition of an extra pitch, D-natural, in the note-row that follows soon after at Fig. 5, b11 (Example 15.15).

Example 15.14

Example 15.15

The Quartet's second movement shows a host of extensions of note-row practice. For the first time, the mordent is prolonged into a trill, and a note-row may be shared between several parts. There are instances of two unrelated note-rows being heard concurrently, and note-rows used in inversion. But no doubt because, for Shostakovich, the note-row would always remain essentially a melodic entity, he almost never risked endangering its audible identity by using it in retrograde or retrograde-inversion.[20]

Two note-rows in particular seem to presage later developments. The row at Fig. 42, b8 (first violin) has eleven pitches only and, like the row with the extra pitch in the first movement, is on the borderline between the orthodox note-row and a type of compatible writing that is to creep progressively into his music. The other note-row prefigures a growing freedom of usage, for in the climactic bars beginning at Fig. 58 is found Shostakovich's first extension of the mordent exception on pitch repetition, with the second now replaced by the minor third. Also of interest are the repeated 12-note chords, resulting in an unusual linking of horizontal and vertical application,[21] and, for the first time in Shostakovich, the overlapping of two successive note-rows (Example 15.16).

Example 15.16

The Twelfth Quartet established serial technique as a substantial part of a work, but the Violin Sonata, composed soon after in the summer of 1968, demonstrated an increased range and resourcefulness in its application, for here Shostakovich was already beginning to insinuate it into his own style by applying it to his favored passacaglia. As already mentioned, the piano sets out a hugely arched, eight-bar passacaglia theme, consisting of a three-bar 12-note series plus a free bar, with all four forthwith repeated in inversion (Example 15.17).

Example 15.17

Although the note-row portion is atonal, the ordering of its pitches proves to be far from arbitrary, for the prominent positioning of E and B at the center of the row in bar 2 hints at the respective tonic and dominant of the movement. Couple these with the B-flat and E-flat placed at that bar's flanks, and there is a foreshadowing of the E/E-flat tensions of the violin's opening theme. In the row's inversion (bars 5–7), the functions are reversed. The piano's twofold repetition of the passacaglia theme in counterpoint with a new violin melody reinforces the E/B tonal function and the E/E-flat tensions. An isolated return of this opening row at Fig. 6, heard in counterpoint with the violin's first four bars (but with the instruments' roles now reversed), is preceded by a different, overlapping note-row that infringes serial orthodoxy by both admitting the perfect fourth to the permitted mordent exception on pitch repetition and incorporating an extra maverick pitch (Example 15.18). In context, it seems unnatural and unmusical to exclude the initial eighth note D of Example 15.18 from this melodic line; perhaps this note-row should therefore be viewed as having two maverick pitches.

Example 15.18

Shostakovich's very first note-rows in the Blok settings had possessed tonal echoes through their use of sequence or scalic movement. Many of the note-rows in the Twelfth Quartet and the Violin Sonata have "cadential" intervals of a fourth or fifth or they may employ sequence, and some use triadic or scalic contours with explicit tonal features. An example of the latter is the row that begins the second theme in the Violin Sonata's first movement (Fig. 10); except for a single chromatic note (G-sharp), its first eight pitches form a D major ascent.

The unrelated note-rows of the Blok cycle had provided early and decisive proof of a wish for melodic variety that now becomes more sharply focused in the dozen-or-so highly contrasting note-rows of the Violin Sonata. It is this burgeoning preoccupation with diversity that will characterize Shostakovich's later 12-note works and take him down a path of growing divergence from Schoenberg.

Neither of the two main themes of the Violin Sonata's second movement is a note-row, though one is used to introduce the second subject (Fig. 34, b3). As with the first subject of the Twelfth Quartet, an atonal note-row prefigures a tonal theme and, as in that quartet, the note-row will participate in counterpoint with the theme. Its first eight pitches form a wedge with gradually broadening intervals, a characteristic melodic contour of Shostakovich and one that transfers readily to a note-row. At the same time, the pitches of the row are carefully positioned so as not to compromise the newly established key of B-flat (Example 15.19).

Example 15.19

This row is crucial to the motivic generation of the movement. Its two intervallic characteristics, the wedge and the semitonal close, may act together or individually in this. Here is one instance where Shostakovich does echo Schoenberg by permitting smaller groups of pitches within the note-row to operate independently of it, though with a freedom that would never have been countenanced by Schoenberg.

The third movement is a fully formed passacaglia, thus fulfilling the promise of the first movement and creating a frame for the whole work. This time the theme has no serial element, and although two rows precede it in the introduction and several more occur later, Shostakovich's license in serial usage is not extended further in this movement.

The increasing preoccupation with diversity traced above hardly anticipates the explosion of new methods to be discovered in the eleven verse-settings that constitute the Fourteenth Symphony (1969). For the first time, canon occurs and, through a sweeping enlargement of the mordent exception that draws in all the remaining intervals, a significant expressive dividend is yielded. The first instance of a favorite melodic contour occurs in the very opening note-row where, in a pattern closely related to the "wedge," intervals widen from a fixed pitch (Example 15.20).

Example 15.20

But for all the breadth of serial resource that may appear in individual movements, there is an underlying motivic thread resulting from the contour of the first four pitches of that opening row. Amongst the roughly eighty different rows scattered across the Symphony, many are derived from this contour.[22] The soprano's opening phrase of the fourth movement, in which she reflects decoratively on the *Dies irae* allusion contained in the row's first four notes, is just one example of the subtle connections of interval.

The expressive consistency of the Symphony is promoted not only by this note-row and by the poetry itself, with its unchanging subject of death; equally important is a blending of row and non-row, in strong contrast to their usual segregation in Shostakovich's immediately preceding works. For while note-row usage is intensive in the Fourteenth Symphony, there is also a type of compatible but free melodic writing, which, although noted above in isolated cases, now becomes a prevailing factor, with many phrases ranging from eight to eleven pitches. Indeed, Shostakovich's melodic inventiveness seems to have gained a new breadth and freedom, resulting in a growing ascendancy of melody and, correspondingly, a receding role for harmony, prophetic of his final works. True, there is, in the climactic *Presto* of the Symphony's third movement, a run of successive, unlike note-rows deployed in canonic entries in the strings that saturate the texture and generate a complex harmonic web (Example 15.21). But such instances are rare in Shostakovich, as is the total atonality that often, as here, is to be associated with moments of extreme expressive intensity. Yet even here, the note-rows are cunningly housed within hints of B-flat as a tonal center, encapsulated in the broken triad at their start and the solitary B-flat bell that follows in their wake. Tonality keeps watch.

The Fourteenth Symphony is profoundly significant in Shostakovich's evolution. Never before had the marks of serialism so stamped themselves upon his own established melodic style. Nevertheless his profitable engagement with serialism was not yet over, for the fruits of this synthesis are perhaps even more evident in the Fifteenth Symphony (1971) which, though containing only a relatively small number of orthodox note-rows, displays, especially in the first movement, a preponderance of melody whose character would surely have been less richly chromatic, but for Shostakovich's experiments with 12-note writing. The first

Example 15.21

movement's opening strand of melody, a non-row but still employing ten different pitch classes, is not untypical. Melody is the very life of this extraordinary movement, and the work that springs to mind as its natural precursor is one that was written well over thirty years before—the Fourth Symphony. There, the opening movement had also been a perpetual stream of melodic generation; now once again, but with its style subtly enriched by this plundering of serial resource, melody is granted supremacy.

Shostakovich's final works—the last two quartets, the three late song cycles, and the Viola Sonata—contain a shift of emphasis towards melody. Although a few rows do still occur—in the first song of the *Tsvetayeva* cycle, for example—this new melodic world is inhabited less by rows than by melodies with a capacity for greatly enhanced chromaticism. The note-row as such has all but disappeared.

There are two other points worth pondering. In the Fifteenth Symphony's finale, there are further signs of melodic synthesis as Shostakovich admits Wagner into his world. Quotations of the "Fate" motif from *Götterdämmerung* and the first notes of *Tristan* occupy the opening, while the tonal simplicity and spaciousness of the ensuing melody allow further infiltration by those same Wagnerian fragments. But ingeniously, the quotations are also insinuated into note-rows that occur during the first three of six varied exposition statements of the first theme (Examples 15.22a–c).

Example 15.22a

Example 15.22b

Example 15.22c

Thus Shostakovich's serialism is briefly invaded by melody of another composer. And in this finale's passacaglia (Fig. 125), Shostakovich turns to the march theme from his own Seventh Symphony, converting its first four bars to form part of a note-row (with one extra pitch) that provides the passacaglia's recurring ground.

Shostakovich's serial usage was light-years away from Schoenberg's. But perhaps his highly individual treatment reflected his Russian identity. David Brown has observed that many Russian folksongs unfold as successive variations around a tiny melodic protoshape, with protoshapes recurring from folksong to folksong.[23] This can be heard also in the works of Glinka or Tchaikovsky, for example, the six-note descending "Fate" motif in *Eugene Onegin*, whose contour may be discerned not only within many very unlike themes of that opera but also in significant contexts in later Tchaikovsky works. As we have noted, in any one Shostakovich movement there may be multiple note-rows, some of them occurring maybe only once as a single melodic entity. But could it be that, just as the earlier Russian composers' melodic faculties had found fertile stimulus in the constraint of a brief protoshape, Shostakovich's found a stimulus in operating within the restriction of the twelve pitch classes, each used once only, these being constantly reshuffled and rhythmically restructured? And so: was Shostakovich's affair with serialism not just a brief submission to the control of a very Western creative procedure but an expression of his profound Russianness?

CHAPTER 16

THE MOVING IMAGE: TIME AND NARRATIVE IN THE FIFTEENTH QUARTET[1]

Richard Burke

Shostakovich's Fifteenth String Quartet, his last, was written in 1974, almost one hundred years after Tchaikovsky's Third Quartet, also in E-flat minor. Besides their key, an unusual and in some ways problematic choice for strings, the two works share an elegiac tone, largely confined to the funeral march in the Tchaikovsky but pervasive and unrelenting in the Shostakovich. Tchaikovsky's quartet, however, is a straightforward work in four movements, its unusual features easily accounted for by its dedication to the memory of violinist Ferdinand Laub. Shostakovich's quartet is another matter. Its six movements are linked by transitions and are all marked *adagio*. In addition, the key signature of six flats and the E-flat tonal center are maintained through most of the piece. There is little about this quartet that is straightforward. Paul Griffiths declared it "the strangest of all" the quartets;[2] Hugh Ottaway called it "an austere, cryptic utterance."[3]

But though it may seem strange or cryptic to even the most experienced listener, there is something tantalizingly communicative about the work, as if it were speaking a strange dialect of a familiar language, requiring only that the ear become accustomed to its sound and rhythm to reveal its meaning. Certainly, the titles of its six movements need not be translated. The first five are common musical genres: Elegy, Serenade, Intermezzo, Nocturne, and Funeral March; the last, Epilogue, is a standard literary designation. And though the exact starting and ending points of individual movements are occasionally obscured by transitions, strong generic characteristics make each movement, once under way, easily discernible. The Serenade consists of a songlike melody supported by a simple suggestion of strumming. The Nocturne is propelled by an arpeggiated accompaniment figure that immediately calls to mind the left-hand patterns of nineteenth-century piano nocturnes. And the Funeral March inches forward in the heavy dotted rhythms traditionally associated with the genre. The Intermezzo, however, is different.

The Serenade ends with a recitative for the cello that comes to rest on a low E-flat. It is here that the Intermezzo begins. The entire movement, consisting largely of a soaring, angular cadenza for violin, is played out over this sustained E-flat. Toward the end of the movement, the cello twice briefly abandons the E-flat (Figs. 44, b2 and 45, b3), ultimately returning to it in the last measure. From there, the persistent E-flat finally descends to a D, where the next movement, the Nocturne, begins. This odd, twenty-seven-measure movement might be considered merely a transition from the Serenade to the Nocturne. But a transition, at least in traditional usage, is a passage that provides continuity, taking the listener from one place to another in a logical and convincing manner. The Intermezzo in Shostakovich's Quartet is boldly discontinuous, even disruptive, and when we reach its end, we are in a place emotionally indistinguishable from where we began. In this respect, it bears little resemblance to the most famous transition of all, the one connecting the third and fourth movements of Beethoven's Fifth Symphony, where a great deal of energy is accumulated and finally released in a big blast of finale. In fact, Shostakovich's transitions rarely fit this dark-to-light, struggle-to-triumph paradigm—a striking exception being the connection between the last two movements of the programmatic Twelfth Symphony, or, in a different vein, in the Eighth Symphony, where the bleak march of the passacaglia is brought to a halt as it slides into the soft, hopeful C major of the last movement. More common in Shostakovich is the transition where one movement quietly and almost undetectably fades into the next. The prototype is also found in Beethoven, between the "Storm" and the "Hymn of Thanksgiving" in the *Pastoral* Symphony. Here, the material of the fourth movement gradually fades away as the storm recedes. And unlike the finale of the Fifth Symphony, the new movement begins with its ideas not yet fully formed: the new key has not yet been established; the intervals of the tune are still too big. The transition is incomplete.

Something similar happens in Shostakovich's Fifth Quartet. Even before the B minor slow movement comes to a close, its materials seem to be breaking up. The main theme is fragmented and a prominent outlining of a C minor triad (Fig. 77, b2) slightly weakens the final B minor chord. As the third and last movement begins (Example 16.1), the first violin, viola, and cello refuse to give up B minor, obstructing the modulation to the new key, B-flat. Meanwhile, the second violin introduces an idea built around the pitches B, D, and E-flat. E-natural (from the old key of B minor) still has a place (m. 10, m. 26, and mm. 28–30), but E-flat, whose status in mm. 2–16 is that of chromatic neighbor tone to the D, eventually becomes more prominent. Similarly, starting in m. 17, B-flat begins to take the place of B-natural; in m. 23, the latter now appears as a chromatic C-flat. But even after m. 33, where F-natural firmly establishes itself in the bass, remnants of B minor still linger (for example, mm. 41–42, essentially replaying mm. 31–32), making the identity of the G-flat in the viola and cello at m. 43 slightly questionable. Finally, the dominant of B-flat is reached in m. 47, followed two measures

Example 16.1

later by the tonic. In this remarkable modulation, B minor is painstakingly transformed into B-flat, the old key slowly dissolving as the new key emerges. The effect is similar to the fading of the old material at the end of the storm in the *Pastoral* Symphony, with one important difference. In the Shostakovich transition, there is a point at which both the old and the new seem to exist simultaneously.

Transitions of this type, though often involving thematic material rather than tonality, can be found between the second and third movements of, respectively, the
Seventh, Ninth, and Fourteenth Quartets.

Shostakovich uses another, somewhat similar kind of transition, in which a single pitch from one movement intrudes into the next. In the Eighth Quartet, for
example, the A-sharp from the third movement persists well into the fourth. The
first violin obstinately refuses to let go of the pitch in spite of the angry, dissonant
chords that challenge it. The other instruments eventually give in to the
A-sharp—an F-sharp major chord may be the sign of surrender—and the movement proceeds. Other works to use this kind of transition include the Fourth,
Ninth, and Tenth Quartets, the *Seven Romances on Poems of Alexander Blok*, the
Suite on Poems of Michelangelo, and the Thirteenth Symphony.

A third type of transition is so abrupt that the word transition may seem inappropriate. Just before the *attacca* between the Humoresque and the Elegy in the Eleventh Quartet, the listener may well think a transition is in progress. This impression
probably comes less from the actual music than from expectations established by the
previous four movements, all of which are connected rather neatly. But between the
Humoresque and the Elegy, the connection is sudden and jarring as the repeated,
rather ridiculous cuckoo gesture played by the violin is suddenly replaced by the
slow, dignified dotted rhythm of the new movement. The contrast between the two
movements is extreme in every way: the dynamic shift from *piano* to *fortissimo*; the
tempo *allegro* to *adagio*; the register high to low; and the key C major to F-sharp
minor. These contrasts only broaden the enormous gap between the two genres: a
humoresque, a character piece with a light, almost silly connotation (though here, as
in most of Shostakovich's humorous movements, possessing a dark, disturbing side),
and an elegy, with its traditional implications of eloquence, gravity, and sorrow.

All three types of transition bear a striking resemblance to techniques found in
film. The first connection is like a dissolve, a narrative device in which one image
slowly fades out as a new one fades in. As with the keys in the Fifth Quartet modulation, there is a brief moment at which the old and the new exist simultaneously. The second kind of connection, where a single pitch is sustained into the
following movement, is similar to an overlap, a device in which one aspect of a
scene continues into the next, as when dialogue is heard even after the characters
speaking it are no longer visible. And the third connection is an abrupt shift in
content, commonly known as a cut.

Shostakovich and Film

Shostakovich's association with film began early in his life, in the 1920s, during
what was arguably the most significant and exciting decade of Soviet film history.
In the early years of the decade, the director Lev Kuleshov showed that a story
could be told far more effectively by abandoning the pedestrian narrative
techniques of earlier films. His goal was, as he put it, "to try the tricks that the
pre-revolutionary and early Soviet cinema could not achieve."[4] In 1922, he made

a series of experimental films that demonstrated that editing was the most important element in film narrative. Vsevolod Pudovkin described one of these experiments, involving a close-up of a famous Russian actor:

> In the first combination the close-up of Mosjukhin [Mozzhukhin] was immediately followed by a shot of a plate of soup standing on a table. It was obvious and certain that Mosjukhin was looking at his soup. In the second combination the face of Mosjukhin was joined to shots showing a coffin in which lay a dead woman. In the third the close-up was followed by a shot of a little girl playing with a funny toy bear. When we showed the three combinations to an audience which had not been let into the secret, the result was terrific. The public raved about the acting of the artist. They pointed out the heavy pensiveness of his mood over the forgotten soup, were touched and moved by the deep sorrow with which he looked on the dead woman, and admired the light, happy smile with which he surveyed the girl at play. But we knew that in all three cases the face was exactly the same.[5]

In another experiment, using a clip from an American film, Kuleshov was able to show two men shaking hands in front of the monument to Gogol in Moscow, and then turning and climbing the steps of the White House.[6] There was no superimposition of images, just a simple juxtaposition of shots that the viewer perceived as a single narrative, something that has come to be known as the "Kuleshov effect." Kuleshov in part created his new narrative techniques by doing away with the establishing shot, the shot that would provide the audience with a frame of reference for the ensuing montage. (Although an establishing shot provided clarification of what was to come, it also greatly limited the flexibility of the montage.) This technique was summed up and expanded in Pudovkin's 1925 essay on film theory, which exerted an extraordinary and immediate influence on Soviet film. Many of the films of the period—Kuleshov's own *The Death Ray*, Eisenstein's *Strike* and *Battleship Potemkin*, and Kosintzev and Trauberg's *The Overcoat*—are still startlingly fresh and bold in their use of narrative techniques.

Contemporary with the technical breakthroughs in film, the so-called Russian Formalists were exploring similar ideas in literary criticism. One of the chief concerns of the group was the analysis of narrative, which, in a famous distinction between "plot" and "story," divorced what was being told from the way it was related. Not surprisingly, the paths of the new Soviet directors and literary critics converged, culminating in 1927 in a collection of essays on film by leading formalist critics Tynyanov, Eikhenbaum, Kazansky, Pyotrovsky, and Shklovsky.[7] The Formalists saw some of their theories realized in the new films. Shklovsky, for example, points to one connection between Formalist theory and film theory in a 1927 essay in which he discusses Kuleshov's famous experiments:

> But the fact is that for the professional the man in the shot does not laugh or cry or mourn, he only opens and shuts his eyes and his mouth in a specific way. He is raw material. The meaning of a word depends on the phrase I place it in. If I place the word properly in another phrase it will have a different meaning.[8]

It was also clear to Shklovsky and his colleagues that the defamiliarization of the ordinary, a concept at the heart of Formalist theory, was exactly what the camera did whenever it viewed an ordinary object from an unusual angle. And the distinction between plot and story in Formalist narrative analysis could also be seen as a critical element in montage.

It is hard to imagine that the young Shostakovich was not in some way aware of the work of the new film directors and critics. He may not have read Formalist theory or Pudovkin's pamphlets, but he would certainly have seen or, during his days as silent-film pianist, even accompanied some of the films that experimented with narrative and montage. And Kozintsev and Trauberg, the directors for whom Shostakovich would write his first film score, *New Babylon* (1929), were deeply involved in Kuleshov's innovations, had worked with Tynyanov, and were the subject of a number of critical writings by Shklovsky.[9] Shostakovich was clearly aware of the contribution that music could make to film narrative. In 1929, he wrote, in reference to *New Babylon*: "At the end of reel 2, the important moment is the German cavalry's advance on Paris, but the reel ends in a deserted restaurant. But the music, in spite of the fact that the German cavalry is no longer seen on the screen, continues to remind the audience of the approach of that fierce power."[10] In short, Shostakovich created what may very well be the earliest example of an overlap between the screen image and the score.

There is additional evidence of this awareness in Shostakovich's music of the 1920s and 1930s. There are times in the dramatic works where the influence of film is obvious, for example, in the often-mentioned similarity between the Keystone Kops of American silent-film comedy and the police in *Lady Macbeth*; or in the second scene of the third act of *The Nose*, staged as if a camera were cross-cutting, to use the film term, between two separate apartments, and then immediately moving out to the street for an exterior shot. And other, perhaps more subtle cinematic influences appear in Shostakovich's instrumental music as early as 1925, shortly after his first professional contact with films. His works begin to exhibit greater formal freedom in comparison to the textbook forms of the earlier pieces. The odd juxtaposition of a lament with elements of the scherzo in the first of the Two Pieces for Octet, and the sectional construction of the First Piano Sonata seem to imitate montage, as do many passages in the Second and Third Symphonies, where strongly contrasting kinds of music are often juxtaposed like film shots. These juxtapositions are even more striking in the two sprawling outer movements of the Fourth Symphony, where unpredictable, unrelated kinds of music—a wild fugato, a strange dance, a number of marches (including a funeral march) and a waltz—collide. Not surprisingly, as the Symphony draws to a close, it takes more than two hundred measures of a tonic chord to convince the ear that what it has heard has been a unified whole. Such a work would perhaps be better analyzed in terms of montage than, say, sonata form, for, to borrow from Eisenstein writing about film, the different kinds of music in the piece "placed together, combine into a new concept, a new quality, arising out of that juxtaposition."[11]

The Fifteenth Quartet

Narrative devices do not in themselves suggest narratives. Just as a film director may attempt to duplicate the effect of four-part polyphony in dialogue or in the visual image without necessarily bringing along historical or compositional implications of the technique, a composer may use a musical analogue to a film or literary device without implying the presence of a narrative. In the transition between the last two movements of Shostakovich's Fifth Quartet, the device that I have called a "dissolve" is probably nothing more than an effect. On the other hand, the cut from the fourth to the fifth movement in the Eleventh Quartet encourages interpretation because of additional information from one of the strongest sources in music, genre. A Humoresque abruptly juxtaposed with an Elegy is discursive, strongly suggesting the presence of a narrative. Add to this Shostakovich's dedication of the work to the memory of Vasily Shirinsky, the recently deceased second violinist of the Beethoven Quartet, and the interpretation becomes even more specific. Other elements of the work fall into place. The presence of an etude in the middle of the Quartet, for example, suddenly makes sense.

In the Fifteenth Quartet, a number of different factors combine to suggest a narrative: the dissolve transitions that connect the movements, the strong generic characteristics, and the highly unusual unity of tempo and tonality. But in addition, the four central movements, progressing from a Serenade to a Funeral March, form a chronology. A Serenade is often a love song, bringing with it images of youth and hope, or at least anticipation, and even suggestions of place, usually outdoors, and time, more than likely evening. The Serenade is followed by the Intermezzo and then the Nocturne. At the same time lyrical and bleak, sentimental and cold, this Nocturne takes place in the dead of night. Its chromatic tune barely seems able to move, confined to a midrange by arpeggios that span two octaves. The melody is notably similar to that of the first song of *From Jewish Folk Poetry,* "The Lament for the Dead Child."[12] There is a tragic tone in this strange night-piece that leads very convincingly into the Funeral March, which almost always takes place in the morning.

If this is indeed a chronology, then the connection at the beginning of the Quartet, Elegy to Serenade, does not fit. The Elegy, a lament or expression of mourning, would, of course, make sense after the Funeral March. And it does in fact appear there, for the final movement, the Epilogue, eventually leads back to the last five measures of the Elegy. At this point, the Formalist distinction between *fabula* and *syuzhet,* or story and plot, might prove useful. The story is the actual order of events. In the Quartet, this is the progression from the Serenade to the Funeral March and Epilogue, ultimately leading to the Elegy. The plot is the way in which the story is actually told. In the Quartet, the Elegy, which comes at the end of the narrative sequence, is heard first, as in the common narrative device called analepsis or, in film, flashback.

The flashback is a familiar plot device in fiction and film. It can be a brief segment of a narrative or the entire narrative itself. Numerous films and novels begin with a significant event—often, a funeral, a memorial tribute, or some kind of tragedy—which triggers a recollection of the events that led up to it. The flashback ends, of course, when we once again reach the present. The Fifteenth Quartet does something like that. At the end of the opening Elegy, a digression very much like a flashback begins. At the end of the Quartet, after the Serenade, Intermezzo, Nocturne, and Funeral March, the Epilogue makes its way back to the same point where the digression began, that is, the final measures of the Elegy.

The transition from the Elegy to the Serenade is one of the strangest passages in Shostakovich. As the Elegy fades away, the Serenade begins with a twelve-note row moving, one long note at a time, from instrument to instrument. Each note is slightly over a measure in length and overlaps briefly with the start of the next one; each note is also marked with a lunging crescendo from *pianissimo* to quadruple *forte*. The twelve-note passage is followed by an equally disruptive series of gestures made up of strummed pizzicato chords (m. 13) and disjunct melodic fragments played by the cello (mm. 13-17), like pieces of recitative overheard through a door. While this remarkable transition connects the Elegy to the Serenade, it also distances the Elegy from the rest of the work, destroying the Elegy's tonal, harmonic, and formal stability. The twelve-note series is similar in design to a particular kind of film montage used to show accelerated time, in which each shot overlaps the previous one, often coming into focus as if from a distance. These montages, popular in the 1930s and 40s, often show a series of calendar pages, shots of the seasons changing, or train wheels against a shifting background. The twelve-note chain achieves a similar temporal distancing of the Elegy from the rest of the piece. In a flashback, there is also an initial feeling of disorientation, sometimes suggested by a blurring of the image on the screen. The strange chords and the fragmented, indistinct bits of recitative have a similar effect. It is almost as if Shostakovich were trying to distance the Elegy from the Serenade by avoiding anything that might be misconstrued as music.

The string of pitches, the pizzicato chords, and the recitative are immediately repeated. This time, the passage is abbreviated: the twelve-note chain is replaced by an unrelated sequence of eight pitches. This repetition may simply be a confirmation of what just occurred, or, to continue the narrative that is being sketched, a deepening of the distancing of the Serenade. The Serenade melody grows out of the shreds of recitative, as if these blurry, distant vocalizations suddenly come into focus as a melody, with the curious strummed chords now forming its accompaniment. The song section of the Serenade is interrupted by another string of pitches, this time eleven and starting in the cello. This may again suggest temporal motion, for the second rendition of the tune is played by the cello, as if the voice were deepening or, one might even say, maturing. The flashback, as expected, is now moving forward in time.

The Intermezzo, built on the last note of the Serenade, seems to suspend the action of the narrative, just as an intermezzo, in its traditional theatrical usage, suggests an interruption of the action of a drama. The sustained E-flat in the cello intensifies the sense of suspension, while the violin cadenza begins by playing with fragments of the Serenade. As the Intermezzo ends, the scene of the Serenade, still present in the sustained E-flat of the cello, has darkened. The E-flat descends to a D and the Nocturne begins. The tragic tone established at the beginning of the movement intensifies, leading easily into the Funeral March, which in turn dissolves into the Epilogue. Here, in the final movement, themes from earlier in the work drift in and out, separated by an eerie tremolo figure. The tremolo passages, played *fortissimo*, at first recall the violin cadenza from the Intermezzo, especially in the wide range outlined by their rise and fall. At Fig. 68, a twelve-note chain drifts by, played loudly and quickly by violins and viola pizzicato. The interval structure of this chain replicates exactly that of the twelve-note chain that started the Serenade, although the minor second formed by the first two pitches is here inverted. Thus, the gesture with which the Quartet's flashback began now signals its end. During the three measures leading up to Fig. 73, the tremolos grow shorter and softer, confining themselves to a very limited range, eventually dissolving into quiet trills from Fig. 73. Finally, the last measures of the Elegy are played again—flashbacks must return to the exact place where they began—and the Elegy, the narrative, and the Quartet all come to an end.

Shostakovich's last quartet is clearly a memorial of some sort. In this sense, it follows in a singularly Russian tradition of chamber works written *in memoriam*: piano trios by Tchaikovsky, Rachmaninov, Arensky, and Shostakovich himself, quartets by Tchaikovsky and Shostakovich (both mentioned earlier), and Schnittke's Piano Quintet. But all of these works have clearly stated dedicatees. For whom was Shostakovich's Fifteenth Quartet written?

The narrative I have sketched is really only half a narrative, a plot with no story. But that is enough. A search through Shostakovich's life to find a specific event that would fit this narrative would probably be easy. Tragedy abounds. But uncovering a specific incident to account for the Elegy or supplying a corpse for the Funeral March would be like giving an establishing shot to Kuleshov's montage—it would ruin the effect by limiting it. What this sketch of a narrative does, perhaps, is explain why the work works, why it seems to speak a familiar language. But it is probably the most obvious feature of this quartet that says the most about it—the unchanging tempo marking and key signature. This is not a work in six movements, but one in a single movement, an elegy, interrupted by a recollection of the events that inspired it.

Although few are actually so named, there are many great instrumental elegies in music. This is not surprising: music is especially good at depicting and expressing grief. But Shostakovich's last quartet may be the greatest elegy of all. It plays with time. And in so doing, it goes under the surface and beyond the sorrow to depict the elemental, inescapable force that creates every narrative and motivates every lament—memory.

PART **IV**

ASPECTS OF SHOSTAKOVICH

CHAPTER 17

SHOSTAKOVICH AND THE CINEMA

John Riley

As a student, Shostakovich worked as a cinema pianist, and between 1929 and 1970 wrote almost forty film scores. Yet because most of these scores are regarded as propaganda, this work is almost completely ignored. Although hardly an unbroken series of masterworks, there are certainly outstanding pieces amongst them. In any case, this music constitutes a surprisingly large part of his output, and to ignore it risks distorting our view of him.[1]

Lenin rejected the idea of art-for-art's-sake, insisting that its political role was paramount: "All Social-Democratic literature must become Party literature."[2] Cinema was the perfect medium. Its newness paralleled the new Soviet society, its technological base reflected Soviet technophilia, and it circumvented the still-endemic illiteracy. It was these attributes that led to the legendary Leninism that cinema was "of all the arts, for us the most important."[3] The industry was nationalized in 1919 but many cinemas remained in private hands. The industry was clearly in a cycle of decline, with home-produced films in the minority, and cinemas closing and being asset-stripped by their near-bankrupt departing owners. Despite this, the mid-1920s saw a flowering in Soviet cinema as a flood of new talent was attracted to the state-supported industry, and many films now regarded as classics were made between 1924 and the end of the decade.

The release of *The Jazz Singer* in October 1927 is generally seen as marking the beginning of the end of "silent cinema" in the West, though this description is misleading; from the earliest days the aural void was filled with music or sound effects, and there had been attempts to develop synchronized sound systems. These experiments presented filmmakers simultaneously with an opportunity and a problem: they could now control the relationship between image and sound, but the crudity of the technology limited what was possible. Nevertheless, the debate about *how* sound should be used entered a new phase. In 1928, Eisenstein, Pudovkin, and Alexandrov opposed realistic sound, proposing instead a "counterpoint" between it and the image: "the first experiments in sound must aim at a sharp discord with the visual images."[4] Musical counterpoint generally comprises two or more *interdependent* voices, but, in the case of film, the image would set the parameters and the soundtrack would either reflect or set up a "sharp contrast" to it. Although the precise relationship of the two was still being worked out and Eisenstein's own ideas would change, the proposals still centered on the primacy of the image.

Shostakovich would probably have met Eisenstein's circle through Meyerhold, but he was also associated with FEKS (the Factory of the Eccentric Actor) led by Leonid Trauberg, Grigory Kozintsev, Sergei Yutkevich, and professional gambler Georgy Kryzhitsky. Their 1922 manifesto is an exuberant piece of impudence, full of America- and mechanophilia, and praise for the circus, Chaplin and demotic art.[5] Eccentrism subverted automatic responses by defamiliarizing everyday things through surreal juxtapositions and having ordinary human impulses and emotions magnified, distorted, or arise from improbable sources. FEKS' first theater work was a production of Gogol's *The Marriage*, subtitled *A Gag in Three Acts*, with interpolated clips of Chaplin films and a poster promising "the electrification of Gogol" (a reference to Lenin's famous slogan, "the electrification of the entire country").[6] Unfortunately, FEKS' defamiliarization program was linked to Formalism, which was later to become the most serious charge that could be made against a Soviet artist.

Shostakovich was in many ways the ideal composer for FEKS' new film about the Paris Commune, *New Babylon*. One of the things that had most offended Shostakovich in the cinema pit was cliché, and this seemed like an opportunity to develop a considered and original film score. But Soviet film technology lagged behind the West, and synchronized sound had not yet arrived. Not every cinema had the requisite forces, so orchestral scores could only be used at a limited number of venues if additional players were not to be hired, making performances of such scores expensive. Since avant-garde films, despite critical praise, were unpopular, and since Shostakovich and the directors were known avant-gardists, Sovkino was brave to commission a modernist score to be played by a large ensemble in synchronization with a politically sensitive film that would probably turn out also to be extremely avant-garde. But though the makers managed to get it past the studio, they underestimated the political and practical difficulties that the film and its music would cause.

The directors had been working on *New Babylon* since February 1928, but Shostakovich only signed the contract on 28 December. With the film set to open on 18 March 1929, he had just eleven weeks to compose ninety minutes of music in orchestral, piano trio, and piano solo versions. He was suffering from flu and was also committed to writing music for Meyerhold's Moscow production of Mayakovsky's play, *The Bedbug*. Commuting back and forth between Leningrad and Moscow, he dashed off the twenty-three numbers of *The Bedbug* in less than a month and, after watching the film twice and receiving a breakdown of the timings for each section, the score for *New Babylon* was ready by 20 February 1929.[7] Unsurprisingly, the two projects share material. Shostakovich also drew on existing music by himself and others.

In March, *New Babylon* opened to general consternation. Communist Youth International denounced it as counter-revolutionary, though the Russian Association of Proletarian Writers (RAPP) defended it. Factory workers argued about it and there were calls for public debates. Newspapers were divided, with some calling for the makers to be tried for "jeering at the heroic pages of revolutionary history and the French proletariat."[8]

The directors always insisted that the music was integral to the film but that it was "linked with the inner meaning rather than the external action and would develop contrary to the events, independent of the construction of the scene."[9] But critics felt that the film's deliberately confusing sense of time and space would alienate the masses. In December 1928, just before Shostakovich had joined the production, the Sovkino Workers' Conference called for experimental art to be "intelligible to the millions." In return, Trauberg accused the Conference of demanding "NEP style ideology" and mere "agreeableness in this battle with public taste."[10] A week before the premiere, Shostakovich wrote an article decrying the standard of film music: "It's time to take cinema music in hand, to eliminate the bungling and the inartistic and to thoroughly clean the Augean stable. The only way to do this is to write special music."[11] He also complained about the conditions under which films were shown—for example, the habit of projecting popular films at a faster speed so that they could be shown twice a night, thus ruining the music.

Perhaps anticipating the puzzlement that the film and its music might cause, Shostakovich explained how he did *not* always illustrate what was on the screen:

For example at the end of the second reel the important episode is the German cavalry's advance on Paris though the scene ends in an empty restaurant. Silence. But the music, in spite of the fact that the cavalry is no longer on screen, continues to remind the audience of the approaching threat. I constructed a lot of the music on the principle of contrast. For example when Jean comes across Louise at the barricades he is filled with despair. The music becomes more and more cheerful, finally resolving into a giddy, almost "obscene" waltz reflecting the Versailles army's victory over the people of the commune. An interesting process is used at the beginning of the fourth reel. While the rehearsal of the operetta is on screen the music plays variations of Hanon's exercises differently nuanced in relation to the action; sometimes gay, sometimes

irritating, sometimes languid and sometimes frightening.... Based on a wide variety
of sources, the music maintains an unbroken symphonic tone throughout. Its basic
function is to suit the tempo and rhythm of the picture and make the impressions it
produces more lasting.[12]

New Babylon was marked by its use of quotations, including revolutionary songs
and fragments of Offenbach and Shostakovich. Earlier composers (perhaps Shostakovich too in his time in the cinema pit) had used these to get a knee-jerk reaction; the *Internationale* or the *Marseillaise* could be guaranteed to get an audience
to its feet. Similarly, folk songs would encourage the audience to join in, and this
may have been Ippolitov-Ivanov's intention in his music for the 1908 film *Stenka
Razin*. Few of Shostakovich's film scores are completely devoid of quotations, either from folk music or from his or other composers' work. But in *New Babylon*,
they are neither simply time-savers used by a hard-pressed composer, nor quick
fixes for scene painting: they add layers of meaning to the film in a way that creates a truly audio-visual experience.

The music brilliantly comments on the action of the film, yet is in itself completely satisfying and independent. Thus, tragic images can be accompanied by
jolly music (or vice versa) as when scenes of the Paris onslaught are accompanied
by Offenbach. This was one of the high points not only of Shostakovich's career
(and not just in film) but also of dramatic music in general, while the imagery
and editing of the film reach a high-water mark of Formalism. Shostakovich may
have been aiming for a "symphonic tone," but *New Babylon* is more akin to an
opera without words, one whose rapidly changing moods echo *Wozzeck*, which
Shostakovich had enjoyed in 1927. There is also the extraordinary moment when
he counterpoints the *Marseillaise* with the "Can-Can" from *Orpheus aux enfers*.[13]
Echoing the momentarily unbalanced Second Empire, this could be read as the
Communards' complacency and failure to build on early victories leading to their
downfall, just as it had endangered the regime they were attempting to overthrow.
But the increasingly prevalent Stalinist view, reflecting the dictator's own ambi-
tions, was that the problem was the lack of centralized control.

If the film was questionable politically, its musical performance was abominable.
Part of the problem was that the film had been substantially re-edited after the
score was written. Whether this happened, to cite conflicting sources, "less than
three weeks" or "three days" before the film's opening,[14] Shostakovich could not
ensure that the changes he made were all carried through into the orchestral parts.
At the premiere, he ended up playing some portions of the film on the piano in
order to save the performance.

The controversy surrounding the film continued for many years even in the absence of the music. Although it closed almost immediately, Viktor Shklovsky
wrote a cautiously supportive article in 1930.[15] In 1967, Pyotr Sobolevsky, who
had played the soldier Jean, criticized the film for its unintelligibility,[16] and in
1971, President Pompidou denounced the film as an incitement to riot and
banned its broadcast. Gennady Rozhdestvensky rediscovered the score in 1976

and Trauberg attended some of the accompanied screenings that began to restore the film's reputation. This version was prepared by the British Film Institute and Boosey and Hawkes, but there are still disagreements about the film's restoration. It was broadcast in Russia in 2000 with Shostakovich's music completely re-edited; Marek Pytel's video and accompanying book explain the rationale behind his synchronization.[17] Even the score itself was for a long time a matter of contention.[18]

After the debacle of *New Babylon*, the makers had to prove that its failure was a one-off and that their hearts did indeed beat, as Pavel Petrov-Bytov demanded, "in unison with the masses."[19] Kozintsev and Trauberg announced their next film, *Alone*, as the story of a woman going unwillingly to teach in a distant republic but meeting such resistance from the locals that she gives up hope and commits suicide. However, two major changes were overtaking the directors. Soviet sound-film technology had lagged behind the West, but in 1930, a usable sound recording system was developed. Now, the soundtrack could be placed on the film itself, thus foregoing systems that relied on live performance or on synchronizing records with film. At the same time, the Soviet avant-garde was drawing in its horns, and not necessarily entirely under duress.[20] Although Socialist Realism had yet to be defined,[21] art was becoming increasingly positivist and "accessible to the millions," extolling Soviet moral and physical strength. The ending of *Alone* was changed and the villagers, after leaving the teacher to die of exposure, have a change of heart, and she comes to see the value of her work. Nevertheless, the film was still criticized for its pessimism and for its sympathetic portrayal of a shaman.

Although Kozintsev and Trauberg were moving away from Eccentrism and had abandoned the FEKS label, *Alone* still had some strange effects. For example, the cutting between Altai villagers and Leningrad street tannoys served metaphorically to fill the entire country with the Soviet message. (Such an overlap of the soundtrack from one scene into the next is often used to ease continuity, but such extremes have other purposes. For example, the factory hooter's signal in *The Golden Mountains* continues over shots of both St. Petersburg and Baku, urging the whole country to strike. And in *The Youth of Maxim*, the officer's recitation of oblasts from which the hero is banned continues satirically over his doleful exit.) With Stalin intensifying the class struggle and forcing the country into total submission, *Alone's* hit song, "How Good Life Will Be!," hardly seems to reflect current events.[22] Rather, in association with a title card reading "Time to Get Up!," it is used in a consciously ironic way. First, it describes the teacher Kuzmina's *current* ecstasy at the prospect of her *future* wedding. Next, it accompanies Kuzmina watching the sleeping village head and his wife, and realizing that their political ignorance parallels her *past* in Leningrad. Finally, as Kuzmina is rescued, there is a repeat of the "Time to get up!" title card that awoke her at the beginning of the film, apparently underlining the metaphorical meaning and alerting us to her truly changed attitude and joy in her work for a *future* where life will be beautiful. However, as her plane leaves, we see the still-drying horse skin, the symbol of rural superstition that she had encountered when she first arrived. Yet for all that it might be seen as rubbing the audience's face in their privations, the song seems to have been popular, with its catchy tune. But its lyric—the poor recording quality led the directors to reduce it to simple repetitions of the title—may have given a glimpse of the goal to which the nation's suffering was intended to lead.

Alone was shot in Leningrad, the Altai, and Kiev, and though Shostakovich took little account of indigenous music, the soundtrack does include sounds of a shaman; in the Altai, the recording had failed and the shaman had to be brought to Leningrad to repeat his performance.[23] Realizing that part of the problem for *New Babylon* was the long cues, Shostakovich completely changed his method for *Alone*, producing small pieces that could be easily cut, altered, and shuffled around, a technique he would use often in his later film scores. (Incidentally, Prokofiev came to the same conclusion in his cinema work and argued the point with director Gendelshtein before abandoning work on *Lermontov* (1942).[24]) Meanwhile, the kaleidoscope of sounds that *Alone* uses—a clever interleaving and layering of music, sound effects, and speech—marks it out as one of the more innovative early sound films. Later, Shostakovich was more dismissive, stating that "the way to a truly artistic combination of sound and image was still being sought,"[25] a comment in all likelihood made to distance himself from the film's "formalism." Indeed, the film was banned until changes were made to the soundtrack, though it was released shortly thereafter.[26] Having seen it, Stalin decided to increase funding for the sonorization of the film industry.[27] Nonetheless, had the clampdown on the arts not happened shortly afterwards, *Alone* could have shown one way forward for the aesthetics of sound film.

As Shostakovich later noted, filmmakers were trying to decide how to combine sound and images, and one question was the relationship between cinematic and musical forms. If in the wake of *The Nose*, the seven "acts" of *New Babylon* form a quasi-opera without voices, *Alone's* kaleidoscope of many short pieces is perhaps more balletic, reflecting *The Age of Gold* and *The Bolt*, though its sound world often veers close to his new opera *Lady Macbeth* and the anguished Fourth Symphony that he was to write six years later.

The one major form that had not yet been reflected in his film output was the symphony, but he would approach that in 1931 with his next project, *The Golden Mountains*, a "proper" sound film with the synchronized speech that *Alone* had largely avoided, and an improved recording system. Directed by his friend and lodger Sergei Yutkevich, it tells of a peasant coming to the city to work but becoming embroiled in a strike. Shostakovich adapted the catchy popular song, "If Only I Had Mountains of Gold," which helped ensure the film's success, though the novelty of a sound film would have attracted audiences in any case. By now, Shostakovich was adamant that film scores should not be "mere illustration" and felt fortunate that the directors with whom he worked agreed. Later, he would praise Ermler and Yutkevich for recognizing the role that music should play in films.[28]

By 1932, *New Babylon* was long forgotten and Shostakovich was asked to score Ermler and Yutkevich's *The Counterplan*, the only film commissioned for the 15th anniversary of the Revolution, and one so important that Leningrad Party chief

Sergei Kirov took an interest in it.[29] Perhaps Ermler was also expected to draw on his experience in the Cheka (forerunner of the NKVD and subsequently KGB) to keep an eye on things. After two successful film songs, Shostakovich saw no reason to alter his game plan and worked hard on the "Song of the Counterplan." After several attempts, he struck gold with a song that became and would remain immensely popular. "Finally the melody's author becomes anonymous, something of which he can be proud," Shostakovich later observed, laconically echoing the 1930s drive against individualism. On a more practical note, he added, "'The Song of the Counterplan' has taught me that music composed as an integral part of a film must not lose its artistic value, even outside it."[30]

Yet, *The Counterplan* is a troubling and ambiguous film. Wreckers endanger the work of a Leningrad factory, but their sabotage is discovered and corrected by good communists. In the context of show-trials and the "unmasking of wreckers," *The Counterplan* seems supportive of the regime's tactics, though the makers probably had little choice in the matter. Against that was the inclusion of what some saw as a redundant "love interest." Shostakovich must have had mixed feelings about the project, which would have been intensified when it was held up as a model for Soviet film making, and further confused when lyricist Boris Kornilov was purged in 1938. Having worked hard on the song, Shostakovich made the song work hard for him, and much of the film's score is based on variants of it. As in *The Golden Mountains*, there are orchestral pieces as well, but it was the song that would continue to be an important element in his career, reverberating for many years. He reused it several times, perhaps hoping to remind the regime that he could come up with the goods.[31] Following the purging of Kornilov, which included the destruction of many of his papers, "The Song of the Counterplan" became officially described as a setting of an anonymous folk text.

By now, Shostakovich was seen as an asset to a film and was approached to write more scores. So far, he had worked with only four directors but he was about to add a fifth to the roster and move into a new genre with his first cartoon, Mikhail Tsekhanovsky's *The Tale of the Priest and his Worker Balda*, based on Pushkin's verse-story. Because it was animated, Shostakovich was able to write the music first so the images could be fitted to it—his first chance to completely overturn the hegemony of the image. Giving full rein to his grotesque side, he wrote most of the thirty-four numbers in late 1934 but re-orchestrated parts of it in 1935, an unusual instance of his returning to a work after completion. After making slow progress with the animation, Tsekhanovsky was sacked and the film was never finished, though according to Tsekhanovsky, Shostakovich's involvement contributed to the problem. Most of what was completed was destroyed in the bombing of Leningrad in 1941; only a few minutes survive.

If this was reminiscent of the problems surrounding *New Babylon*, his next film, Gendelshtein's semi-expressionist *Love and Hate*—with an equally turbulent score—was no palliative, creeping out in 1935 with hardly a ripple. But that had less to do with its quality than with what else was available to Soviet cinema-goers, who were being treated to the first two true masterpieces of socialist realist cinema:

the Vasilyev Brothers' *Chapayev* and Kozintsev and Trauberg's *The Youth of Maxim*, the first part of a trilogy. Given their friendship, it was natural that Kozintsev and Trauberg should ask Shostakovich to score the trilogy, and the enormous success of its first part bolstered his reputation. Maxim is a kind of Soviet everyman, who rises from political ingénue to head the National Bank. The trilogy begins in 1910, so the team looked for a contemporary song to serve as Maxim's theme tune; "Whirling and Twirling" ("Krutitsya-Vertitsya") became so closely associated with the character that when Boris Chirkov was persuaded to reprise the role in *The Great Citizen*, the song announced his presence even when he was in revolutionary disguise. Shostakovich's contribution was mostly to select and adapt various folk and revolutionary songs, and though the law of diminishing returns generally applies through the trilogy, he began with it a bang. If *New Babylon* had surprised the audience by counterpointing two tunes, in the prologue to *The Youth of Maxim* Shostakovich trumps that by paralleling the edge-of-the-seat opening nighttime sleigh-ride with a brilliant combination of the *Oira Polka*, the *Krakowiak*, and *Dark Eyes*, cunningly using the orchestration to separate the three.

Both *The Youth of Maxim* and *Chapayev* were released around the same time and vied for popularity and political acclaim. *Maxim* had the more difficult birth: the directors had proposed it as their first project after *New Babylon*, but it was rejected. Even when it was completed, there were questions about its political stance. The directors wrote a defensive article claiming that any success would be due to a variety of reasons including "the people whose lives we found so moving."[32] But in the end, it was a tie as the films' title-role protagonists both became popular folk heroes. In the popular mind, Chapayev bore the visage of the actor Boris Babochkin and images of him atop his tank with a Lenin-like outstretched arm appeared everywhere. Meanwhile, Maxim became so popular that people began to write to him asking advice on their problems, and one Siberian town even voted for him to be their parliamentary representative.[33] Both films relied on song to drive and define the narrative, and this may have been one of the things that fed their popularity.

In 1934, Shostakovich embarked on Lev Arnshtam's film *Girlfriends*. Arnshtam's career had begun similarly to Shostakovich's. They met as piano students at the Petrograd Conservatory and Arnshtam had gone on to work as a pianist at Meyerhold's theatre. After this, he had moved into films as a sound recordist and worked on *Alone*, but was also beginning to develop a directing career. *Girlfriends*, the story of three wartime nurses, was his first solo effort. Shostakovich wrote a substantial score for the film but much of it was lightly scored, including early essays for string quartet, while the girls' transformation into nurses is accompanied by a slow processional for brass and organ, an instrument Shostakovich used only rarely. There are also some quirky fanfares like those he would write for *King Lear* thirty-five years later, as well as a snatch of youthful irreverence as the "Internationale" is played on what sounds like a cross between a theremin and an out-of-control short-wave radio.

Girlfriends was released in February 1936, just thirteen days after the second *Pravda* denunciation of Shostakovich, but the film passed relatively unnoticed in the storm surrounding *Lady Macbeth* and *The Limpid Stream*.[34] The dearth of work following the 1936 denunciations had left Shostakovich struggling for money. The prospect of the remaining two-thirds of the *Maxim* trilogy (1937 and 1939) must have been welcome, and other friends offered film work as well. This period marked his first intensive engagement with cinema—the 1948 denunciation would have a similar effect on his career. The eight films he had scored to date were varied and he had brought an inventive approach to them, but his film work over the next few years would generally become musically more cautious and include some of his cinematic low points. Nevertheless, Shostakovich was probably happy to see the 1936 re-release of *The Golden Mountains*. Although shorn of about a third of its length—for example, the fugue, a dangerous "formalist" abstraction, had been removed—it still served as a reminder that he could write popular and politically acceptable works. In 1936, many Soviet films (including classic silent titles) were being banned, so the re-release of *The Golden Mountains* may have been due less to its popularity than to the acceptance that something had to be provided for Soviet screens even if it was re-releases of old films suitably revised for a new age. The film ends with the last bars of the Third Symphony accompanying shots of marching strikers from various angles. This music was "introduced into the Finale" of the suite that Shostakovich drew from the score, suggesting that the original 1931 version of the film may have had different ending music from the 1936 revision.[35] Although the revised version seems to be the only version of the film currently available, the original score's fugue can be heard in the suite.

In 1936–1937, Shostakovich wrote scores for *The Return of Maxim* and *Volochayev Days*. Along with the Fifth Symphony, these films began the process of rehabilitation. In 1938, more films that he had worked on in the depths of the crisis appeared on Soviet screens: *The Great Citizen (Part One)* (with *Part Two* following the next year), *Friends*, *The Man with the Gun*, and *The Vyborg Side*. The years 1938–1939 saw two recordings of the Fifth Symphony, and a film of at least part of it, in a performance conducted by Mravinsky.[36] This period also saw the rise of a new film genre, "kinoleniniana"—films about Lenin that increasingly sanctified the revolutionary. Both *The Man with a Gun* and *The Vyborg Side* include scenes of Lenin demonstrating his beneficence and omniscience. But he is not alone. At his side is his right-hand man and natural successor, Stalin. As the style developed, Stalin's importance increased until the living Lenin could be largely replaced with the omnipresent pictures on the walls and references to his philosophy as a justification for current policy. When these films were re-released post-1956, Stalin was largely excised, and it is only now that attempts are being made to restore the films to something like their original states.

Shostakovich did not write particularly lengthy (or distinguished) scores for most of these films, although we need not read too much into that—many films around this time had nothing more than opening and closing title music and a few cues or songs in between. Arnshtam's *Friends*, which advocated friendship between Soviet peoples (i.e., discouraging nationalism), is different in this regard, a strange hybrid work, a sound film with strong traces of a silent film aesthetic, giving Shostakovich room to write quite a substantial score. This may have been why it featured so many written intertitles to explain the action in still-silent cinemas. Yet, Arnshtam went further; the intertitles have a strange relationship to the soundtrack, sometimes reinforcing it, sometimes simply scene setting, and sometimes posing a question that the film will go on to address. The score is similarly perched on a crux, a mixture of Shostakovich's current and older styles alongside local folk music recorded in the area. One of *Pravda's* criticisms of the ballet *The Limpid Stream* was that it had taken insufficient account of the folk music of the Kuban, where it was set. Shostakovich was not going to make that mistake again.

The next two projects were definitely more to his taste. *The Silly Little Mouse* (1940) was another animated film by the now-rehabilitated Tsekhanovsky. Shostakovich wrote the score first, turning Marshak's poem into a charming little mini-opera. The baby mouse won't go to sleep; various animal neighbors try to help and the cat joins in, seeing a lunch opportunity before the dog's intervention saves the mouse. With its verse/chorus structure the story is a natural for a musical setting, and Shostakovich took the opportunity to paint the animal-characters as vividly as Prokofiev had in *Peter and the Wolf* in 1936, producing one of his most lovable scores. Then, in 1941, Shostakovich recaptured his early vigor in the short Chaplinesque comedy *The Adventures of Korzinkina*. As with *Alone*, Shostakovich wrote a score whose individual numbers could be cut up as necessary so that, brief as the published score is, there is more there than in the film. Particularly mysterious is why the filmmakers did not make more use of the hilarious two-piano chase, which fits the frenetic middle of the film as perfectly as the gently lachrymose final chorus does the sentimental ending. The talent-show setting allows Shostakovich to bulk things out with musical items, including a chunk of Glinka's *Capriccio brillante*.

"The most important art" took on a new significance in the war years, being mobilized in various ways, and Shostakovich's film scores changed accordingly. The Motherland expected every citizen to contribute to the effort with self-sacrifice, exemplified in films such as *She Defends Her Motherland* (1943), *The Rainbow*, and *Zoya* (both 1944), all three featuring female leads. Shostakovich's "war work" included joining the Art Council of the Committee for Cinema Affairs alongside twenty-four cinema workers and two military advisors. On the lighter side, he also played the waltz from *The Golden Mountains* in a surprisingly elaborate little film by Ilya Trauberg (Leonid's brother) though, despite the music's wit, Shostakovich wears a glum stare throughout.

Shostakovich's cinema style still ran parallel to his concert works, but whereas in the late 1930s he had often contributed very little music to films—sometimes only ten minutes—the later work usually involved bigger scores, typically thirty to forty minutes. This may have been partly a fashion (other composers' scores, particularly those from Hollywood, were sometimes very extensive) and partly a reflection of the improved quality of recording techniques. By now, he had abandoned the "song-score" of *The Counterplan* and was developing the more symphonic strand that had started with *Golden Mountains*. But in many cases, it seemed more a question of yardage. Although *Zoya,* the highly mythologized life-story of the partisan Zoya Kosmodemyanskaya who was killed by the Nazis, has a song, many of the other cues run out of breath after a few seconds. In common with many scores of the time, *Zoya* uses pre-existing music to flag emotions in a simple way. One example is the C major "Glory" chorus from Glinka's *A Life for the Tsar* (Sovietized as *Ivan Susanin*), whose theme of self-sacrifice the film echoes. Another example can be seen early on in the film, where Arnshtam, who incorporated archive footage to give a more "documentary" feel, showed footage of Lenin's funeral. Shostakovich reinforced this by accompanying the scene with the song "You Fell as a Victim," music that had been heard at the actual event.

In 1946, the film industry would fall victim to Zhdanov's purges. After problems at the production stage, Kozintsev and Trauberg's *Simple People* (1945) was cited in the same Resolution that hit Lukov's *The Great Life*, the second part of Eisenstein's *Ivan the Terrible*, and Pudovkin's *Admiral Nakhimov*.[37] Although only *The Great Life* was explicitly banned, all the films were withdrawn. Shortly thereafter, Trauberg began to be smeared as a "rootless cosmopolitan" (i.e., a Jew), and had to rely on pseudonymous writing to earn money. It was the end of a directing partnership that had lasted since the early 1920s. Most of the team's regular actors and technicians, including Shostakovich, chose to continue with Kozintsev rather than Trauberg.[38] *Simple People* was finally released in 1956, but so heavily re-edited that the makers disowned it. Gerasimov's *The Young Guard* (1948) fared better, though like Alexander Fadeyev's novel upon which it was based, it had to be revised before being hailed.

Following the 1948 denunciations, Shostakovich resorted to cinema work in order to survive financially, just as he had in 1936. The late 1940s and early 1950s saw a slew of Soviet biopics on the lives of Soviet pioneers or Russian precursors of the Revolution. Composers, scientists, writers—anyone who could be depicted as aiding the Revolution was so honored. Shostakovich contributed scores to Alexander Dovzhenko's celebration of the agronomist *Michurin* (1949) as well as Kozintsev's biopics of the surgeon *Pirogov* (1947) and the literary critic *Belinsky* (1950, released 1953). Dovzhenko had started adapting his stage play *Life in Bloom* in 1945, but it had been sent back for endless rewrites and the film was not completed until 1948. Stalin rejected it. Dovzhenko had a breakdown but, after a stay at a sanatorium, reworked the film with his wife Yuliya Solntseva. Following its release in 1949, *Michurin*, as it was now called, was awarded a Stalin Prize, a move typical of the regime's alternation of praise and condemnation.

Shostakovich had not been the producer's first choice, but Gavriil Popov's score had been criticized for its "formalism and excessively complicated musical language" so that "even correctly reproduced Russian songs were distorted by the composer's harmonic refinements."[39] In contrast, Khrennikov opined that Shostakovich's score "makes one glad of its warmth and humanity."[40] Despite his extremely politicized work, Dovzhenko is seen as the great poet of Soviet cinema with his lyrical contemplations of nature. He manages to include several such

interludes, and even experiments with time-lapse photography to show spring flowers opening. But he also had to add cruder material, lampooning the botanist's visitors from America and the church. As these are dialogue-heavy scenes, Shostakovich
could concentrate, unusually for him, on the pastoral scenes. *Michurin* is gloriously
photographed but sometimes the attempted grandeur of the music makes it all a little too much and, generally speaking, it is the quieter cues that work better.

Shostakovich did not particularly admire Dovzhenko's work,[41] and was annoyed
that his music was drowned by the dialogue and sound effects. Worse was to come
with *Meeting on the Elbe* (1949), *The Fall of Berlin* (1950) and *The Unforgettable
Year 1919* (1952). Despite (and because of) these films' saturation levels of propaganda, they have some interesting aspects. Shostakovich had previously written
pieces that were classed as, or aspired to be, jazz, but up to this point few had
been "jazzy" in any Western sense. But *Meeting on the Elbe* is notable for having
some of the most convincing jazz that he ever wrote, portraying the bourgeois and
perfidious post-war Americans. Nevertheless, by the end of 1948, Shostakovich
was writing to Isaak Glikman, complaining of exhaustion after a year of writing
film music and of his difficulty getting to grips with *Meeting on the Elbe*; Glikman
ascribed this difficulty in part to the wretched artistic quality of the film.[42]

But the most extraordinary of these films is *The Fall of Berlin*.[43] Soviet film production in the early 1950s was at a historic low, releasing between nine and twenty
films a year. Despite the events of 1948, Shostakovich was a favored film composer just as he had been at the introduction of sound, though now perhaps for
different reasons. In 1946, the Georgian Mikhail Chiaureli had directed *The Vow*,
a hymn to Stalin, and in the run-up to the leader's seventieth birthday in 1950,
Mosfilm "decided" he should make a cinematic present in the form of *The Fall of
Berlin*. Andrei Balanchivadze had scored *The Vow*, but now, for whatever reason,
Shostakovich took over. The basic premise is that while Stalin's military genius
alone won the Great Patriotic War, he still found time to take a paternalistic interest in the lives of each of his subjects. Shostakovich set the embarrassingly poor
texts of party poet Yevgeny Dolmatovsky praising Stalin and the vernal innocence
of the pre-war Soviet Union. And again, Shostakovich produced the traditional ac-
clamation, setting the simple message, "Glory to Stalin."

The 160-minute film demanded quite a lot of music—in the end Shostakovich
wrote about forty-five minutes—but not all of it was so crude. Alexei, the Stakhanovite steel-worker and soon-to-be hero of the Red Army, worries about his relationship with schoolteacher Natasha, and takes a walk to a nearby lake to the
accompaniment of a gentle and affecting nocturne. Other sequences are more
obvious, and there are, as usual, a couple of quotations. Shostakovich does not
miss the opportunity to recycle part of the first movement of his Seventh Symphony to accompany the German attack, though this is much cruder than anything in *New Babylon*, lacking the ironic edge, being a simple symbol of "German
attack." But another quotation deserves some attention.

The marriage of the deranged Hitler is intercut with scenes of the flooding of
the metro and the overrun streets of Berlin. All this is accompanied by alternations

of Shostakovich and, bizarrely, the wedding march from *A Midsummer Night's Dream*. The Jewish Mendelssohn was, for the Nazis, *entartete*—degenerate. At the end of the sequence, a strange silence descends over the bunker as Eva Braun hides a cyanide capsule in a pastry to test it on a favorite dog. Is Chiaureli using this to mock the Nazi's inability to recognize the music that they themselves banned, or to underline their ultimate failure by accompanying this most important ceremony with their most hated music? This puzzling moment becomes even more confusing when we see the storming of the Reichstag, which Chiaureli, an opponent of Eisenstein, intended as a parodic reversal of the famous Odessa steps sequence of *The Battleship Potemkin* (1927). That this iconic moment of Soviet film should be mocked is strange, but then the arrival of Stalin in Berlin—an event that never happened—is very clearly based on the arrival of Hitler in Nuremburg at the beginning of *Triumph of the Will* (1934), while Chiaureli based the last shot of the film on a scene in the 1945 Nazi film *Kolberg*.

Compare the satirical view of the mad Führer with the portrayal of Stalin. The latter is always calm and in control. When we first see the Great Gardener he is tending his orchard. At the threshold of audibility is a choir, yet so heavenly and saccharine that we might be tempted to wonder if it is ironic; if so, it was entirely the composer's doing. With Shostakovich reusing "When the War was Over" from *The Song of the Forests*, perhaps this is a tongue-in-cheek reference to the baton of Soviet agronomy having been passed on to Stalin.

Mikheil Gelovani gives a wooden performance of Stalin (his face barely moves, perhaps out of fear of getting it wrong), while Boris Andreyev (who put in similar turns in *The Unforgettable Year 1919* and *Meeting on the Elbe*) mugs as the proletarian par excellence. Shostakovich was careless of the way the music was used in the film; it is edited extremely crudely with rapid fades up and down and inappropriate cuts. He also wrote a miniature piano concerto for it, but the material is unmemorable, going off at half cock. Being cut into several chunks further hinders its effectiveness in the film. When Atovmyan compiled the suite, he did not reconstitute the fragments. One can only infer that neither he nor Shostakovich felt it would really work. But Shostakovich would later return to the piano concerto idea, producing a very enjoyable example for *The Unforgettable Year 1919*.

Nevertheless, *The Fall of Berlin* contains much evocative photography and, whatever Shostakovich intended, some effective musical moments—some of the ideas would be developed later in the Preludes and Fugues and the Tenth Symphony. It is one of the most fascinating documents of its time, the quintessence of the Stalin personality cult and Soviet kitsch, in some ways well made and in others terrible, even ignoring its offensive message. But in the post-Stalin era, it had become an embarrassment.[44] Chiaureli's star waned, while some of the actors and technicians quietly dropped the film from their biographies. Shostakovich's music had been published and recorded, and remained visible even as the exact nature of the project was forgotten.[45] Rarely if ever shown for many years, it was restored in 1994.[46]

Through the rest of the decade, Shostakovich worked on a series of films that were more or less satisfying and/or profitable. Kozintsev's *Belinsky* (1950)

emphasized the nineteenth-century critic's importance in the early days of the populist movement, and Shostakovich underlined this by inserting folk songs. But it
was heavily criticized and not released until 1953. Kozintsev did not go as far as
disowning it, as he had *Simple People*, but he nevertheless expressed his dislike for
it. *The Unforgettable Year 1919* (1951) was a different affair. The last of Chiaureli's
Stalin biographies, it is as misleading as the others, but was naturally proclaimed a
great film in the cinema press. Shostakovich again produced some evocative music,
and it may be the subject matter that has dissuaded people from recording what is
an effective suite.[47]

Dutch director Joris Ivens' documentary *The Song of the Rivers* (1954) was the
first Soviet/East German co-production. Describing the first congress of the World
Trades Union Congress in Vienna, it uses the conceit of workers from the banks
of six of the world's great rivers coming together to form a seventh river. Shostakovich wrote some new music for it, adding recycled parts of his Eighth Symphony
and other scores. But his greatest popular film success of the time was *The Gadfly*
(1955), Faintsimmer's melodrama about a nineteenth-century Italian revolutionary. The "Romance" became a hit and became well known in the West as the
theme music to the BBC television drama *Reilly, Ace of Spies*. *The Gadfly* became
Shostakovich's most frequently recorded film score.

In 1956, Shostakovich scored Kalatozov's *The First Echelon*. Meanwhile, the
long-banned *Simple People* was released, though neither film attracted much attention. Then, in 1958, Vera Stroyeva asked Shostakovich to edit Musorgsky's *Khovanshchina* for a film version she was producing. Shostakovich gladly accepted and
ended up collaborating on the screenplay also. Rather than cut entire scenes, he
chose to snip lines and sections to keep the larger structure intact, a different
course than he would later take on the film adaptations of his own, *Moscow, Cheryomushki* and *Katerina Izmailova*, both of which saw more wholesale cuts, additions, and revisions.

September 1960 brought what he saw as his greatest capitulation to the regime
when, under pressure, he became a provisional member of the Communist Party,
achieving full membership in October 1961. Yet, from this point, he began to
write pieces that more outspokenly tackled the problems of the Soviet Union or
that ran head on against the ideas of Socialist Realism, notably the Thirteenth and
Fourteenth Symphonies (1962 and 1969) and *The Execution of Stepan Razin*
(1964). He also began to withdraw from the cinema, and in the fifteen years left
to him, worked on only seven more films. Existing Shostakovich scores were used
in films such as the 1967 anniversary release of Eisenstein's *October*, but the composer took little or no part in these productions.

If the films were fewer in number, they often meant something more than usual
to him; five were works by close friends while the other two were adaptations of
his stage works, *Cheryomushki* (1962) and *Katerina Izmailova* (1967). Kozintsev
directed *Hamlet* (1964) and *King Lear* (1970), while Grigory Roshal's *A Year Is
Worth a Lifetime* (1965) was loosely based on Galina Serebryakova's biographical
novel about Marx. Arnshtam directed *Five Days, Five Nights* (1961) and *Sofia*

Perovskaya (1968). Of these seven films, *Katerina Izmailova* and Kozintsev's films were the most important to Shostakovich. His participation in *Sofia Perovskaya* was partly an act of charity in the wake of the death of Arnshtam's wife. He wrote the whole score without having seen any of the film, taking the opportunity to include some cheekily banal military music in what is otherwise a quite conventional film.

Hamlet had long fascinated both director and composer, and the film was the culmination of decades of engagement with the play. In the 1920s, Kozintsev proposed it as a FEKS project; in 1932, Shostakovich wrote music for Akimov's notorious comic production, and in 1954, Kozintsev had staged it, using Shostakovich's music from their 1941 staging of *King Lear*, adding three new pieces. Fresh from the Thirteenth Symphony, Shostakovich was shortly to write the "vocal-symphonic poem" *The Execution of Stepan Razin*, and there are musical and thematic links between the three scores, particularly in their contemplation of leadership, conscience, and honor. Kozintsev's claim that Hamlet's encounter with the ghost embodies "the noble theme of social duty"[48] is reminiscent of Shostakovich's comment that the Thirteenth Symphony is about "the problem of civic, repeat civic morality."[49] Even though *Hamlet* is not a vocal work, some of it sounds like a late Shostakovich setting of hidden texts. Overturning the usual interest in concert over film music, *Stepan Razin* has been relatively ignored, while *Hamlet* has enjoyed several recordings.

Kozintsev had been planning the film for about a decade, and we can assume that Shostakovich was keen to collaborate. A British article in early 1962 claimed he had already started work,[50] although he had merely accepted the commission at this point. In October 1962 he announced its near-completion.[51] However, in a 1963 radio interview, he said he was about to start it, having seen some clips from the film.[52] And in October 1963 he declared that both *Hamlet* and *A Year Is Worth a Lifetime* (at that point known as *Karl Marx*): "await my attention (I have seen some of the first sequences for *Hamlet* and they seem to be excellent). These are important pictures and will naturally require a lot of serious thought."[53] Shostakovich wrote much of Hamlet's music based on test footage of Smoktunovsky that was eventually used in the film. *Hamlet* was filmed in Estonia and the Crimea, while Shostakovich wrote most of the music in Moscow, finishing it off in Gorky in early 1964 while attending a festival of his music. One of the concerts included some excerpts—one of the few times his film music was heard in the concert hall before the cinema.

The whole conception was utterly different from Akimov's 1932 version. Whereas the 1932 score is light and satirical, this is grim and serious, its humor blacker as in the court fanfare, a constipated alternation of two notes. Rather than accompanying the ghost with quiet, eerie music, Shostakovich provides a full-on brass and percussion chorale-fanfare, underlining Hamlet senior's grandeur and the sheer terror that he produces, while the slow-motion images move the event out of normal time. As well as this extremely masculine music, there is tenderness and a painful wit in Ophelia's music lesson, as she moves mannequin-like to the brittle harpsichord. Whereas Hamlet father and son have themes associated with them, she is portrayed by this instrumental color.

Kozintsev was concerned not to set the film in too identifiable a period, but it is a severe view of the Soviet Union of the time, with its struggles for supremacy and the questionable validity and viability of its rulers. Although careful to avoid making a filmed play, he echoes the theories of stage director Gordon Craig, boiling the visuals down to an elemental level, and there are many shots of water, fire, and stone.[54] This approach chimed with Shostakovich's increasingly timeless and elemental simplicity, increasingly reliant upon gesture.

Hamlet was extremely successful, winning awards at several film festivals. In 1965, Kozintsev and Smoktunovsky were awarded Lenin Prizes, and in 1966 a ten-kopeck stamp was issued featuring a still from the film (the previous year, a similar honor had gone to *The Young Guard*). Shostakovich was satisfied enough to go to see the film eight or nine times after it was released, and wrote congratulating Kozintsev on it.[55] His contribution was widely recognized by the press both at home and abroad, and won an award for best film music at an all-Union film festival. It was later used for several *Hamlet* ballets. Deservedly it is one of his most popular and frequently recorded film scores.

Katerina Izmailova, the revised version of *Lady Macbeth of the Mtsensk District*, had received its stage premiere in 1963. The Kiev production had been Shostakovich's favorite, and it was that company that recorded the soundtrack for the film version that director Mikhail Shapiro began shooting in mid-June 1965. Sadly, the soundtrack has never been commercially released. With Vishnevskaya in the lead role, it makes a fascinating comparison with her 1978 recording of the original version.[56]

Many opera films employ cuts, replace theatre sets with location filming, and have actors mime to existing recordings. Although *Katerina Izmailova* follows the first two conventions, Vishnevskaya both sings and acts. As well as overseeing Glikman's revision to the screenplay, Shostakovich took charge of editing the music. Apart from rewriting the interludes, he cut the whole of the scene where the police brag about their corruption. *Katerina Izmailova* is more innovative than most entrants in the genre: for instance, when the peasant runs to report Izmailov's murder to the police, the screen is split diagonally while the characters' daydreams are brought to life through superimpositions. Although not conceived as such, this seems to be another attempt at his occasionally voiced wish of writing a film-opera, yet *Testimony* reports that: "Directors treat the music in opera as something of minor importance. That's how they ruined the film version, *Katerina Izmailova*. The actors were magnificent, particularly Galina Vishnevskaya, but you can't hear the orchestra at all. Now, what is the point of that?"[57] Vishnevskaya was similarly critical of the sound balance, not to mention the filmmakers' attempts to go still further in desexualizing the drama,[58] but Shostakovich's letters to Glikman trace his journey from apprehension at the prospect to general satisfaction with the result.[59] Whatever the merits of *Testimony*, this passage does reflect Shostakovich's concern that music takes its proper place in the drama—in the case of opera, the pre-eminent one. Sometimes, he was not particularly involved in the work—witness *The Fall of Berlin*. But in those projects where he was concerned about his music, the sympathetic ears of certain directors made them important collaborators and encouraged him to take the projects more seriously.

King Lear was the last film for both Shostakovich and Kozintsev, but it was not intentionally a "last statement"; Kozintsev considered other projects, but, in common with many artists' late works, there is a sense of both director and composer sloughing off irrelevances. Kozintsev's rate of film production had slowed down in later years. Between the war and his death in 1973, he made only five films. After *Pirogov* and *Belinsky*, critically mauled and unsatisfactory for all involved, came three literary adaptations: *Don Quixote* (1957),[60] *Hamlet*, and finally *Lear*. He considered *Lear* as early as 1967, but even when production started it took some time to make, not least because of difficulties over casting the lead. Lear needed two very clear qualities; expressive eyes for close-ups and a short frame so he was surrounded by large people. Eventually, Yury Yarvet was chosen. But there was another problem. Yarvet was Estonian and spoke poor Russian. But rather than be dubbed, he insisted on improving his accent. *Lear*, made when he was 51, boosted his career, and the next year he appeared in Tarkovsky's *Solaris* with his *Lear* co-star Donatas Banionis, who plays Albany.

By this time, Kozintsev was popularly seen as having left behind the avant-garde and taken the role of "grand old man." But however "normal" *Lear* is on the surface compared to some of his earlier films, it still has uncomfortable things to say politically. Plays such as *Hamlet*, *Lear*, and *Macbeth* have a particular importance in a country that has been led by Ivan the Terrible, Boris Godunov, Catherine the Great, Peter the Great, and Stalin. Eighteenth-century Westernizers made Shakespeare central to Russian intellectual life, and authors used his plots and characters as reference points and templates for their own works. *Hamletism* was a recognized psychological state, and an accusation that was leveled at Shostakovich, whose Fifth Symphony attracted the appellation. And for Akhmatova, *Macbeth* was simply too close to the bone—"only this one we do not have the strength to read."[61]

Shostakovich wrote the music in summer 1970, though the fact that he would be separated from the crew during filmmaking had made him consider turning the commission down. "But my love of Shakespeare, of cinema, and my friend Grigory Kozintsev got the upper hand. It was a long and painstaking task. Kozintsev and I had hour-long telephone conversations between Leningrad and Moscow, and I received all the necessary material from him by post. Still, I had to go to Leningrad to round off the work."[62] Kozintsev wrote that Shostakovich "expressed pity like a force.... I would not be able to make a Shakespeare film without [his music], just as I would not be able to without Pasternak's translation.... In Shostakovich's music I can hear a ferocious hatred of cruelty, the cult of power and the oppression of justice."[63] In their correspondence about the film music, there are repeated requests and promises that the music should be "sadder."[64]

Shostakovich wrote enthusiastically, eventually producing seventy cues, though less than half of them made it into the film. Often fragmentary and dislocated, many items last only a few seconds, and though there are some extended sequences, the music used in the film totals just half an hour, in over thirty cues. Shostakovich seems to have written some of the music without having particular sequences in mind, giving them arbitrary numbers, and titling them afterwards, having seen the film.[65] Again, Shostakovich carries ideas over from recent works and also projects forward to the future. In "The First Sighting of Lear's Castle," we hear the cautious tread of pizzicato strings with slow, meandering flute and clarinet lines (a texture that reappears in the last movement of the Fifteenth Symphony), the strings here outlining a twelve-note row of the type that had become common in Shostakovich's work at around this time. "Lunch at Goneril's" half-echoes Ophelia's music from *Hamlet* and the first movement of the Second Piano Concerto, though these seem to be fingerprints rather than deliberate references. Similarly, the choral vocalise, "People's Lamentation," is as motivically tight as the Eighth String Quartet, the main theme, later used as the opening of the Thirteenth Quartet, even playing with the intervals that form the DSCH monogram. Yet, at the same time, like cues from films such as *Alone*, the chorus was conceived in separate sections to allow the director to pick whichever ones he wanted.[66]

Lear's brief cues and emphasis on flexibility marked another advance in Shostakovich's film music as he moved further towards producing gestural cues rather than the thematic and melodic ones that had marked his earlier work, in particular the wartime scores. Two important ideas are the fool's music and the three-note "Voice of Truth" motif. The latter is as stark as anything in his late works, and was used to open "To Anna Akhmatova," the last of the Tsvetayeva songs he wrote three years later. (It had, incidentally, also started the Fugue op. 87, no. 19.) "The Songs of the Fool" are reminiscent of the 1941 stage production, though Oleg Dal sings them in such a cracked voice, hovering between speech and singing, that they are hardly recognizable. As Shostakovich said: "Music suits both vaudeville and heroic tragedy. In vaudeville you have to sing the existing couplets and sing them as merrily as possible, whereas in great tragedy the music must, in my opinion, only speak at the moments of highest dramatic tension."[67] Echoing his comments about *New Babylon*, he quipped: "It is not the composer's job to be a musical illustrator. This can be done far more easily by the staff of a music library."[68]

One thing that fascinated both Kozintsev and Shostakovich was "foolishness" and the difference between its various types: the amusing behavior of the clown-fool, the foolish, that is naïve, behavior of Lear and Gloucester, and the feigned madness of Edgar who "acts the fool," just as Hamlet may (or may not) be doing. The "fool's" role is not only to point to paradoxes of sense and power, but to throw up questions of morality and, specifically, honesty. He is also a kind of alter ego to Lear, mouthing, with impunity, the unpalatable truths that the king dare not admit to himself. Translating that into Russian terms, it is hard to avoid the *yurodivye*, the "holy fool" who had just such a relationship with the Tsar. A *yurodivye* has the last word in Musorgsky's *Boris Godunov*, probably Shostakovich's favorite opera. The fool's pipe bookends Lear and accompanies the burial of Lear and

Cordelia, pointing to a similarity between the two stories. It may even be that Vera Stroyeva's 1955 film version of *Boris* had some influence; both films end with the *yurodivye* sitting amidst the ruins and preparations for war. Shostakovich's music for Lear's fool echoes Musorgsky's two-note sighing figure ("Flow, flow, bitter tears!"), and the choice of E-flat clarinet is reminiscent of the *yurodivye's* whining, high-pitched voice. Stroyeva ended her film with these two repeated notes fading away, implying that "times of trouble" were the recurrent lot of Russians (perhaps she saw the post-Stalin interregnum as another of these). Shostakovich's music ends similarly inconsequentially, finishing almost arbitrarily, perhaps implying that it is only the end of the film, not of the situation. Although in 1970 there was no power struggle in the wake of a ruler's death, the country was in the grip of stagnation following a backlash against Khrushchev's reforms. The years that Kozintsev worked on the film had seen, amongst other things, in 1968 the trial of Ginsburg and Galanskov for publishing details of the Sinyavsky-Daniel trial, and the invasion of Czechoslovakia.

The adjacent opus numbers of the Twelfth and Thirteenth Symphonies (opp. 112 and 113) seem to be a pointed comment, one bearing a dedication to Lenin, the other condemning the Soviet system's failures. In a similar but earlier move, Shostakovich seems to have consciously linked his "other" *King Lear* (Kozintsev's 1941 staging) and his orchestration of *Boris Godunov* by giving them the respective opus numbers 58a and 58. The plots of both have similarities; as with many tragic figures, both Lear and Boris are slowly overtaken by events they have initiated but over which they have lost control. And a fool reminds both of their folly.

Coincidentally, Peter Brooke was working on his *Lear* at the same time, and the two directors corresponded during their work. Their books discuss the landscape in which *Lear* should be set, Kozintsev choosing a post-apocalyptic, or rather a landscape out of time, both past and future, "so very far in the past that it could be some post-neutron-bomb, post-Christian future." Continuing the paring down he had begun in *Hamlet*, he likened the landscape to an abandoned cemetery. To this, Kozintsev added other cultures, particularly Japanese. In 1928, he had seen every production of the Kabuki Theater's tour of Russia, and he knew the director Akira Kurosawa who made several Shakespeare films.[69] Later, he visited Japan and was struck not only by Noh theater and Japanese gardens but also by the museum of Hiroshima. Traces of all of these appear in the film. Yet, "There is no 'desert' in Lear, the world of tragedy is densely populated."[70] As so often, the adaptation of a "classic" text has more to do with the Soviet Union's recent and not so recent past than might be immediately apparent. Not only does Kozintsev compress geography, but he collapses time to bring together a leader out of control (such as Boris or Stalin) and the barren landscape and rampant corruption of contemporary Brezhnevian stagnation. Despite his unprepossessing appearance, a paradoxically child-like wizened old man, Lear retains his "kingliness" in the eyes of his followers, just as the pock-marked, shrivel-armed Stalin held the country in thrall. Perhaps, like institutionalized patients, some preferred the false security of totalitarianism.

After *Hamlet* and *King Lear*, Kozintsev considered adding *The Tempest* to make a Shakespearean trilogy, but eventually wrote *St. Petersburg Nights*, a screenplay based on themes from short stories by Gogol. Shostakovich's range of cinema collaborators had been shrinking but he was happy to take this commission, especially as it was a Gogol project. The early 1970s brought the deaths of several of Shostakovich's close friends and collaborators. But Kozintsev's death in 1973 was a particularly devastating blow, bringing both the film and Shostakovich's cinema career to an end. It closed the loop with the director who, with Leonid Trauberg, had been his first cinema collaborator, and with the writer (Gogol) who had brought them together.

Unlike some composers, Shostakovich's film scores kept stylistic pace with his concert works. Ustvolskaya, for example, drained off her own personality to produce film scores in a wholly acceptable Soviet style from which she could completely disassociate herself. Schnittke used them to test ideas for his concert works. His film and concert works from quite different periods could share material, whereas Shostakovich's film and concert works tend to revolve around each other much more closely. Shared materials usually come from the same era, and even when there is no contemporary material in common, there is a common style so that the music for *Zoya* or *Michurin* largely speaking sounds like late 1940s Shostakovich, if without the intensity of the concert works.

The trajectory of Shostakovich's cinematic career is parabolic, starting with great and innovative scores that explored the role of music in the cinema and acted as an incentive to improve the technical side of the industry. During this period, he also helped to set in motion and develop the two strands of Soviet film score writing: the symphonic and the song-score. And with scores such as *The Golden Mountains*, he managed to bring them together in a single film. The *Maxim* trilogy saw the beginning of an accommodation with Socialist Realism, evidenced both in the films themselves and in his music. *The Youth of Maxim* retains a FEKS-like exuberance, but as the trilogy continued, the political necessities became more obvious. Even through this period, some of his film scores try to innovate, but in the wake of the *Pravda* editorials, the cinema became largely a way to get by financially. Shostakovich hoped that the results would be favorably looked on, but there was always the danger of adverse political fall-out even from these projects, and such excursions became more difficult. The idea that this was a safe area to withdraw into is disproved by the problems that attended many of the films he worked on. Increasingly, he seemed to be saving his strength for a few major statements, none of which were films, though ironically it was after the 1936 and 1948 denunciations that the sheer quantity of his film work reached its peaks. Between these moments, the war brought its own necessities, and in the cinema his voice was diluted just as were those of many with whom he worked. This seems to have encouraged him to use film work more actively just as he had in the early part of his career, and after the war the relationship between his concert and film work grew closer again. But after 1960, there was yet another development as he began to withdraw from the cinema, choosing projects more carefully but often investing more in them. Shostakovich was an evolutionary, not a revolutionary, and not only do the late films show an interest in an evolving audio-visual landscape but in the last two, *Hamlet* and *King Lear*, we see flaring up again the uncompromising anger and wit of the younger man, producing a final condemnation of the regime under which he had spent most of his life.

CHAPTER 18

SHOSTAKOVICH THE PIANIST

Sofia Moshevich

I am very well aware of how my audience perceives my music—and not after, but during the actual performance. I am clearly helped in this by the fact that I myself am a performer, and used to appear in public until 1958. If it were not for my incapacitated hand, I would still be playing today.[1]

(Dmitry Shostakovich)

From the outset, Shostakovich had prepared himself for a career as a pianist, and until his mid-twenties was unable to choose between composition and performance as his main pursuit. At the age of almost nine, he took his first steps under his mother's guidance. Sofia Shostakovich had studied piano at the St. Petersburg Conservatory under a former student of Balakirev, Alexandra Rozanova (1876–1942). Although not a professional music teacher, Sofia taught her young children, as well as those of her friends, with insight. Witnessing Dmitry's phenomenal progress after only a month of lessons, she took him to audition for the famous Petersburg pedagogue Ignaty Glyasser (1862–1925) on 15 August 1915. The Polish-born Glyasser had studied in Germany with Theodor Kullak and Karl Klindworth, and was a close friend of Ignacy Paderewsky. A strong technician, Glyasser had written a number of books on piano technique, including a collection of exercises that, according to Glyasser, were played by such eminent figures as Rachmaninov.[2]

Having finished in six months the one-year introductory course taught by Glyasser's wife, Olga, Dmitry graduated in 1916 to Glyasser's own class. He later recalled that at one of his first-year exams, he played the entire *Children's Album* by Tchaikovsky and, the following year, sonatas of Mozart and Haydn.[3] In Glyasser's school, he also learned Beethoven's Sonata in C minor, op. 10, No. 1,[4] and Third Piano Concerto.[5] Then, in 1917, after only two years of study, the eleven-year-old performed all the Preludes and Fugues of Bach's *Well-Tempered Clavier*, an outstanding achievement for this precocious young musician. According to Sofia Khentova, Glyasser demanded "a 'natural' attack, based on a precise finger action with a strictly horizontal wrist," a manner fully adopted by Shostakovich:

> Then, as later on, typically "Glyasserian" characteristics were apparent in Shostakovich's playing—restricted shoulder movements as well as a prevalence of hand movement along the keyboard combined with limited wrist flexibility—qualities of "inhibited movement" not common in the modern technique, but ones that nevertheless guaranteed the precision, clarity, and idiosyncratic dexterity of Shostakovich's performances. Like many other of Glyasser's students Shostakovich [thus] developed velocity and finger strength, exactness of tone, and dexterity in leaps.[6]

Dmitry's technique blossomed and his repertory expanded, but his composition was neglected by Glyasser, who considered it a useless pursuit for such a budding virtuoso. Aware of Dmitry's growing resentment and boredom, Sofia Shostakovich in 1917 transferred him and his sister Mariya to her own former teacher, Alexandra Rozanova.[7] Cultured, sensitive, and patient, Rozanova taught Shostakovich to strive for greater refinement and subtlety. And unlike Glyasser, Rozanova encouraged his attempts at composition and suggested that he seek professional instruction. The young Shostakovich took lessons in improvisation from Georgy Bruni during the spring and summer of 1919. At the time, he resented these sessions and the seemingly silly assignments he was given (to write such pieces as "On the Lawn" or "Round Dance"[8]). However, a few years later, as a pianist for silent movies, these improvisation lessons would prove quite useful.[9]

Even after he was accepted as a composition and piano student at the Petrograd Conservatory in the autumn of 1919, Shostakovich remained in Rozanova's class for one more year. During his years at the Conservatory, Shostakovich met and studied under many extraordinary musicians, among them Maximilian Shteinberg, who became his composition teacher, Alexander Glazunov, theorist Nikolai Sokolov, conductor Nikolai Malko, musicologist Alexander Ossovsky, and, most influential of all during these formative years, Leonid Nikolayev (1872–1942). A broadly educated and charismatic person, Nikolayev combined the intuition of a gifted teacher with the vast experience of a performer, conductor, and composer.

To audition for Nikolayev, Shostakovich performed Grieg's Piano Concerto, with Nikolayev accompanying him from memory, as well as his own piano works. Impressed by his capacities, the professor avidly welcomed him as his new pupil. While Nikolayev was initially cautious in his choice of repertory for Dmitry, he later added more substantial works, such as Schumann's *Faschingsschwank aus Wien*. A year and a half later, Shostakovich was learning Beethoven's *Hammerklavier* Sonata, and in the spring of 1922, the fifteen-year-old performed this sonata at Nikolayev's class recital "with an astonishing grasp of the work's grandiose concept, rhythmic will of steel, and most profoundly lyrical insight."[10] Under Nikolayev's guidance, Shostakovich mastered a vast and varied repertory, including many contemporary works.[11] Nikolayev instilled in his students a keen awareness and clear understanding of musical form. Especially invaluable for Shostakovich, however, were his teacher's pertinent suggestions concerning the structure and harmony of his own pieces, which by 1922 already included the orchestral Scherzo, op. 1, Theme and Variations, op. 3, *Two Fables of Krylov*, op. 4, nine Piano Preludes,[12] and *Three Fantastic Dances*, op. 5.

In June 1923, Shostakovich took his final piano exam. This consisted of two public concerts—a solo recital and a concerto performance. On 28 June, Shostakovich played a program of Bach's Prelude and Fugue in F-sharp minor (*Well Tempered Clavier*, Book 1); Beethoven's *Waldstein* Sonata, op. 53; Mozart's Variations in C major ("Ah vous dirai-je, maman"); Chopin's Ballade No. 3; Schumann's *Humoresque;* and Liszt's "Venice and Naples" from *Années de pèlerinage*. For the second concert, he performed Schumann's Piano Concerto. Josef Shvarts, Dmitry's classmate and the dedicatee of his *Three Fantastic Dances*, reminisced that "I have always remembered—and it still sounds in my ears—his interpretation of all the movements of Schumann's Concerto and *Humoresque, op. 20*."[13] Shostakovich, however, was not satisfied with his performance of the Concerto, lamenting that he was ill at the time.

Following his graduation in piano, Shostakovich continued his studies in composition at the Conservatory, while at the same time embarking on a performing career. The critic Alexei Kholodnyi wrote in June 1923:

A short young man, dressed in a jacket instead of the traditional tails, appeared on the stage. His fingers, moving quickly and surely, demonstrated his evidently strong technique and serious training. His performance of Schumann's *Humoresque*, and of Liszt's *Funerailles* and *Gnomenreigen*, was confident and clear, but not yet mature; in some places, it lacked nuances. However, the excitement and temperament were both felt, as well as his strong and sure attack.[14]

Six months later, the renowned critic and violinist Viktor Valter wrote a rather more glowing review of Shostakovich's recital of 16 December:

The other day, seventeen-year-old pianist Dmitry Shostakovich played Bach-Liszt's Prelude and Fugue, Beethoven's *Appassionata,* and a number of his own works at his concert: the Theme and Variations, Preludes, Dances, Scherzo. I take upon myself the courage of greeting this young man with the same words as the ones with which I greeted the young Heifetz. In Shostakovich's playing, one is struck by that same exuberantly serene self-confidence of genius. I am referring to not only Shostakovich's exceptional playing, but also his compositions. What a wealth of creativity and amazing conviction are present in his own work (especially in the Variations) at the tender age of seventeen! Moreover, in this young man, these qualities are combined with the most modest of manners and an almost childish appearance. Shostakovich has enormous tasks in front of him. Let us hope that this boy, who has defeated the cold and hunger of the past years, will victoriously overcome all the trials ahead.[15]

Other critics were not quite so enthusiastic. When, on 10 December 1923, Shostakovich substituted for Nikolayev in Bach's Brandenburg Concerto in D, critic Dmitry Mazurov opined, "the only thing that marred the performance was the wooden tone produced by the player of the piano part, D. Shostakovich."[16] In the same review, we read of another Shostakovich performance, given on 27 May 1924: "Shostakovich performed Tchaikovsky's First Piano Concerto. The young pianist played very confidently, technically secure and in strict rhythm. He has a powerful attack and clean pedaling. But ... how awful if this is all we can say about him as a pianist!"[17]

In March 1924, despite his established reputation, Shostakovich was not accepted for postgraduate studies in piano (then called "academic courses") at the Leningrad (Petrograd) Conservatory. The reasons for this decision remain unclear, although the official explanation given by the Conservatory Board at the time was "immaturity and young age."[18] Nikolayev protested the decision and continued to teach Shostakovich free of charge.

Over the next four years, Shostakovich undertook a heavy load of engagements, appearing not only in numerous solo recitals and concertos, but also as an ensemble player. He accompanied the singer Lidiya Vyrlan, participated in a trio with the violinist Venyamin Sher and the cellist Grigory Pekker, played Mozart's Concerto for Two Pianos with Gavriil Popov, accompanied the contemporary dancer Mariya Ponna, and participated in a performance of Bach's Brandenburg Concerto in D, and in the Russian premiere of Stravinsky's *Les noces*. A fantastic sight-reader and a quick learner, Shostakovich was invaluable to the premieres of his friends' compositions.

Throughout this period, following the death in 1922 of Dmitry senior, the Shostakovich family struggled financially. In the autumn of 1924, Shostakovich was forced to seek employment as a pianist-improviser for silent films, and over the next two years played regularly at the Bright Reel, Splendid, and Piccadilly cinemas.[19] Whether playing solo or with the small ensembles that were sometimes used, Shostakovich's cinematic improvisations were markedly different from the standard menus of musical clichés (books of ready-made music "for all occasions"—happiness, despair, a chase scene, etc.) provided by most pianists. Although some enjoyed Shostakovich's unorthodox music, many moviegoers disliked it, some even complaining to the management. Shostakovich attempted to handle these situations with humor, but more often than not, he experienced frustration and exhaustion. Ultimately, it proved a serious drain on his time, health, and energy, and it was with few regrets that, in March 1926, he was able to cease this line of work forever.

In 1925, Shostakovich had submitted his First Symphony for his graduation exam in composition. The work enjoyed an unprecedented success, bringing international recognition to the young composer. On 1 October 1926, Shostakovich was accepted, with unanimous recommendation, to the Leningrad Conservatory's "aspirantura" program, the postgraduate course in composition. One of his first works as an "aspirant" was the technically challenging one-movement First Piano

Sonata, op. 12. At the Moscow premiere, he performed this difficult work twice, "for the sake of a better understanding of this music."[20] His playing revealed an idiosyncratic performance style, which was, according to Dmitry Kabalevsky, "somewhat dry, toccata-like, but flawless in terms of the pianism."[21] Conductor Nikolai Malko recalled, "[Shostakovich's] fingers miraculously played everything and succeeded in everything. His performance of his own First Sonata always produced amazement.... On the occasions when I would introduce Shostakovich to musicians who were guests from abroad and would request him to play his sonata, the effect was always the same. 'How does he do it?'"[22]

By this time acknowledged as one of the finest Soviet pianists, Shostakovich was chosen to participate in the First International Chopin Piano Competition, held in Warsaw in January 1927. His program featured the compulsory Concerto in E minor, op. 11, Polonaise in F-sharp minor, op. 44, Preludes in F-sharp minor and B-flat minor, op. 28, and the Ballade in A-flat major, op. 47. The remaining pieces were of his own choice: the Nocturnes in F-sharp major, op. 15, No. 2 and in C-sharp minor, op. 27, No. 1; the Etudes in C-sharp minor, op. 10, No. 4 and in A-flat major, op. 25, No. 1; and the Mazurkas in B minor, op. 33, No. 4 and in C-sharp minor.[23]

No recordings of Shostakovich's Chopin have been preserved. However, the pianist and teacher Nathan Perelman, who heard Shostakovich's concert in Leningrad prior to his departure for the Warsaw competition, reminisced:

> His Chopin playing didn't resemble anything I have heard before or since. It reminded me of his performances of his own music, very direct and without much plasticity, and very laconic in expression.... He never allowed himself the slightest hint of 'Chopinesque' sentiment, and this in its own way had much charm. He had a wonderful technique, with fantastic octaves. He played Tchaikovsky's First Piano Concerto excellently, with brilliant octave passages.... If he chose to use little pedal, it wasn't because he did not know how to use it, but because he heard the music this way. It didn't at all coincide with our notions and expectations of piano playing.... Shostakovich emphasized the linear aspect of music and was very precise in all the details of performance. He used little rubato in his playing, and it lacked extreme dynamic contrasts. It was an 'antisentimental' approach to playing which showed incredible clarity of thought.... But it made less impression in Warsaw, where Oborin's more decorative, charming and "worldly" approach, albeit somewhat militaristic, was the order of the day. However, Shostakovich seemed to foresee that by the end of the twentieth century, his style of playing would predominate, and in this his pianism was truly contemporary.[24]

At the competition itself, Shostakovich played, as he put it, "forgetting about everything else on earth, played, as they say, with inspiration."[25] Failing to win a prize, he was awarded a diploma. The outcome upset the young Shostakovich and to some extent influenced his eventual decision to abandon his career as a piano virtuoso, a decision that his early and steady successes as a composer, as well as his passion for writing music, would only have reinforced. In 1956, however, looking back and evaluating his life, the fifty-year-old Shostakovich expressed certain regrets about this career direction: "After graduating from the Conservatory, I faced the dilemma of what to become—a pianist or a composer? The latter won out, but to tell the truth, I should have been both. It is too late now to blame myself for such a categorical decision."[26] Nevertheless, over the next couple of years, Shostakovich continued to appear as a soloist and received encouraging reviews. For instance, on 18 March 1928, in Moscow, Shostakovich played in one of a series of concerts featuring Nikolayev's students. The critic Grigory Kogan wrote:

> The wonderful, yet still very young, pianist Shostakovich, nourishes great hidden potential, the eventual fruits of which not only he himself [but also others] will probably enjoy. His performance of the entire Liszt cycle "Venice and Naples" (*Gondoliera, Canzone,* and *Tarantella*) was on an extraordinarily high level, both artistically and musically. His rhythm creates a particularly strong impression: unlike Rachmaninov's "iron" or Paderewski's "whimsical" rhythms, Shostakovich's rhythm, possessing a "flowing" logic of its own, is natural, free, and saturated with intense musical expression.[27]

By 1929, Shostakovich's performances were becoming rarer. He appeared with an orchestra only once that year, on 3 February, playing Prokofiev's First Piano Concerto under Georgy Sheidler. Reminiscing many years later, Alexander Rozanov wrote of this performance that "Shostakovich's interpretation was not joyful as much as it was sarcastic. He played the fast sections with a somewhat dry, toccata-like tone, abrasively rather than mirthfully or boldly, and the slow ones with a reserved feeling that reflected a lyrical emotion instead of reproducing it. The integrity of his interpretation was remarkable."[28] For this performance, Shostakovich retouched several details of Prokofiev's orchestration.[29]

A year later, in early February 1930, he played the same Prokofiev concerto, conducted by Grigory Yakobson, in Rostov-on-Don. This was to be his last appearance as a soloist with a composition that was not his own. After this, with the exception of the occasional chamber performance, he performed only his own music. Following his Rostov-on-Don appearance, Shostakovich took a three-year break from public performance, and did not write for the piano for some five years—from the completion of *Aphorisms* in April 1927, until December 1932, when he started work on the Twenty-four Preludes, op. 34. However, the break from public performance was by no means a break from the piano. The composer would demonstrate all his new symphonic compositions, his music for films, theater, and ballet, even entire operas, singing and playing them at the piano.

Shostakovich's desire to appear once again as a performer prompted him to write the Twenty-four Preludes and the First Piano Concerto, and led to many concert engagements, starting from 17 January 1933 when he premiered eight of the new Preludes. Touring extensively between 1933 and 1936, he played in Voronezh, Kharkov, Baku, and Batumi, in addition to many Moscow and Leningrad recitals. As a rule, his performances were enthusiastically received. Of the premiere performances of his First Piano Concerto in Moscow, conducted by Alexander Gauk, on 9 and 14 December 1933, A. K. Smis wrote:

> With elasticity, ease, and precision, Shostakovich overcame all technical difficulties. It was wonderful; he played as only a composer can—inimitably. Even those who do not entirely agree with his compositions have not even the slightest doubt about his virtuosity as a pianist.[30]

The most exciting event of these years, however, was his spring 1935 tour of Turkey (13 April to 24 May). One of a select few at that time permitted to travel to a capitalist country, Shostakovich played many concerts during this five-week whirlwind journey, giving solo recitals in Ankara and Istanbul, and two concerts in Izmir.

Following *Pravda's* notorious 1936 editorial "Muddle Instead of Music," Shostakovich withdrew from public performance for almost two years. On 16 November 1937, five days before the successful premiere of his Fifth Symphony, he reappeared in the public eye, playing his First Piano Concerto, conducted by Nikolai Rabinovich. Over the next three years, Shostakovich's appearances became more frequent, his repertoire now including the Piano Quintet (with the Beethoven and Glazunov Quartets) and the Cello Sonata (with Viktor Kubatsky and Arnold Ferkelman—these recitals often featuring the Grieg and Rachmaninov Cello Sonatas). The musicologist Arnold Alshvang wrote that Shostakovich's "compositions are so poignant and have elicited so much debate that audiences tend to overlook his incredible talent as a pianist. Nevertheless, Shostakovich remains one of the most gifted and original of Soviet pianists. Never giving in to mere showmanship or empty virtuosity, Shostakovich's path is one of heartfelt emotion. . . . His performance of his own compositions . . . is exceptional and merits further study."[31]

During the war years, Shostakovich gave concerts in Kuibyshev, Novosibirsk, Ufa, and Belebei. On his return from evacuation, he played in Moscow and Leningrad, and included his new Second Piano Sonata, *Romances*, op. 62 (with the baritone Efrem Flaks), and Second Piano Trio (with Dmitry Tsyganov and Sergei Shirinsky). Participating in the Prague Spring Festival in May 1947, Shostakovich performed and recorded the Second Trio with David Oistrakh and the Czech cellist Milos Sadlo.

Shostakovich's concertizing experienced its second involuntary break following Zhdanov's 1948 campaign against formalism. In March 1949, he performed his piano arrangement of the Fifth Symphony's scherzo at New York's Madison Square Garden, part of his visit to the Cultural and Scientific Congress for World Peace to which Stalin had dispatched him as a delegate. However, this political showcase constituted his only public appearance during almost two years of silence. After 1950, Shostakovich's concerts would again become more frequent, as he played his old compositions and promoted his new cycle of Preludes and Fugues. In addition to Moscow and Leningrad, he toured the capitals and other major cities of Lithuania, Latvia, Byelorussia, Armenia, Georgia, Azerbaijan, and Ukraine. The year

1954 proved unproductive both in his compositional output and in his performing activities, Shostakovich managing only one public appearance.

Following the sudden death of his wife Nina Varzar in December 1954, Shostakovich began appearing publicly more regularly, partly to improve his family's des-
titute material circumstances. Among other works, he performed his song cycle
From Jewish Folk Poetry (with Nina Dorliak, Zara Dolukhanova, and Alexei Mas-
lennikov), the composition that had waited seven years to be played openly on the
concert stage. Between 1955 and 1957, he made public appearances in Minsk,
Riga, Tallinn, Vilnius, Kaunas, Gorky, Voronezh, Tambov, Sverdlovsk, Lvov, Kiev,
Odessa, Kishinev, and repeatedly in Moscow and Leningrad. This began to take
its toll on Shostakovich, who articulated his frustrations in a letter to his student,
Kara Karayev: "I am living a hectic life. I am concertizing a lot, but without any
particular pleasure. I am still unable to get used to the stage. It causes me a great
many anxieties and affects my nerves. As soon as I reach the age of fifty, I'll stop
concertizing."[32]

In 1958, Shostakovich went on his two final concert tours overseas—to Bulgaria
in January and France in May. In Bulgaria, he performed the Second Piano Concerto under Konstantin Iliev, Preludes and Fugues, and chamber works with the
Beethoven Quartet. In Paris, he appeared only as a soloist, playing and recording
both Piano Concertos under André Cluytens, as well as the *Fantastic Dances* and the
Preludes and Fugues. It was here that Shostakovich first experienced severe pain in
his right hand—the onset of a serious condition that would soon curtail his concert
career. Despite deteriorating health, he played sporadically during the early to mid-
1960s, and on 28 May 1966, gave his last recital, accompanying his vocal works
with Galina Vishnevskaya and Yevgeny Nesterenko. The following night, he suffered
his first heart attack. Unable to play publicly any more, Shostakovich continued to
perform privately for and with friends and students, sight reading various pieces and
demonstrating new compositions. Even up until 1971, he continued to believe that
he would once again play publicly. However, this was not to be.

Interpretation

The commercially released recordings, dating from 1946 to 1958, are listed in
Table 18.3 (see page 480). They represent the primary source of our understanding
of Shostakovich's performance style. Some fascinating details can also be discovered
by comparing different recordings of the same pieces. And although he rarely made
alterations to completed works, certain departures from the score can be found here.
For example, in his recording of "Birthday" from the *Children's Notebook*, he plays
only forty bars of this fifty-three-bar-long piece, excising thirteen bars of the coda.

One criticism often leveled against Shostakovich's playing concerned his apparent penchant for swift, sometimes hectic, tempi. What the recordings show, however, is that this tendency was generally confined to music at the faster end of the
tempo spectrum. By contrast, slower movements (*Largo, Adagio, Lento, Andante,* or
Moderato) tended to be played as marked or very often slower; rarely were they

played faster. Table 18.1 compares the marked tempi in selected slower movements of the Preludes and Fugues, op. 87, with those found in Shostakovich's recordings.[33]

Table 18.1
Tempi in Shostakovich's Recordings of Selected Preludes (P) and Fugues (F), op. 87: Movements marked *Adagio*, *Andante*, or *Moderato*.

Title/Key	Printed Tempo ($\downarrow$=)	Performance Tempo ($\downarrow$=)
P1/C maj	Moderato/92	81 (1951), 83 (1958)
F1/C maj	Moderato/$\downarrow$ = 92	96 (1951), 86 (1958)
P4/E min	Andante/100	69 (1952), 77 (1958)
F4/E min	Adagio/80	60 (1952), 72–74 (1958)
F6/B min	Moderato/100	86 (1952), 85 (1958)
F8/F-sharp min	Andante/84	57—tempo rubato (1952)
P18/F min	Moderato/88	69 (1958)

maj = major; min = minor

By contrast, the faster works tend to support the conventional wisdom; he generally does play them more quickly, in some cases by a considerable margin, than is indicated in the score. Table 18.2 shows this tendency in selected *Allegretto* and *Allegro* movements of the Preludes and Fugues.

Table 18.2
Tempi in Shostakovich's Recordings of Selected Preludes (P) and Fugues (F), op. 87: Movements marked *Allegretto* or *Allegro*.

Title/Key	Printed Tempo ($\downarrow$=)	Performance Tempo ($\downarrow$=)
P2/A min	Allegro/$\downarrow$ = 92	106 (1952)
F2/A min	Allegretto/116	135 (1952)
F3/G maj	Allegro molto/$\downarrow$. = 126	130 (1952)
P5/D maj	Allegretto/120	165 (1951), 177 (1958)
F5/D maj	Allegretto/138	158 (1951), 182 (1958)
F12/G-sharp min	Allegro/152	171 (1952)

maj = major; min = minor

The tendencies noted in the Preludes and Fugues apply generally to Shostakovich's other solo recordings. However, in his chamber performances, the tempo choice is quite unpredictable because of Shostakovich's accommodating attitude towards his partners. His two recordings of the D-minor Prelude, op. 34, illustrate this clearly. In his 1947 solo recording of the piece, Shostakovich plays at an extremely rapid tempo—$\downarrow$ = 106, instead of the printed $\downarrow$ = 76. But in his 1956 recording of the violin/piano transcription with Leonid Kogan, Shostakovich follows Kogan's more moderate tempo ($\downarrow$ = 76). Similar examples can be found in the two recordings of the Cello Sonata (Shafran, Rostropovich) and in those of the Second Piano Trio (Tsyganov/Shirinsky, Oistrakh/Sadlo).

A master of large-scale composition, Shostakovich also demonstrates an unfailing sense of form in his performances of such works. In fact, this quality was noted even at an early age. His friend Lidiya Zhukova described an early performance of a Beethoven sonata as displaying a mature "grasp of the whole grandiose work. Even then he already thought in symphonic dimensions and large boulder-like sections."[34] This command of form is revealed in his recording of the piano duet arrangement of his Tenth Symphony, performed with Mieczysław Weinberg (Moisei Vainberg). Despite its duration of twenty-one minutes, the Symphony's monumental first movement does not seem long. Its balanced proportions and naturally flexible tempi create an emotionally charged, captivating, and deeply exciting drama.

Shostakovich begins the introduction at ♩ = 72–76. Although much slower than indicated in both the piano and orchestral scores (♩ = 96), this is exactly the tempo originally indicated in the autograph of the piano arrangement. Eight bars before Fig. 5, the tempo (♩ = 90) is still slower than indicated, although the marked ♩ = 108 is reached shortly after Fig. 5. A considerable speeding up, induced by Shostakovich, occurs two bars before Fig. 10 (♩ = 126) and again at Fig. 11 (♩ =144). Here, as so often in his solo performances, he presses forward as the intensity of the music increases.

The second subject (Fig. 17) is calmer with its speed (♩ =126, close to the indicated ♩ = 120) prepared by Weinberg through an easing of the tempo before Fig. 15. However, the second subject gains momentum from Fig. 22 onwards. Shostakovich's tempo at Fig. 24 is ♩ = 152, slowing down only in the approach to the development (Fig. 28). The development (Fig. 29) starts slightly slower than indicated: ♩ = 92 instead of ♩ = 108. Throughout this section, there is a gradual increase in speed matching the dynamic growth and intensification of texture. Whereas the first and second subjects subside dynamically after their climactic peaks, the development itself has no decrease of volume, its peak functioning as the start of the recapitulation. A significant reduction in tempo on Shostakovich's part is felt in the recapitulation (eight bars before Fig. 55), where the volume is also reduced to *piano.*

The reprise of the second subject (Fig. 57) points up another discrepancy between orchestral and piano scores. In the orchestral score, the tempo here is indicated faster than the corresponding passage in the exposition. In the piano score, it is identical (♩ = 120). Starting at ♩ = 132, Weinberg keeps intact the tempo proportions suggested by the orchestral score. In the coda (Fig. 65), Shostakovich re-establishes almost the same tempo as the introduction, ♩ = 80.

Yet another editorial discrepancy occurs in the second movement, marked 𝅗𝅥 = 116 in the piano score, an extremely fast tempo, though just about playable. By contrast, the orchestral score (edited by Weinberg in the *Collected Works*),[35] gives an impossible 𝅗𝅥 = 176. In the Shostakovich/Weinberg recording, the tempo starts at ♩ = 174–176, possibly suggesting that it is the orchestral score that gives the correct marking (176), albeit with the wrong durational value.

Like all great pianists, Shostakovich's sense of rhythmic energy and pulsation is highly individual. We can easily recognize this "Shostakovichian" rhythm from the very first sounds of any of his recordings. His rhythm feels unique largely because of his rubato, which is flexible yet always natural and faultlessly balanced. In the Prelude in E-flat, op. 34, No. 19, his rubato is especially pronounced in bars 28–31. He treats the repeated E-flats (playing *poco rit.* then *accel.*) in bar 30 as any good singer would—freely, yet tastefully—adding even more warmth to this charming music. The same unfailing sense of proportion shapes his *ritenuti* in the cadences in bars 12–13 and 24–25.

Shostakovich's recordings also provide information about the subtler aspects of interpretation, for example, pedaling and touch. In the Prelude in A-flat major, op. 34, we sense the sincerity of *dolce, espressivo,* and *amoroso,* Shostakovich's interpretation lacking the ironic flavor that others find. Through his refined pedaling and touch, he creates a slow, poetic waltz of illusive and delicate tenderness—we could easily imagine Shostakovich interpreting Chopin. Sometimes, he sustains pedals further than indicated. For example, the score shows a long pedal covering bars 1–4. The release is indicated on the fourth bar's final beat, causing this one note to sound without pedal. But in performance, Shostakovich changes the pedal on the first beat of the fifth bar, thus avoiding a "dry" final beat in bar 4. A similar approach can be found with the long pedal in bar 8, and that spanning bars 24–26. In two instances, he releases the pedal early: in bar 31 (instead of 33); and in bar 37 where, by stopping the pedal on the second beat of the bar, he enhances the "newness" of the concluding A-flat major harmony after the preceding A-flat minor.

Shostakovich's command of tone color is evident in his recording of the tranquil F major Prelude, op. 34, No. 23. In the final four bars, he uses a subtle half-pedal nuance that allows him both to sustain the long held bass notes and to create the impressionistic effect of a glimmering *morendo.* At this point, we hear clearly that he does not use the middle pedal, enjoying instead the colorful resources of the damper pedal.

Unlike the Preludes, op. 34, which abound in pedal markings, the set of Preludes and Fugues, op. 87, contains only one pedal indication—in the Prelude in C-sharp minor, no. 10, bar 49. Nevertheless, Shostakovich's recordings demonstrate when and how he intended the pedal to be utilized. Even when pedaling a melodic line, clarity is always the priority. Comparing his presentation of the A-major Fugue subject to that in Tatyana Nikolayeva's 1987 recording,[36] we note that while Nikolayeva keeps the dampers raised for the duration of the theme, Shostakovich employs the pedal minimally in order to provide a subtle timbral enrichment while maintaining the overall effect of an unblurred single voice (Example 18.1; both pedal indications are mine).

Example 18.1

Because Shostakovich's hands were quite small, he was usually forced to break or roll chords embracing an interval of a ninth or wider. For example, he arpeggiates the left hand chord (D–G–B-flat–E-flat) in bar 24 of the D minor Prelude, op. 87, even though this is not indicated in the score. Moreover, his manner of executing such extended chords is often unorthodox, as at the start of bar 54 of the B-flat minor Fugue, op. 87, where he first plays the B-flat in the bass, then the F in the top voice, and finally the D-flat in the middle voice. Another idiosyncratic treatment of a wide chord can be found in the two final bars of the E minor Fugue (Example 18.2a). Shostakovich breaks the last chord in a manner typical for string instruments, but not so common for the piano (Example 18.2b). In both the 1952 and 1958 recordings, he renders this chord the same way. This, along with the unwritten "syncopation" before the penultimate bar's final beat, enhances the ending of this spectacular Fugue.[37]

Example 18.2a - Score

Example 18.2b - Shostakovich's recordings (1952 and 1958)

In both solo and ensemble works, Shostakovich often breaks ties, reiterating long notes to maintain sonority. For example, in his recording of the Tenth Symphony arrangement with Weinberg, he reiterates the tied bass note (E) that underpins the movement's second theme at Figs. 5, b8, 5, b12, and 6, and again at the theme's reappearance at 15, b7 and 15, b11. [Interestingly, the bass note reiteration seems arbitrary relative to the phrasing of the theme that it accompanies, occurring one bar earlier after Fig. 15 (seventh and eleventh bars) than after Fig. 5 (eighth and twelfth bars)—Ed.] Of course, given the need to recreate the sustaining power of orchestral instruments, this practice is common in a piano arrangement of a symphonic work. But for Shostakovich, it made little difference whether it was an original piano piece or an arrangement. For instance, in the C minor Prelude, op. 87, he breaks the tie in bars 9–13 and repeats the bass octaves in bars 32–34 (Example 18.3a) earlier than indicated (Example 18.3b).[38]

Example 18.3a - Score

Example 18.3b - Shostakovich's recording (1952)

Shostakovich's relationship with the piano was never free from contradictions. Although it was his first instrument, as well as the only one over which he had complete command, the piano was not "an extension of himself" as it had been with, say, Chopin, Rachmaninov or Medtner. For Shostakovich the composer, his real "instruments" were the orchestra, the string quartet, and the human voice. He himself admitted this when discussing the violin transcriptions of the Preludes, op. 34, with their arranger, Dmitry Tsyganov. Shostakovich confessed, "You have probably noticed that I have not written a lot for the piano. I am not particularly fond of this instrument. I don't even know why I wrote the Preludes as piano pieces; I think they sound better on the violin."[39]

Although an excellent pianist, Shostakovich did not think solely in terms of pianistic perfection. He cared less about technical flawlessness and instrumental effects than about the spontaneity of musical communication. Certainly, his recordings contain many wrong notes as well as other faults of execution. Yet they remain unique, a world unto themselves. We can find other recordings of Shostakovich's music that are more polished, but probably none more soulful, sincere, and inspiring than the composer's own.

Table 18.3
Commercially Released Recordings Featuring Shostakovich as Pianist[40]

Op.	Title	Collaborating Artists	Location, Date
5	*Three Fantastic Dances*		Prague, 1947[41]
5	*Three Fantastic Dances*		Paris, 1958[42]
22	Polka (from *The Age of Gold*)		Prague, 1947[43]
34	Preludes: 8, 14-19, 22, 24		Prague, 1947[44]
34	Preludes: 8, 22, 23		Moscow, 1950[45]
34	Preludes: 10, 15, 16, 24 (arr. Dmitry Tsyganov for violin and piano)	Leonid Kogan	Moscow, 1956[46]
35	Piano Concerto No. 1	Josif Volovnik (trumpet) Moscow PO/Samuil Samosud	Moscow, 1954[47]
35	Piano Concerto No. 1	Ludovic Vaillant (trumpet) Orch. Nat. de la Radiodiffusion Française/André Cluytens	Paris, 1958[48]
40	Cello Sonata	Daniil Shafran	Moscow, 1946[49]
40	Cello Sonata	Mstislav Rostropovich	Moscow, 1957[50]
57	Piano Quintet	Beethoven Quartet	Moscow, 1940[51]
57	Piano Quintet	Beethoven Quartet	Moscow, 1955[52]
67	Piano Trio No. 2	Dmitry Tsyganov (violin) Sergei Shirinsky (cello)	Moscow, 1946[53]
67	Piano Trio No. 2	David Oistrakh (violin) Milos Sadlo (cello)	Prague, 1947[54] Prague, 1947[55]
69	*Children's Notebook*		
79	*From Jewish Folk Poetry*	Nina Dorliak (soprano) Zara Dolukhanova (mezzo-soprano) Alexei Maslennikov (tenor)	Moscow, 1956[56]
87	Preludes & Fugues: 1, 3, 5, 23		Moscow, 1951[57]
87	Preludes & Fugues: 2, 4, 6-8, 12-14, 16, 20, 22, 24		Moscow, 1952[58]

Continued

Table 18.3
Continued

Op.	Title	Collaborating Artists	Location, Date
87	Preludes & Fugues: 1, 4-6, 13, 14, 18, 23		Paris, 1958[59]
93	Symphony No. 10 (arr. piano, four hands)	Mieczysław Weinberg	Moscow, 1954[60]
94	Concertino for Two Pianos	Maxim Shostakovich	Moscow, 1956[61]
97	*The Gadfly* (fragment, arr. DS)		Moscow, 1955[62]
102	Piano Concerto No. 2	Moscow Radio SO/ Alexander Gauk	Moscow, 1958[63]
102	Piano Concerto No. 2	Orch. Nat. de la Radiodiffusion Française/André Cluytens	Paris, 1958[64]
134	Violin Sonata	David Oistrakh Tatyana Nikolayeva	Moscow, 1968[65]
—	Bach: Concerto in D minor for Three Pianos, BWV 1063	Pavel Serebryakov Berlin Radio Symphony/Kirill Kondrashin	Leipzig, 1950[66]

CHAPTER 19

THE SHOSTAKOVICH LEGACY

Louis Blois

The list of great composer-pedagogues of the twentieth century includes such distinguished names as Paul Hindemith, Ralph Vaughan Williams, and Alexander Glazunov. In this tradition, Shostakovich brought his talents to the classrooms of the Moscow and Leningrad Conservatories where he taught generations of younger composers and shepherded their compositional skills. The roster of his students includes some of the most distinguished names in contemporary Russian music: Revol Bunin, Kara Karayev, Yury Levitin, Georgy Sviridov, Boris Tchaikovsky, Boris Tishchenko, Vladislav Uspensky, Galina Ustvolskaya, and many more. Each of these composers absorbed, to one degree or another, some aspects of Shostakovich's musical language in the pursuit of their own artistic identity. Some, as in the case of Boris Tishchenko, adopted certain devices and gestures as a permanent part of their own mature language. For others, such as Galina Ustvolskaya, Shostakovich's influence served in a transitional phase until that composer's work took a completely different creative direction.

Shostakovich the Teacher

Shostakovich's teaching career is split into two phases. In 1937, he was appointed to the faculty of the Leningrad Conservatory, and in 1943, he accepted a similar position at the Moscow Conservatory. In 1948, in the wake of the Zhdanov purges, he was dismissed from both posts. Invited by one of his former students at the Leningrad Conservatory, composer and academic Orest Yevlakhov (1912–1973), Shostakovich returned to the institution in 1961 to conduct a series of postgraduate seminars in composition, where his students included Gennady Belov, Alexander Mnatsakanyan, German Okunev, Boris Tishchenko, and Vladislav Uspensky.[1]

Shostakovich enjoyed an excellent reputation as a teacher, often winning worshipful admiration among his students. He strongly advocated the detailed study of the classics, both Russian and non-Russian, and would join his students in playing four-hand piano arrangements of Haydn, Schubert, Brahms, and others. A voracious explorer of new music in his own conservatory days, he encouraged his students to bring to class unfamiliar scores for examination. He impressed upon his students values of musical integrity—in particular, the notion that every piece of music must have a conceptual basis—and technical mastery: "Real mastery means that the composer's professional technique never comes to the forefront. Sometimes it is even imperceptible."[2] Shostakovich placed priority on the creative process. Karen Khachaturian recalls, "He required that we showed him a large span of composition—either a whole movement or at least the whole exposition—even if all the details were not filled in. Shebalin, on the other hand, preferred to work on small sections, maybe only a theme."[3]

Perhaps because of the reactionary nature of his own education at the Petrograd Conservatory, his teaching style avoided a strict, dogmatic approach, despite his insistence on technical mastery. Yury Levitin recalls that Shostakovich "was one of our 'unobtrusive' professors, so to speak—no dogmas; no stereotyped principles; brief remarks, sometimes sharp and picturesque, but usually mild and seemingly incidental. However, they sank deeply into the mind of the responsive student to grow in time into what was incomparably greater: principles, conviction and taste."[4] Boris Tishchenko shares a similar recollection: "there was no formal teaching or tutoring as such. Shostakovich never dreamt of such an approach. When we became his students he simply said to us 'You're grown up, you're mature composers.' And so in this way he didn't deal with the usual mechanics of teaching. But of course his eye and ear were perfect, so he would pick out all the shortcomings in our works."[5]

Shostakovich sought to foster the individuality of his students. Vladislav Uspensky recalls, "Shostakovich never imposed anything upon anyone, looking to develop each musical identity separately. If he showed us his music, it was as if he was addressing his colleagues, not his students, asking whether 'You like that or not?'"[6] Gennady Belov acknowledges the unavoidable impact of Shostakovich's own music: "we were certainly all under his influence—and sometimes without meaning to, we included short references to his works in ours. Shostakovich made a particular effort to try to ensure that the works of his students remained very much their own. He didn't like eclecticism."[7]

The influence of Shostakovich on his students was, on occasion, reciprocated—sometimes in a very concrete manner (the Ustvolskaya quotations in Shostakovich's Fifth String Quartet and the *Suite on Verses of Michelangelo Buonarroti*), at other times in a more conceptual way.[8] Examples of the latter include the *Six Poems of Marina Tsvetayeva* (1973) following Tishchenko's *Three Tsvetayeva Songs* (1970); *From Jewish Folk Poetry* (1948) following Weinberg's *Jewish Songs* (1943–1944); Shostakovich's first forays into twelve-tone writing (Twelfth String Quartet, 1968) following Levitin's Suite for Cello and Chamber Orchestra and Boris Tchaikovsky's *Partita* (both 1966); and, possibly, the format of all slow movements for the Fifteenth String Quartet (1974) following a similar format in Boris Tchaikovsky's Third Quartet (1967).

The Shostakovich Influence

Well before he assumed an official teaching role, Shostakovich had exerted an immeasurable influence on the music of his fellow Soviet composers. His First Symphony (1925) had catapulted him to world fame, and the mystique of its unprecedented success would linger in the halls of the major conservatories. The work was a triumphant assimilation of Western European trends and the Russian classics, and an irresistible model for other Soviet composers to emulate. Vladimir Shcherbachov (1889–1952), the leading pedagogue at the Leningrad Conservatory, evidently wrote his Third Symphony (1926–1931) under its influence. Although in later years Shcherbachov receded into enforced conservatism, at the time he was known for his exploratory diversity of styles.

When Dmitry Kabalevsky (1904–1987) graduated from the Moscow Conservatory in 1931, his diploma work, the First Piano Concerto, was "hailed in advance as Moscow's answer to Leningrad's Shostakovich."[9] Unfortunately, its haphazard construction proved disappointing, and it hardly stands alongside the work that would subsequently flow from that composer's exquisitely lyrical pen. The pretenses made of Kabalevsky's Concerto pointed to the professional rivalry that now and then arose between Shostakovich and some of his colleagues. Kabalevsky seemed to keep a career-conscious eye on Shostakovich's output, not wishing to compete with him *mano a mano*, as it were. He wrote the first three of his four symphonies between 1931 and 1937, when Shostakovich had apparently taken a hiatus from the form. And after the 1936 *Pravda* attack on *Lady Macbeth of the Mtsensk District* had put a dead halt to Shostakovich's operatic career, Kabalevsky took up the slack with his stylistically more acceptable work, a masterpiece nevertheless, *Colas Breugnon* (1938).

The effort to reproduce another Shostakovich First is egregiously evident in the First Symphony (1934–1935) by the young, ambitious Moscow student, Tikhon Khrennikov (1913–2007). Everything about its first movement rings similar to the first movement of the Shostakovich, from its grotesque dance material and sparse instrumental textures to the textbook sonata structure with reverse-order recapitulation. Admittedly, Khrennikov's development section only momentarily hints at the dark menace of its model. At the climax, the escalation of tension abruptly vanishes and runs headlong into the detached march theme at the onset of the recapitulation. The sudden transition from hair-raising tension to utter nonchalance is the most macabre juxtaposition in all of Khrennikov's music, no doubt the result of an awkward assembly of sonata parts rather than a deliberate attempt to horrify. The similarity to Shostakovich ends after the first movement, but this well-promoted symphony launched a composing career that would soon find its own charismatic lyricism. A perhaps unlikely supporter of the Symphony was Elliott Carter, who described it as "appealing and fresh and full of melodic interest. It is better music than Shostakovich's *First Symphony* with which it has many points in common."[10]

The 1930s saw various attempts to establish an identity for the Soviet symphony. Myaskovsky's Twelfth ("Collective Farm," 1931–1932), the first Soviet attempt in the genre of "topical" symphonism, launched a variety of similar, if none too successful, issues. These included Shcherbachov's Fourth ("Izhora," 1932–1935); Polovinkin's Fourth ("The Red Army," 1933); Vasilenko's Fourth ("Arctic," 1934); and Krein's symphonic dithyramb *The USSR: Vanguard of the World Proletariat* (1931-32). Likewise, the genre of the "Song-Symphony" achieved brief popularity during the 1930s, marked by the singular success of Lev Knipper's Fourth Symphony ("Poem about a Fighter Komsomol," 1934). Within this climate of hollow grandiloquence, it would fall upon Shostakovich's Fifth Symphony of 1937 to lead symphonic music "out of its crisis."[11]

Several of Shostakovich's works from the following decade would prove just as influential as the First Symphony had been. The monumental Seventh Symphony (1941) served as the prototype for a genre of "war symphonies," a phenomenon that peaked during the 1940s but that was being pursued by Russian composers even into the 1980s. Such works include Aram Khachaturian's Second, Gavriil Popov's Second, Prokofiev's Fifth, Myaskovsky's 22nd, 23rd, and 24th, Karayev's First, Shalva Mshvelidze's First and Second, and Andrei Balanchivadze's First. If Shostakovich's Seventh Symphony had comprised a virtual eyewitness account of the siege of Leningrad, the Eighth contained a more anguished, psychological reflection on the horrors experienced. With its extraordinary degree of thematic brutalization (in the opening two movements) and its aggressive use of short motivic material (in the second and third), the Eighth was the more profoundly influential. Shostakovich's student, Georgy Sviridov, fell under its spell in his wartime Piano Trio. And we hear reverberations of its pages ringing in the works of composers from far-flung Soviet republics: the near-contemporary Second Symphony in C minor (1946, revised 1969–1970) by the prominent Azerbaijani composer Sultan Hajibeyov (or Gadzhibekov, 1919–1974), the Fourth Symphony (1952–1956) by the Azerbaijani composer and Shostakovich student Ahmet Hajiev (or Akhmed Gadzhyev, born 1917),[12] and the First Symphony (1961) by the Tatar composer Fasil Akhmetov (born 1935).

With the Piano Quintet (1940) and the Second Piano Trio (1944), Shostakovich laid down the foundations of his mature chamber music. The influence of these landmark works, each a Stalin Prize winner, on Soviet music cannot be overestimated. Of the many stylistic features that emerge from them, one in particular—the ostinato—merits attention. Both works use the device for prolonged periods. Indeed, the device dominates their metric flow to the point of being recognizable as a Shostakovich mannerism. Ostinato was neither new to the twentieth century nor to Russian music. However, whereas Stravinsky's ostinato, say, with its spiky rhythms and pointed dissonances, redefined the term in a neoclassical context, that of Shostakovich established a defining turf in a neo-romantic context. The Shostakovich ostinato is a feature that can readily be identified in many Soviet chamber works. The mature styles of two of Shostakovich's most prominent pupils, Galina Ustvolskaya and Boris Tchaikovsky, make extensive use of it.

Shostakovich's influence at the Leningrad and Moscow Conservatories became a target of the 1948 anti-Formalist denunciations. A contemporary cartoon published in *Sovetskaya muzyka* depicts a parade of little "Shostakovich clones" emerging from their combined halls. The cartoon is accompanied by a derogatory poem, which in Laurel Fay's translation reads: "Year after year these glorious portals, Disgorge a stream of inglorious mortals, They keep on coming—in vain one bemoans, All the Shostakovich clones!"[13] Shostakovich, Shebalin, and other accused Formalists were dismissed from their teaching posts by a bureaucracy afraid of having such influential promoters of "Formalist" values "corrupting" the next generation of composers. Former students of Shostakovich, such as German Galynin and Boris Tchaikovsky, were censured and required to submit conformist diploma works. The ordeal seriously derailed Galynin, while Tchaikovsky went on to pursue a distinguished creative career. However, his just-completed opera, *The Star* (1947), was harshly dealt with and he never returned to the genre again—a course of events gravely reminiscent of Shostakovich's aborted operatic career.

The denunciations inhibited the experimentation of composers at every level and changed the complexion of Soviet music for many years. The subsequent run of inflated, patriotic works was only broken with Shostakovich's Tenth Symphony (1953), a score of brooding intensity and a paramount accomplishment in twentieth-century music. In its wake appeared a number of similarly tragic symphonies, works that would have been ideologically unacceptable just a few years before. Prominent among them were Kabalevsky's Fourth Symphony, his last (1956), and the Third Symphony (1957) of Nikolai Peiko. Several symphonies from other republics dealt with what was described as "the struggle for peace." They include the Latvian Adolfs Skulte's First (1954), a pair of second symphonies by the Estonian cousins Eugen and Villem Kapp (1954 and 1955, respectively), the outstanding Sixth Symphony (1954) by the Estonian Eduard Tubin, and the second version (1954) of the impassioned Third Symphony of Ukrainian composer Boris Lyatoshinsky—the latter premiered in 1955 by Yevgeny Mravinsky, who had premiered the Shostakovich Tenth in 1953.

From the same period came Shostakovich's mammoth cycle of Twenty-four Preludes and Fugues (1950–1951). It was his most significant contribution for solo piano. Not surprisingly, it inspired several similar efforts. Although Kabalevsky's initial reaction was negative, he had become a staunch admirer by 1952 and before the end of the decade had produced his own fairly substantial Six Preludes and Fugues (1958–1959), offering virtuosity and lyrical grace in a somewhat less rigorous context. With its unadorned progression of block chords in dotted rhythm, the first Prelude conspicuously pays homage to the nearly identical texture and rhythm of the opening page of the Shostakovich score. As if to avoid the accusations of Formalism that initially met Shostakovich's cycle, Kabalevsky adorned each of his prelude/fugue pairs with a programmatic, if overtly socialistic, subtitle

("The Story of a Hero," "At the Young Pioneer Summer Camp," etc.). Another interesting case is Aram Khachaturian's Seven Recitatives and Fugues. Although the fugues were composed in 1928, they lay dormant until the 1960s, when they were revised, apparently with Shostakovich in mind,[14] and coupled with the newly composed recitatives. Also noteworthy are a collection of Twenty-four Preludes and Fugues from the 1980s by the Moscow-based composer/pedagogue Alexander Flyarkovsky (born 1931) and the Twenty-four Preludes and Fugues (1994) by Sergei Slonimsky. Slonimsky in particular was heavily influenced by Shostakovich's example, and seems to pay direct homage at various points, such as in the homophonic chords in the first Prelude.

The most substantial of this pedigree is Rodion Shchedrin's Twenty-four Preludes and Fugues for piano, written between 1964 and 1970. The order of keys is directly modeled after the Shostakovich cycle, as distinct from Bach's, proceeding clockwise around the circle of fifths. This engaging cycle takes the form further into the twentieth century with a more radical approach to tonality and motivic material. Tonal centers are most often used as passing points of reference, in contrast to their somewhat more stable appearance in the Shostakovich. A number of the preludes, especially from the latter half of the cycle (specifically nos. 14, 15, 17, and 20), almost totally sacrifice motivic definition to sonority and expressionistic gesture. The fugues, which vary from two to five voices, are for the most part written with a satisfying internal logic. Only rarely is a Shostakovichian characteristic suggested, as in the modulation schemes of the Tenth Fugue. At around this period, Shchedrin was somewhat preoccupied with the prelude form. His Second Symphony (1962–1965) is built around and subtitled "Twenty-five Preludes." There also followed a *Polyphonic Notebook: Twenty-five Preludes for Piano* in 1972.

Most recently, Dmitry Smirnov has completed his *Well-Tempered Piano*, a set of twenty-four preludes and fugues composed between 1968 and 2000. Smirnov acknowledges that his decision to attempt a cycle was a result of playing some of the Shostakovich op. 87 as a student in the mid-1960s. He cites his Prelude No. 10 and Fugues 2, 7, 9, 10, and 16 as containing "elements ... that could be regarded as stylistically influenced by Shostakovich."[15]

The early 1960s saw the revival of two major Shostakovich works abandoned for a quarter of a century: the opera *Lady Macbeth of the Mtsensk District*, now revised as *Katerina Izmailova*, and the withdrawn Fourth Symphony, whose blazing intensity seemed to outshine Shostakovich's more recent work. Written in 1936 but premiered only in 1961, the Symphony unveiled a vocabulary of dazzling effects whose reverberations would be felt in a host of Soviet works that followed. For example, one of the recurring motives in the first movement of Tishchenko's Second Symphony (1964), written at the outset of his studies with Shostakovich, is almost identical in rhythm, contour, and orchestration to a short, distinctive rhythmic transitional passage in the first movement of Shostakovich's Fourth (the four bars before Fig. 79). Hints of the Shostakovich Fourth can be heard in later works of Tishchenko, as well as in the frenzied thematic abundance of the Second Symphony of Boris Tchaikovsky, which appeared in 1967 and which, incidentally, was dedicated to Kirill Kondrashin, the conductor of the premiere of Shostakovich's Fourth.

Shostakovich's Students

What follows are brief musical portraits of Shostakovich's most prominent students, showing an overview of their paths to artistic maturity and the manner in which the influence of Shostakovich affected that process.

Boris Tishchenko (born 1939)

As Jupiter attracts other planets so Shostakovich influences other composers.—Boris Tishchenko[16]

Of all Shostakovich's students, Boris Tishchenko stands out as having made the most important contributions to the large-scale forms propounded by his teacher. He studied composition under Galina Ustvolskaya at the Leningrad Music College from 1954 to 1955, and under Vadim Salmanov and Orest Yevlakhov at the Leningrad Conservatory between 1957 and 1963. Ustvolskaya and Yevlakhov were themselves students of Shostakovich. Tishchenko's postgraduate studies with Shostakovich at that institution date from 1962 to 1965.

To date, he has written seven numbered and four unnumbered symphonies, two concerti each for violin and cello, a harp concerto, a piano concerto, five string quartets, plus many works in almost every other genre. True to the all-inclusive aspect of his postmodern aesthetic, Tishchenko is perhaps the most brilliant assimilator of musical styles in the modern era. The range and scope of his influences are nothing less than virtuosic while still remaining within the boundaries of tonality. Inasmuch as he is regarded as Shostakovich's favorite pupil, the stylistic affinities between the two composers are readily apparent. If Tishchenko has embraced Shostakovich's aesthetic frame of reference, he has done so with purpose, absorbing his influences as a foundation and expanding upon them with depth and originality. Variously associated with a group of modernists of the same generation, such as Edison Denisov, Alfred Schnittke, Rodion Shchedrin, and Sergei Slonimsky, he nevertheless stands apart from any fixed label or particular school. As if to demonstrate that Shostakovich was not the last representative of time-honored traditions, Tishchenko freely combines advanced procedures with conservative principles, maintaining the integrity of the symphonic process in the late twentieth and early twenty-first centuries.

Neither Tishchenko nor Shostakovich is known as an outstanding melodist in the traditional sense. Both are more concerned with the manipulation and interaction of musical ideas than with their intrinsic appeal as articulated forms. This is especially true of Tishchenko, whose lyricism is the more varied and unconventional. At times his material may sound overtly Tchaikovskian, as in his Seventh Symphony, or Schubertian, as in his Fifth String Quartet, or even make reference to various forms of jazz. Yet, the processes to which it is subjected and the classical forms to which it adheres prevents such heterogeneous material from sounding stylistically out of place.

Shostakovich's influence is especially apparent in Tishchenko's Second Violin Concerto (1981), whose finale contains a Shostakovich-style set of variations (passacaglia), and in the Second Cello Concerto (1969), where the vaulting rise and fall of perfect fifths in the lower strings at the start echo the rhythm, instrumentation, and overall character of the opening of Shostakovich's Fifth Symphony. And the main theme of the final movement of his Seventh Piano Sonata (with bells, 1982) hints at Shostakovich's piano Prelude in D minor, op. 34, No. 24. Yet, it is the first movement of that sonata that provides the most interesting parallel. Formally, it follows the model of the first movement of Shostakovich's Fifth Symphony, albeit with more traditional tonal relationships between first and second subjects (the movement is based loosely around the tonality of C, with an exposition second subject based around G), and a rather old-fashioned exposition repeat. Using both main themes, the development displays a somewhat simplified version of Shostakovichian "brutalization," interspersed with toccata-like passages, and comes, like the Shostakovich Fifth, to a broad, powerful climax based, also like the Shostakovich, on the reiteration of double-dotted rhythms. The climax is capped by the sound of the bells, reserved by Tishchenko for important structural points and reminiscent perhaps of the tam-tam used by Shostakovich to cap his climax. And like the Shostakovich Fifth, the next thing we hear is the recapitulation of the second theme, now based around the tonic. There are also parallels in harmonic style between the two composers. The sonata's second subject, for example, begins with a G major "vamp" in the left hand set against a right-hand melody in G minor. Moreover, the presence of both A and A-flat in this melody gives an intermittent Phrygian coloring (Example 19.1). Both the bimodality and the "Phrygian" flattened second were characteristic of Shostakovich.

Example 19.1

It is in the developmental process that Tishchenko's music reveals a musical mind of extraordinary flexibility. Indeed, the degrees of thematic distortion and transformation as employed by Shostakovich provide points of departure for a more extensive, vividly diverse set of practices in Tishchenko. His primary material typically undergoes a wide range of deformation, sometimes to the point of total destruction. At every moment, however, the music is guided by an uncompromising sense of logic and an uncanny sense of sustained drama worthy of Shostakovich. Tishchenko places a high priority on strategies of motivic integration, often employing in his orchestral music devices similar to those used in the later quartets of Shostakovich. An entire work may be based on germinal material presented in the opening bars, as in the First Cello Concerto (1963), scored for seventeen winds with percussion and harmonium (reorchestrated, incidentally, in 1969 by Shostakovich in a more conventional setting as a thirtieth birthday present for Tishchenko). In other works, all thematic material may derive from a common intervallic or rhythmic reservoir, for example, the Second Cello Concerto (1969), scored for forty-eight celli and twelve double basses, whose movements derive their material from a common perfect fifth interval.

Another outstanding work is the five-movement Concerto for Harp and Chamber Orchestra (1977). Avoiding the angelic arpeggiations that one usually finds in bravura works for harp, Tishchenko places the instrument in a more assertive, even percussive, role akin to a piano solo. The range of expression and lyrical variety is impressive, from the deranged piano clusters that completely disintegrate the theme of the second movement Scherzo to the haunting vocals in the penultimate movement. The xylophone (accompanied by woodblock) solo that opens the third movement seems to recall the xylophone that starts the fifth movement ("On the Alert") of Shostakovich's Fourteenth Symphony, and the scoring of the movement's climax is reminiscent of the percussiveness of the eighth song ("Creativity") of the *Michelangelo Suite*. Also reminiscent of Shostakovich's late-period scoring is Tishchenko's use of registral polarization. Compare, for example, his use of high violins and low double basses in the fourth movement of his Concerto for Flute, Piano, and Chamber Orchestra (1972) with Shostakovich's use of the same instruments at the end of the first movement ("De Profundis") of his Fourteenth Symphony (1969). In both cases, the spare, haunting atmosphere is created by the two polarized sets of voices—the lack of any other instruments depletes the texture of its center. (In the case of the Shostakovich, there is a gap averaging about three octaves between the upper double basses—the bass part is *divisi*—and the second violins.)

The framing works of Tishchenko's cycle of numbered symphonies, the First (1961) and Seventh (1994), form a pair of matching bookends of sorts. Each is cast in five self-contained movements that draw upon broad thematic material of a deceptively Romantic nature. The treatment of the material, however, lies well beyond the scope of Romanticism and exhibits a pan-stylistic exuberance where brilliance can at times border on slickness. In between these works we find just as resourceful a variety of form and expression.

The chamber textures and developmental procedures of the Third Symphony (1966) are reminiscent of the episodic relays between small groups of instruments found in early Shostakovich. The first and principal movement, *Meditation*, contains some striking timbral effects and culminates in the same kind of frantic overlay of activity (or "ultrapolyphony") that occurs on a much larger scale in the Shostakovich Second, and to a lesser extent in *The Nose*.

Tishchenko reaches the apex of formal experimentation with his blisteringly intense Fourth Symphony (1974). A work of Mahlerian proportions, each of its five movements is labeled "Sinfonia" and hinges upon a number of straightforward structural devices that are scaled up to monumental proportions. The bitonally inflected gestures of the opening movement, "Sinfonia di forza," recall the metal and thunder conflicts of the opening movement of the Shostakovich Eighth. The "Sinfonia rabbia" movement is based on the climactic convergence of competing lines and rhythms wherein a series of quirky interjections gradually fuses with its syncopated accompaniment. The third movement, "Sinfonia di tristezza," is built monolithically around a succession of short, detached phrases.

Tishchenko's Second (1964) and Sixth (1988) Symphonies are dominated by the human voice, and one finds in them a more tamed set of developmental schemes. The Second, "Marina," scored for mixed chorus and orchestra, is based on texts by Marina Tsvetayeva. Here Tishchenko's lively choral writing embraces a Carl Orff-like diatonicism for the most part and shares almost equal time with the purely instrumental sections. The Sixth, which calls for soprano and contralto with orchestra, features lyrically expressive vocal lines that are very much attached to the Russian tradition. The settings draw upon texts of Naiman, Akhmatova, and again, Tsvetayeva. Tishchenko's *Requiem* (1966), scored for soprano, tenor and orchestra, to words by Akhmatova, offers a lyrical style of greater emotional severity, one that may have influenced Shostakovich in his Fourteenth Symphony (1969), also scored for male and female soloists. The single-movement purely instrumental *Blockade Chronicle Symphony* (1984) again shows Tishchenko embracing explicit narrative objectives on a large scale.

The Fifth Symphony (1976) is Tishchenko's memorial tribute to Shostakovich, written the year after his death. In the opening movement, Shostakovich's DSCH monogram forms a series of dissonant, explosively anguished outbursts. The third movement incorporates a number of allusive quotations from the scherzi of Shostakovich's Eighth and Tenth Symphonies and, later, sonorities taken from the Eleventh. Some may feel that the use of the borrowed material in this case compromises the work's formal clarity. However, there is no denying the depth and sincerity of Tishchenko's monumental effort on behalf of his beloved teacher.

Mieczysław Weinberg (Moisei Vainberg) (1919–1996)[17]

I am a pupil of Shostakovich. Although I never had lessons from him, I count myself as his pupil, his flesh and blood.—Mieczysław Weinberg[18]

Mieczysław Weinberg's staggering output ranks him as one of the most prolific composers of the twentieth century: twenty-two symphonies, four chamber symphonies, seven operas, seventeen string quartets, and a large inventory of other chamber works. Shostakovich regarded him as one of the most important composers of the time. In aesthetic orientation, in humanitarian concerns as musically expressed, and in the forms to which he was drawn, Weinberg comes closer than any other composer to constituting a spiritual and artistic mirror of Shostakovich. It is not surprising that the two developed a close personal and professional relationship. Although there is a clear distinction between their styles, the work of each seemed at times to draw inspiration from that of the other.

Weinberg's artistic conscience was shaped by the Holocaust: after the German invasion of his native Poland in 1939, his entire family was exterminated. Forced to flee to the Soviet Union, he found friendship and professional support in Shostakovich. He too suffered the tyranny of the Zhdanovshchina, and was subsequently jailed as part of the stepped up anti-Semitic campaign of Stalin's last years. These experiences met a spirit of resilience. Composing became an article of faith, a healing of the soul, a moral as well as an artistic destiny. Possessing a profound lyrical gift, he proceeded to write symphonies and other works that often are concerned with war and oppression. Yet, in the tradition of Beethoven, they also deal with the struggle, reconciliation, and regeneration of the human spirit.

The musical works of Weinberg and Shostakovich have often been compared, but their similarities are often overstated in the presence of major distinctions. Both composers are drawn to traditional forms generated with free linear polyphony. Both employ comparable techniques of thematic development, including brutalization, parody, and transformation. Both share a certain amount of emotional volatility. In Weinberg's music, however, the symphonic thread is less jarred by cataclysm and contradiction than in Shostakovich's; its experiences of anguish, violence, and despair take place in a more continuously lyrical framework.

Weinberg's lyricism lies at the core of his symphonic thinking. In faster tempi it has a nervous, often fidgety quality, marked by quirky repetition of individual notes, intervals, and scale fragments in the melodic stream. A number of other features, such as accented acciaccaturas and certain scale patterns, associate it with Jewish music. In slower movements it has a tendency toward broad cantilena. Like Shostakovich and Prokofiev, Weinberg incorporates a variety of dance forms, often of a patently rustic quality, into his symphonies. In the 1940s, he wrote several explicitly ethnic works that reflect the Slavic and Jewish orientation of his lyricism: *Jewish Songs* (two sets, 1943 and 1944—in order to get printed, the former cycle was re-named *Children's Songs*), Sinfonietta No. 1 (1948), *Moldavian Rhapsody* (1949), and *Polish Tunes* (1949). Within a year of the first set of *Jewish Songs*, and of the initial meeting of the two composers, inflections of Jewish folk music began to appear prominently in Shostakovich's music, most notably the Second Piano Trio (1944) and the song cycle *From Jewish Folk Poetry* (1948)—one of the many parallelisms that one finds between the two composers, though the influence of Shostakovich's Jewish student Venyamin Fleishman in this regard must also be acknowledged. Weinberg's string quartet style also exhibits textural similarities to that of Shostakovich, though there is no mistaking his stamp of originality. Shostakovich, incidentally, dedicated his Tenth String Quartet (1964) to Weinberg.

The symphonies form the backbone of Weinberg's creative output. Those from the late 1950s and early 1960s already show a broad, encompassing vision, and are characterized by their tight, neoclassical construction. The Fourth (1957/1961) and Fifth (1962) Symphonies and the Violin Concerto (1959), each cast in four movements, form a trilogy of clarity and potency, particularly in their first movement sonata-allegros. They recall Shostakovich in their schematic treatment of thematic material without in any way being imitative. The Violin Concerto's leading theme indelibly impresses with its passionate double stops and hard-driven Slavic rhythms. The aggressive contrapuntal texture in the opening movement of the Fourth Symphony seethes with boundless energy. Prokofiev's influence is sensed in Weinberg's preference at this time for broad, diatonic melody, floating cantilena, and his choice of instrumental timbre. The Fifth Symphony opens with a set of opposing ideas—a military trumpet call set against a grotesquely stylized dance theme—that are brought to a rousing confrontation. Written a year after the premiere of Shostakovich's Fourth, it is dedicated to Kirill Kondrashin, the conductor of the Shostakovich premiere, and shares some characteristics with that work, including the use of quadruple winds. The Symphony's mysterious ending recalls the Shostakovich in its use of a solo celesta over an ostinato and, as with Shostakovich, the celesta's final note creates a dissonance with the surrounding harmony. Also from this period is the Flute Concerto (1961), the slow movement of which is composed in that favorite Shostakovichian form, the passacaglia, and uses string textures reminiscent of those that accompany the slow movement of Shostakovich's First Cello Concerto (1959). The first movement of Weinberg's own Cello Concerto (also 1959) appears to quote the first four notes of the Shostakovich concerto—two appearances, both transposed into the key of E, and with the first note raised a half-step.

Weinberg's Sixth Symphony (1963) was written one year after the appearance of two monumental Soviet works, Shostakovich's powerfully defiant Thirteenth Symphony ("Babi Yar") and Kabalevsky's mighty *Requiem*. A common thread of wartime subjects connects the three works, as does their scoring for voices and orchestra. Shostakovich's Thirteenth had spurred notorious disfavor in official circles for its critique of the Soviet government's institutional anti-Semitism. Weinberg's symphony raises no such red flags. Yet it reflects its solidarity with Shostakovich by examining the theme of Jewish children as the victims of the Nazi terror. Given the emotional volatility of the subject, it is handled with remarkable restraint and sensitivity. Its haunting message is made even more poignant through its setting for children's voices—a scoring detail borrowed from the Kabalevsky. The texts derive from three twentieth-century Soviet poets: Lev Kvitko, Samuil Galkin, and Mikhail Luokin. The Sixth would be the first of five Weinberg symphonies to include the human voice.

During the 1960s, Weinberg explored a number of other variations on symphonic form, as witnessed by his Seventh Symphony (1964), scored for strings and harpsichord. The harpsichord is used sparingly, though its presence as an occasional commentator establishes key points of repose and reference against the more active material in the strings. Interestingly, the Seventh is exactly contemporaneous with Shostakovich's score to Kozintsev's *Hamlet*, which also features a part for the harpsichord. The 1960s saw the start of a mini harpsichord revival in the Soviet Union, one that would continue into the 1990s, with composers such as Boris Tchaikovsky, Edison Denisov, Sofia Gubaidulina, Alfred Schnittke, and Sergei Slonimsky, among others. Such "retrofitting" can also be found in Weinberg's Tenth Symphony (1968) whose movements are gilded with historical names: Concerto Grosso (another Soviet 1960s favorite), Pastoral, Canzone, Burlesque, Inversion. In what must have been Weinberg's acknowledgement of the modernist movement of the 1960s, the Tenth, scored for strings, employs an uncharacteristically advanced, almost Bartokian language. The opening Concerto Grosso sports a waggishly dissonant version of its Baroque counterpart. The expressive nucleus of the work, however, is the set of highly chromatic, anguished solo string cadenzas that dominate the middle movements. The sense of disorientation so created is only tentatively relieved in the dance tune of the Burlesque and in the final return to the work's opening decorum.

The Twelfth Symphony (1976) is Weinberg's musical offering to Shostakovich. Unlike other musical tributes written around the same time, the work shuns direct quotation, even the overt use of the DSCH monogram. One does find oblique suggestions of Shostakovich's style, for example, the empty, "middle-less" texture of high, wandering violin lines set against low-register cellos and double basses in the first movement. There are also references to Shostakovich's characteristic anapest rhythmic cell in the final movement, which features a part for a most un-Shostakovichian instrument, the marimba. But Weinberg is careful to leave a tribute to his dear friend in his own voice. For the most part, subtlety of expression is suspended throughout the Symphony in favor of material that bears its grief in more physically demonstrative ways.

The Twelfth Symphony stands at a stylistic crossroad in the course of Weinberg's symphonic cycle, ushering in a new phase marked by expansion and synthesis. In the symphonies that follow, we find a more relaxed approach to form, roomier and more malleable thematic material, and, in order to accommodate an increased emphasis on instrumental color, a luxuriously extended orchestral palette. In a formal sense they mirror the later quartets of Shostakovich in their striving toward greater unity through linked movements or single-movement structures. But in their spontaneous, broadly flowing narratives, their all-inclusive range of experience, and their lofty but ruminative quest for spiritual understanding, they are more allied to the universe of Gustav Mahler. These traits are already present in the Fourteenth Symphony (1977), wherein one finds an opulent journey of the soul through lyrical detours both radiant and fantastic, even including a passing quotation from Stravinsky's *Petrushka*. Their greater flexibility allows Weinberg to embrace a new grandiloquence of expression, one that he applies with impressive results in his trilogy of war symphonies, nos. 17, 18 ("War—There Is

No Word More Cruel"), and 19. Composed between 1982 and 1985, the trilogy forms one of the major achievements of his career. The now songful, now eruptive lyricism, the emotionally wide-ranging drama, the final transcendence achieved in each, all recall the directness of Shostakovich and the transcendence of Mahler, yet without their self-absorbed suffering.

Galina Ustvolskaya (1919–2006)

Galina Ustvolskaya is one of those self-invented figures that defy all catego-ries. Her small catalogue of works—with a total back-to-back duration of less than six hours—stands apart from anything in the Western music tradition. In order to arrive at its remote artistic destination, her music has traveled along the widest possible arc, passing through, in its early stages, the influential orbit of Shostakovich. Ustvolskaya's music is decidedly an acquired taste. In its spiritual goals and technical means there is a willful nonconformity mixed with a puri-tanical austerity: its motivic material is generally nondescript, its harmonies neu-tral gradations of add-on dissonance, its rhythm often reduced to a steady, undifferentiated pulse. And yet it is music of intense passion and incorruptible integrity, wedged within the confines of an aesthetic that is uncompromisingly, sometimes agonizingly narrow. It takes the listener into solitary, even disturbing regions of experience that implicitly demand total surrender to its absolute authority. It is music that is at once either utterly trivial or unfathomably deep as it relentlessly, and with paradoxical defiance, aspires to the pious, the devo-tional, the hypnotic.

Ustvolskaya's renegade music has always remained as resistant to tradition as it has to the avant-garde. Although she chooses titles such as Sonata and Symphony, there is a patent avoidance of the forms associated with those terms. Those pre-cepts, as she uses them, are unconstrained by the small ensembles for which she writes, and she has commented, "My music is never chamber music, not even in the case of a solo sonata." Her music has an ascetic intensity that aspires, in the later works, to the condition of ritual.

Ustvolskaya graduated from the Leningrad Conservatory in 1947. The role that Shostakovich, her composition teacher, had played in her musical development prompted her publisher Viktor Suslin to compare their "intimate spiritual and artis-tic relationship" with that of Schoenberg and Webern.[19] Rostropovich considered Ustvolskaya one of Shostakovich's "faithful friends" who "certainly regarded [him] very highly," and described their relationship as "very 'tender.'"[20] Graduating at the onset of Zhdanov's cultural purges, she found few supporters to defend her against the derogations of her superiors. It has often been mentioned that Shostakovich came to her defense at this point. Yet, in a recent interview, Suslin, speaking on Ust-volskaya's behalf and in her presence, claimed that it was Mikhail Gnesin who defended her, and that Shostakovich's defense amounted to a single letter written to composer Edison Denisov. Suslin says that Ustvolskaya was "astounded and deeply disappointed by [Shostakovich's] conspicuous silence" at the time.[21]

How reciprocal their influence was on each other's music remains to be fully explored. For her part, it apparently took "almost superhuman strength to avoid [Shostakovich's] influence."[22] In a letter to her publisher, she wrote, "then, as now, I determinedly rejected his music, and unfortunately his personality only intensified this negative attitude.... One thing remains as clear as day: a seemingly eminent figure as Shostakovich, to me, is not eminent at all, on the contrary, he burdened my life and killed my best feelings."[23] Nonetheless, her earliest acknowledged work, the heroic Concerto for Piano, Strings, and Timpani (1946), contains echoes of her teacher's first work in that form, with which it shares almost identical instrumentation. In the process of capturing some of the atmosphere and pyrotechnic elegance of the Shostakovich Concerto, it also employs a similar mordent-like motive.

On the other hand, Shostakovich appears to have attached great value to the relationship: "It is not you who are influenced by me: rather it is I who am influenced by you."[24] One of the themes from the finale of Ustvolskaya's Clarinet Trio (1947) is quoted in two works of Shostakovich from widely separated points in his career.[25] In the first movement of Shostakovich's Fifth String Quartet (1952), Ustvolskaya's theme is given structural prominence when it appears as an episode of reconciliation after the combative confrontation of the development section. It was a disappointment to Shostakovich when Ustvolskaya turned down his marriage proposals to her, made shortly after the death of his first wife Nina in December 1954 and again after his divorce from Margarita in 1959. In 1974, Ustvolskaya's theme would reappear as the basis of the ninth song, "Night," of his *Suite on Verses of Michelangelo Buonarroti*. Here the mood is resigned and darkly melancholic, the verses cryptically suggestive of love rejected.

Although the long polyphonic lines of the Clarinet Trio (1947) show a graceful lyricism, they also show several anarchistic impulses. In the finale, a traditional parlay of themes suddenly dissolves into a coda of defiantly repeated piano strokes. The strokes anticipate the incessantly hammering rhythms of her mature style. By the early 1950s, Ustvolskaya's range of expression both narrowed and intensified, with a corresponding distillation of technical means. Repetition becomes a principal developmental feature, embodying a rhythmic obsessiveness that stands apart from folkloric or minimalist associations. Yet, it is a repetitiveness of expressive flexibility, allowing a spontaneity of line that is disciplined and propelled forward by incessant ostinato rhythms. There is also a proclivity for short material and aphoristic gesture. Such an astringency of means and methods is apparently intended to direct the listener's attention away from the surface and toward the underlying musical processes.

We find these features deployed in the Octet for two oboes, four violins, timpani, and piano (1949–1950). The work establishes the composer's preference for unusual combinations of instruments as well as her peculiar manner of thematic development. Each of its four movements consists of two or three short rhythmic motives that participate in a steadily pulsed, highly repetitive polyphonic argument of successive alternations and overlaps. The shifts in metric emphasis are achieved through a different time signature in almost every measure; in later works, Ustvolskaya made a practice of eliminating the bar line altogether. The metric shifts are most stirring in the second movement where anguished tritones propel the music to a demonic frenzy. Through fluctuations in the level of dissonance and repetitive accumulation, the music passes through a number of severe, striking psychological states. The work is brought to an arresting conclusion with a set of apocalyptic timpani strokes, raging against an indifferent firmament.

The decade culminates with the very effective *Grand Duet* for cello and piano (1959). The influence of Shostakovich is evident in the character of its lyricism. At the same time, it is a summary of Ustvolskaya's work to this point. Where the ideas in the Octet seem to derive monolithically from a common pool, the *Grand Duet* is dialectic of vivid motivic contrasts. Rhythmic ideas emerge with such compelling force that one almost hears them as a fully orchestral setting. The music treads the same tormented trails as the Octet, yet its wager between the anxious-propulsive and the redemptive-lyrical is pursued through a greater variety of cross-reactive sections. Like the Octet, the Duet terminates in the inconclusive, now with an impenetrable fading into the distance rather than a terminal jolt. At the same time, its articulation of a broader range of experience yields a more satisfying overall result.

Ustvolskaya's few public comments offer a glimpse into her working methods. It was her practice to let her finished compositions "rest" for long periods before they were presented publicly—or else destroyed. Furthermore, she declared, "I only write when I am in a state of grace."[26] This may explain the fact that she composed very little during the decade of the 1960s, save a duet for violin and piano (1964).

She regained her composing stride in the 1970s with a set of three "Compositions," the bizarre scorings of which seem to have been chosen with a proselytizing vengeance. Their religious subtitles do not refer to any explicit content in the liturgical sense, but the composer has remarked about them, "They are full of religious spirit, and they would come out best in a church, without any introduction or scientific analyses." The territory of register extremes is explored in Composition No. 1, "Dona Nobis Pacem" (1970–1971), scored for tuba, piccolo, and violin. The Shostakovichian absurdity of the instrumental combination drops a rare hint of a sense of humor, yet piccolo and tuba seem to take on the symbolic roles of irreconcilable extremes in the ongoing quest for peace. Composition No. 2, "Dies Irae" (1972–1973), is scored for eight double basses, a piano without its lid, and a wooden cube (specifically, forty-six centimeters per side) struck with timpani mallets. Composition No. 3, "Benedictus qui venit" (1974–1975), calls for four flutes, bassoon, and piano, and makes chilling, at times ominous, use of timbre contrasts.

Over the succeeding decade, Ustvolskaya focused on writing "symphonies," completing her Second through Fifth between 1979 and 1990. These short works, lasting between seven and sixteen minutes, are in no way connected to the symphony as it is conventionally understood. They differ from her previous works in their greater emphasis on hammering percussive strokes and the incorporation of short, repeated phrases spoken by a reciter. Their subtitles include "True and Eternal Bliss" (Symphony No. 2) and "Jesus Messiah, Save us!" (Symphony No. 3). Symphony No. 5, "Amen," is a brooding setting of the Lord's Prayer, an ironic choice of text because the music seems to convey the exasperation of prayers left unanswered. In the score, Ustvolskaya provides details of instrument placement and performance style that invoke ritualistic associations. The narrator is to be dressed in black and is to recite with "inner emotion"; the violinist is to play like a "voice from under the ground." The imploring, world-weary ambience gives way to moments of intensity amid the indifferent, ever-present rappings of the wooden box. In the end, the music withdraws into the cryptically unconsoled cosmos that is singularly Ustvolskaya's.

Boris Tchaikovsky (1925–1996)

Shostakovich imposed nothing upon me, rather he gave me direction. When I had achieved, in his opinion, the necessary level of professionalism, he allowed me much creative freedom.—Boris Tchaikovsky[27]

No one in his generation was as prolific or industrious in the manipulation of abstract forms as Boris Tchaikovsky. His name is revered in Russian contemporary music circles for a distinguished corpus of works known for their originality and impeccable craftsmanship. Tchaikovsky amassed a formidable catalogue of works that includes four symphonies, four concerti, six string quartets, a variety of chamber and orchestral music for variously composed ensembles, piano and vocal music, and an abundance of music for the cinema. His music reflects a concern for internal logic, expressive finesse, and in the final analysis, clear communication with his audience.

A native Muscovite, Tchaikovsky was trained at the Moscow Conservatory (1943–1949) during the most arduous of times: Stalin's postwar assault on the arts. To his credit he refused to participate in the official condemnations of the much-abused Shostakovich, who was banned from the Conservatory at the time and whose former students, Tchaikovsky among them, were branded as "contaminated." He graduated not totally unscathed, having studied with the most prominent composers of instrumental music of the time—Myaskovsky, Shebalin, and Shostakovich.

Tchaikovsky's works of the 1950s exhibit fresh and sensitive lyricism enveloped in a Romantic ethos allied to the music of his teachers. The rhapsodically flowing *Sinfonietta for Strings* and the youthfully exuberant Piano Trio, both of 1953, boast ripe craftsmanship and made positive impressions on Shostakovich.

Some characteristics of his mature style can be heard in the Sonata for Cello and Piano (1957), a work whose restless patterns seem to pay stylistic tribute to its dedicatee, Weinberg. And the essential idiosyncrasies of his music are united in the profoundly conceived Piano Quintet (1962), perhaps his finest work in the

chamber genre. The work's poise and contemplative dignity recall the same qualities in Shostakovich's Piano Quintet (1940), not to mention the typically Shostakovichian texture of simple octaves that begins the opening *Moderato*. Yet, its
depth and originality stake Tchaikovsky's claim as a unique creative force.

The freer creative environment in which Soviet composers found themselves
during the 1960s led to a dramatic metamorphosis in Tchaikovsky's style. A
tendency toward shorter motivic material and increased levels of dissonance bear
the stamp of Shostakovich's influence. Although Tchaikovsky's lyricism continued to embrace the eloquent cantilena found in the Violin Sonata of 1959,
rhythm would now become the vital generating force of his music. A set of
ideas is typically subject to an almost mechanically repetitive treatment where
unyielding, declamatory rhythmic patterns give way to intervallic, harmonic,
and other alterations. Related to aspects of Russian folk music, the striking ri-
gidity of these utterances, and the rhythmically obsessive framework in which
they are embedded, mark something of a departure from Shostakovich. Thematic development proceeds not in the conventional sense, but rather by
schemes of alternation and contrast. Enough flexibility is built around these
somewhat unyielding building blocks to allow a wide range of expression and
formal design.

This newly evolved language propelled Tchaikovsky toward new forms and
fresh approaches to old forms. In this sense he inherited Shostakovich's ceaseless
quest for formal variety as embodied in his symphonies. In the Cello Concerto
(1964), Tchaikovsky produced a lyrical bravura work that challenges the notion of
thematic identity. In each of its four contrasting movements, melodic material is
either constantly transformed, implied, or subverted altogether. In the remarkable
first movement, the most experimental music Tchaikovsky ever wrote, soloist and
orchestra appear preoccupied with what sounds like raw materials—isolated intervals, scale patterns, rhythmic vamps, broken triads. From these inchoate elements
Tchaikovsky assembles new and recurring points of reference into a broadly
unfolding, theme-free dramatic arch. Oblique references to the familiar late-
Romantic rhetoric tantalize the informed listener with a blend of the familiar and
unfamiliar. With the opening movement's chamber-like transparency and improvisatory expanse followed by shorter movements of lighter content, the Cello Concerto must have reminded Shostakovich of the similar layout of his own Sixth
Symphony. Upon hearing the Concerto Shostakovich asked for the full score,
remarking, "I want to study these unearthly beauties."[28]

The Piano Concerto (1971) explores a different classical form in each of its five
movements and uses rhythm as the defining element of construction as well as the
springboard for all its thematic material. Another significant departure is found in
the one-movement Violin Concerto (1969) where, throughout the work's entire
forty-minute duration, a fresh supply of thematic material is continually introduced, sidestepping one of the most basic principles of classical form, repetition.
Shostakovich also experimented with a similar schema in his Third Symphony
(1929).

In Tchaikovsky's music one frequently finds a sectional or multi-movement approach to musical architecture. The focus on a handful of shorter forms within a larger form, akin to the suites of the Baroque period, opened up for the composer a number of expressive and technical possibilities. Examples of this multiple short movement design include the six-part *Partita for Cello, Harpsichord, Piano, Electric Guitar and Percussion* (1966), the six-part *Chamber Symphony* (1967), *Six Etudes for Strings and Organ* (1976), the seven-part *Music for Orchestra* (1984), and the five-part *Symphony with Harp* (1993). In the colorful *Partita,* the opening movement, "Twelve Notes," anticipates the opening bars of Shostakovich's Twelfth Quartet (1968) in its sequential juxtaposition of major scale and twelve-tone row—in the Shostakovich, it is also the cello that bears the twelve-tone message. Both works proceed in a manner that, as a seeming manifesto, patently rejects the confines of strict serialism in favor of a flexible, hybrid diatonicism. (Interestingly, the "Toccata" section of the first movement of the *Suite for Cello and Chamber Orchestra* by another Shostakovich student, Yury Levitin, also contains twelve-tone writing in the cello part. Composed in 1966, Levitin's work predates both the Tchaikovsky and the Shostakovich.)

We find similar paths of innovation in the symphonic works. The three-movement Second Symphony (1967) takes Tchaikovsky's rhythmic idiosyncrasies into new formal territory. The opening movement, cast in sonata form with double exposition, presents a runaway succession of ideas and shifting accents. Textures are occasionally reminiscent of the 1960s Polish school (chord clusters and the like), and the dramatic contrasts in orchestral color and mood, and even the use of quadruple winds, recall the fugitive abundance of the Shostakovich Fourth Symphony, whose premiere earlier the same decade could not have escaped Tchaikovsky's notice. The material is fresh, lively and sophisticated and makes astonishing demands on winds and brass. The first movement's cornucopia of themes includes a final series of quotations from the classical literature: Mozart's Clarinet Quintet, first movement, second subject (Fig. 113); the opening of Beethoven's Quartet, op. 18, no. 4 (Fig. 115); the aria "Erbarme dich" from Bach's *St. Matthew Passion* (Fig. 117), and Schumann's "Des Abends" from the *Fantasiestücke,* op. 12 (Fig. 118). These do not become a structural part of the work as do Shostakovich's quotations of Rossini, Wagner, and Glinka in his Fifteenth Symphony, written seven years later. Yet they do bear both personal and cultural relevance. The phenomenon of referential quotation had been a part of Shostakovich's music since his youth, and had found new currency in Soviet music during the vogue of "pan-stylism."

Composed in 1980, the Third Symphony ("Sevastopol") has a more convincing sense of unity and takes a completely different expressive direction. It commemorates the victims of the city that was twice under siege, during the Crimean and Second World wars, and which remains a symbol of courage and endurance. There is here something of the nobility, cathartic grief, and reflective anguish of other Soviet works commemorating the ravages of war, such as Shostakovich's monumental Eighth Symphony and Khachaturian's Symphony No. 2 ("The Bell"), both of 1943.

Tchaikovsky's string quartets—at least the latter four that have been recorded—occupy a small but striking corner of his catalogue. They are an attractive collection of miniatures, the last three not exceeding a quarter of an hour apiece. Each boasts the same thematic integrity, vitality, and craftsmanship found in the rest of the composer's chamber music, yet on an even more compressed scale. They are more like polished poems, effective, poignant, distinctive. The recurring oscillating fourths and rising and falling glissandi in the Third String Quartet (1967) are very Shostakovichian and create an arresting atmosphere. Both Sofia Khentova and Dorothea Redepenning have speculated that the format of all slow movements in the Third Quartet was to influence Shostakovich in his Fifteenth Quartet, though others, such as David Fanning, are less convinced.[29] Tchaikovsky never returned to the form after 1976. In the realm of chamber music, Tchaikovsky's fondness for novel instrumental groupings is again represented in his very effective Sextet for Winds and Harp (1990).

No survey of Tchaikovsky's music would be complete without mention of an undisputable masterpiece, the cantata *Signs of the Zodiac* (1974), a setting of four poems by Tyutchev, Blok, Tsvetayeva, and Zabolotsky, for soprano, harpsichord and strings. In this deeply Russian, broadly philosophical work, with organically interlinked movements, the cantilena aspect of the composer's lyricism shines brightly.

Georgy Sviridov (1915–1998)

[Sviridov] always recognized the great ethical meaning of our art—and he cannot stand people looking for tone without meaning, although he never tires of always trying new forms and creating a new musical language to express his own ideas.—Shostakovich[30]

The reputation of Georgy Sviridov as one of the giants of Russian vocal music is richly deserved. Early on, he carved a niche for himself, exalting Russian culture through contemporary settings of classic Russian poetry that hark back to its varied singing traditions. His songs and choral works, many of them staples of the Russian repertoire, demonstrate that a conservative language in the twentieth century need not be devoid of vitality or originality.

Sviridov was one of Shostakovich's first composition students at the Leningrad Conservatory, graduating in 1941. His cantata *Poem in Memory of Sergei Yesenin* (1955) was his first major success, establishing his independent standing and catapulting him to the front ranks of Soviet music. Scored for solo tenor, large chorus and augmented orchestra, it is based on the texts of the Russian poet (1895–1925) whose "village poetry" had recently been made available. Merging folk influence, a touch of Borodin, and modern sensibilities, the cantata is a luxurious setting of nine poems that paint various impressions of Russia, taking the listener from tsarist ruralities to the Revolution.

Sidestepping personal revelations, Sviridov's music is more concerned with the epic sweep, the collective essence of his poetic subjects. His deceptively straightforward technical apparatus—the homophonic textures, the modal and chromatic progressions of block harmony, the flowing diatonic lines—is considerably more sophisticated than has often been given credit by Western critics. His music derives much of its novelty from a powerful lyricism that averts, or rather modifies, standard Romantic phrase and cadence structures. A Sviridov melody is typically built out of small subphrases, or unit cells, each of which has strong rhythmic characteristics. Repetition, especially in accompaniment patterns, is a frequent feature, very suggestive of patterns found in folk music. Cadential phrases are shortened or completely absent. While the Dargomyzhsky-Musorgsky inheritance is an inevitable part of his Slavic demeanor, Sviridov's clear, pithy melodies are unmistakably his own. Still, it has to be said that much of the impact of Sviridov's work, including the *Yesenin* cantata, derives from stylistic features that do not surrender readily to technical analysis: the grandly opulent gestures, the strategic shifts of atmosphere and texture within and between movements, the preternatural sense of folkloric fantasy. His fresh, contemporary approach within the folkloric, operatic, and liturgical genres is remarkable in that it transcends the barriers of both language and time.

Where Sviridov established his own stylistic ground in the vocal genres, it was in the realm of instrumental music that he struggled to find his own stamp, and where he fell intensely under the spell of Shostakovich. The 1940 Chamber Symphony displays much lyrical imagination, but also the student Sviridov's difficulty in organizing his musical materials. The Piano Trio of 1945 (revised 1955) reflects a mature craftsmanship and at the same time a pronounced Shostakovich influence. The Scherzo of Sviridov's Trio unblushingly lifts the main tune from the second movement of Shostakovich's Eighth Symphony written two years previously, and places it into the context of a fiery *Ländler*-scherzo type familiar from Shostakovich's Piano Quintet (1940) and Second Piano Trio (1944). And the manner in which the slow movement's cantilena floats over a strolling pizzicato bass line clearly echoes the Intermezzo movement of Shostakovich's Stalin Prize-winning Piano Quintet. Conformist to the letter, and arguably with a vengeance, Sviridov's Trio elicited what was no doubt the anticipated outcome, his own Stalin Prize.

The incident reflected not only a creative crisis but also the professional jealousy that Sviridov reportedly harbored toward Shostakovich, perhaps understandable at a time when high-profile masterworks were tripping off Shostakovich's pen. Sviridov's solo piano works of the same period, which include a Piano Sonata (1944) and a pair of partitas, are attractive concert pieces, though none are blessed with the originality of his vocal music. His persistence in the chamber music genre, however, delivered one remarkable payoff, the three-movement *Music for Chamber Orchestra* for strings, horn, and piano (1964), a reworking of a piano quintet that he had abandoned some twenty years earlier. Faint echoes of the teacher remain, but style and form are ingeniously tailored to the unique character of Sviridov's cellular melodic thinking. The second movement merges half-a-dozen short, imaginative motives into a gloriously synoptic climax; the material in the final *Largo*

gradually builds to a moving peroration. One laments Sviridov's subsequent abandonment of the genre, for *Music for Chamber Orchestra* remains one of the finest
chamber works of the Soviet repertoire.

German Galynin (1922–1966)

German Galynin was another composer of striking individuality. Unfortunately,
his life was more deeply affected by the events of 1948 than any other Shostakovich student. His works were held in the highest esteem by Shostakovich and
Myaskovsky, his teachers at the Moscow Conservatory, and were performed by the
most prominent musicians of the day. He rose to prominence as a student with
his brilliantly original First Piano Concerto (1946), which remains in the repertoire both in Russia and internationally. A clear stylistic debt to Shostakovich can
be found, particularly in the first movement. Its first theme recalls Shostakovich's
liking for lowered thirds and lowered sixths (minor-key implication), lowered seconds ("Phrygian implication), and raised seconds ("leading note" to the major
third) within an otherwise major-key context, sometimes emphasizing or dwelling
on these "wrong" notes to uproarious effect. Galynin favors simple two-part
melody-and-accompaniment textures, or melodies in octaves, as preferred by Shostakovich in his piano concertos. Inserted into the final movement of the Concerto
are two consecutive, conspicuously exposed utterances of Shostakovich's DSCH
monogram: at Fig. 56, b10 (transposed to start on A-sharp) and Fig. 56, b13
(starting on B). We can only speculate as to whether this is indeed the origin of
DSCH. Interestingly, it predates by at least a year the first appearance of the
motive in Shostakovich's own work, specifically, in the scherzo of the First Violin
Concerto (1947–1948), where the motive also appears transposed.[31]

Almost all of Galynin's celebrated works date from his student days at the Conservatory. One of these is his deeply felt Suite for String Orchestra (1949), whose
haunting strains pay homage to Myaskovsky. This period also produced a notable
First String Quartet (1946) and a distinguished Piano Trio (1948), the latter har-
boring echoes of Shostakovich's widely influential Piano Quintet (1940) and Second Piano Trio (1944). A group of piano works, including six piano sonatas
(1939–1941) and a substantial Piano Suite (1945), again show a richly inventive
personal lyricism. After Shostakovich had been dismissed from the Moscow Conservatory in 1948, Galynin's graduation was delayed for two years so that he could
fulfill the requirement of composing works that demonstrated his 'reeducation' after being 'contaminated' by the teachings of Shostakovich. The two works that
Galynin submitted for this assignment were an oratorio, *Death and the Maiden*
(1951), and the folkloric *Epic Poem* (1950), for which he won a 1951 Stalin Prize.
While each work boasts its lyrical charms, the musical language in both is rather
guarded and reactionary. The ordeal seriously affected Galynin's creativity, which,
tragically, fell almost totally silent for more than a decade, only to be revived but a
few years before his premature death at the age of 44.[32] During the brief second
flowering, he revised a quantity of works from his student days, wrote a number

of incidental pieces, and produced two works of significance: an *Aria* for Violin and Orchestra (1963) and a Second Piano Concerto (1965). The Concerto reveals a lucid imagination, with earlier idiosyncrasies revived. Its restless modulations, metric shifts, and quirky themes, some of which are borrowed from his earlier period, offer an impressive, if disturbing, testimony to the shattered path of his creative life.

Karen Khachaturian (born 1920)

Karen Khachaturian enjoyed a brief moment of fame in the West with his Myaskovskian Violin Sonata (1947), championed by such luminaries as Oistrakh, Kogan, and Heifetz. His music has a more cosmopolitan character than that of his famous uncle, Aram Khachaturian, though it is not totally divorced from the latter's exotic folklore-based style. He studied at the Moscow Conservatory under Shebalin, Myaskovsky, and Shostakovich, and graduated in 1949. His First Symphony (1954) is colorful, if standard issue, with some genuine flashes of inspiration. His next two symphonies (1968 and 1982) display an increasing tendency toward coloristic effects in place of conventional development, and exhibit clear if superficial similarities to Shostakovich. His Cello Concerto (1983) prominently incorporates the DSCH motif as demarcation points in between its three main sections, evidently a belated tribute to the master. The motif's first few appearances are based on G-sharp, thus matching its debut in Shostakovich's First Violin Concerto. His oratorio about the assassination attempt on Lenin, *An Instant in History* (1971), does not quite live up to—nor do many of his other later works—the youthful promise of the Violin Sonata. His popular ballet, *Chippolino* (1974), whose principals are farm vegetables, consists of charming, if innocuous, dance numbers.

Kara Karayev (1918–1982)

Kara Karayev assumed a leadership role in Azerbaijani music as a composer and educator who brought Azerbaijani concert music up to date with contemporary European trends. He was drawn to Moscow during the 1940s from his native Baku, and there studied with Shostakovich. His First Symphony (1943), written at the outset of his student years at the Moscow Conservatory, appears to reflect a heavy Shostakovich influence. His diploma piece, however, the *mugam*-inflected Second Symphony (1946), already shows a shift toward his mature style, while his Third Symphony (1964) flirts with twelve-tone technique in the context of a Stravinskian neoclassicism. Karayev was an outspoken admirer of Shostakovich, to whom his folkloric Second String Quartet (1947) was dedicated. Shostakovich, in kind, praised his work more than once in public forums. Karayev's finest achievements are the balletically conceived works that incorporate ravishing Azerbaijani lyricism, such as *Leli and Mejnun* (1947), *Seven Beauties* (1949), which Shostakovich praised,[33] and not least, the award-winning *Path of Thunder* (1957), whose South African setting introduces an additional element of exoticism.

NOTES

Preface

1. Data from approximately three hundred American and Canadian orchestras reported to the League of American Orchestras, http://www.americanorchestras.org/knowledge_center/orchestra_repertoire_reports.html (accessed March 3, 2008).

2. The question was first brought to light by Simon Karlinsky, "Our Destinies are Bad," *The Nation*, November 24, 1979, 535. Further research was presented by Laurel Fay in April 1980 in "Will the Real Dmitri Shostakovich Please Stand Up?" (paper presented at the Midwest Chapter of the American Musicological Society in Columbus, OH). Subsequently published, Laurel E. Fay, "Shostakovich versus Volkov: Whose *Testimony?*" *Russian Review* 39, No. 4 (1980): 484–93. Reprinted in *A Shostakovich Casebook*, ed. Malcolm Hamrick Brown (Bloomington: Indiana University, 2004), 11–21.

3. Elizabeth Wilson, *Shostakovich: A Life Remembered*, new ed. (London: Faber and Faber, 2006), xiii.

4. Patrick McCreless, "The Cycle of Structure and the Cycle of Meaning: the Piano Trio in E minor, op. 67," in *Shostakovich Studies*, ed. David Fanning (Cambridge: Cambridge University Press, 1995), 114.

5. Fanning, ed. *Shostakovich Studies*.

6. Rosamund Bartlett, ed., *Shostakovich in Context* (Oxford: Oxford University Press, 2000).

7. Laurel Fay, ed., *Shostakovich and His World* (Princeton: Princeton University Press, 2004).

8. David Fanning, *Shostakovich: String Quartet No. 8* (Aldershot: Ashgate, 2004); Pauline Fairclough, *A Soviet Credo: Shostakovich's Fourth Symphony* (Aldershot: Ashgate, 2006).

9. David Fanning, *The Breath of the Symphonist: Shostakovich's Tenth* (London: Royal Musical Association, 1989).

10. Nicolai Malko, *A Certain Art* (New York: W. Morrow, 1966), 180.

11. Elizabeth Wilson, *Shostakovich: A Life Remembered*, original ed. (Princeton: Princeton University Press, 1994), 314.

12. This reverse influence is explored in David Fanning, "Shostakovich and His Pupils," in *Shostakovich and His World*, ed. Laurel Fay, 275–302.

13. Ibid., 282–283.

Chapter 1

1. *Pravda*, August 12, 1975, 3. Also in *Sovetskaia muzyka* (1975, No. 9): 6–7. German translation appears in Ernst Kuhn and Günter Wolter, eds., *Volksfeind Dmitri Schostakowitsch: Eine Dokumentation der öffentlichen Angriffe gegen den Komponisten in der ehemaligen Sowjetunion* (Berlin: E. Kuhn, 1997), 212–14.

2. Speech given on October 26, 1932. Quoted in A. Kemp-Welch, *Stalin and the Literary Intelligentsia, 1928–39* (New York: St. Martin's Press, 1991), 131.

3. "Sumbur vmesto muzyki: ob opere 'Ledi Makbet Mtsenskogo Uezda' D. Shostakovicha," *Pravda*, January 28, 1936, 3; "Baletnaia fal'sh," *Pravda*, February 6, 1936, 3.

4. Elizabeth Wilson, *Shostakovich: A Life Remembered*, original ed. (Princeton: Princeton University Press, 1994), 190–1. For a cartoon of the Shostakovich "clones," see Rosamund Bartlett, ed., *Shostakovich in Context* (Oxford: Oxford University Press, 2000), front cover.

5. David Rabinovich, *Dmitry Shostakovich—Composer*, trans. George Hanna (London: Lawrence and Wishart, 1959), 10.

6. Recollection of Mark Lubotsky. In Elizabeth Wilson, original ed., 475. Khrennikov would repeat the quote in a 1986 interview. See Joel W. Spiegelman, "The Czar of Soviet Music," *High Fidelity*, March 1986, 55.

7. *Collected Works* 20 (1985, full score); 22 (1985, piano/vocal score): "Editor's Note," np.

8. *Collected Works* 16 (1985).

9. *Collected Works* 1 (1987); *New Collected Works* 1 (2002).

10. *The New York Times*, February 6, 1935, 23.

11. Letter to Ernest Ansermet dated April 4, 1935. Robert Craft, ed., *Stravinsky: Selected Correspondence*, vol. 1 (New York: Knopf, 1982), 224.

12. Aaron Copland, "From the '20s to the '40s and Beyond," *Modern Music* 20 (1943): 82.

13. Gerald Abraham, *Eight Soviet Composers* (London: Oxford University Press, 1943), 27–9.

14. Glenn Gould, "Music in the Soviet Union," in *The Glenn Gould Reader*, ed. Tim Page (New York, Knopf, 1984), 177.

15. Pierre Boulez, "Eventually ...," in *Notes of an Apprenticeship*, trans. Herbert Weinstock (New York: Knopf, 1968), 148.

16. Telegram to Olin Downes, March 11, 1949, in *Arnold Schoenberg Correspondence*, comp. Egbert Ennulat (Metuchen, NJ: Scarecrow, 1991), 259.

17. Arnold Schoenberg, *Criteria for the Evaluation of Music, Style and Idea*, ed. Leonard Stein (London: Faber, 1975), 136.

18. Interview, September 1993. Frans C. Lemaire, *La musique du xxe siècle en Russie* (Paris: Fayard, 1994), 207. In *Composers on Music—Eight Centuries of Writings*, 2nd ed., ed. Josiah Fisk (Boston: Northeastern University Press, 1997), 429.

19. Interview with Hugh Canning, *The Sunday Times* [London], January 9, 2000.

20. Robin Holloway, "The Shostakovich Horrors," *The Spectator*, August 26, 2000, 42.

21. Interview with Oksana Dvornichenko, in "DSCH: The Life and Works of Dmitri Shostakovich," *Cultural Heritage Series*, vol. 1 (Chandos Multimedia DVD-ROM, CHAN 550011).

22. Solomon Volkov, *Testimony: The Memoirs of Dmitri Shostakovich*, trans. Antonina W. Bouis (New York: Harper and Row), xvii.

23. See Herbert Mitgang, "Shostakovich Memoir, Smuggled Out, Is Due," *The New York Times*, September 10, 1979, C14; and Craig R. Whitney, "Shostakovich Memoir a Shock to Kin," *The New York Times*, November 13, 1979, C7.

24. Volkov, *Testimony*, 3.

25. Volkov, *Testimony*, 257.

26. Kirill Kondrashin, "Talking about Shostakovich," trans. Tatjana Norbury, in *Shostakovich Reconsidered*, ed. Allan B. Ho and Dmitry Feofanov (London: Toccata Press, 1998), 520.

27. Central Committee Minutes, "Concerning Measures for Propagandizing and Preserving D.D. Shostakovich's Creative Legacy," December 14, 1978. In Alla Bogdanova, "Notes from the Soviet Archives on Volkov's *Testimony*," in *A Shostakovich Casebook*, ed. Malcolm Hamrick Brown (Bloomington: Indiana University, 2004), 94.

28. *Govorit Dmitrii Shostakovich*. Melodiya M40 41705–12 (LP only).

29. Mikhail Iakovlev, *D. Shostakovich o vremeni i o sebe: 1926–1975* (Moscow: Sovetskii kompozitor, 1980).

30. Lev Grigoryev and Yakov Platek, *Dmitry Shostakovich: About Himself and His Times*, trans. Angus and Neilian Roxburgh (Moscow: Progress Publishers, 1981).

31. "Zhalkaia poddelka. O tak nazyvaemykh 'memuarakh' D.D. Shostakovicha," *Literaturnaia gazeta*, November 14, 1979, 8. Quoted in Ho and Feofanov, eds., *Shostakovich Reconsidered*, 61.

32. Elena Basner, "The Regime and Vulgarity," in Brown, ed., 138. See also Allan B. Ho and Dmitry Feofanov, *The "Shostakovich Wars"* (London: Toccata Press, forthcoming).

33. Irina Nikolskaya, "Shostakovich Remembered—Interviews with His Soviet Colleagues," in Brown, ed., 155.

34. Louis Blois, "A Town Hall Interview with Maxim Shostakovich," *DSCH Society Newsletter* XIV (November 1989): 5–6.

35. Maxim Shostakovich, "Six Lectures on the Shostakovich Symphonies," in Ho and Feofanov, eds., *Shostakovich Reconsidered*, 402.

36. Volkov, *Testimony*, 38.

37. D.D. Shostakovich, "Moi tvorcheskii otvet," *Vecherniaia Moskva*, January 25, 1938, 30. Quoted in Richard Taruskin, "Public Lies and Unspeakable Truth: Interpreting Shostakovich's Fifth Symphony," in *Shostakovich Studies*, ed. David Fanning (Cambridge: Cambridge University Press, 1995), 33.

38. Volkov, *Testimony*, 183.

39. *Sovetskoe iskusstvo*, November 7, 1944. In Grigoryev and Platek, 111.

40. Volkov, *Testimony*, 140–1.

41. Ibid., 257.

42. Ibid., xiv-xv.

43. Quoted in Boris Schwarz, *Music and Musical Life in Soviet Russia, 1917–1981*, Enlarged ed. (Bloomington: Indiana University Press, 1983), 645.

44. Speech to commemorate the bicentennial of Bach's death (Leipzig, 1950); speech on Beethoven (Berlin, 1952); article "About Certain Vital Questions in Musical Creativity: A Composer's Remarks," (*Pravda,* June 17, 1956); and speech to the Second All-Union Congress of Composers (1957).

45. Daniil Zhitomirsky, "Shostakovich," trans. Véronique Zaytzeff and Frederick Morrison, in Ho and Feofanov, eds., 431–2.

46. Edward Rothstein, "A Labour of Love," *The Independent Magazine*, November 12, 1988, 50. (Italics original)

47. Alexander Werth, *Musical Uproar in Moscow* (London: Turnstile, 1949), 40.

48. See in particular Wilson, original ed., Ho and Feofanov, eds., *Shostakovich Reconsidered*, and Ho and Feofanov, eds., *The "Shostakovich Wars."*

49. Maxim Shostakovich. Quoted in Schwarz, 645.

50. Henry Orlov, "A Link in the Chain," in Brown, ed., 196.

51. Joseph Horowitz, "A Moral Beacon Amid the Darkness of a Tragic Era," *The New York Times*, January 6, 2000, Section 2, 1.

52. Gerard McBurney, "Whose Shostakovich?" in Brown, ed., 284.

53. "Brave Words, Brave Music," BBC Radio 3, broadcast August 16, 1998. (British Library catalogue number H10605/2)

54. For example, Eric Roseberry, "Some thoughts after a re-reading of *Testimony*," *Melos* 4–5 (1993): 24; Taruskin in Fanning, ed., 47; Laurel E. Fay, *Shostakovich: A Life* (New York: Oxford University Press, 2000), 4.

55. Volkov, *Testimony*, xvii.

56. Simon Karlinsky, "Our Destinies are Bad," *The Nation*, November 24, 1979, 535; Laurel E. Fay, "Shostakovich versus Volkov: Whose *Testimony*?" *Russian Review* 39, No. 4 (1980): 484–93. Reprinted in Brown, ed., 11–21.

57. See, for example, statements of Lev Lebedinsky, Edison Denisov, Yury Lyubimov. In Wilson, original ed., 337–8, 432–5.

58. In Wilson, original ed., 307.

59. Alexander Solzhenitsyn, *The Oak and the Calf* (New York: Harper and Row, 1979), 221.

60. Zhitomirsky, in Ho and Feofanov, eds., *Shostakovich Reconsidered*, 432–3.

61. In Wilson, original ed., 337.

62. Ian MacDonald, *The New Shostakovich*, original ed. (Boston: Northeastern University Press, 1990), 11.

63. Isaak Glikman, ed., *Story of a Friendship: The Letters of Dmitry Shostakovich to Isaak Glikman, 1941–1975* (Ithaca: Cornell University Press, 2001), 72–3.

64. Richard Taruskin compares the interchanging of Kirilenko and Kirichenko in the second recitation to "the Ukrainian nomenklatura's Dobchinsky and Bobchinsky, the tweedledee-tweedledum bureaucrats in Gogol's farce, *The Inspector General*." Richard Taruskin, "Shostakovich and Us," in Bartlett, ed., 2.

65. Letter dated November 17, 1935. Lyudmila Mikheyeva-Sollertinskaya, "Shostakovich as Reflected in His Letters to Ivan Sollertinsky," in Bartlett, ed., 75.

66. Taruskin, "Public Lies and Unspeakable Truth," 18.

67. Ibid., 47.

68. Solomon Volkov, "Universal Messages: Reflections in Conversation with Günter Wolter," *Tempo* 200 (1997, No. 4): 16.

69. Mark Aranovskii, "Inakomysliashchii," *Muzykal'naia akademiia* (1997, No. 4): 2–3.

70. David Fanning, *Shostakovich: String Quartet No. 8* (Aldershot: Ashgate, 2004), 11.

71. Taruskin, "Public Lies and Unspeakable Truth," 47.

72. In Wilson, original ed., 337.

73. Quoted by Malcolm Hamrick Brown, "Ian MacDonald's *The New Shostakovich*," in Brown, ed., 261.

74. Quoted in Ludmila Kovnatskaya, "An Episode in the Life of a Book—An Interview with Henry Orlov," in Brown, ed., 108–9.

75. Kirill Kondrashin, in Wilson, original ed., 359.

76. Malcolm MacDonald, "Words and Music in Late Shostakovich," in *Shostakovich: The Man and His Music*, ed. Christopher Norris (Boston: Marion Boyars, 1982), 136.

77. Interview with Marina Sabinina. Irina Nikolskaya, "Shostakovich Remembered—Interviews with His Soviet Colleagues," in Brown, ed., 152.

78. Quoted in Norman Lebrecht, *The Sunday Times Magazine* [London], April 15, 1984, 26.

79. Georgii Khubov, "Piataia simfoniia D. Shostakovicha," *Sovetskaia muzyka* (1938, No. 3): 14. (Trans. Tatyana Buzina for this volume).

80. Ibid., 16.

81. Ibid., 27.

82. Ibid., 25.

83. Volkov, *Testimony*, 257–64.

84. See Solomon Volkov, *Shostakovich and Stalin: The Extraordinary Relationship between the Great Composer and the Brutal Dictator*, trans. Antonina W. Bouis (New York: Knopf, 2004), 82.

85. Volkov, *Testimony*, 183.

86. Ibid., 141.

87. Ibid., 156.

88. Quoted in Lebrecht, *The Sunday Times Magazine*, April 15, 1984, 26.

89. Christopher Norris, "Shostakovich: Politics and Musical Language," in Norris, ed., 186. Also, "Music Matters," BBC Radio 3, broadcast February 15, 1998.

90. Christopher Norris, "Ambiguous Shostakovich," *Gramophone*, February 1983, 892.

91. Norman Lebrecht, "Shostakovich—Dissident Notes," *Lebrecht Weekly* (*La Scena Musicale* online), January 19, 2000, http://www.scena.org/columns/lebrecht/000119-NL-Dissident.htm (accessed June 17, 2007).

92. In Wilson, original ed., 139.

93. Yevgenii Mravinskii, "Tridzat let s musikoi Shostakovicha," in *D. Shostakovich*, ed. Lev Danilevich (Moscow: Sovetskii kompozitor, 1967), 106–7. Quoted in Gregor Tassie, *Yevgeny Mravinsky—The Noble Conductor* (Lanham, MD: Scarecrow Press, 2005), 130.

94. In Wilson, original ed., 315.

95. Ian MacDonald, *The New Shostakovich*, original ed., 5–6.

96. Galina Vishnevskaya, *Galina: A Russian Story*, trans. Guy Daniels (San Diego: Harcourt Brace Jovanovich, 1984), 213.

97. Ian MacDonald, *The New Shostakovich*, original ed., 115–6. See also Volkov, *Testimony*, 119.

98. In Wilson, original ed., 225.

99. Ian MacDonald, *The New Shostakovich*, original ed., 171 and 169.

100. Quoted in Werth, 71–2.

101. Solomon Volkov, "Universal Messages," 15. Later, Volkov would quip that "For some critics, the names Ian MacDonald and Solomon Volkov became virtually interchangeable. Nothing can be farther from reality. We agreed on many things, disagreed about others." Letter to Raymond Clarke dated September 1, 2005. Quoted in Ian MacDonald, *The New Shostakovich*, new ed., rev. Raymond Clarke (London: Pimlico, 2006), xvi.

102. Ian MacDonald, *The New Shostakovich*, new ed., xvi.

103. See, for example, Pauline Fairclough, "The Old Shostakovich: Reception in the British Press," *Music and Letters*, 88/2 (2007), 266–298.

104. Ian MacDonald, *The New Shostakovich*, new ed., xvii.

105. Compare Ian MacDonald, *The New Shostakovich*, original ed., 167–72; and Ian MacDonald, *The New Shostakovich*, new ed., 190–4.

106. Ian MacDonald, *The New Shostakovich*, original ed., 127. (Italics original)

107. Maxim Shostakovich, "Six Lectures on the Shostakovich Symphonies," 409.

108. In Wilson, original ed., 426.

109. Volkov, "Universal Messages," 17.

110. Gerard McBurney, "Surviving Stalin," *Index on Censorship* 27 (1998): 57.

111. Fay, *Shostakovich: A Life*, 111.

112. See http://home.clara.net/istrachan/DSCH/ (link not currently active; last accessed June 17, 2007).

113. Elizabeth Wilson, lecture at Manhattan School of Music, September 28, 1998. *An Inter-Disciplinary Symposium on Dmitri Shostakovich* (Manhattan School of Music cassette tape 9899 L5).

114. "Brave Words, Brave Music."

115. Lev Mazel' and V. Tsukkerman, *Analiz musikal'nykh proizvedenii: elementy muzyki i metodika analiza malykh form* (Moscow: Muzyka, 1967), 748, n1. Quoted in Manashir Iakubov, commentary to *New Collected Works* 20 (2003): 125.

116. Beneditsky's unpublished thesis is summarized in *New Collected Works* 20 (2003): 125–9. His examples include a connection between the balletic descending theme in the Symphony's second movement (Fig. 53) and the descending oboe melody in the Prelude to Act 4 of *Carmen*, and a connection between the melodic pattern based on pitch degrees 5-1-2-3 found in the Symphony's first movement (Fig. 14), the introductory theme to the finale, and at Fig. 119 with a similar shape found in Bizet's Seguidilla and parts of the Habanera. Of course, given the prevalence of the 5-1-2-3 pattern in music, including its presence in the "Barbarian Artist" from the *Four Pushkin Romances*, establishing clear lines of influence can be difficult.

117. Manashir Yakubov, "Shostakovich Feature—A Journey into Light," BBC Radio 3, broadcast August 20, 2006. Interview also appears at http://www.bbc.co.uk/radio3/shostakovich/feature.shtml (accessed June 17, 2007). Shostakovich's use of this diminutive can be seen, for example, in a letter dated December 31, 1934 ("Dearest Lyalya!"). DSCH DVD-ROM.

118. *New Collected Works* 20: 126.

Chapter 2

1. Interview with Oksana Dvornichenko. "DSCH: The Life and Works of Dmitri Shostakovich," *Cultural Heritage Series*, vol. 1 (Chandos Multimedia DVD-ROM, CHAN 550011).

2. Letter dated June 15, 1950. DSCH DVD-ROM.

3. Irina Nikolskaya, "Shostakovich Remembered," in *A Shostakovich Casebook*, ed. Malcolm Hamrick Brown (Bloomington: Indiana University, 2004), 161.

4. Interview with Oksana Dvornichenko. DSCH DVD-ROM.

5. Michael Ardov, *Memories of Shostakovich*, trans. Rosanna Kelly and Michael Meylac (London: Short, 2004), 58–9.

6. Interview with Oksana Dvornichenko. DSCH DVD-ROM.

7. Ardov, 63.

8. Elizabeth Wilson, *Shostakovich: A Life Remembered*, original ed. (Princeton: Princeton University Press, 1994), 436.

9. Andrea Olmstead, ed., *Conversations with Roger Sessions* (Boston: Northeastern University Press, 1982), 238–9.

10. Wilson, original ed., 462–3.

11. Nelly Kravetz, "A New Insight into the Tenth Symphony of Dmitry Shostakovich," in *Shostakovich in Context*, ed. Rosamund Bartlett (Oxford: Oxford University Press, 2000), 171.

12. Wilson, original ed., 229.

13. Kravetz, in Bartlett, 173.

14. Wilson, original ed., 165.

15. Letter to Marietta Shaginyan dated April 4, 1941. DSCH DVD-ROM. See also "Marietta Shaginyan—Fifty Letters from Dmitri Shostakovich," *Soviet Literature* 1 (1984): 68–99.

16. Wilson, original ed., 463.

17. Letter dated September 24, 1968. Isaak Glikman, ed., *Story of a Friendship: The Letters of Dmitry Shostakovich to Isaak Glikman, 1941–1975*, trans. Anthony Phillips (Ithaca: Cornell University Press, 2001), 154–5. In his footnote, Glikman notes the starkness of this statement with its, for Shostakovich, rare use of the exclamation mark. Glikman, 301–2, n60.

18. Wilson, original ed., 426.

19. Grigorii Kozintsev, *Sobranie sochinenii v 5 tomakh*, vol. 2 (Leningrad: Isskustvo, 1982), 423. In Wilson, original ed., 370–1.

20. Letter dated August 28, 1950. DSCH DVD-ROM.

21. Interview with Elizabeth Wilson. Wilson, original ed., 9.

22. Letter dated September 6, 1944. Quoted in Wilson, original ed., 196.

23. Maxim Shostakovich, "Six Lectures on the Shostakovich Symphonies," in *Shostakovich Reconsidered*, ed. Allan B. Ho and Dmitry Feofanov (London: Toccata Press, 1998), 411.

24. Glikman diary entry dated February 24, 1975. Glikman, 201.

25. Kozintsev, 430. In Wilson, original ed., 371.

26. Viktor Yuzefovich, "Besedi s masterami ... s Daniilom Shafranom," *Sovetskaia muzyka* (1978, No. 1): 80. In Sofia Moshevich, *Dmitri Shostakovich, Pianist* (Montreal and Kingston: McGill-Queen's University Press, 2004), 86.

27. Wilson, original ed., 454.

28. Interview with David Lloyd Jones, 1964. In Shostakovich Symphony No. 8, Leningrad Philharmonic/Mravinsky. BBC Legends BBCL 4002–2.

29. Wilson, original ed., 407.

30. Gennady Rozhdestvensky. Interview with Oksana Dvornichenko. DSCH DVD-ROM.

31. Wilson, original ed., 190–1.

32. L. Chalova, "Takoi on byl ...," in *Vospominaniia o Mikhaile Zoshchenko*, ed. Iu. Tomashevskii (St. Petersburg: "Khudozh. literature," Sankt-Peterburgskoe otd-nie, 1995), 339. Quoted in Laurel E. Fay, *Shostakovich: A Life* (New York: Oxford University Press, 2000), 110.

33. Glikman, xxviii.

34. Rodion Shchedrin, interview with Oksana Dvornichenko. DSCH DVD-ROM.

Chapter 3

1. Simon Karlinsky, "Our Destinies Are Bad," *The Nation*, November 24, 1979, 535.

2. Laurel E. Fay, "Shostakovich versus Volkov: Whose *Testimony?*" *Russian Review* 39, No. 4 (1980). Reprinted in *A Shostakovich Casebook*, ed. Malcolm Hamrick Brown (Bloomington: Indiana University, 2004), 17.

3. Craig R. Whitney, "Shostakovich Memoir a Shock to Kin," *The New York Times*, November 13, 1979, C7.

4. Irina Shostakovich, "The Dead Are Defenseless?" *DSCH Journal* 14 (2001): 7.

5. Solomon Volkov, *Testimony: The Memoirs of Dmitri Shostakovich*, trans. Antonina W. Bouis (New York: Harper and Row, 1979), xvi–xvii.

6. Ian MacDonald, *The New Shostakovich*, original ed. (Boston: Northeastern University Press, 1990), 264.

7. Elizabeth Wilson, *Shostakovich: A Life Remembered*, original ed. (Princeton: Princeton University Press, 1994).

8. Allan B. Ho and Dmitry Feofanov, "Shostakovich's *Testimony*: Reply to an Unjust Criticism," in *Shostakovich Reconsidered*, ed. Allan B. Ho and Dmitry Feofanov (London: Toccata Press, 1998), 33–311.

9. Ibid., 80.

10. Volkov, *Testimony*, 3.

11. Volkov, *Testimony*, xvii.

12. Solomon Volkov, "Shostakovich Conference," Mannes School of Music, February 15, 1999, http://www.siue.edu/~aho/musov/man/mannes4.html (accessed June 17, 2007).

13. Laurel E. Fay, "Volkov's *Testimony* Reconsidered," in Brown, ed., 29.

14. Ibid., 34–9.

15. Ibid., 39.

16. Ibid., 39–40.

17. Orlov's report appears in Ludmila Kovnatskaya, "An Episode in the Life of a Book," in Brown, ed., 107–16.

18. Allan B. Ho and Dmitry Feofanov, *The "Shostakovich Wars"* (London: Toccata Press, forthcoming).

Chapter 4

1. Letter to Lev Shulgin, no date, but almost certainly early-to-mid-1927. "DSCH: The Life and Works of Dmitri Shostakovich," *Cultural Heritage Series*, vol. 1 (Chandos Multimedia DVD-ROM, CHAN 550011).

2. Elizabeth Wilson, *Shostakovich: A Life Remembered*, original ed. (Princeton: Princeton University Press, 1994), 5.

3. Shostakovich, "Avtobiografiia, 1927" *Sovetskaia muzyka* 9 (1966, No. 9). DSCH DVD-ROM.

4. A few compositions survived the house-cleaning and are scheduled for publication in volumes 54, 55, and 109 of the *New Collected Works*. See http://www.devinci.fr/chostakovitch/BILINGUE/150.htm (accessed June 17, 2007).

5. Victor Seroff (with Nadezhda Galli-Shohat), *Dmitri Shostakovich: The Life and Background of a Soviet Composer* (New York: Knopf, 1943), 72–3.

6. Boris Losskii, "Novoe o Shostakoviche," *Russkaia Mysl'*, no. 3771, April 24, 1989. In Wilson, original ed., 12.

7. Liudmila Mikheeva, *Zhizn' Dmitriia Shostakovicha* (Moscow: Terra, 1997), 20. Quoted in Solomon Volkov, *Shostakovich and Stalin*, trans. Antonina W. Bouis (New York: Knopf, 2004), 51.

8. Losskii. In Wilson, original ed., 19–20.

9. Zoya Shostakovich. In Wilson, original ed., 6.

10. Losskii. In Wilson, original ed., 20.

11. Wilson, original ed., 19.

12. Solomon Volkov, *Testimony: The Memoirs of Dmitri Shostakovich*, trans. Antonina W. Bouis (New York: Harper and Row, 1979), 7 (Italics added).

13. Dmitrii Shostakovich, "Zhisneopisanie," TsGALI, Moscow, F.2048, op. 1, ed. khr. 66. In Wilson, original ed., 11–2.

14. Losskii. In Wilson, original ed., 14–5.

15. Roman Ilich Gruber, "Responses of Shostakovich to a Questionnaire on the Psychology of the Creative Process," trans. Malcolm Hamrick Brown, in *Shostakovich and His World*, ed. Laurel E. Fay (Princeton: Princeton University Press, 2004), 30.

16. Vladimir Mayakovsky, "Order No. 2 to the Armies of Arts," in *The Bedbug and Selected Poetry*, ed. Patricia Blake, trans. Max Hayward and George Reavy (London: Weidenfeld and Nicholson, 1960), 145–9.

17. Vladimir Mayakovsky, "Order to the Armies of Arts," in *Mayakovsky and His Poetry*, rev. ed., comp. Herbert Marshall (London: The Pilot Press, 1945), 44–5.

18. Leo Arnshtam, "Bessmertie," in *Shostakovich: Stat'i i materialy*, ed. G. Shneerson (Moscow: Sovetskii kompozitor, 1976), 105–9. In Wilson, original ed., 22.

19. Letter to Anatoly Lunacharsky dated August 16, 1921, in N.S. Zelov, "Scholarships of the Commissariat of Enlightenment," *Iunost'* (1967, No. 10): 101–2. In Wilson, original ed., 28.

20. Conversation with Maxim Gorky. In Viktor Shklovskii, *Zhili-byli; vospominaniia, memuarnye zapisi, povesti o vremeni: s kontsa xix v po. 1964 g* (Moscow: Sovetskii pisatel', 1966), 164. In DSCH DVD-ROM.

21. Olga Digonskaya, "Unknown Shostakovich Manuscripts" (paper presented at the symposium *Shostakovich 100*, Deptford Town Hall, London, September 27, 2006). Also, private correspondence from Olga Digonskaya to the author dated February 19, 2007.

22. Letter to an unknown correspondent, 1926 (date not given). DSCH DVD-ROM.

23. Michael Ardov, *Memories of Shostakovich*, trans. Rosanna Kelly and Michael Meylac (London: Short Books, 2004), 48.

24. Translation by Joan Pemberton Smith. *Shostakovich—The Orchestral Songs*, vol. 1, Deutsche Grammophon, 439: 860–2.

25. Nicolai Malko, *A Certain Art* (New York: W. Morrow, 1966), 186.

26. Letter to Glivenko dated November 14, 1923. Quoted in Ian MacDonald, "His Misty Youth: The Glivenko Letters and Life in the '20s," in *Shostakovich Reconsidered*, ed. Allan Ho and Dmitry Feofanov (London: Toccata Press, 1998), 540, n20.

27. Letter to Glivenko dated November 29, 1923. Quoted in MacDonald, "His Misty Youth," 536.

28. Letter to his mother dated August 3, 1923. R.S. Sadykhova and D.V. Frederiks, "Shostakovich: Letters to his Mother, 1923–1927," in Fay, ed., *Shostakovich and His World*, 4–5.

29. See MacDonald, "His Misty Youth," 539–40, 545–6. The New Economic Policy (1921–1928) introduced limited free trade into the Soviet economy.

30. Letters to Glivenko dated April 26 and June 3, 1924. Quoted in MacDonald, "His Misty Youth," 547.

31. Letter to Glivenko dated January 2, 1924. Quoted in MacDonald, "His Misty Youth," 546, n36.

32. MacDonald, in Ho and Feofanov, eds., 546.

33. See Chapter 18, footnote 19 for discussion on when exactly Shostakovich began working in the cinema.

34. Letter to his mother dated April 8, 1924. Sadykhova and Frederiks, in "Shostakovich: Letters to His Mother," 9.

35. Letter to his mother dated March 8, 1925. Sadykhova and Frederiks, in "Shostakovich: Letters to His Mother," 11.

36. Letter to Lev Oborin dated April 17, 1925. M. Kozlova, "'Mne ispolnilos' vosemnadtsat' let': Pis'ma D.D. Shostakovicha L.N. Oborinu," in *Vstrechi s proshlym, vyp. 5* (Moscow: Sovetskaia Rossiia, 1984), 247. Quoted in Wilson, original ed., 46.

37. His letter to his mother written the following day puts a rather optimistic spin on events. See Sadykhova and Frederiks, "Shostakovich: Letters to His Mother," 12–3.

38. Letter to Glivenko dated April 8, 1925. Quoted in MacDonald, "His Misty Youth," 549, n40.

39. MacDonald, "His Misty Youth," 548–9.

40. Letter to Lev Oborin. Kozlova, 241. Quoted in Laurel E. Fay, *Shostakovich: A Life* (New York: Oxford University Press, 2000), 26.

41. *Rostropovich—Three Friends*. BBC2 TV, broadcast November 27, 1988. (British Library catalogue number V2694/3).

42. Letter to Boris Yavorsky, November 29, 1925. DSCH DVD-ROM.

43. Wilson, original ed., 47.

44. D. Shostakovich, *Sovetskaia muzyka* (1962, No. 9): 103–4. Quoted in Manashir Iakubov, commentary, *New Collected Works* 1 (2002): 147.

45. Malko, 166.

46. Ibid., 174.

47. Quoted in Sof'ia Khentova, *V mire Shostakovicha* (Moscow: Kompozitor, 1996), 291. In Laurel E. Fay, "Shostakovich, LASM, and Asafiev," in *Shostakovich in Context*, ed. Rosamund Bartlett (Oxford: Oxford University Press, 2000), 58 (Italics original).

48. Interview with Edison Denisov. Wilson, original ed., 303. See also Laurel E. Fay, "Shostakovich, LASM, and Asafiev," 56–66.

Chapter 5

1. See letters to Yavorsky dated July 29 and October 21, 1926. "DSCH: The Life and Works of Dmitri Shostakovich," *Cultural Heritage Series*, vol. 1 (Chandos Multimedia DVD-ROM, CHAN 550011).

2. Ronald Stevenson, "The Piano Music," in *Shostakovich: The Man and His Music*, ed. Christopher Norris (Boston: Marion Boyars, 1982), 89.

3. Sofia Moshevich, *Dmitri Shostakovich, Pianist* (Montreal and Kingston: McGill-Queen's University Press, 2004), 43.

4. David Fanning, "Shostakovich: The Present-Day Master of the C Major Key," *Acta Musicologica* 73 (2001): 119.

5. Letter to Yavorsky dated December 11, 1926. DSCH DVD-ROM.

6. Agitotdel = Propaganda division of the State Music Publishers

7. Fig. 6, b3 and Fig. 7 (first trumpet).

8. Other contemporary works employing this formula include Mikhail Gnesin's *1905–1917, Symphonic Monument* (1925) and Alexander Krein's *Mourning Ode to Lenin* (1926).

9. Letter to Boleslav Yavorsky. See Laurel E. Fay, "Shostakovich, LASM, and Asafiev," in *Shostakovich in Context*, ed. Rosamund Bartlett (Oxford: Oxford University Press, 2000), 52. LASM's top two positions were held by Yugis Karnovich, a student of Rimsky-Korsakov's son-in-law Shteinberg, and Yuliya Veisberg, Rimsky-Korsakov's daughter-in-law. Rimsky-Korsakov's grandson, Andrei, was another founding member.

10. See Neil Edmunds, *The Soviet Proletarian Music Movement* (Bern: Peter Lang, 2000), 105–107.

11. "Oktiabr i novaia muzyka," *Novaia muzyka* 5 (1927). Quoted in Nicholas Slonimsky, "The Changing Style of Soviet Music," *Journal of the American Musicological Society* 3/3 (Autumn 1950): 237.

12. Joseph E. Darby, "Dmitri Shostakovich's Second, Third, and Fourth Symphonies: Problems of Context, Analysis, and Interpretation" (Ph.D. diss., City University of New York, 1999), 45.

13. David Haas, *Leningrad's Modernists: Studies in Composition and Musical Thought, 1917–1932* (New York: Peter Lang, 1998), 193.

14. Maximilian Shteinberg, diary, November 2, 1927, RoRIII, f. 28, yed. khr. 1106. Quoted in Laurel E. Fay, *Shostakovich: A Life* (New York: Oxford University Press, 2000), 44.

15. Letter to Lev Shulgin dated June 6, 1927. DSCH DVD-ROM.

16. Ian MacDonald, "Recent Commentary on Symphonies 1–5," *DSCH Journal* 7 (1997): 9.

17. Proletkult = Proletarian Culture. This movement was active between 1917 and the early 1920s.

18. Katerina Clark describes the "stage" for the 1927 Leningrad spectacle *Ten Years*: "The set designer, Valentina Khodasevich, identified as the 'proscenium' a large stretch of the Neva River between two bridges, while she called the 'main stage' the Peter and Paul Fortress, with the Mint nominated as the 'rear stage' and the Kronkversky Canal functioning as 'wings'. The auditorium, she claimed, was 'the entire population of Leningrad'." Katerina Clark, *Petersburg, Crucible of Cultural Revolution* (Cambridge, MA: Harvard University Press, 1995), 244.

19. Clark, 246–7.

20. See Clark, 225.

21. Richard Taruskin, *Defining Russia Musically* (Princeton: Princeton University Press, 1997), 94.

22. Darby, 59.

23. David Fanning, "Shostakovich," *The New Grove Dictionary of Music and Musicians*, ed. Stanley Sadie and John Tyrrell (London: Macmillan, 2001), xxiii, 288.

24. Haas, 193–4.

25. Iurii Tiulin, "Iunie gody D.D. Shostakovicha," in *Dmitrii Shostakovich*, ed. L. Danilevich (Moscow: Sovetskii kompozitor, 1967), 36–8. In Elizabeth Wilson, *Shostakovich: A Life Remembered*, original ed. (Princeton: Princeton University Press, 1994), 34.

26. Ibid. In Wilson, original ed., 35.

27. Mikhail Druskin, *Ocherki, stat'i, zametki* (Leningrad: Sovetskii kompozitor, 1987), 45–59. In Wilson, original ed., 44.

28. Haas, 179.

29. Druskin. In Wilson, original ed., 44.

30. Nicolai Malko, *A Certain Art* (New York: W. Morrow, 1966), 196–7.

31. Interview with Elizabeth Wilson. In Wilson, original ed., 64.

32. Malko, 187–8.

518 Notes

33. Ivan Sollertinskii, "*Nos*": orudie dal'noboinoe," *Rabochii i teatr* (1930, No. 7): 7. Quoted in Geoffey Norris, "The Operas," in Christopher Norris, ed., 109.

34. Boris Asaf'ev, "O tvorchestve Shostakovicha i ego opere 'Ledi Makbet'," in *Ob opere: Izbrannye stat'i*, 2nd ed. (Leningrad: Muzyka, 1985), 314. Quoted in Caryl Emerson, "Shostakovich and the Russian Literary Tradition," in *Shostakovich and His World*, ed. Laurel E. Fay (Princeton: Princeton University Press, 2004), 186.

35. Letter to Smolich dated June 7, 1929. In Gavriil Iudin, "Vasha rabota dlia menia sobytie na vsiu zhizn'," *Sovetskaia muzyka* (1983, No. 6): 90. Quoted in Fay, *Shostakovich: A Life*, 54.

36. For example, D. Shostakovich, "Pochemu 'Nos'?" the composer's preface to the published libretto, *NOS. Polnyi tekst opery* (Leningrad: Teakinopechat', 1930), 3–4. Quoted in Emerson, "Shostakovich and the Russian Literary Tradition," 191.

37. Grigorii Kozintsev, *Sobranie sochinenii v piati tomakh* (Leningrad: Isskustvo, 1982), vol. 1, 156–7. In Wilson, original ed., 75.

38. Levon Hakobian, "*The Nose* and the Fourteenth Symphony: An Affinity of Opposites," trans. Dimitri Shapovalov, in Fay, ed., *Shostakovich and His World*, 173–4.

39. "Kukryniksy" was an acronym incorporating the names of Mikhail Kupriyanov, Porfiry Krylov, and Nikolai Sokolov.

40. For example, Trial of the Syrtsov-Lominadze Plot (1930), Trial of the Industrial Party (1930), Trial of the Bacteriologists (1930), Trial of the Historians (1931), Trial of the Mensheviks (1931), Trial of Metro-Vickers Spies (1933).

41. *Pravda*, December 4, 1929. Quoted in Boris Schwarz, *Music and Musical Life in Soviet Russia, 1917–1981*, enlarged ed. (Bloomington: Indiana University Press, 1983), 58.

42. See Darby, 86. As Darby points out, most musical activity in Leningrad between 1929 and 1933 was covered not by a dedicated musical journal but by *Rabochii i teatr* (Worker and Theater).

43. Transcript of the discussion of *The Nose*, January 14, 1930, SPgGMTMI, kn. 7755/4143 oru. 5365. In Fay, *Shostakovich: A Life*, 55.

44. S. Gres, "Ruchnaia bomba anarkhista," *Rabochii i teatr* (1930, No. 10). Quoted in Fay, *Shostakovich: A Life*, 55.

45. Letter to Zakhar Lyubimsky dated April 16, 1930. In V. Kislev, "Iz pisem 1930-kh godov," *Sovetskaia muzyka* (1987, No. 9): 89. Quoted in Fay, *Shostakovich: A Life*, 56.

46. Report to Leningrad Conservatory, October 31, 1929. In Manashir Iakubov, "Ia pytalsia peredat' pafos bor'by i pobedy," *Sovetskaia muzyka* (1986, No. 10): 55–6. Quoted in Darby, 29.

47. Darby, 96.

48. Iakubov, 55–6. Quoted in Darby, 30.

49. Clark, 268.

50. Ibid., 271.

51. Letter to Smolich, October 30, 1930, in Gavriil Iudin, "Vasha rabota dlia menia sobytie na vsiu zhizn'," *Sovetskaia muzyka* (1983, No. 6): 91–2. Quoted in Wilson, original ed., 89.

52. Iurii Brodersen, "Legalizatsiia prisposoblenchestva," *Rabochii i teatr* (1930, No. 60–1): 8–9. Quoted in Manashir Yakubov, "*The Golden Age*: The True Story of the Première," in *Shostakovich Studies*, ed. David Fanning (Cambridge: Cambridge University Press, 1995), 200.

53. *Proletarskii muzykant* (1930, No. 3): 25. English translation of the full article appears in Darby, 185–7.

54. See Darby, 184–5.

55. Letter dated February 10, 1930. Lyudmila Mikheyeva-Sollertinskaya, "Shostakovich as Reflected in his Letters to Ivan Sollertinsky," in Bartlett, 73.

56. See Tat'iana Bruni, "O balete s neprekhodiashchei liubov'iu," *Sovetskii balet* 5 (1991): 36. Quoted in Simon Morrison, "Shostakovich as Industrial Saboteur," in Fay, ed. *Shostakovich and his World*, 122.

57. Most sources cite a single performance, including Shostakovich himself in a letter to Sollertinsky dated August 24, 1934. DSCH DVD-ROM. In a 1961 reminiscence, Alexander Gauk recalled a second performance. See Aleksandr Gauk, "Tvorcheskie vstrechi," in *Aleksandr Vasilievich Gauk: Memuary, izbrannie stat'i, vospominaniia sovremmenikov,* ed. L. Gauk, R. Glezer, and Y. Milstein (Moscow: Sovetskii kompozitor, 1975), 128. Quoted in Wilson, original ed., 93.

58. See *Rabochii i teatr* (1931, No. 12): 22. Quoted in Fay, *Shostakovich: A Life,* 62.

59. Letter to Vissarion Shebalin dated October 1931. DSCH DVD-ROM.

60. The closest to a literal translation of the Russian title, *Uslovno ubityi,* is *Conditionally Killed,* though it has been more frequently translated as *Declared Dead* or *Hypothetically Murdered.*

61. Dmitrii Shostakovich, et al., "Bolezni muzykalnoi kritikii," *Rabochii i teatr* (1929, No. 14): 4. Quoted in Darby, 181.

62. Dmitrii Shostakovich, "Deklaratsiia obiazannostei kompozitora," *Rabochii i teatr* (1931, No. 31): 6. The full article is translated in Darby, 190–2.

63. Ibid.

64. Ibid.

65. "Plenum Soveta Vserokomdrama. Fragment stenogrammy, posviashchennyi muzykalnym voprosom," December 18–19, 1931, *Muzykal'naia akademiia* (1993, No. 2): 160–77. Quoted in Darby, 198. English translation of the full article appears in Darby, 197–9.

66. Rose Lee, "Dimitri Szostakovich—Young Russian Composer Tells of Linking Politics with Creative Work," *The New York Times,* December 20, 1931, Section 8, 8.

Chapter 6

1. See A. Kemp-Welch, *Stalin and the Literary Intelligentsia, 1928–39* (New York: St. Martin's Press, 1991), 108–13.

2. See Iurii Keldysh, *100 let Moskovskoi konservatorii, 1866–1966* (Moscow: Muzyka, 1966), 128. Quoted in Neil Edmunds, *The Soviet Proletarian Music Movement* (Bern: Peter Lang, 2000), 106.

3. See Keldysh, 129. Quoted in Edmunds, 107.

4. Central Committee Resolution, "On the Reformation of Literary-Artistic Organizations," April 23, 1932. *Pravda,* April 24, 1932. Quoted in Kemp-Welch, 115.

5. A. Kut, "Kompozitory u tov. A.S. Bubnova: zadachi muzykal'nogo fronta," *Sovetskoe iskusstvo* (April 1932). Quoted in David Haas, *Leningrad's Modernists: Studies in Composition and Musical Thought, 1917–1932* (New York: Peter Lang, 1998), 31.

6. Dmitrii Shostakovich, et al., "Polnotsennymi proizvedeniiami: otvechaem na postanovleni TsK," *Rabochii i teatr* (1932, No. 16): 5–6. In Joseph E. Darby, "Dmitri Shostakovich's Second, Third, and Fourth Symphonies: Problems of Context, Analysis, and Interpretation" (Ph.D. diss., City University of New York, 1999), 204.

7. As Hamlet tells Rosencrantz and Guildenstern that he will not be manipulated, he waves a recorder and asks, "Do you think I am easier to be played on than a pipe? Call me

what instrument you will, though you can fret me, you cannot play upon me" (Act III, Scene 2). In Akimov's production, Hamlet holds the flute to his rear, farting through it the tune of Davidenko's mass song, which Shostakovich scores for piccolo, double bass, and drum.

8. Between five and eight million people perished in the great Ukrainian famine alone. The "Holodomor" (Famine-Genocide) of 1932–1933 was officially explained as the tragic result of having to export most of Ukraine's produce to keep the country afloat. In fact, it was a deliberate act of genocide by Stalin to punish the Ukrainians for their resistance to collectivization.

9. An English translation of Stalin's report, "The Results of the First Five-Year Plan," delivered on January 7, 1933 to the Central Committee can be found at http://www.marx2-mao.com/Stalin/RFFYP33.html (accessed June 17, 2007).

10. *Literaturnaia gazeta*, November 11, 1932. Quoted in Régine Robin, *Socialist Realism: An Impossible Aesthetic*, trans. Catherine Porter (Stanford, CA: Stanford University Press, 1992), 41.

11. A "District" was a term indicating a primarily rural area centered on one town. The designation is frequently dropped (i.e., *Lady Macbeth of Mtsensk*), an error that undermines the opera's specifically rural setting and culture.

12. D. Shostakovich, "Moe ponimanie 'Ledi Makbet'." Program book, *Ledi Makbet Mtsenskogo Uezda. Opera D. Shostakovicha*. Gosudarstvennyi Akademicheskii Malyi Opernyi Teatr (1934), 7. Quoted in "Editor's Note," *Collected Works* 20 (1985): np.

13. D. Shostakovich, "Tragediia-satira," *Sovetskoe iskusstvo*, October 16, 1932. Quoted in "Editor's Note" to *Collected Works* 20: np, note 1.

14. Interview with L. and P. Tur. *Vecherniaia kraznaia gazeta*, February 10, 1934. Quoted in "Editor's Note" to *Collected Works* 20: np, note 1.

15. "The main character of the next opera will be a heroine [Sofia Perovskaya] of the People's Will revolutionary group. Then will come a woman of our century. And finally I will portray our Soviet heroine, a generalised image of the woman of today and tomorrow, combining the characteristics of Larisa Reisner and Zhenya Romanko, the best worker at the concrete plant of the Dnieper Hydropower Project." Interview with L. and P. Tur.

16. D. Shostakovich, "Tragediia-satira."

17. See "Novaia opera Shostakovicha," *Vecherniaia Moskva*, December 21, 1932. Quoted in "Editor's Note" to *Collected Works* 20: np.

18. David Fanning, "Leitmotif in *Lady Macbeth*," in *Shostakovich Studies*, ed. David Fanning (Cambridge: Cambridge University Press, 1995), 145–9.

19. Eckart Kröplin, *Frühe Sowjetische Oper: Schostakowitsch, Prokofjew* (Berlin: Henschelverlag, 1985), 220–1; Bernd Feuchtner, *Dimitri Schostakowitsch: "Und Kunst geknebelt von der groben Macht"* (Kassel: Bärenreiter, 2002): 48–9, 145.

20. For example, Seventh Symphony, first movement "invasion theme"; First Violin Concerto, third movement passacaglia theme; First Cello Concerto, second movement; and Fifteenth Symphony, fourth movement passacaglia theme.

21. Fanning, "Leitmotif in *Lady Macbeth*," 146.

22. Letter to an unknown correspondent dated April 13, 1933. "DSCH: The Life and Works of Dmitri Shostakovich," *Cultural Heritage Series*, vol. 1 (Chandos Multimedia DVD-ROM, CHAN 550011).

23. Letter to Smolich dated February 28, 1934. In Gavriil Iudin, "Vasha rabota dlia menia sobytie na vsiu zhizn'," *Sovetskaia muzyka* (1983, No. 6): 92. Quoted in Elizabeth Wilson, *Shostakovich: A Life Remembered*, original ed. (Princeton: Princeton University Press, 1994), 100, n90.

24. See Chapter 4.

25. Letter to Yelena Konstantinovskaya dated August 9, 1934. DSCH DVD-ROM.

26. Liudmila Mikheeva-Sollertinskaia, "D.D. Shostakovich v otrazhenii pisem k I.I. Sollertinskomu. Shtrikhi k portretu," in *D.D. Shostakovich: sbornik statei k 90-letiiu so dnia rozhdeniia*, comp. Liudmila Kovnatskaia (St. Petersburg: Kompozitor, 1996), 92. Quoted in Laurel E. Fay, *Shostakovich: A Life* (New York: Oxford University Press, 2000), 80.

27. See Chapter 5.

28. He had used it previously in the "Finale" that he had provided in 1929 for Erwin Dressel's opera, *Der Arme Columbus*, in the "Foxtrot" from *The Golden Age*, and in the "Archangel Gabriel" tune from *Declared Dead*. The tune is sometimes misattributed to the not dissimilar Austrian song "Ach, du lieber Augustin."

29. *Sovetskoe iskusstvo*, November 5, 1934. Quoted in "Editor's Note" to *Collected Works* 12 (1982): np.

30. For example, the second movement of Mozart's Piano Concerto No. 20, K. 466, or the fifth movement of the Serenade for Thirteen Wind Instruments, K. 361.

31. D. Shostakovich, "Mysli o muzykal'nom spektakle," *Sovetskoe iskusstvo*, December 5, 1935. Quoted in "Editor's Note" to *Collected Works* 20: np.

32. Solomon Volkov, *Shostakovich and Stalin*, trans. Antonina W. Bouis (New York: Knopf, 2004), 98.

33. *Sovetskaia muzyka* (1933, No. 6). Quoted in Boris Schwarz, *Music and Musical Life in Soviet Russia (Enlarged Edition, 1917–1981)* (Bloomington: Indiana University Press, 1983), 120.

34. A.A. Ostretsov. Quoted in Victor Seroff (with Nadezhda Galli-Shohat), *Dmitri Shostakovich: The Life and Background of a Soviet Composer* (New York: Knopf, 1943), 197.

35. Letter to Ernest Ansermet dated April 4, 1935. Robert Craft, ed., *Stravinsky: Selected Correspondence*, vol. 1 (New York: Knopf, 1982), 224.

36. Olin Downes, "New Soviet Opera Is Presented Here," *The New York Times*, February 6, 1935, 23.

37. *New York Sun*, February 9, 1935.

38. Diary entry dated March 18, 1936, in *Letters from a Life. The Selected Letters and Diaries of Benjamin Britten, 1913–1976*, vol. 1, ed. Donald Mitchell (Berkeley: University of California Press, 1991), 409.

39. Derek C. Hulme, *Dmitri Shostakovich: A Catalogue, Bibliography, and Discography*, 3rd ed. (Lanham, MD: Scarecrow Press, 2002), 132.

40. A clip can be seen in DSCH DVD-ROM.

41. Lyudmila Mikheyeva-Sollertinskaya, "Shostakovich as Reflected in his Letters to Ivan Sollertinsky," in *Shostakovich in Context*, ed. Rosamund Bartlett (Oxford: Oxford University Press, 2000), 73.

42. Ibid., 74.

43. Ian MacDonald, *The New Shostakovich*, original ed. (Boston: Northeastern University Press, 1990), 96.

44. First plenary session of the Organizing Committee, May 19, 1932. Quoted in Robin, 38–9.

45. *Literaturnaia gazeta*, November 11, 1932. Quoted in Robin, 41.

46. Stalin had first aired this slogan in a speech given on October 26, 1932. (Quoted in Kemp-Welch, 131.) Stalin's industrial moniker in turn reflected Lenin's belief that writers were "a cog and a screw of one single great Social-Democratic mechanism." V.I. Lenin,

"Party Organization and Party Literature," in *Marxism and Art: Writings in Aesthetics and Criticism*, comp. Berel Lang and Forrest Williams (New York: McKay, 1972), 55–9.

47. Andrei Zhdanov, "Soviet Literature—the Richest in Ideas, the Most Advanced Literature," in *Problems of Soviet Literature—Reports and Speeches at the First Soviet Writers' Congress*, ed. H.G. Scott (Westport, CT: Greenwood, 1979), 21.

48. Karl Marx and Friedrich Engels, *Literature and Art: Selection from Their Writings* (New York: International, 1947), 44–5.

49. The Stakhanovite "shock-worker" movement began in 1935 to promote competition and record-breaking in industrial production. It was named after the miner, Alexei Stakhanov, who purportedly set a record on August 31, 1935 by mining 102 tonnes of coal in less than six hours, only to break his own record on September 19 with 227 tonnes of coal in one shift. It has since been claimed that Stakhanov had been helped in his feats by other miners, but for publicity value, it was considered more effective to have a single "record breaker."

50. Pauline Fairclough, "Texts and Contexts—Mahler Reconstructed: Sollertinsky and the Soviet Symphony," *The Musical Quarterly* 85 (2001): 375–6.

51. A summary of this study can be found in Eric Roseberry, *Ideology, Style, Content, and Thematic Process in the Symphonies, Cello Concertos, and String Quartets of Shostakovich* (New York: Garland, 1989), 507–20.

52. Fairclough, "Texts and Contexts," 376–80.

53. Nikolai Chelyapov, Opening Speech to Moscow Composers' Union, February 10, 1936. Quoted in Seroff, 211.

54. "Vystuplenie tov. Shostakovicha" ("Diskussiia o sovetskom simfonizme"), *Sovetskaia muzyka* (1935, No. 5): 31–3. In Darby, 380–1.

55. *Izvestiia*, April 3, 1935. Reprinted in Lev Grigoryev and Yakov Platek, *Dmitry Shostakovich: About Himself and His Times*, trans. Angus and Neilian Roxburgh (Moscow: Progress Publishers, 1981), 58.

56. "Vystuplenie tov. Shostakovicha." In Darby, 381–2.

57. "Vystuplenie tov. Shostakovicha." In Darby, 383.

58. D. Shostakovich, "Schast'e poznaniia," *Sovetskoe iskusstvo*, November 5, 1934. DSCH DVD-ROM.

59. Pauline Fairclough, "The 'Perestroyka' of Soviet Symphonism: Shostakovich in 1935," *Music and Letters* 83 (2002): 271.

60. See Kiril Tomoff, *Creative Union—The Professional Organization of Soviet Composers, 1939–1953* (Ithaca: Cornell University Press, 2006), 21.

61. Fairclough, "Perestroyka," 263.

62. Stalin to composer Yury Shaporin. M. Rutman, "Melodiia dlia dvoikh," *Sankt-Peterburgski e Vedomosti*, November 7, 1998, 10. Quoted in Caroline Brooke, "Soviet Musicians and the Great Terror," *Europe-Asia Studies* 54 (2002): 397.

63. The fragments of this symphony appear in Shostakovich, *New Collected Works* 3 (2002).

64. Pauline Fairclough, *A Soviet Credo: Shostakovich's Fourth Symphony* (Aldershot: Ashgate, 2006), xix.

65. Levon Atovm'ian, "Iz vospominanii," *Muzykal'naia akademiia* (1997, No. 4): 71. Quoted in Elizabeth Wilson, *Shostakovich: A Life Remembered*, new ed. (London: Faber and Faber, 2006), 128.

66. See Volkov, *Shostakovich and Stalin*, 101–2.

67. See Sergei Radamsky, "Lady Macbeth Put On for Stalin—but Shostakovich Waited in Vain for a Call," *The Times* [London], November 18, 1963.

68. Recalling the event thirty-five years later, Radamsky states that Shostakovich was not called to take a bow at the end of the opera (Radamsky). However, in a letter to Sollertinsky, Shostakovich states that he had gone out on stage, and that he had only regretted not having taken a bow at the end of the third act too. (Letter dated January 28, 1936. Liudmila Mikheeva, "Istoriia odnoy druzhby," *Sovetskaia muzyka* (1987, No. 9): 79. Quoted in Wilson, original ed., 108—9.)

69. Elizabeth Wilson reports the government delegation leaving after the third act (Wilson, original ed., 109). Radamsky claims they stayed to the end of the opera (Radamsky).

70. Atovm'ian, quoted in Wilson, new ed., 128.

71. "Sumbur vmesto muzyki: ob opere 'Ledi Makbet Mtsenskogo Uezda' D. Shostakovicha," *Pravda,* January 28, 1936, 3. Quoted in Seroff, 204–7.

72. Oleg V. Naumov and Andrei Artizov, *Vlast'i khudozhestvennaia intelligentsia. Dokumenty TsK RKP(b)-VKP(b), VChK-OGPU-NKVD o kul'turnoi politike. 1917–1953 gg.* (Moscow: Mezhdunarodnyi fond "Demokratiia," 1999), 290–5. See Volkov, *Shostakovich and Stalin,* 113.

73. Solomon Volkov, *Testimony: The Memoirs of Dmitri Shostakovich*, trans. Antonina W. Bouis (New York: Harper and Row, 1979), 113–4.

74. For example, Galina Vishnevskaya. *Galina: A Russian Story,* trans. Guy Daniels (San Diego: Harcourt Brace Jovanovich, 1984), 207–10.

75. Janet Hyer, abstract to Leonid Maximenkov, "New Archival Evidence on the Soviet Committee on Arts Affairs, 1936–1938: Stalin's Ministry of Culture" (paper presented at the University of Toronto, September 19, 1996). http://www.utoronto.ca/crees/serap/bull96.htm (link no longer available). See also Leonid Maksimenkov, *Sumbur vmesto muzyki: Stalinskaia kul'turnaia revoliutsiia 1936–1938* (Moscow: Iuridicheskaia kniga, 1997).

76. "Sumbur vmesto muzyki." Quoted in Seroff, 206.

77. Ostretsov. Quoted in Seroff, 120.

78. "Sumbur vmesto muzyki." Quoted in Seroff, 207.

79. Isaak Glikman, *The Story of a Friendship: The Letters of Dmitry Shostakovich to Isaak Glikman, 1941–1975*, trans. Anthony Phillips (Ithaca: Cornell University Press, 2001), 214.

80. Ian MacDonald, "Laurel E. Fay's *Shostakovich: A Life*," part 3, http://www.siue.edu/~aho/musov/fay/fayrev3.html (accessed June 17, 2007).

81. Radamsky.

82. Fay, *Shostakovich: A Life*, 89–90.

83. "Baletnaia fal'sh," *Pravda*, February 6, 1936, 3. Quoted in Seroff, 207–8.

84. RGALI, f. 962, op. 10s, ed. khr. 14, 1. 16. Quoted in Brooke, 406.

85. *Sovetskaia muzyka* (1936, No. 5): 27. German translation appears in Ernst Kuhn and Günter Wolter, eds., *Volksfeind Dmitri Schostakowitsch: Eine Dokumentation der öffentlichen Angriffe gegen den Komponisten in der ehemaligen Sowjetunion* (Berlin: E. Kuhn, 1997), 15.

86. Kuhn and Wolter, eds., 47.

87. Ibid., 43.

88. Radamsky.

89. Kuhn and Wolter, eds., 21.

90. Naumov and Artizov, 290–5. Quoted in Volkov, *Shostakovich and Stalin*, 115.

91. Maksim Gorkii, "Dva pis'ma Stalinu," *Literaturnaia gazeta*, March 10, 1993, 6. Quoted in Fay, *Shostakovich: A Life*, 91.

92. Glikman, 222.

93. Ian MacDonald, "Laurel E. Fay's *Shostakovich: A Life*," part 3.

94. *Sovetskaia muzyka* (1956, No. 9): 9–15. Quoted in Schwarz, 170.

95. Aleksandr Gauk, "Tvorcheskie vstrechi," in *Aleksandr Vasilievich Gauk: Memuary, izbrannie stat'i, vospominaniia sovremmenikov*, ed. L. Gauk, R. Glezer, and Y. Milstein (Moscow: Sovetskii kompozitor, 1975), 223. Quoted in Wilson, original ed., 115.

96. Liudmila Mikheeva, *Zhizn' Dmitriia Shostakovicha* (Moscow: Terra, 1997), 196. Quoted in Fairclough, *A Soviet Credo*, 28.

97. Volkov, *Testimony*, 120. In all probability, the comment "no one would have spared him either" refers to the fact that the conductor of the Bolshoi production of *Lady Macbeth*, Alexander Melik-Pashayev, had also been a target during the subsequent scandal.

98. Mikheeva, *Zhizn' Dmitriia Shostakovicha*. Quoted in Fairclough, *A Soviet Credo*, 28.

99. Glikman, xxiii. Ten years previously, Shostakovich had shared his high opinion of Stiedri (a "fine fellow" and a "splendid" conductor) in a letter to Boleslav Yavorsky dated October 21, 1926.

100. The ninety-four extant bars of this sketch are to be published in *New Collected Works* 115.

101. Tim Souster, "Shostakovich at the Crossroads," *Tempo* 78 (1966): 2.

102. Somewhat idiosyncratically, Ottaway refers to the bassoon theme at Fig. 31 as the third theme, "which is introduced at an early stage in the development." Hugh Ottaway, "Looking Again at Shostakovich 4," *Tempo* 115 (1975): 19–20.

103. Roseberry, 390.

104. Karen Kopp, *Form und Gehalt der Symphonien des Dmitri Schostakowitsch* (Bonn: Verlag für systematische Musikwissenschaft, 1990), 160.

105. Darby, 302.

106. Fairclough, *A Soviet Credo*, 104.

107. Richard Longman, *Expression and Structure: Processes of Integration in the Large-Scale Instrumental Music of Shostakovich* (New York: Garland Publishing, 1989), 11.

108. Bill Thaddeus Stanley, Jr., "The Relationship of Orchestration to Formal Structures in the Non-Programmatic Symphonies of Shostakovich" (Ph.D. diss., Florida State University, 1979), 14.

109. Richard Taruskin, "Shostakovich and Us," in Bartlett, ed., 26.

110. See Chapter 12.

111. Longman, 15.

112. Fairclough, *A Soviet Credo*, 104.

113. Ibid., 74.

114. Marian Koval', "Tvorcheskii put'" D. Shostakovicha," *Sovetskaia muzyka* (1948, No. 3): 39. German translation in Kuhn and Wolter, eds., 166–7.

115. David Fanning and Pauline Fairclough are two commentators to have noted the connection between Shostakovich and Mahler at this point. David Fanning, "Shostakovich: 'The Present-Day Master of the C Major Key'," *Acta musicologica* 73 (2001): 121; Fairclough, *A Soviet Credo*, 218–20.

116. Taruskin, "Shostakovich and Us," 25.

117. Fanning, "Shostakovich: 'The Present-Day Master of the C Major Key'," 124.

118. Ibid., 123.

119. Ibid., 131.

120. Mahler would go on to use this major-minor chord progression as a leitmotif in the Sixth Symphony.

121. Boris Gasparov, *Five Operas and a Symphony—Word and Music in Russian Culture* (New Haven: Yale University Press, 2005), 164–5, 168.

122. Gasparov, 166. See also Valentin Kataev, *Time Forward!* trans. Charles Malamuth (New York: Farrar and Rinehart, 1933), 3.

123. Gasparov, 166.

124. Translation by Joan Pemberton Smith. *Lady Macbeth of Mtsensk*, EMI CDS 7 49955 2, 77.

125. Gasparov, 178.

126. Ibid., 182.

127. Fay, *Shostakovich: A Life*, 96.

128. Lev Atovm'ian, "Iz vospominanii," *Muzykal'naia akademiia* (1997, No. 4): 74. Quoted in Fay, *Shostakovich: A Life*, 306, n34.

129. Mark Aranovskii, "Inakomysliashchii," *Muzykal'naia akademiia* (1997, No. 4): 2–3. See discussion in Chapter 1.

130. See http://www.marxists.org/history/ussr/government/law/1936/moscow-trials/index.htm. Accessed December 10, 2007. Also, Robert Conquest, *The Great Terror: A Reassessment* (New York: Oxford University Press, 1990). Trotsky himself, then exiled in Norway, was convicted *in absentia*. On Stalin's orders, he was assassinated in Mexico City in 1940.

131. Boris Khaikin, *Besedy o dirizhirovanii*, 89. Quoted in Wilson, original ed., 27.

132. Fairclough, "Texts and Contexts," 384.

133. Gerard McBurney, liner note to recording of the orchestral version conducted by Mark Elder, United, CD-88001.

134. Translation by Gerard McBurney. Ibid.

135. Venyamin Basner, interview with Elizabeth Wilson. Wilson, original ed., 123–5.

136. Manashir Iakubov, "The Fifth Symphony. The Story of How It Was Composed and Its First Performances," *New Collected Works* 5 (2004): 170.

137. Hugh Ottaway, *Shostakovich's Symphonies*, BBC Music Guides, No. 39 (London: BBC, 1978), 27–8.

138. Klaus Meyer, appendix to Timothy Jackson, "Dmitry Shostakovich: The Composer as Jew," in *Shostakovich Reconsidered*, ed. Allan B. Ho and Dmitry Feofanov (London: Toccata Press, 1998), 638–40.

139. Jackson, in Ho and Feofanov, eds., 610–11.

140. Ibid., 610.

141. Taruskin, "Public Lies and Unspeakable Truth," 40.

142. For example, Stanley, 26; Joseph Huband, "The First Five Symphonies of Dmitri Shostakovich" (D.A. dissertation, Ball State University, 1984), 44–5.

143. For a comparison between the slow movements of Shostakovich's Fifth Symphony and Bruckner's Seventh, see Michael Mishra, "Soviet Musical Criticism and Shostakovich's Fifth Symphony" (D.A. diss., University of Northern Colorado, 1997), 112–13.

144. Longman, 305.

145. Preston Stedman, *The Symphony* (Englewood Cliffs, NJ: Prentice Hall, 1979), 316.

146. Gerard McBurney, "Hidden Agenda," BBC Radio 3, broadcast February 26, 1993.

147. David Rabinovich, *Dmitry Shostakovich—Composer*, trans. George Hanna (London: Lawrence & Wishart, 1959), 49.

148. *Shostakovich Symphonies 5 and 9.* New York Philharmonic Orchestra, cond. Leonard Bernstein (1959). Sony Classical 61841. *Shostakovich Symphonies 5 and 9.* Russian National Orchestra, cond. Yakov Kreizberg (2007). Pentatone 5186 096.

149. The Fifth Symphony has been published six times in Russia: 1939, 1947, 1956, 1961, 1980, and 2004 (with a piano four-hand version in 2003). The 1939 score, along with its many Western derivatives (e.g., Kalmus miniature (No. 165), Kalmus/Bellwin Mills octavo (No. K00165), Boosey and Hawkes (American edition, No. 575), Edition Musicus (No. 16313), and Dover), gives the faster tempo of quarter = 188. This was corrected to the slower tempo (eighth = 184) in both the 1947 and 1956 editions and their derivatives: the Leeds Music score (dated, surely incorrectly, as 1945), the dateless Kalmus full score, and the 1967 Eulenburg edition (No. 579). The 1961 edition reinstated the original faster marking, a mistake that was carried over into the 1980 Muzyka *Collected Works* score. The 2004 DSCH *New Collected Works* score gives the corrected slower marking. Incidentally, the standard mechanical metronome does not have a setting for 188; 184 and 192 are the only available choices here. See also Manashir Iakubov, "Comments, Shostakovich Symphony No. 5," *New Collected Works* (2004): 173–4.

150. Sir Charles Mackerras, "Slow Shostakovich," letter to *Classic CD*, November 1995, 14.

151. Maxim Shostakovich, "Six Lectures on the Shostakovich Symphonies," ed. John-Michael Albert. In Ho and Feofanov, eds., 410.

152. Letter dated July 19, 1960. In Sof'ia Khentova, *V mire Shostakovicha*, 321. Quoted in Fay, *Shostakovich: A Life*, 309, n83.

153. Stedman, 315.

154. O.P. Lamm, *Pages from Myaskovsky's Diary*, Moscow, 1989, 265. Quoted in Manashir Iakubov, "Shostakovich's Fifth Symphony. Assessment by the Composer and His Critics," *New Collected Works* 20 (2003): 125.

155. Some performances, such as Leonard Bernstein (1959) or Leonard Slatkin, replace this final cymbal crash with a suspended cymbal roll through the entire bar, a gesture that falsifies the effect at the very end, replacing Shostakovich's dull "thud" with a spurious splash of sound. (Shostakovich was generally clear when he wanted the suspended cymbal, usually notating the part as a roll and including the instruction "colla bacchetta di Timpani.")

156. Barsova cites connections with Strauss' *Till Eulenspiegel* and Berlioz' *Symphonie fantastique*, and the Last Judgment in Mahler's Second Symphony. Inna Barsova, "Between 'Social Demands' and the 'Music of Grand Passions'—The Years 1934–37 in the Life of Dmitry Shostakovich," in Bartlett, ed., 86–91.

157. Ibid., 91, 94.

158. Maxim Shostakovich, "Six Lectures on the Shostakovich Symphonies," 409.

159. Quoted in Wilson, new ed., 152.

160. "Vpechatleniia slushatelei," *Muzyka*, November 26, 1937. Quoted in Taruskin, "Public Lies and Unspeakable Truth," 27.

161. Gauk, 129. Quoted in Wilson, original ed., 134, n39.

162. Shostakovich's contempt for these two officials can be witnessed in his satire *Rayok*, in which both their names were altered so as to give them scatological overtones.

163. Mikhail Chulaki, "Segodnia ia rasskazhu o Shostakoviche," *Zvezda* (1987, No. 7): 190–2. Quoted in Wilson, original ed., 135.

164. Aleksei Tolstoi, "Piataia simfoniia Shostakovicha," *Izvestiia*, December 28, 1937, 5. Quoted in Taruskin, "Public Lies and Unspeakable Truth," 32.

165. D.D. Shostakovich, "Moi tvorcheskii otvet," *Vecherniaia Moskva*, January 25, 1938, 30. Quoted in Richard Taruskin, "Public Lies and Unspeakable Truth," 33.

166. Ibid., 33–4, n28.

167. Henry Orlov, "A Link in the Chain," in *A Shostakovich Casebook*, ed. Malcolm Hamrick Brown (Bloomington: Indiana University Press, 2004), 195.

168. Volkov, *Shostakovich and Stalin*, 154.

169. Taruskin, "Public Lies and Unspeakable Truth," 24.

170. Ian MacDonald, "Naïve Anti-Revisionism," in Ho and Feofanov, eds., 674, 677.

171. Georgii Khubov, "Piataia simfoniia D. Shostakovicha," *Sovetskaia muzyka* (1938, No. 3): 14. Translated for this volume by Tatyana Buzina.

172. Ibid., 27.

Chapter 7

1. Isaak Glikman, *The Story of a Friendship: The Letters of Dmitry Shostakovich to Isaak Glikman, 1941–1975*, trans. Anthony Phillips (Ithaca: Cornell University Press, 2001), xxvi.

2. Laurel E. Fay, *Shostakovich: A Life* (New York: Oxford University Press, 2000), 107–8.

3. *The Vyborg District, The Friends, The Great Citizen (Part 1)*, and *The Man with a Gun*.

4. The three-movement Second Suite for Jazz Orchestra was composed in 1938 for the new USSR State Jazz Band. The score has since been lost. However, following the discovery of piano sketches during the 1990s, Gerard McBurney made a reconstruction and orchestration that was premiered in 2000 (BBC Symphony Orchestra/Andrew Davis). Confusingly, however, an eight-movement Suite for Variety Stage Orchestra, containing arrangements by an unknown hand of Shostakovich film score excerpts, has also appeared under the title of Second Suite for Jazz Orchestra. This misattributed work was premiered in 1988 (London Symphony Orchestra/Mstislav Rostropovich) and received its first recording in 1991 (Concertgebouw Orchestra/Riccardo Chailly). See Derek C. Hulme, *Dmitri Shostakovich: A Catalogue, Bibliography, and Discography*, 3rd ed. (Lanham, MD: Scarecrow Press, 2002), 181–3.

5. Dmitri Shostakovich, "My Current Works," *Rabochi'i i teatr* (1937, No. 111). Translation in "DSCH: The Life and Works of Dmitri Shostakovich," *Cultural Heritage Series*, vol. 1 (Chandos Multimedia DVD-ROM, CHAN 550011).

6. Solomon Volkov, *Testimony: The Memoirs of Dmitri Shostakovich*, trans. Antonina W. Bouis (New York: Harper and Row, 1979), 257.

7. "Program in Music, True and False," *Sovetskaia muzyka* (1951, No. 5): 77. Quoted in Shostakovich, *Collected Works* 35 (1979): "Editor's Note," np.

8. Glenn Gould, "Music in the Soviet Union," in *The Glenn Gould Reader*, ed. Tim Page (New York: Knopf, 1984), 177.

9. "Dmitry Shostakovich's New Works," *Leningradskaia pravda*, August 28, 1939. Quoted in Shostakovich, *Collected Works* 3 (1980): "Editor's Note," np.

10. For example, the end of the slow introduction to Beethoven's Fourth Symphony, where, following what sounds like a half-cadence in the key of D minor (A, C-sharp, E), the A alone is held while F is suddenly inserted a third underneath to form part of the V7 chord (F, A, C, E-flat) in the real key of B-flat.

11. Richard Taruskin, "Shostakovich and Us," in *Shostakovich in Context*, ed. Rosamund Bartlett (Oxford: Oxford University Press, 2000), 18.

12. "The Soviet People Will Not Forgive or Forget the Bloody Crimes of the Band of Fascist Killers, Spies and Wreckers," *Ogonek* 623 (March 2, 1938), http://www.cyberussr.com/rus/ogon380302-e.html (accessed June 17, 2007).

13. "Report of Court Proceedings in the Case of the Anti-Soviet 'Bloc of Rights and Trotskyites' heard before the Military Collegium of the Supreme Court of the USSR,

Moscow, March 2–13, 1938" (Moscow: People's Commissariat of Justice of the USSR, 1938), http://art-bin.com/art/obukharin.html (accessed June 17, 2007).

14. Fay, *Shostakovich: A Life*, 119.

15. "Marietta Shaginyan—Fifty Letters from Dmitri Shostakovich," *Soviet Literature* 1 (1984): 72. Also Hulme, 562.

16. Fay, *Shostakovich: A Life*, 119.

17. Ian MacDonald, *The New Shostakovich*, original ed. (Boston: Northeastern University Press, 1990), 135.

18. In a letter to his friend Levon Atovmyan, dated 20 November, Shostakovich anticipates the first performance "tomorrow" under Mravinsky's baton (DSCH DVD-ROM). However, the date of the premiere has sometimes been given as 5 November, e.g., by Isaak Glikman (in Glikman, xxxii; reproduced in Elizabeth Wilson, *Shostakovich: A Life Remembered*, original ed., (Princeton: Princeton University Press, 1994), 130; and new ed. (London: Faber and Faber, 2006), 164 and by Ian MacDonald (MacDonald, original ed., 292), though Raymond Clarke makes the correction ("Premiered two years to the day after the Fifth [Symphony]") in his posthumous revision of MacDonald (Ian MacDonald, *The New Shostakovich*, new ed., rev. Raymond Clarke [London: Pimlico, 2006], 168). Both Roy Blokker and Robert Dearling mistake the 3 December Moscow premiere for the world premiere. (Roy Blokker [with Robert Dearling], *The Music of Dmitri Shostakovich—The Symphonies* [London: The Tantivy Press, 1979], 75; Robert Dearling, "The First Twelve Symphonies: Portrait of the Artist as a Citizen–Composer," in *Shostakovich: The Man and His Music*, ed. Christopher Norris [Boston: Marion Boyars, 1982], 61.)

19. Henry Orlov, "A Link in the Chain: Reflections on Shostakovich and His Times," in *A Shostakovich Casebook*, ed. Malcolm Hamrick Brown (Bloomington, Indiana University Press, 2004), 202.

20. For example, Handel's *Messiah* ("And with His Stripes"), Mozart's *Requiem* ("Kyrie"), or the Adagio and Fugue in C minor, K. 546.

21. Ian MacDonald, *The New Shostakovich*, original ed., 141–2.

22. Ibid., 145.

23. Ibid., 142–3.

24. Ibid., 146.

25. David Fanning, "Shostakovich," in *The New Grove Dictionary of Music and Musicians*, ed. Stanley Sadie and John Tyrrell (London: Macmillan, 2001), xxiii, 295.

26. Blokker, 75.

27. Dearling, "The First Twelve Symphonies," 62.

28. Ibid., 63.

29. Iu. Fedosiuk, "Zhivu v serdtsakh vsekh liubiashchikh ...," *Sovetskaia muzyka* (1991, No. 9): 34. In Fay, *Shostakovich: A Life*, 120.

30. For further details, see Victor Dvortsov, "Rediscovered: a Forgotten Composition by Shostakovich—Suite on Finnish Themes (1939)," *DSCH Journal* 15 (2001): 6–8.

31. Glikman, xxxiii.

32. Moisei Grinberg, "Proizvedenie Shostakovich—gluboko zapadnoi orientatsii," *Staraia ploshchad': vestnik* 5 (1995): 156. In Fay, *Shostakovich: A Life*, 117.

33. Sof'ia Khentova, *Dmitrii Shostakovich v gody Velikoi Otechestvennoi voiny* (Leningrad: Muzyka, 1979), 51–52. Quoted in Sofia Moshevich, *Dmitri Shostakovich—Pianist* (Montreal: McGill-Queen's University Press, 2004), 100.

34. See Fay, *Shostakovich: A Life*, 126–7.

35. See Glikman, 3–5.

36. Interview in *The War Symphonies: Shostakovich against Stalin* (1997), dir. Larry Weinstein. DVD released by Philips (2005).

37. Extended transcript of "Shostakovich Feature—A Journey into Light," BBC Radio 3, broadcast August 20, 2006, http://www.bbc.co.uk/radio3/shostakovich/feature.shtml (accessed June 17, 2007).

38. See Fay, *Shostakovich: A Life*, 133.

39. "Shostakovich feature—A Journey into Light."

40. *Time*, July 20, 1942.

41. Harvey Sachs, *Toscanini* (Philadelphia: J.P. Lippincott, 1978), 279.

42. Letter dated June 29, 1942 from Bruno Girato to David Grunes. New York Philharmonic Orchestra Archive, Box 011-11-01-05, file 17.

43. Letter dated July 1, 1942 from David Grunes to Bruno Girato. New York Philharmonic Orchestra Archive, Box 011-11-01-05, file 17.

44. See Christopher H. Gibbs, "'The Phenomenon of the Seventh': A Documentary Essay on Shostakovich's 'War' Symphony," in *Shostakovich and His World*, ed. Laurel E. Fay (Princeton: Princeton University Press, 2004), 64.

45. George R. Marek, *Toscanini* (London: Vision, 1975), 234.

46. *New York Herald Tribune*, October 15, 1942.

47. Ernest Newman, "The New Shostakovich," *The Sunday Times* [London], June 28, 1942, 2. I am grateful to Constance Dee for pointing me to this reference.

48. Ernest Newman, "The 'Leningrad' Again," *The Sunday Times* [London], January 30, 1944, 2.

49. D. Shostakovich, "V dni oborony Leningrada," *Sovetskoe iskusstvo*, October 9, 1941, 3. Quoted in "Editor's Note" to *Collected Works* 4 (1981): np.

50. Shostakovich's only previous sonata form movements in a major key were the outer movements of the First Quartet, where mediant rather than dominant relationships apply. Even in minor key works, the classical "relative major" relationship was also a rarity, for example, the First Symphony, first movement.

51. D. Shostakovich, "V dni oborony Leningrada."

52. Volkov, *Testimony*, 156.

53. In Wilson, original ed., 159.

54. David Hurwitz, *Shostakovich Symphonies and Concertos—An Owner's Manual* (Pompton Plains, NJ: Amadeus Press, 2006), 86.

55. Glikman, xxxiv.

56. In Wilson, original ed., 148.

57. Irina Nikolskaya [Nikolska], "Shostakovich Remembered," in Brown, ed., 159.

58. Timothy Jackson, "Dmitry Shostakovich: The Composer as Jew," in *Shostakovich Reconsidered*, ed. Allan B. Ho and Dmitry Feofanov (London: Toccata Press, 1998), 617–9.

59. Ian MacDonald, *The New Shostakovich*, original ed., 160.

60. Liudmila Mikheeva and Alla Kenigsberg, *111 simfonii: spravochnik-putevoditel'* (St. Petersburg: Kul't Inform Press, 2000), 618. In Solomon Volkov, *Shostakovich and Stalin* (New York: Knopf, 2004), 171.

61. O. Gladkova, *Galina Ustvol'skaia—muzyka kak navazhdenie* (St. Petersburg: Muzyka, 1999), 31. In Volkov, *Shostakovich and Stalin*, 170.

62. *Novyi mir* (1990, No. 3): 267. In Volkov, *Shostakovich and Stalin*, 172.

63. D. Shostakovich, "V dni oborony Leningrada."

64. Ibid.

65. Here, the "dominant" scale of C-sharp minor (G-sharp, A, B-sharp, C-sharp, D-sharp, E, F-sharp) corresponds exactly to the scale of G-sharp *freygish*.

66. Volkov, *Testimony*, 184.

67. Taruskin, "Shostakovich and Us," 18.

68. In the Fourth Symphony, the funeral march that comprises the slow introduction to the finale subsequently returns in the coda. Technically, of course, this is not inter-movement cyclism. However, the effect of that long slow introduction is almost that of a separate movement. When the funeral march returns towards the end, it certainly feels as if an entirely new movement has passed in the interim.

69. The following lists the standard Western modes in ascending order of "brightness." Each mode contains one note raised from the previously listed mode: Locrian (m2, m3, P4, D5, m6, m7); Phrygian (m2, m3, P4, P5, m6, m7); minor/Aeolian (M2, m3, P4, P5, m6, m7); Dorian (M2, m3, P4, P5, M6, m7); Mixolydian (M2, M3, P4, P5, M6, m7); major/Ionian (M2, M3, P4, P5, M6, M7); Lydian (M2, M3, A4, P5, M6, M7). M = major, m = minor, P = perfect, D = diminished, A = augmented.

70. Rendered in their Russian translations "The Wood, the Weed, the Wag" (trans. Boris Pasternak) and "MacPherson before His Execution" (trans. Samuil Marshak), respectively.

71. The writer Dipak Nandy recalls Pasternak's own recording: "His deep voice nearly cracked when he came to the line, 'And art made tongue-tied by authority.' There was no scope for delight in the sound or texture of the original, but every word was freighted with a burden of personal meaning." Letter to the *London Review of Books* 20/4 (February 19, 1998).

72. Marina Frolova-Walker, "Shostakovich's Songs: Meanings Lost and Found." Paper given at the Symposium Shostakovich Song-Cycles: A New Appreciation, London, Pushkin House, September 29, 2007.

73. Note to CD *Shostakovich—The Orchestral Songs, vol. 1*. Deutsche Grammophon 439 860–2

74. Discussion at the Plenary Session of the Organizing Committee of the Soviet Composers' Union, April 1944. In Manashir Yakubov, "Inside the Second Piano Sonata," trans. Sofia and Avital Moshevich, *DSCH Journal* 14 (2001): 60.

75. Letter to Isaak Glikman dated December 8, 1943. Glikman, 22.

76. For example, Ian MacDonald, *The New Shostakovich*, original ed., 169–70. Later, MacDonald would tone down his criticisms. See Ian MacDonald, *The New Shostakovich*, new ed., 192–3.

77. David Fanning, *The Breath of the Symphonist: Shostakovich's Tenth* (London: Royal Musical Association, 1989), 36.

78. See ibid., 36–7.

79. See Ellon D. Carpenter, "Russian Theorists on Modality in Shostakovich's Music," in *Shostakovich Studies*, ed. David Fanning (Cambridge: Cambridge University Press, 1995), 91.

80. Hurwitz, 103.

81. Ibid., 104.

82. Dearling, "The First Twelve Symphonies," 69.

83. See Kiril Tomoff, *Creative Union—The Professional Organization of Soviet Composers, 1939–1953* (Ithaca: Cornell University Press, 2006), 78.

84. According to Khachaturian, there were "around 500 anthems" submitted, including his and Shostakovich's individual efforts as well as their combined venture (Sof'ia Khentova, "Shostakovich i Khachaturian: ikh sblizil 48-y god," *Muzykal'naia zhizn'* (1988, No. 24): 11. In Wilson, original ed., 179). Kiril Tomoff cites 165 composers (Tomoff, 77), while Laurel Fay puts it at "nearly 200 competitors" and reports that Shostakovich submitted two

anthems of his own (one using a text of Yevgeny Dolmatovsky and one using "a variant" of what would turn out to be the winning text, set to Alexandrov's music, by Sergei Mikhailov and G. El-Registan) in addition to the joint entry (Fay, *Shostakovich: A Life*, 139). Khachaturian goes on to relate how he and Shostakovich broke a match to decide who should orchestrate their joint effort. As the loser, Khachaturian was charged with this task (Wilson, original ed., 180). According to *Testimony*, however, Shostakovich was the loser, Khachaturian having correctly guessed in which hand Shostakovich held the matchstick (Volkov, *Testimony*, 259).

85. Khentova. In Wilson, original ed., 180.

86. See Leonid Maximenkov, "Stalin and Shostakovich: Letters to a 'Friend'," in Fay, ed., *Shostakovich and His World*, 51.

87. Patrick McCreless rightly points out that at the end of this second passage, just before Fig. 16, the strings and the piano left-hand fudge the otherwise strong B-flat cadence in the right hand, though one might disagree with his assertion that this creates a "simultaneous E-flat cadence," obscuring the B-flat tonicization. Patrick McCreless, "The Cycle of Structure and the Cycle of Meaning: the Piano Trio in E minor, op. 67," in Fanning, ed., 132.

88. Fay, *Shostakovich: A Life*, 143.

89. A slightly different, though equally valid, labeling comes from Patrick McCreless, who views what I have termed the two "A" themes as "A" and "B" and what I have described as the two "B" themes as a single theme "C." McCreless, in Fanning, ed., 121.

90. Solomon Volkov, "Dmitri Shostakovich's 'Jewish Motif': A Creative Enigma," in *Dmitri Schostakowitsch und das jüdische musikalische Erbe*, ed. Dethlef Arnemann, et al. (Berlin: Kuhn, 2001), 5.

91. Timothy L. Jackson, "Dmitry Shostakovich: The Composer as Jew," in Ho and Feofanov, eds., 597–640.

92. Marina Ritzarev, "When Did Shostakovich Stop Using Jewish Idiom?" in Arnemann, ed., 130.

93. Esti Sheinberg, "Shostakovich's 'Jewish Music' as an Existential Statement," in Arnemann, ed., 90–101.

94. RTsKhIDNI, f. 17, op. 125, d. 123, l. 21–23. See Gennadi Kostyrchenko, *Out of the Red Shadows: Anti-Semitism in Stalin's Russia*, trans. H.T. Willetts (Amherst, NY: Prometheus Books, 1995), 15–17.

95. Judy Kuhn, "Looking Again at the Jewish Inflections in Shostakovich's String Quartets," in Arnemann, ed., 192.

96. Ritzarev, "When Did Shostakovich Stop Using Jewish Idiom?" 122.

97. Alan George, note to CD *Shostakovich Quartets 2, 5, and 7*. Olympia OCD 532, p. 4.

98. Richard Longman, mistakenly I believe, describes this as a false recapitulation. In his view, the recapitulation is of the "reverse order" type, starting with the reprise of the second subject at Fig. 26 and proceeding to the first subject, doubling as coda, at Fig. 28. Richard M. Longman, *Expression and Structure: Processes of Integration in the Large-Scale Instrumental Music of Dmitri Shostakovich* (New York: Garland, 1989), 60.

99. Fay, *Shostakovich: A Life*, 140.

100. *Sovetskoe iskusstvo*, November 7, 1944. Reprinted in Lev Grigoryev and Yakov Platek, *Dmitry Shostakovich: About Himself and His Times*, trans. Angus and Neilian Roxburgh (Moscow: Progress Publishers, 1981), 111.

101. David Rabinovich, *Dmitry Shostakovich—Composer*, trans. George Hanna (London: Lawrence and Wishart, 1959), 97.

102. Glikman, 242, n184.

103. Ibid.

104. Volkov, *Testimony*, 141.

105. In Wilson, original ed., 178. (Orlov's first name is here mistakenly given as Georgi.)

106. Olga Digonskaya, "Unknown Shostakovich Manuscripts" (paper presented at the symposium *Shostakovich 100*, Deptford Town Hall, London, September 27, 2006).

107. See Fay, *Shostakovich: A Life*, 147.

108. Memo dated April 19, 1946. DSCH DVD-ROM.

109. See, for example, the end of the slow introduction of Haydn's Symphony No. 92 ("Oxford"), where to the ear, at least, a dominant seventh chord in the "wrong" key turns out, with a couple of bars hindsight, to be a German sixth chord in the "right" key.

110. Sir Charles Mackerras recalls being coached by Shostakovich specifically on this point in Edinburgh in 1962. According to Mackerras' biographer, Nancy Phelan, Shostakovich "emphasized particularly that the slow movement should be played slightly rubato and not quite as originally written, but although Charles carried out the instructions so faithfully that Shostakovich was pleased, one critic complained that the slow movement had been played at the wrong tempo." Nancy Creagh Phelan, *Charles Mackerras: A Musician's Musician* (London: Victor Gollancz, 1987), 132.

111. See Judy Kuhn, "Looking Again at the Jewish Inflections in Shostakovich's String Quartets," 191–5.

112. Letter to Edison Denisov dated April 22, 1950. DSCH DVD-ROM.

113. Longman, 61; Christopher Rowland, "Interpreting the String Quartets," 20.

114. Eric Roseberry, *Ideology, Style, Content, and Thematic Process in the Symphonies, Cello Concertos, and String Quartets of Shostakovich* (New York: Garland, 1979), 264.

115. In a case of mistaking a dominant for a tonic, Richard Longman gives C major as the recapitulation's starting key. Longman, *Expression and Structure*, 62.

116. Ibid., 63.

117. Ibid.

118. Printed in *Kul'tura i zhizn'*, August 20, 1946. Translation at http://www.cyberussr.com/rus/zvezda-e.html (accessed June 17, 2007).

119. In Wilson, original ed., 201.

120. See Fay, *Shostakovich: A Life*, 151–2.

121. A report filed by Shostakovich twenty years later, when he was serving as Deputy for the city of Gorky, gives an idea of the work involved. In the period 1966–1968, he had dealt with 105 letters about housing, twenty letters from prisoners requesting pardons, and fifty dealing with miscellaneous social and domestic issues. Report dated November 2, 1968. In DSCH DVD-ROM.

122. *Poem of the Motherland* was recorded and broadcast, although sources disagree on whether it was actually performed live. See Fay, *Shostakovich: A Life*, 154. Derek Hulme gives the live premiere as 1956. Hulme, 262–3.

123. Tomoff, 131–2.

Chapter 8

1. The meeting convened Saturday 10, Monday 12, and Tuesday 13 January.

2. Alexander Werth, *Musical Uproar in Moscow* (London: Turnstile, 1949), 47. Werth provides an English translation of much, although not all, of the conference transcript that was published in March 1948. The transcript itself appears to have been retroactively

doctored in parts to reflect more closely the Resolution published in February. See Laurel E. Fay, *Shostakovich: A Life* (New York: Oxford University Press, 2000), 156.

3. Werth, 82.

4. By 1948, Shostakovich had received Stalin Prizes for his Piano Quintet and Seventh Symphony (both First Class), and the Second Piano Trio (Second Class). Several films for which he had composed scores had also received Stalin Prizes. For details of the dacha and the 60,000 ruble award, see letter from Shostakovich to Stalin dated May 27, 1946. Quoted in Leonid Maximenkov, "Stalin and Shostakovich: Letters to a 'Friend'," in *Shostakovich and his World*, ed. Laurel Fay (Princeton: Princeton University Press, 2004), 43.

5. Werth, 50.

6. Ibid., 83.

7. Ibid., 58.

8. Ibid., 85.

9. Kiril Tomoff, *Creative Union—The Professional Organization of Soviet Composers, 1939–1953* (Ithaca: Cornell University Press, 2006), 103–106.

10. Werth, 54–5.

11. Ibid., 62, 68.

12. Resolution of the Central Committee of the All-Union Communist Party (Bolsheviks), "On V. Muradeli's Opera, *The Great Friendship*," February 10, 1948. Jonathan Walker and Marina Frolova-Walker, "Newly Translated Source Documents" (presented at the symposium *Music and Dictatorship: Russia under Stalin*, New York, February 2003), 11–12.

13. Glavrepertkom, Order No. 17, February 14, 1948. The complete list of banned works appears in *Dmitri Schostakowitsch und das jüdische musikalische Erbe*, ed. Dethlef Arnemann, et al. (Berlin: Kuhn, 2001), 344–7.

14. See Maximenkov, "Stalin and Shostakovich," 51–3.

15. In a 2006 interview, the 93-year-old Khrennikov admitted that he had enjoyed and was flattered by the power that Stalin had given him: "My word was law. People knew I was appointed personally by Stalin and they were afraid that … I would go and tell Stalin about them. I was Stalin's Commissar. When I said No! (he shouts), it meant No." Yet, in the same interview, Khrennikov claims that he too was a pawn in the system—"They made me do it"—and that both Shostakovich and Prokofiev understood this: "I did everything I could to help them financially while they were banned and repressed … and they were grateful to me." Interview with Martin Sixsmith, *The Guardian*, July 15, 2006. Also online at http://books.guardian.co.uk/review/story/0,,1819763,00.html (accessed June 17, 2007). Similar sentiments are expressed in a 1998 interview. See Marcus Warren, "Soviet Music's Apparatchik," *Sunday Telegraph*, December 27, 1998, Review, 7.

16. Jeremy Eichler, "The Denouncer—A meeting with Stalin's music man, who outlived them all," *The Boston Globe*, September 2, 2007.

17. Kiril Tomoff, *Creative Union—The Professional Organization of Soviet Composers, 1939–1953* (Ithaca: Cornell University Press, 2006), 280.

18. See ibid., 170–5.

19. Transcript of the April 1948 conference. A German translation of excerpts appears in Ernst Kuhn and Günter Wolter, ed., *Volksfeind Dmitri Schostakowitsch: Eine Dokumentation der öffentlichen Angriffe gegen den Komponisten in der ehemaligen Sowjetunion* (Berlin: E. Kuhn, 1997), 121–3.

20. Ibid., 124.

21. Werth, 88.

22. Ibid., 102–3.

23. Perhaps the most notorious case was German Zhukovsky's opera *From All One's Heart,* which only weeks after receiving a Stalin Prize was suddenly withdrawn, along with the prize, after *Pravda* attacked its "weak and colorless" score and its "false" libretto. *Pravda,* April 19, 1951. Quoted in Boris Schwarz, *Music and Musical Life in Soviet Russia (Enlarged Edition, 1917–1981)* (Bloomington: Indiana University Press, 1983), 264. The opera was eventually rehabilitated in the 1958 Resolution, "On Rectifying Errors in the Evaluation of the Operas *Great Friendship, Bogdan Khmelnitsky,* and *From All One's Heart.*"

24. Marian Koval', "Tvorcheskii put' D. Shostakovicha," *Sovetskaia muzyka* (1948, No. 2): 47–61; (1948, No. 3): 31–43; (1948, No. 4): 8–19. A German translation can be found in Kuhn and Wolter, eds., 126–93.

25. Michael Ardov, *Memories of Shostakovich,* trans. Rosanna Kelly and Michael Meylac (London: Short, 2004), 68.

26. *Sovetskaia muzyka* (1948, No. 1): 79. Walker and Frolova-Walker, 17–9.

27. Elizabeth Wilson, *Shostakovich: A Life Remembered,* original ed. (Princeton: Princeton University Press, 1994), 294–5.

28. For an explanation of the puns, see Manashir Yakubov, "Shostakovich's Anti-Formalist Rayok—A History of the Work's Composition and its Musical and Literary Sources," in *Shostakovich in Context,* ed. Rosamund Bartlett (Oxford: Oxford University Press, 2000), 135–57.

29. Ibid., 136–41.

30. Lev Lebedinsky, "The Origin of Shostakovich's 'Rayok'," *Tempo* 173 (1990): 31–2.

31. Elizabeth Wilson, "Understanding Shostakovich Today" (address to the symposium *Shostakovich 100,* Queen Elizabeth Hall, London, September 25, 2006).

32. Shostakovich conversation with Viktor Liberman, concertmaster of the Leningrad Philharmonic. In Vladimir Spivakov, "The Voice of All Voiceless," *DSCH Journal* 24 (2006): 8.

33. I.M. Dobrushin and A.D. Iuditskii, eds., *Evreiskie narodnye pesni* (Moscow: Gos. izd-vo khudozh. literatury, 1947).

34. The date for the orchestration of *From Jewish Folk Poetry* is often given, erroneously, as 1963 or 1964. It is probable that these dates apply only to the orchestrations of the final three songs in preparation for the premiere of the orchestral version on 19 February 1964.

35. See, for example, Rostislav Dubinsky, *Stormy Applause: Making Music in a Workers State* (London: Hutchinson, 1989), 4–5. Perets Markish's poem "An Eternal Light at the Coffin," read at Mikhoels' funeral, made reference to the director's murder. See Arno Lustiger, *Stalin and the Jews—The Red Book* (New York: Enigma Books, 2003), 192–3.

36. Wilson, original ed., 228.

37. Joachim Braun, "Shostakovich's Song Cycle *From Jewish Folk Poetry*: Aspects of Style and Meaning," in *Russian and Soviet Music: Essays for Boris Schwarz,* ed. Malcolm Hamrick Brown (Ann Arbor: UMI Research Press, 1984), 261.

38. The truth emerged in 1951 when, under interrogation, the deposed Minister of State Security, Viktor Abakumov, admitted his involvement. The details were revealed in a letter from Lavrenty Beriya to Georgy Malenkov dated April 2, 1953, four weeks after Stalin's death. Meanwhile, Stalin's daughter, Svetlana Alilluyeva, recalls the day of the murder. She had walked into her father's room at the end of a phone conversation: "Something was being reported to him and he was listening. Then, as a summary of the conversation, he said, 'Well, it's an automobile accident.' I remember so well the way he said it: not a question but an answer, an assertion. He wasn't asking; he was suggesting: "an automobile

accident." When he got through, he greeted me; and a little later he said: 'Mikhoels was killed in an automobile accident'." Svetlana Alliluyeva, *Just One Year*, trans. Paul Chavcha- vadze (New York: Harper and Row, 1969), 154. See also Arkady Vaksberg, *Stalin against the Jews* (New York: Knopf, 1994), 159–82.

39. Laurel Fay, "The Composer Was Courageous, But Not as Much as in Myth," *The New York Times*, April 14, 1996, section 2, 32.

40. Braun, "Shostakovich's Song Cycle," 260.

41. Ibid., 263.

42. Wilson, original ed., 229.

43. Braun, "Shostakovich's Song Cycle," 268.

44. Ibid.

45. Daniil Zhitomirskii, "Shostakovich," *Muzykal'naia akademiia* (1993, No. 3): 29. Quoted in Fay, *Shostakovich: A Life*, 168.

46. Liudmila Karagicheva, ed., *Kara Karaev: stat'i, pis'ma, vyskazyvaniia* (Moscow: Sovet- skii kompozitor, 1978), 49. Quoted in Fay, *Shostakovich: A Life*, 168.

47. Fay, *Shostakovich—A Life*, 176.

48. This story, along with the perception of its participants, has become somewhat con- fused. Rostislav Dubinsky, the Borodin Quartet's first violinist, recalls playing the Fourth Quartet twice on that occasion, in what turned out to be a futile attempt to "obtain per- mission to perform the work in public." According to Dubinsky, they played it first "emphasiz[ing] everything that socialist realism requires to be concealed," and a second time in a less "anti-Soviet" interpretation: "Even our faces tried to look optimistic. We lied! We presented the foreboding mood of the first movement as hope for a brighter future; the plaintive lyricism of the second as a pleasant little waltz; the sinister muted scherzo became a cheerful dance; and the tragic Jewish themes of the finale took on a traditional Oriental coloring." Rostislav Dubinsky, *Stormy Applause: Making Music in a Workers State* (London: Hutchinson, 1989), 279. Berlinsky dismisses Dubinsky's account as a "pretty invention," claiming in any case that the audition was for the purposes of securing a commission for Shostakovich rather than permission for performance. Wilson, original ed., 246.

49. Judy Kuhn, "Looking Again at the Jewish Inflections in Shostakovich's String Quar- tets," in Arnemann, ed., 195.

50. See Fay, *Shostakovich: A Life*, 175.

51. "Galina Ustvolskaya 1919–2006," *DSCH Journal* 26 (2007): 52.

52. *The New York Times*, March 27, 1949, 44.

53. Letter to Leonid Ilyichov (Agitprop) dated March 7, 1949. See Maximenkov, "Stalin and Shostakovich," 54.

54. Memo to Central Committee member Mikhail Suslov dated March 10, 1949. See "DSCH: The Life and Works of Dmitri Shostakovich," *Cultural Heritage Series*, vol. 1 (Chandos Multimedia DVD-ROM, CHAN 550011).

55. Sources disagree on the date. However, it was almost certainly 16 March. Shostako- vich's letter of thanks to Stalin, dated 17 March, refers to the "conversation that took place yesterday." See Maximenkov, "Stalin and Shostakovich," 55.

56. Order No. 3197 declared the previous year's repertoire ban (Order No. 17) "illegal," and recommended the reprimand of Glavrepertkom for publishing an illegal order. See Eliza- beth Wilson, *Shostakovich: A Life Remembered*, new ed. (London: Faber and Faber, 2006), 246.

57. Khentova, *V mire Shostakovicha* (Moscow: Kompozitor, 1996), 34–5. Wilson, new ed., 273.

58. DSCH DVD-ROM.

59. Ardov, 73.

60. Letter to Robert Craft dated March 16, 1949. Igor Stravinsky, *Selected Correspondence*, vol. 1, ed. Robert Craft (London: Faber and Faber, 1982), 359.

61. Ibid., 358.

62. Nicolas Nabokov, *Old Friends and New Music* (London: Hamish Hamilton, 1951), 204. This passage is omitted from the US edition (Boston: Little, Brown, 1951).

63. Ibid., 205.

64. Wilson, original ed., 211.

65. David Fanning, "Shostakovich: The Present-Day Master of the C Major Key," *Acta musicologica* 73 (2001): 137.

66. Wilson, original ed., 250.

67. Ibid., 253.

68. See Isaak Glikman, ed., *Story of a Friendship: The Letters of Dmitry Shostakovich to Isaak Glikman, 1941–1975* (Ithaca: Cornell University Press, 2001), 288, n140.

69. Translation by Marina Ter-Mikaelian. *Shostakovich—The Song of the Forests/The Sun Shines Over the Motherland*. Russian Disc, RD CD 11 048.

70. See Fay, *Shostakovich: A Life*, 183.

71. For example, Louis Blois, "Shostakovich and the Ustvolskaya Connexion: A Textual Investigation," *Tempo* 182 (1992): 10–18; David Fanning, *Shostakovich: String Quartet No. 8* (Aldershot: Ashgate, 2004), 37–8.

72. Arkadii Klimovitskii, "Eshche raz o teme-monogramme *D-Es-C-H*," in *D.D. Shostakovich: sbornik statei k 90-letiiu so dnia rozhdeniia*, ed. Liudmila Kovnatskaia (St. Petersburg: Kompozitor, 1996), 265. Quoted in Fanning, *Shostakovich: String Quartet No. 8*, 36.

73. Fanning, *Shostakovich: String Quartet No. 8*, 36–8.

74. Wilson, new ed., 295, n66.

75. Dorothea Redepenning, "Shostakovich's Song Cycles," in *Shostakovich Studies*, ed. David Fanning (Cambridge: Cambridge University Press, 1995), 207.

76. Wilson, new ed., 296.

77. Georgii Khubov, "Muzyka i sovremennost' (o zadachakh razvitiia sovetskoi muzyki)," *Sovetskaia muzyka* (1953, No. 4): 20. Quoted in Fay, *Shostakovich: A Life*, 186.

78. Anonymous memo dated May 8, 1953. DSCH DVD-ROM.

79. Wilson, original ed., 260–1.

80. Tatyana Nikolayeva claims to have heard Shostakovich demonstrate the Tenth Symphony on the piano in 1951 (see Wilson, original ed., 256–7). However, no further corroboration of an earlier composition date has come to light.

81. David Fanning, *The Breath of the Symphonist: Shostakovich's Tenth* (London: Royal Musical Association, 1989), 8.

82. Solomon Volkov, *Testimony: The Memoirs of Dmitri Shostakovich*, trans. Antonina W. Bouis (New York: Harper and Row, 1979), 141.

83. A somewhat arcane speculation concerns Benjamin Britten's festival cantata *Rejoice in the Lamb*, written in 1943, in which Britten sets the words of the eighteenth-century poet Christopher Smart, who wrote from his lunatic asylum: "For the officers of the peace are at variance with me and the watchman smites me with his staff. For silly, silly fellow is against me." Derek Hulme points out that Britten uses the DSCH motif during this section, particularly on the words "silly fellow." Hulme believes that "It is surely not coincidental that when Shostakovich was in disgrace in Russia with 'officers of the peace,' Britten should introduce this secret message of sympathy. Did, then, Benjamin Britten discover and

initiate the use of the DSCH motto in 1943?" Derek C. Hulme, *Dmitri Shostakovich: A Catalogue, Bibliography, and Discography,* 3rd ed. (Lanham, MD: Scarecrow Press, 2002), 568.

84. Fanning, *Shostakovich: String Quartet No. 8,* 35.

85. Fanning, *The Breath of the Symphonist,* 53.

86. Nelly Kravetz, "A New Insight into the Tenth Symphony of Dmitry Shostakovich," in Bartlett, ed., 163.

87. Fanning, *The Breath of the Symphonist,* 64.

88. Eric Roseberry, *Ideology, Style, Content, and Thematic Process in the Symphonies, Cello Concertos, and String Quartets of Shostakovich* (New York: Garland, 1989), 98.

89. Speech to the Music Section of the Stalin Prize Committee, April 1, 1954. DSCH DVD-ROM.

90. Aram Khachaturian, "Desiataia simfoniia D. Shostakovicha," *Sovetskaia muzyka* (1954, No. 3): 25. Quoted in Fay, *Shostakovich: A Life,* 189.

Chapter 9

1. Elizabeth Wilson, *Shostakovich: A Life Remembered,* original ed. (Princeton: Princeton University Press, 1994), 264–5.

2. Letter to Kara Karayev dated March 11, 1956. Liudmila Karagicheva, ed., *Kara Karaev: stat'i, pis'ma, vyskazyvaniia* (Moscow: Sovetskii kompozitor, 1978), 54. Quoted in Laurel E. Fay, *Shostakovich: A Life* (New York: Oxford University Press, 2000), 195.

3. Letter to his mother dated August 3, 1923. R.S. Sadykhova and D.V. Frederiks, "Shostakovich: Letters to his Mother, 1923–1927," in *Shostakovich and his World,* ed. Laurel E. Fay (Princeton: Princeton University Press, 2004), 5.

4. Peter Maniura, *Shostakovich: A Career (The Public and Private Voice of Dmitri Shostakovich).* BBC2 TV, broadcast November 7, 1987.

5. Wilson, original ed., 230.

6. Conversation with Isaak Glikman dated December 23, 1954. Isaak Glikman, ed., *Story of a Friendship: The Letters of Dmitry Shostakovich to Isaak Glikman, 1941–1975* (Ithaca: Cornell University Press, 2001), 57.

7. Letter dated March 21, 1955. Glikman, 56.

8. The "Thaw" referred to the period between 1953 (the death of Stalin) and 1964 (the ousting of Khrushchev and his replacement by Leonid Brezhnev), during which a certain amount of cultural liberalization took place. The term itself was taken from Ilya Ehrenburg's 1954 novel, *The Thaw.*

9. See Laurel E. Fay, "From *Lady Macbeth* to *Katerina*—Shostakovich's Versions and Revisions," in *Shostakovich Studies,* ed. David Fanning (Cambridge: Cambridge University Press, 1995), 160–77.

10. Glikman, 261, n30.

11. Michael Ardov, *Memories of Shostakovich,* trans. Rosanna Kelly and Michael Meylac (London: Short, 2004), 110.

12. Glikman, 261, n30.

13. Ibid., 262, n30.

14. Zinaida Gayamova diary entry dated November 1956. "DSCH: The Life and Works of Dmitri Shostakovich," *Cultural Heritage Series,* vol. 1 (Chandos Multimedia DVD-ROM, CHAN 550011).

15. Zinaida Gayamova diary entry dated 1958. DSCH DVD-ROM.

16. Nikita Khrushchev, speech to the 20th Congress of the CPSU, http://www.marxists. org/archive/khrushchev/1956/02/24.htm (accessed June 17, 2007).

17. David Fanning, *Shostakovich: String Quartet No. 8* (Aldershot: Ashgate, 2004), 40–1.

18. Glikman, 262–3, n40.

19. Ian MacDonald, *The New Shostakovich*, original ed. (Boston: Northeastern University Press, 1990), 214.

20. Ibid.

21. The "Young Pioneers" was a Scout-like youth movement that inculcated Soviet educational values.

22. Gerard McBurney, "Spinning Tales and Tunes to Remember a Friend," *The New York Times*, April 21, 2002, Section 2, 28.

23. In David Caute, *The Dancer Defects: The Struggle for Cultural Supremacy during the Cold War* (Oxford: Oxford University Press, 2003), 457.

24. See Wilson, original ed., 320.

25. As his student Boris Tishchenko recalls, Shostakovich was a stickler for correct notation, insisting that notes on the page reflect their true tonal function. "Remembering Shostakovich ... with Boris Tishchenko," *DSCH Journal* 23 (2005): 7.

26. Roy Blokker (with Robert Dearling), *The Music of Dmitri Shostakovich—The Symphonies* (London: The Tantivy Press, 1979), 126.

27. Central Committee Resolution, "On the Correction of Errors in the Evaluation of the Operas *The Great Friendship, Bogdan Khmelnitsky,* and *From All One's Heart,* 28 May 1958," *Pravda*, June 8, 1958. Quoted in Boris Schwarz, *Music and Musical Life in Soviet Russia (Enlarged Edition, 1917–1981)* (Bloomington: Indiana University Press, 1983), 311.

28. Galina Vishnevskaya, *Galina: A Russian Story*, trans. Guy Daniels (San Diego: Harcourt Brace Jovanovich, 1984), 244.

29. Wilson, original ed., 293–4.

30. Ian MacDonald, "Laurel E. Fay's *Shostakovich: A Life*," part 4, http://www.siue.edu/ ~aho/musov/fay/fayrev4.html (accessed June 17, 2007).

31. Gerard McBurney, "Fried Chicken in the Bird-Cherry Trees," in Fay, ed., *Shostakovich and His World*, 229.

32. Ibid., 254.

33. Letter dated December 19, 1958. Glikman, 79.

34. Shostakovich's orchestration of *Khovanshchina* can be heard in recordings conducted by Emil Tchakarov (Sofia National Opera, 1986, Sony), Claudio Abbado (Vienna State Opera, 1989, Deutsche Grammophon), and Valery Gergiev (Kirov Opera, 1991, Philips), though Abbado replaces Shostakovich's ending with Stravinsky's final chorus and uses Musorgsky's own orchestration of the Act III portions. As of 2007, Shostakovich's re-orchestration of *Boris Godunov* has never been recorded, although a live 1967 performance from Venice with Belgrade National Opera forces conducted by Dušan Miladinovic has been sporadically available on several small labels.

35. Eric Roseberry, *Ideology, Style, Content, and Thematic Process in the Symphonies, Cello Concertos, and String Quartets of Shostakovich* (New York: Garland, 1989), 429–30.

36. Joachim Braun, "The Double Meaning of Jewish Elements in Dimitri Shostakovich's Music," *The Musical Quarterly* 71 (1985): 70. Braun mistakenly refers to the finale as the third movement.

37. For example, Fay, *Shostakovich: A Life*, 216; Fanning, *Shostakovich: String Quartet No. 8*, 41.

38. I am excluding vocal music, incidental stage works, film scores, and children's pieces, because altogether different agendas operate in those realms. I have also excluded the

Twenty-four Preludes and Fugues, which, although forming a cycle in one sense, remain, ultimately, a series of individual pieces.

39. The table cites only examples of obvious thematic cyclism, not the cyclism created by motivic development or tonal planning. So, for example, only the appearances of the Eleventh Symphony's "Timpani Triplet motif" in movements 1 and 2 are listed, even though Shostakovich goes on to use the figure in a more motivic manner in movements 3 and 4.

40. Membership of the Accademia di Santa Cecilia (Rome); Commandeur de l'Ordre des arts et lettres (Paris); Doctor *honoris causa* (Oxford University); Membership of the Royal Academy of Music (London); International Sibelius Prize (Helsinki).

41. Andrea Olmstead, ed., *Conversations with Roger Sessions* (Boston: Northeastern University Press, 1982), 238–9.

42. Letter dated May 5, 1958. Glikman, 74–5.

43. Abraam Gozenpud. Wilson, original ed., 333.

44. Ian MacDonald, "Laurel E. Fay's *Shostakovich: A Life*," part 4.

45. Glikman, 92.

46. Wilson, original ed., 337.

47. Glikman, 91–2.

48. Vishnevskaya, 269.

49. Ardov, 158. Interestingly, in this interview, Galina implies that the Quartet was finished at Shostakovich's Zhukovka dacha, where he had been residing after his return from Dresden. This would put the completion a few days later than the commonly accepted date of 14 July.

50. Letter dated July 19, 1960. Glikman, 90–1.

51. Fay, *Shostakovich: A Life*, 219.

52. Glikman, 276, n36.

53. In common with most authors, I am defining quotation as a reference that is clearly recognizable at the most superficial level. The quotations in the Eighth Quartet are: Shostakovich's First Symphony, Second Piano Trio, First Cello Concerto (and its subsidiary, *The Young Guard*), *Lady Macbeth*, and the Revolutionary song "Tormented by Harsh Captivity." Allusion implies a looser connection, e.g., a melodic contour or a rhythmic gesture. Inevitably, identifying allusions is rather trickier and involves greater subjective latitude. The Fifth Symphony and Tchaikovsky *Pathétique* examples were cited by Shostakovich himself. (Letter dated July 19, 1960. Glikman, 91.) For a comprehensive listing of possible allusions, see Fanning, *Shostakovich: String Quartet No. 8*, 54–5.

54. See *Izvestiia*, September 25, 1960. Quoted in Lev Grigoryev and Yakov Platek, *Dmitry Shostakovich: About Himself and His Times*, trans. Angus and Neilian Roxburgh (Moscow: Progress Publishers, 1981), 215. The journalist Hermann Werner Finke has claimed that Shostakovich's 1960 visit was not in fact his first exposure to the ruins of Dresden. According to Finke, Shostakovich had made a quick side-trip there in 1950 during his visit to Leipzig. *Sächsische Neueste Nachrichten*, August 13, 1975. Cited in Ian MacDonald, "The Legend of the Eighth Quartet," in *Shostakovich Reconsidered*, ed. Allan B. Ho and Dmitry Feofanov (London: Toccata Press, 1998), 588.

55. Yury Keldish, "An Autobiographical Quartet," trans. Alan Lumsden, *The Musical Times* 102 (April 1961): 226.

56. Fanning, *Shostakovich: String Quartet No. 8*, 60.

57. Ibid., 89.

58. Ibid., 92.

59. Ibid.

60. Liner note to *Shostakovich String Quartets 1–15*, Emerson Quartet. DG 463284, p. 32.

61. Fanning, *Shostakovich: String Quartet No. 8*, 56.

62. Richard Taruskin, "Shostakovich and Us," in *Shostakovich in Context*, ed. Rosamund Bartlett (Oxford: Oxford University Press, 2000), 27.

63. Fanning, *Shostakovich: String Quartet No. 8*, 139.

64. "Tvorcheskie plany Dmitriia Shostakovicha," *Sovetskaia kul'tura*, June 6, 1959, 4. Quoted in Fay, *Shostakovich: A Life*, 221.

65. *Muzykal'naia zhizn'* (1960, No. 21): 10. Quoted in Fay, *Shostakovich: A Life*, 221–2.

66. In Wilson, original ed., 346.

67. Fay, *Shostakovich: A Life*, 223.

68. David Hurwitz, *Shostakovich Symphonies and Concertos—An Owner's Manual* (Pompton Plains, NJ: Amadeus Press, 2006), 159.

69. See Hurwitz, 161–3.

70. Letter dated August 15, 1961. Glikman, 97.

71. Wilson, original ed., 346–7.

72. Fumiko Hitotsuyanagi, "The New Face of the Twelfth Symphony," trans. Véronique Zaytzeff and Frederick Morrison, *DSCH Journal* 13 (2000): 59–63.

73. Isaak Glikman diary entry dated October 5, 1961. Quoted in foreword to Shostakovich, "Unfinished Quartet" (Moscow: DSCH, 2005), 6–7.

74. Letter dated November 18, 1961. Glikman, 99. Laurel Fay presents the possibility that this letter may in fact have dated from 1962 since it was "distinctly improbable" that Shostakovich could have scrapped two quartets (Fay, *Shostakovich: A Life*, 337, n92–338, n92). However, the newly revealed Glikman diary entry from October 5, 1961, made during rehearsals for the Twelfth Symphony's premiere, would seem to corroborate the November 1961 date for the letter and suggest that Shostakovich did in fact scrap two "ninth" quartets during 1961–1962.

75. Shostakovich, "Unfinished Quartet," 6–7.

76. Ibid., 7–8.

77. Zinaida Gayamova diary entry dated December 31, 1961. DSCH DVD-ROM.

78. "Russian Declines Philharmonic Bid," *Musical America* (September 1942): 9. Quoted in Christopher H. Gibbs, "'The Phenomenon of the Seventh': A Documentary Essay on Shostakovich's 'War' Symphony," in Fay, ed., *Shostakovich and His World*, 87.

79. Wilson, original ed., 378–9; also Anna Fortunova, "Shostakovich the Conductor" (paper presented at the symposium *Shostakovich 100*, Deptford Town Hall, London, September 27, 2006).

80. An American LP of the Tenth Symphony in which a "National Philharmonic Orchestra" was purportedly conducted by Shostakovich (Colosseum CRLP 173) turned out to be a misattributed reissue of Mravinsky's pioneering 1954 recording with the Leningrad Philharmonic.

81. Kirill Kondrashin. Wilson, original ed., 359.

82. Yevtushenko has since made alterations to "Fears." The revised text received its premiere in New York in February 2003 (Czech Philharmonic Orchestra/Vladimir Ashkenazy).

83. Glikman, 281, n93.

84. Wilson, original ed., 367–8.

85. Ibid., 368.

86. Gregor Tassie, *Yevgeny Mravinsky—The Noble Conductor* (Lanham, MD: Scarecrow Press, 2005), 198–9.

87. Ibid., 198.

88. "Smert'ne strashus', no k zhizni privyazan," *Sovetskaia kul'tura* (June 8, 1991). Quoted in Fay, *Shostakovich: A Life*, 233.

89. Tassie, 199.

90. See Priscilla Johnson and Leopold Labedz, eds., *Khrushchev and the Arts—The Politics of Soviet Culture, 1962–1964* (Cambridge, MA: The MIT Press, 1965), 101–105.

91. Ibid., 120–1.

92. Wilson, original ed., 360–1.

93. Schwarz, 367.

94. A live recording of the second performance (20 December) was briefly available on Russian Disc RDCD 11191.

95. Wilson, original ed., 361–2. Kirill Kondrashin, "Talking About Shostakovich," in Ho and Feofanov, eds., 516.

96. See Albert Todd, "The Many Literary Worlds of 'Babi Yar'" (paper presented at *Brown Symposium XVII*, Southwestern University, Georgetown, Texas, February 25, 1995). Recording on file with the author.

97. Memo dated May 15, 1963. DVD-ROM.

98. For example, Vitaly Katayev (Minsk, March 1963), Igor Blazhkov (Leningrad, December 1966) and, apparently, Yury Temirkanov (Leningrad, date not given). See Fay, *Shostakovich: A Life*, 236; Tassie, 199; and Yury Temirkanov, panel discussion at Manhattan School of Music, September 28, 1998, *An Inter-Disciplinary Symposium on Dmitri Shostakovich* (Manhattan School of Music cassette tape 9899 L5).

99. Letter to Isaak Glikman dated September 15, 1964. Glikman, 118.

100. Jeffrey Baxter, "A Descriptive Analysis of the Yevtushenko Settings of Dmitri Shostakovich" (D.M.A. diss., University of Cincinnati, 1988), 15.

101. The song translates literally as "Ah you entrance hall, my entrance hall," though *seni* is sometimes rendered simply as "hall" or "porch." Occasionally, it is confused with *seno*, meaning "hay," and the song gets mistranslated, referring to "hayloft" or "attic."

102. Richard Longman, *Expression and Structure: Processes of Integration in the Large-Scale Instrumental Music of Shostakovich* (New York: Garland Publishing, 1989), 331; Malcolm MacDonald, "Words and Music in Late Shostakovich," in *Shostakovich: The Man and His Music*, ed. Christopher Norris (Boston: Marion Boyars, 1982), 129; Elizabeth Wilson, "Understanding Shostakovich Today" (address to the symposium *Shostakovich 100*, Queen Elizabeth Hall, London, September 25, 2006).

103. Wilson, "Understanding Shostakovich Today."

104. Braun, "The Double Meaning of Jewish Elements in Dimitri Shostakovich's Music," 76–7.

105. Esti Sheinberg, "Shostakovich's 'Jewish Music' as an Existential Statement," in *Dmitri Schostakowitsch und das jüdische musikalische Erbe*, ed. Dethlef Arnemann, et al. (Berlin: Kuhn, 2001), 92.

106. For example, both the Thirteenth and Fourteenth Symphonies later appeared in German translations authorized by Shostakovich. As he told the conductor Thomas Sanderling, "it is absolutely awful when you hear everybody at the concert turning their programme pages simultaneously." See Wilson, original ed., 420.

107. Baxter, 30.

108. Malcolm MacDonald, "Words and Music in Late Shostakovich," in *Shostakovich: The Man and His Music*, ed. Christopher Norris (Boston: Marion Boyars, 1982), 136.

109. Longman, 338.

110. Malcolm MacDonald, "Words and Music in Late Shostakovich," 129.

111. Ian MacDonald, *The New Shostakovich*, original ed., 230.

112. Sof'ia Khentova, *Shostakovich, zhizn' i tvorchestvo*, vol. 2 (Leningrad: "Sovetskii kompozitor," Leningradskoe otd-nie., 1986), 444. Quoted in Ardov, 116.

113. Letter to Smolich dated February 28, 1934. Gavriil Iudin, "Vasha rabota dlia menia sobytie na vsiu zhizn'," *Sovetskaia muzyka* (1983, No. 6): 92. Quoted in Wilson, original ed., 100, n90.

114. Khentova, 445–6. Ardov, 117.

115. Letter dated September 6, 1958. Glikman, 76.

116. Fiona Ford, "The Role of Ophelia's Unaccompanied Songs in Kozintsev's *Hamlet*," *DSCH Journal* 26 (2007): 24–32.

117. A full investigation into the use of the tritone, the pedal, and the octatonic scale (referred to by Smith as an "alternating scale") can be found in Arthur Duane Smith, "Recurring Motives and Themes as a Means to Unity in Selected String Quartets of Dmitri Shostakovich" (D. Mus. Ed. diss., University of Oklahoma, 1976), 187–306.

118. Smith, 369.

119. Fanning, *Shostakovich: String Quartet No. 8*, 50–1.

120. Smith, 359.

121. Glikman, 287, n133.

122. Letter to Glikman dated September 15, 1964. Glikman, 118.

123. Letter to Glikman dated September 24, 1964. Glikman, 119.

124. Letter to Glikman dated September 15, 1964. Glikman, 118.

125. Letter to Glikman dated May 31, 1962. Glikman, 101.

126. Letter to Glikman dated September 15, 1964. Glikman, 118.

127. Baxter, 85.

128. Caryl Emerson, "Shostakovich and the Russian Literary Tradition," in Fay, ed., *Shostakovich and His World*, 194.

129. Malcolm MacDonald, "Words and Music in Late Shostakovich," 134.

130. Bassoons, contrabassoon, timpani, bass drum, tam-tam, harp, pizzicato cellos and double basses.

131. Bass clarinet, bassoons, contrabassoon, horns, trombones, tuba, timpani, tam-tam, tubular bells, harps, piano, and pizzicato strings.

132. Henry Orlov, "A Link in the Chain—Reflections of Shostakovich and His Times," in *A Shostakovich Casebook*, ed. Malcolm Hamrick Brown (Bloomington: Indiana University Press, 2004), 210.

133. Translation by Sergey Suslov. *Shostakovich—Complete Songs*, vol. 2. Delos 3307.

Chapter 10

1. Paul Eugene Dyer, "Cyclic Techniques in the String Quartets of Dimitri Shostakovich," Ph.D. diss., Florida State University, 1977, 242–3.

2. Solomon Volkov, *Shostakovich and Stalin*, trans. Antonina W. Bouis (New York: Knopf, 2004), 33.

3. Isaak Glikman, *The Story of a Friendship: The Letters of Dmitry Shostakovich to Isaak Glikman, 1941–1975*, trans. Anthony Phillips (Ithaca: Cornell University Press, 2001), 131.

4. Laurel E. Fay, *Shostakovich: A Life* (New York: Oxford University Press, 2000), 251.

5. For example, letter dated November 10, 1966. Glikman, 134–5.

6. Letter to Dmitri Shepilov dated September 21, 1966, in *Tak eto bylo: Tikhon Khrennikov o vremeni i o sebe*, ed. V. Rubtsova (Moscow: Muzyka, 1994), 142. Quoted in Fay, *Shostakovich: A Life*, 247.

7. Eric Roseberry, *Ideology, Style, Content, and Thematic Process in the Symphonies, Cello Concertos, and String Quartets of Shostakovich* (New York: Garland, 1979), 451.

8. Other examples include: Fifth Symphony, fourth movement (Fig. 129, b3–4); Thirteenth Symphony, fourth movement (Fig. 103, b2 et seq.), and several places in the Tenth Symphony, first movement (e.g., b13–14). See David Fanning, *The Breath of the Symphonist: Shostakovich's Tenth* (London: Royal Musical Association, 1989), 11.

9. Hard to translate, *bubliki* fall somewhere between bread rolls and bagels.

10. The idea of percussion interjections in cadenzas can be traced at least as far back as Beethoven's arrangement for piano and orchestra of his Violin Concerto, in which timpani complement the piano in the first movement cadenza.

11. Roseberry, *Ideology, Style, Content*, 463.

12. Eric Roseberry's statement that the cadenza is in G major is surely a mistake, one that may have been created by a misreading of clefs. Ibid., 465.

13. See Fay, *Shostakovich: A Life*, 250.

14. The *Blok* cycle is often referred to as *Seven Romances on Poems of Alexander Blok*, but the designation "Romances" does not appear in Shostakovich's score.

15. Dorothea Redepenning, "Shostakovich's Song Cycles," in *Shostakovich Studies*, ed. David Fanning (Cambridge: Cambridge University Press, 1995), 217.

16. Translation by Sergey Suslov. *Shostakovich—Complete Songs,* vol. 2. Delos 3307.

17. Fay, *Shostakovich: A Life*, 253.

18. Norman Kay, "First Performances—Shostakovich's Second Violin Concerto," *Tempo* 83 (Winter 1967–1968): 23.

19. See Fay, *Shostakovich: A Life*, 254.

20. Elizabeth Wilson, *Shostakovich: A Life Remembered*, original ed. (Princeton: Princeton University Press, 1994), 398.

21. Memo sent to Pyotr Denisov dated October 20, 1966. DSCH DVD-ROM.

22. Christopher Rowland and Alan George, "Interpreting the String Quartets," in *Shostakovich: The Man and His Music*, ed. Christopher Norris (Boston: Marion Boyars, 1982), 31.

23. Dmitrii Shostakovich, "Shirokie massy verny nastoiashchei muzyke," *Sovetskaia muzyka* (1959, No. 11): 7. Quoted in Fay, *Shostakovich: A Life*, 214.

24. Peter J. Schmelz, "Shostakovich's 'Twelve-Tone' Compositions and the Politics and Practice of Soviet Serialism," in *Shostakovich and His World*, ed. Laurel E. Fay (Princeton: Princeton University Press, 2004), 303–54.

25. Reported by Sergey Girshenko, panel discussion at Manhattan School of Music, September 28, 1998, *An Inter-Disciplinary Symposium on Dmitri Shostakovich* (Manhattan School of Music cassette tape 9899 L5). See also Louis Blois, "Manhattan School of Music Seminar," *DSCH Journal* 10 (1998): 47.

26. Richard M. Longman, *Expression and Structure: Processes of Integration in the Large-Scale Instrumental Music of Dmitri Shostakovich* (New York: Garland, 1989), 216.

27. Letter dated February 1, 1969. Glikman, 158.

28. Letter dated February 17, 1969. Glikman, 159.

29. Lorca was murdered by Franco's "Escuadra Negra" during the Spanish Civil War; Apollinaire succumbed to the Spanish flu epidemic in Paris in 1918; Küchelbecker died in

a Siberian labor camp, to which he had been exiled for his part in the 1825 Decembrist uprising; Rilke died of septicemia contracted from a rose thorn.

30. Gerard McBurney, "Marking the Graves," BBC Radio 3, broadcast February 25, 1993. (British Library catalogue number H1222/03)

31. Solomon Volkov, *Testimony: The Memoirs of Dmitri Shostakovich*, trans. Antonina W. Bouis (New York: Harper and Row, 1979), 182.

32. Longman, 350.

33. "Burning blood" was changed from Lorca's "Women's blood." Shostakovich worried that "Women's blood" would probably carry "menstrual and gynaecological association[s]" for the more prudish elements of the audience. See letter to Glikman dated 19 March 1969. Glikman, 161.

34. Glikman, 305, n85.

35. McBurney, "Marking the Graves."

36. Longman, 362.

37. For a performance that presents the texts in their original languages, see Shostakovich, Symphony No. 14, Concertgebouw Orchestra, cond. Bernard Haitink. However, the texts used here are not the original poems, but back-translations of the Russian versions.

38. Italics added for emphasis.

39. McBurney, "Marking the Graves."

40. Ibid.

41. Castanets, woodblock, tom-toms (soprano, alto, tenor), whip, tubular bells, vibraphone, xylophone, and celesta.

42. The vibraphone had been used three times before in non-concert works: the cartoon *The Priest and His Servant Balda* (1934), the film *The First Echelon* (1956), and the so-called Suite for Variety Stage Orchestra (often referred to, incorrectly, as the Suite for Jazz Orchestra No. 2).

43. Roy Blokker (with Robert Dearling), *The Music of Dmitri Shostakovich—The Symphonies* (London: The Tantivy Press, 1979), 147.

44. *Rostropovich—Three Friends.* BBC2 TV, broadcast November 27, 1988. (British Library catalogue number V2694/3)

45. Letter to Boris Tishchenko dated August 23, 1963. In "DSCH: The Life and Works of Dmitri Shostakovich," *Cultural Heritage Series*, vol. 1 (Chandos Multimedia DVD-ROM, CHAN 550011).

46. Fay, *Shostakovich: A Life*, 263.

47. Eric Roseberry, "A Debt Repaid? Some Observations on Shostakovich and His Late-Period Recognition of Britten," in Fanning, ed., *Shostakovich Studies*, 244.

48. Levon Hakobian, "*The Nose* and the Fourteenth Symphony: An Affinity of Opposites," in Fay, ed., *Shostakovich and His World*, 178.

49. Roseberry, "A Debt Repaid?," 229.

50. Ibid., n1.

51. Quoted in Fay, *Shostakovich: A Life*, 261.

52. Letter dated June 24, 1969. Glikman, 165.

53. Rudolf Barshai. In Wilson, original ed., 416.

54. Volkov, *Testimony*, 184.

55. See Fay, *Shostakovich: A Life*, 262.

56. See Robert M. Pascuzzi, "Shostakovich and Amyotrophic Lateral Sclerosis," *Seminars in Neurology* 19 (1999): 63.

57. Letter to Glikman dated November 23, 1969. Glikman, 169.

58. Letter to Glikman dated March 28, 1970. Glikman, 177.

59. Letter to Glikman dated May 11, 1970. Glikman, 177.

60. Kozintsev. In Wilson, original ed., 424.

61. The Thirteenth Quartet and Fifteenth Symphony are separated only by the minute-and-a-half-long march for wind band, *Soviet Militia*, and the orchestral reworking of the *Six Romances on Words of W. Raleigh, R. Burns, and W. Shakespeare.*

62. See Rowland and George, "Interpreting the String Quartets," 29; Wilson, original ed., 441.

63. David Fanning, "Shostakovich and His Pupils," in Fay, ed., *Shostakovich and His World*, 297.

64. See Wilson, original ed., 438–9.

65. Richard Taruskin, "Double Trouble," *New Republic*, December 24, 2001, 26–34. Reprinted ("When Serious Music Mattered") in *A Shostakovich Casebook*, ed. Malcolm Hamrick Brown (Bloomington: Indiana University, 2004), 363–4.

66. Maxim Shostakovich, "Six Lectures on the Shostakovich Symphonies," in *Shostakovich Reconsidered*, ed. Allan B. Ho and Dmitry Feofanov (London: Toccata Press, 1998), 416.

67. Ibid.

68. Interview with Boris Tishchenko, *DSCH Journal* 23 (2005): 9.

69. N.V. Lukyanova, *Shostakovich*, trans. Yuri Shirokov (Neptune City, NJ: Paganiniana, 1984), 93.

70. See Fay, *Shostakovich: A Life*, 273–4.

71. Fyodor Druzhinin. In Wilson, original ed., 440.

72. Ibid.

73. Like "Elmira," "Seryozha" relies on a mix of standard Russian (i.e., German) musical nomenclature and solfège syllables, with the note D-sharp enharmonically respelled as E-flat, the pitch "G" interpreted as a French-style soft "G" corresponding to the Russian "ж" ("zh"), and the letter "e" taking both the "e" and "yo" pronunciations. Hence S-e-r-yo-zh-a becomes, musically, Es–E–Re–E–G–A, or D-sharp–E–D–E–G–A. See Laurel E. Fay, "The Last Quartets of Dmitrii Shostakovich: A Stylistic Investigation" (Ph.D. diss., Cornell University, 1978), 42–3.

74. Shostakovich sailed to the USA on the maiden voyage of the "Mikhail Lermontov." Footage of this voyage can be seen in *A Journey of Dmitry Shostakovich*, dir. Oksana Dvornichenko and Helga Landauer (2006).

75. Sofia Khentova, *Shostakovich, Tridtsatiletie 1945–1975* (Leningrad: Sovetskii kompozitor, 1982), 318. Quoted in Caryl Emerson, "Shostakovich, Tsvetaeva, Pushkin, Musorgsky," in *Shostakovich in Context*, ed. Rosamund Bartlett (Oxford: Oxford University Press, 2000), 193.

76. Malcolm MacDonald, "Words and Music in Late Shostakovich," in Norris, ed., 139.

77. Translation by Sergey Suslov. *Shostakovich—Complete Songs*, vol. 2. Delos 3307.

78. Emerson, "Shostakovich, Tsvetayeva, Pushkin, Musorgsky," 193.

79. Ibid., 211.

80. Ibid., 197.

81. The six poems were written in 1913, 1916, 1923, 1931, 1931, and 1916, respectively.

82. "Interview with western correspondents," August 21, 1973. In *Sakharov Speaks*, ed. Harrison E. Salisbury (London, Collins 1974), 194–207.

83. "Pozorit zvanie grazhdanina," *Pravda*, 3 September 1973, 2.

84. *Mstislav Rostropovich and Galina Vishnevskaya: Russia, Music, and Liberty—Conversations with Claude Samuel*, trans. E. Thomas Glasow (Portland, OR: Amadeus Press, 1995), 98–9.

85. Wilson, original ed., 429–30.

86. Irina Shostakovich, "The Dead Are Defenseless?," *DSCH Journal* 14 (2001): 7.

87. John Rockwell, "Rostropovich: 'I Feel Like a Native'," *The New York Times,* January 18, 1981, Section 2, 17.

88. Glikman, 192.

89. Wilson, original ed., 470.

90. Jonathan Drury, "Traditionalism in Shostakovich's Fifteenth String Quartet," *South African Journal of Musicology* 10 (1990): 17.

91. Longman, 395.

92. Ibid.

93. Redepenning, "Shostakovich's Song Cycles," 221.

94. For several examples of this motive, see ibid., 219.

95. Unless otherwise indicated, text citations are taken from Efros' translation rather than Michelangelo's original. English translation of Efros by Sarah White and Eric Walter White, *Shostakovich's Songs*. Decca 475 7441.

96. The completion date of the orchestration is usually given as November 5, 1974. However, the pianist Yevgeny Shenderovich, who partnered Yevgeny Nesterenko at the premiere of the cycle, reports that at a subsequent private performance on January 8, 1975, Shostakovich told Khachaturian that he had no intention of orchestrating the cycle. Wilson, original ed., 456.

97. Redepenning, 221.

98. Wilson, original ed., 455.

99. Letter to Glikman dated August 23, 1974. Glikman, 197. Also remarks to Shenderovich. Wilson, original ed., 458.

100. Glikman, 201–2.

101. Glikman, 206.

102. Wilson, new ed., 528–9.

103. Wilson, original ed., 470.

104. Ivan Sokolov, "The Riddle of Shostakovich's Viola Sonata op. 147" (paper presented at the symposium *Shostakovich 100*, Deptford Town Hall, London, September 27, 2006).

Chapter 11

1. The first section of this chapter (*The Nose*) is a modified reprint of James Morgan, "Interview with 'The Nose': Shostakovich's Adaptation of Gogol," in *Intersections and Transpositions: Russian Music, Literature, and Society*, ed. Andrew Wachtel (Evanston: Northwestern University Press, 1998), 111–37. Reprinted with permission. The second section of this chapter (*Lady Macbeth of the Mtsensk District*) is published here for the first time.

2. Carl Dahlhaus, "What Is a Musical Drama," trans. Mary Whittall, *Cambridge Opera Journal* 1 (1989): 100.

3. Bakhtin sees the novel as a radically synchronic work in which history, whether public or personal, plays a role only inasmuch as it has direct impact on the present. There is little teleological development of situation or character. Each personage is a fluid

combination of voice, personality and idea, the sum of which is "unfinalizable," that is, irreducible to a simple element of authorial design. Rather each character has, in the framework of the novel, a fully independent existence, outside of the author's rhetorical or ideological voice. All the events of the novel emerge from the characters' subordination of themselves to this knot of personality and ideology. The characters live in a dialogic relationship with one another and the interaction of their various voices forms the polyphonic fabric of the novel. Thus the novel is more concerned with the synchronic play of multiple voices than with the ultimate outcome of the plot. See Mikhail Bakhtin, *Problems of Dostoevsky's Poetics*, ed. and trans. Caryl Emerson (Minneapolis: University of Minnesota Press, 1984).

4. Herbert Lindenberger, *Opera: The Extravagant Art* (Ithaca: Cornell University Press, 1984), 95.

5. Caryl Emerson, *Boris Godunov: Transpositions of a Russian Theme* (Bloomington: Indiana University Press, 1986), 8.

6. In order to avoid confusion, I will refer to Gogol's story as "The Nose" and to Shostakovich's opera as *The Nose*. According to the composer, the famous Soviet satirist Yevgeny Zamyatin prepared the libretto for the first scene in Kovalyov's bedroom (Act I, Scene 3, No. 5). The composer himself wrote the remainder of the first act and the entire second act. For the third act, Shostakovich had two collaborators, Georgy Ionin and Alexander Preis. See D. Shostakovich, "K prim'ere 'Nosa'," *Rabochii i teatr* (1929, No. 24): 12. See "Editor's Note" in *Collected Works* 18 (1981): np. For convenience, I will refer to Shostakovich himself as the librettist.

7. The excerpt is Smerdyakov's song from Book 5, Chapter 2.

8. This East-West tension provides a further example of how Russian culture, in opera as in literature and history, sets itself apart from the Western tradition even as it draws from it and compares itself to it. See, for instance, Michael Holquist's penetrating discussion of this problem in the first chapter of his book, *Dostoevsky and the Novel* (Princeton: Princeton University Press, 1977), 3–34. Geoffrey Norris places Shostakovich's operas in the context of Soviet music of the twenties and thirties in "The Operas," in *Shostakovich, the Man and His Music*, ed. Christopher Norris (Boston: M. Boyars, 1982), 105–24, while the connections between *The Nose* and the Russian operatic tradition, especially Musorgsky, are exhaustively detailed in Galina Grigor'eva, "Pervaia opera Shostakovicha—'Nos'," in *Muzyka i sovremennost', vyp. 3* (Moscow: Muzyka, 1965), 68–103. More recently, Katerina Clark discusses *The Nose* as a salient example of a "new" Soviet opera, placing it in the context of the revolutionary culture of the 1920s, in *Petersburg: Crucible of Cultural Revolution* (Cambridge: Harvard University Press, 1995), 224–41.

9. For a concise account of the opera's composition and production history, see Laurel Fay, "The Punch in Shostakovich's Nose," in *Russian and Soviet Music: Essays for Boris Schwarz*, ed. Malcolm Hamrick Brown (Ann Arbor: UMI Research Press, 1984), 229–43. Fay also offers an admirable distillation of the opera's main features and a useful synopsis in "The Nose," in *The New Grove Dictionary of Opera*, ed. Stanley Sadie (New York: Macmillan, 1992), iii, 621–23. For a detailed account of Meyerhold's influence on Shostakovich, see Larisa Bubennikova, "Meierkhol'd i Shostakovich: iz istorii sozdaniia opery 'Nos'," *Sovetskaia muzyka* (1973, No. 3): 43–8.

10. Letter dated March 27, 1928. See Paul Schmidt, ed., *Meyerhold at Work* (Austin: University of Texas Press, 1980), 149. Quoted in Fay, "The Punch in Shostakovich's Nose," 233.

11. Quoted in Bubennikova, 44.

12. For another view of Meyerhold's impact on Shostakovich, see Clark, 230.

13. V.M. Bogdanov-Berezovskii, *Sovetskaia opera* (Leningrad and Moscow: Izdanie Leningradskogo otdeleniia VTO, 1940), 114–5.

14. Review of 1964 Florence production. David Drew, "The Nose," *New Statesman*, June 12, 1964, 922.

15. See Caryl Emerson, "Back to the Future: Shostakovich's Revision of Leskov's 'Lady Macbeth of Mtsensk District'," *Cambridge Opera Journal* 1 (1989): 69–70.

16. Norris lists several of Gogol's works that pop up in the libretto. Norris, 110.

17. This process differs greatly from that of Musorgsky or Dargomyzhsky, who, in their operatic versions of Gogol's *The Marriage* and Pushkin's *The Stone Guest*, respectively, attempted to set the words of the source text without alteration. In their anticipation of twentieth-century *Literatur-Oper*, the two earlier composers were dealing with dramatic works and were determined to retain the dramatic genre. Making an opera from a play is perhaps more challenging than making one from a novel, and the results of the earlier composers' work, especially in light of their strict imposition of "fidelity," would be evidence to support such a claim. Musorgsky never finished *The Marriage*, while *The Stone Guest* is merely a historical footnote. It is interesting that Shostakovich himself later attempted this more restrictive approach in his unfinished setting of another of Gogol's plays, *The Gamblers*. On this issue, see Norris, 113–4. [According to Isaak Glikman, Shostakovich stated that "'In *The Nose* I treated Gogol's text with great freedom, but in *The Gamblers* I plan to be absolutely faithful to the author. I shall keep in every word of every line, as Dargomïzhsky did in *The Stone Guest*. My librettist will be none other than Gogol himself.' ... The eventual fate of *The Gamblers* is well known. Shostakovich reluctantly came to the conclusion that if the text of Gogol's one-act play were to be uncut it would far exceed the limits of contemporary operatic convention." Isaak Glikman, *The Story of a Friendship: The Letters of Dmitry Shostakovich to Isaak Glikman*, trans. Anthony Phillips (Ithaca, NY: Cornell University Press, 2001), xlii-xliii.—Ed.]

18. *The Nose* consists of ten scenes (numbered sequentially) and sixteen numbers (also numbered sequentially). These fall into three acts and an epilogue. Thus: Act I contains an introduction followed by Scenes 1–4 (corresponding to Nos. 1–7); Act II contains an Introduction followed by Scenes 5 and 6 (Nos. 8–11); Act III contains Scenes 7 and 8 (Nos. 12–14); and the Epilogue contains Scenes 9 and 10 (Nos. 15 and 16). I will refer to a given scene by act, scene, and number. When a number does not correspond to a given scene (e.g., the entr'actes), I will refer to it by act, title, number.

19. N.V. Gogol', *Sobranie sochinenii v shesti tomakh* (Moscow: Gos. izd-vo khudozh. Literatury, 1952), vol. 3, 44.

20. Dmitrii Shostakovich, *Nos: Opera v 3-x deystviiakh, 10-ti kartinakh po N.V. Gogoliu* (Leningrad: Teakinopechat', 1930), 9. The libretto, along with synopsis and commentary, is also available in French: "Dimitri Chostakovitch, Lady Macbeth de Mzensk; Le nez," *L'Avant-Scène Opéra*, 141 (1991). In this edition, the quoted passage is found on p. 124. Unless otherwise indicated, all translations are my own.

21. Dahlhaus, 101.

22. Shostakovich, *Nos*, 16; *Le nez*, 140. See Fyodor Dostoevsky, *The Brothers Karamazov*, trans. Constance Garnett, rev. and ed. Ralph Matlaw (New York: Norton, 1976), 205 (translation adjusted for accuracy). Dostoyevsky claimed that Smerdyakov's song was "not his own composition, but a popular song." See letter to Nikolai Lyubimov dated May 10, 1879; quoted in Victor Terras, *A Karamazov Companion* (Madison: University of Wisconsin Press, 1981), 17. It is interesting to note the narrator's comments about Smerdyakov's tune: "A young man's voice suddenly began singing in a sugary falsetto, accompanying himself on the guitar.... It was a lackey's tenor and a lackey's song." Except the change from guitar,

most likely the Russian seven-stringed version, to the balalaika, Shostakovich seems to have retained Dostoyevsky's "stage directions" for Ivan's song.

23. Personal correspondence with the author.

24. M. Iankovskii, "'Nos' v Malom opernom teatre," *Rabochii i teatr* (1930, No. 5): 6; quoted in Sof'ia Khentova, *Shostakovich: Zhizn' i tvorchestvo*, vol. 1 (Leningrad: Sovetskii kompozitor, 1985), 207.

25. Gogol, vol. 4, 118.

26. Shostakovich, *Nos*, 23; *Le nez*, 156.

27. See Shostakovich, *Nos*, 9; *Le nez*, 124.

28. In the play, Agafiya Tikhonovna, caught in her dressing gown by a sudden influx of prospective suitors, retires to her room to change. Their interest understandably piqued, the suitors follow one another to her door and attempt to see her through the keyhole. One of the suitors, Zhevachkin (Mr. Chewer), caught behind his rivals, politely requests that they allow him a peek. See Gogol, vol. 4, 125.

29. Bogdanov-Berezovskii, 121.

30. For the original text of Katerina's lascivious aria, which was changed in the opera's second version, see Royal S. Brown, "The Three Faces of Lady Macbeth," in *Russian and Soviet Music*, ed. Malcolm Hamrick Brown, 247.

31. These included *Wozzeck* (premiered 1925; Leningrad premiere, 1927), Krenek's *Der Sprung über den Schatten* (premiered 1924; Leningrad premiere, 1927) and *Jonny spielt auf* (premiered 1927; Leningrad premiere, 1928; Moscow premiere, 1929), Schreker's *Der ferne Klang* (premiered 1912; Leningrad premiere, 1927) and Prokofiev's *Love for Three Oranges* (premiered 1919; Leningrad premiere, 1926). See Norris, 107, and Clark, 227–8.

32. See Solomon Volkov, *Testimony: The Memoirs of Dmitri Shostakovich*, trans. Antonina W. Bouis (New York: Harper & Row, 1979), 42–3.

33. Gennadii Fedorov, "U poroga teatra Shostakovicha," *Teatr*, October 1976, 26.

34. Drew, 922. In an example of cross-cultural non-comprehension, Drew takes literally Kovalyov's misleading use of a military title. Kovalyov is in fact a petty bureaucrat, whose civil rank of "kollezhskii assessor" (college assessor) was equivalent to the military rank of major, the eighth in a hierarchy of fourteen. According to Leonard Kent, civil servants could technically use the corresponding military title, but this was rare outside the highest ranks. For the table of ranks, see *The Collected Tales and Plays of Nikolai Gogol*, ed. Leonard J. Kent, trans. Constance Garnett (New York: Pantheon Books, 1964), xli. Drew has thus missed an important element of Gogol's satire—like Joseph Sedley in *Vanity Fair*, Kovalyov is a civilian who appropriates military trappings to gain social status.

35. On the musical structure of Wozzeck, see Douglas Jarman, *Alban Berg: Wozzeck*, Cambridge Opera Handbooks (New York: Cambridge University Press, 1989), 41–51.

36. See Alla Bretanitskaia, "O muzykal'noi dramaturgii opery 'Nos'," *Sovetskaia muzyka* (1974, No. 9): 47–53. Bretanitskaya argues that the opera is constructed in sonata form, with Scenes 1–4 stating the theme, Scenes 5–13 constituting the development, and Scenes 14–15 and the epilogue serving, respectively, as recapitulation and coda.

37. Carolyn Roberts Finlay, "Operatic Translation and Šostakovič: *The Nose*," *Comparative Literature* 35 (1983): 198–9.

38. In a 1927 article, Berg states: "I simply wanted to compose good music; to develop musically the contents of Georg Büchner's immortal drama; to translate his poetic language into music. Other than that, when I decided to write an opera, my only intention, as related to the technique of composition, was to give the theatre what belongs to the theatre.

The music was to be so formed that at each moment it would fulfill its duty of serving the action." (Alban Berg, "A word about 'Wozzeck'," in Jarman, 152.) Berg here promises to serve not only the drama, but also the theater, that is, the performative aspect of the opera, the action on the stage.

39. For a comparison of Shostakovich's recitative with that of Musorgsky's "The Marriage," see Grigor'eva, 80–2.

40. Bretanitskaia, 50. For a different view of Shostakovich's setting of Gogol's text, one that emphasizes the composer's fidelity to the rhythm of regular speech, see Alexander N. Tumanov, "Correspondence of Literary Text and Musical Phraseology in Shostakovich's Opera *The Nose* and Gogol's Fantastic Tale," *The Russian Review* 52 (1993): 397–414 (especially 404–5 and 413–4).

41. Drew cannot imagine anyone but Shostakovich making an opera of "The Nose," "the famous story of little Major Kovalev who lost his nose and didn't know where to find it.... If Shostakovich had not made an opera of the story, no one else would have done." Drew, 922. Similarly, Gary Schmidgall remarks that "[Büchner] was also obliged to wait for nineteenth-century operatic conventions to be replaced by ones more congenial to his art." Gary Schmidgall, *Literature as Opera* (New York: Oxford University Press, 1977), 290.

42. Emerson, "Back to the Future," 74.

43. Georg Büchner, *Complete Works and Letters*, ed. Walter Hinderer and Henry J. Schmidt, trans. Henry J. Schmidt, The German Library, vol. 28 (New York: Continuum, 1986), 209–10.

44. Ann Shukman, "Gogol's 'The Nose' or the Devil in the Works," in *Nikolay Gogol: Text and Context*, ed. Jane Grayson and Faith Wigzell (London: Macmillan, 1989), 78.

45. See Schmidgall, 316. It is curious, however, that in *Woyzeck*, Büchner lists the Feast of the Annunciation as July 20 rather than March 25. See Büchner, 217.

46. Gogol, vol. 3, 50.

47. See Tumanov's interesting remarks on this issue. Tumanov, 405–6.

48. Schmidgall, 301.

49. Shostakovich, "Pochemu 'Nos'?," in Shostakovich, *Nos*, 4.

50. For an interesting refutation of Shostakovich's remarks on the opera, see Bogdanov-Berezovskii, 112–5.

51. Joseph Kerman, "Reading Opera," *New York Review of Books* 25 (February 9, 1978): 30.

52. The idea of orchestra as narrator in *Lady Macbeth* was proposed by Caryl Emerson ("Back to the Future," 69–70.) Related to this is what Tumanov calls orchestral or symphonic *skaz* (Tumanov, 401). *Skaz* is the slippery term the Russian formalist critic Boris Eikhenbaum coined to describe how Gogol's narrative voice mimics oral performance. Shostakovich's use of symphonic *skaz*, in Tumanov's view, "could have been, and apparently was" derived from the formalists' view of Gogol's narrator (Tumanov, 401). I disagree. Shostakovich's interest in Gogol and his participation in the cultural scene of post-revolutionary Leningrad make his passing familiarity with contemporary literary theory inevitable; I would hesitate to reduce Shostakovich's adaptation of "The Nose" to a programmatic application of formalist principles. By contrast, although Reed Merrill believes that *skaz* exerted influence on Shostakovich, he allows for the composer's independent appropriation of Gogol's narrative technique. "It appears," he writes, "that Shostakovich was aware of the *skaz* technique, if not the term itself, when he was working on the score." Reed Merrill, "The Grotesque in Music: Shostakovich's *Nose*," *Russian Literature Triquarterly* 23 (1990): 307.

53. See Lindenberger, 34–5.

54. Grigor'eva, 83–4.

55. As Norris points out, it is significant that the police sergeant is a non-commissioned officer. Norris, 112.

56. Act I, Introduction, No. 1; most of the barber's race down the embankment (Act I, Scene 2, No. 3); the percussion interlude (Act I, Entr'acte, No. 4); Kovalyov's galop (Act I, Galop, No. 6); the fugue Entr'acte (Act II, Entr'acte, No. 10); the Police Captain's galop at the end of the scene in the Petersburg Post Station (Act III, Scene 7, No. 12); the beginning of Kovalyov's walk—his nose regained—along Nevsky Prospect (Epilogue, Scene 10, No. 16).

57. Valentina Rubtsova, "Zametki ob orkestre v operakh S. Prokof'eva 'Liubov k trem apel'sinam', 'Duen'ia' i D. Shostakovicha 'Nos'," *Voprosy teorii i estetiki muzyki, vyp. 15* (Leningrad, 1977), 128. Note that the exceptions are Kovalyov's laments and Ivan's song.

58. Auden, 472.

59. Bubennikova, 45.

60. In the 1974 Moscow recording, a multiplicity of human voices accompanies, or rather, obscures Ivan's canon. Passers-by call out to Ivan Yakovlevich, mocking him. This device, which Shostakovich did not include in his score, externalizes Ivan's tension, makes it more rigorously dramatic (although not any more theatrical) by placing its expression in spoken voices. These voices lead the audience to believe that Ivan's tension stems at least in part from the mocking catcalls that whirl around him and obscure the internal tension of the orchestra's invidious canon.

61. Bubennikova, 46.

62. In fact, Lev Kuleshov's popular 1924 farce "Neobychainye prikliucheniia Mistera Vesta v strane Bol'shevikov" [The Extraordinary Adventures of Mister West in the Land of the Bolsheviks] contains a preposterous chase scene involving a gun-toting American cowboy in a horse-drawn sled, the police, and several passing muzhiks. Several commentators, among them Emerson, Grigoryeva, and Vladimir Hoffmann, note Shostakovich's reliance on cinematic techniques in *The Nose*, but none offer concrete examples. See Emerson, "Back to the Future," 74; Grigor'eva, 99; Hoffmann, cited by Merrill, 309. As Katerina Clark has pointed out to me in correspondence, "'cinefication' was a general slogan for Soviet literature and theatre in the mid-1920's."

63. Lindenberger, 95.

64. Boris V. Asaf'ev, *Izbrannye trudy*, vol. 5 (Moscow: Izd-vo Akademii Nauk SSSR, 1957), 65.

65. Asaf'ev, 118.

66. Lev Anninskii, *Leskovskoe ozherelie*, 2nd ed. (Moscow: Kniga, 1986), 76.

67. Solomon Volkov, *Petersburg: A Cultural History*, trans. Antonina W. Bouis (New York: Free Press, 1995), 409–10.

68. See Catherine Clément, *Opera, or the Undoing of Women*, trans. Betsy Wing (Minneapolis: University of Minnesota Press, 1988).

69. Leskov to N.N. Strakhov dated December 7, 1864; quoted in Hugh MacLean, *Nikolai Leskov: The Man and His Art* (Cambridge, MA: Harvard University Press, 1977), 146.

70. See I.V. Stoliarova, "Tragicheskoe v povesti Leskova 'Ledi Makbet Mtsenskogo uezda'," *Russkaia literatura* (1981, No. 4): 77–84; Kenneth Lantz, *Nikolay Leskov* (Boston: Twayne's, 1979), 44–5.

71. In his disputed memoirs, *Testimony*, Shostakovich claims that his collaborator on his opera libretti, Alexander Preis, "created a marvelous opera plot especially for me: the life of

women who want to be emancipated. It was to be a serious opera. But nothing came of it, nothing." Volkov, *Testimony*, 206. [See also Chapter 6.—Ed.]

72. D.D. Shostakovich, "Tragediia—satira," *Sovetskoe iskusstvo*, October 16, 1932. Quoted in Laurel Fay, *Shostakovich: A Life* (New York: Oxford University Press, 2000), 69.

73. Introduction to a 1934 libretto of *Katerina Izmailova*; quoted in Elizabeth Wilson, *Shostakovich: A Life Remembered*, original ed., (Princeton: Princeton University Press, 1994), 96.

74. Anninskii, 75. Also see Richard Taruskin, *Defining Russia Musically: Historical and Hermeneutical Essays* (Stanford: Stanford University Press, 1997), 504–5.

75. "Moe ponimanie 'Ledi Makbet'," in *Ledi Makbet Mtsenskogo uezda: Opera D.D. Shostakovicha* (Leningrad: Gosudarstvennyi Akademicheskii Malyi Opernyi Teatr, 1934), 6. Quoted in Emerson, "Back to the Future," 63.

76. Taruskin, 509.

77. "Sumbur vmesto muzyki: ob opere 'Ledi Makbet Mtsenskogo uezda' D. Shostakovicha," *Pravda*, January 28, 1936, 3. Quoted in Norris, 121.

78. See Emerson, "Back to the Future," 75. Also see Marina Tcherkashina, "Gogol and Leskov in Shostakovich's Interpretation," *International Journal of Musicology* 1 (1992): 239.

79. Anninskii, 91.

80. See Emerson, "Back to the Future," 74–5.

81. MacLean, 149.

82. Dahlhaus, 95–111.

83. Emerson, "Back to the Future," 68.

84. Norris, 118.

85. Taruskin, 503.

86. Compare Sylvia Harvey, who writes that "film noir offers us again and again examples of abnormal or monstrous behavior, which defy the patterns established for human social interaction, and which hint at a series of radical and irresolvable contradictions buried deep within the total system of economic and social interactions that constitute the known world." Sylvia Harvey, "Women's Place: The Absent Family of Film Noir," in *Women in Film Noir: New Edition*, 2nd ed., ed. E. Ann Kaplan (London: British Film Institute, 1998), 35.

87. N.S. Leskov, *Povesty i rasskazy* (Moscow: Russkii iazyk, 1985), 17–8. I have translated the quoted passages myself. For a full translation, see Nikolai Leskov, *Lady Macbeth of Mtsensk and Other Stories*, trans. David McDuff (New York: Penguin, 1987). All references to "Leskov" are to the Russian version.

88. Ibid., 18.

89. D.D. Shostakovich and A. Preis, libretto to *Lady Macbeth of Mtsensk*, trans. Joan Pemberton Smith, in booklet to sound recording conducted by Mstislav Rostropovich (EMI CDS 7 49955 2), 28. Hereafter referred to as "Libretto." In this and subsequent references to the libretto, I have adjusted the translation for accuracy and emphasis.

90. An early version of the libretto made an unambiguous reference to Zinovy's impotence in Scene 3, after Sergei's seduction/rape of Katerina. In his response—later deleted—to Katerina's protest that she is a married women, Sergei said, "Ho, ho. Seems I have never seen married women give themselves to me so quickly. Ho, ho. Zinovy heh Borisovich. Ho-ho-ho-ho … he couldn't [****] his wife … ho-ho-ho-ho." Translated by and quoted in Laurel E. Fay, "From *Lady Macbeth* to *Katerina*: Shostakovich's versions and revisions," in *Shostakovich Studies*, ed. David Fanning (Cambridge: Cambridge University Press, 1995), 166.

91. Libretto, 62.
92. Ibid., 30.
93. Ibid., 34.
94. Alla Bogdanova, *Opery i balety Shostakovicha* (Moscow: Sovetskii kompozitor, 1979), 179.
95. Libretto, 90.
96. Ibid., 94.
97. Ibid., 94.
98. Leskov, 34.
99. Alexander Ostrovsky, *Plays*, trans. Margaret Wettlin (Moscow: Progress, 1974), 238.
100. Leskov, 35.
101. Ibid., 19.
102. Ibid., 20.
103. Libretto, 36–8.
104. Ibid., 40.
105. Ibid., 46,
106. Ibid., 44–6.
107. Tcherkashina, 240.
108. Emerson, "Back to the Future," 75.
109. Barbara Evans Clements, "The Birth of the New Soviet Woman," in *Bolshevik Culture: Experiment and Order in the Russian Revolution*, ed. Abbott Gleason, Peter Kenez, and Richard Stites (Bloomington: Indiana University Press, 1985), 220.
110. Taruskin, 501.
111. Ibid., 503.
112. Galina Vishnevskaya, *Galina: A Russian Story*, trans. Guy Daniels (San Diego: Harcourt Brace Jovanovich, 1984), 355.
113. Libretto, 104.
114. Ibid., 112.
115. Emerson, "Back to the Future," 73.
116. Ibid., 77.
117. Libretto, 128.
118. Emerson, "Back to the Future," 64.

Chapter 12

1. *Sovetskaia muzyka* (1935, No. 3): 33.
2. Ibid.
3. [However, see Chapters 11 and 15 of the present volume.—Ed.]
4. Alban Berg, "A Lecture on 'Wozzeck'," in Douglas Jarman, *Alban Berg: Wozzeck* (Cambridge: Cambridge University Press, 1989), 161.
5. On the structural significance of the six-pitch "whole-tone plus one" set (a five-pitch whole-tone segment plus an odd note), see George Perle, *Serial Composition and Atonality*, 6th ed. (Berkeley: University of California Press, 1991), 38–9; and Douglas Jarman, *The Music of Alban Berg* (Berkeley: University of California Press, 1979), 57–8.
6. Pauline Fairclough, *A Soviet Credo: Shostakovich's Fourth Symphony* (Aldershot: Ashgate, 2006), 90.
7. Karen Kopp, *Form und Gehalt der Symphonien des Dmitri Schostakowitsch* (Bonn: Verlag für systematische Musikwissenschaft, 1990), 158.

8. Joseph E. Darby, "Dmitri Shostakovich's Second, Third, and Fourth Symphonies: Problems of Context, Analysis, and Interpretation" (Ph.D. diss., City University of New York, 1999), 302.

9. Marina Sabinina, *Shostakovich: Simfonist: Dramaturgiia, estetika, stil'* (Moscow: Muzyka, 1976), 104–5.

10. Eric Roseberry, *Ideology, Style, Content, and Thematic Process in the Symphonies, Cello Concertos, and String Quartets of Shostakovich* (New York: Garland, 1989), 405.

11. Richard M. Longman, *Expression and Structure: Processes of Integration in the Large-Scale Instrumental Music of Dmitri Shostakovich,* vol. 1 (New York: Garland, 1989), 10.

12. Aleksandr Naumovich Dolzhanskii, "O ladovoi osnove sochinenii Shostakovicha," *Sovetskaia muzyka* (1947, No. 4): 65–74; reprinted in *Cherty stilia D. Shostakovicha,* ed. Liubov' Berger (Moscow: Sovetskii kompozitor, 1962), 24–42.

13. Ellon D. Carpenter, "Russian Theorists on Modality in Shostakovich's Music," in *Shostakovich Studies,* ed. David Fanning (Cambridge: Cambridge University Press), 91.

14. The six variants are: 1) Dolzhansky's eight-note "Alexandrian" scale; 2) Adam's nine-note "mediant-derived mode"; 3) Burda's "melodic nine-note mode"; 4) Dolzhansky's "Alexandrian decachord"; 5) Adam's nine-note "submediant-derived mode"; and 6) Burda's "nine-note mode." See Carpenter, 91.

15. Because Clifton Callender has recently drawn attention to the "Prometheus" or "Mystic" chord's containment in the acoustic collection, it is reasonable to ask if Shostakovich may not have inherited the collection from Scriabin. But the removal of that one pitch to transform the acoustic collection into Scriabin's six-note "Mystic" chord (i.e., removing the D from the collection C-sharp–D–E–F–G–A–B) results in the net loss of a half-step and two minor thirds, and curtails the potential for generating minor-mode melodic material, thus rendering this six-note collection irrelevant to Shostakovich's practice. See Clifton Callender, "Voice-leading Parsimony in the Music of Alexander Scriabin," *Journal of Music Theory* 42 (Fall 1998): 219–34.

16. [The Interval Class Vector of a pitch collection is a tally of each interval class, in ascending order, contained within that collection. For example, the Interval Class Vector for a major scale [254361] indicates a scale containing two minor seconds, five major seconds, four minor thirds, three major thirds, six perfect fourths, and one tritone. The remaining intervals do not appear in the vector, since they generate no further information—a scale with two minor seconds will, by definition, have two major sevenths; five major seconds equate to five minor sevenths; etc.—Ed.]

17. For Schoenberg's explanation of the term, see the chapter "Vagrant Harmonies," in Arnold Schoenberg, *Structural Functions of Harmony,* ed. Leonard Stein (New York: Norton, 1969), 44–50.

18. The soloist's dramatic opening passage in the first movement begins with three C minor scales that ascend from C to C in typical "melodic minor" fashion. However, in an F minor passage for piano during the development, a transformed version of the scale makes a more unusual ascent: from a leading tone on the downbeat. And although the rondo's main theme suggests the harmonic minor pitch vocabulary, the coda—ostensibly in C major—contains a melodic G-sharp, whose salience in the coda's opening scalar passage might be taken as an incursion into diatonic C major of a six-pitch fragment of the acoustic collection (G-sharp, A, B, C, D, E).

19. The rapid scalar rips in mm. 30, 46, and later are functionally explained as a dominant preparation (i.e., a scalarization of a first-inversion dominant chord) for a tonicization of B-flat. Yet by using a linear segment consisting of pitches A–B-flat–C–D-flat–E-flat–F in

lieu of a chord, Chopin shows that basic harmonic information in tonal music can be conveyed by means of a dramatic linear gesture, even an unaccompanied or unharmonized line, as later occurs frequently in Shostakovich.

20. In mm. 1–8 of "Samuel Goldenberg and Schmuyle," Musorgsky begins a phrase three times with the leading tone A from the tonic key of B-flat minor, a tonality that is simultaneously being turned into a folk mode, due to augmented intervals.

21. Although there is far less harmonic ambiguity in the oboe's opening phrase of the Fourth Symphony's second movement in the key of B-flat minor, the plagal range of the melodic line results in an unconventional use of all seven pitches of the ascending melodic minor scale, i.e., the acoustic collection.

22. In this exceptional example, the ascending "Phrygian second" is lacking, yet the scalar usage is every bit as unconventional. Although much of the splendor of the scene's D-flat theme is owed to the effective oscillation of D-flat major and A-major triads, the scalar melody itself features a pronounced five-pitch whole-tone segment (F–E-flat–D-flat–B–A) and—major triads notwithstanding—would actually present the full seven pitches of the melodic minor scale (!), were the missing A-flat and G-flat to be supplied. In Tatyana's last phrase ("Slova nadezhdi mne shepnul") prior to the emergence of the D-flat theme, six of the seven pitches of the collection do occur (at a different transposition) and the more usual minor-mode potential of the collection is suggested.

23. Allen Forte, "The Mask of Tonality: Alban Berg's Symphonic Epilogue to 'Wozzeck'," in *Alban Berg: Historical and Analytical Perspectives,*" ed. David Gable and Robert Morgan (Oxford: Clarendon Press, 1991), 199.

24. Igor Glebov [pseud., Boris Asafyev], "Muzyka Votstseka," *Novaia muzyka* 1 (1927): 35.

25. Vladimir Dranishnikov, "Votstsek," *Novaia muzyka* 1 (1927): 18–28.

26. Berg, 155.

27. George Perle, *The Operas of Alban Berg*, vol. 1, "Wozzeck" (Berkeley: University of California Press, 1980), 133.

28. A translation appears in Jarman, *Alban Berg: Wozzeck*, 143–8.

29. Berg, 161.

30. Ibid., 155.

31. Perle, 161–2.

32. Shteinberg later maintained that the break occurred in the spring of 1927, when Shostakovich showed him his newly composed *Aphorisms* for Piano, op. 13. For Sofia Khentova's discussion of the process of alienation between teacher and student, see Sof'ia Mikhailovna Khentova, *D. Shostakovich: Zhizn' i tvorchestvo* (Leningrad: Sovetskii kompozitor, 1985–86), 1, 161–2, 184, and 530–1.

33. For commentary on Asafyev's assessment of Shostakovich in 1927 and citations from Asafyev's essay "Ten Years of Russian Symphonic Music," see David Haas, *Leningrad's Modernists* (New York: Peter Lang, 1998), 40–1.

34. Mikhail Ivanovich Chulaki, "O V. Shcherbacheve i ego shkole," in *Shcherbachev: Stat'i, materialy, pis'ma*, ed. Raisa Slonimskaia (Leningrad: Sovetskii kompozitor, 1985), 85.

35. Extensive descriptions, excerpts of the melodic lines, and stylistic commentaries on both the Second Symphony and the Septet are found in Haas, 123–54 and 197–213.

36. Valerian Bogdanov-Berezovsky acknowledged that Shostakovich repeatedly "showed his works … to Shcherbachov, Ryazanov, [Nikolai] Malko, and Asafyev." Quoted in Haas, 178–9.

37. Sheinberg's treatment of harmony is limited to an extended analysis of a single work, the Prelude in A minor, op. 34, No. 2, which happens to be among the most harmonically

baffling of the set. It is also anomalous with respect to the use of the acoustic collection, probably because the dense commingling of four pitch vocabularies (elegantly captured in Sheinberg's quadra-color plates!) precludes full seven-pitch statements of it. On the other hand, subsets extracted from it could easily interface with all four of Sheinberg's layers, according to her criteria. This illustration of Bakhtinian "plurivocal parody" is found in Esti Sheinberg, *Irony, Satire, Parody and the Grotesque in the Music of Shostakovich* (Aldershot: Ashgate, 2000), 176–85.

    38. [See Chapter 15 of the current volume for a use of Berg's tone row in Shostakovich's Violin Sonata.—Ed.]

Chapter 13

    1. [See Chapter 6.—Ed.]

    2. The sketch has been published in *New Collected Works* 3. The first page of the autograph score is also reproduced in *Collected Works* 2: frontispiece.

    3. Eric Roseberry, *Ideology, Style, Content, and Thematic Process in the Symphonies, Cello Concertos, and String Quartets of Shostakovich* (New York: Garland, 1979), 44–45.

    4. The first four pitches of the first subject are an exact quotation from the trio (Fig. 123) of the second movement of the Fourth Symphony.

    5. For a description of how this second subject functions harmonically, see Joseph Huband, "The First Five Symphonies of Dmitri Shostakovich" (D.A. diss., Ball State University, 1984), 60–3.

    6. Richard M. Longman, *Expression and Structure: Processes of Integration in the Large-Scale Instrumental Music of Dmitri Shostakovich* (New York: Garland, 1989), 75. Roy Blokker also makes a comparison between the melodic style of the first subject's second strain and that of Berlioz. Roy Blokker, *The Music of Dmitri Shostakovich—The Symphonies* (London: The Tantivy Press, 1979), 67.

    7. For example, Bill Thaddeus Stanley, Jr., "The Relationship of Orchestration to Formal Structures in the Non-Programmatic Symphonies of Shostakovich" (Ph.D. diss., Florida State University, 1979), 21.

    8. Quarter = 92 (Fig. 17), *poco animando* (Fig. 18, b4), 104 (Fig. 19), 126 (Fig. 22), and 132 (Fig. 25, b4).

    9. David Fanning, *The Breath of the Symphonist: Shostakovich's Tenth* (London: Royal Musical Association, 1988), 34.

    10. David Fanning, "Introduction. Talking about Eggs: Musicology and Shostakovich," *Shostakovich Studies* (Cambridge: Cambridge University Press, 1995), 10–12.

    11. Jacques Wildberger, *Dmitri Schostakowitsch 5. Symphonie D-Moll op. 47* (Munich: Wilhelm Fink, 1989), 22; Hugh Ottaway, *Shostakovich Symphonies*, BBC Music Guides, No. 39 (London: BBC Publications, 1978), 27.

    12. Fanning, *The Breath of the Symphonist*, 34.

    13. Joseph Huband, "Shostakovich's Fifth Symphony: A Soviet Artist's Reply ...?," *Tempo* 173 (1990): 15, n25.

    14. Stanley, 21.

    15. Souster does not give a starting point, but his statement that the themes "re-emerge ... in a different order" implies Fig. 39. Tim Souster, "Shostakovich at the Crossroads," *Tempo* 78 (Autumn 1966): 6.

    16. Roseberry, 147–8 and 154–6.

17. Ottaway, 27.

18. Longman, 30.

19. Fanning, *The Breath of the Symphonist*, 29.

20. In this example, one element of resolution, namely that of harmonic inversion, is delayed. The blazing return of the first subject in the tonic (bar 208) is mitigated by the presence of a dominant pedal. As the music winds down, tonic (E minor) harmony is presented in second and in first inversions, but conspicuously not in root position. With this tension unresolved, the second subject is restated in E major, again avoiding reference to the tonic chord in root position. Remarkably, other than a fleeting arpeggio at bar 246, the full resolution does not arrive until the restatement of the third subject (bar 251), in the tonic major and over root position harmony—forty-four bars into the recapitulation. This long-awaited moment of true resolution is made still more poignant by the altered presentation of this third theme—now *piano* and exquisitely rescored.

21. Karen Kopp, *Form und Gehalt der Symphonien des Dmitri Schostakowitsch* (Bonn: Verlag für systematische Musikwissenschaft, 1990), 195.

22. *Shostakovich Symphonies 4 and 5*, Chicago Symphony Orchestra, cond. André Previn. EMI CZS 5 72658 2

23. *Shostakovich Symphony No. 5*, Scottish National Orchestra, cond. Neeme Järvi. Chandos CHAN 8650

24. Ian MacDonald, *The New Shostakovich*, original ed. (Boston: Northeastern University Press, 1990), 129.

25. Roseberry, 159.

26. Ibid., 98. Other examples include: Fourth Symphony, first movement; Fifth Symphony, second movement; Seventh Symphony, first movement; and Tenth Symphony, first and fourth movements.

27. Michael Steinberg, *The Symphony: A Listener's Guide* (New York: Oxford University Press, 1995), 543–4.

28. The marking of eighth = 69 at Fig. 103 should surely read quarter = 69. (Cf. exposition at quarter = 92.)

29. A term used by Jacques Wildberger. Wildberger, 25.

30. For a more detailed discussion of this finale's structure, see Michael Mishra, "Soviet Musical Criticism and Shostakovich's Fifth Symphony" (D.A. diss., University of Northern Colorado, 1997), 119–37, 148.

Chapter 14

1. Jeffrey Kallberg, "The Rhetoric of Genre: Chopin's Nocturne in G minor," *19th Century Music* 11 (1988): 243.

2. One difference between Bach's and Shostakovich's cycles lies in the order in which the twenty-four keys are presented. The *Well-Tempered Clavier* is organized in chromatically ascending order – No. 1, C major; No. 2, C minor; No. 3, C-sharp major, etc. Shostakovich's op. 87 moves through a circle of fifths, addressing each major key, then its relative minor – No. 1, C major; No. 2, A minor; No. 3, G major, etc.

3. [See Chapter 12—Ed.]

4. [This motive is identical in rhythm, and very close in melodic contour, to a short passage in the Fourth Symphony, first movement, Fig. 54.—Ed.]

5. [A similar reassignment of a major second to a minor second had been seen two years previously in the finale of the First Violin Concerto, where the opening melody— E-A-B-A—is transformed at the start of the recapitulation into E–A–B-flat–A (Fig. 102).–Ed.]

Chapter 15

1. The first section of this chapter, "Shostakovich and the Passacaglia: Breaking New Ground?" Is an Expanded Version of "Shostakovich and the Passacaglia: Old Grounds or New?" *The Musical Times* 141 (Spring 2000). Reprinted with permission.

2. Some editions omit Fig. 5. This bar corresponds to Fig. 4, b5.

3. For example, in the wake of her husband Zinovy's murder, dotted rhythms predominate in the closing bars of Act II, and an orchestral fugato introduces the main characters' wedding scene (Act III).

4. I am dissuaded from my earlier choice of D minor by David Fanning. See David Fanning, "Shostakovich in Harmony: Untranslatable Messages," in *Shostakovich in Context*, ed. Rosamund Bartlett (Oxford: Oxford University Press, 2000), 34.

5. Three years after the Eighth Symphony, its passacaglia was almost certainly consciously echoed in the parallel movement of the Third Quartet (1946), with a strong similarity in their opening bars and a similar harmonic sleight of hand leading into the finale. But because the Quartet movement possesses two distinct melodic limbs, and repetition within it is very free, its form seems closer to variation than passacaglia.

6. Eric Roseberry's contention that passacaglia also occurs in the final Prelude and Fugue seems unfounded. See Eric Roseberry, "A Debt Repaid? Some Observations on Shostakovich and His Late-Period Recognition of Britten," in *Shostakovich Studies*, ed. David Fanning (Cambridge: Cambridge University Press, 1995), 241.

7. For example, the "Dirge" from the Serenade for Tenor, Horn and Strings (1943).

8. Shostakovich's union of serialism and passacaglia, a straightforward instance of a row temporarily functioning as a ground, is somewhat different to Britten's. In the final scene of *The Turn of the Screw*, there are eight iterations of a ground bass using the first six pitches of a row that was first stated in the opera's prologue and that had formed the basis of its fifteen following variation-interludes. As the final scene unfolds, the row gradually "re-assembles" itself (with eight-, nine-, and ten-note versions) while still functioning as the ground. Only in its last two contrasting statements does the row declare itself fully, although by this point its status as ground has somewhat evaporated.

9. For example, the monumental *Podvizhnoi kontrapunkt strogogo pis'ma* (Invertible Counterpoint in the Strict Style) by Sergei Taneyev, published in Leipzig and Moscow in 1909.

10. Example preserved in the British Museum, Add. Ms. 305130. Printed in *The Mulliner Book*, ed. Denis Stevens, published as *Musica Britannica*, 1 (London: Stainer & Bell, 1951), 5.

11. Significantly, perhaps, these are re-used as pitches 2–5 of the second row of this thirty-six-note multiple theme.

12. [See Chapter 12 of this volume for a possible use of Berg's note-row in Shostakovich's Fifth Symphony.—Ed.]

13. Hans Keller, "Shostakovich's Twelfth Quartet," *Tempo* 99 (Autumn 1970): 6–15.

14. Eric Roseberry, *Ideology, Style, Content, and Thematic Process in the Symphonies, Cello Concertos, and String Quartets of Shostakovich* (New York: Garland, 1989), 470–501.

15. Jacques Wildberger, "Ausdruck lähmender Angst," *Neues Zeitschrift für Musik* 151 (1990): 4–11.

16. Peter Child, "Voice-Leading Patterns and Interval Collections in Late Shostakovich: Symphony No. 15," *Music Analysis* 12 (1993): 71–88.

17. Peter J. Schmelz, "Shostakovich's 'Twelve-Tone' Compositions and the Politics and Practice of Soviet Serialism," in *Shostakovich and His World*, ed. Laurel E. Fay (Princeton: Princeton University Press, 2004), 303–54.

18. [More specifically, Shostakovich may have been inspired by his students, Boris Tchaikovsky and Yury Levitin, both of whom had written serial pieces in 1966, the year before Shostakovich. See Chapter 19 in this volume.—Ed.]

19. Because of the large number of note-rows in Shostakovich, discussion is generally confined to those that are of particular significance in the development of Shostakovich's technique. Of the rest, some adhere strictly to the tenets of serialism in their construction, while others repeat certain freedoms that are found in earlier examples. In no way would consideration of these have affected this study's basic conclusions.

20. [A notable exception can be found in the Thirteenth Quartet, at Fig. 20, b4, where the row that has been reiterated over the previous nine bars then appears, for one time only, in retrograde. See Chapter 10.—Ed.]

21. Although the Fourth Symphony's first movement contains a famous pair of twelve-note chords (Fig. 90, b13), these were employed purely for their sonority and, as such, could not be said to represent a precursor of serial technique.

22. Many of these rows are listed in Erin Michael Rettig, "Melodic, Harmonic, and Formal Analysis of Symphony No. 14, op. 135 (1969) by Dmitri Shostakovich" (B.M. thesis, James Madison University, 1995).

23. David Brown, *Tchaikovsky: A Biographical and Critical Study.* vol. 4, *The Final Years, 1885–1893* (London: Victor Gollancz, 1991), 422–3.

Chapter 16

1. This chapter is a modified reprint of Richard Burke, "Film, Narrative, and Shostakovich's Last Quartet," *The Musical Quarterly* 83 (1999): 413–29. Reprinted with permission.

2. Paul Griffiths, *The String Quartet: A History* (New York: Thames and Hudson, 1983), 215.

3. Hugh Ottaway, notes to Shostakovich, *String Quartets Nos. 5 and 15*. Borodin String Quartet. EMI CDC 7 49270 2.

4. In Jay Leyda, *Kino: A History of Russian and Soviet Film*, 3rd ed. (Princeton: Princeton University Press, 1983), 173.

5. V.I. Pudovkin, *Film Technique and Film Acting*, trans. Ivor Montagu (New York: Bonanza Books, 1949), 140.

6. Leyda, 164.

7. See Herbert Eagle, *Russian Formalist Film Theory* (Ann Arbor: Michigan Slavic Publications, 1981).

8. Viktor Shklovsky, "The Film Factory," in *The Film Factory: Russian and Soviet Cinema in Documents*, ed. Richard Taylor and Ian Christie, trans. Richard Taylor (Cambridge, MA: Harvard University Press, 1988), 169.

9. For the use of the Kuleshov effect and other narrative devices in *New Babylon*, see David Bordwell's fascinating analysis of the film in *Narration in the Fiction Film* (Madison, WI: University of Wisconsin Press, 1985), 249–68.

10. *Sovetskii ekran*, March 12, 1929; quoted in Leyda, 259.

11. Sergei Eisenstein, *The Film Sense*, trans. Jay Leyda (New York: Harcourt, Brace and World, 1942), 4.

12. Dorothea Redepenning also points out an important resemblance between this arpeggio figure and the one in the song "Night" from the *Suite on Poems of Michelangelo*, op. 145. Dorothea Redepenning, "Shostakovich's Song Cycles," in *Shostakovich Studies*, ed. David Fanning (Cambridge: Cambridge University Press, 1995), 224.

Chapter 17

1. For a fuller study, see John Riley, *Dmitri Shostakovich: a Life in Film* (London: I.B. Tauris, 2005).

2. V.I. Lenin, "Partiinaia organizatsiia i partiinaia literatura," *Novaia zhizn,'* No. 12, November 13, 1905. Reprinted in V.I. Lenin, *Collected Works*, vol. 10 (Moscow: Progress Publishers, 1965), 44–49.

3. Anatoli Lunacharsky, "Conversation with Lenin," in *Lenin i kino*, ed. G.M. Boltianskii (Moscow: Gosudarstvennoe izd-vo, 1925), 16–19; quoted in R. Taylor, ed. and trans., and I. Christie, ed., *The Film Factory: Russian and Soviet Cinema in Documents 1896–1939*, (Cambridge, MA: Harvard University Press, 1988), 56–7. Note that Lunacharsky's report of this conversation was published only after Lenin's death.

4. "Statement on Sound," in *S.M. Eisenstein: Selected Works*, vol. 1. *Writings 1922–1934*, ed. Richard Taylor, trans. William Powell (London: British Film Institute, 1996), 113–4.

5. For an annotated translation, see Taylor and Christie, 58–64. For a different, unannotated version, see Marek Pytel and Giovanni Dadomo, *Eccentrism* (London: The Eccentric Press, 1992).

6. Such multimedia experiments were popular in the 1920s. The Dadaist film *Entr'acte* (1923), with music by Satie, began life as cinematic interlude in the ballet *Relâche*, and Eisenstein at one point considered having the prow of a ship burst through the screen at the end of *The Battleship Potemkin* (1927).

7. *New Collected Works* 122 (2004): 533 (Russian), 544 (English).

8. Grigorii Kozintsev, *Glubokii ekran* (Moscow: Iskusstvo, 1971), 101.

9. Grigorii Kozintsev, *King Lear: The Space of Tragedy*, trans. Mary A. Mackintosh (London: Heinemann, 1977), 243.

10. For translations of some of the conference speeches, see Taylor and Christie, 241–5 and 250–1.

11. *Sovetskii ekran*, vol. 11, No. 29, 3. This is one of the most important texts on Shostakovich's film work and his general aesthetic at the time, yet it has rarely been reproduced in full and the first complete English translation only appeared in Marek Pytel, *New Babylon* (London: The Eccentric Press, 1999), 24, 26.

12. Ibid.

13. More than once, Trauberg claimed the counterpoint Was his idea. "When Film Making Was All About Circus and Scandal," *The Times* [London], January 20, 1983, 8. Theodore van Houten, *Leonid Trauberg and his Films: Always the Unexpected* ('s-Hertogenbosch: Art & Research, 1989), 151.

14. The estimates are taken, respectively, from *Iz istorii Lenfil'ma vyp.* 1 (Leningrad: Iskusstvo, 1968), 256; and Pytel, *New Babylon*, 28. Pytel believes that Trauberg may have

misremembered or confused the pre- and post-censorship versions, or that it was possibly a simple slip of the tongue.

15. Viktor Shklovsky, "The Film Language of 'New Babylon'," in Taylor and Christie, 311, 313.

16. Petr Sobolevskii, *Iz zhizni kinoaktera* (Moscow: Iskusstvo, 1967), 85–116.

17. Pytel, passim.

18. Conductor Mark Fitz-Gerald discusses some of the problems in John Riley, "New Babylon in Rotterdam," *DSCH* 16 (2002): 50–1. Rozhdestvensky produced a suite (Sovetskii kompozitor, 4191) that he then altered in his own recording. Boosey and Hawkes' edition, although used as the basis of the 1980s performances, was never published. The Sikorski edition is the basis of the only complete recording to date (Capriccio 10 341/2. Berlin Radio Symphony Orchestra, conductor James Judd). The *New Collected Works* 123 (2005) resolves some of these issues, though it introduces other problems.

19. Pavel Petrov-Bytov had repeatedly criticized *New Babylon* and other avant-garde films. "We Have No Soviet Cinema," *Zhizn' iskusstva*, April 21, 1929, 8. Taylor and Christie, 259–62.

20. For the argument that the split between the "avant-garde" and the "proletarians" was less pronounced than has been suggested in the past, see Neil Edmunds, "The Ambiguous Origins of Socialist Realism and Musical Life in the Soviet Union," in *Socialist Realism and Music*, ed. Mikuláš Bek, et al. (Prague: Koniasch Latin Press, 2004), 115–30.

21. The phrase seems first to have appeared in a speech by *Izvestiya* editor Ivan Gronsky on May 20, 1932.

22. Trauberg claimed to have thought up the tune and that Shostakovich had merely transcribed it. "I wrote the song and instructed Shostakovich how to compose it, and he wrote it right away, a very good song." van Houten, 144.

23. In 1928, Pudovkin had gone to Tuva to make *Storm over Asia* (*Potomok Chingiz-Khana*). Arriving too late to film a particular religious ceremony he managed to persuade the locals to repeat it even though it was only supposed to be performed on a set date.

24. See Harlow Robinson, *Sergei Prokofiev: A Biography* (New York: Paragon House, 1988), 407–8.

25. Shostakovich, "Kino kak shkola kompozitora," in *30 let sovetskoi kinematografii: sbornik stat'ei*, ed. D. Eremin (Moscow: Goskinoizdat, 1950), 354.

26. CSALA St Petersburg rec. gr 257, inv. 16, f 192, sheets 152, 153. See *New Collected Works* 123 (2004): 320 (Russian), 332–3 (English).

27. Boris Shumiatskii, *Kinematografiia millionov* (Moscow: Kinofotoizdat, 1935), 117.

28. Eremin, 355.

29. *The Encounter* is the most accurate of a bewildering array of translated titles, including *Shame*, *Coming Your Way*, *The Passer-by*, and *Turbine 50,000*. The most common translation, *The Counterplan*, refers to the contemporary slogan "Let's have a counterplan to the industrial and financial plan," as factories autonomously "decided" to exceed their production quotas by a set amount. The working title was *Greeting the Future*.

30. Eremin, 355.

31. Shostakovich reused it in the cantata *The Poem of the Motherland* (1947), the score to the films *Michurin* (1948) and *The Song of the Rivers* (1954), and the operetta *Moscow, Cheryomushki* (1958, filmed in 1962 with the name of the city dropped from the title).

32. Kozintsev and Trauberg, "The Youth of Maxim," *Izvestiia*, December 14, 1934. In Taylor and Christie, 338.

33. Actor Boris Chirkov published a collection of the letters. He also appeared in the role in Sergei Gerasimov's wartime propaganda short *Meeting with Maxim* (1941).

34. It may have been simple carelessness that led to both this film and *The Youth of Maxim* sharing an opus number (op. 41), or it may have been a reflection of how unimportant Shostakovich felt them to be.

35. *Collected Works* 41 (1987).

36. The original fourteen 78-rpm sides (06820/33) have been released on CD (BMG (Japan) B0CC 3) as a bonus disc in a four-disc set. A brief report of a screening of the film at the Academy Cinema in London on 26 November 1939 appears in the annual report of the Society for Cultural Relations, 1940. It may be that the 78s were taken from the film soundtrack.

37. "The Decree on the Film 'The Great Life'," in *S.M. Eisenstein: Selected Works*, vol. 3: *Writings 1934–47*, 295–8.

38. Kozintsev and Shostakovich said little or nothing about the break. Trauberg claimed it was due to a mixture of the anti-cosmopolitan campaign, Kozintsev's ambition to carve out a solo career, and an argument over having Kozintsev's wife Sophie Magarill star in Trauberg's solo film *The Actress* (1943). Trauberg broke with Shostakovich in 1950, feeling that the composer had backed out of collaborating on an operetta based on *The Youth of Maxim*. (See van Houten, 146–7, 153–8, 167–8). Yet letters show that Shostakovich had only lent his support to the project to help get Trauberg's libretto accepted, hoping Sviridov would write the music. See Isaak Glikman, *The Story of a Friendship: The Letters of Dmitry Shostakovich to Isaak Glikman*, trans. Anthony Phillips (London: Faber and Faber, 2001), 40, 250.

39. L. Schwarz, "On Modern Film Music," *Sovetskaia muzyka* (1948, No. 3): 6. Quoted in Tatiana Egorova, *Soviet Film Music* (Amsterdam: Harwood Academic Press, 1997), 291.

40. Tikhon Khrennikov, "Muzyk v kino," *Iskusstvo kino* (1950, No. 1): 27.

41. In 1967 he wrote to Glikman: "I really cannot understand why Eisenstein, and for that matter Dovzhenko, are considered such geniuses. I don't much like their work." Having seen *October* with selections from his music, Shostakovich was of the opinion that "overall my music has by and large added to it." Glikman, 146, 298–9, n29.

42. Ibid., 34, 245, n16.

43. For a detailed synopsis and discussion of the film, see Richard Taylor, *Film Propaganda: Soviet Russia and Nazi Germany* (London: I.B. Tauris, 1998), 99–122.

44. Director and film are mentioned in Nikita Khrushchev, *Khrushchev Remembers*, trans. Strobe Talbott (London: Sphere Books, 1971), 306.

45. The deletion of Stalin from Soviet art was by no means comprehensive after 1956. *The Fall of Berlin's* song "Beautiful Day" was published in 1958, and in the same year, among a small rash of Lenin films, Sergei Vasilyev directed *In the Days of October* in which Andro Kobaladze played Stalin. Although not so industrious in portraying the leader as Gelovani, Kobaladze played him several times.

46. There is a monochrome clip from *The Fall of Berlin* in Márta Mészáros' autobiographical *Napló zerelmeimnek* [Diary for my Loves] (1987), in which the young film student is shown the film. The restoration is generally to a very high quality, but there are sections where the original materials have become extremely degraded. It has since been released on DVD, in Russia and in the West.

47. So far there has only been one complete recording of the suite. Marco Polo 8.223897.

48. Grigorii Kozintsev, *Shakespeare: Time and Conscience*, trans. Joyce Vining (New York: Hill and Wang, 1966), 150.

49. Quoted in Marietta Shaginian, *O Shostakoviche: Stati* (Moscow: Muzyka, 1979), 12.

50. *Soviet News*, April 5, 1962.

51. *Pravda*, October 21, 1962.

52. Radio interview, September 2, 1963; reprinted in Lev Grigoryev and Yakov Platek, *Dmitry Shostakovich—About Himself and His Times*, trans. Angus and Neilian Roxburgh (Moscow: Progress Publishers, 1981), 241, 243. It appears on the four-disc set of LPs of speeches by Shostakovich, *Govorit Dmitrii Shostakovich* [Dmitry Shostakovich speaks]. Melodiya M40 41705-12 (record 2, side 1).

53. *Literaturnaia gazeta*, October 12, 1963. The Marx film was one he seemed unable to get started on. During 1965, he wrote to Glikman complaining about it several times. Glikman, 120–2.

54. Kozintsev, *Shakespeare: Time and Conscience*, 266.

55. Kozintsev. "Spasibo za schast'e, kotoroe on mne prinosil," *Sovetskaia muzyka* 9 (1990): 93–9.

56. EMI 77 49955 2.

57. Solomon Volkov, *Testimony: The Memoirs of Dmitri Shostakovich*, trans. Antonina W. Bouis (New York: Harper & Row), 107–8.

58. Galina Vishnevskaya, *Galina: A Russian Story*, trans. Guy Daniels (San Diego: Harcourt Brace Jovanovich, 1984), 358–60.

59. See Glikman, 125, 291, n170.

60. *Don Quixote* is the only major film by Kozintsev that Shostakovich did not score. Kara Karayev filled the breach. Like many other FEKS and Kozintsev films, one of its major themes is foolishness.

61. The last line of "To the Londoners."

62. "Budni i Prazdniki Muzyki: Interviuiu s Dmitrii Shostakovichem," *Izvestiia*, December 7, 1970; reprinted in Grigoryev and Platek, 296.

63. Kozintsev, *The Space of Tragedy*, 254.

64. Ibid., 204, 244.

65. Selections are published in vol. 42 of the *Collected Works*, including some that were not used in the film but excluding some that were, although the selection is not explained. The numbering of the cues is also puzzling; for example, "The First Sighting of Lear's Castle," an early moment in the film, is number 51.

66. Kozintsev, *The Space of Tragedy*, 251.

67. Quoted in the London Symphony Orchestra festival program, *Shostakovich 1906–1975*, 66.

68. Ibid.

69. Kozintsev thought Kurosawa's *Kumonosu-Jo* [Throne of Blood] (1957) the best film version of Macbeth.

70. Kozintsev, *The Space of Tragedy*, 82.

Chapter 18

1. *Muzykal'naia zhizn'* (1966, No. 17): reprinted in Lev Grigoryev and Yakov Platek, *Dmitry Shostakovich—About Himself and His Times*, trans. Angus and Neilian Roxburgh (Moscow: Progress Publishers, 1981), 272.

2. See Sof'ia Khentova, *Shostakovich: zhizn' i tvorchestvo, kniga pervaia* (Leningrad: Sovetskii kompozitor, 1985), 72.

3. Dmitrii Shostakovich, "Avtobiografiia, 1927," *Sovetskaia muzyka* (1966, No. 9): 24.

4. Sof'ia Khentova, *Molodie gody Shostakovicha, kniga pervaia* (Leningrad: Sovetskii kompozitor, 1975), 79.

5. Evgenii Makarov, "Ia bezgranichno uvazhal ego," *Muzykal'naia akademiia* (1993, No. 1): 154.

6. Khentova, *Shostakovich: zhizn' i tvorchestvo, kniga pervaia*, 71.

7. [It is not clear when exactly Shostakovich made the transfer from Glyasser to Rozanova. Shostakovich's own "Avtobiografiia, 1927" states that "in February 1917 I got bored with studying with Glyasser.... From 1917–1919 I studied with A. Rozanova." However, Shostakovich's childhood friend Boris Lossky has claimed that the move was not made until the very end of 1918. He recalls Shostakovich's performance in one of Glyasser's examination concerts in April 1918, his appearance in a group photograph of Glyasser's class the following month, and his attendance at a music theory lesson given by Glyasser in November 1918. How much of this actually precludes Shostakovich from having made the transfer in 1917 is hard to say. It is certainly possible that he was studying with both teachers during 1917–1918. In fact, given his mother's characteristic diplomacy, it is quite likely that this transition was engineered gradually rather than suddenly. See Elizabeth Wilson, *Shostakovich: A Life Remembered*, original ed. (Princeton: Princeton University Press, 1994), 13–14.—Ed.]

8. Aleksandr Rozanov, "Obodriaiushchaia prostota," *Sovetskaia muzyka* (1981, No. 10): 34.

9. Sof'ia Khentova, *V mire Shostakovicha* (Moscow: Kompozitor, 1996), 24.

10. Josef Shvarts, "Neskol'ko sobitii i faktov," in *L. V. Nikolaev, Stat'i i vospominaniia sovremennikov, pis'ma*, comp. Lev Barenboim and Nathan Fishman (Leningrad: Sovetskii kompozitor, 1979), 122.

11. Including: Bach-Liszt Organ Prelude and Fugue in A minor; Beethoven *Waldstein* and *Appassionata* Sonatas; Brahms *Variations on Theme by Handel*; Liszt *Dante* Sonata, "Funerailles" and "Venice and Naples" from *Années de pèlerinage, Spanish Rhapsody, Gnomenreigen, Waldesrauschen,* and *Grand galop chromatique*; Chopin *Krakowiak*, op. 14, First and Second Piano Concertos, Ballades Nos. 1, 2, and 3, Etudes, and numerous miniatures; Schumann *Humoreske* and Sonata in F-sharp minor; Tchaikovsky First Piano Concerto; Scriabin Sonatas Nos. 2, 3, and 4; Prokofiev Third Sonata and First Piano Concerto; plus works of Lyadov and Rachmaninov.

12. Comprising the Eight Preludes, op. 2 (four of which—G, A minor, F minor, and D-flat—were also used for a cycle of preludes composed in collaboration with his friends Pavel Feldt and Georgy Klements), plus an additional prelude in E minor written expressly for the collaborative project.

13. Shvarts, 122.

14. Quoted in Larisa Kazanskaia, "Kruzhok druzei kamernoi muzyki," *Muzykal'naia akademiia* (1996, No. 1): 206.

15. Ibid., 206–7.

16. Ibid., 207–8.

17. Ibid., 208.

18. Letter from Sofia Shostakovich to Leonid Nikolayev dated March 12, 1924. Barenboim and Fishman, 256.

19. Shostakovich's "Avtobiografiia, 1927" gives the autumn of 1923, and there is evidence to suggest that Shostakovich did appear as a cinema pianist as early as this. For example, a poster indicating an appearance at the *Svetlaya lenta* cinema on 23 December 1923 is

reproduced in Sof'ia Khentova, *Zhizn' Shostakovicha v illiustratsiiakh i slove* (Moscow: Maktsentr, 1999), 28. However, letters and other documents point to Shostakovich beginning regular employment in the autumn of 1924. See Laurel Fay, *Shostakovich: A Life* (New York: Oxford University Press, 2000), 23.

20. See Dmitrii Kabalevskii, "Neskol'ko slov o Dmitrii Shostakoviche," in *Dmitrii Shostakovich: sbornik stat'ei*, comp. Givi Ordzhonikidze (Moscow: Sovetskii kompozitor, 1967), 89.

21. Ibid.

22. Nicolai Malko, *A Certain Art* (New York: W. Morrow, 1966), 180.

23. Shostakovich letter to Boleslav Yavorsky dated January 27, 1927. "Khorosho bilo bi ne dymat'," *Muzykal'naia akademiia* (1997, No. 4): 39. The identity of the C-sharp minor Mazurka (op. 50, No. 3 or op. 63, No. 3) is not known.

24. Wilson, original ed., 58–9.

25. Letter to Yavorsky.

26. Dmitrii Shostakovich, "Dumi o proidennom puti," *Sovetskaia muzyka* (1956, No. 9): 11.

27. Grigorii Kogan, *Voprosi pianizma* (Moscow: Sovetskii kompozitor, 1968), 428–9.

28. Rozanov, 34.

29. See Krzysztof Meyer, notes to *Shostakovich Piano Concertos, etc.*, trans. Mary Whittall. EMI CDC 7 54606 2, p. 6.

30. A.K. Smis (alias Konstantin Kuznetsov), "Muzykalno-kriticheskie fragmenti," *Sovetskaia muzyka* (1934, No. 2): 62.

31. Quoted in Vladimir Grigoryev, notes to the LP set *Dmitry Shostakovich—Pianist*, vol. 1. Melodiya, M10-39073-80, p. 5.

32. Letter dated October 4, 1955. Liudmila Karagicheva, ed., *Kara Karaev: stat'i, pis'ma, vyskazyvaniia* (Moscow: Sovetskii kompozitor, 1978), 53.

33. [Tables 18.2 and 18.3 give the tempi heard at the start of each piece. In the faster pieces (*Allegretto* and *Allegro*), Shostakovich had a tendency to accelerate, sometimes at an early stage and often to a quite drastic degree. For example, the 1951 recording of the D major Fugue (marked qtr. = 138) starts at 158, passes through 176 at bar 8 (the entry of the second voice), and 188 at bar 19 (the entry of the third), reaching 196 at bar 42. The tempo then settles in the upper-190s/lower-200s, other than a brief *accelerando* between bars 89 and 107, where it momentarily peaks at about 215. In the slower pieces (*Adagio* and *Andante*), Shostakovich often accelerates as well, although here the upper limit usually remains short of the indicated tempo (e.g., both performances of the E minor Prelude or the 1952 E minor Fugue), only occasionally reaching it (the 1958 E minor Fugue). The movements marked *Moderato* do, in a very few cases, end up faster than the metronome indication as the result of acceleration (e.g., both performances of the C major and B minor Fugues). An examination of the entire op. 87 cycle shows the considerable extent to which our generalization holds true: in none of the slow pieces does Shostakovich play faster than marked, and in only one of the fast pieces (the E-flat minor Fugue) does he play slower. The pieces marked *Moderato* only occasionally end up faster—the aforementioned C major and B minor Fugues; also the G major Prelude and the 1951 performance of the F major Fugue. (Sections marked *più mosso* in the E minor and D minor Fugues have not been considered.)—Ed.]

34. Lidiia Zhukova, *Epilogi, kniga pervaia* (New York: Chalidze, 1983), 27.

35. *Collected Works* 5 (1979): 170.

36. Melodiya 74321 19849-2

37. [The pre-empting of the low B is heard in both performances. The early arrival of the preceding C, notated as a tied grace note in Example 18.2b, is more noticeable on the 1958 recording.—Ed.]

38. [Incidentally, Tatyana Nikolayeva, "after consultation with the composer, and with his approval" (see notes to her 1989 recording on Hyperion CDA66441/3, p. 6), similarly reiterates the bass octaves and, moreover, follows Shostakovich in the aforementioned "syncopation" and broken chord at the end of the E minor Fugue.—Ed.]

39. Khentova, *V mire Shostakovicha*, 208.

40. [The availability of Shostakovich's recordings in the West has traditionally been patchy. The 1990s witnessed several isolated, and usually short-lived, CD reissues of certain pieces on a variety of labels including EMI, Melodiya, Russian Disc, and several smaller labels. In 1997–1998, an attempt was made by the British label Revelation to issue a more-or-less comprehensive series of Shostakovich's Russian and Czech recordings under the title "Shostakovich Plays Shostakovich," but by early 1999, Revelation was forced to suspend operations because of a legal dispute with its Russian suppliers. As of late 2007, all of Shostakovich's performances, with the exception of the 1940 account of the Piano Quintet, the Russian recordings of the Piano Concertos, and the French recordings of the Preludes and Fugues 6, 13, 14, and 18, are back in the catalogue—the French recordings (other than the Preludes and Fugues exceptions already noted) and the Cello Sonata with Rostropovich on EMI, the remainder on smaller and sometimes harder to find labels such as Doremi, Eclectra, Metropole, and Symposium. The notes below give each performance's availability on CD, as of December 2007, together with details of the relevant deleted Revelation issue, the latter noted in parentheses and italics. The 1940 recording of the Piano Quintet was never released by Revelation, so the deleted Multisonic and Danté-Lys issues are given instead. Misattribution of dates and provenance amongst Soviet recordings was quite common; where necessary, these have been corrected in Table 18.3. In this regard, we would like to thank Vladimir Gabyshev for his research at Ostankino and Vsesoyuznaya Studiya Gramzapisi (All-Union Studio of Sound Recording). Additionally, four short film excerpts of Shostakovich the pianist are available on DVD-ROM: First Piano Concerto, third movement (live performance, 1940?); Piano Quintet, fourth movement (live performance with the Borodin Quartet, 1964); Second Piano Trio, first movement (piano part only, at the composer's home, 1944); Seventh Symphony, third movement (at the composer's home, 1941). "DSCH: The Life and Works of Dmitri Shostakovich," *Cultural Heritage Series*, vol. 1 (Chandos Multimedia DVD-ROM, CHAN 550011). A new documentary by Oksana Dvornichenko, *Shostakovich—Pianist*, including all surviving film footage of Shostakovich the pianist, was released at the end of 2006.—Ed.]

41. Doremi DHR-7787 or Symposium 1314. (*Revelation RV70008*). Date mistakenly given on Doremi and Revelation as 1946.

42. EMI 7243 5 62646 2.

43. Symposium 1314. (*Revelation RV70008*). Date mistakenly given as 1946.

44. Symposium 1314. (*Revelation RV70007*). Preludes Nos. 8 and 22 appear on Doremi DHR-7787. Date mistakenly given on Doremi and Revelation as 1946.

45. (*Revelation RV70007*)

46. Eclectra ECCD-2067. (*Revelation RV70002*)

47. (*Revelation RV70006*). Date mistakenly given as 1956.

48. EMI 7243 5 62646 2.

49. Eclectra ECCD-2046 or Brilliant Classics 93096. (*Revelation RV70008*). Eclectra's transfer omits the first movement repeat.

50. EMI CZS 572016-2 or CZS 572295-2. (*Revelation RV70005*)

51. (Multisonic 310179-2 or Danté-Lys 369-370)

52. Eclectra ECCD-2067 or Doremi DHR-7787. (*Revelation RV70005*). Date mistakenly given on Doremi as 1949 and on Revelation as 1950.

53. Doremi DHR-7787. (*Revelation RV70007*). Date mistakenly given on Doremi as 1945.

54. Symposium 1314 or Eclectra ECCD-2046. (*Revelation RV70006*)

55. Symposium 1314 or Doremi DHR-7787. (*Revelation RV70007*). Date mistakenly given on Doremi and Revelation as 1946.

56. Eclectra ECCD-2067. (*Revelation RV70007*)

57. Metropole Mono 008 (*Revelation RV70001 includes Nos. 1, 3, and 5, and Revelation RV70003 includes No. 23*). In the case of Nos. 1, 3, and 5, the date is mistakenly given as 1952.

58. Metropole Mono 008 (*Revelation RV70001 includes Nos. 2, 4, 6–8, and 12–14, and Revelation RV70003 includes Nos. 16, 20, 22, and 24*). Date of No. 16 is mistakenly given as 1951. This 1952 performance of No. 24 also appears alongside the 1958 French recordings of Nos. 1, 4, 5, and 23 on EMI 7243 5 62646 2. Although included on Revelation RV70003, Nos. 17 and 18 are not played by Shostakovich—see Sofia Moshevich, "Russian Revelation a Forgery: Who is Really Playing Shostakovich's F minor Prelude and Fugue?" *DSCH Journal* 12 (2000): 66–9.

59. Recorded in France in 1958, Shostakovich's performances were issued there on LP (*French Columbia FCX 771*). The CD reissue, EMI 7243 5 62646 2, contains only Nos. 1, 4, 5, and 23, plus the 1952 Russian account of No. 24. The French performances of Nos. 6, 13, 14, and 18 have, to date, not appeared on CD.

60. Metropole Mono 008. (*Revelation RV70002*)

61. (*Revelation RV70006*)

62. Eclectra ECCD-2067. (*Revelation RV70002*)

63. (*Revelation RV70006*). Date mistakenly given by Revelation as 1959.)

64. EMI 7243 5 62646 2.

65. Eclectra ECCD-2046. (*Revelation RV70008*). This is a private recording that predates the first performance. Sources vary as to whether it was made at Shostakovich's home or Oistrakh's.

66. Cassette tape—Regent Records MG 5020.

Chapter 19

1. For a complete list of Shostakovich's "official" students, see David Fanning, "Shostakovich and His Pupils," in *Shostakovich and His World,* ed., Laurel E. Fay (Princeton: Princeton University Press, 2004), 277.

2. *Sovetskaia kul'tura*, December 20, 1956. Reprinted in Lev Grigoryev and Yakov Platek, *Dmitry Shostakovich—About Himself and His Times*, trans. Angus and Neilian Roxburgh (Moscow: Progress Publishers, 1981), 184.

3. Elizabeth Wilson, *Shostakovich: A Life Remembered*, original ed. (Princeton: Princeton University Press, 1994), 184.

4. Yury Levitin, "The Teacher," 1976. Quoted in N.V. Lukyanova, *Shostakovich* (Neptune City, NJ: Paganiniana, 1984), 91.

5. *DSCH Journal* 13 (2000): 35.

6. *DSCH Journal* 12 (2000): 8.

7. *DSCH Journal* 14 (2001): 45.

8. For further information on this aspect of Shostakovich's relationship with his students, see Fanning, "Shostakovich and His Pupils," 275–302.

9. Stanley Dale Krebs, *Soviet Composers and the Development of Soviet Music* (London: George Allen and Unwin Ltd., 1970), 236.

10. Else Stone and Kurt Stone, eds., *The Writings of Elliott Carter* (Bloomington: Indiana University Press, 1977), 10.

11. Lukyanova, 86.

12. Moments of the Gadzhyev contain not so much reverberations as outright plagiarism of Shostakovich's Eighth. See Fanning, "Shostakovich and His Pupils," 282–3.

13. A. Kostomolotsky, "Pedagogical Humor," *Sovetskaia muzyka* (1948, No. 4): 89. In Laurel E. Fay, *Shostakovich: A Life* (New York: Oxford University Press, 2000), 163.

14. See Victor Yuzefovich, *Aram Khachaturyan*, trans. Nicholas Kournokoff and Vladimir Bobrov (New York: Sphinx Press, 1985), 48–9.

15. E-mail message to the author, June 29, 2006.

16. *DSCH Journal* 13 (2000): 35.

17. The composer is better known through recordings as Moisei Vainberg, the surname being the English transliteration of the Russian transliteration of Weinberg. However, the name given to him by birth was Mieczysław Weinberg, and the composer's biographer, the late Per Skans, advocated this as the preferred spelling.

18. Per Skans, liner notes to Olympia's series of CDs of the music of Weinberg (Vainberg). This quotation appears as part of the introductory section common to all the issues in this series.

19. Viktor Suslin, *Galina Ustvolskaya: Catalogue*, trans. Alfred Clayton (Hamburg: Musikverlag Hans Sikorski, 1990), 4.

20. Wilson, original ed., 216–7.

21. Thea Derks, "Galina Ustvolskaya: 'Sind Sie Mir Nicht Böse!' (Very Nearly an Interview)," *Tempo* 193 (1995): 32.

22. Ibid.

23. Ibid.

24. Suslin, 5.

25. For further details, see Louis Blois, "Shostakovich and the Ustvolskaya Connexion: a Textual Investigation," *Tempo* 182 (1992): 10–18.

26. Frans C. Lemaire, liner notes to Ustvolskaya, "Preludes and Compositions," MDC 7867 (1994).

27. From interviews conducted with Tchaikovsky from the following sources: L. Mikhailova (*Literaturnaia Rossiia*), G. Ovsiankina (*Muzykal'naia akademiia*), and V. Kelle (*Muzykal'naia zhizn*). The interviews were indistinguishably combined into one poorly translated essay at http://www.mmv.ru/p/bt/english.htm (website no longer available—last accessed August 26, 2006).

28. Unreferenced remark made to the author by the Boris Tchaikovsky Society, Moscow.

28. Sof'ia Khentova, *Shostakovich*, vol. 2 (Leningrad, Sovetskii kompozitor, 1986), 522. Dorothea Redepenning, liner notes for Brodsky String Quartet recording of Shostakovich Complete String Quartets. Teldec 9031 71702-2. Fanning, "Shostakovich and His Pupils," 296.

30. *Sovetskaia muzyka* (1965, No. 12). Quoted in Louis Blois, "The Music of Georgi Sviridov," *Kastelmusick* 8 (1983): 10–11.

31. [See Chapter 8.—Ed.]

32. While the composer's son, Dmitry Galynin, acknowledges the mental breakdown that his father underwent post-1948. he strongly refutes Marina Sabinina's claim of "schizophrenia," stating that no such clinical diagnosis was ever made. (See Wilson, original ed., 224). I am grateful to Dmitry Galynin and to Igor Prokhorov for providing clarification on this point.

33. *Pravda*, December 18, 1952. Reprinted in Grigoryev and Platek, 144–5.

SELECT BIBLIOGRAPHY

Compiled by Michael Mishra

Books and Articles

Abdel-Aziz, Mahmud. *Form und Gehalt in den Violoncellowerken von Dmitri Schostako-witsch*. Regensburg: G. Bosse, 1992.

Abraham, Gerald. *Eight Soviet Composers*. London: Oxford University Press, 1943, rev. 1970.

Akopian (Hakobian), Levon. *Dmitrii Shostakovich: Opyt fenominologii tvorchestva*. Saint Petersburg: Dmitrii Bulanin, 2004.

Antokoletz, Elliott. *Twentieth-Century Music*. Englewood Cliffs, NJ: Prentice Hall, 1992.

———. *Memories of Shostakovich: Interviews with the Composer's Children*. Translated by Rosanna Kelly and Michael Meylac. London: Short, 2004.

Ardov, Mikhail. *Shostakovich: v vospominaniiakh syna Maksima, docheri Galiny i protoiereia Mikhaila Ardova*. Moscow: Zakharov, 2003.

Avrutin, Lilia. "Film as Metatext and Myth: Shostakovich on Screen." *The Russian Review* 56, No. 3 (1997): 402–24.

"Baletnaia fal'sh" [Balletic Falsehood], *Pravda*, February 6, 1936, 3. Also *Sovetskaia muzyka* (1936, No. 2): 6–8.

Barry, Malcolm. "Ideology and Form: Shostakovich East and West." In *Music and the Politics of Culture*, edited by Christopher Norris, 172–86. London: Lawrence & Wishart, 1989. New York: St. Martin's Press, 1989.

Bartlett, Rosamund. *Shostakovich in Context*. Oxford: Oxford University Press, 2000.

Berger, Liubov', ed. *Cherty stilia D. Shostakovicha*. Moscow: Sovetskii kompozitor, 1962.

Bernatchez, Hélène. *Schostakowitsch und die Fabrik des Exzentrischen Schauspielers*. Munich: M Press, Martin Meidenbauer, 2006.

Biesold, Maria. *Dmitrij Schostakowitsch: Klaviermusik der Neuen Sachlichkeit*. Wittmund: Edition Musica et Claves, 1988.

Blois, Louis. "Shostakovich and the Ustvolskaya Connexion: A Textual Investigation." *Tempo* 182 (1992): 10–18.

Blokker, Roy (with Robert Dearling). *The Music of Dmitri Shostakovich—The Symphonies.* London: The Tantivy Press, 1979. Rutherford, NJ: Fairleigh Dickinson University Press, 1979.

Bobrovskii, Viktor. *Kamernye instrumental'nye ansambli Shostakovicha: issledovanie.* Moscow: Sovetskii kompozitor, 1961.

Bogdanova, Alla. *Opery i balety Shostakovicha.* Moscow: Sovetskii kompozitor, 1979.

Bouscant, Liouba. *Les quatuors à cordes de Chostakovitch: Pour une esthétique du sujet.* Paris: L'Harmattan, 2003.

Braun, Joachim. *Shostakovich's Jewish Songs: From Jewish Folk Poetry, op. 79: Introductory Essay with Original Yiddish Folk Text Underlay.* Tel-Aviv: World Council for Yiddish and Jewish Culture/Institute Yud Lezlilei Hashoa, 1989.

———. "Shostakovich's Song Cycle *From Jewish Folk Poetry*: Aspects of Style and Meaning." In M.H. Brown, ed. *Russian and Soviet Music: Essays for Boris Schwarz*, 259–86.

———. "The Double Meaning of Jewish Elements in Dimitri Shostakovich's Music." *The Musical Quarterly* 71 (1985): 68–80.

Brentanitskaia, Alla. *'Nos' D.D. Shostakovicha.* Moscow: Muzyka, 1983.

Brockhaus, Heinz. *Dmitri Schostakowitsch.* Leipzig: Breitkopf & Härtel, 1962.

Brown, Malcolm Hamrick, ed. *Russian and Soviet Music: Essays for Boris Schwarz.* Ann Arbor: UMI Research Press, 1984.

———, ed. *A Shostakovich Casebook.* Bloomington: Indiana University Press, 2004.

Brown, Royal S. "The Three Faces of Lady Macbeth." In M.H. Brown, ed. *Russian and Soviet Music: Essays for Boris Schwarz*, 245–52.

Buske, Peter. *Dmitri Schostakowitsch: Leben und Schaffen des Sowjetischen Komponisten.* Berlin: Zentralvorstand der Gesellschaft für Deutsch-Sowjetische Freundschaft, Abteilung Kultur, 1975.

Calvocoressi, Michel D. *A Survey of Russian Music.* Harmondsworth, Middlesex: Penguin, 1944. Reprinted Westport, CT: Greenwood Press, 1974.

Carroll, Mark. *Music and Ideology in Cold War Europe.* Cambridge: Cambridge University Press, 2003.

Child, Peter. "Voice-Leading Patterns and Interval Collections in Late Shostakovich: Symphony No. 15." *Music Analysis* 12 (1993): 71–88.

Clark, Katerina. *Petersburg, Crucible of Cultural Revolution.* Cambridge, MA: Harvard University Press, 1995.

Conquest, Robert. *The Great Terror—A Reassessment.* New York: Oxford University Press, 1990.

Craft, Robert, ed. *Stravinsky: Selected Correspondence.* New York: Knopf, 1982 (vol. 1), 1984 (vol. 2).

Danilevich, Lev. *D.D. Shostakovich.* Moscow: Sovetskii kompozitor, 1958.

———. *Dmitrii Shostakovich.* Moscow: Sovetskii kompozitor, 1967.

———. *Dmitrii Shostakovich: zhizn' i tvorchestvo.* Moscow: Sovetskii kompozitor, 1980.

Del'son, Viktor. *Fortepiannoe tvorchestvo D.D. Shostakovicha.* Moscow: Sovetskii kompozitor, 1971.

———. "Molodoi Shostakovich, o pianiste 20ykh i 30ykh gg." *Voprosy muzykal'no-ispolnitel'skogo iskusstva* 5 (1969): 193–228.

Dermoncourt, Bertrand. *Dimitri Chostakovitch.* Arles: Actes sud, 2006.

Devlin, James. "Dmitri Shostakovich—Pianist." *The Anglo-Soviet Journal,* September 1980: 18–20.

———. *Shostakovich.* Sevenoaks: Novello, 1983.

———. "Shostakovich's Re-orchestration of the Schumann Cello Concerto in A Minor." *The Anglo-Soviet Journal,* May 1980: 19–20.

Dmitri Schostakowitsch: Interpretationen, Programme, Dokumente: Wissenschaftliche Beiträge 1984/85. Duisburg: Stadt Duisburg, Dezernat für Bildung und Kultur, 1984.

Dolinskaia, Elena, ed. *Shostakovichu posviashchaetsia: sbornik statei k 90-letiiu kompozitora (1906–1996).* Moscow: Kompozitor, 1997.

Dolzhanskii, Aleksandr. *Izbrannye stat'i.* Leningrad: Muzyka, 1973.

———. *Dvadtsat chetyre preliudii i fugi D. Shostakovicha,* 2nd ed. Leningrad: Sovetskii kompozitor, 1970.

Downes, Olin. "New Soviet Opera Is Presented Here." *The New York Times,* February 6, 1935.

Drury, Jonathan. "Traditionalism in Shostakovich's Fifteenth String Quartet." *South African Journal of Musicology* 10 (1990): 9–32.

Dubinsky, Rostislav. *Stormy Applause: Making Music in a Workers State.* London: Hutchinson, 1989.

Dvornichenko, Oksana. *Dmitrii Shostakovich: Puteshestvie.* Moscow: Tekst, 2006.

Edmunds, Neil, ed. *Soviet Music and Society under Lenin and Stalin.* London: Routledge Curzon, 2004.

———. *The Soviet Proletarian Music Movement.* Bern: Peter Lang, 2000.

Egorova, L.N. *D.D. Shostakovich, 1906–1975: informatsionnyi biulleten' kinovideomaterialov.* Moscow: Gos. kom-t SSSR po televideniiu i radioveshchaniiu, 1990.

Egorova, Tatiana. *Soviet Film Music: An Historical Survey.* Translated by Tatiana A. Ganf and Natalia A. Egunova. Amsterdam: Harwood Academic Publishers, 1997.

Ellestrom, Lars. "Some Notes on Irony in the Visual Arts and Music: The Examples of Magritte and Shostakovich." *Word and Image* 12 (1996): 197–208.

Emerson, Caryl. "Back to the Future: Shostakovich's Revision of Leskov's 'Lady Macbeth of the Mtsensk District'." *Cambridge Opera Journal* 1 (1989): 59–78.

Fairclough, Pauline. "Mahler Reconstructed: Sollertinsky and the Soviet Symphony." *The Musical Quarterly* 85 (2001): 384.

———. "The Old Shostakovich: Reception in the British Press." *Music and Letters* 88/2 (2007): 266–98.

———. "The 'Perestroyka' of Soviet Symphonism: Shostakovich in 1935." *Music and Letters* 83 (2002): 259–73.

———. *A Soviet Credo: Shostakovich's Fourth Symphony.* Aldershot: Ashgate, 2006.

Fanning, David. *The Breath of the Symphonist: Shostakovich's Tenth.* London: Royal Musical Association, 1988.

———, ed. *Shostakovich Studies.* Cambridge: Cambridge University Press, 1995.

———. *Shostakovich: String Quartet No. 8.* Aldershot: Ashgate, 2004.

———. "Shostakovich: The Present-Day Master of the C Major Key." *Acta Musicologica* 73 (2001): 101–40.

———. Untitled commentary accompanying exhibit of manuscripts of Shostakovich's Fifth String Quartet and Ustvolskaya's Trio for Clarinet, Violin, and Piano. In *Settling New Scores: Music Manuscripts from the Paul Sacher Foundation,* edited by Felix Meyer, 235–9. Mainz: Schott, 1998.

Fay, Laurel E. "The Composer Was Courageous, But Not as Much as in Myth." *The New York Times*, April 14, 1996, section 2.

———. "The Punch in Shostakovich's *Nose*." In M.H. Brown, ed. *Russian and Soviet Music: Essays for Boris Schwarz*, 229–43.

———. *Shostakovich: A Life*. New York: Oxford University Press, 2000.

———, ed. *Shostakovich and His World*. Princeton: Princeton University Press, 2004.

———. "Shostakovich versus Volkov: Whose Testimony?" *The Russian Review* 39/4 (1980): 484–93. Reprinted 2004 in Brown, ed. *A Shostakovich Casebook*, 11–21.

Fedosova, Eleonora. *Diatonicheskie lady v tvorchestve D. Shostakovicha*. Moscow: Sovetskii kompozitor, 1980.

Fenton, John. "Thematic Unity in Shostakovich's Eighth Quartet." *Music Teacher* 5 (1979): 18–21.

Ferenc, Anna. "Music in the Socialist State." In *Russian Cultural Studies: An Introduction*, edited by Catriona Kelly and David Shepherd. Oxford: Oxford University Press, 1998, 109–119.

Feuchtner, Bernd. *Dmitri Schostakowitsch: "Und Kunst geknebelt von der groben Macht."* Kassel: Bärenreiter, 2002; Stuttgart: Metzler, 2002.

Fielden, Jan, ed. *Composers' Letters*. London: Marginalia Press, 1994.

Finlay, Carolyn Roberts. "Operatic Translation and Sostakovic: *The Nose*." *Comparative Literature* 35 (1983): 195–214.

Fisk, Josiah, ed. *Composers on Music: Eight Centuries of Writings*, 2nd ed. Boston: Northeastern University Press, 1997.

Fitzpatrick, Sheila. *The Commissariat of Enlightenment: Soviet Organization of Education and the Arts under Lunacharsky, October 1917–1921*. Cambridge: Cambridge University Press, 1970, 2002.

Frei, Marco. *Chaos statt Musik: Dimitri Schostakowitsch, die Prawda Kampagne von 1936 bis 1938 und der Sozialistische Realismus*. Saarbrücken: Pfau, 2006.

Fuchs, Martina. *Ledi Makbet Mcenskogo uezda: Vergleichende Analyse der Erzählung N.S. Leskovs und der gleichnamigen Oper D.D. Sostakovics*. Heidelberg: J. Groos, 1992.

Gasparov, Boris. *Five Operas and a Symphony: Word and Music in Russian Culture*. New Haven: Yale University Press, 2005.

Gerstel, Jennifer. "Irony, Deception, and Political Culture in the Works of Dmitri Shostakovich." *Mosaic: a Journal for the Comparative Study of Literature* 32 (1999): 35–51.

Glicksman, Marlaine. "Citizen Artist: On Shostakovich and the Soviets." *Film Comment* 24 (1988): 50–1.

Glikman, Isaak. *Pis'ma k drugu: Dmitrii Shostakovich-Isaaku Glikmanu*. Moscow: DSCH, 1993; St. Petersburg: Kompozitor, 1993. *The Story of a Friendship: The Letters of Dmitry Shostakovich to Isaak Glikman, 1941–1975*. Translated by Anthony Phillips. Ithaca: Cornell University Press, 2001. *Chaos statt Musik?: Briefe an einen Freund*. Translated by Thomas Klein and Reimar Westendorf. Berlin: Argon, 1995. *Dmitri Chostakovitch: lettres à un ami*. Translated by Luba Jurgenson. Paris: Albin Michel, 1994.

Gojowy, Detlef. "Dimitri Schostakowitsch: Briefe an Edison Denissow." In *Musik des Ostens*, edited by Hubert Unverricht, 181–206. Kassel: Bärenreiter, 1986.

———. *Dmitri Schostakowitsch: Mit Selbstzeugnissen und Bilddokumenten*. Reinbek bei Hamburg: Rowohlt, 1983. *Chostakovitch*. Translated by Catherine Métais-Bührendt. Arles: B. Coutaz, 1989.

———. *Schostakowitsch in Deutschland*. Berlin: E. Kuhn, 1998.

Greenberg, Robert. *Great Masters. Shostakovich, his Life and Music.* Chantilly, VA: Teaching Company, 2002. (CD, Cassette, VHS, or DVD)

Grigoryev, Lev, and Yakov Platek. *Dmitri Shostakovich: About Himself and His Times.* Translated by Angus and Neilian Roxburgh. Moscow: Progress Publishers, 1981. (Modified version of Iakovlev, below)

Gubanow, Jakow. "Der Stil Dimitrij Schostakowitschs in den Zwanziger Jahren: Harmonik, Polyphonie, Instrumentation." In *Musik der Zwanziger Jahre*, edited by Werner Keil, 135–65. Hildesheim: G. Olms, 1996.

Haas, David. *Leningrad's Modernists: Studies in Composition and Musical Thought, 1917-1932.* New York: Peter Lang, 1998.

Hakobian (see also Akopian), Levon. *Music of the Soviet Age, 1917–1987.* Stockholm: Melos Music Literature, 1998.

Hayward, Max, and Leopold Labedz, eds. *Literature and Revolution in Soviet Russia.* London: Oxford University Press, 1963.

Heikinheimo, Seppo. "Tikhon Khrennikov in Interview." Translated by Jeremy Parsons. *Tempo* 173 (1990): 18–20.

Hellmundt, Christoph, and Krzysztof Meyer. *Erfahrungen: Aufsätze, Erinnerungen, Reden, Diskussionsbeiträge, Interviews, Briefe.* Leipzig: Reclam, 1983.

Henderson, William J. Review, *New York Sun*, February 9, 1935.

Hinrichsen, Hans-Joachim, and Laurenz Lütteken. *Zwischen Bekenntnis und Verweigerung: Schostakowitsch und die Sinfonie im 20. Jahrhundert: Symposium Zürcher Festspiele 2002.* Kassel: Bärenreiter, 2005.

Hitotsuyanagi, Fumiko. "Novyi lik devenadtsatoi: chto skryto v nespravedlivo nizko otsenennoi simfonii." *Muzykal'naia akademiia* (1997, No. 4): 87. English translation in *DSCH Journal* 13 (1997): 59–63.

Ho, Allan B., and Dmitry Feofanov, eds. *Shostakovich Reconsidered.* London: Toccata Press, 1998.

———. *The "Shostakovich Wars."* London: Toccata Press, forthcoming.

Hopkins, George William. "Shostakovich's Ninth String Quartet." *Tempo* 75 (Winter 1965–66): 23–5.

Huband, Joseph. "Shostakovich's Fifth Symphony: A Soviet Artist's Reply …?" *Tempo* 173 (1990): 11–16.

Hulme, Derek. *Dmitri Shostakovich: A Catalogue, Bibliography, and Discography*, 3rd ed. Lanham, MD: Scarecrow Press, 2002.

Hurwitz, David. *Shostakovich Symphonies and Concertos: An Owner's Manual.* Pompton Plains, NJ: Amadeus, 2006.

Hussey, William. "Triadic Post-Tonality and Linear Chromaticism in the Music of Dmitri Shostakovich." *Music Theory Online* 9 (2003).

Iakovlev, Mikhail. *D. Shostakovich o vremeni i o sebe: 1926-1975.* Moscow: Sovetskii kompozitor, 1980. (For English translation, see Grigoryev and Platek, above.)

Jackson, Russell. *The Cambridge Companion to Shakespeare on Film.* Cambridge: Cambridge University Press, 2000.

Jackson, Stephen. *Dmitri Shostakovich: An Essential Guide to His Life and Works.* London: Pavilion Books, 1997.

Jellinek, George. "Shostakovich: *The Nose* and *The Gamblers.*" *The Opera Quarterly* 16 (Fall 2000): 680.

Johnson, Priscilla, and Leopold Labedz, eds. *Khrushchev and the Arts—The Politics of Soviet Culture, 1962-1964.* Cambridge, MA: MIT Press, 1965.

Jorgens, Jack J. *Shakespeare on Film*. Bloomington: Indiana University Press, 1977.

Karagicheva, Liudmila, "'Pishete kak mozhno bol'she prekrasnoi muzyki …': iz pisem D.D. Shostakovicha K.A. Karaevu." *Muzykal'naia akademiia* (1997, No. 4): 202–11.

Karl, Gregory, and Jenefer Robinson. "Shostakovich's Tenth Symphony and the Musical Expression of Cognitively Complex Emotions." *Journal of Aesthetics and Art Criticism* 53 (Fall 1995): 401–15. Reprinted in Jenefer Robinson, *Music and Meaning*, 154–78. Ithaca: Cornell University Press, 1997.

Karlinsky, Simon. "Our Destinies are Bad." *The Nation*. November 24, 1979, 533–6.

Kay, Norman. *Dmitri Shostakovich*. London: Oxford University Press, 1971.

———. "Shostakovich's Fourteenth Symphony." *Tempo* 92 (1970): 20–1.

———. "Shostakovich's Fifteenth Symphony." *Tempo* 100 (1972): 36–40.

———. "Shostakovich's Second Violin Concerto." *Tempo* 83 (1967–1968): 21–3.

Keldish, Yury. "An Autobiographical Quartet." Translated by Alan Lumsden. *The Musical Times* 102 (1961): 226–8.

Keller, Hans. "The Crisis of Commitment: Second-Round Marxism in the Western Musical World." *Musical Newsletter* 5 (Winter 1975): 3–7, 18–22.

———. "Shostakovich's Twelfth Quartet." In *Hans Keller: Essays on Music*, edited by Christopher Wintle. Cambridge: Cambridge University Press, 1994, 93–102.

Kemp-Welch, A. *Stalin and the Literary Intelligentsia, 1928–39*. New York: St. Martin's Press, 1991.

Kettle, Christopher J. "Brian, Mahler, Shostakovitch and Schoenberg: Some Idle Thoughts. With comments by Larry Alexander and Malcolm MacDonald." In *HB: Aspects of Havergal Brian*, edited by Jürgen Schaarwächter. Aldershot: Ashgate, 1997.

Khentova, Sof'ia. *D.D. Shostakovich v gody Velikoi Otechestvennoi voiny*. Leningrad: Muzyka, 1979.

———. *Molodye gody Shostakovicha, kniga pervaia*. Leningrad: Sovetskii kompozitor, 1975.

———. *Molodye gody Shostakovicha, kniga vtoraia*. Leningrad: Sovetskii kompozitor, 1980.

———. "Shostakovich i kino." *Muzykal'naia zhizn'* (1996, Nos. 5 and 6): 41–5.

———. *Shostakovich—Pianist*. Leningrad: Muzyka, 1964.

———. *Shostakovich: tridtsatiletie, 1945-1975*. Leningrad: Sovetskii kompozitor, 1982.

———. *Udivitel'nyi Shostakovich*. St. Petersburg: Variant, 1993.

———. *V mire Shostakovicha*. Moscow: Kompozitor, 1996.

———. *Shostakovich: zhizn' i tvorchestvo*, 2nd ed. Moscow: Kompozitor, 1996.

Khubov, Georgii. "Piataia simfoniia D. Shostakovicha." *Sovetskaia muzyka* (1938, No. 3): 14–28. Revised in Khubov, *O muzyke i muzykantakh*, 224–40. Moscow: Sovetskii kompozitor, 1959.

Klemm, Sebastian. *Dmitri Schostakowitsch, das zeitlose Spätwerk*. Berlin: E. Kuhn, 2001.

Koball, Michael. *Pathos und Groteske: Die Deutsche Tradition im Symphonischen Schaffen von Dmitri Schostakowitsch*. Berlin: E. Kuhn, 1997.

Kolesnikoff, Nina, and Walter Smyrniw, eds. *Socialist Realism Revisited: Selected Papers from the McMaster Conference*. Hamilton, Ontario: McMaster University, 1994.

Kondrashin, Kirill. Statement read at a symposium sponsored by Bucknell University, September 9, 1980. Translated by Antonina W. Bouis. *DSCH* XIX (1991): 34–5.

Kopp, Karen. *Form und Gehalt der Symphonien des Dmitri Schostakowitsch*. Bonn: Verlag für Systematische Musikwissenschaft, 1990.

Körner, Klaus. "Schostakowitschs Vierte Symphonie." *Archiv für Musikwissenschaft* 31 (1974): 116–36, 214–36.

Koussevitsky, Serge. *The Serge Koussevitsky Archive 1920–1976 (Bulk 1924–1951).* Music Division, Library of Congress. Material pertaining to Shostakovich (1929–1945) in Folders 56/6, 56/7, and 56/8.

Koval', Marian. "Tvorcheskii put' D. Shostakovicha." *Sovetskaia muzyka* (1948, No. 2): 47–61; (1948, No. 3): 31–43; (1948, No. 4): 8–19. Translated in Ernst Kuhn and Günter Wolter. *Volksfeind Dmitri Schostakowitsch*, 126–93.

Kovnatskaia, Liudmila, ed. *D.D. Shostakovich: sbornik statei k 90-letiiu so dnia rozhdeniia.* St. Petersburg: Kompozitor, 1996.

———. *Pis'ma I.I. Sollertinskomu.* St. Petersburg: Kompozitor, 2006.

———. *Shostakovich: mezhdu mgnoveniem i vechnost'iu: dokumenty, materialy, stat'i.* St. Petersburg: Kompozitor, 2000.

———. (Kovnatskaya, Ludmila). "Shostakovich and the LASM." *Tempo* 206 (1998): 2–6.

Kozintsev, Grigorii. *King Lear: The Space of Tragedy.* Translated by Mary A. Mackintosh. London: Heinemann Educational, 1977.

Kozlova, Miralda. "'Mne ispolnilos' vosemnadtsat' let ...': pis'ma D.D. Shostakovicha k L.N. Oborinu." *Vstrechi s proshlym* (1984, No. 5): 232–60.

———. "Vsegda dorozhu vashem mneniem ..." In *Vstrechi s proshlym, sbornik materialov,* edited by N. Volkova (1978, No. 3): 253–9. Translation in "Prokofiev's Correspondence with Stravinsky and Shostakovich." In *Slavonic and Western Music: Essays for Gerald Abraham,* edited by Malcolm Brown and R. Wiley, 271–92. Ann Arbor: UMI Research Press, 1985.

Kramer, Lawrence. *Musical Meaning: Toward a Critical History.* Berkeley: University of California Press, 2002.

Kremer, Anastasiia. *Vokal'nye tsikly D. Shostakovicha.* Moscow: Rossiiskaia akademiia muzyki im. Gnesinykh, 2005.

Kröplin, Eckart. *Frühe Sowjetische Oper: Schostakowitsch, Prokofjew.* Berlin: Henschelverlag, 1985.

Kuchinke, Norbert, and Felix Schmidt. "[Maxim] Shostakovich: Why I Fled from Russia." Translated by Gillian Macdonald. *The Sunday Times* [London], May 17, 1981, 35A.

Kuhn, Ernst, Jaschas Nemtsov, and Andreas Wehrmeyer. *Schostakowitsch und die Folgen: Russische Musik zwischen Anpassung und Protest: Ein internationales Symposium.* Berlin: E. Kuhn, 2003.

Kuhn, Ernst, and Günter Wolter. *Volksfeind Dmitri Schostakowitsch: Eine Dokumentation der öffentlichen Angriffe gegen den Komponisten in der ehemaligen Sowjetunion.* Berlin: E. Kuhn, 1997.

Langen, Tim, and Jesse Langen. "Music and Poetry: The Case of Shostakovich and Blok." In *Intersections and Transpositions: Russian Music, Literature, and Society,* ed. Andrew Wachtel, 138–64. Evanston: Northwestern University Press, 1998.

Lawson, Peter. "Shostakovich's Second Symphony." *Tempo* 91 (1969–70): 14–17.

Lebedinsky, Lev. "The Origin of Shostakovich's 'Rayok'." *Tempo* 173 (1990): 31–2.

Lebrecht, Norman. *The Sunday Times Magazine* [London], April 15, 1984, 24–8.

Lee, Rose. "Dimitri Szostakovitch." *The New York Times,* December 20, 1931, Section 8, 8.

Lehrman, Phillip. "A Schoenberg Note about Prokofiev, Shostakovich, Stravinsky and Koussevitzky." *Journal of the Arnold Schoenberg Institute* 11, No. 2 (1988), 174–180.

Leie, Tat'iana. *D. Shostakovich: Problemy stilia.* Moscow: Rossiiskaia akademiia muzyki im. Gnesinykh, 2003.

Leikin, Anatole. "Decoding the Twenty-Four Preludes of Shostakovich: a Hermeneutic Approach." *American Journal of Semiotics* 13, No. 1-4 (Fall 1996), 165-181. Reprinted in *Signs in Musical Hermeneutics*, edited by Siglind Bruhn. Pensacola: Semiotic Society of America, 1998.

Leskov, Nikolai. *Povesty i rasskazy.* Moscow: Russkii iazyk, 1985. For an English translation of *The Lady Macbeth of the Mtsensk District*, see Nikolai Leskov, *Lady Macbeth of Mtsensk and Other Stories.* Translated by David McDuff. Harmondsworth, Middlesex: Penguin, 1987.

Liebert, A. "Anmerkungen und Ergebnisse zum Verhältnis Mahler-Sostakovic." In *Theorie der Musik: Analyse und Deutung.* Laaber: Laaber-Verlag, 1995, 223–52.

Longman, Richard M. *Expression and Structure: Processes of Integration in the Large-Scale Instrumental Music of Shostakovich.* New York: Garland Publishing, 1989.

Luk'ianova, Nataliia (Lukyanova, N.V.). *Dmitrii Dmitrievich Shostakovich.* Moscow: Muzyka, 1980. *Shostakovich.* Translated by Yuri Shirokov. Neptune City, NJ: Paganiniana, 1984. *Dmitri Dmitrijewitsch Schostakowitsch.* Translated by Nina Sohr and Beate Petras. Berlin: Verlag Neue Musik, 1982. 2nd. ed. Mainz: Schott, 1993 and Munich: Piper, 1993. *Sostakovic.* Translated by Ivan Slimak. Bratislava: Opus, 1984.

MacDonald, Calum. "The Anti-Formalist 'Rayok'—Learners Start Here!" *Tempo* 173 (1990): 23–30.

MacDonald, Ian. "Common Sense about Shostakovich: Breaking the 'Hermeneutic Circle'." *Southern Humanities Review* 26 (Spring 1992): 153–67.

———. "Fay versus Shostakovich: Whose Stupidity?" *East European Jewish Affairs* 26 (1996): 5–26.

———. "Laurel E. Fay's *Shostakovich: A Life.*" *Music Under Soviet Rule.* http://www.siue.edu/~aho/musov/fay/fay.html. Accessed February 24, 2008.

———. *The New Shostakovich.* Boston: Northeastern University Press, 1990.

———. *The New Shostakovich*, 2nd edition. Revised by Raymond Clarke. London: Pimlico, 2006.

Mackerras, Charles. "Slow Shostakovich." Letter to *Classic CD,* November 1995: 14.

Maksimenkov, Leonid. *Sumbur vmesto muzyki.* Moscow: Iuridicheskaia kniga, 1997.

Malko, Nicolai. *A Certain Art.* New York: W. Morrow, 1966.

Martynov, Ivan. *Dmitrii Shostakovich.* Moscow: Muzgiz, 1946.

———. *Dmitri Shostakovich: The Man and His Work.* Translated by T. Guralsky. New York: Philosophical Library, 1947. Reprinted New York: Greenwood Press, 1969.

———. *Dmitrij Schostakowitsch.* Translated by Ina Tinzmann. Berlin: B. Henschel, 1947.

———. *Chostakovitch.* Translated by Rostislav Hofmann. Paris: Éditions du Chêne, 1946.

Marx, Karl, and Friedrich Engels, *Karl Marx and Friedrich Engels on Literature and Art: A Selection of Writings.* New York: International, 1974.

Mason, Colin. "Form in Shostakovich's Quartets." *The Musical Times* 103 (1962): 531–3.

Mazel', Lev. *Etiudii o Shostakovich: stat'i i zametki o tvorchestve.* Moscow: Sovetskii kompozitor, 1986.

———. *Simfonii D.D. Shostakovicha—putevoditel,* 2nd ed. Moscow: Sovetskii kompozitor, 1981.

McBurney, Gerard. "Soviet Music after the Death of Stalin: The Legacy of Shostakovich." In *Russian Cultural Studies: An Introduction*, edited by Catriona Kelly and David Shepherd. Oxford: Oxford University Press, 1998, 120–137.

———. "Surviving Stalin." *Index on Censorship* 27 (1998): 52–61.

McCreless, Patrick, "Dmitri Shostakovich: The String Quartets." In *Intimate Voices: Aspects of Construction and Character in the Twentieth-Century String Quartet*, edited by Evan Jones. Rochester: University of Rochester Press, forthcoming.

Merrill, Reed. "The Grotesque in Music: Shostakovich's *Nose.*" *Russian Literature Triquarterly* 23 (1990): 303–14.

Meskhishvili, Erna. *Dmitrii Shostakovich: Notograficheskii spravochnik.* Moscow: Orekhovo-Zuevskaia tipografiia, 1995.

Meyer, Krzysztof. *Dmitri Chostakovitch.* Paris: Fayard, 1994. *Schostakowitsch: Sein Leben, Sein Werk, Seine Zeit.* Translated by Nina Kozlowski. Bergisch Gladbach: Gustav Lübbe Verlag, 1995.

———. *Shostakovich: zhizn', tvorchestvo, vremia.* Translated by E. Guliaevoi. St. Petersburg: DSCH Kompozitor, 1998.

Mikheeva, Liudmila. "Pis'ma Shostakovicha k Sollertinskomu." *Zhurnal liubitelei iskusstva* (1996, No. 2): 9–15; (1996, No. 3): 6–13; (1996, No. 4): 6–12; (1997, No. 1): 16–20; (1997, No. 4 and 5): 16–30; (1997, No. 6 and 7): 47–50; (1997, No. 8 and 9): 59–65; (1997, No. 10 and 11): 44–51; (1998, No. 1): 43–47.

———. *I.I. Sollertinskii: zhizn' i nasledie.* Leningrad: Sovetskii kompozitor, 1988.

———. *Zhizn' Dmitriia Shostakovicha.* Moscow: Terra, 1997.

Moisenko, Rena. *Realist Music: 25 Soviet Composers.* London: Meridian, 1949.

Morton, Brian. *Shostakovich: His Life and Music.* London: Haus, 2006.

Moshevich, Sofia. *Dmitri Shostakovich: Pianist.* Montreal: McGill-Queen's University Press, 2004.

Muñoz, Gustave. *Dimitri Chostakovitch: guide des quatuors à cordes.* Nîmes: C. Lacour, 2000.

Murphy, Edward. "A Programme for the First Movement of Shostakovich's Fifteenth Symphony: a Debate about Four Musical Styles." *The Music Review* 53 (1992): 47–62.

Nabokov, Nicolas. *Old Friends and New Music.* London: Hamish Hamilton, 1951. Boston: Little, Brown, 1951. (The US edition omits certain references to Shostakovich found in the British edition.)

Niemöller, Klaus. *Bericht über das Internationale Dmitri-Schostakowitsch-Symposion, Köln, 1985.* Regensburg: G. Bosse, 1986.

Norris, Christopher. "Ambiguous Shostakovich." *Gramophone.* February 1983: 892.

———. "Shostakovich and Cold War Cultural Politics: A Review Essay." *Southern Humanities Review* 25/1, 54–77.

———, ed. *Shostakovich: The Man and His Music.* Boston: M. Boyars, 1982.

Norris, Geoffrey. "An Opera Restored. Rimsky Korsakov, Shostakovich and the Khovansky Business." *The Musical Times* 123 (1982): 672–5.

Olkhovsky, Andrey. *Music under the Soviets: The Agony of an Art.* New York: Praeger, 1955.

O'Loughlin, N. "Shostakovich's String Quartets." *Tempo* 87 (Winter 1968–9): 9–16.

Ordzhonikidze, Givi. *Dmitrii Shostakovich.* Moscow: Sovetskii kompozitor, 1967.

Orlov, Genrikh. *Dmitrii Dmitrievich Shostakovich: Kratkii ocherk zhizni i tvorchestva.* Moscow: Muzyka, 1966.

———. *Simfonii D. Shostakovicha.* Leningrad: Muzgiz, 1962.

Osthoff, Wolfgang. "Leeres Tönespiel oder gefährdeter Frieden mit liturgischem Bittruf? Zum Finale der 8. Symphonie von Dmitri Schostakowitsch." In *Symphonik 1930-1950*, edited by Wolfgang Osthoff and Giselher Schubert, 243–58. Mainz: Schott, 2003.

Ottaway, Hugh. "Looking Again at Shostakovich 4." *Tempo* 115 (1975): 14–24.

———. *Shostakovich Symphonies.* London: BBC Publications, 1978.

Parrot, Jasper, and Vladimir Ashkenazy. *Beyond Frontiers.* London: Collins, 1984.

Pascuzzi, Robert M. "Shostakovich and Amyotrophic Lateral Sclerosis." *Seminars in Neurology* 19 (1999): 63.

Plotnikov, Boris. "On Dialectical Structure Creating Process in Shostakovich's Prelude op. 34, no. 20." *Eunomios: an Open Online Journal for Theory, Analysis, and Semiotics of Music* (January 5, 2001), http://www.eunomios.org/contrib/plotnikov1/plotnikov1. html. Accessed February 24, 2008.

Pulcini, Franco. *Sostakovic.* Turin: EDT Musica, 1988.

Rabinovich, David. *Dmitry Shostakovich: Composer.* Translated by George Hanna. London: Lawrence and Wishart, 1959.

Radamsky, Sergei. "Lady Macbeth Put On for Stalin—But Shostakovich Waited in Vain for a Call." *The Times* [London], November 18, 1963.

Redepenning, Dorothea. "Mahler und Schostakowitsch." In *Das Gustav-Mahler-Fest, Hamburg, 1989. Bericht über den Internationalen Gustav-Mahler-Kongress,* edited by Matthias Theodor Vogt. Kassel: Bärenreiter, 1991.

Riley, John. *Dmitri Shostakovich: A Life in Film.* London: I.B. Tauris, 2005.

Robin, Régine. *Socialist Realism: An Impossible Aesthetic.* Translated by Catherine Porter. Stanford: Stanford University Press, 1992.

Robinson, Harlow, ed. *Selected Letters of Sergei Prokofiev.* Boston: Northeastern University Press, 1998.

Roseberry, Eric. *Ideology, Style, Content, and Thematic Process in the Symphonies, Cello Concertos, and String Quartets of Shostakovich.* New York: Garland, 1989.

———. *Shostakovich: His Life and Times.* Tunbridge Wells: Midas, 1982. Reprinted London: Omnibus, 1986.

Sabinina, Marina. *Dmitrii Shostakovich.* Moscow: Sovetskii kompozitor, 1959.

———. *Shostakovich—simfonist: dramaturgiia, estetika, stil'.* Moscow: Muzyka, 1976.

Salisbury, Harrison E. "Visit with Dmitri Shostakovich." *The New York Times Magazine,* August 8, 1954, 9, 44 (with response by Julie Whitney, "Music 'in a Cage'." 43).

Schmalenberg, Hilmar, ed. *Schostakowitsch in Deutschland.* Berlin: E. Kuhn, 1998.

Schwarz, Boris. *Music and Musical Life in Soviet Russia, 1917–1981.* Enlarged edition. Bloomington: Indiana University Press, 1983.

Scott, H.G., ed. *Problems of Soviet Literature: Reports and Speeches at the First Soviet Writers' Congress.* Westport, CT: Greenwood, 1979.

Seehaus, Lothar. *Dmitrij Schostakowitsch, Leben und Werk.* Wilhelmshaven: F. Noetzel, 1986.

Seroff, Victor, and Nadezhda Galli-Shohat. *Dmitri Shostakovich: The Life and Background of a Soviet Composer.* New York: Alfred A. Knopf, 1943.

Shaginyan, Marietta. "Fifty Letters from Dmitri Shostakovich." *Soviet Literature* 1 (1984): 68–99.

Shebalina, Alisa, ed. "Eto byl zamechatel'nyi drug: iz pisem D.D. Shostakovicha k V.Ia. Shebalinu." *Sovetskaia muzyka* (1982, No. 7): 75–85.

Sheinberg, Esti. *Irony, Satire, Parody and the Grotesque in the Music of Shostakovich: A Theory of Incongruities.* Aldershot: Ashgate, 2000.

Shirinsky, Vasily. "Iz kvartetnogo zhurnala." *Muzykal'naia akademiia* (1997, No. 4): 137–48.

Shneerson, Grigorii Mikhailovich. *D. Shostakovich: stat'i i materialy.* Moscow: Sovetskii kompozitor, 1976.

Shostakovich, Dmitrii. "Avtobiografiia, 1927." *Sovetskaia muzyka* (1966, No. 9): 24–5.

———. "Deklaratsiia obiazannostei kompozitora." *Rabochii i teatr* 31 (November 20, 1931): 6. English translation in Darby, 190–2 (see Theses and Dissertations below).

———. "Moy tvorcheskii otvet." *Vecherniaia Moskva,* January 25, 1938, 3.

———. "An Open Letter from Dmitri Shostakovich." *Music Journal* (November 1965): 31, 62.

———. "Otvet amerikanskomu muzykal'nomu kritiku." *Sovetskaia muzyka* (1956, No. 3): 142–3.

―――. *Pis'ma Dmitriia Dmitrievicha Shostakovicha Borisu Tishchenko: s kommentariiami i vospominaniiami adresata.* St. Petersburg: Kompozitor, 1997.

―――. *Letters of Dmitri Dmitriyevich Shostakovich to Boris Tishchenko: With the Addressee's Commentaries and Reminiscences.* Translated by Asya Ardova. St. Petersburg: Compozitor (Kompozitor) Publishing House, 2001.

―――. *The Power of Music.* New York: Music Journal, 1968. (Reprints of *Music Journal* articles dating from between 1962 and 1968)

―――. "Sovetskaia muzykal'naia kritika otstaiot." *Sovetskaia muzyka* (1933, No. 3): 120–1.

―――. *Dmitrii Shostakovich: Stranitsy zhizni v fotografiiakh.* Moscow, DSCH, 2006.

Shostakovich, Dmitrii Dmitrievich, and Irina Bobykina. *Dmitrii Shostakovich: v pis'makh i dokumentakh.* Moscow: RIF "Antikva," 2000.

Shostakovich, Dmitri, and Tikhon Khrennikov. "Impressions of American Music." *Music Journal* (March 1960): 10–11, 90.

Shostakovich, Dmitrii, et al. *Russian Symphony: Thoughts about Tchaikovsky.* New York: Philosophical Library, 1947.

Sollertinsky, Dmitri, and Ludmilla Sollertinsky. *Pages from the Life of Dmitri Shostakovich.* New York: Harcourt Brace Jovanovich, 1980. London: Robert Hale, 1981.

Sollertinskii, Ivan. *Von Mozart bis Schostakowitsch: Essays, Kritiken, Aufzeichnungen.* Translated by C. Rüger. Leipzig: P. Reclam, 1979.

Souster, Tim. "Shostakovich at the Crossroads." *Tempo* 78 (Autumn 1966): 2–9.

Steinberg, Michael. *The Concerto: A Listener's Guide.* New York: Oxford University Press, 1998.

―――. *The Symphony: A Listener's Guide.* New York: Oxford University Press, 1995.

Steiner, Jörg. *Wer tanzt schon zu Musik von Schostakowitsch.* Frankfurt: Suhrkamp, 2000.

Stetina, Edmund. *Die Vierte Symphonie von Dmitrij Sostakovic: Ein Zurückbehaltenes Bekenntnis.* Aachen: Shaker-Verlag, 1997.

"Sumbur vmesto muzyki: ob opere 'Ledi Makbet Mtsenskogo Uezda' D. Shostakovicha [Muddle Instead of Music: On Shostakovich's Opera 'Lady Macbeth of the Mtsensk District']. *Pravda,* January 28, 1936. Reprinted in *Sovetskaia muzyka* (1936, No. 2). 4–5.

Svarts, Betti *Shostakovich. Kakim zapomnilsia.* St. Petersburg: Kompozitor, 2006.

Tairova, Farakh. *Dmitrii Shostakovich i Azerbaidzhanskaia muzykal'naia kul'tura.* Baku: Nurlan, 2006.

Tammaro, Ferruccio. *Le sinfonie di Sostakovic.* Turin: G. Giappichelli, 1988.

Taruskin, Richard. Review of facsimile edition of Shostakovich Symphony No. 7 (see under Yakubov, below). *Notes - Quarterly Journal of the Music Library Association* 502 (1993): 756–61.

―――. *Defining Russia Musically.* Princeton: Princeton University Press, 1997.

―――. "The Opera and the Dictator." *New Republic* 200 (1989): 34–40.

Taubman, Howard. "A Big Boy Now: Shostakovich Deserves a Little Freedom." *The New York Times,* January 8, 1956, Section 2, 9.

Taylor, Clifford. *Musical Idea and the Design Aesthetic in Contemporary Music.* Lewiston, NY: Edwin Mellen Press, 1990.

Tcherkashina, Marina. "Gogol and Leskov in Shostakovich's Interpretation." *International Journal of Musicology* 1 (1992): 229–44.

Terry, Paul. "Shostakovich, String Quartet No. 8." *Music Teacher* 811 (2002): 27–31.

Tomoff, Kiril. *Creative Union: The Professional Organization of Soviet Composers, 1939-1953.* Ithaca: Cornell University Press, 2006.

Tosser, Grégoire. *Les dernières oeuvres de Dimitri Chostakovitch: une esthétique musicale de la mort, 1969-1975*. Paris: L'Harmattan, 2000.

Tret'iakova, Liliia. *Dmitrii Shostakovich*. Moscow: Sovetskaia Rossiia, 1976.

Tumanov, Alexander N. "Correspondence of Literary Text and Musical Phraseology in Shostakovich's Opera, *The Nose* and Gogol's Fantastic Tale." *The Russian Review* 52/3 (1993): 397–414.

Vishnevskaya, Galina. *Galina: A Russian Story*. San Diego: Harcourt Brace Jovanovich, 1984.

Volkov, Solomon. *St. Petersburg: A Cultural History*. Translated by Antonina W. Bouis. New York: Free Press, 1995.

———. *Shostakovich i Stalin: khudozhnik i tsar'*. Moscow: EKSMO, 2004.

———. *Shostakovich and Stalin: The Extraordinary Relationship between the Great Composer and the Brutal Dictator*. Translated by Antonina W. Bouis. New York: Knopf, 2004.

———. *Testimony: The Memoirs of Dmitri Shostakovich*. Translated by Antonina W. Bouis. New York: Harper & Row, 1979.

———. "Universal Messages: Reflections in Conversation with Günter Wolter." *Tempo* 200 (1997): 14–9.

von Geldern, James, and Richard Stites. *Mass Culture in Soviet Russia: Tales, Poems, Songs, Movies, Plays, and Folklore, 1917-1953*. Bloomington: Indiana University Press, 1995.

Wagner, Bettina. *Dmitri Schostakowitschs Oper Die Nase: Zur Problematik der Kategorie des Grotesken in der Musik*. Frankfurt: P. Lang, 2003.

Walsh, Stephen, "Shostakovich's 'Seven Romances [on Poems of Alexander Blok]'." *Tempo* 85 (Summer 1968): 27–8.

Wang, Dajue (with response by Ronald Henson). "Shostakovich: Music on the Brain?" *The Musical Times* 124 (January 1983): 347–8.

Wehrmeyer, Andreas, ed. *Schostakowitschs Streichquartette: ein Internationales Symposium*. Berlin: E. Kuhn, 2002.

Weiner, Jack. "The Destalinization of Dmitri Shostakovich's '*Song of the Forests*,' op. 81 (1949)." *Rocky Mountain Review* 38 (1984): 214–22.

Weiss, Stefan. "Text und Form in Schostakowitschs 2. Sinfonie op. 14." *Archiv für Musikwissenschaft* 51 (1994): 145–60.

Weitzman, Ronald. "Fleischmann, Shostakovich, and Chekov's 'Rothschild's Fiddle'." *Tempo* 206 (1998): 7–11.

Werth, Alexander. *Musical Uproar in Moscow*. London: Turnstile, 1949. Reprinted Westport, CT: Greenwood, 1973.

Whitney, Craig R. "Shostakovich Memoir a Shock to Kin." *The New York Times,* November 13, 1979, C7.

Wildberger, Jacques. *Dmitri Schostakowitsch, 5. Symphonie D-Moll op. 47*. Munich: Wilhelm Fink, 1989.

Wilson, Elizabeth. *Shostakovich: A Life Remembered*. London: Faber and Faber, 1994. Princeton, NJ: Princeton University Press, 1994.

———. *Shostakovich: A Life Remembered*, new ed. London: Faber and Faber, 2006.

Wolter, Günter, Marco F. Frei, and Ernst Kuhn. *Dmitri Schostakowitsch: Komponist und Zeitzeuge*. Berlin: E. Kuhn, 2000.

Wolter, Günter, Ernst Kuhn, and Andreas Wehrmeyer. *Dmitri Schostakowitsch und das jüdische musikalische Erbe*. Berlin: E. Kuhn, 2001.

Yakubov, Manashir, ed. *Dmitri Shostakovich Symphony No. 7: "Leningrad," op. 60, 1941*, facsimile edition. Tokyo: Zen-On Music, 1992.

Yelagin, Yuri. *Taming of the Arts*. New York: Dutton, 1951.

Yevtushenko, Yevgeny. *Fatal Half Measures: The Culture of Democracy in the Soviet Union*. Translated by Antonina Bouis. Boston: Little, Brown, 1991, 292–99.

———. *Symphony No. 13 on Its Prison Uniform: The Adventures of the Most Famous Symphony of the 20th Century*. Baltimore: Baltimore Symphony Orchestra, 2000.

Zaderatskii, Vsevolod. *Polifoniia v instumentalnykh proizvedeniiakh D. Shostakovicha*. Moscow: Muzyka, 1969.

Zak, Vladimir. *Shostakovich i evrei?* New York: Izdatel'stvo "Kiev," 1997.

Zhdanov, Andrei. *On Literature, Music and Philosophy*. London: Lawrence and Wishart, 1950.

———. *Essays on Literature, Philosophy and Music*. New York: International Publishing, 1950.

Zukowska, Anna. *Forma Sonatowa w Symfoniach Dymitra Szostakovicza*. Gdansk: Akademia Muzyczna, 1973.

Documentary Films

Dmitri Shostakovich: Sonata for Viola (1981), directed by Semyon Aranovich and Alexander Sokurov. DVD released by Ideale Audience International (2005).

DSCH: The Life and Works of Dmitri Shostakovich, compiled by Oksana Dvornichenko. *Cultural Heritage Series*, vol. 1. Chandos Multimedia DVD-ROM, CHAN 550011.

A Journey of Dmitry Shostakovich (2006), directed by Oksana Dvornichenko and Helga Landauer.

Testimony: The Story of Shostakovich (1987), directed by Tony Palmer. DVD released by Digital Classics (2005).

The War Symphonies: Shostakovich Against Stalin (1997), directed by Larry Weinstein. DVD released by Philips (2005).

Theses and Dissertations

Adams, Robert Michael. "Dmitri Shostakovich and the Fugues of op. 87: A Bach Bicentennial Tribute." M.M. thesis, North Texas State University, 1981.

Bates-Crouch, Karen Anne. "Formal Structure in the Cello Concerto No. 1, Opus 107 by Dmitri Shostakovich." M.M. thesis, University of Nebraska-Omaha, 1990.

Baxter, Jeffrey William. "A Descriptive Analysis of the Yevtushenko Settings of Dmitri Shostakovich." D.M.A. diss., University of Cincinnati, 1988.

Bennet, Evan. "The Treasons of Image: Bach, Irony, and Shostakovich's Preludes and Fugues, op. 87." Ph.D. diss., Princeton University, 2004.

Brown, Stephen C. "Dual Interval Space in Twentieth-Century Music." Ph.D. diss., Yale University, 1999.

Cassidy, Robert. "A Comparison of Passacaglias in Piano Trios by Ravel and Shostakovich from a Historical and Theoretical Perspective." D.A. diss., Ball State University, 2006.

Castro, David. "Sonata Form in the Music of Dmitri Shostakovich." Ph.D. diss., University of Oregon, 2005.

Darby, Joseph Eugene. "Dmitri Shostakovich's Second, Third and Fourth Symphonies: Problems of Context, Analysis, and Interpretation." Ph.D. diss., City University of New York, 1999.

D'hoe, Jeroen. "Manifestations of Structural Dualism in the Twentieth-Century Symphony." D.M.A. diss., Julliard School of Music, 2003.

Downes, Michael. "The Politics of Musical Criticism: A Study of Some Works by Dmitri Shostakovich." M.Phil. thesis, University of Cambridge, 1991.

Drury, Jonathan Daniels. "Pitch Class Pairs in the Form of Dmitry Shostakovich's String Quartets." M.A. thesis, University of Illinois, 1973.

Dyer, Paul Eugene. "Cyclic Techniques in the String Quartets of Dmitri Shostakovich." Ph.D. diss., Florida State University, 1977.

Fankhauser, Gabe. "Cadential Intervention and Tonal Expansion in Select Works of Shostakovich." Ph.D. diss., Florida State University, 1999.

Fay, Laurel E. "The Last Quartets of Dmitrii Shostakovich: A Stylistic Investigation." Ph.D. diss., Cornell University, 1978.

German, Lyudmila. "The Constructive Role of Polyphony in the Second, Fourth, and Eleventh Symphonies of Dmitri Shostakovich." D.M.A. diss., Manhattan School of Music, 2003.

Gould, Stephany Lynn. "Romantic Literary Narrative into Opera: Towards a Poetics of Transposition." Ph.D. diss., University of Wisconsin–Madison, 1997.

Grönke, Kadja. "Studien zu den Streichquartetten 1 bis 8 von Dmitrij Sostakovic." Ph.D. diss., Christian-Albrechts-Universität Kiel, 1993.

Gunter, Sheila Dewing. "Chernyi and Shostakovich: Parallel Satires." M.A. thesis, University of Texas, 2002.

Heine, Erik. "The Film Music of Dmitri Shostakovich in The Gadfly, Hamlet, and King Lear." Ph.D. diss., University of Texas, 2005.

Hibberd, Kristian. "Shostakovich and Bakhtin: A Critical Investigation of the Late Works (1974-1975)." Ph.D. diss., Goldsmiths College (University of London), 2005.

Hovland, Denise A. "Dmitri Shostakovich's Wartime Works and Socialist Realism with an Emphasis on the Piano Trio, opus 67 in E minor." M.M. thesis, University of North Dakota, 1987.

Huband, Joseph. "The First Five Symphonies of Dmitri Shostakovich." D.A. diss., Ball State University, 1984.

Jemian, Rebecca Ann. "Tonality in the String Quartets of Dmitri Shostakovich." M.M. diss., University of Texas, 1983.

Jones, Catherine. "The Importance of the Solo Piano Music of Shostakovich." M.Mus. thesis, University of Sheffield, 1993.

Kazakova, Tatyana. "Orchestral Style Development in the Symphonies of Dmitri Shostakovich." M.A. thesis, California State University–Fullerton, 1983.

Khalatova, Karina. "Polyphonic Innovations in the Piano Music of Dmitry Shostakovich: Twenty-four Preludes and Fugues." D.M.A. diss., University of Cincinnati, 2000.

Klefstad, Terry Wait, "The Reception in America of Dmitri Shostakovich, 1928–1946." Ph.D. diss., University of Texas at Austin, 2003.

Kroetsch, Terence R. "A Baroque Model in the Twentieth Century: The Preludes and Fugues, op. 87 of Dmitri Shostakovich (Russia)." M.A. thesis, University of Western Ontario, 1997.

Kuhn, Judith. "Shostakovich's Intimate Voice: An Approach to Language and Meaning in the Fourth Quartet." M.A. thesis, University of Wisconsin–Milwaukee, 2000.

Lee, Tze Fung Alfred. "Tonal Perspectives in the Selected Piano Preludes of Shostakovich (op. 34, nos. 1, 3, 6, 14, and 24)—an Analytical Study." M.A. thesis, University of North Texas, 1994.

MacKeon, Edward John. "Socialist Realism and the Revolutionary Music of Dmitri Shostakovich." M.A. thesis, University of Sussex, 1995.

McCall, Sarah. "The Symphonic Scherzos of Dmitri Shostakovich: The Individualizing of a Traditional Form." M.M. thesis, University of Kansas, 1984.

McNeely-Zissman, April. "Biography of an Opera: Lady Macbeth of the Mtsensk District by Dmitri Shostakovich." M.A. thesis, California State University–East Bay, 2006.

Mechell, Harry Anthony. "Dmitri Shostakovich (1906–1975): A Critical Study of the Babi Yar Symphony with a Survey of His Works Involving Chorus." D.M.A. diss., University of Illinois, 1985.

Mishra, Michael. "Soviet Musical Criticism and Shostakovich's Fifth Symphony." D.A. diss., University of Northern Colorado, 1997.

Moshevich, Sofia. "Shostakovich as Interpreter of His Own Music: A Study of Recorded Performances." Ph.D. diss., University of the Witwatersrand, 1988.

Myer, Frederick Geer. "Historical Survey and Analysis of the Symphony No. 4, op. 43, by Dmitri Shostakovich." M.M. thesis, George Washington University, 1983.

O'Brien, Kelly Elizabeth. "Shostakovich: Preludes and Fugues." M.A. thesis, University of Virginia, 1992.

Odegaard, David. "Sonata Form and Deformation in Dimitri Shostakovich's Seventh Symphony." M.M. thesis, Southern Methodist University, 2000.

Reichardt, Sarah. "Composing the Modern Subject: Four String Quartets by Dmitri Shostakovich." Ph.D. diss., University of Texas, 2003.

Rettig, Erin Michael. "Melodic, Harmonic, and Formal Analysis of Symphony No. 14, op. 135 (1969) by Dmitri Shostakovich." B.M. thesis, James Madison University, 1995.

Seo, Yun-Jin. "Three Cycles of 24 Preludes and Fugues by Russian Composers—D. Shostakovich, R. Shchedrin, and S. Slonimsky." D.M.A. diss., University of Texas, 2003.

Shelton, Shelby Sue. "Symphony No. 5 by Dmitri Shostakovich: A Historical and Analytical Study." M.M. thesis, Southern Illinois University Carbondale, 1984.

Smith, Arthur Duane. "Recurring Motives and Themes as a Means to Unity in Selected String Quartets of Dmitry Shostakovich." D.M.E. diss., University of Oklahoma, 1976.

Spencer, William Brockway. "The Fourth Symphony of Dmitri Shostakovich: An Analysis, Including Its Inception in Earlier Symphonic Thought, and Its Relationship to His Later Style." Thesis, Boston University, 1985.

Stanley, Bill Thaddeus, Jr. "The Relationship of Orchestration to Formal Structures in the Non-Programmatic Symphonies of Shostakovich." Ph.D. diss., Florida State University, 1979.

Tentser, Alexander. "The Second Piano Sonata by Dmitrii Shostakovich: A Style Analysis." Ph.D. diss., University of Arizona, 1996.

Titus, Joan Marie. "Montage Shostakovich: Film, Popular Culture, and the Finale of the Piano Concerto No. 1." M.A. thesis, Ohio State University, 2002.

Wilson, Kenyon D. "Recurring Themes as a Means to Unity in Shostakovich's String Quartet No. 11 with a Comparative Analysis of Beethoven's op. 131." M.M. thesis, Baylor University, 1995.

Wilson, Miranda. "Shostakovich's Cello Sonata: Its Genesis Related to Socialist Realism." D.M.A. diss., University of Texas, 2005.

MUSICAL EXAMPLES PERMISSIONS

INDEX OF SHOSTAKOVICH WORKS

*Sections in which a given work forms a major focus of the discussion are indicated in **bold** numbering.*

INDEX OF NAMES AND SUBJECTS

ABOUT THE AUTHOR AND CONTRIBUTORS

About the Author

Michael Mishra (USA/UK) is currently Professor and Director of Orchestral Studies at Southern Illinois University Edwardsville, IL. He was the First Prize winner of the 2003 Vakhtang Jordania International Conducting Competition in Ukraine and frequently performs in the Czech Republic, where he has conducted the Karlovy Vary Philharmonic, the Hradec Kralove Philharmonic, and at the Silesian State Opera. In 2001, he made his debut with the Bulgarian National Radio Symphony Orchestra in Sofia and has recently appeared with orchestras in Russia, Ukraine, Argentina, Austria, and in South Korea, where he conducted the first performance by a Korean orchestra of Bruckner's Symphony No. 2. He has presented papers at Shostakovich conferences in Glasgow, Cambridge, and London.

About the Contributors

Louis Blois (USA) is a writer, lecturer, and collector, with a specialization in Russian and Soviet music. His articles have been published in *Tempo, Kastelmusick, Sovetskaya kultura, Journal of the British Music Society,* and *American Record Guide,* where he was a member of the reviewing staff for a number of years. He is a regular contributor to the *DSCH Journal* and author of CD liner notes. He teaches at the College of Staten Island (City University of New York).

Richard Burke (USA) is an Associate Professor of Music at Hunter College of the City University of New York. His main interests are music of the nineteenth and twentieth centuries and the history of opera. He has written articles on

Shostakovich, Beethoven, and Prokofiev, and is a frequent contributor to *Opera News*. He is also a composer and has worked extensively in theater and television.

Andrew Grobengieser (USA) holds degrees from Millikin University and the University of Texas–Austin and is an Adjunct Professor of Music Theory at Pace University in New York City. He has worked as a musical director and conductor for several Broadway musicals, including *The Lion King, Lestat, The Radio City Christmas Spectacular,* and *The Little Mermaid.* He is a freelance transcriber and engraver for the Hal Leonard Corporation, and his original jazz compositions and arrangements are published through UNC Jazz Press.

David Haas (USA) is Professor of Musicology at the University of Georgia, specializing late Romantic and early twentieth-century music. He is the author of *Leningrad's Modernists* (Peter Lang, 1998). His translation and commentary of Boris Asafyev's classic volume of Russian opera criticism entitled *Symphonic Etudes* was published by Scarecrow Press in 2007. He has also published essays on Tchaikovsky, Shostakovich, Sibelius, Russian opera, and Russian symphonic theory.

Lyn Henderson (UK) is a freelance researcher whose special interests are Shostakovich and Prokofiev. Her several articles include a detailed comparative study of Prokofiev's opera *The Fiery Angel* and his Third Symphony, and she has also devised a scenario for an entertainment in dance based on the opera's storyline, to be accompanied by the orchestral piece. In recent years, she has been investigating the music of Arvo Pärt, and her survey of his early period will be published in the near future.

James Morgan (USA) received his Ph.D. in Slavic Languages and Literatures from Yale University in 1998 and taught for several years at Oberlin College and Bates College. In addition to his work on Shostakovich's operas, he has published articles on the poetry of Alexander Pushkin, Konstantin Batyushkov, and Marina Tsvetayeva. He will receive Rabbinical ordination from Hebrew College (Newton, MA) in 2008. He lives in the Boston area with his wife and two young sons.

Sofia Moshevich (Canada) is an independent scholar and pianist. After graduating in Moscow, she continued her studies in Israel and was awarded her Ph.D. in South Africa, where she was also active as a pianist and teacher. Since settling with her husband and two children in Toronto in 1991, she has published numerous articles and has presented papers on Glenn Gould, Russian composer-performers, and Shostakovich at international conferences. Her book *Shostakovich, the Pianist* was published in 2004 by the McGill-Queens University Press (Montreal). She is now working on her second book, *Music for Piano Solo by Dmitri Shostakovich,* for Indiana University Press.

John Riley (UK) is a writer, lecturer, film programmer, and broadcaster, specializing in music, film, and Russian and Soviet culture. His book *Dmitri Shostakovich: a Life in Film* (I.B. Tauris, 2005) is the first English-language study of the composer's cinema career. He has also contributed to books from Routledge and Cambridge University Press. He has curated film seasons at various cinemas including the Barbican, which hosted Britain's largest ever retrospective of films scored by Shostakovich, and has contributed to radio programs for the BBC and in The Netherlands. He has also made a film, and his evening-length entertainment based on Shostakovich's film work was premiered by the City of Birmingham Symphony Orchestra at London's South Bank Centre.